New Directions in California History. A Book of Readings

New Directions in California History: A Book of Readings

Edited by

James J. Rawls
Diablo Valley College

McGraw-Hill Book Company

New York St. Louis San Francisco Auckland Bogotá Caracas Colorado Springs
Hamburg Lisbon London Madrid Mexico Milan Montreal New Delhi
Oklahoma City Panama Paris San Juan São Paulo Singapore Sydney Tokyo Toronto

This book was set in Times Roman by the College Composition Unit in cooperation with Crane.
The editor was Phillip A. Butcher;
the designer was Charles Carson;
the production supervisor was Denise L. Puryear.
Project supervision was done by The Total Book.
R. R. Donnelley & Sons Company was printer and binder.

The cover photograph of the Santa Cruz Mountains was taken by Alexander Lowry/ Photo Researchers, Inc.

NEW DIRECTIONS IN CALIFORNIA HISTORY: A BOOK OF READINGS

1 2 3 4 5 6 7 8 9 0 DOCDOC 8 9 2 1 0 9 8 7 8

ISBN 0-07-051253-1

Library of Congress Cataloging-in-Publication Data

New directions in California history : a book of readings / edited by
  James J. Rawls.
      p. cm.
    ISBN 0-07-051253-1.   ISBN 0-07-051255-8 (instructor's manual)
    1. California—History.   I. Rawls, James J.
  F861.5.N49 1988
  979.4—dc19   87-31162
                                        CIP

For Linda,
Benjamin, and Elizabeth

Contents

Preface

California history is alive and well. Scholars around the state and across the nation are making major contributions to the field each year, yet few attempts have been made to collect these contributions, to make them readily available to the general reader or to the thousands of students who enroll annually in California history classes. *New Directions in California History* is a collection of readings drawn from the latest scholarship. It reflects the excitement of new work being done in the field and presents new directions in historical interpretation, areas of inquiry, and methods of analysis.

The book is organized chronologically and covers a wide range of topics in social, political, cultural, and economic history. It does not attempt to force California history into an adversarial pro and con framework—a standard format for historical anthologies—but seeks rather to identify those works which best present the state's history in a fresh and lively way.

Several of the readings offer bold new paradigms or schemes of periodization for California history. The first selection, for example, provides a synthesis of what Joseph L. Chartkoff and Kerry Kona Chartkoff call California's "Pacific Period." The Chartkoffs are anthropologists who have divided all of California's past into four major periods. A later selection by historian Michael Kazin offers a new interpretation of the relationship between California labor and politics and outlines a three stage periodization for the state's labor history. Likewise Donald J. Pisani, in a seminal study of California water policy, divides the state's agricultural history into three distinct periods.

New research on a number of familiar topics in California history is presented in other selections. Harry Kelsey provides new insights into the sixteenth-century voyage of discovery of Juan Rodríguez Cabrillo. Basing his work on original research in Spanish archives, Kelsey relocates the likely site of Cabrillo's final and fatal anchorage along the California coast. Francis F. Guest uses the theological manuals of Spanish Franciscans to reconstruct the world view of the missionaries who labored on the California frontier. Guest argues that to understand the missionaries' policy of forcing Indians to reside at the missions, one must first understand the missionaries' theology. As a counterpoint to the ''inside view'' provided by Father Guest, James J. Rawls offers an interpretation of the views of foreign visitors who came to California in the late eighteenth and early nineteenth centuries. Rawls finds that these observations were often remarkably hostile and reflected both the ideology and self-interest of the outside observers. David J. Weber, in a new study of mission secularization, notes that ideology and self-interest continued to inform attitudes toward the missions during the Mexican era. Norman A. Graebner, a senior diplomatic historian, argues in a subsequent article that the United States acted out of a clear sense of self-interest in seizing California during the Mexican War of 1846–48. Graebner presents a mature judgment on the causes of the war and draws parallels with events in the Vietnam war and other American conflicts. One of the liveliest topics in the history of early American California is vigilantism in San Francisco. Robert M. Senkewicz, in a major new book on the subject, surveys recent interpretations of the San Francisco vigilantes.

Among the many new areas of inquiry in California history perhaps none is as rich in potential as the history of women and the family. Representative of this exciting new field is Gloria E. Miranda's study of child-rearing practices in Hispanic California. Miranda finds that during the Spanish and Mexican periods differences in social class were a major factor in determining patterns of fertility, socialization, adolescence, and education. Likewise Jacqueline Baker Barnhart, in a study of prostitution in gold-rush San Francisco, emphasizes that differences in rank and status were also important among the city's ''fair but frail.'' Robert L. Griswold uses divorce records from the late nineteenth century to reexamine relations between the sexes in Victorian California. He finds that the institution of marriage underwent a fundamental change as women became increasingly independent in both thought and deed. His account of the sexual activities of California women presents a striking contrast to the familiar image of repressed sexuality among the Victorians.

Another major new field of inquiry, growing in importance over the past quarter century, is the history of California's ethnic minorities. A selection from the work of Douglas Henry Daniels traces the residential pattern of black San Franciscans from 1850 until the advent of World War II. In an effort to capture the quality of life and urban identity of these ''pioneer urbanites,'' Daniels draws upon oral histories as well as more conventional sources. Likewise Ricardo Romo uses marriage records, city directories, and manuscript censuses to plot the occupational and spatial mobility of Mexicans in East Los Angeles during the twentieth century. The most flagrant racist abuse in California in the twentieth century, the relocation of Japanese Americans during World War II, is the subject of a selection by Roger Daniels. Daniels discusses the changing perception of relocation over the past forty years and speculates on the prospects of redress for those who were relocated.

One of the newest fields of investigation in California studies is environmental history. Environmental historians often conduct research on the background of contemporary public policy issues. Douglas H. Strong, for example, recounts the problems caused by rapid growth at Lake Tahoe and chronicles the emergence of one of the state's earliest efforts at environmental protection, the Tahoe Regional Planning Agency.

California historians are not only active in new fields of inquiry, they are also engaged in developing new methods of analysis. David Rich Lewis has adopted from literary criticism the technique of content- or value-analysis. Applying this technique to diaries kept by gold-seekers on the overland trail, Lewis offers a systematic account of the experiences of the argonauts. More common borrowings are from the social sciences. Andrew Rolle applies the technique of psychoanalysis to the enigmatic explorer John Charles Frémont. Rolle probes deeply into Frémont's psyche, seeking answers to basic questions about the Pathfinder's character and motivation.

Historians have also adopted from the social sciences various methods for analyzing quantitative data. Known generally as practitioners of the new social history, these historians are interested in understanding the processes that affected the great majority of people alive at any given time. History for too long, they believe, has been simply an account of the lives of the elite. The new social historians, therefore, pay special attention to the inarticulate, the anonymous masses in society who leave little or no literary records of their existence. These historians often turn to bare quantitative data—and sophisticated statistical analysis—to "get at" the lives of the common people. Critics of the new social history have charged that it is not really so new, its arrival having been heralded early in the century by James Harvey Robinson under the very label of the "new history." Critics also have denigrated much of the writing of the new social historians as pedestrian in style and lacking in connection to broader historical themes.

Several selections in this anthology are representative of the best of the new social history in California studies. Ralph Mann, for example, analyzes the changing social structure of two gold-mining towns, Grass Valley and Nevada City. Likewise Sucheng Chan uses quantitative methods often employed in the new social history to analyze the structure of Chinese livelihood or occupation in rural California during the late nineteenth century. Ricardo Romo's analysis of occupational mobility in East Los Angeles during the twentieth century is also based on quantitative analysis.

The broad range of interests of contemporary California scholars is reflected in this volume. In addition to the works cited above, social history is represented by James N. Gregory's study of California's Okie subculture in the 1930s and W. J.

Rorabaugh's account of the student movement on the Berkeley campus of the University of California in the 1960s. The continuing controversy over California's system of higher education is described in the selection by William Zumeta and Priscilla Wohlstetter. Political history is represented by Spencer C. Olin's assessment of the "politics of antimonopoly" in the late nineteenth century and by Jacqueline R. Braitman's biographical sketch of progressive reformer Katherine Philips Edson. Several selections are important contributions to the state's cultural history. Kevin Starr describes the consolidation of a mythic identity for southern California in the 1880s, while Gerald D. Nash demonstrates that the migration of European exiles during World War II had an enormous impact on the southland's regional culture. Hollywood and its role in shaping American popular culture during the cold war are discussed in the selection by Lary May. Recent economic history is the subject of Jack Citrin's article on the legacy of the tax revolt and Michael B. Teitz's analysis of the contemporary California economy.

Although not intended to be comprehensive, *New Directions in California History* offers a remarkably thorough introduction to major developments in the history of the Golden State.

A word or two may also be in order about the authors whose works appear here. The majority are scholars who completed their doctoral studies in the 1970s and 1980s. Two are still in graduate school. Thus the authors are for the most part a relatively young group, many of whom are at the beginning or midpoint of their careers. With one exception, all of the selections included here first appeared in the 1980s and several are drawn from an author's first major publication. Three of the selections are original works not previously published—James N. Gregory's article on the Okie subculture, W. J. Rorabaugh's study of the Berkeley Free Speech Movement, and Lary May's essay on Hollywood during the cold war.

About half of the authors are currently on the faculty of a California college or university. Each segment of the state's system of higher education is represented. As one might expect, the largest representation is from the various campuses of the University of California. Included are the works of scholars at Berkeley, Irvine, Los Angeles, Santa Barbara, and Santa Cruz. The California State University system is represented by selections from scholars at San Diego and Chico. The work of historians at the 106 California community colleges is exemplified by selections from instructors at Los Angeles Valley College and Diablo Valley College. Articles by scholars at the University of Southern California, University of San Francisco, and Santa Clara University are representative of the state's private institutions of higher learning.

California history is not a parochial subject. Scholars at universities across the country are conducting research and writing books and articles on the state's history. Indicative of this wide interest in the field are selections from researchers at American University, Michigan State University, Southern Methodist University, Texas A&M University, the University of Cincinnati, and the Universities of Colorado, Minnesota, New Mexico, Oklahoma, Texas, Virginia, and Washington.

Nor is the interest in California history limited to the ranks of professional historians. Many of the new directions represented in this anthology come from scholars who serve in disciplines other than history, and it is precisely this inter-disciplinary quality that makes California studies a lively and innovative field. Thus the ''California historians'' included here come from academic departments as diverse as American Studies, Communication Arts, Political Science, Anthropology, Public Affairs, Chicano Studies, Black Studies, Public Administration, and City and Regional Planning.

A final note should be added on the editorial method. Most of the selections included in this reader are adapted from larger works, therefore deletions and other revisions were necessary in nearly every case. Subheads have been inserted in each of the texts, and notes, tables, and graphs have been renumbered and re-positioned. Full citations to the original works are included at the beginning of each selection.

Editorial introductions precede each of the selections and serve a variety of purposes. They often summarize the larger work from which a selection is drawn, providing a context for better understanding. Some describe briefly the historical period or topic under discussion, again with the purpose of providing context. Others summarize alternate points of view on the topic or provide an overview of recent historiography. The introductions generally identify the new interpretations, areas of inquiry, or methods of analysis contained in the following selection. The introductions also provide a sense of continuity from selection to selection, tying together common threads and connecting themes as they appear in various readings. Each introduction ends with a brief note about the author of the selection.

I acknowledge with gratitude the individuals who reviewed the prospectus for this reader and who offered many helpful suggestions for improvement: Dennis Berge, San Diego State University; David W. Eakins, San Jose State University; and Eugene C. Lee, University of California—Berkeley. Special thanks are also due to each of the scholars whose works appear in the following pages and without whose encouragement and good wishes this book would not exist.

James J. Rawls

THE PACIFIC PERIOD

EDITOR'S INTRODUCTION

California's prehistory, when it is thought of at all, is often imagined as a kind of frozen tableau in which native people lived out their lives in a timeless and unchanging natural world. While it is true that the cultural landscape of what would be California appeared virtually static in the millennium before white contact, the archaeological record of this area reveals a process of dynamic change and innovation.

Archaeologists Joseph L. Chartkoff and Kerry Kona Chartkoff, in their book *The Archaeology of California* (1984), have divided California's past into four major periods: *Paleo-Indian, Archaic, Pacific,* and *Historical.* California's Paleo-Indian Period began at least 12,000 years ago with the arrival of the first *Homo sapiens.* The Chartkoffs characterize the Paleo-Indians as true pioneers, a people who continued in a new land to follow their old ways of life as long as they could. For the Paleo-Indians this meant continuation of a focal economy based on big-game hunting and reliance on a universal technology. (A *focal economy* is one in which peoples' lives depend on relatively few resources. *Universal technology* refers to the generalized nature of the tool kit that the Paleo-Indians developed.)

As the great herds of grazing animals dwindled in what was to become California, the Paleo-Indian Period came to a close about 11,000 years ago. During the Archaic Period, lasting for 7,000 years, the people of this area developed a diffuse economy which included the use of hundreds of plant species and dozens of species of animals. The Archaic people developed a specialized technology, creating entirely new kinds of tools and techniques. Their diffuse economy and technological sophistication allowed them to penetrate many new ecological niches, moving into areas previously uninhabited.

Beginning around 4,000 years ago and continuing to 1769, California passed through what the Chartkoffs call the Pacific Period. During these years, the California

1

cultures underwent a transformation from small groups of hunters and gatherers to larger, more sedentary groups which developed the beginnings of a cash economy and more complex political organizations. The Pacific people returned to a focal economy, concentrating on a few primary staples. In most areas two or three resources served as staples, which were collected in surplus quantities and stored throughout the year. The most impressive quality of the Pacific people was their achievement of cultural complexity without the development of agriculture.

The term "Pacific Period" was created by the Chartkoffs to emphasize that the cultural developments then taking place in California were similar to those occurring elsewhere along the Pacific coast. They also chose this term to call attention to the growing importance of maritime resources. The Pacific Period began gradually and undramatically at different times in different parts of this area: As people developed new patterns of subsistence, they became part of the new epoch.

Although the Pacific Period began gradually, it ended climactically with the arrival of the first Europeans. Spanish explorers sailed along the California coast in the mid-sixteenth century and permanent settlement began in 1769 with the coming of the Spanish missionaries. Thus began the Historical Period, an era of permanent disruption of the Pacific way of life. The major themes of this period from an archaeological perspective are the breakdown of the Pacific Period economy and cultures, the emergence of a new pioneer settlement pattern, and the later rise of an urban, industrial, and multiethnic society.

In the selection that follows, the Chartkoffs describe some of the major developments during the Pacific Period. The selection begins with an imaginative scenario, a brief reconstruction of the everyday life of the Pacific people.

Joseph L. Chartkoff and Kerry Kona Chartkoff are archaeologists who have done extensive fieldwork in California, surveying archaeological sites throughout the northwestern part of the state and in the Central Valley. Joseph Chartkoff received his Ph.D. from the University of California, Los Angeles, in 1974 and is currently a Professor of Anthropology at Michigan State University. Kerry Kona Chartkoff, a third-generation Californian, is a consulting archaeologist.

READING 1

The Pacific Period

Joseph L. Chartkoff
Kerry Kona Chartkoff

A low, grassy terrace faces the ocean along the Santa Barbara Channel. The terrace parallels the shore and slopes gently upward away from the beach. A rocky point of land juts out into the water to the west of the beach, sheltering it from the prevailing winds and currents. East of the beach, a stream descends from the nearby coastal mountains and cuts across the terrace, where it empties into the sea. At its mouth is a sizable tidal estuary and lagoon. Shorebirds wade in and out among the thickets of reeds and cattails. Cries of the gulls that wheel above the sandbar sound through the rolling of the surf beyond. Behind the lagoon, oaks line the sides of the small canyon through which the stream drains, and chaparral blankets the slopes of the hills beyond. A ridge of coastal hills rises to define the horizon to the north; southward out to sea the spines of the distant Channel Islands punctuate the ocean's line.

A village settlement spreads out over the sloping terrace. There are perhaps 30 huts in all, grouped in several irregular clusters. Most of the huts are about 15 feet across and built almost wholly above ground, but in the center of the settlement is a much larger structure, almost 30 feet across. The common huts are made with frames of saplings lashed into bee-hive shapes and covered with layers of reed mats and thatching for their walls and roofs. The larger hut, though outwardly similar, re-

Adapted from *The Archaeology of California,* by Joseph L. Chartkoff and Kerry Kona Chartkoff, pp. 140–146, 227–242. The preliminary report was prepared under a grant from the Forest Service, U.S. Department of Agriculture, and is in the public domain. The revisions and new matter are copyright © 1984 by The Board of Trustees of the Leland Stanford Junior University.

quires the support of several heavy posts set into its subterranean floor to support its roof beams.

At one edge of the settlement, near the creek, stands a large roofless enclosure whose interior is a bare earthen floor. Not far from it, but much closer to the beach, is a small, low-roofed, semi-subterranean struc-ture, in front of which are heaps of ashes. A thatched hut stands at the opposite end of the village, so small that only a few people can enter it at a time. Along the beach, above the high-tide mark, a half-dozen plank canoes are drawn up onto the sand.

Nearly 250 people live in the village. A family lives in each hut, and the groups of huts represent four different lineages. It is spring, past the rainy season and warm enough for outdoor work. In the morning hours the women of most households are doing chores at the hearths next to their huts. At this time of year houses are used mainly for sleeping, as shelter during foul weather, and to store the family's belongings. Now that winter has passed, the indoor fireplace, used for cooking and heating, has been cleaned out in each house, and the food preparation and cooking are done at the outdoor hearths. Women and older girls move back and forth among the houses, visiting, carrying firewood or bundles of reeds, hauling water in basketry canteens, bringing acorns from the granaries, or tending babies. Children run around the settlement. Dogs can be seen prowling between the houses, looking for dis-carded bits of fish and meat.

The low-roofed, semi-subterranean structure near the beach is the village sweathouse. Smoke rises from the sweathouse's smoke hole. Some of the older men have stoked a fire inside, in which they are heating rocks. When enough stones have been heated, the men will spread them around the hearth. The men will lie on the floor, perspiring from the heat that radiates from the stones. After soaking up all the heat they can bear, the men will crawl out through the sweathouse's low door, hurry down to the creek, and complete their bath by plunging into the chilly water. While they are inside the sweathouse, the only sign of activity visible from the outside is the column of smoke rising from the smokehole, and the fresh pile of old coals, ashes, and fire-cracked rocks outside the door.

Along the beach several of the older boys dig for clams in the sand. One young man has swum offshore from the rocky point and dives in search of abalones on the channel bottom. Several other boys clamber along the rocks at the point to harvest mussels from the boulders in the splash zone. A young woman with her baby in a carrier on her back can be seen making her way along a path up the terrace to a small spring above the village where she can collect some spring greens.

Several plank canoes are rounding the point and making for the shelter of the estuary mouth where they can be drawn up onto the beach. A number of men from the village went out to sea before dawn to hunt schools of skipjack and yellowfin. Now they are returning. Each of the 30-foot-long boats rides low in the water, burdened by the sodden nets, stone net sinkers, and piles of fish. The bearskin cloaks of the boat captains glisten with spray. Bailers have worked steadily throughout the voyage to remove the water that leaks in between the canoe planks, since even the best-fit boards are never completely watertight in spite of their sewn lashings and caulking of asphaltum. The paddlers have to work especially hard to bring the heavy craft to shore. Tired boat crews pull their nets onto the beach to stretch them out to dry. Later, each net owner will have his wife or the village netmaker repair any damage to the netting he owns.

The fish from each boat are laid out above the beach. Here they will be gutted and scaled. Women come down from their houses to meet the boats and help with the catch. Several groups begin to process the fish, while others set up green-wood drying racks, under the direction of senior boat captains. The cleaned fish will be laid out on the racks to be dried or smoked. When the processing is complete, the catch will be divided according to shares. Each crew member gets a share, with extra shares going to the helmsman, captain, and owner of each boat. The day's catch can feed the village for more than a week, as well as providing a surplus to feed the community and visitors during future festivals. As the fish cleaning proceeds, some women begin to bring down piles of firewood that the headman had asked them to collect for the smoking racks.

The headman walks down from his large house in the center of the village to watch the landing of the boats. He directs the cleaning operation, calling on people to work well and take care. His house dominates all others, as befits his station. He is the most important figure in his village, and this village is the largest and politically most important for several miles in each direction along the coast. His village dominates this district and the dozen other settlements in it, making him the richest and most important individual in the entire area. In the village, his position is symbolized by the fact that the doorways of all other houses face his house, even though he belongs to only one of the four lineages in the village. Each of these kin groups has relatives who live in surrounding settlements, or even on the offshore islands, for most of the wives in the village were born elsewhere and were brought here by their husbands.

The headman asks one of his children to hike up the terrace out to the point to watch for another canoe. This canoe has carried a trading party to the area now known as the Palos Verdes Peninsula. One of the headman's younger brothers heads this expedition. It left two weeks before to trade for steatite, a highly desirable raw material used for the manufacture of stone cooking pots, frying griddles, beads, pipes, pendants, funeral offerings, and religious items. Santa Catalina Islanders quarry the rock, carving some pieces into finished artifacts and leaving some in rough, unfinished form. They then export their products by canoe to the great trading port villages around the Palos Verdes Peninsula, where they exchange the steatite with village headmen for shell money and goods. The headmen in turn trade with delegations from all over southern California. Some traders come from as far away as Arizona, bringing pottery and turquoise to exchange for the steatite, abalone shell, asphaltum, and other coastal products.

The canoe trip to Palos Verdes from the village normally takes four or five days. Stops are made along the way to visit kinsmen and engage in some small-scale trading. The canoe left the village packed with goods to exchange for the steatite: baskets filled with lumps of asphaltum, blocks of Monterey chert and fused shale (flintlike rocks used for toolmaking), bundles of pismo clam shells, and bales of sea-otter pelts acquired from villages farther up the coast. The trade goods had to be protected well during the voyage, so the canoe had to be bailed continually and beached during heavy seas.

The headman is starting to be concerned about the canoe's return, because it has been away a day or more longer than might be expected. The trading crew might be expected to have stayed at Palos Verdes for two or three days, since trading is an occasion for feasting and negotiations are not completed in haste. Expeditions are invariably risky, however, and delayed returns cause concern.

Trading trips are made in spite of the risks. Steatite is highly prized for its many uses and ease of carving. No other available material can substitute for it. Its acquisition makes the

time, effort, and dangers of the trading trips worthwhile, and the trips offer chances for profit as well. Those who contributed the most to the trading expedition will be best rewarded when the canoe returns and the headman divides up the steatite. He himself will keep a larger share as compensation for having organized the expedition and for backing it with supplies from the resources stored in his house.

The headman is well respected for having organized a number of expeditions and for having rewarded his supporters with proceeds from the trips. His main source of prestige has been his skill and valor as the village's war leader, however. Only the year before a party of raiders attacked the village one morning before dawn to steal a woman. The headman led his fighters across the mountains after the raiders. His war party launched a revenge raid against the raiders' settlement, burning it to the ground, rescuing the kidnapped woman from her would-be husband, and killing two enemies. Since then the village has been peaceful and the headman's stature as a war leader has become widely know along the coast.

Not all the villagers are at work cleaning fish. In the tiny hut at the village outskirts, a young girl is in seclusion in commemoration of her first menstrual period. She is fasting while being prepared for her initiation into womanhood. She has been isolated in the hut for nearly three weeks now, and during that time she has worked to make her initiation costume. She has also received many long hours of instruction from her older female relatives on the proper conduct of a person in her new status.

Later in the day, the large, roofless ceremonial house near the sweathouse will be the scene of a comparable activity for boys. Here, the village shaman and some of the senior men in the religious society of the community are training a group of boys for the rituals that mark their entry into manhood, teaching them the extensive bodies of lore and ritual they must memorize before their circumcision ceremony. Even though they come from all different kin-groups in the village, the boys who go through their circumcision experience together will share lifelong bonds.

As some of the heavier work of the fish cleaning comes to a close, the headman directs a team of young men to another part of the beach, where a partially dismembered whale skeleton lies. Since the whale was beached during a storm the previous fall, the villagers have long since removed the meat. During the winter, the skeleton was cleaned by scavengers. The work party will now cut out some of the whale's ribs and carry them to the village. Some of the ribs will be used as support posts for new house construction. Others will be cut into sections and carried to the village cemetery to be used for tomb-stones and grave covers.

Village life will continue in this fashion throughout the year. The village will never be totally abandoned at any time. During the summer, some families will camp in the nearby coast ranges for a few months to hunt and to gather the resources peculiar to that area. But other families will remain in the village, along with people too old or ill to travel and mothers with newborn babies. If the village were left unoccupied, someone might steal or destroy the ritual costumes stored there that are necessary for the proper conduct of the village's ceremonial life. Such a calamity would have terrible consequences for the well-being of every member of the community.

During the year, groups will make trips into the surrounding hills to collect particular resources. Ten or twelve men might go out for a week to quarry fused shale from an outcrop in a particular canyon. Several kinswomen might travel to the ridge crest for three or four days to gather basketry materials. Autumn is a good time for teams of men to cut trees in the hills and drag the logs back to the village to be split into planks for more canoes. Early autumn is

also the time for groups of women and children to go into the hills and canyons to collect acorns. People will spend much of the late summer and fall filling the granaries near their houses with acorns, storing them for the rest of the year. Seeds, collected during the summer, will also be stored in baskets kept in each house. Extra trips will be made to fill the headman's granaries, so that he can host and sponsor ceremonies. When a headman is famed for his hospitality, he brings prestige to his kinsmen and village.

By excelling in war and ritual, the headman had become almost as notable as his father, who was headman before him. The memory of his father is still honored. When the father died, his funeral was one of the most lavish in memory. Representatives came from all the surrounding villages to attend the ceremony, bringing with them gifts to contribute to the burial offerings. To mark his high status, his grave was excavated in an area of the village cemetery separate from the ones regularly used by each kin group. After preparation, the body was placed in the grave fully extended; the bodies of ordinary people were prepared for the grave by being drawn up and tied into a fetal position. More than 200 strings of shell beads accompanied the body of the former headman. Other contributions included carved steatite bowls inlaid with shell and filled with food, and two dozens baskets filled with food and shell ornaments. The headman's ceremonial costumes and finest weapons were placed in the grave with him. A whale scapula was placed over the grave before it was covered with dirt, and a long section of whale rib was stuck upright at the head of the grave. It still stands there, bleached white by the sun and turning chalky from the elements.

The funeral was accompanied by more than a week of feasting. The old headman's widows mourned in public, singeing off their hair and smearing themselves with soot. Nearly a year later, they still wear ashes in *respect and tribute to their husband. Now his son, the new headman, is rising to similar prominence. His valor in war has confirmed the judgment of the village elders that he should succeed his father. Since then his generosity in hosting feasts, his piety in leading ceremonies, and his skill in helping lead the village have brought prestige to him, his family, and the whole village.*

This scenario of life in a late prehistoric village along the southern California coast describes a way of life that embodied the climax of several thousand years of development away from the Archaic pattern. Archaeologists have recognized climaxes of this sort in many parts of the state but have not agreed on a term to embrace them all. Since we feel that the climax cultures around California have many general features in common, we have decided to create a general term to refer to them. The last four millennia of prehistory we have called the *Pacific Period*.

Many of the ideas archaeologists have about Pacific Period society are based on ethnographic accounts. Since survivors of more or less intact California cultures—at least in the more remote parts of the state—were still alive throughout the nineteenth and early twentieth centuries, the state has a particularly rich literature covering these traditional cultures. Archaeologists have used these writings to model late prehistoric cultures. Ethnographic ideas have also influenced our thinking about Archaic and Paleo-Indian cultures, but the immediacy and amount of literature that deals with the final stages of prehistory are so much greater that its influence on archaeological thought has been correspondingly greater. This ethnographic model has not yet been found to be in serious conflict with archaeological evidence, but a great deal of work still needs to be done to confirm and refine it, especially for the earlier stages of the Pacific Period.

POPULATION GROWTH

Pacific Period societies supported large populations by means of their focal economies, augmented by trading, the accumulation of surplus food and goods, and the avoidance of wholesale seasonal migration. Just how large the population of that time became is still debated, but authorities think that around A.D. 1770 California held about 310,000 people (plus or minus 30,000), which, we might note, is six times the size of the Spanish capital of Madrid on the eve of Cortés's conquest of Mexico.[1] It is harder to make good population estimates for earlier periods, but some figures can be suggested that show the consequences of economic change for California populations.

At the end of the Pleistocene 12,000 years ago (10,000 B.C.), there may have been no more than 1,000–2,000 people in the whole state. During the Archaic that figure may have grown slowly to several times the Paleo-Indian population, but the actual numbers were still small. We feel that around 7,000 years (5000 B.C.) the state may have held no more than about 10,000–15,000 people. By the end of the Archaic, about 4,000 years ago (2000 B.C.), the population may have risen to 25,000–30,000. During the next 3,000 years, the increased productivity of Pacific Period economies may have allowed populations a three- to six-times growth, to 100,000–150,000. The stage was set for a final, rapid spurt in population growth, starting sometime after A.D. 1200 (800 years ago), because of the development of efficient deep-sea fishing, anadromous fishing, surplus collection, storage, trade, and money.

Although population growth was obviously stimulated by economic improvements, it in turn affected the economy. As populations grew, they placed more demands on the economy for food, products, and services, and greater stress on the social fabric of communities. Population size and the economy should be seen as interrelated factors rather than as causes or results.[2]

For example, one result of population growth in prehistoric California was the development of territoriality. Prehistoric groups probably always had some sense of territoriality, since free access by a group to the resources it needed was necessary for its survival and unrestricted competition with other groups for the same resources would have worked against survival. During Archaic times, however, groups were small and spread far apart, and people from one group could wander temporarily into the range of another group with little chance of contact or retaliation. Pacific Period populations were much denser, however, which meant that more people were packed into the same space. As the land became more fully populated, the distance between settlements decreased, pressures on resources increased, border violations were more likely to occur, and competition between groups increased.

A predictable result would have been that borders were formalized somewhat and guarded more jealously. In particular, the key food and trade resources in each territory were most likely defended strenuously. We would also expect that armed conflict in Late and Final Pacific times would have been greater than ever before, and in fact the number of burials showing signs of violent death rises sharply during the Pacific Period. Evidence shows that the Pacific was the time when the ethnographically known groups became established in their historically recognized territories. Ethnographic accounts describe warfare for every group, and reprisals for territorial violations were a frequent cause of war.[3]

Besides the rising importance of territoriality, the development of more complex societies accompanied population growth. More settlements occurred in each region than earlier. In general there were more people in the average settlement, and greater differences in size between large and small communities.[4] And be-

cause the kinds of informal, democratic relationships that had governed Archaic communities were less effective in these larger, more complex communities, new degrees of internal division developed.

The headman of a large Pacific community had more formal authority, more economic power, and consequently greater social status than his Archaic counterpart. Other bases for social status were also beginning to emerge, including social rank, wealth, and rights to certain rituals and equipment. These rights and privileges were largely inherited through families, so that social position began to take on some characteristics of a class system.

Some of the individuals and families enjoying higher status were the special task leaders mentioned earlier. In a large community, comparatively few people could hold such leadership positions. As a result they gained disproportionately large shares of the community's resources. Wealthy families or individuals often owned important food sources, such as groves of oak trees or favored fishing places, or important pieces of capital equipment, such as canoes. In many cultures the owners of such resources allowed others to use them on request for a fee (normally a share of the yield), which gave the system some of the features of capital investment. In this manner, the sharing ethic of earlier times began to give way to a system of personal acquisition in keeping with the Pacific strategy of surplus storage and trade. Trade opportunities also created means for individuals or families to become wealthier than their neighbors. Wealthy people could put their wealth to use to gain greater prestige and power within their communities.

Cemetery remains provide one line of evidence for the rise in social stratification. In contrast to Archaic practices, Pacific burials displayed greater and greater differentiation as time went on. Most people were buried modestly, but a few individuals were buried with lavish offerings. Large cemeteries often had distinct areas for family or kin groups, and within each kin area were often a small number of clearly prestigious, or "elite," burials. These possessed not only a much larger number of burial offerings than those of other individuals, but also many more exotic and elaborate offerings.

SPECIALIZATION

Another feature of social development during the Pacific Period was the appearance of special task groups to perform economic activities through cooperative labor. In earlier times, the nuclear family was not just the basic work unit, but substantially the only work unit. The family continued to be an important work force in Pacific society, but other organizations were developed as well. They increased economic productivity by performing tasks beyond the scope of the nuclear family. Offshore net fishing, for example, was accomplished by boat crews that were not nuclear family units. Their members were drawn from the whole community, and might or might not have been members of the same larger kin group. Trade expeditions might include dozens of men, each representing a different nuclear family. Some kinds of tasks, such as antelope drives or the construction of fish dams, might draw the cooperative labor of several neighboring communities. Some of these special task groups were organized along lines of kinship, but others were organized according to residence or skill. This distinction depended more on the circumstances of the moment than on the task at hand. The leaders of such tasks enjoyed extra power and prestige while performing their leadership functions. Their leadership helped to organize work and make it more productive and efficient. Both the productivity of special task groups and the fact that they were able to accomplish tasks beyond the abilities of individual families helped to enrich Pacific Period economies.

Accompanying the rise of cooperative labor organizations was the development of individual specialists, who acquired skills beyond the level expected of ordinary householders. Those with expert abilities enriched group life and earned social and economic rewards. Craft specialists worked in this way through the production of craft goods on a part-time or full-time basis. There were other kinds of specialists as well during the Pacific Period. Their contributions lay in the provision of services rather than products.

The headman is perhaps the most dramatic example of a service specialist. He provided organization, planning, and decision-making skills to make the work of others more productive. Leaders of special task groups provided similar services, though in more restricted circumstances. Other specialists included singers, storytellers, and herb doctors, who received payment for providing their particular skills. Anthropologists Lowell Bean and Sylvia Vane note that senior leaders in many religious societies also served as teachers for craft and service professions; teaching itself was a specialty.[5]

Pacific societies had several kinds of religious specialists, including healing spiritualists or doctors, leaders of public rituals, diviners, "white" or beneficial magicians, were-doctors (shamans with the reputed ability to take animal form), and sorcerers. They indicate the variety and complexity of Pacific society, and the significance of religious institutions in the operation of these societies.

The recognition of the individual skills of such specialists in Pacific society counterbalanced the tendency toward a social class system based on the inherited control of wealth and political power. Pacific cultures maintained a great deal of flexibility by allowing considerable latitude for individual abilities. For example, although the headman position was generally inherited, it was maintained only if the individual displayed the necessary leadership ability. Otherwise, a headman might be removed by his constituency and replaced by a more able individual. Skilled young craftsmen could hope to rise to positions of prominence even if they came from poor backgrounds.[6] Among the Yurok of northwestern California, a wealthy man often adopted an able but relatively poor young male relative as his heir, giving him the training, skills, social standing, and access to wealth necessary to validate a high position in society.[7] Religious specialists might also draw their apprentices from the community at large, depending on an individual's ability and proclivities.

One of the most dramatic features of California's ethnographically known cultures is the occurrence of great public ceremonies featuring elaborate costumes, music, rituals, and choreography. Although most information about these ceremonies comes from ethnographic sources, corroboration is provided by some archaeological manifestations, such as the ritual sites of northwestern California, the great dance houses of central California, and the brush-ringed dance floors of southern California.[8]

Four great regional patterns or traditional systems of religious movements arose in California during the Pacific Period: the World Renewal movement in northwestern California, the Kuksu Cult of the Sacramento Valley and North Coast Ranges, the Chingichgich movement of coastal southern California, and the Toloache Cult, which was widespread in the region south of the Delta. Though the details of these movements varied considerably, they also shared certain features: their ceremonies were conducted by religious societies that existed within communities; membership was usually restricted to those adult males who passed initiation tests; and shamans played important roles in these societies.

A man's ability to be admitted to a religious society, and to achieve high rank within it, generally depended on his wealth and social standing in the community at large, as well as on his personal skills. Religious societies often served important political roles, drawing together communities of different sizes and degrees of wealth or economic rivalry. They were also important economically, often serving as the intermediaries in trade. They also controlled some of the skilled crafts, provided for the specialized training for craft apprentices, and oversaw the distribution of goods within communities. All this was done in accordance with prescribed rituals to sanctify and legitimize the proceedings. Ritual systems thus provided the more complex Pacific societies with much of the organization that kinship alone was able to provide in Archaic societies.[9]

In historical times, two other ritual movements appeared in California as outgrowths of "ghost dance" movements that swept through the American West in the 1870's and 1890's. These movements, which sought to eliminate Europeans and restore pre-contact life through spiritual and magical means, bore many ceremonial similarities to the more traditional religious movements. Some of the largest central California dance houses were built during the "ghost dance" development.[10] In addition, some denominations of more widespread Christian churches have developed distinctively Native American forms among some Native Californian communities. These religious institutions are still in existence but have not been the subjects of archaeological study.

GROWING COMPLEXITY

Besides the rise of complex mechanisms to organize and control the people living within communities, Pacific times also saw the rise of mechanisms that controlled the relationship between communities. Kinship, trade, and religion provided some of these ties, but during the Late and Final Pacific there arose a new form of political organization that united communities into a more complex form, the tribelet.

Some writers have likened this organization to that of a true chiefdom, ruled by a powerful, authoritarian leader, but most anthropologists do not believe that California tribelets were that centralized or were ruled by authoritarian leaders who could compel their subjects to obey their decisions.[11] The leader of the tribelet did seem to control more resources and power than the headman of any other settlement in the tribelet, a fact that was reflected in Pacific burial practices.

The members of a family in one settlement within a tribelet might have kin in several other communities. In this way, kinship ties cross-cut community organization and helped to hold the tribelet together. The value of the tribelet to Pacific Period society lay in just this ability to tie together into cooperative organizations, with political, religious, social, and economic links, communities that otherwise might be rivals. Through cooperation, communities were better able to fulfill their needs in the Pacific strategy.

Just how much more complex and sophisticated Native Californian cultures might have become and what directions they might have taken will never be known. With the arrival of the Europeans came an end to the autonomous Native Californian way of life. Starting with occasional contacts by land and sea in 1539–40, and then with permanent settlement in 1769, the foreigners brought with them new technology, new diseases, new religions, new economies, and the physical destruction of the old order.

Notes

1 Sherburne F. Cook, *The Population of the California Indians 1769–1970* (Berkeley, 1976), 42–44; Cook, "Historical Demography," in Robert F. Heizer, ed., *California*, Handbook of North American Indians, vol. 8 (Washington, D.C., 1978), 91.

2 Kent V. Flannery, "Archaeological Systems Theory and Early Mesoamerica," in Betty J. Meggers, ed., *Anthropological Archaeology in the Americas* (Washington, D.C., 1968), 67–87.

3 Alfred L. Kroeber, *Handbook of the Indians of California*, Bureau of American Ethnology Bulletin, no. 78 (Washington, D.C., 1925); Thomas McCorkle, " Intergroup Conflict," in Heizer, ed., *California*, 694–700.

4 Lowell J. Bean, "Social Organization," in Heizer, ed., *California*, 673–82.

5 Lowell J. Bean and Sylvia B. Vane, "Cults and their Transformations" in Heizer, ed., *California*, 662–72.

6 For an illustration, see Theodora Kroeber, *Ishi in Two Worlds* (Berkeley, 1959), 196.

7 Dorothea Theodoratus, Joseph L. Chartkoff, and Kerry K. Chartkoff, eds., "Cultural Resources of the Gasquet-Orleans (G-O) Road, Six Rivers National Forest, California" (unpublished manuscript, 1979).

8 Lowell J. Bean and Sylvia B. Vane, "Cults and Their Transformations," in Heizer, ed., *California*, 662–672.

9 Ibid.; Lowell J. Bean and Thomas F. King, eds., *Antap: California Indian Political and Economic Organization*, Ballena Press Anthropological Papers, no. 2 (Socorro, N.M., 1974).

10 Cora A. DuBois, *The 1870 Ghost Dance*, University of California Anthropological Records, vol. 3 (Berkeley, 1939), 1–151.

11 See Thomas F. King, *The Dead at Tiburon*, Northwest California Archaeological Society Occasional Papers, no. 2 (Daly City, Calif., 1971).

EUROPEAN DISCOVERY

EDITOR'S INTRODUCTION

One of the most familiar names to students of California history is that of Juan Rodríguez Cabrillo, yet there is much that is unknown or in dispute about this remarkable man. For centuries historians maintained that Cabrillo was Portuguese, but recently scholars have concluded that he was more likely a Spaniard.[1] No one knows for certain the year or place of his birth, or whether he came from a humble family or a noble lineage. Even the course of his famous voyage along the California coast remains unclear.

We do know that Juan Rodríguez Cabrillo was the leader of a Spanish expedition that sailed north from Navidad in June, 1542, to explore the Pacific coast of New Spain. Cabrillo became the first European to visit what is now San Diego Bay, San Pedro, and the Santa Barbara Channel. The expedition reached as far north as the Russian River and, after the captain's death, it continued northward to the present California-Oregon border.

The latest scholar to study this voyage of discovery is Harry Kelsey, whose meticulously researched biography, *Juan Rodríguez Cabrillo* (1986), offers a new interpretation of Cabrillo's last days in California. The traditional view has been that Cabrillo and his men spent the winter of 1542 at a sheltered cove on San Miguel Island, one of the many islands they discovered in the Santa Barbara Channel. Kelsey, however, concludes that the expedition wintered far to the south on the island today known as Santa Catalina. This was the island Cabrillo named San Salvador, after his flagship, and which Sebastián Vizcaino later rechristened with its present

[1]W. Michael Mathes, "The Discoverer of Alta California: João Rodrigues Cabrilho or Juan Rodríguez Cabrillo," *Journal of San Diego History,* 19 (Summer 1973), 1.

name. It was on Santa Catalina, Kelsey maintains, that Cabrillo fell and broke his arm
or leg on Christmas Eve, and it was here that the captain died about a week later and
was buried.

Most earlier versions of Cabrillo's expedition have relied on the research of the
revered bibliophile Henry Raup Wagner. Wagner's accounts of Cabrillo's voyage,
published in *Spanish Voyages to the Northwest Coast of America in the Sixteenth
Century* (1929) and *Juan Rodríguez Cabrillo, Discoverer of the Coast of California*
(1941), are directly challenged by Kelsey. Kelsey notes that while the original
narratives of the voyage are often unclear in their references to particular islands,
Wagner "only adds to the confusion." As for Wagner's mistaking the identity of the
island then known as San Salvador, Kelsey offers the rejoinder: "I do not think he is
correct."

In identifying Santa Catalina as the final resting place of Cabrillo, Kelsey also
indirectly challenges the interpretation of an inscribed stone metate found around the
turn of the century on Santa Rosa Island. Soon after its discovery, the stone was duly
cataloged and stored away at the University of California museum of anthropology in
Berkeley. Seventy years later, anthropologist Robert F. Heizer reexamined the stone
and insisted that its inscription should be read as "JRC." The metate, Heizer
concluded, was in fact a marker from the grave of Juan Rodríguez Cabrillo and thus
should be accepted as "California's oldest historical relic." Heizer believed further that
California Indians had moved the stone from the site of Cabrillo's grave, then believed
to be on San Miguel, to its point of discovery on nearby Santa Rosa.[2]

Like that other famous artifact from the age of discovery, Francis Drake's "Plate of
Brass," the Santa Rosa metate was placed on public display at the university. And
just as the authenticity of the Drake plate has been challenged by recent metallurgical
analysis, so too has Harry Kelsey's archival research diminished the likelihood that
the Santa Rosa metate is indeed the gravestone of the discoverer of California.

The following selection from Kelsey's biography of Cabrillo begins with the arrival
of the expedition in San Diego Bay in September, 1542. Kelsey offers a careful
accounting of the voyage northward, identifying the islands and other features of the
landscape visited by Cabrillo. Of special interest is the account of the natives of the
Santa Barbara Channel, the same area described by the Chartkoffs in the opening
scenario of the previous selection.

Harry Kelsey received his Ph.D. from the University of Denver in 1965 and is
currently serving as Chief Curator of History at the Los Angeles County Museum of
Natural History.

---

[2]Robert F. Heizer, "A Probable Relic of Juan Rodríguez Cabrillo," *The Masterkey*, 47
(April–June 1973), 62–67; Heizer, *California's Oldest Historical Relic?* (Berkeley, 1974), 6–8.

European Discovery

Harry Kelsey

The expedition continued to sail north and west, and on 28 September 1542 the explorers discovered "a sheltered port and a very good one, to which they gave the name San Miguel," as the next day would be the feast of Saint Michael. This was the first landfall in the area that was to become known as Upper California. The name given to the new port seems to have caused some grumbling among the crew members, for San Miguel was also the name of the smallest ship in the expedition. The crews of the other ships evidently demanded similar honor, so the next important discoveries were named after the other two ships, *San Salvador* and *La Victoria*.[1]

Captain Juan Rodríguez Cabrillo estimated the latitude of the port at thirty-four and a third degrees. After anchoring at the entrance to the bay, a party went ashore and found a few Indians, most of whom fled. For three of the natives avarice outweighed fear, and they stayed to receive some gifts. The presents must have been a disappointment, for that night, when the men went ashore to fish with a net, some of the Indians returned, armed with bows and arrows and shot three of the Spaniards,[2] but the wounds must have been minor, and relations with the Indians here soon began to improve.

The next morning another shore party rowed up the bay in a boat, perhaps the *San Miguel*, sounding the depth of the water and looking for other natives. Spying two children on the beach, they landed, captured them, and brought them back to the fleet. They were talkative children, but try as they might, no one could understand the language, and signs were useless. Consequently, the commander gave the children some shirts, a very generous gift, and sent them back ashore.[3]

The good treatment accorded the Indian children seems to have strengthened the resolve of the adults. Three of them came out to the ships on the following morning and managed a lengthy conversation in sign language. They reported that further inland there were bearded men dressed just like those on the ships, armed with crossbows and swords. "They made gestures with the right arm as though they were using lances, and they ran about as though they were riding horses." According to the Indians, the bearded men had killed many natives. This, they said, was the reason they had fled in fear when Cabrillo and his men approached them two days earlier. The Indians had a curious name for the Spaniards, who thought it sounded something like "Guacamal."[4]

This port, now called San Diego, was the finest on the West Coast and the first landfall made by Cabrillo in Upper California. During their five day sojourn here there was a great storm, but the fleet had sailed farther up the harbour and felt scarcely a tremor of movement.[5]

Leaving port on Tuesday, 3 October, the armada sailed slowly up the coast, noting many interesting valleys, broad savannahs, high mountains a few miles inland, and a great pall of smoke that told them the area was heavily inhabited. After two days of this, they sailed out toward some islands that lay about seven leagues, or twenty miles offshore.[6]

Reaching the nearest island on Saturday the seventh, they named it San Salvador, after the expedition's flagship. This is the island now called Santa Catalina. The second island (now named San Clemente) they called Victoria, after the third ship in the armada.[7]

They went ashore on the nearer one, San Salvador, and as the boat approached, a great crowd of armed Indians appeared. Shouting and gesticulating, the Indians made it clear that they wanted the strangers to come ashore. But the women suddenly fled, and for a time it seemed as though this might be a trap. Finally, the Indians put down their weapons, and eight or ten of them piled into a canoe and paddled boldly out to the ships.[8]

As usual, the commander gave the visitors beads and other gifts that pleased them. A little later all went ashore, the best of friends. As the narrative has it, "They felt very secure, the Spaniards, the Indian women, and everyone." During this brief visit an old man came up to the visitors and said that he had heard reports of bearded men dressed like the Spaniards somewhere on the mainland.[9]

Anxious to continue exploring the vastly improved coastline, Juan Rodríguez Cabrillo and his men made a hasty departure from the islands, and the next morning they were in San Pedro Bay. The burning chaparral raised such thick clouds of smoke that they named the place Baya de los Fumos (the Bay of Smoke). Cabrillo called this place "a good port and a good land with many valleys and plains and wooded areas." A few Indians came out to visit them in a canoe and repeated the now familiar story that bearded men just like the Spaniards lived somewhere to the north. Since this was Sunday, they decided to remain for the day in port.[10]

On Monday, the ninth of October, they left the Baya de los Fuegos (the Bay of Fire), as they also called it, and sailed a few miles up the coast. Seeing another large cove, they anchored overnight in what is now called Santa Monica Bay.[11]

On Tuesday the tenth they sailed up the coast another twenty miles. In one of the few direct quotations from Juan Rodríguez Cabrillo, the narrative gives a little glimpse of the countryside. "We saw an Indian town on the land next to the sea, with large houses built much like those of New Spain." On the beach were many fine canoes, each capable of carrying twelve or thirteen Indians. There were so many of these impressive vessels that the men christened the place Pueblo de las Canoas. This was very probably the large village at Mugu Lagoon, the same place visited half a century later by Vizcaíno.[12] Canoeloads of Indians came out to visit the ships and talk to the men. By this time the explorers were almost bored by the repeated story of bearded Christians marching through the interior. The local name for the Christians sounded to Spanish ears like "Taquimine."[13]

The manuscript sources used by royal historian Antonio de Herrera y Tordesillas at the end of the sixteenth century led him to believe that these Indians were "gentle" people.[14] This did not necessarily mean they were pacifists, as we shall see, but they made Juan Rodríguez and his men feel so welcome that they distributed gifts here for the first time since leaving the island of San Salvador. This pleased the Indians so much that they repeated their stories about Spaniards who traveled in the interior, adding that they were near a great river and that they were only seven days' travel away.[15]

Realizing that these Spaniards could be Alarcón's second voyage, Juan Rodríguez very nearly decided to send two men to find out whether these persistent reports were true. Finally, he decided not to do so, and instead dispatched another letter in care of some Indians who were going in that direction.[16]

SANTA BARBARA CHANNEL

For the next few days the expedition sailed along the channel that runs between the nearby islands and the mainland, an area known now as the Santa Barbara Channel, with a southern extension called the San Pedro Channel. The islands themselves are now named the Channel Islands. Juan Rodríguez later called them the Islas de San Lucas, after the Apostle Luke, because he took formal possession of the islands on the feast of St. Luke. He seems to have recognized that these islands can be subdivided into two groups, those near Santa Barbara being in one group of San Lucas Islands (now called San Miguel, Santa Rosa, Santa Cruz, and Anacapa), and those near San Pedro (now called Santa Barbara, Santa Catalina, San Clemente, and San Nicolas) constituting the "other islands of San Lucas."[17]

The main narrative of the expedition is almost hopelessly confusing and repetitious at this point, having been derived from several sources, each account somewhat different from the other. The seeming contradictions are probably due to the fact that the various islands and the towns on the mainland were visited on different days by various vessels in the expedition. As a result, what purports to be a list of village names in the narrative for 15 October is really a composite of several lists, with a good deal of repetition. The same holds true for a second list of that date, as well as the list dated 1 November, one following comments made for 3 January 1543, and one dated 12 January. For more than a century historians have disputed the exact locations of these places. But now with more information available than was previously the case, it is possible to clear up some of the confusion and to be reasonably certain about the whereabouts of the expedition.

On Friday the thirteenth the ships sailed further up the channel. Passing Quelqueme (Hueneme), Misinagua (Ventura), and Xuco (Rincón), they noticed the Anacapa Islands on the port side.[18] From Indians who came out from the mainland they learned that these were uninhabited. The mainland was a country of broad savannahs, dotted with groves of trees. Passing the Rincón, where the lowlands of Carpinteria begin, they anchored on Saturday the fourteenth at Carpinteria Valley, a place that was both "very beautiful and filled with people, a level country with many trees."[19] This proved to be one of the most

pleasant spots on the voyage. Indians in canoes swarmed out to the ships with newly-caught fish to trade with the men of the armada.[20]

Sunday, 15 October, the armada continued its slow voyage up the heavily populated coast, passing Coloc, in the Carpinteria estuary, Xabagua near present Montecito, and Cicacut near present Santa Barbara.[21] On 16 October the fleet sailed further westward, passing Potoltuc, Anacbuc, and Gwa, the latter two of which were located on small islets adjoining the mainland.[22]

The next day, Tuesday the seventeenth, they continued sailing west, still encountering canoeloads of Indians with fresh sardines to trade for the beads and other gifts the ships carried for that purpose.[23] Anchoring for the night off Gaviota Pass, they noted the Indians still clothed themselves in skins, still tied their hair in cords, with little daggers of flint, bone, and wood stuck into the braids. As with the Indians in Xucu, these people knew about maize or *oep*, but did not raise it themselves. Some alleged that there was corn in the interior and "cattle," or elk, which they called *cae*. Juan Rodríguez Cabrillo said the country was "more than excellent."[24]

The wind blew stronger on the morning of 18 October, as the ships of the armada neared Point Conception. Sailing west, as they were, the coastline appeared so long and low that it reminded the sailors of a galley, so they named it Cabo de Galera. As the northwest wind freshened, the ships found it impossible to sail around the cape. Coming about, they headed south toward the Channel Islands, landing and taking possession on San Miguel. In a singular failure of imagination they named this island La Posesión, still calling the whole group Las Islas de San Lucas, as we have seen. The sudden foul weather forced the ships to remain for a week in the islands, anchored most of that time in the harbour at La Posesión, the place now called Cuyler Harbor on San Miguel Island.[25]

While anchored here the captain made some effort to sort out the geography of the islands, most of which had been visited by one or another of his vessels while the rest of the armada made its way along the coast. At every island, cape, and point visited by the flagship, the captain general took possession in the name of the king, "naming them and placing markers there." We have this from the testimony of Lázaro de Cárdenas. Cárdenas also confirmed a fact that was common knowledge among the men but somewhat muddled in the summary report we now have: that the principal island in the San Lucas group was called Capitana.[26] This was the familiar name of the expedition's flagship, which was more formally called *San Salvador* and less formally called *Juan Rodríguez.*

As though to add to our confusion, the Spaniards also called this island La Posesión, just as they did the one we now call San Miguel and probably others as well. No wonder the compiler of the expedition's narrative got so many place names confused! Historians formerly thought San Miguel was the only one with the name, but a careful reading of the sources makes it clear that the island called San Salvador also was "one of those called La Posesión."[27] It was also called Juan Rodríguez and Capitana.

By Wednesday, 25 October, when the storm abated, they were in the harbor at San Miguel, one of the islands named Posesión. From this point it was possible to see the Cabo de Galera, but there was insufficient wind to take them around the point. Instead they drifted in the entrance to the channel, so that when a heavy storm struck again at midnight the onshore wind very nearly blew them aground. On the evening of the twenty-sixth, with a fresh breeze from the south, the fleet was able to round the cape and explore the coast for a few leagues north of Point Arguello. But the treacherous winds and the strong west-flowing currents kept driving them toward the rocky coastline, and

they were unable to land at the village they called Nocos (near present Jalama).[28]

The Indians told them stories of a great river to the north, and one of the accounts has given a name to the river, el Rio de Nuestra Señora.[29] The river in question was probably the Rio de Buena Guia, named by Alarcón in honor of Nuestra Señora de Buena Guia whose motto was on Mendoza's coat of arms. Some of Ulloa's men thought the river flowed into the Pacific as well as the gulf, and Alarcón had said it reached the sea and "those islands," presumably the Spice Islands.[30] Of course, it did neither, but the expedition was doubtless instructed to look for evidence and settle the matter once for all.

After several days of fighting the elements, the ships turned back toward the channel villages, finally coming to rest just about midnight of 1 November at a village below Cabo de Galera. Because it was the Feast of All Saints, they called the village Todos Santos, but the natives called it Xexo. The next day they sailed on to the Pueblos de Sardinas, anchoring at Cicacut, where they stayed for a few days taking on wood and water.[31]

VISITORS

The Indians at Cicacut were delighted to have the Spaniards back. The canoe masters came on board, dressed in their official capes and followed by Indian oarsmen. Indian musicians brought out their pipes and rattling reeds, and the sailors played Spanish bagpipes and tambourines. Dancing and feasting began. The elderly woman who was chief of this province stayed on board the flagship for the next two nights, along with a good many of her loyal subjects.[32] These Indians were party-goers of great dedication, it would seem. Father Juan Crespí reported a similar celebration at the same place two centuries later. With a few details changed, it could very easily describe the party of November 1542.[33]

In the afternoon the chief men came from each town, one after the other, adorned according to their usage, painted and loaded with plumage and some hollow reeds in their hands, to the movement and noise of which they kept time with their songs and the cadence of the dance, in such good time and in such unison that it produced real harmony. These dances lasted all afternoon, and it cost us much trouble to rid ourselves of the people. They were sent away, charged with emphatic signs not to come in the night and disturb us; but it was in vain, for as soon as night fell they returned, playing on some pipes whose noise grated on our ears.

Finally, a squad of soldiers was sent out with some small gifts, telling the Indians that they were no longer welcome, and that if they came again the reception would not be so pleasant. Juan Rodríguez and his men also loved a party, it seems, for they remained at the Pueblos de Sardinas until Monday, November 6.

The Indians here lived in round dwellings, made of reeds tied to a wooden framework over a dirt floor.[34] Herrera printed a report of the expedition that describes these dwellings as having "dos aguas," a gabled roof from which water drains in two directions.[35] This is an interesting error that no doubt came from seeing Oviedo's pictures and descriptions of houses in New Spain.[36] His statement that they were "large...like those in New Spain"[37] is more nearly correct and matches the description given by Juan Rodríguez, who reported seeing one village where fifty Indians lived in one house.[38] Crespí reported seeing lodges big enough to hold sixty people comfortably. They were "round like half oranges," he said, the typical dwelling of the Chumash.[39]

In the middle of each village there was usually "a great plaza," surrounded by a plant fence and a stone curbing three palms high. Inside the enclosures were mastlike posts covered with paintings. The Indians danced around the enclosures in such a way as to lead the Spaniards to conclude they were of great religious significance, though no one could determine their exact meaning.[40]

The captain general was impressed with the abundant food supplies in this semi-agricultural economy. During good years the wooded hillsides, lush grasslands, and coastal marshes furnished rich harvests of seeds and nuts, including acorns (from the *quercus agrifolia*), grass seeds, and cattail (*typha*) seeds used in preparing atole, pinole, and the mush cakes that Juan Rodríguez described as tamales and "good to eat." One of the seeds, probably the acorn, was "as large as maize and white," but maize itself was not grown or eaten there.[41] Herrera saw one account that described hazelnuts as part of the diet, but is not clear what this meant. As would be expected, the Indians ate fish, both cooked and raw, and maguey.[42]

The Channel Indians painted and decorated themselves with beads and daggers of bone and stone and shell. Colorful feathers were stuck here and there in their coiffures, as style and taste dictated, but no detailed descriptions by the men of the expedition survive. Canoe owners and the leading chiefs wore capes of elk hide or bearskin, but most of the people wore nothing at all, a fact that brought no complaint from the men on the ships.[43]

With full stomach and full water casks, the armada weighed anchor on Monday 6 November, sailing again toward Cabo de Galera and the elusive Rio de Nuestra Señora.[44]

PROGRESS AND RETREAT

By 11 November they were running along the coast around Point Sal in the neighborhood of San Luis Obispo. With a stiff wind from the southwest and no sign of shelter along the coast they dared not attempt to anchor. In any case, they saw no sign of habitation and decided the mountainous area was not so pleasant a place as the channel they had just left. As it was the feast of Saint Martin, they named the range of mountains that runs north from Point Sal the Sierras de San Martín and called the big cape of Piedras Blancas the Cabo de San Martín. They estimated the latitude of the cape to be 38 degrees, about a degree and a half too high.[45]

That night, while they were lying to several miles off the coast, a severe storm struck the fleet and drove the vessels northwest. Running before the wind, with only a small sail on their foremasts, the ships became separated in the rain and wind. Perhaps at the urging of the chaplain, the men on the *San Salvador* said special prayers to the Virgin, calling her Our Lady of the Rosary and the Blessed Mother of Piety. They vowed to make a pilgrimage to her shrine if she would return them home safely. Those on the *Victoria* may have been too busy to pray. Herrera reports that they lost all their deck cargo, and there was doubtless much damage to masts and rigging.[46]

The *San Salvador* had run out to sea, in order to avoid being driven onto the rocky shore, and when the storm abated on the thirteenth, the vessel took advantage of a shift in the wind to make its way back to shore. The sea remained high and the wind strong, shifting a bit more to the west and allowing the flagship to run north. The men sighted Point Reyes, where the pilot measured the sun's position with an astrolabe and called the latitude forty degrees. They named the place Cabo de Pinos because of the great stands of Douglas fir and other evergreens that covered the hillsides.[47]

Still searching for the great river, the lookouts missed the entrance to San Francisco Bay, which everyone else did too for the next two centuries and more. Instead, the ship rounded the point and sailed up the coast for another thirty-five or forty miles to the Russian River. This was obviously not the great watercourse they sought, so the commander ordered the pilot to turn back.[48]

South of the Cabo de Pinos the mountains (Santa Cruz) were covered with snow, evidently from a fresh storm the night of the fourteenth. The weather was so cold the seamen could scarcely man the sails. Then, on the morning of the fifteenth, they suddenly came upon the other ships lying at anchor, one of them leaking badly, with the entire crew exhausted and half frozen.[49]

Continuing south, the fleet rounded the point at Santa Cruz on November 16 and entered the bay they had missed in the storm, now called Monterey Bay. Here again they failed to find the great river. In fact, the surf was so high the boats could not be sent ashore. Instead, the ships cast anchor in forty-five fathoms, while the captain general named the place Baya de los Pinos, computed the latitude at a bit more than thirty-nine degrees, and took formal possession in the name of the king of Spain and the viceroy of Mexico, as he had done at all the other capes and points and bays he discovered and named.[50]

The leaky vessel stayed at anchor for another day, making hasty repairs, while the *San Salvador* beat about the bay looking for the river. The following day, Saturday, 18 October, the fleet sailed on south looking for a safer anchorage. Cypress Point was covered with snow, so the men called it Cabo de Nieve. The northwest wind cleared away the clouds, so they measured the altitude of the sun and computed the latitude at thirty-eight degrees and forty minutes, about two degrees too high.[51]

The mountainous coastline south of Monterey Bay was covered with a blanket of snow, which lay so thick on the trees and cliffs that the men called the mountains the Sierras Nevadas, or the Snowy Mountains.[52] The kind of snowy winter of these years is totally unknown in central and southern California today, but it was the prevailing weather pattern in the sixteenth century. This was the middle part of a cool-moist weather cycle that began about 1370, reached an extreme in 1770, and finally changed to the present warm-dry trend about 1860.[53]

The high, rugged mountains along the coast were an imposing sight, covered with snow and ice. Sailing close to shore, as the narrative says they did, the shivering sailors thought the cliffs "were about to fall on the ships." Why they clung so close to the cliffs is still something of a mystery, for there was a heavy swell with breakers crashing on offshore reefs, and still no place to anchor. South of Cabo de Martín they again noticed signs of Indian settlements, but the high wind and heavy seas kept them headed for the islands.[54]

The voyage ended on Thursday, 23 November 1542, when the tattered armada arrived "at the Islands of San Lucas, at one of those called Posesión."[55] This was doubtless the one now called San Miguel Island, where there is a good harbor, though a small one with a narrow entrance. The fragata *San Miguel* was by this time leaking so badly that the sailors on board thought it would sink at any time. They quickly hauled the small vessel ashore and began to recaulk the hull and repair the sprung planking.[56] Their refuge, called Cuyler Harbor, opens to the north, and the heavy swells that accompany the northwest winds make it a treacherous anchorage for much of the year.[57] The other ships probably did not remain there for long, but sought shelter in the other islands.

It is difficult to make much sense of the lists of islands and village names in this part of the narrative. The island called Limu, for example, is said to contain eight towns, though ten names are given. It is said to be a close neighbor of Ciquimuymu (or Posesión) and Nicalque.[58] Linguistic evidence supports the conclusion that Nicalque is the one now called Santa Rosa Island. Another island, mentioned earlier in the narrative as San Lucas, is pretty clearly the one now called Santa Cruz Island.[59] Limu and Ciquimuymu are not so easy to identify.

Limu is not even in the same island group. Rather, it is the one now called Santa Catalina Island.[60] The captain general gave this one the name San Salvador, after his flagship, which the crewmen called *Juan Rodríguez* and *La Capitana*. There can scarcely be any doubt that this is the island that sailors Lázaro de Cárdenas and Francisco de Vargas referred to as *la isla Capitana,* calling it the most important island discovered on the expedition and the headquarters for all the fleet.[61]

THE DEATH OF CABRILLO

Here it was that the fleet wintered, according to Vargas and Cárdenas. The Indians who lived there quickly tired of the Spaniards and began a series of running battles with them. Vargas recalled that "all the time the armada was in the Isla Capitana the Indians there never stopped fighting us."[62] On Christmas Eve or thereabouts the captain sent a party ashore for water, and the Indians attacked. The soldiers, outnumbered and sorely pressed, called out to the ship for help. Juan Rodríguez Cabrillo himself determined to rescue them, quickly gathered a relief party and rowed ashore in one of the launches. "As he began to jump out of the boat," said Vargas, "one foot struck a rocky ledge, and he splintered a shinbone." Somehow dragging himself ashore, the captain general refused to leave the island until all of his men were rescued.[63]

There is some conflicting evidence about the nature of the injury. The younger Juan Rodríguez Cabrillo said in 1560 that his father had a broken leg, and Lázaro de Cárdenas verified this.[64] The Urdaneta copy of the narrative says, "He broke an arm close to the shoulder."[65] In a fall such as this, it is certainly possible that he broke both his arm and his leg. Vargas, however, insists that the injury was a shattered shinbone. "The witness knows this," said Vargas, "because he was right there." Juan León, the notary who took the testimony in 1543 also took the testimony in 1560, and he saw no reason to question either account.[66]

Juan Rodríguez Cabrillo was taken back aboard ship, where the surgeon tried to treat the wound. However, the injury could not be helped with the medical knowledge then available. The wound quickly turned morbid and became infested with gangrene. Knowing death was near, Juan Rodríguez called in his chief pilot to hand over command of the armada. He then proceeded to put his papers in the best order possible, though he was not able to summon enough strength to complete that part of his account that recorded the voyage of the Channel Islands. This section of the narrative remains singularly lacking in detail, having none of the enlightening comments that enliven the earlier pages.[67]

Unable to complete the voyage himself, Juan Rodríguez charged Bartolomé Ferrer with responsibility for doing so and further ordered him to make a complete report to the viceroy. Once this was done, according to Cárdenas, "He called Captain Ferrer and gave him command as captain general of the armada, by the authority of the royal commission that he held."[68] Juan Rodríguez Cabrillo died on 3 January 1543, and was buried on the island Capitana.[69] "Because he died here," said Cárdenas, "the island retained the name Capitana."[70]

Notes

1 Archivo General de Indias, Seville, Spain (A.G.I.), *Patronato* 20, no. 5, ramo 13, fol. 3–3v.
2 A.G.I., *Patronato* 20, no. 5, ramo 13, fol. 3.
3 A.G.I., *Patronato* 20, no. 5, ramo 13, fol. 3.
4 A.G.I., *Patronato* 20, no. 5, ramo 13, fol. 3–3v.
5 A.G.I., *Patronato* 20, no. 5, ramo 13, fol. 3v.
6 A.G.I., *Patronato* 20, no. 5, ramo 13, fol. 3v.
7 Henry Wagner first thought that both names, San Salvador and Victoria, were originally applied to Santa Catalina Island, which has a sort of figure-eight appearance and could perhaps be mistaken for two islands. See his *Spanish Voyages to the Northwest Coast of America in the Sixteenth Century* (San Francisco: California Historical Society, 1929), 333–34, n. 72. He changed his mind

about this after seeing Homem's map, which shows them as two distinct islands at some distance from each other. See his *Juan Rodríguez Cabrillo, Discoverer of the Coast of California* (San Francisco: California Historical Society, 1941), 17.
8 A.G.I., *Patronato* 20, no. 5, ramo 13, fol. 3v.
9 A.G.I., *Patronato* 20, no. 5, ramo 13, fol. 3v.
10 A.G.I., *Patronato* 20, no. 5, ramo 13, fol. 3v. George E. Davidson, "Voyages of Discovery," U.S. Coast and Geodetic Survey *Annual Reports* (1887), 196, says the bay was Santa Monica, rather than San Pedro.
11 A.G.I., *Patronato* 20, no. 5, ramo 13, fol. 3v. Davidson, "Voyages of Discovery," 196, identifies the place as Laguna Mugu.
12 A.G.I., *Patronato* 20, no. 5, ramo 13, fol. 3v. Davidson, "Voyages of Discovery," 198, identifies the site as Ventura.
13 A.G.I., *Patronato* 20, no. 5, ramo 13, fol. 4.
14 Antonio de Herrera, *Historia general de Los hechos de Los Castellanos* (Madrid: Tipografía Archivos, 1934–1953), 4:fol. 113.
15 A.G.I., *Patronato* 20, no. 5, ramo 13, fol. 3v–4.
16 A.G.I., *Patronato* 20, no. 5, ramo 13, fol. 3v.
17 A.G.I., *Patronato* 20, no. 5, ramo 13, fol. 4, 6.
18 A.G.I., *Patronato* 20, no. 5, ramo 13, fol. 4. Chester King and Thomas Blackburn, "The Names and Locations of Historic Chumash Villages," *Journal of California Anthropology 2* (Winter 1975): 176. Alan K. Brown, "The Aboriginal Population of the Santa Barbara Channel," *University of California Archaeological Survey Reports,* no. 69 (January 1967): 42–44.
19 A.G.I., *Patronato* 20, no. 5, ramo 13, fol. 4. Brown, "Aboriginal Population," 39–41.
20 Herrera, *Historia general,* 4:fol. 113.
21 A.G.I., *Patronato* 20, no. 5, ramo 13, fol. 4. King and Blackburn, "Chumash Villages," 176. Brown, "Aboriginal Population," 36–37.
22 A.G.I., *Patronato* 20, no. 5, ramo 13, fol. 4. King and Blackburn, "Chumash Villages," 176. Brown, "Aboriginal Population," 24–28. Campbell Grant, "Eastern Coastal Chumash," *Handbook of North American Indians,* edited by William C. Sturtevant, vol. VIII, *California,* edited by Robert F. Heizer (Washington: Smithsonian Institution, 1978), 510.

23 A.G.I., *Patronato* 20, no. 5, ramo 13, fol. 4.
Testimony of Lázaro de Cárdenas, 26 April 1560,
Justicia 290, fol. 68v.

24 A.G.I., *Patronato* 20, no. 5, ramo 13, fol. 4. H. W.
Henshaw thought these ''cattle'' might be bison.
See his notes to the translation by Richard Stuart
Evans, ''Translation from the Spanish of the ac-
count of the Pilot Ferrel of the Voyage of Cabrillo
along the West Coast of North America in 1542,''
*Report of the U.S. Geographical Surveys West of
the One Hundreth Meridian,* vol. VII. *Archaeology*
(Washington: G.P.O, 1879), 307.

25 A.G.I., *Patronato* 20, no. 5, ramo 13, fol. 4.

26 A.G.I., *Justicia* 290, fol. 68–68v.

27 ''On Thursday the 23rd day of the month they
neared the end of their voyage in the islands of
San Lucas *at one of those* called Posesión.''
Italics mine. The phrase is *''a una dellas llamada
la posesión.''* A.G.I., *Patronato* 20, no. 5, ramo
13, fol. 5v.

28 A.G.I., *Patronato* 20, no. 5, ramo 13, fol. 4v.

29 Herrera, *Historia general,* fol. 114.

30 Buckingham Smith, *Colección de varios documentos para la historia de la Florida y tierras
adyacentes* (London: Casa de Trubner, 1857), 4.
In 1574 Juan Fernández de Lladrillero spoke of
the search for a passage to the North Sea along
these coasts, but it is wrong to interpret his
testimony as evidence that Juan Rodríguez Cabrillo was looking for such a strait. Lladrillero,
''Declaracion,'' 15:fol. 179–179v. More likely,
the testimony was prompted by Gastaldi's recent
map and pamphlet suggesting that there was a
Strait of Anian connecting the Mar del Sur to the
Mar del Norte.

31 A.G.I., *Patronato* 20, no. 5, ramo 13, fol. 4v–5.

32 Herrera, *Historia general,* 4:fol. 113. A.G.I.,
Patronato 20, no. 5, ramo 13, fol. 4v–5.

33 Herbert E. Bolton (ed.), *Fray Juan Crespi, Missionary Explorer on the Pacific Coast, 1769–1774*
(Berkeley: Univ. of California Press, 1927), 168.

34 A.G.I., *Patronato* 20, no. 5, ramo 13, fol. 5.

35 Herrera, *Historia general,* 4:fol. 113.

36 Oviedo, *Primera parte de la general y natural
historia de las Indias* (Seville: Imprenta de Juan
Cromberger, 1535), fol. viii verso and lix.

37 Herrera, *Historia general,* 4:fol. 113.

38 A.G.I., *Patronato* 20, no. 5 ramo 13, fol. 6.

39 Quoted in Brown, ''Aboriginal Population,'' 4.

40 A.G.I., *Patronato* 20, no. 5, ramo 13, fol. 5.

41 A.G.I., *Patronato* 20, no. 5, ramo 13, fol. 5.
Grant, ''Eastern Coastal Chumash'', 516–17. Lo-
well John Bean and Harry W. Lawton, ''Some
Explanations for the Rise of Cultural Complexity
in Native California with Comments on Proto-
Agriculture and Agriculture,'' *Native Califor-
nians: A Theoretical Retrospective,* edited by
Lowell John Bean and Thomas C. Blackburn
(Socorro, N.M.: Ballena Press, 1976), 35–38.

42 Herrera, *Historia general,* 4:fol. 113. A.G.I.,
Patronato 20, no. 5, ramo 13, fol. 3v.

43 A.G.I., *Patronato* 20, no. 5, ramo 13, fol. 5.
Grant, ''Eastern Coastal Chumash,'' 510,
514–16.

44 Herrera, *Historia general,* 4:fol. 114. A.G.I.,
Patronato 20, no. 5, ramo 13, fol. 5. King and
Blackburn, ''Chumash Villages,'' 176–77,
Brown, '' Aboriginal Population,'' 16–24.

45 A.G.I., *Patronato* 20, no. 5, ramo 13, fol. 5.

46 A.G.I., *Patronato* 20, no. 5, ramo 13, fol. 5.
Herrera *Historia general,* 4:fol. 114.

47 Herrera, *Historia general,* 4:fol. 114 A.G.I., *Pa-
tronato* 20, no. 5, ramo 13, fol. 5–5v. John
Thomas Howell, *Marin Flora: Manual of the
Flowering Plants and Ferns of Marin County,
California,* 2nd edition (Berkeley: Univ. of Cali-
fornia Press, 1970), 7–10.

48 A.G.I., *Patronato* 20, no. 5, ramo 13, fol. 5v.

49 A.G.I., *Patronato* 20, no. 5, ramo 13, fol. 5v.
Herrera, *Historia general,* 4:fol. 114.

50 A.G.I., *Patronato* 20, no. 5, ramo 13, fol. 5v.
Herrera, *Historia general,* 4:fol. 114.

51 A.G.I., *Patronato* 20, no. 5, ramo 13, fol. 5v.
Herrera, *Historia general,* 4:fol. 114.

52 A.G.I., *Patronato* 20, no. 5, ramo 13, fol. 5v.

53 Michael J. Moratto, Thomas F. King, and Wallace B. Woolfenden, ''Archaeology and California's Climate,'' *Journal of California
Anthropology* 5 (Winter 1978): 151.

54 A.G.I., *Patronato* 20, no. 5, ramo 13, fol. 5v.

55 A.G.I., *Patronato* 20, no. 5, ramo 13, fol. 5v.

56 Herrera, *Historia general,* 4:fol. 114.

57 Davidson, ''Voyages of Discovery,'' 226.

58 A.G.I., *Patronato* 20, no. 5, ramo 13, fol. 6.

59 King and Blackburn, ''Chumash Villages,'' 177-
178.

60 King and Blackburn, "Chumash Villages," 178.
A.L. Kroeber, *Handbook of the Indians of California,* Bureau of American Ethnology Bulletin 78 (Washington: Smithsonian Institution, 1925), 554–55. For identification of some of the village names on Limu-Catalina see C. Hart Merriam, "Village Names in Twelve California Mission Records," edited by Robert F. Heizer, University of California Archaeological Survey Reports, No. 74 (July 1968): 97, 128–37. See also Henry Wagner, "The Names of the Channel Islands," Historical Society of Southern California *Annual Publication,* 15 (1933): 16–18.

61 A.G.I., *Justicia* 290, fol. 69, 72v.
62 A.G.I., *Justicia* 290, fol. 72v–73.
63 A.G.I., *Justicia,* 290, fol. 73.
64 A.G.I., *Justicia* 290, fol. 68v.
65 A.G.I., *Patronato* 20, no. 5, ramo 13, fol. 6.
66 A.G.I., *Justicia* 290, fol. 73.
66 A.G.I., *Justicia* 290, fol. 73.
67 Testimony of Francisco de Vargas, A.G.I., *Justicia* 290, fol. 72–73v. A.G.I.
68 A.G.I., *Justicia* 290, fol. 68v.
69 A.G.I., *Patronato* 20, no. 5, ramo 13, fol. 6.
70 A.G.I., *Justicia* 290, fol. 69. See also the family tradition recounted in the questions in fol. 46v.

THE FRANCISCAN WORLD VIEW

EDITOR'S INTRODUCTION

More than two centuries passed between the time of Cabrillo's voyage of discovery and the establishment of European settlement in Alta California. In the spring of 1769 a bedraggled party of Franciscan priests and Spanish soldiers arrived in San Diego to begin the arduous process of conquest and colonization.

The central institution of this imperial outpost of Spain was the mission, an instrument designed to bring about a rapid and thoroughgoing transformation of the native people. The missions established in California were known as *reducción* or *congregación* missions, of the kind developed in the late sixteenth century for use where Indian populations were not already densely concentrated in native pueblos. By various means the Indians were congregated around the missions, where they were "reduced" from their "free, undisciplined" state to become regulated and disciplined members of colonial society.

Inside the missions, the priests exercised an absolute authority over the Indians in matters both spiritual and temporal. Resistance to this authority was met with reproof and, if it continued, with the lash, stocks, irons, and other means of punishment. Soldiers garrisoned at the missions or at one of the nearby presidios assisted in the enforcement of discipline and in the recapture of runaway Indians. Once Indians became neophytes, or converts, they were considered no longer free to reject their vows and return to their former lands or way of life.

Scholarly opinion about the missions has long been divided in one of the great debates in California historiography. The leading critic of the mission system is the late Sherburne Friend Cook, professor of physiology and anatomy at the University of California, Berkeley. In a four-volume study, *The Conflict between the California Indian and White Civilization* (1943), Cook presents a devastating critique of the missions. He asserts that the greatest single effect of the missions was to reduce the number of Indians through the introduction of alien diseases, a suboptimum diet, and the disruption of native society. The missions were oppressive institutions, Cook argues, because they denied the Indians liberty, subjected them to cruel punishments, and established a system of forced labor. Furthermore, Cook maintains that during the later mission period forced recruitment of neophytes became a common practice.

In recent years Fr. Francis F. Guest, O.F.M., has emerged as the most articulate defender of the missions. Author of the definitive biography of Fermín Francisco de Lasuén, successor to Junípero Serra as Father-President of the California missions, Guest attacks directly the research and conclusions of S. F. Cook in a series of tightly reasoned articles. Guest refutes Cook's thesis that the missionaries engaged in forced recruitment and he argues that the entire mission experience must be judged in the context of its time.[1] Cook, he argues, engages in "newsreel history" by failing to consider the cultural background of either the Spanish priests or their Indian wards. "One cannot judge eighteenth-century people," Guest reminds us, "by twentieth-century standards."[2]

Guest's views of the missions, however, have not remained unchanged. A careful reading of his work reveals a progressive willingness on his part to acknowledge that errors in judgment were made by the missionaries and that the missions do present a number of troublesome contradictions. In the following selection, Guest attempts to reconstruct the eighteenth-century *weltanschauung* of the Franciscan missionaries. Only by considering their world view, he argues, can we understand one of the thorniest problems of mission history, the missionaries' policy of enforced residence of the neophytes at the missions.

Francis F. Guest, a native Californian, has served as a professor in Church History at the Franciscan Theological Seminary, Berkeley; and as director of the Academy of American Franciscan History in Washington, D.C. Currently he is Archivist for the Santa Barbara Mission Archive-Library.

[1]Francis F. Guest, O.F.M., "An Examination of the Thesis of S. F. Cook on the Forced Conversion of Indians in the California Missions," *Southern California Quarterly*, LXI (Spring 1979), 1–78.

[2]Guest, "Cultural Perspectives on California Mission Life," *Southern California Quarterly*, LXV (Spring 1983), 1, 58. See also Guest, "Junípero Serra and His Approach to the Indians," ibid., LXVII (Fall 1985), 223–261.

The Franciscan World View

Francis F. Guest, O.F.M.

Gilbert Keith Chesterton, a prominent Englishman of letters early in the present century,
advises his readers to study a familiar object
until it looks different. In his novel *Manalive,*
he exemplifies this principle in one of the characters, Innocent Smith, who travels all the way
around the globe so that, when he comes back
to England, he will see his country differently
than he ever had before. Actually, Mr. Smith
sees in a different light, not only his country,
but his own wife, falling in love with her all over
again and eloping with her.[1]

If anything in California is a familiar object to
us, it is the Franciscan missions founded by
Fray Junípero Serra and his successors. We
have often seen them, at least in paintings and
photographs, and have often had them portrayed for us by travelers, by men of letters, or
by professional scholars representing various
branches of learning, e.g. history, geography,
economics, anthropology, archaeology, sociology, architecture, and art. So we know what the
missions have looked like to all sorts of people
who have observed them from different points
of view. But nobody has asked, as yet, what the
missions looked like to the Franciscan *padres*
who worked in them. Nobody has asked, as
yet, how the friars pictured the missions to
themselves. In this context, then, let us try to
see the missions through the eyes of the missionaries, a task that will be rendered relatively
easy if we but read the books they were accustomed to use as guides in their work.

Adapted from "New Look at California's Missions," by
Francis F. Guest, O.F.M., in *Some Reminiscences about
Fray Junípero Serra,* edited by Francis J. Weber, pp. 77–88.
Copyright © 1985 by the California Catholic Conference.

SPANISH THEOLOGY

An excellent source for material of this kind is
the *Itinerario para parochos de Indios* by
Alonso de la Peña Montenegro, Bishop of Quito
from 1653 to 1687.[2] This volume was first issued
from the press in 1668, but the edition the
California *padres* used was the ninth, dated
1754. A manual of pastoral theology originally
written for pastors of Indian parishes in Peru,
this book, profusely footnoted, presupposes a
general knowledge of the scholastic theology of
the Counter-Reformation and of the Spanish
Golden Age. It instructs, admonishes and coun-
sels Spanish missionaries on the proper way to
deal with Indian converts and parishioners.

One of the pastoral principles to which the
Bishop of Quito devotes careful attention in his
manual is that of inculpable ignorance. The
bishop argues that, although Indians had an
obligation in the objective order to accept
Christianity and to observe the precepts of the
natural moral law, nevertheless, in the subjec-
tive order, the order of the mind, the order of
conscience, they were excused from sins
against the faith and from many other sins as
well because of inculpable ignorance, or at least
because, when they performed a given immoral
act, they did not advert to its culpability.[3]

Let us take two examples of the application
of this principle of inculpable ignorance. In
1795, when some recently converted Indians at
Mission San Buenaventura became involved in
the murder of some other Indians, Fray Fermín
Francisco de Lasuén, the *Presidente* of the
missions, wrote, "...it [the murder] is the work
of those who little realize its gravity."[4] Again,
in 1817, when parties of one Indian faction at
Mission San José murdered parties of another,
Fray Narciso Durán, the head missionary,

wrote of "these unfortunate people who have no realization of what they have done."[5] One recalls at this point the words of Lasuén in paragraph 74 of his Refutation of Charges, dated 1801: "They [the Indians] look on their own most barbarous and cruel actions with an indifference foreign to human nature, and death is their customary way of avenging injuries."[6] Because of inculpable ignorance, however, they were often guiltless of any really grave offense against the moral law, and the missionaries took due notice of this fact.

Secondly, the Franciscan missionaries of Hispanic California, for a number of reasons, were accustomed to look upon the Indians as adult children. First of all, the friars of the various mendicant orders in sixteenth-century New Spain commonly took the view that the Indians they dealt with resembled children.[7] And the Indians they were endeavoring to evangelize were much further advanced in culture than those of the California coast. Junípero Serra and his companions, through their acquaintance with *Monarquía Indiana* by Juan de Torquemada, would normally have been aware of this fact.[8] Secondly, a jurist, Gaspar de Villaroel, in his *Gobierno Eclesiástico-Pacífico, Unión de los dos Cuchillos Pontificio y Regio,* dated 1738, explains that Indian commoners in colonial Spanish America were categorized, in Spanish law, as *personas miserables,* a legal term which comprised, besides Indians, the poor, the orphans, the blind, the lame, and the leprous—in a word, the unfortunate and disadvantaged, those in need of protection and aid, especially legal assistance in cases of litigation. Bishops were authorized by law to transfer the cases of such people from a civil to an ecclesiastical court, if necessary, and to aid needy plaintiffs or defendants with alms. Indians were bracketed as *personas miserables* because of their poverty, timidity, continual labor, personal services, simplicity, ignorance, and weakness of understanding.[9] It must be remembered that, in those days, when some races might be considered brighter than others, and when the lower classes within a given race might be regarded as less richly endowed than the upper classes, Indian commoners, when compared to Spaniards, were often held to be intellectually inferior, although Bishop Palafox y Mendoza and Benito Feyjóo, in this context, wrote in defense of the Indian.[10] Finally, the Spanish jurist, Juan de Solórzano Pereira, in Book II, Chapter IX of his *De Indiarum Jure,* observes that, because of their childlike mentality, barbaric and uncivilized races, including the Indians of the American wilderness, should be treated as children.[11] Catholic theologians, both in Europe and in the New World, appealed to this principle to bundle safely into Heaven a very high percentage of Indian unbelievers both in past centuries and in their own times.[12] In the course of their training in the apostolic missionary colleges of Spanish America, Franciscan missionaries, looking forward to their evangelical work among the aborigines, were not likely to miss the significance of this concept. As a matter of fact, the Franciscan missionaries of Alta California, in Spanish law, stood to their Indian converts as legal guardians to their wards.[13] Missionized Indians, then, were regarded as minors, not as adults. The way the neophytes were taught their *doctrina,* reciting it twice a day every day of their lives for a lifetime, implies that, in the eyes of the missionaries, they did not have the maturity or intelligence of European adults.

In their reply to one of the questions of the *Interrogatorio* sent to the missionaries of Alta California by the Spanish government, 1812–1815, Fray Juan Bautista Sancho and Fray Pedro Cabot of Mission San Antonio wrote as follows: "Behold how these poor Indians, fathers of families, if not entirely, at least in part, are held excused before both God and man."[14] In the light of the principles that have here been treated, it is not difficult to understand why the missionaries should have taken this view of their neophytes.

ENFORCED RESIDENCE

Now then, let us bear these two principles in mind as we ask ourselves why the Laws of the Indies required that all converted Indians make their residence at the mission to which they were attached and why the Franciscan missionaries, where their own missions and neophytes were concerned, insisted on the observance of this law.[15]

First of all, the *Itinerario,* the manual of pastoral theology used by the *padres,* makes it very clear that their most important obligation as missionaries was to instruct their Indian converts in the faith.[16] To the friars, this meant that the neophytes should recite their *doctrina* twice daily just as Indian converts had done in Spanish missions since the sixteenth century. But the priests in Hispanic California, regarding missionized Indians as adult children, could hardly have expected them, if left free to come and go as they wished, to show up regularly of their own volition twice a day for this educational and spiritual exercise which was the cardinal feature of mission routine. Hence it is evident that the only thing the *padres* could do to be certain that their gravest obligation with respect to their converts would be fulfilled was to insist, as their legal guardians, that they make their residence at the mission to which they were attached, ever subject to the summons of the mission bell.

Fray Francisco Palóu, in Chapter 55 of his biography of Junípero Serra, gives three reasons why it was necessary for the neophytes to make their residence at the missions. He expressed the first of these reasons in the following terms: "They [the Indians] can be conquered first only by their interest in being fed and clothed, and afterwards they gradually acquire a knowledge of what is spiritually good and evil. If the missionaries had nothing to give them, they could not win them over."[17] Palóu's observations can easily be harmonized with the information obtained from the *Itinerario.* For

one thing, the Indians were customarily engaged each day in an interminable search for food and had no set time for meals. As hunters and food-gatherers, they were accustomed to eat whenever they felt hungry. Hence it was necessary for the friars to gather a group together and feed them before attempting to sit them down and convey to them some portion of the Gospel message. Repeated daily, this process of feeding the Indians who came to visit the missions soon necessitated the farms, fields of grain, *ranchos,* livestock, crops, and crafts characteristic of mission life. Furthermore, it was perfectly true that, as a general rule, gifts of food and bright-colored clothing provided an inducement for Indians to visit the missions and even to consider undertaking mission life. On the other hand, Palóu does not explain the role played by music and song in attracting curious inquirers from among the aborigines. It is in the *Itinerario* that we find the material on the importance of the more receptive and responsive boys chosen from each of the three or four linguistic groups at a given mission, on the training they were given by the friars in Spanish and Latin, on their usefulness as choristers, altar boys, interpreters, and catechists, and on the help they gave the friars in attracting Indians to the mission, in mastering the rudimentary elements of the various Indian languages, and in working out a summary of Christian doctrine in each so that the converts could memorize and recite their lessons in religion every day.[18]

Evidence that the friars used this method is to be found in several of Serra's early letters.[19] Palóu's observation that after joining the mission the Indians "gradually acquire a knowledge of what is spiritually good and evil" implies two things: first, that they were slow to learn, and secondly, that the lessons imparted to them were elementary in character and importance.[20] Taking the *Itinerario* and Palóu together, one observes at once the paramount reasons why the *padres* insisted that Indian converts make their residence at the mission. It is evident that the neophytes, even if they had remained in their villages in the forest and visited the mission from time to time, could ultimately have acquired the religious knowledge they needed. But the process of education would have been much slower, more gradual, and more exposed to error, the missionaries would have had to learn by trial and error the three or four languages spoken at each mission, and the end result of all their work would, from their standpoint, have been less certain. In a word, the fundamental principle that led ultimately to the elaborate organization of each mission with all its grain production, herds of livestock, workshops and the like seems to have been the importance of giving religious instruction to the Indian converts every day twice a day. If any one aspect of mission life may be said to have been the foundation stone upon which all the rest was based, it was the daily recitation of the *doctrina* by the neophytes and the religious directives given by the friars.

The second reason Palóu gives for keeping the Indian converts at their missions is that, if they continued to follow their village life instead of being segregated from it, the missionaries would be unable to induce them to relinquish "their vicious pagan practices."[21] Among these objectionable customs of the Indians, the following may be noted: (a) their religious beliefs and observances insofar as they were at variance with Christianity; (b) their aboriginal habit of taking property from those who lived outside the tribal unit; (c) the prevalence of divorce and re-marriage; (d) indulgence in promiscuity and, in some tribelets, in homosexuality; (e) the sometimes inadequate regard for the sacredness of human life, as in aborting unwanted infants and in avenging injuries with death.[22] When the missionaries spoke of teaching the Indians to live a rational life, what they meant was training them to observe the principles of the natural moral law. This meant correcting in them the above-mentioned

violations of this law, a procedure they could follow more efficiently by keeping the Indian converts at the mission than by leaving them to continue their village life in the forest. Governor Pablo Vicente de Solá observed that, among the neophytes, theft and concubinage were the offenses for which they were most frequently punished.[23]

Thirdly, said Palóu, it was necessary to keep the Indian converts at the mission in order to civilize them.[24] It is not difficult to see that the friars would not have succeeded very well in teaching given Indians to be farmers, ranchers, carpenters, blacksmiths, weavers, tailors, leather workers and the like if the students kept disappearing into the wilderness at odd intervals and turning up again whenever the fancy struck them. Incidentally, civilizing the Indians included training them in Spanish home life, accustoming them to living in Spanish cottages, to using beds, chairs, tables, kitchen utensils, privies and the like. With great care and much patience, missionized Indians were taught habits and customs in which Spanish parents had instructed Spanish children from time immemorial. It is little wonder that Lasuén, in his Refutation of Charges, paragraph 121, describes missionary work as hard work involving much effort and many annoyances.[25] But in paragraph 54 of the same document he writes, "It is well known that many facilities are lacking here for the civilization of these Indians, and that those we have up to the present are being availed of to such an extent that unprejudiced and well-informed men have ranked our Indians as more civilized than those of many very old *pueblos* in America."[26]

At this point it will be appropriate to note briefly that the Spanish *padres* separated the Indians from their native habitat and culture without realizing that, in doing so, they were making an educational error. Today the Catholic Church requires that, when aborigines are evangelized, Catholicism is to be integrated with their aboriginal culture, which is to remain as undisturbed as possible. In other words, the Church no longer conducts missions among aboriginal peoples as the Franciscan *padres* did in Hispanic California two hundred years ago.[27]

But the friars had other reasons for keeping the Indians at the missions, reasons that call for some small measure of explanation and analysis.

On June 16, 1802 Lasuén wrote a letter to Fray José Gasol, Guardian of the College of San Fernando, on the question whether or not converted Indians should be left free to come and go at the missions as they pleased, an issue that had first been introduced by Governor Felipe de Neve (1777–1782) in his *Reglamento* for the Province of California, had been defeated by the friars, but had arisen often since that time. Lasuén opposed the idea because, if the Indians were instructed and baptized and then allowed to remain in their *rancherías*, they would be confronted daily with dangers to their faith. In their villages, he said, the non-Christian Indians kept alive at all hours the memory of their native religion.[28]

But the non-Christian Indians in the forest were a danger, he explained, not only to the faith of the neophytes but also to their morals. At Mission San Diego, where Lasuén had been head missionary for eight years, groups of Indian converts rotated in residing at the mission. Because mission farms could not produce enough food for all the converts to live at the mission at one time, one group stayed for a few weeks while the rest remained with their relatives in the forest. Commenting on the unsatisfactory results of this method, Lasuén wrote as follows: "Oh, my revered Father! What anxieties! What disappointments! What vigilance! What anguish of mind! What labors day and night for the missionaries! What liberties! What excesses! What irregularities! What ignorance! What disorders! How Christian civilization and pagan barbarity can give way to one another in the same neophytes!"[29] From these lines it is evident that, in the minds of the missionaries,

the neophytes had to be forbidden to associate freely and for prolonged periods of time with non-Christian Indians in their villages in the forest. The reason for this was that these villages, for the neophytes, were an occasion of sin. That is to say, Indian village life easily led the neophytes back into the moral faults and deficiencies which the missionaries were trying to correct in them. Because of the fourth commandment (Honor thy father and thy mother), the missionaries had to allow their converts to visit parents, relatives, and friends in their native villages for a brief period of five or six weeks each year.[30] Besides, as Lasuén observed in his Refutation of Charges, paragraph 57, "We must remember that the majority of our neophytes are so attached to the mountains that if there were an unqualified prohibition against going there, there would be danger of a riot."[31]

Spanish moralists argued that he who could prevent a given sin and failed to do so was actually cooperating in the offense committed against God and therefore shared in the guilt.[32] For the missionaries, what did this mean? It meant that they regarded themselves as bound in conscience to shelter and protect their Indian converts from any spiritually harmful association with non-Christian Indians in the forest. And since, in Alta California, the missionaries stood to their converts as guardians to wards, they had the responsibility, not only of pastors, which was heavy enough, but of parents, which was even more binding.

The Franciscans in Alta California were by no means the first missionaries in Spanish America to follow the line of reasoning that has here been briefly outlined. Missionaries much earlier in the colonial period must surely have recognized the same responsibilities and arrived at the same conclusions. Whatever the reasons the members of the Council of the Indies may have had for enacting the law of February 4, 1604, which required that converted Indians make their residence at the mission to which they were attached, all that was really necessary for them to reach the conclusion they arrived at was the line of argumentation sketched above.[33] To the Spanish missionaries, segregation of converted Indians from their non-Christian brethren in the forest was necessary for daily religious instruction, for effective moral training, for education in the arts of civilization, and for successful avoidance of the occasion of sin. The same chain of logic which provided for a union of Church and state, for Catholicism as the established religion, for the exclusion of all other religions, and for government protection of Catholic subjects (including Indian subjects) in all religious matters led inevitably to the clause in the Laws of the Indies which provided that converted Indians reside in the mission where they belonged.

In the eyes of the Spanish missionaries, the Indians of the forest, though certainly not deprived of divine grace and by no means irretrievably lost, lived in the darkness of ignorance and heathenism, guiltless of serious sin though many of them often were. By means of the missions, Indian converts were to be brought closer to God than they otherwise would be, closer to the truth, to reason, to the observance of the natural moral law, to salvation, to the arts of civilization and to adulthood as it was understood by Europeans. The friars saw their Indian converts as children of the Church and subjects of the Spanish state. They saw the Indians of the forest as children of God, at least potentially. And they saw the missions as enclaves of Spanish Catholicism, culture, and civilization in an alien and barbaric world. They saw the death-rate, too, of course, and helplessly wrung their hands over it, unable to understand why their surgeons and their medicines were unavailing.[34]

In addition to the four reasons given above (daily religious instruction, effective moral training, education in the arts of civilization, and avoidance of the occasion of sin), the friars

had a further reason for insisting that the law which required converted Indians to reside at the missions be observed. It was this. Other things being equal, the longer a given neophyte lived at a mission, the more he learned about Christian conduct and the moral law and the more deeply he absorbed the spirit of the Gospel. In other words, the longer he stayed at a mission, the less able he was to take advantage of the saving principle of inculpable ignorance. Hence, if he were allowed to make his residence somewhere in the wilderness away from the mission, especially a great distance away, and if he should violate the moral law in grave matter, how much shelter would the principle of inculpable ignorance afford him? How serious would his guilt be? Who would know that he needed a priest? Who would hear his confession and absolve him? The *padres* were gravely concerned about Indian converts who returned to the wilderness to live. On July 20, 1775, Fray Junípero Serra wrote to Fernando de Rivera y Moncada, Commander of the *Presidios* of Alta California, as follows: "Now, my dearest Sir, I state to you that those wayward sheep [fugitive neophytes] are my burden, and I am responsible for them not at the treasury in Mexico but at a much higher tribunal than that, and so you should not be surprised if I should be a little importunate in the matter."[35] Other texts of a similar character could easily be quoted.[36]

As for the Indians, they had a perfectly normal tendency to tire of the novelty of mission life after a while and go back to the ways of their ancestors in the forest. Even if, at the missions, there had been no workshifts, no physical punishments and no deaths from white men's diseases, the Indians would have tended to drift back to aboriginal ways anyhow. If some of the neophytes escaped and became fugitives, the *padres*, anxious about the spiritual welfare of their converts, their wards, did their best to get them back. Since the *padres* were the legal guardians of their converts, they were as responsible for them as parents would have been for their children. In other words, Indians who took French leave from their missions were, in the eyes of their legal guardians, in the same position as children who had run away from home. As for the missionaries, their manual of pastoral theology, the *Itinerario*, taught them this principle: if they did not strive perseveringly to correct in their converts faults that were intrinsically wrong (*e.g.*, concubinage, incest, sexual perversion, murder), then they themselves would incur the same guilt the Indians had in committing them.[37] So the *padres* did what they could to return fugitive neophytes to their missions. In doing so, they were trying to fulfill their personal responsibilities as pastors and legal guardians. They were trying to discharge obligations they regarded as serious. They were trying to avoid sins of omission and neglect.

CONCLUSION

In the latter half of the eighteenth century the Catholic Church in Spain was divided. A strong minority of the clergy are now described by historians as "Enlightened Catholics." Open to much of the science and philosophy of the Enlightenment, they espoused the principles of freedom and toleration in the religious sphere and developed an ecumenical spirit.[38] But the majority of the clergy, traditionalist and scholastic, regarded the above-mentioned principles as harmful to religious unity in Spain and the Spanish empire. To the Franciscans of Hispanic California, who seem clearly to have belonged to the latter group, these enlightened concepts would normally have been unwelcome, and to expect the friars to have applied them in the case of fugitive neophytes would be anachronistic.

Without at least a bowing acquaintance with Spanish theology as it was in the eighteenth century, it is impossible to acquire a balanced appreciation of either the missions or the missionaries of Hispanic California. If we leave the

theological manuals of the *padres* unconsulted, the more enigmatic aspects of mission life either remain undecipherable or become the subjects of misconception and anachronism. In obedience to G. K. Chesterton's maxim, it is sometimes useful, even in the academic order, to study familiar objects until they look different.

Notes

1 G. K. Chesterton, *Manalive* (New York: John Lane, 1912).
2 Alonso de la Peña Montenegro, *Itinerario para parochos de Indios* (9th ed.; Amberes: Hermanos de Tournes, 1754).
3 Ibid., Libro I, Tratado X, Sección III, pp. 140–143. Libro II, Tratado VIII, Sección VII, pp. 278–281.
4 Finbar Kenneally, O.F.M. (ed. and trans.), *Writings of Fermín Francisco de Lasuén* (2 vols.; Washington, D.C.: Academy of American Franciscan History, 1965), I, 363.
5 Narciso Durán to the Very Reverend Father Prefect, Santa Cruz Mission, December 28, 1817, Archive of the Archbishop of San Francisco.
6 Kenneally, *Lasuén*, II, 220.
7 Lino Gómez Canedo, "Evangelización y política indigenista. Ideas y actitudes franciscanas en el siglo xvi," *Estudios sobre política indigenista española en América* (3 vols.; Universidad de Valladolid, Semanario de Historia de América, 1975–1977), II, 21–46. Juan de Solórzano Pereira, *De Indiarum Ture* (2 vols.; Lyons, 1672), Vol. I, Book II, Chapter IX, pp. 197–198.
8 Juan de Torquemada, *De los veinte i un libros rituales i monarchia indiana, con el origen y guerras, de los indios occidentales, de sus poblaçones, descubrimiento, conquista, conversion, y otras cosas maravillosas de la mesma tierra distribuydos en tres tomos* (Madrid, 1723), III, Book 18, Chapter 4, pp. 292–3.
9 Gaspar de Villaroel, *Govierno Eclesiástico-Pacífico. Unión de los dos Cuchillos Pontificio y Regio* (2 vols.; Madrid, 1738), II, 192–196.
10 Harry C. Payne, *The Philosophes and the People* (New Haven and London: Yale University Press, 1976), pp. 20–30. Alejandro Filgueira Alvado, "Capacidad intelectual y actitud del indio ante el castellano," *Revista de Indias*, Año xxxix (enero-

diciembre, 1979), Nos. 155–158, pp. 163–186. Juan de Pala-Fox y Mendoza, *Virtudes del Indio* (Madrid: Imprenta de T. Minuesa de los Ríos, 1893), pp. 66–67. Benito Gerónimo Feyjóo, *Teatro critico universal, ó Discursos varios en todo genero de materias, para desengaño de errores comunes* (8 vols.; Madrid, 1765–1779), II, 350–351.

11 Solórzano, *De Indiarum Iure*, Vol. I, Book II, Chapter IX, p. 194.

12 Jerome P. Theisen, O.S.B., *The Ultimate Church and the Promise of Salvation* (Collegeville, Minn.: St. John's University Press, 1976), p. 31.

13 Kenneally, *Lasuén*, II, 216.

14 Maynard Geiger, O.F.M., and Clement W. Meighan, *As The Padres Saw Them: California Indian Life and Customs as Reported by the Franciscan Missionaries, 1813–1815* (Santa Barbara, California: Santa Barbara Mission Archive Library, 1976), p. 25.

15 *Recopilación de leyes de los reinos de las Indias, ley* xix, *título* iii, *libro* vi.

16 Montenegro, *Itinerario, Libro* I, *Tratado* IV, *Sección* I, p. 78.

17 Maynard J. Geiger, O.F.M., Ph.D., *Palou's Life of Fray Junípero Serra* (Washington, D.C.: Academy of American Franciscan History, 1955), p. 232.

18 Montenegro, *Itinerario, Libro* II, *Tratado* X, *Sección* III, pp. 139-140.

19 Antonine Tibesar, O.F.M. (ed.), *Writings of Junípero Serra* (4 vols.; Washington, D.C.: Academy of American Franciscan History, 1965–1975), I, 209, 257, 313, 315, 347, 363; II, 197.

20 Geiger, *Palóu's Life*, p. 232.

21 Ibid.

22 Kenneally, *Lasuén*, II, 276–279, 220. Geiger and Meighan, *As The Padres*, pp. 105–106. Sherburne F. Cook, *The Conflict Between the California Indian and White Civilization* (Berkeley and Los Angeles: University of California Press, 1976), pp. 103–107.

23 Pablo Vicente de Solá to the Viceroy, Monterey, June 2, 1816, Santa Barbara Mission Archive–Library.

24 Geiger, *Palóu's Life*, p. 232.

25 Kenneally, *Lasuén*, II, 231.

26 Ibid., p. 214.

27 Francis F. Guest, O.F.M., "Cultural Perspectives on California Mission Life," *Southern California Quarterly*, Vol. LXV (Spring, 1983), pp. 1–65. Compare pp. 23–24 and Notes 81–84.

28 Kenneally, *Lasuén*, II, 276.

29 Ibid., II, 277.

30 José Señán to Lasuén, Mission San Buenaventura, October 21, 1800, Archivo General de la Nación, Mexico, Provincias Internas 216. Cited hereinafter as AGN. Estevan Tapis to Lasuén, Mission Santa Barbara, October 30, 1800, AGN, Provincias Internas 216. Otto von Kotzebue, *A Voyage of Discovery into the South Sea and Bering's Straits, for the purpose of exploring a northeast passage, undertaken in the years 1815–1818 . . . in the ship Rurik* (3 vols.; London, 1821), III, 43–47.

31 Kenneally, *Lasuén*, II, 215.

32 Antonio a San Joseph, *Compendium Salmanticense* (4th ed.; 2 vols.; Pampeluna, 1791), I, 208–210. Nos. 192–203.

33 Compare Note 15. The date of the law is February 4, 1604.

34 Mariano Payeras to the Father Guardian and the Discretorium of the College of San Fernando, La Purísima, February 2, 1820, AGN, Historia de Mexico, Primera Serie, Tomo 2. Narciso Durán to the Mexican Government, San José Mission, May 22, 1826, AGN, Colección de Documentos para la Historia de Mexico, Segunda Serie, Tomo 4, ff. 178–183.

35 Tibesar, *Serra*, II, 285.

36 Ibid., II, 43; III, 407–415.

37 Montenegro, *Itinerario, Libro* I, *Tratado* IV, *Sección* II, pp. 80–81. The sins mentioned in the text, *viz.*, concubinage, incest, sexual perversion, and murder, are given as examples of offenses that, in Catholic doctrine, are considered intrinsically evil. There is no implication, in this context, that all the tribelets of Alta California practiced or even tolerated incest.

38 María Giovanna Tomsich, *El Jansenismo en España: Estudio sobre ideas religiosas en la segunda mitad del siglo xviii* (Madrid: siglo veintiuno, 1972), *passim*. William J. Callahan, "Two Spains and Two Churches," *Historical Reflections*, II (Winter, 1976), 157–182.

VIEWS FROM THE OUTSIDE

EDITOR'S INTRODUCTION

The earliest views we have of California and its people come from the journals of those hearty Europeans, such as Juan Rodríguez Cabrillo, who sailed along the Pacific coast in the sixteenth and early seventeenth centuries. Unfortunately, these views are fragmentary and incomplete. More thorough accounts began in the eighteenth century with the arrival of the Spanish missionaries. In their writings we find fascinating glimpses of the California landscape, but frustratingly little information about the culture of the Indians in their charge.

One of the richest sources for the study of early California history is the body of travel literature produced by geographers, diplomats, sea captains, and traders from England, France, and Russia who visited California during the years when the region was a Spanish and Mexican province. These outside observers were often highly literate and acute, and the official accounts of their sojourns in California constitute the first sustained attempt to describe the region and its inhabitants.

California often appears in these early travel narratives as a place of abundance and great potential, while the people of California are portrayed as somehow unworthy of the land they possessed. The California Indians are pictured as incredible primitives; the Spanish-speaking residents as both cruel and incompetent. Special criticism is reserved for the missions and their alleged oppression of the natives.

The images of Indians and missions in this European travel literature initiated a tradition of perception and description that was later shared by Anglo-American visitors to California. To a remarkable extent early visitors from the United States ordered their impressions of California along the lines established by their European predecessors. Anglo-American visitors continued the tradition of portraying the California Indians as hapless primitives, victims of Hispanic exploitation and cruelty.

The policy of enforced residence at the missions, discussed by Francis F. Guest in the previous selection, was especially troubling to many outside observers. European and American visitors frequently criticized the Hispanos in California for their use of armed force to recapture escaped mission Indians. In the winter of 1833–1834, for example, a group of neophytes escaped from Mission San Juan Bautista, taking with them about three hundred horses. The local authorites sent a group of soldiers to recapture the runaway Indians and to retrieve the missing horses. A party of American beaver trappers happened to observe the work of the expedition as it attacked the camp of mission runaways. As the soldiers came upon the fugitives' camp they found that it was nearly deserted; the horses were mostly killed, and their meat was stretched to dry. Beaver trapper Zenas Leonard described the scene: "By way of revenge... the Spaniards fell to massacring indiscriminately those helpless creatures who were found in the wigwams with the meat, and cutting off their ears. Some of them were driven into a wigwam, when the door was barricaded, and a large quantity of combustible matter thrown on and around the hut, for the purpose of setting fire to it, and burning them all together."[1] The American trappers attempted unsuccessfully to prevent the slaughter, and Leonard denounced the soldiers for their "barbarous treatment" of the Indians.

James J. Rawls, in his *Indians of California: The Changing Image* (1984), demonstrates that while white observers consistently described the California Indians as primitives, their attitudes toward these "primitives" changed dramatically over the generations of contact. He argues that the driving force in this evolution of attitudes was the changing needs of the white observers. In the following selection, Rawls describes the earliest images of the Indians and missions which appeared in the European travel literature of the late eighteenth and early nineteenth centuries. The hostile images of the missions in this literature stand as a rejoinder to Fr. Guest's contention that to judge the missions by the standards of the Enlightenment would be anachronistic. These contemporary views also remind us of the abiding importance of self-interest in the shaping of all such imagery.

James J. Rawls, editor of this volume, received his Ph.D. from the University of California, Berkeley, in 1975. He teaches California and American history at Diablo Valley College, Pleasant Hill.

[1]Zenas Leonard, *Narrative of the Adventures of Zenas Leonard* (Chicago, 1934), 190.

Views From the Outside

James J. Rawls

When Jean François Galaup de La Pérouse and the crews of the *Boussole and Astrolabe* anchored their ships in Monterey Bay in September, 1786, they became the first foreign visitors to call on the Spanish frontier outposts in Alta California. Even before disembarking, La Pérouse, the leader of this official round-the-world voyage of exploration and discovery, was impressed by the abundance of life in California. He recorded in his journal that the ships were surrounded by a herd of spouting whales and that the surface of the bay was covered with cavorting pelicans. After putting in to Monterey for several weeks, La Pérouse cataloged the extraordinary abundance of California wildlife: seals, hares, rabbits, stags, bears, foxes, wolves, wildcats, partridges, woodpeckers, sparrows and titmice. Conditions in California seemed ideal for the flourishing of living things: "There is not any country in the world, which more abounds in fish and game of every description," La Pérouse observed. The abundance of flourishing wildlife, the unusually salubrious climate, the "inexpressible fertility," and the breathtaking natural beauty, seemed to La Pérouse (and later to a host of others) the outstanding characteristics of California.[1]

Reflecting growing international interest in California, such descriptions were often followed by remarks on the apparent failure or inability of the Spanish-speaking colonists properly to appreciate or exploit the natural riches of California. As if the implications of such comments were not clear enough, some visitors went on to note the vulnerability of

Adapted from *Indians of California: The Changing Image,* by James J. Rawls, pp. 26–43. Copyright © 1984 by the University of Oklahoma Press.

California, its sparse population, and its weak defenses.[2] "At first one is astonished," wrote Captain Cyrille Pierre La Place, of the frigate *l'Artémise,* in 1837, "that this...country, so beautiful, so fertile and at the same time so easy to take, has not yet become the prey of the great nations of the Old World." The present owners of the area he viewed with disgust as both ignorant and lazy.[3] Likewise, British visitors, such as George Vancouver and Frederick Beechey, found it incredible that a land of such beauty, fertility, good climate, and capacious harbors should be allowed to lie fallow. The remarks of Francis Simpkinson, a midshipman aboard the *HMS Sulphur,* were typical: "In possession of a beautiful and fertile country where anything might be produced, and blessed with a climate like that of Italy, the Californians might if they pleased soon raise themselves to wealth and importance, but that unfortunate spirit of indolence which alike pervades all classes completely destroys these blessings."[4]

Nothing was more striking to these early visitors than the contrast between the land of California and its unworthy, indolent population. California, with all its abundance, fertility, natural beauty, and potential for wealth, required a population worthy of developing it. These early visitors might disagree over who among them was worthy of this land, but most could agree that the present colonizers were inadequate.

THE PRIMITIVES OF CALIFORNIA

What of the California Indians? What place do they occupy in these early accounts of life in California? Almost invariably the natives of California were described in these early travel accounts as exceedingly primitive in comparison not only with Europeans but also with other Indian cultures. The familiar (and often incorrect) contrasts were made between the wandering and nonagrarian nature of Indian "savagery" and European sedentary and agrarian "civilization." What stands out, however, is the degree of primitiveness attributed to the California Indians.[5]

Several elements of aboriginal culture were repeatedly cited by these early visitors as evidence of the extreme primitiveness of the California Indians. The near nudity of the natives, for example, frequently elicited comparisons between Indians and other "wild beasts" of the forest.[6] The conical reed houses and tule-reed boats that were common along the central California coast were considered evidence of the Indians' inability to fashion more sophisticated structures. Captain Vancouver, for example, upon sighting tule boats on San Francisco Bay, commented that they were without exception "the most rude and sorry contrivances" that he had ever seen. La Pérouse described the native houses around Monterey—made of long poles stuck in the earth and pulled together to form arches and covered with bundles of thatch—as "the most miserable that are to be met with among any people."[7] The Indians' watertight cooking baskets, feathered arrows, and headdresses evoked more positive comments, but such items were usually regarded as impressive exceptions to the general barrenness of Indian culture.[8] "However dull and heavy, however filthy, ugly, and disgusting, these people appear," wrote Georg Heinrich von Langsdorff in his narrative of the California voyage of Count Nikolai Petrovich Rezanov in 1806, "yet they show a great fondness for ornaments and sports."[9]

Many of the early European visitors viewed the complexion, physiognomy, and stature of the California Indians as the most damning evidence of their extreme "brutishness" and "stupidity."[10] During his visit to San Francisco in 1817, Lieutenant Camille de Roquefeuil

stated that the Indians of California were short and squat with neither grace nor vigor and that "their faces bear the imprint of apathy and stupidity."[11] Abel Du Petit-Thouars, captain of the *Venus* on a voyage of scientific and commercial exploration in the 1830s saw the Costanoans at Mission San Carlos Borromeo as having unusually dark skin, black hair, large mouths and "a stupid air which in general corresponds to their intelligence, not much higher than that of animals."[12] Langsdorff likewise described the Indians of San Francisco as badly proportioned with a dull, heavy, and neglected appearance. Neither he nor the crew could recall having seen "the human race on such a low level."[13]

These early visitors often wondered how to account for the presence of peoples whom they considered to be among the world's most primitive in a country possessing such an ideal climate, rich abundant wildlife, and fertile soil. Although outside observers regarded the Spanish and Mexican populations as unworthy of such a land, the Hispanos were, after all, relatively recent arrivals in California. It was contemptible that they had failed to develop California or appreciably to benefit from its landscape, but it was not nearly as puzzling as the supposed anomaly of the California Indians. The Europeans wondered how it was that they after hundreds of generations had not benefited more from their environment. This question—or, more broadly, the problem of accounting for the extreme primitiveness of most of the California tribes—was the prime intellectual problem posed by the Indians of California in the minds of their early European observers. It was stated most clearly by the German-born physician Georg Heinrich von Langsdorff. After his stay in San Francisco in the spring of 1806, during which he had time for considerable observation and comment on the local Indian population, Langsdorff was left puzzled:

Although it must be allowed generally, as facts incontestible, that a moderate climate is the most favorable to the human species, and that the mild regions of the globe are those which nature points out to man as the most friendly for his habitation, yet here we find a most striking exception to the general rule.

Here, on this western coast of North America, in the thirty-eighth degree of north latitude, where the aborigines live in a very moderate and equable climate, where there is no lack of food and no care about habitations or clothing...where an abundance of roots, seeds, fruits, and the products of the sea, in many varieties are at their hands,— these people are, notwithstanding, small, ugly, and of bad proportion in their persons, and heavy and dull in their minds....I frankly acknowledge that the phenomenon of these Californian pigmies, in such a mild climate, and with an abundance of food, is to me a puzzle.[14]

Two separate solutions were suggested to this problem, one of which may be termed environmental, and the other historical. The environmentalists argued that the primitiveness of California Indians was a natural product of their idyllic environment. This was an interesting local expression of the larger controversy during the late eighteenth and early nineteenth centuries over the origins of the diversity of mankind. As the horizons of European knowledge had expanded, the multiplicity of new plants, animals, and human beings had created an acute problem for the natural scientists of the Enlightenment. The preferred explanation for the diversity came to be environmental: different climates and physical landscapes were believed to be responsible for different forms of life and different human cultures. Specifically, the environment of North America was responsible for the peculiar flora, fauna, and people of the New World.

Further debate raged, however, over the nature of that environment and the quality of the life that it had produced. The great French naturalist Comte Georges de Buffon argued that

the insalubrious physical environment of the Western Hemisphere was responsible for the deficiencies both of American wildlife and of the American Indian. Thomas Jefferson denied that analysis and argued for the superiority of the American environment and of its natural products, human and otherwise. There was a curious twist to the dispute in California, in that the European visitors argued that the *superior* natural environment of California had somehow created an *inferior* people. They argued that the abundance of wildlife and the temperate climate of the area had made life too easy for the California Indians.[15]

Claude François Lambert, for example, praised the region's fertility, abundance, and climate. The soil was so rich, he noted, and the seasons were so perfect that plants bore three times a year instead of just once. In all its natural products California was flourishing; Lambert even stated that in the spring a "kind of manna" fell that was as sweet as sugar. Yet in this ideal setting the California Indians remained primitive. Lambert found the explanation in the natural abundance of California: "Tho' heaven has been so bountiful to the [California Indians], and tho' their soil spontaneously produces what does not grow elsewhere without a great deal of trouble and pains, yet they have no regard to the riches and abundance of their life, they are little solicitous about everything else." In such a setting only the most primitive devices were necessary to survive. Weapons remained simple; clothing was unnecessary; housing was of only casual concern. "The trees defend them from the heat of the sun by day," Lambert observed, "and of the branches and leaves they make a kind of bower, to screen themselves from the injuries of the nocturnal air."[16]

The environmental solution to Langsdorff's puzzle found its fullest development in the memoirs of Russian visitor Kirill Timofeevich Khlebnikov. Seeking to account for the primitiveness of the California Indians, whom he acknowledged were often described as stupid, Khlebnikov argued that their circumstances did not require them to be intelligent. Among the circumstances that he described were the "climate and environment" of California, which so readily supplied the natives with food: "The oak produces acorns, which comprise the chief provision; in many places wild rye grows, the grain of which is gathered by the Indians. In the ground they find many hamsters, Siberian marmots, mice, frogs, etc., which make up their diet." Khlebnikov then proceeded to describe the abundance of larger game as well—geese, ducks, mountain sheep, goats, and deer. Furthermore, since the climate was so mild, the natives had no need of elaborate shelters and thus could "find refuge in the hollows of big trees, in mountain clefts or in tents made of twigs." Likewise, Khlebnikov observed, "The climate does not compel them to dress in skins or textile fabrics. Men and women go around nude." After cataloguing these and other examples, Khlebnikov concluded:

> Since the native in his primitive condition readily finds his chief needs, food and shelter, everywhere, there is consequently no reason for exerting his intellectual capacities in improving his state; he thinks that of all the inhabitants of the entire world, those of neighboring territories or territories rumored of, he is the happiest. Perhaps it is this mode of life that is responsible for his deep ignorance.[17]

In contrast to Khlebnikov, other visitors to California speculated that the condition of the California tribes was caused more by historical than by environmental factors. Visitors often noted the contrasts between the "heavy and dull" mission neophytes and the more "lively" unconverted Indians.[18] Captain Du Petit-Thouars, for example, was struck by the difference between "the entirely independent Indians who live far from the missions" and the "dull and unintelligent" mission neophytes. "One cannot help thinking," he concluded,

"that perhaps the state of idiocy in which they are found may be due to the cloistered life and to the slavery to which they have been bound since infancy."[19] Where others had found in the natural conditions an explanation for the primitiveness that they perceived in the California Indians, Du Petit-Thouars speculated that the explanation lay in that "unnatural" feature of the landscape the mission.

THE CALIFORNIA MISSIONS

Beginning with La Pérouse in 1786, a description of the missions and a judgment on their effectiveness was de rigueur for early visitors to California. For better or worse, the early image of the California Indians and that of the California missions were intimately joined. There was always disagreement over the nature of the missions, but most observers viewed them critically and expressed a considerable degree of sympathy for the Indians. In this critical view the California Indians figured as victims of an oppressive institution, as slaves who possessed rights that were violated and whose limited potential was not being developed. The Indians' natural rights to private property and to liberty were denied; their daily lives were made miserable by frequent and harsh corporal punishment. Some observers charged that not only were the Indians held to the missions by force but also many had been originally recruited by force. In spite of the often-noted productivity of the missions, critics maintained that the mission Indians were receiving inadequate instruction in practical skills and that their religious instruction was shallow and ineffective. Later visitors concluded that the rapid depopulation of coastal California was a direct result of Spanish efforts at missionization.

La Pérouse's *Voyage Round the World*, published in 1797, was the first account of Hispanic California by an outsider, and accurately foreshadowed the sensibilities of many subsequent visitors. In a familiar passage La Pérouse de-

scribed the scene at Mission San Carlos Borromeo, which reminded him of a slave
plantation in the West Indies: "The men and
women are assembled by the sound of the
bell, one of the religious conducts them to
their work, to church, and to all other exer-
cises. We mention it with pain, the resemblance is so perfect, that we saw men and
women loaded with irons, others in the
stocks; and at length the noise of the strokes
of a whip struck our ears." La Pérouse,
however, was careful to distinguish between
the missionaries who were "individually humane and good" and the institution of the
mission, which he regarded as reprehensible.
What most disturbed him was the delegation
to the missionaries of absolute temporal and
spiritual power over the neophytes, which he
judged to be a violation of the Enlightenment
ideals of equality and "the rights of man." He
condemned the missions for inflicting corporal punishments for acts that were not considered criminal offenses in Europe and for not
allowing the neophytes to renounce their
vows and freely return to their native villages.
Those who attempted to leave the mission, he
noted, were forced to return by squads of
soldiers and then publicly flogged. Even
within the mission the neophytes' freedom
was restricted. For example, the single men
and women were locked in separate dormito-
ries at night.[20]

La Pérouse questioned whether the
authoritarian structure of the missions, the
corporal punishments, and the denial of freedom
were necessarily the most effective means to deal
with the Indians. He argued that "even these"
backward people perhaps had a sense of justice,
which, when violated, rendered all efforts to
"civilize" them a failure. He asked whether it
would be possible to convince at least some of
the Indians of "the advantages of a society
founded on the rights of the people." La Pérouse
suggested that perhaps the missionaries were
underestimating the potential of the California
Indians. Their efforts at "civilizing" the natives
were undercut by their own prejudice: persuaded
that "the reason of these men is never clear," the
padres considered themselves justified in treating
the Indians like children. As they were
constituted, La Pérouse concluded, the California
missions were "by no means calculated" to free
the Indians from their "state of ignorance."[21]

That La Pérouse was not alone in his criticisms of the missions should be clear to anyone
who reads through the subsequent European
travel literature of the late eighteenth and early
nineteenth centuries.[22] For example, the narrative of Auguste Bernard Duhaut-Cilly's voyage
in the 1820s contains an extensive critique of
the mission system. Duhaut-Cilly asked, "What
do the padres demand from the Indians of
Upper California?" and replied, "A little labor
in exchange for abundant nourishment, good
clothing and the benefits of civilization." He
concluded, "In spite of these evident advantages the instinct of liberty is there crying to
them to prefer to this quiet, though monotonous, state, the poor and uncertain life of their
woods and their marshes."

Duhaut-Cilly pictured the California Indians
as engaged in a heroic struggle against the
mission system. When asked by Mexican authorities to transport three Indians who were
charged with some unspecified crime, Duhaut-
Cilly reluctantly agreed but then allowed them
to escape. While on board the *Héros*, Duhaut-
Cilly reported proudly, the Indians were given
their freedom—for France had no slavery, and
they were then on French soil. He noted that
they "at no time failed to conduct themselves
most exemplarily; but they knew that, in a few
days they should again find their fetters and
their tyrants." Duhaut-Cilly described several
instances in which Indians had escaped from
"bad treatment" in the missions and had been
pursued and punished by their "oppressors."
The expeditions to recover mission runaways
were condemned by Duhaut-Cilly as an "atro-
cious system."[23]

Duhaut-Cilly's belief that the California Indians were victims of a system of oppression is most clearly revealed in his description of Pomponio, an escaped Costanoan from Mission Dolores. In this remarkable passage a California Indian emerges as a truly heroic figure.

Among the Indians, of whom the larger part seem to be so submissive, there are some who know the prize of liberty, and who seek to gain it by flight. They easily succeed in escaping, but they are often retaken by emissaries sent in their pursuit by the missionaries and the commandants of the soldiers; and without considering that these men have done nothing but make use of the most natural right, they are generally treated as criminals, and pitilessly put in irons.

One of these unfortunate creatures, after several attempts to flee from his oppressors, had at last been condemned to die in irons by the commandant of San Francisco. It is true Pomponio, so he was called, had added to the offense of his numerous desertions, thefts and even murders of some of those appointed to bring him back to his prison. He bore upon each leg an enormous iron ring, riveted on in such a way as to leave him no hope of freeing himself from it; but this man, gifted with an energy and a courage proof against the most frightful tortures, conceives yet once more the plan of freeing himself, and he carries it out. When all his watchers are plunged in sleep, he sharpens a knife, cuts off his heel and slips off one of his fetters; thus, without uttering the least sigh, he mutilates himself in a nervous and sensitive part. But imagine what strength of mind he needs to begin again this cruel operation; for he has yet gained only half of his freedom! He hesitates not; he takes off the other heel and flees, without fearing the acute pain which each step adds to his sufferings: it is by his bloody tracks that his escape is discovered the next day.[24]

Like La Pérouse forty years earlier, Duhaut-Cilly wondered whether a more humane method of dealing with the Indians might not be possible.[25]

Other elements of La Pérouse's critique can be seen throughout the subsequent travel literature. Some observers, for example, criticized the use of military force to recruit or capture neophytes and the use of corporal punishment within the missions.[26] The criticism was sometimes mild, sometimes scathing. Dr. John Coulter, a British visitor, reported the possibility of forced recruitment or "kidnapping" of Indians for the missions and described in a tone of bemused indifference the whipping of neophytes who were late for mass.[27] In contrast, the Russian otter hunter Vassilli Petrovitch Tarakanoff described similar scenes—and worse—with suppressed horror. Tarakanoff had been captured by the Spaniards at San Pedro and held captive for over a year at Santa Barbara or San Fernando. His narrative of that experience includes scenes of vicious torture and cruelty: "From all I saw," he wrote, "I must say the Spaniards are bad men." At one point he described a group of neophytes who had left the mission and were being brought back by soldiers and priests:

They were all bound with rawhide ropes and some were bleeding from wounds and some children were tied to their mothers.

The next day we saw some terrible things.

Some of the run-away men were tied on sticks and beaten with straps. One chief was taken out to the open field and a young calf which had just died was skinned and the chief was sewed into the skin while it was yet warm. He was kept tied to a stake all day, but he died soon and they kept his corpse tied up.[28]

Perhaps the most serious charge made against the missions was that they were responsible for ill health and death among the Indians of California.[29] Du Petit-Thouars, for example, described the "cruel ravages" of fevers, smallpox, measles, and dysentery among the neophyte populations. "The state of ill health does not extend to the uncivilized Indians," observed Beechey, and Du Petit-Thouars also noted that the "independent Indians" were "less subject to disease than those who live at the missions."[30] The poor health, disease, and high mortality rate among the neophytes led some visitors to speculate whether it was possible for the Indians to survive the process of being "civilized" at the missions: Would the ultimate result of the missions be Indian "civilization" or Indian extinction?[31]

Before leaving this consideration of early European views of the California Indians, we should note that not all comment on the missionary enterprise in Alta California was hostile. The missions had their defenders and, after secularization, a long line of eulogizers. In this more positive view the Indians were pictured not as exploited victims but rather as beneficiaries of the blessings of Hispanic civilization. The emphasis was on uplift and amelioration. The major concerns of mission defenders were either to demonstrate that the California Indians had in fact benefited from the missions or, less frequently, to explain why they had not much benefited. In either case the aboriginal cultures of the natives were described almost wholly in negative terms. On the one hand, the missions were to be admired for their success in substituting an obviously superior culture for an inferior one, yet, on the other hand, any failure to accomplish their noble enterprise was no fault of the missionaries but due instead to the hopeless primitiveness of the California Indians. Thus the defenders of the missions might deny that the California Indians were victims, but they shared the view of the mission critics that the natives of California were indeed primitive.

Shortly after La Pérouse's visit in 1786, California welcomed one of the mission system's most enthusiastic defenders, Captain Alejandro Malaspina. Malaspina's voyage of scientific discovery, including his visit to California in 1791, has been described as "probably Spain's greatest exploratory contribution to the age of enlightenment."[32] Although both Malaspina and La Pérouse may be considered products of the Enlightenment, their reactions to the mission system were considerably different. In describing Alta California, Malaspina felt compelled to refute the "ridiculous inventions of many foreign authors, who confusing at times the system with the abuses, and ignoring always the primary object of such establishments, have painted all our missions in America as horrible and oppressive." There was no question in Malaspina's mind that the missionaries had accomplished a great good. The Spanish priests had brought to the Indians, "without the slightest shedding of blood, the end of a thousand local wars that were destroying them, social beginnings, a pure and holy religion, [and] safe and healthy foods." He considered these accomplishments even more impressive because of the extreme backwardness of the local Indians, whom he described as "certainly little ready for rapid progress in civilization." He reported that with the exception of the Chumash of Santa Barbara the natives of California demonstrated an incredible ineptitude in learning the simplest tasks taught them by the missionaries. In his view, the missionaries' work was so difficult and their accomplishment so remarkable because the California Indian was so nearly a beast—the subject of "animal instincts" which "degrade him, make him stupid, and almost convert his life into a living picture of that of irrational beings."[33]

CONCLUSION

The early chroniclers of Hispanic California invariably focused their attention on the relations between the Indians and the Spanish-speaking colonists, and generally their sympathies lay with the former rather than the latter. Many of these early visitors judged the Spaniards and Mexicans as unworthy of California and vigorously criticized the most conspicuous institution of their colonization, the mission. The dominant image of California Indians in this early travel literature is of a primitive people who were victims of Hispanic mistreatment and exploitation.

How are we to account for this image? Part of the explanation is that the missions of California were indeed paternalistic and authoritarian institutions. Outside observers, bringing with them values shaped by the Enlightenment, judged the missions to be incompatible with their ideals of equality, liberty, and justice. The image, however, was also a clear reflection of the self-interest of the observers.

Long before settlement of Alta California the imperial rivals of Spain had been condemning Spaniards elsewhere for their mistreatment of the Indians of the Americas. The unflattering comments of La Pérouse and the other critics of Hispanic California were latter-day manifestations of a tradition of criticism of Spanish colonialism that began in the sixteenth century. In 1552, Bartolomé de Las Casas had published his scathing indictment of his countrymen's relations with the Indians of the New World. Although Las Casas hoped that his book would influence the Spanish crown to provide effective protection for the Indians, its most lasting result was to supply the enemies of Spain with ammunition in their verbal assaults on the Spanish empire. French, Dutch, and English propagandists over the next two and a half centuries produced a considerable literature, inevitably citing Las Casas as one of their sources, which described in bloody detail the horrors of Spanish mistreatment of the Indians. Collectively this literature formed a part of what came to be known as "La Leyenda Negra," or "the Black Legend," in which the Spaniards stood accused of gross misconduct in their relations with the Indians.[34]

The Black Legend, which had its roots in European rivalries that existed even before the discovery of America, flourished as the imperial competitors of Spain sought to establish their own claims to the New World. Because Spain was the earliest European power to lay claim to the hemisphere, it was incumbent upon later arrivals to discredit in some fashion the Spanish presence. The Black Legend thrived among those who needed a rationale to challenge or evict Spaniards from their possessions. The argument was plain enough: because the Spaniards had demonstrated such unconscionable cruelty and exploitation in their dealings with the native peoples of the New World, their claims should be invalidated, and more humane colonizers should take over, rescue the Indians, and develop the land in a proper way. By the late sixteenth century, with the growing ideological division of Europe into Protestant and Catholic, the anti-Hispanicism of the Black Legend had become heavily mixed with anti-Catholicism. Thus the church within the Spanish empire came under particular attack for either permitting or perpetuating cruelties toward the Indians.

Of course, not all visitors to Latin America came away with a negative impression of the Spaniards and their treatment of the native peoples. As we have seen in California, observers disagreed among themselves in evaluating Spanish intentions and accomplishments. The positive view of Spanish-Indian relations became part of a so-called White Legend, in which Spaniards were pictured as especially humane, just, enlightened, and energetic. One finds, however, that during times of conflict between Spain and its rivals images in the tradition of the Black Legend predominated. Such conflicts were particularly common during the early years of colonization, but Black Legend propaganda flourished as late as the mid-eighteenth century.[35]

The early European criticisms of the Hispanic enterprise in California and the image of California Indians as the victims of oppression are best understood when placed in the larger context of the Black Legend tradition. The expeditions initiated by La Pérouse in 1786 demonstrated the growing international interest in California, and the image of the mistreated and exploited California natives proved useful to those who wished to discredit the Spanish or Mexican presence in California.

Notes

1 Jean François Galaup de La Pérouse, *A Voyage Round the World in the Years 1785, 1786, 1787, and 1788*, ed. M. L. A. Milet-Mureau, 2:195–96, 202–204, passim. See also Claude François Lambert, *Curious Observations upon the Manners, Customs, Usages...of the Several Nations of Asia, Africa, and America* 1:123–33; George Verne Blue, ed., "The Report of Captain La Place on His Voyage to the Northwest Coast and California in 1839," *California Historical Society Quarterly*, 18 (March, 1939): 319–23; Abel Du Petit-Thouars, *Voyage of the Venus: Sojourn in California*, trans. Charles N. Rudkin, pp. 33–37; William Finley Shepard, ed., "California Prior to Conquest: A Frenchman's Views," *California Historical Society Quarterly* 37 (March, 1958): 71; August C. Mahr, *The Visit of the "Rurik" to San Francisco in 1816*, pp. 77–79; Georg Heinrich von Langsdorff, *Langsdorff's Narrative of the Rezanov Voyage to Nueva California in 1806*, ed. and trans. Thomas C. Russell, pp. 62–64; Frederick William Beechey, *Narrative of a Voyage to the Pacific and Beering's Strait ...in the Years 1825, 26, 27, 28* 2:66-67; Francis Guillemard Simpkinson and Edward Belcher, *H.M.S. Sulphur at California, 1837 and 1839*, ed. Richard A. Pierce and John W. Winslow, pp. 21–22; Albert M. Gilliam, *Travels in Mexico During the Years 1843 and 44*, p. 288; Alejandro Malaspina, *Malaspina in California*, ed. Donald C.Cutter, p. 53.

2 Beechey, *Narrative of a Voyage* 2:66–67; Gilliam, *Travels in Mexico*, p. 288. On the growing imperial interest in California see Robert Glass Cleland, *The Early Sentiment for the Annexation of California: An Account of the Growth of American Interest in California from 1835 to 1846;* Abraham P. Nasatir, *French Activities in California: An Archival Calendar Guide;* Rufus Kay Willys, "French Imperialists in California," *California Historical Society Quarterly* 8 (June, 1929): 166–219; and the several articles on Rus-

sian interest in the same journal, vol. 12 (September, 1933).

3 As quoted in Blue, "The Report of Captain La Place," pp. 319, 323.

4 Simpkinson, *H.M.S. Sulphur at California*, pp. 21–22.

5 See La Pérouse, *Voyage Round the World* 2:197. See also Simpkinson, *H.M.S. Sulphur at California*, p. 17; Adelbert von Chamisso in Mahr, ed., *Visit of the "Rurik,"* p. 83; Malaspina, *Malaspina in California*, p. 53; Eugene Duflot de Mofras, *Duflot de Mofras' Travels on the Pacific Coast*, ed. and trans. Marguerite Eyer Wilbur, vol. 2, p. 188; and George Vancouver, *Vancouver in California, 1792–1794: The Original Account of George Vancouver*, ed. Marguerite Eyer Wilbur, pp. 11, 26, 42.

6 See, for example, Beechey, *Narrative of a Voyage* 2:17, 51, 77; Langsdorff, *Langsdorff's Narrative*, pp. 55–57; Simpkinson and Belcher, *H.M.S. Sulphur at California*, pp. 17, 39, 45; Edmond Le Netrel, *Voyage of the Héros Around the World with Duhaut-Cilly in the Years 1826, 1827, 1828 & 1829*, trans. Blanche Collet Wagner, p. 39. Alfred Kroeber has noted that in many parts of California "all men went wholly naked except when the weather enforced protection" (Kroeber, *Elements of Culture in Native California*, p. 260).

7 Vancouver, *Vancouver in California*, pp. 11, 26–28, 65; La Pérouse, *Voyage Round the World* 2:211.

8 Beechey, *Narrative of a Voyage* 2:57, 75; Chamisso and Louis Choris, in Mahr, ed., *Visit of the "Rurik,"* pp. 85, 99–101; Langsdorff, *Langsdorff's Narrative*, p. 58; Du Petit-Thouars, *Voyage of the Venus*, pp. 48–49; Kirill T. Khlebnikov, "Memoirs of California," trans. Anatole G. Mazour, *Pacific Historical Review* 9 (Sept., 1940): 333; August Bernard Duhaut-Cilly, "Duhaut-Cilly's Account of California in the Years 1827-1828," trans. Charles F. Carter, *California Historical Society Quarterly*, 8 (December, 1929): 314; Alexander Markoff, *The Russians on the Pacific Coast*, trans. Ivan Petroff, p. 60.

9 Langsdorff, *Langsdorff's Narrative*, pp. 57–59. Cf. Beechey, *Narrative of a Voyage* 2:74–77.

10 Vancouver, *Vancouver in California*, p. 26; Duhaut-Cilly, "Duhaut-Cilly's Account of Cali-

fornia," pp. 313–314; Otto von Kotzebue, in Mahr, ed., *Visit of the "Rurik,"* p. 61.

11 Camille de Roquefeuil, *Camille de Roquefeuil in San Francisco, 1817–1818,* ed. and trans. Charles N. Rudkin, p. 71.

12 Du Petit-Thouars, *Voyage of the Venus,* pp. 48–49.

13 Langsdorff, *Langsdorff's Narrative,* p. 57.

14 Langsdorff, *Langsdorff's Narrative,* pp. 62–63.

15 For a discussion of "environmentalism" see Robert F. Berkhofer, Jr., *The White Man's Indian: Images of the American Indian from Columbus to the Present,* pp. 38–44. On views in California see, for example, Malaspina, *Malaspina in California,* p. 53; José Bandini, *A Description of California in 1828,* trans. Doris Marion Wright, p. 18.

16 Lambert, *Curious Observations* 1:128–131.

17 Khlebnikov, "Memoirs of California," p. 333.

18 Vancouver, *Vancouver in California,* pp. 93–104, 139, 148–149; Du Petit-Thouars, *Voyage of the Venus,* p. 83; Beechey, *Narrative of a Voyage* 2:13, 19, 21, 24, 29–34; George Simpson, *Narrative of a Voyage to California Ports in 1841–42,* pp. 53–54, 60–67, 132.

19 Du Petit-Thouars, *Voyage of the Venus,* p. 77.

20 La Pérouse, *Voyage Round the World* 2:201–206, 212–214, 218–220.

21 Ibid., 2:205, 213–216, 220, 225.

22 Chamisso, in Mahr, ed., *Visit of the "Rurik,"* p. 81; Du Petit-Thouars, *Voyage of the Venus,* p. 40; Rosamel, in Shepard, "California Prior to Conquest," p. 66; Heinrich Künzel, *Upper California,* trans. Anthony and Max Knight, p. 45.

23 Duhaut-Cilly, "Duhaut-Cilly's Account of California," pp. 214–215, 242, 317.

24 Ibid., 215, 242.

25 Ibid., 215, 317.

26 Kotzebue, Chamisso, and Choris, in Mahr, ed., *Visit of the "Rurik,"* pp. 61–63, 81–83, 95;

Khlebnikov, "Memoirs of California," pp. 312, 334; Langsdorff, *Langsdorff's Narrative,* pp. 47–48, 66–68; Beechey, *Narrative of a Voyage* 2:17–19, 21–33; Thomas Coulter, *Notes on Upper California: A Journey from Monterey to the Colorado River in 1832,* pp. 24–27.

27 John Coulter, *Adventures on the Western Coast of South America and in the Interior of California* 1:168–170.

28 Vassilli Petrovitch Tarakanoff, *Statement of My Captivity Among the Californians,* trans. Ivan Petroff, pp. 15–18.

29 Coulter, *Notes on Upper California,* p. 26; Le Netrel, *Voyage of the Héros,* pp. 36–37; Kotzebue, in Mahr, ed., *Visit of the "Rurik,"* p. 59; Duhaut-Cilly, "Duhaut-Cilly's Account of California," p. 228; Beechey, *Narrative of a Voyage* 2:71; Roquefeuil, *Camille de Roquefeuil in San Francisco* 2:18, 71.

30 Du Petit-Thouars, *Voyage of the Venus,* p. 85; Beechey, *Narrative of a Voyage* 2:71, 78.

31 Roquefeuil, *Camille de Roquefeuil in San Francisco,* p. 21; Coulter, *Notes on Upper California,* p. 26; Simpson, *Narrative of a Voyage,* p. 67; Belcher, *H.M.S. Sulphur at California,* p. 46; Kotzebue, Chamisso, and Choris, in Mahr, ed., *Visit of the "Rurik,"* pp. 61–63, 83, 99; Duhaut-Cilly, "Duhaut-Cilly's Account of California," p. 316.

32 Cutter, "Introduction," *Malaspina in California,* p. v.

33 Malaspina, *Malaspina in California,* pp. 50, 53, 58, 62–65.

34 Philip Wayne-Powell, *Tree of Hate: Propaganda and Prejudice Affecting United States Relations with the Hispanic World,* p. 11.

35 Charles Gibson, *Spain in America,* pp. 136–137; John Francis Bannon, Robert Ryal Miller, and Peter Masten Dunne, *Latin America,* pp. 125–126.

THE COLLAPSE OF THE MISSIONS

EDITOR'S INTRODUCTION

As Herbert Eugene Bolton explained long ago, the Spanish mission was a frontier institution. It was created to advance and consolidate Spanish claims over new territories, first in the epochal struggle against the Moors in Spain and then later against the Indians of the New World. Once the frontier had passed, the mission was obsolete.[1]

Thus the missions of California, like those on all Spanish frontiers, were temporary institutions. When the work of Christianization and civilization was finished, the missionaries were expected to move on to new frontiers. The missions gradually were to be turned over to secular clergy, and the common mission lands distributed among the former neophytes.

There were, however, ideological and economic forces in Spain and Spanish America that pressed for immediate secularization of all the missions. The ideological pressures were rooted in the same values of the Enlightenment that had led La Pérouse and other visitors to criticize the California missions. Spanish liberals, including the "Enlightened Catholics" referred to by Francis F. Guest in a previous selection, regarded the missions as autocratic institutions that violated the rights of the Indians. In 1813 the liberal Spanish Cortes, or parliament, adopted a democratic constitution and ordered the immediate secularization of all the missions. This short-lived secularization order was nullified the following year when more conservative forces returned to power under Ferdinand VII. The 1813 decree, although it was not enforced, continued to haunt the Francisans in California and served as a portend of things to come.

[1]See Herbert Eugene Bolton, "The Mission as a Frontier Institution in the Spanish American Colonies," *American Historical Review*, XXIII (October 1917), 42–61.

Following the establishment of Mexican independence in 1821, secularization was both supported and opposed as liberals and conservatives vied for power in Mexico City. The constitution of the Republic of Mexico, adopted in 1824, endorsed the equality of *all* Mexicans regardless of race. Mexican liberals concluded, with fair justification, that the missions were henceforth unconstitutional. In 1831, for example, a Mexican philosopher denounced the missions as "a monstrous regime suited to the era of fanaticism of the Spanish people [which] cannot fit in with modern politics and much less with our social institutions."[2] Yet, because the liberals held power in Mexico City only sporadically, secularization was not pursued as a consistent policy.

The most important secularization decree was adopted on April 16, 1834, during the liberal administration of Valentín Gómez Farías. The decree ordered the immediate end to all the missions in the republic. Gómez Farías soon fell from power, and—with one major exception—his decree had little effect. As we shall see, that one exception was California.

The following selection, from David J. Weber's *The Mexican Frontier, 1821–1846: The American Southwest Under Mexico* (1982), describes the general impact of Mexican independence on the frontier missions. Weber argues that to understand secularization we must consider the substantial differences in local circumstances on each of the frontiers. Secularization proceeded at a different pace and with different results in Arizona, New Mexico, and Texas. The process was especially problematical in California, where powerful economic and political interests pushed hard for secularization and the struggle over mission spoils was intense.

David J. Weber, Dedman Professor of History at Southern Methodist University, is the leading interpreter of the American Southwest. Among his many books on the subject are *Foreigners in Their Native Land: Historical Roots of the Mexican Americans* (1973) and *New Spain's Northern Frontier: Essays on Spain in the American West, 1540–1821* (1979).

---

[2]Quoted in David J. Weber, *The Mexican Frontier, 1821–1846: The American Southwest Under Mexico* (Albuqurque, 1982), 47.

READING 5

The Collapse of the Missions

David J. Weber

The [government] wants the Indians to be private owners of lands and of the other property; this is just. The Indians, however, want the freedom of vagabonds. The [non-Indians] want the absolute liberation and emancipation of the neophytes...in order that they may avail themselves of their lands and other property as well of their persons. I do not see how these opposing interests can be harmonized.

—Fray Narciso Durán, *Alta California*, 1833

"It seems likely," one California Franciscan wrote in 1822, "that these missions will fall to pieces within, a few years."[1] His words were prophetic. Within a decade and a half, the last missions of Arizona, New Mexico, and Texas, as well as those of California, had slipped from Franciscan control. Indians deserted the missions, buildings began to decay, fields lay fallow, orchards went untended, and the once common sight of the robed and sandaled Franciscans became little more than a memory in many frontier communities.

Although missions had been the key institution for expansion of the frontier under Spain, they began to decline in the late eighteenth century and their complete collapse occurred under independent Mexico. Much has been written about the establishment and operation of the missions and their vital role in pushing the frontier north, but little has been said about their disintegration. An examination of their demise sheds considerable light on social, economic, political, and ideological forces in Mexico and especially on its northern frontier where most missions were located in 1821.[2] The long-term effects of divesting the missionaries of control over mission lands were profound, especially in California where the missions were

most vigorous and where efforts to dismantle them were most strenuous and complex.

INDEPENDENCE AND IDEOLOGY

At the dawn of Mexican independence, the future of the frontier missions seemed bleak. Most immediately, the ten-year struggle for Mexican independence had disrupted the mission economies. Government aid to the distant northern missions had all but stopped by the mid-1810s as Spanish officials diverted resources to crushing rebel forces and stopped sending the padres' annual stipends (*sínados*) and monies for supplies. Following independence, the economic situation remained dismal. The national treasury was often empty and traditional sources of funds, such as income from estates, mortgages, and contributions from wealthy and pious individuals, had become undependable.[3]

Loss of income was not the only cross the padres bore as a result of the turbulent struggle for independence. Government aid no longer reached the frontier military garrisons, so troops appropriated supplies and food from the missions and depleted still further the Franciscans' dwindling resources. At the already impoverished Texas missions, the few remaining friars claimed to be near starvation by 1822; most of their neophytes had left. In Alta California, where relatively young missions prospered more than anywhere else on the northern frontier, troops drained the mission economies but did not destroy them. By 1820, according to their own reckoning, Franciscans in Alta California had furnished nearly one half million pesos in supplies to the military and to government officials.[4] "Words are hardly adequate to describe the sacrifices and hardships of the missions since the year 1810," Fray José Señán wrote in 1819. The missions, he said, "have been the support and pillar of the province."[5]

The war for independence also hindered the Franciscans' ability to enlist new recruits. Instead of training Mexicans for the priesthood, the Order had depended almost entirely on Spain as a source of new priests. By 1820, however, few Spaniards wanted to go to the rebellious colony. That year the Franciscan College of Querétaro sent a representative to Spain in search of thirty new priests, but found only four willing to return to Mexico with him.[6]

Strained relations between Spain and Mexico in the 1820s probably made recruiting difficult. The shortage of priests in Mexico grew critical in the late 1820s, as aftershocks of the independence struggle heightened Mexican xenophobia against Spaniards. In 1827 and again in 1829 the government ordered Spanish residents of the republic, with few exceptions, to leave.[7] On the frontier, the expulsion of the Spaniards hit hardest at the Pimería Alta missions of present Arizona, leaving it practically without priests. Yet, the expulsion had no effect on Texas, which was served by only two Mexican-born Franciscans. In California and New Mexico the orders did not strike with full force because local officials balked at enforcing them. To expel the Spanish-born Franciscans would have been easy, but who would replace them? Three of New Mexico's five Spanish-born friars left the province voluntarily. Some of Alta California's twenty-five Spanish-born friars would have left, too, but Governor José María Echeandía refused to issue them passports.[8]

The departure of most Spanish-born Franciscans during the revolt and its aftermath made its greatest impact on Mexico's five Franciscan colleges. The College of San Fernando in Mexico City, which had furnished all of the padres for Alta California's twenty-one coastal missions up to that time, and the College of Santa de Querétaro, which staffed the Pimería Alta missions, were both nearly closed by the end of the 1820s for lack of priests. Those colleges could no longer send replacements to the frontier for friars who grew aged, infirm, or died. Only the College of Guadalupe at Zacatecas, the largest of the five, seems to have recruited enough Mexican-born priests to continue operations in Texas and take up some of the slack in California.[9]

The impact of the struggle for independence on funds and priests constituted a serious threat to the continuance of missions on the frontier of independent Mexico. More profoundly threatening, however, were ideological pressures, which had been building up for decades.

A humanistic tradition that urged against the natural inferiority of Indians and in favor of the equality of Indians with other men had powerfully influenced Spanish thought since the sixteenth century. In the glow of the Enlightenment, eighteenth-century Spanish liberals rekindled the spark of humanism and combined it with an anticlericism that spelled trouble for the frontier missions.[10] The most dramatic manifestation of this new spirit had been the Crown's 1767 order to expel the Jesuits throughout Spain and her empire—an action inspired more by politics, however, than by ideology. As a result, officials removed Jesuits from their missions in Pimería Alta and replaced them with Franciscans, who inadvertently acquired a monopoly of the entire mission field from California to Texas.

In the late eighteenth century the Franciscans came under increasing pressure to secularize their missions. Secularization had always been the eventual goal of missionization, although the law specified no precise time for that to occur.[11] Secularization meant the replacement of state-supported missionaries from religious orders (regular clergy), whose task had been to propagate the faith, with parish-supported priests or *curas* (secular clergy), who would be responsible for the preservation of the faith. As missions became parishes, Indians would cease being awards and become parishioners and taxpayers—no small matter for the royal exchequer. Moreover, parishioners would assume support of the priest through the payment of *diezmos* or tithes, and other fees, thereby ending the government's responsibility to send annual *sínados* to the missionaries. Secularization also implied that Indian communal property, held in trust by missionaries, would be returned to the Indians and the surplus would enter the public domain.

In theory, secularization seemed compatible with the goals of the Franciscans who saw their purpose, as one put it, in "denaturalizing" the Indians and transforming "a savage race...into a society that is human, Christian, civil, and industrious."[12] Having "civilized" the Indians, the Franciscans would turn them over to parish priests and move on to work among a new group of "savages."

In practice this seldom occurred. Franciscans consistently pronounced neophytes unfit and unready to take their place in Hispanic society. Indians, the padres reported, did not place sufficient value on private property, thrift, or hard work and would either "eagerly return to their former unrestricted habits" or become victimized by rapacious settlers.[13]

Whether the Franciscans' goal of Hispanizing Indians could have succeeded is another matter. Some contemporaries argued that acculturation would not take place because the missions kept Indians apart from other members of society.[14] Certainly the fact that the padres represented a minority trying to "denaturalize" a majority made the padres' task of directing cultural change more difficult. When they failed to alter Indian culture, some Franciscans blamed Indian obstinacy rather than questioning the goal. After forty years of experience with California Indians, Fray Narciso Durán wrote in 1845: "The Indians, in my opinion, do not deserve to be directed by a missionary. A slavedriver is what they ought to have."[15] The padres commonly compared Indians with "children" and termed them inferior and incapable of change. Fray Vicente Francisco de Sarría, for example, described the California Indians as possessing "congenital idleness" and a "natural repugnance...for work."[16] Such negative attitudes by persons who today we would identify as role models and teachers for Indians might have constituted what educators now term a "self-fulfilling prophecy." That is to say that regardless of a student's ability, his achievements seldom exceed his teacher's expectations.

In practice, then, many of the Indians who accepted the faith had to be forcibly held in missions through corporal punishment and few seemed ready to live as equals among non-Indians.[17] Franciscans gave up missions only in areas where the lack of cooperation by Indians or the decimation of their numbers by European diseases—a commonplace occurrence—made mission communities unworkable.

SECULARIZATION IN CALIFORNIA

In New Mexico, Arizona, and Texas, the decline of the Franciscan missions under independent Mexico occurred quietly in comparison to their spectacular demise in Alta California. There, missions and missionaries remained a force to be reckoned with in the 1820s. In contrast to other provinces on the northern frontier, California's missions still possessed considerable vitality. The first of twenty-one Alta California missions had been built on San Diego Bay in 1769, just two years after the expulsion of the Jesuits from the Spanish Empire and at the same time that officials were pressuring Franciscans to secularize missions elsewhere. This contradiction arose out of necessity. The unoccupied California coast seemed menaced by the British and Russians, and some enlightened officials still regarded a modified form of missions as the most effective institution for extending the frontier. Not all officials shared that viewpoint. Just a decade after the founding of San Diego mission in 1769, some officials began to call for secularization of the Alta California missions. Such calls continued to be heard in the late colonial period but they had little effect in California where the vigorous grayrobes from the College of San Fernando continued to plant missions along with citrus and olive trees in temperate valleys along the Pacific.[18]

By 1823, shortly after independence, the *fernandinos* (Franciscans from the College of San Fernando) had established their twenty-first and final mission in California, at Sonoma, north of San Francisco Bay. At about the same time, the number of Indians attached to those missions reached its zenith, over 21,000.[19] In the names of those neophytes, Franciscans held a near monopoly over the temperate coastal lands from San Diego to Sonoma. Mission orchards, fields, pastures, and shops, all operated by Indian labor, produced most of the food and manufactured goods for the isolated province.

The California Franciscans, despite their travails during the recent wars for independence, presided over the most prosperous missions on the frontier at the dawn of Mexican independence, and they fought to preserve them. In general, California Franciscans opposed the conversion of missions to parishes for the classic reasons: Indians were not yet prepared to assume the role of citizens and needed the protection of the padres, or pobladores would exploit them.[20] Some Franciscans apparently did not oppose secularization in itself. Those who were ill or "wearisome," such as the partially paralyzed Fray Felipe Arroyo la Cuesta of Mission San Juan Bautista, would have happily relinquished responsibility for farming, ranching and construction in order to tend to spiritual matters exclusively. Before surrendering control over their neophytes, however, most Franciscans wanted safeguards established so that Indians would not be exploited or return to their so-called pagan ways.[21]

One bold and ingenious plan came from Fray Narciso Durán. The genial, blue-eyed, Spanish-born padre, who had served at San José since 1806 and twice acted as father president of the California missions, suggested that construction of a new inland chain of missions accompany secularization of the coastal missions. In resurrecting this idea, which had been discussed in the first years of the century, Durán recognized the necessity of opening coastal lands to colonization if California was to attract immigrants and grow. At the same time, he argued, inland missions built to the east of the coastal ranges would block former mission Indians from fleeing into the interior. "They would either have to join the new missions or lead a rational life in the [coastal] pueblos."[22] Indians, who seemed unsuited for life among the gente de razón could be relocated to the new missions as the old were abandoned. Too costly to implement (as Durán acknowledged), the idea of building an inland chain of missions continued to receive serious discussion as late as 1845, and one prelate even suggested that missions be extended north to Oregon.[23] The idea continued to receive attention because it represented the only way for the California mission to survive.

California's coastal missions met stiffer opposition than any other missions on the frontier, and the stakes were higher for all parties involved. Ideology aside, *californios* and federal officials alike saw missions as an obstacle to the economic development of the province. The missions' near monopoly over California's coastal strip and over the indigenous labor force hindered badly needed immigration and retarded growth of private ranches and farms. "The clamor for land is greater than ever," one foreign-born merchant reported in 1831. "Many soldiers...do not know how they are going to settle with their growing families."[24] Missions also retarded growth of new towns. Petaluma and Santa Rosa were needed to block the Russian advance from Fort Ross, but their sites occupied lands claimed by a mission.[25]

Thus, secularization seemed to represent the key to the prosperity of California and ultimately to its security. Thoughtful observers knew that if Mexico did not populate and develop the coast, another nation would seize it.[26] Because of the importance of these issues, and because California's territorial status brought it under federal jurisdiction, the government in Mexico City involved itself in secularization in California more than anywhere else on the northern frontier.

But the government faced a dilemma. Although long-range development of California seemed dependent upon secularization, the disruption of mission farms and ranches seemed certain to bring immediate ruin to the provincial economy. The military forces stationed in California and her public officials depended upon the missions as a source of food, supplies, "forced loans," and their very salaries, which the perennially impecunious federal treasury usually failed to provide.[27] California officials repeatedly acknowledged this dependence on the missions. Governor José María Echeandía, for example, declined to enforce laws requiring expulsion of the Spanish-born Franciscans, explaining to the federal government that twenty-five of California's twenty-eight padres would be required to leave under the law. This, he argued, would not only ruin the missions, but "the rest of the inhabitants and the troops would perish."[28]

Officials also feared that without Franciscan control, mission Indians might revolt. Mission Indians outnumbered the *californios* by at least six to one. The Chumash had revolted at Santa Barbara in 1824 and talk of secularization encouraged stirrings of revolt in other missions as well, giving prudent men pause about the wisdom of secularization.[29] California, it appeared, could not grow so long as the missions existed, but neither could it survive without them.

Under these circumstances, the government adopted a gradual approach toward secularization, hoping to weaken the power of the padres and make land and labor available for private development while avoiding economic ruin, Indian revolt, and maintaining the allegiance of the powerful Spanish-born Franciscans, whose loyalty was suspect. From 1825, when the prestigious Commission for the Development of the Californias recommended secularization of California's missions, until 1833, successive governments in Mexico City adopted remarkably similar strategies for implementing the secularization law of September 13, 1813 in California. The first three governors sent to California by independent Mexico—José María Echeandía, Manuel Victoria, and José Figueroa—carried instructions to proceed "slowly and prudently."[30]

The unpopular Manuel Victoria, who lasted in the governor's office for less than a year (1831) did nothing to promote secularization, but Echeandía (1825–31) and Figueroa (1832–35) both experimented with a cautious policy, which had been tried earlier by Pablo Sola, the last Spanish-appointed governor. Echeandía and Figueroa permitted select Indians to leave certain missions and granted them land and the full rights of citizens.[31]

Mission Indians did not clamor to be included in the new plan to make them property owners. Juan Bautista Alvarado recalled visiting the mission of San Miguel and making an impassioned speech on the rights of free men while standing in a cart in the middle of the courtyard. He concluded by saying, "those who prefer to be made proprietors and free men, step to my right." Overwhelmingly, the Indians ignored him and stayed with the priest. "It reminded me of the old Roman Lady," Alvarado later wrote "who began to weep when she learned about the death of Nero...[because] it was better to know one known bad person than a good one unknown.[32]

It is not surprising that the few Indians who were released from the restraints of institutional life did not turn into Mexicans overnight. Instead, as one historian has put it, many demonstrated "the kind of psychological disorientation that often accompanies decolonization."[33] Freed mission Indians, according to one British observer, were reduced to beggary and thieving after having "gambled away their clothes, implements, and even their land."[34] Fray Narciso Durán reported that liberated Indians became "slaves or servants of white men."[35] Nonetheless, Governor Echeandía thought the experiment had sufficient merit to extend it to still more missions in 1828, but he also built in more safeguards, one of which prohibited Indians from selling their property for five years. Political turmoil both in California and the nation, however, prevented full implementation of Echeandía's plans.

THE FIGUEROA PLAN

Governor Figueroa, who deplored the missions as a "monastic despotism," also adopted a gradual approach and his program began auspiciously. By 1834 he had established three Indian towns in southern California, at Las Flores, San Juan Capistrano, and San Dieguito. Ironically, it would be Figueroa, who had opposed secularization "at one blow" because "such a cure is worse than the disease," who would preside over the rapid dissolution of the Alta California missions.[36] A sudden shift in federal policy prompted Figueroa to act in a way that he otherwise would have viewed as unwise.

On August 17, 1833, almost a year before it ordered all missions in Mexico secularized, the liberal vice-president Gómez Farías signed into law a bill specifically secularizing all missions in both Alta and Baja California and requiring the immediate replacement of Franciscans by secular clergy. The bill made no provision for the disposition of mission properties, but other legislation, not yet approved by Congress, contained a formula for distributing that property to various groups, including colonists from Mexico and from foreign countries.[37]

Due to faulty communication and poorly drafted legislation the *californios* misunderstood these measures to mean that the Goméz Farías administration intended to grant all of California's mission lands to a group of Mexican colonists led by José María Híjar and José María Padrés. The administration had recently appointed Híjar to replace Figueroa as *jefe político* and also to serve as commissioner of colonization for California. When the colonists led by Híjar and Padrés set out for California in 1834, they carried instructions to "occupy all the property belonging to the missions."[38]

Garbled reports of these matters reached California and alarmed settlers who had long coveted mission properties but now saw them slipping from their grasp. Meanwhile, however, Governor Figueroa had received no formal orders to implement the new secularization law; he expected Híjar, the new governor, to bring those instructions. In an effort to head off Híjar and make the best of a bad situation, Figueroa accepted a secularization program drawn up by the California diputación, and announced it on August 9, 1834, prior to Híjar's arrival. This plan called for the immediate secularization of ten missions and secularization of the remainder soon after. It permitted Franciscans to remain in order to tend to spiritual matters until secular priests arrived. Indians would receive private plots of land, which they could not sell, and would also get tools, seed, and livestock. As in Pimería Alta, a mayordomo, appointed by the governor, would take charge of surplus fields, orchards, and herds. Profits from this surplus property would be used for the expenses of "good government," such as the salary of the priests and the mayordomo, the support of schools, or supplies for the military garrisons. Lest mission ranches and farms cease operating and this income dry up, the plan permitted the governor to require Indians to labor on the surplus lands.[39]

The plan adopted by Figueroa and the diputación served the interests of upper class *californios*. It blocked the acquisition of mission lands by immigrants from Mexico, by foreigners, and by lower class *californios* who would have benefited from the Gómez Farías legislation. Figueroa's plan also kept the mission economy intact and maintained the flow of vital revenues by requiring the forced labor of Indians, even while freeing them in theory. The plan did not provide for *californios* to obtain mission lands directly, but it did the next best thing by opening the way for upper class *californios* to assume positions of mayordomos of mission property. Figueroa and the oligarchs in the legislature, then, seemed to have found an ingenious way to thwart the efforts of the liberal Gómez Farías to integrate the California Indians. The *californios* changed the legal status of mission Indians to conform to republican ideals, without changing their actual status. Instead of remaining neophytes under the padres, Indians would become *peones* under a mayordomo.

Between 1834 and 1836 all twenty-one missions were secularized, but not in the manner Figueroa intended. He did not live long enough to supervise the process, dying in office in September 1835. Meanwhile, Híjar never had a chance to put the Gómez Farías plan into effect, either. In one of those quick shifts of power that increasingly characterized Mexican politics, Antonio López de Santa Anna ousted Gómez Farías and revoked Híjar's governorship. Santa Anna, now the champion of conservatives, hoped to reverse the process of secularization that his predecessor had set into motion, but the independent-minded California oligarchy ignored his instructions to delay and secularized the remaining missions.

Following the death of Figueroa, California government became more choatic. During the turbulence, missions constituted the principal source of revenue for ambitious politicians. Mission overseers, who generally belonged to one faction or another, sold off cattle, grain, and lands that rightly belonged to former neophytes and missions deteriorated under their stewardship. In 1839 Governor Juan Bautista Alvarado tried to check what nearly all writers have termed the "plunder" of the missions, but it was too late. The missions had "entirely gone to ruin," one of Alvarado's agents reported, and non-Indians had moved onto Indian lands.[40] "All is destruction, all is misery, humiliation and despair," wrote one padre in 1840.[41]

The destruction of California mission properties, however, did not come about solely because of the activities of unscrupulous mayordomos. Mission Indians themselves displayed contempt for the system that had kept them forcibly institutionalized and participated actively in destroying it. Under the padres, many Indians had resisted missionization in subtle ways, and one of every ten had attempted to run away. With the authority of the padres gone in the mid-1830s, most Indians refused to labor for the overseers and showed little interest in acquiring land near the missions; some fled civilization entirely to live among independent Indian societies; others drifted into white settlements where they became laborers or servants; and others went to work on the private ranchos that *californios* had begun carving out of former mission properties. The self-governing Indian towns, which Figueroa had begun to establish, disintegrated quickly and the number of Indians remaining on mission lands plummeted.[42]

The number of Franciscans in California also fell. Notwithstanding the arrival of reinforcements from the College of Guadalupe at Zacatecas, which sent eleven Mexican-born padres to California in 1833 to replace the depleted ranks of the Fernandinos, the number of Franciscans declined dramatically. Thirty-six gray-robes had served the province in 1820; twenty-one remained in 1836; and only eleven in 1846.[43] The last of the missionaries had no missions. In dire need of funds to run his government, Governor Pío Pico had put most of the remaining mission property—including the crumbling buildings and the chapels themselves—up for public auction in 1845. The central government and the Franciscans tried to prevent this sale, but the independent and desperate frontier governor proceeded nonetheless. The United States government would later judge Pico's action illegal, but at the outbreak of war between Mexico and the United States, California mission property had been secularized, nearly destroyed, and lost completely to the Church. Little wonder, then, that one Catholic historian has termed the Church in California "near extinction" in 1846.[44]

ECONOMIC FORCES

A consideration of local circumstances, from California to Texas, suggests that the frontier missions came to an end as a result of complex causes, both national and regional. If any one of these stand out, it may be that economic forces played the largest role in ending the mission era. For years pobladores had coveted the choice sites that the padres held in trust for the neophytes. Weakened by a loss of income, personnel, and influence following the struggle for independence, the padres could no longer hold out against the growing population of gente de razón. In this respect, events on the frontier followed a national pattern. "If there is one linear tendency which can be documented throughout Mexican history from 1527 to 1910," one historian has written, "it is the constant expansion of private property at the cost of communal property."[45] In their efforts to maintain the missions, the padres fought a holding action against a seemingly inexorable economic force.

National policies, however, did not determine how and when secularization took place on the frontier. On this issue, as on many others, frontiersmen modified or ignored national directives to suit what they perceived as their own interests.

Except in New Mexico, secularization enabled the pobladores to obtain title to former mission lands and Indian labor, thereby shifting the center of production to the private sector. But those gains came at a price. In areas such as Alta California and Pimería Alta, which had relied heavily on missions for Indian control, some officials doubted the wisdom of losing the missions and wished for their return. "To deny the utility of the missions in a country inhabited largely by barbarians, would be absurd," California's representative argued in Congress in 1844.[46] Secularization also cost the frontiersmen the spiritual services of Franciscans, whose stipends had been paid largely by the government and other external sources. With secularization, pobladores became parishioners with the additional obligation of supporting their own priests. Those frontiersmen who had expressed fears that it would be difficult to find curas to replace Franciscans soon learned their fears had been wellfounded.

Notes

1 Fray José Señán to Fray José Gasol, June 4, 1822, Lesley Byrd Simpson, ed., Paul D. Nathan, trans., *The Letters of José Señán, O.F.M. Mission San Buenaventura, 1796–1823* (San Francisco, 1962), p. 155.

2 Moisés González Navarro, "Instituciones indígenas en México independiente," in *Métodos y resultados de la política indigenista en México* (Mexico, 1954), p. 139.

3 Stipends for Pimería Alta missions stopped arriving 1814, for example, and those for Texas stopped in 1816. John L. Kessell, *Friars, Soldiers, and Reformers: Hispanic Arizona and the Sonora Mission Frontier, 1767–1856* (Tucson, 1976), p. 237. Marion A. Habig, *The Alamo Chain of Missions: A History of San Antonio's Five Old*

Missions (Chicago, 1968), p. 107. For the economic situation see the report of Lucas Alamán, November 8, 1823, translated in Joel Roberts Poinsett, *Notes on México Made in the Autumn of 1822* (Philadelphia, 1842), p. 323; C. Alan Hutchinson, "The Mexican Government and the Mission Indians of Upper California, 1821–1835," *The Americas,* XXI (April 1965), p. 336; and Kessell, *Friars, Soldiers, and Reformers,* p. 260.

4 Governor Martínez to the commandant general, April 14, 1822, quoted in William S. Red, *The Texas Colonists and Religion, 1821–1836* (Austin, 1924), pp. 45–46. Hubert Howe Bancroft, *History of California,* 7 vols. (San Francisco, 1886–90), II, 406.

5 Señán to Fr. Baldomero López, Mission San Buenaventura, September 4, 1819, in Simpson, ed., *Letters of José Señán,* p, 129.

6 Kessell, *Friars, Soldiers, and Reformers,* p. 260. Maynard Geiger, *Franciscan Missionaries in Hispanic California, 1769–1848: A Biographical Dictionary* (San Marino, California, 1969), p. x, and Lansing B. Bloom, "New Mexico Under Mexican Administration, 1821–1846," *Old Santa Fe,* I (January 1914), p. 268.

7 The causes and effects of expulsion have been examined by Romeo Flores Caballero, *La contrarrevolución en la independencia: Los Españoles en la vida política, social y económica de México, 1804–1838* (Mexico, 1969), and in Harold D. Sims, *La expulsión de los españoles de México, 1821–1838* (Mexico, 1974). Flores Caballero's study has been translated into English by Jaime E. Rodríguez O., *Counterrevolution* ...(Lincoln, Nebraska, 1974). The decrees, dated December 20, 1827 and March 20, 1829, are in Manuel Dublán and José María Lozano, eds., *Legislación mexicana,* 34 vols. (Mexico, 1876–1904), II, 49–51, 98–99.

8 Bloom, "New Mexico Under Mexican Administration," I, 258, 267–68. Zephyrin Engelhardt, *The Missions and Missionaries of Caliornia,* 4 vols. (San Francisco, 1908–15), III, 273–277. Bancroft, *History of California,* III, 51–52; 95–98. Pimeriá Alta and Texas are discussed later in this chapter.

9 Maynard Geiger, "The Internal Organization and Activities of San Fernando College, Mexico (1734–1858)," *The Americas,* VI (July 1949), 27. Geiger, *Franciscan Missionaries,* pp. ix–x. González Navarro, "Instituciones indígenas," p. 141. Fr. Benedict Leutenegger, trans., *The Zacatecan Missionaries in Texas, 1716–1834...and A Biographical Dictionary* by Fr. Marion A. Habig (Austin, 1973), p. 167.

10 The Bourbons tried various ways to limit the economic power of the religious orders. In 1734, for example, the Crown prohibited Orders in Mexico from taking on new members for a decade. In 1749 the Crown issued a secret instruction that all missions in America be secularized— it was not carried out for lack of priests. C. H. Haring, *The Spanish Empire in America* (New York, 1947), p. 176; Gerald J. Geary, *The Secularization of the California Missions, 1810–1846* (Washington, D.C., 1934), pp. 26–31.

11 The widespread misconception that missions were to be secularized within ten years (see, for example, Charles Gibson, *Spain in America* [New York, 1966], p. 81) may have been the result of an error made by Viceroy Conde de Revillagigedo. The question is discussed in Geary, *The Secularization of the California Missions,* pp. 27–30.

12 Fermín Francisco de Lasuén, Mission San Carlos, June, 19, 1801, quoted in Daniel Garr, "Planning, Politics and Plunder: The Missions and Indian Pueblos of Hispanic California," *Southern California Quarterly,* LIV (Winter 1972), p. 292.

13 Fray Narciso Durán to President Anastasio Bustamante, September 23, 1830, quoted in Engelhardt, *Missions and Missionaries of California,* III, 339–340, is a good exposition of this position, as are two letters from Fray Francisco García Diego y Moreno to José Figueroa, Santa Clara, September 24 and October 15, 1833, in Francis J. Weber, ed. and trans., *Writings of Francisco García Diego y Moreno* (Los Angeles, 1976), pp. 56–60.

14 See, for example, John L. Kessell, ed. and trans., "Anza Damns the Missions: A Spanish Soldier's Criticism of Indian Policy, 1772," *Journal of Arizona History,* 13 (Spring 1972), p. 58.

15 Durán to Pío Pico, December 26, 1845, quoted in Engelhardt, *Missions and Missionaries of California,* IV, 452.

16 Quoted in Hutchinson, "The Mexican Government and the Mission Indians," p. 342. See, too, n. 13 *supra,* and Maynard Geiger, ed. and trans., *As the Padres Saw Them: California Indian Life and Customs as Reported by the Franciscan Missionaries, 1813–1815* (Santa Barbara, 1976), an especially revealing collection.

17 Much has been written about the forcible detention of Indians. See, for example, Billie Persons, "Secular Life in the San Antonio Missions," *Southwestern Historical Quarterly* LXII (July 1958), p. 60; Edward Spicer, *Cycles of Conquest* (Tuscon, 1962), pp. 159; 324–326; Robert Archibald, "Indian Labor at the California Missions: Slavery or Salvation?" *Journal of San Diego History,* XXIV (Spring 1978), pp. 172–182; Francis F. Guest, "An Examination of the Thesis of S. F. Cook on the Forced Conversion of Indians in the California Missions," *Southern California Quarterly,* LXI (Spring 1979), pp. 1–77.

18 José de Gálvez, who directed the settlement of Alta California, had just tried and failed to reorganize the mission Indians of Baja California and Pimería Alta into well-planned secular communities. Ignacio A. del Río Chávez, "Utopia in Baja California, The Dreams of José de Gálvez," *Journal of San Diego History,* XVIII (Fall 1972), pp. 1–13. Modifications of the traditional mission system were attempted in late-eighteenth century California. See Francis Guest, "Mission Colonization and Political Control in Spanish California," ibid, XXIV (Winter 1978), pp. 97–116. Kessell, "Friars vs. Bureaucrats," pp. 152–153. Geary, *Secularization,* pp. 46, 51.

19 J. N. Bowman, "The Resident Neophytes (*Existentes*) of the California Missions, 1769–1834," *Southern California Quarterly,* XL (June 1958), pp. 147–148, puts the neophyte population at over 21,000 in 1820, 1821 and 1824. See, too, the interesting charts and analysis by David Hornbeck, "Mission Population of Alta California," *Historical Geography,* 8 (Spring 1978), Supplement, n.p.

20 For an able articulation of reasons for preserving the missions in California, see Fray Francisco García Diego y Moreno to José Figueroa, Santa Clara, September 24 and October 15, 1833, in Weber, ed. and trans., *Writings of Francisco García Diego,* pp. 56–60.

21 Geiger, *Missionaries,* p. 21; Engelhardt, *Missions and Missionaries,* III, 225–226. On two occasions, in 1821 and 1826, the Fernandinos offered to relinquish the mission, perhaps knowing that the offer would be refused because no one could replace them. See Geary, *Secularization,* pp. 97–98; Hutchinson, "Mexican Government and the Mission Indians," p. 340: and Engelhardt *Missions and Missionaries,* III, 341.

22 Durán outlined his plan in letters to Bustamante, September 23, 1830, and Figueroa, October 3, 1833. They are discussed in Geary, *Secularization,* pp. 119–120, 140–141 and trans. in Engelhardt, *Missions and Missionaries,* III, 337–344; 488–495. The quote is from p. 493. Durán had suggested this at least as early as 1821—see his letter to Fr. Juan Cortés, March 11, 1821, in "Letters of Narciso Durán..." trans. and ed. by Francis Price, *California Historical Society Quarterly,* XXXVII (September 1958), p. 253. For a summary of Durán's views see Neri, "Narcisco [*sic*] Durán," pp. 411–429.

23 Bishop Francisco García Diego to José María Híjar, n.p., August 8, 1845, in Weber, ed. and trans. *Writings of Francisco García Diego,* p. 175. See, too, George William Beattie, *California's Unbuilt Missions. Spanish Plans for an Inland Chain* (Los Angeles, 1930).

24 Heinrich Virmond to Lucas Alamán, Mazatlán, February 1, 1831, in David J. Weber and Ronald R. Young, eds. and trans., "California in 1831," *Journal of San Diego History,* XXI (Fall 1975), p. 4. Other contemporaries noted the problem: José Bandini, *A Description of California in 1828,* trans. by Doris M. Wright (Berkeley, 1951), pp. 6–7; Governor Echeandía, as quoted in Bancroft, *History of California,* III, 104, n. 37. One of the few historians to address this question is Manuel P. Servín, "The Secularization of the California Missions: A Reappraisal," *Southern California Quarterly,* XLVII (June 1965), pp. 135–136.

25 George Tays, "Mariano Guadalupe Vallejo and Sonoma. A Biography and a History," *California Historical Society Quarterly,* XVI (September 1937), p. 235.

26 This, for example, concerned the committee headed by Juan Francisco de Azcárate. "Dicta-

men presentado a la soberana junta gobernative del imperio mexicano," December 29, 1821, published under the title *Un programa de política internacional* (Mexico, 1932).

27 See, for example, Bancroft, *History of California,* II, 517–518, and Fray Francisco García Diego y Moreno to José Figueroa, Santa Clara, June 15, 1883, in Weber, ed. and trans., *Writings of Francisco García Diego,* pp. 53–54.

28 Echeandía to the Ministro de Relaciones, June 30, 1829, quoted in Engelhardt, *Missions and Missionaries,* III, 273–274.

29 I have based this ratio on 21,000 Indians to 3,200 non-Indians. For the 1824 revolt at Santa Barbara, see Maynard Geiger, *Mission Santa Barbara, 1782–1965* (Santa Barbara, 1965), pp. 85–94; Geiger, ed. and trans., "Fray Antonio Ripoll's Description of the Chumash Revolt at Santa Barbara in 1824," *Southern California Quarterly,* LII (December 1970), pp. 345–364; and Thomas Blackburn, ed., "The Chumash Revolt of 1824: A Native Account," *Journal of California Anthropology,* II (Winter 1975), pp. 223–227. For examples of concern about Indian revolt, see Hutchinson, *Frontier Settlement in Mexican California,* p. 152, and Bancroft, *History of California,* III, p. 104, n. 38, quoting Angustias de la Guerra.

30 Hutchinson, "The Mexican Government and the Mission Indians", pp. 346–348. Geary, *Secularization,* p. 96. "Plan for the Administration of the Missions in the Territories of Upper and Lower California. Proposed by the Junta de Fomento of that Peninsula," Mexico, April 6, 1825, trans. in Keld J. Reynolds in "Principal Actions of the California Junta de Fomento," pp. 303–308, and "Final Opinion," May 15, 1827, in ibid., XXV (December, 1946), p. 360. Hutchinson, *Frontier Settlement,* pp. 117–121, 126–127, 143, 156–167.

31 Hutchinson, *Frontier Settlement,* pp. 109–10.

32 Alvarado recalls this incident occurring in early 1831. "History of California," III, pp. 6–7, ms. Bancroft Library, Berkeley. See, too, Bancroft, *History of California,* III, 331–332.

33 George Harwood Phillips, "Indians and the Breakdown of the Spanish Mission System in California," *Ethnohistory,* XXI (Fall 1974), p. 299.

34 Captain Frederick W. Beechey, who took a generally favorable view of the missions, quoted in Hutchinson, "The Mexican Government and the Mission Indians," p. 347.

35 Durán quoted in ibid., p. 350. See, too, Geary, *Secularization,* p. 99, and Bancroft, *History of California,* III, 102–104. Hutchinson provides a good synthesis of these events in *Frontier Settlement in Mexican California,* pp. 128–133.

36 Hutchinson, *Frontier Settlement in Mexican California,* pp. 229, 237. Hutchinson, "The Mexican Government and the Mission Indians," pp. 349–350, 353–354.

37 Dublán and Lozano, *Legislación mexicana,* II, 548–549. Circumstances surrounding the adoption of this bill and its aftermath are best examined in Hutchinson, *Frontier Settlement in Mexican California,* pp. 159–173, 244–245, who sheds new light on this complex question.

38 Hutchinson, *Frontier Settlement,* pp. 182–186, 210–212.

39 The text of this August 9, 1834 plan is translated in Engelhardt, *Missions and Missionaries,* III, 523–530, who labeled it "the crime of the nineteenth century." Bancroft was more sympathetic to the plan, regarding is as "wisely conceived in theory" but difficult to administer (*History of California,* IV, 43–44; III, 342–344). All earlier works have now been supplanted by Hutchinson's summary and analysis of the plan and of Figueroa's quarrel with Híjar, as presented in *Frontier Settlement,* pp. 251–261; 384–391, and in his introduction and translation of Figueroa's *A Manifesto to the Mexican Republic* (1st ed., 1835; Berkeley, 1978), which reinterprets Figueroa's polemic.

40 Englishman William Hartnell, quoted in Lauro de Rojas, ed., "California in 1844 as Hartnell Saw It," *California Historical Society Quarterly,* XVII (March 1938), p. 24.

41 Fray José María de Jesus González Rubio to Fray Rafael Soria, Mission San José, November 3, 1840, quoted in full in Engelhardt, *Missions and Missionaries,* IV, 214–219, describes at length the miserable condition of the missions and the padres. For good general discussions of this period see Bancroft, *History of California,* IV, 42–67, and Daniel Garr, "Planning, Politics, and Plunder," pp. 291–312.

42 Phillips, "Indians and the Breakdown of the Spanish Mission System," pp. 291–302. Sherbourne F. Cook, *The Conflict Between the California Indian and White Civilization* (Berkeley, 1976), pp. 98–134.

43 Geiger, *Franciscan Missionaries in Hispanic California,* pp. ix–xi. Bancroft, *History of California,* II, 393; IV, 63. Weber, ed. and trans., *Writings of Francisco García Diego,* p. 79. Appendix to Francis J. Weber, *Francisco García Diego: California's Transition Bishop* (Los Angeles, 1972), p. 63.

44 John B. McGloin, "The California Church in Transition," *California Historical Society Quarterly,* XLII (March 1963), p. 47. Bancroft, *History of California,* IV, 546–553. Geary, *Secularization,* pp. 185–189. Neri, "Narcisco [*sic*] Durán," pp. 426–28. The missions enjoyed a reprieve in 1843 when Manuel Micheltorena restored the properties of twelve missions of the padres, but a year later the government reversed the order. Bancroft, *History of California,* IV, 368–371, 424.

45 Friedrich Katz, "Labor Conditions on Haciendas in Porfirian Mexico: Some Trends and Tendencies," *Hispanic American Historical Review,* LIV (February 1974), p.39.

46 Speech in Congress, March 30, 1844, in Manuel Castañares, *Colección de documentos relativos al departamento de Californios* (Mexico, 1845), p. 11. Facismile in David J. Weber, ed., *Northern Mexico on the Eve of the United States Invasion: Rare Imprints...*(New York, 1976). See, too, Secretaría de Relaciones, Luis Gonzaga Cuevas, March 1845, quoted in González Navarro, "Instituciones indígenas," p. 144.

FAMILY LIFE IN HISPANIC CALIFORNIA

EDITOR'S INTRODUCTION

One of the great ironies of early California history is that distinctions of rank and class increased during the years when California was a province of the Republic of Mexico. As the proud oligarch of Sonoma, General Mariano Guadalupe Vallejo remarked, there had been more social equality on the California frontier in the Spanish era, "when equality was not known," than in the Republican era "in which all men glory in being equal." Although the Mexican government abolished titles and racial distinctions, differences in social class based on material wealth sharpened.[1]

The new elite that emerged in California was the class of cattle barons known as the *rancheros.* Their wealth was derived from the Mexican government's enormously generous policy of granting huge landholdings to individuals. The grants were given as a means of attracting settlers to the frontier or as rewards for loyal service. The legal maximum of an individual grant was 11 square leagues, or 48,400 acres. Most of the over 600 grants in California were made following the secularization of the missions. Indeed, as suggested in the previous selection by David J. Weber, many of the rancho grants were carved out of former mission lands.

In both northern and southern California great landholding families ruled over their baronies. In the south, for example, the Carrillos held over 320,000 acres. One branch of this family stemmed from Joaquin Carrillo who arrived in San Diego after 1800 and fathered five sons and seven daughters. The Carrillos were typical in their interrelations with other *ranchero* families: One of Joaquin Carrillo's daughters, Francisca Benicia, married General Vallejo; others married scions of the prominent Castro and Pacheco families. From another branch of the Carrillo family came María

---

[1]David J. Weber, *The Mexican Frontier, 1821–1846: The American Southwest Under Mexico* (Albuquerque, 1982), 211. See also Oakah L. Jones, Jr., *Los Paisanos: Spanish Settlers on the Northern Frontier of New Spain* (Norman, 1979), 246–247.

Antonia, the bride of José de la Guerra. The de la Guerras were the leading family of early Santa Barbara, holding rancho lands totaling 326,000 acres.

No thorough study of the rise of the *ranchero* class in California has yet been written.[2] As a consequence, there is much that is unknown about the *californios'* social structure, class and racial attitudes, external relations, and family life. The following selection by Gloria E. Miranda is a pioneering effort to sketch some of the dimensions of family life during the Spanish and Mexican periods. As Miranda points out, what little has been written about families in Hispanic California is based largely on the accounts of foreigners who visited the province. We know from the earlier selection by James J. Rawls that, while these accounts by outsiders are a rich resource for historians, they are often highly colored by prejudice and self-interest. By using original California sources—correspondence, census data, and mission registers—Miranda offers new insights into the private world of the *californios*.

One of Miranda's major conclusions is that differences in social class were important in determining patterns of fertility, socialization, adolescence, and education. She notes, for instance, that while the elite considered having a dozen or more children a mark of status, average family size was no more than three or four children. Differences in educational opportunities were especially striking. The sons of the wealthiest families had private tutors and studied abroad; the majority of poorer Californians remained illiterate.

Gloria E. Miranda is a graduate of California State University, Dominguez Hills, and received her Ph.D. from the University of Southern California in 1978. Currently she is a Professor of Chicano Studies, History, and Humanities at Los Angeles Valley College.

---

[2] The one major study of this class analyzes its decline. See Leonard Pitt, *Decline of the Californios: A Social History of the Spanish-Speaking Californians, 1846–1890* (Berkeley, 1968).

Family Life in Hispanic California

Gloria E. Miranda

Among aspects of California history neglected by researchers in the past was the function of family life as a socializing agent for Hispano-Mexican children in the pre-American era. This major oversight resulted in part because social histories never delved fully into the internal structure of the family unit. Instead, conclusions about family life relied heavily on the observations of nineteenth-century foreign visitors to California who assessed the populace and their cultural values in superficial terms, particularly the group's fertility patterns.[1] Consequently, contemporary study and analysis have yet to explore adequately the depths of familial bonds and traditions in Spanish and Mexican times.

A brief overview of family practices in observance in Santa Barbara prior to statehood should furnish valuable insight into core Hispano-Mexican customs. The geographically isolated and conservative presidial community was a microcosm of the larger provincial society of California during the Spanish and Mexican periods. Foreigners who sojourned in the Channel Islands region recorded their impressions of the *gente de razon* populace as other travelers did about the rest of California.[2] The fecundity of the residents notably impressed many of them.

Yet their estimations of reproduction rates were applicable only to a minority of California families and serve at best as incomplete references for the majority of households. Preliminary statistical analysis of family size for the Spanish and Mexican eras indicates that these

units were on the average not as numerous as many eyewitnesses purported. Census data for 1790, for example, points to a more homogenous pattern in the province at the end of the first phase of the Spanish period. During this time California families averaged between three to four children per household.

As illustrated below, no existing community, presidio, or pueblo averaged over four children per family. Six children to a family in Santa Barbara, eight in Los Angeles and five at San Diego were the largest family units during this period in southern California. The northern communities followed with similar average sizes.[3] The transitory nature of the initial period of growth and settlement in great part is the reason the households were ordinarily small. Yet, as a more permanent society evolved and stabilized in the latter part of the Spanish age, similar patterns prevailed.

Average Number of Children Per Family in 1790

Los Angeles	3.3
Monterey	2.8
San Diego	2.9
San Francisco	3.7
San Jose	3.1
Santa Barbara	3.4
Provincial average:	3.2

By the Mexican era in the 1830s when frontier life had achieved a greater measure of stability, comfort, and ease, fecundity increased in some areas but not in any pronounced upward direction. In Santa Barbara the average family size rose only slightly from 1790. The community had grown to over 900 inhabitants by 1834, up from the 236 residents in 1790. However, the community only aver-

Adaped from "Hispano-Mexican Childrearing Practices in Pre-American Santa Barbara," by Gloria E. Miranda, *Southern California Quarterly*, LXV (Winter 1983), pp. 307–320.

aged 4.4 children per family, an increase of *one* over a forty-four year period.[4] In comparison, Los Angeles to the immediate south, experienced a similar but insignificant rise in household averages by 1836 even though the pueblo's population had grown at a faster rate than Santa Barbara's. The average family size in 1834 was 3.9 children.[5] The largest Santa Barbara family in 1834 listed thirteen children and the smallest units had one child.[6] Similar variations also existed in Los Angeles where twelve was the largest unit.[7]

In Santa Barbara some affluent clans were among the most prolific families in the province. For example, José de la Guerra, the patriarch of the community's most respected family, fathered thirteen children. Yet the illustrious De la Guerra, like other parents, was occasionally surpassed by his own children. De la Guerra's daughter, Teresa, in her marriage to a non-Mexican, William Hartnell, gave her parents eighteen grandchildren.[8] Her famous sibling, Angustias de la Guerra Jimeno had twelve children by her first spouse alone. The younger sisters, Anita and Maria Antonia, were less fertile, with eight children each. Brother Pablo fathered only seven.[9] However, they were not the largest clan in the area. The Ortega surname, another prominent Santa Barbara family, appeared more frequently on mission records during the Spanish and Mexican periods.[10]

For some Californians, having large families was considered a mark of status. According to one visitor, "the larger the family circle the more important the family."[11] Nonetheless, average California family size generally did not reflect such sentiments.

More precisely, several factors contributed to the downward trends in family size. Among the more important were the following: (1) infant mortality, (2) miscarriages, (3) infertility by either spouse, (4) absentee husbands who for economic motives left their families to seek work, (5) marital discord, and (6) personal choice of family size. Certainly the intimate factors in a marital relationship are historically difficult to assess but it is clear they had a direct bearing on fertility patterns in California.

On the average women in California usually conceived during their first or second year of marriage. Expectably since many women married in their middle teens in the Spanish period, they became mothers before they reached their eighteenth birthday. In the Mexican period women on the average wed only sightly later in their teens. By 1834 Santa Barbara women married ideally at age eighteen. By extension, first birth also occurred chronologically later by age twenty for many.[12]

CHILDBIRTH

Diaries and letters maintained by upper class women provide us with information on a number of universal prenatal and postnatal activities in California. Expectant mothers like Angustias de la Guerra Jimeno found food addictions to candied fruit and olives a common response to their condition.[13] For fathers-to-be, both the pregnancy and the period following childbirth diverted their energies to such activities as the construction of useful toys and furniture for their newborn offspring.[14]

For grandparents the arrival of a grandchild usually meant writing congratulatory letters to their children.[15] Women who were literate announced the birth in a similar fashion to family and friends.[16] And as infants grew, parents delighted in revealing each successful achievement of their children. The first steps taken, and the appearance of teeth, were common events recorded by proud parents.[17] Clipping locks of hair and sending them to relatives was a popular practice of the time.[18]

No medical facilities existed in California for expectant mothers but traditionally a midwife attended a mother-to-be when labor commenced.[19] Successful childbirth produced a typical response among new mothers. "Dí a luz un niño" [literally, I gave light to a child] symbolized a religio-philosophical Hispano-Mexican perspective consistent with the biblical story of creation.[20]

But tragedy sometimes marred childbirth. Baptismal registers also recorded infant mortality. As a rule most of these deaths occurred shortly after delivery or within a few months following birth.[21] During the period under study, a total of 272 infants and young children died in Santa Barbara, with greater incidences of male deaths reported.[22] Infant mortality figures for the Spanish era were lower than in the Mexican period. This statistic reflected the generally numerically smaller communities of the former period. With the increase of population in the Mexican era, total infant mortality figures also rose slightly although not in proportion to general growth.[23]

The cause of death among infants, children, or adults is not always cited in community burial registers. But local officials in the Spanish period maintained records on maladies that caused community health problems. In the early 1800s some of the most frequently cited illnesses included pleurisy, numerous viruses, and intestinal disorders which in 1804 were believed to have been caused by extreme climatic heat waves. One of the solar disturbances lasted six to eight months. Officially, at least two deaths were attributed to the heat wave that year.[24] Smallpox always struck with deadly force and occasionally plagued California society. Finally, Indian depredations have been listed as an infrequent cause of death among children.[25]

Because of the familial emphasis found among the Hispano-Mexican population, the death of a child from illness or other tragic circumstances left parents with a profound sense of loss. Consolation for the death of a son or daughter was usually found in the depths of their Catholic beliefs which were central to California culture. A grief-stricken Pablo de la Guerra sought with Christian resignation to comfort his wife on such an occasion when the couple lost a young daughter. He wrote to her:

> ...It is nevertheless a consolation to know that God called her and took her from this world, which every day becomes more corrupt and miserable. Now we have an innocent soul closer to the throne of God who is praying for you and me, prayers which we will need in order to sustain in a Christian manner so many bitter experiences that surround us on this earth.[26]

Santa Barbara records listed a total of 546 deaths of gente de razon children and adults during the Spanish and Mexican eras. However, in spite of the mortality rate live births still outnumbered deaths by three to one. In fact, provincial figures for the late 1820s reported similar three to one birth-death ratios throughout the region.[27] Total Santa Barbara births during the pre-statehood span numbered 1,709; of these 582 of the births occurred in the Spanish period with the additional 1,127 births taking place in the Mexican era. The greatest increase in live deliveries coincided with the rise of Santa Barbara's rancho age, the zenith epoch of frontier stability in California.[28]

Eighteen twin deliveries were included among Santa Barbara's total births for these two periods. Of these multiple births, one set of twins was of illegitimate status. The mother of another pair died during delivery and in a third case the male twin was stillborn.[29] No other multiple births were reported. Mission registers, however, listed three foundling cases. The first known abandoned child was left at the home of one of the presidial families in 1814. The fact that the number of abandoned children was inconsequential adds credence to the generally positive cultural sentiment toward children in California. Even in cases of illegitimacy the mother as a rule was expected to keep her infant and suffer social ridicule rather than part with her offspring. Franciscan missionaries reported only minor episodes of abandoned infants whom they in turn generally placed in foster homes.[30]

SOCIALIZATION

Regardless of circumstances surrounding birth, a child's socialization began as soon as the child became active. The most important role models young infants and children emulated were parents and older siblings. In particular, the example of adults served as an essential component of the socialization process among California's Hispano-Mexican families, regardless of their social standing. However, obvious patterns of deviance in child rearing between rich and poor was evidenced in the type of education families provided their children. Additional social class distinctions nurtured pretentiousness among the upper classes and accounted for the essential difference in lifestyle and outlook between both segments of society. But in terms of cultural values, California families of all classes inculcated basic religious values among the young.

A first step toward inculcating these principles was initiated by parents when they baptized their newborn offspring. This generally took place within a few days after birth. In Santa Barbara, baptismal records document parental diligence in carrying out the initiation of the young into the cultural and religious fraternity of the community. The prompt reception of the baptismal sacrament reflected parental fulfillment of their responsibility as members of the Catholic tradition. Also, it reflected a recognized understanding of the importance of entering the child into the Christian faith as soon as possible.

In accordance with these beliefs, parents frequently selected religious names for their offspring. María, or María in combination with another name, was the most frequently bestowed and popular proper name in Santa Barbara.[31] The choice of proper name for a child often reflected a desire to honor an important person, usually a saint or other religious figure. Occasionally, a parent might honor a particular religious site in this manner. For example, while awaiting the birth of her child in 1846, Angustias de la Guerra Jimeno decided to name the infant after Mission San Carlos.[32] Thus a child's birthdate acquired additional religious importance as a major feast day in the home.[33] In combination with the act of baptism, a child internalized and renewed a central cultural and religious goal of the socialization process each year.

During the Spanish era midwives and soldiers served as baptismal sponsors in Santa Barbara. But with the decline of presidial influence by the Mexican era, selecting relatives and close friends as godparents became more common. Childbirth increasingly took place on ranchos as the community separated itself geographically from the mission center. Because of these residential patterns, godparents frequently took the newborn to the mission for baptism or requested that a friar travel to the ranchos to confer the sacrament.[34]

As a child grew he might also acquire an affectionate nickname which became a part of his or her identity. Conferring nicknames was an Hispano-Mexican practice of singling out unique characteristics of each individual. When a person could not recall a proper name, a nickname served as an acceptable substitute. The De La Guerras are good examples of this custom. Friends and family frequently addressed José de la Guerra as *El Chato*, while his youngest daughter, María Antonia, was nicknamed *La Pantoya*.[35] Other sobriquets in the family included *El Obispo*, a name William Hartnell, Teresa's husband, bestowed with great affection on their second son Nathaniel. *Cuchichito* and *Bebeleche* were names for two other De la Guerra boys.[36] Twins were frequently called *cuate* or *cuata* [also spelled *coate* and *coata*].[37]

Besides obvious familial fondness of children, parental concerns during a child's formative years focused on nurturing responsibility, respect, and future maturity so that he or she could as an adult participate fully in society. The ancient Mexican method of inculcating proper manners and behavior through example served as an adequate model by which to teach children. In this manner as a youngster reached the age of reason, he or she acquired a new depth of knowledge and understanding of family and cultural values. Young boys and girls also learned useful skills that were essential in a frontier setting.

Of the many rugged traits developed by California youngsters, the mastering of riding and horsemanship skills before they could even walk impressed many foreigners. The consequences of early training begot acquisition of riding expertise by the age of ten or twelve.[38] Ability in the use of the lasso among the young also impressed foreigners. In an attempt to appear flattering, Edward Vischer reported that "the lasso is as important a part of their education as reading and writing are with us."[39] Instruction in the art of the lasso included constant practice in roping chickens and kittens with twine.[40] This process of instruction animated boys progressively from "ensnaring tame animals up to wild bulls and ferocious bears."[41] However, the formative years for California children were also directed to teaching them other skills and talents including correct social graces. Many became expert dancers, musicians, and masters of poetry and song.[42]

ADOLESCENCE

As children reached early adolescence a knowledge of adult duties and responsibilities in concert with continued parental respect and allegiance increased in importance. As a rule, decent society viewed disrespect and disobedience of one's elders as a grave offense. A reverent and respectful attitude to all relatives as well as to godparents was expected at all times. Friction between young and old was thus held to a minimum, as it contributed to solidifying family ties. Although disrespectful conduct was a grave social offense, California society deemed corporal punishment of a disobedient child an extreme form of discipline. Yet, respectful behavior by grown children persisted long after they married and became parents themselves. A father expected his matured son to account to him for grave transgressions, and physical punishment remained possible even at a great age.[43]

When young Pablo de la Guerra left his upper class surroundings to enter school at his brother-in-law William Hartnell's residence in Monterey, he found himself in a predicament that required discipline by a person other than his parents. Taking a typical adolescent stance, Pablo attempted to place the blame for his actions on Hartnell. He wrote his father that Hartnell had denied him permission to visit or speak with his sister Teresa. Since the school was located on the family premises, the lad had frequent opportunities to see her. However, according to the Englishman, Pablo had usurped his privileges as a student by assuming that family ties would permit a relaxation of normal student discipline. Justifying his own position, Hartnell informed his father-in-law that

> Pablo has no motive for complaining. Well, he has up to now had the same privileges as the other boys and since the beginning many more. It is untrue that he has been prohibited from speaking to Teresa. What has been forbidden him is to enter the house any time he wants, giving a thousand frivolous pretexts, but with the sole motive of chatting.[44]

The indignant Hartnell informed De la Guerra that Pablo had sufficient time during the day to speak to his sister when he wanted in the garden and was never denied permission to enter the house to visit her. Aware of the youth's efforts to undermine his authority, Hartnell admonished that if young Pablo continued in his abrasiveness, all school discipline would be useless.[45] The family considered the matter of discipline extremely important, but Pablo's mischievous behavior necessitated sterner measures. His pleas to return home made little impression on his father who put aside parental indulging for the sake of insuring that his son learn proper discipline and a more respectful attitude toward other relatives.

The De la Guerra boys had a reputation for mischievous behavior. William Heath Davis found them to be "a little wild" and not adverse to playing pranks. Davis recounted one particularly memorable incident involving the boys and their father's secret hiding place. Apparently they had discovered the location where their father kept his money and soon " devised a plan to secure some of it for their own use."[46] The boys climbed onto the roof of the house, removed some tile from the attic portion and, using a pitchfork took as many gold coins as necessary for their use. De la Guerra eventually detected the scheme and appropriately disciplined the boys. But since the father could not recall the amount of money he had accumulated, he failed to discern how much he had lost to his errant sons.[47]

While pranks were common among boys of all backgrounds, they eventually developed correct modes of behavior as they outgrew stages in which they selfishly manipulated loved ones. By early adolescence enculturation was complete in most children, particularly family pride and religious principles.[48] At this stage of development upper and lower class family practices took different paths. For the latter, learning a skill or a trade prepared them for the responsibilities of their adult life. More fortunate were boys from affluent families who could offer them more formal educational opportunities. José de la Guerra provided several of his young sons with such an education,

sparing no expense in sending them to Mexico City and Europe to acquire instruction. Perhaps one of the most brilliant of his sons was Juan José. Born in 1810, he received his education in England at the insistence of William Hartnell.[49] In keeping with his family's staunch Catholic outlook, he attended a Jesuit college.[50] In one of his numerous letters to his then new brother-in-law, the sixteen-year-old reported on his academic accomplishments at the Liverpool school he was attending. The lad informed Hartnell of his "considerable improvement in Latin," as evidenced by his ability to translate Ovid's *Metamorphoses* and his mastery of such studies as ancient history, geography, chemistry, and natural science.[51]

Like many Catholic fathers, José de la Guerra evidently wished to fulfill a lifelong dream through his eldest son. But despite deep parental love, the young man was adverse to entering the priesthood. The son's behavior was similar to some of his brothers. Uncontrolled youthful tendencies distracted him from developing the necessary discipline or spiritual desire to enter the religious life. Moreover, the lengthy separation from his family had generated a stronger longing to return to the comforts of home rather than to pursue the spiritual life. When he returned to California Juan José put his European schooling to practical use by supporting Hartnell's educational projects. But tragedy interrupted his work. The young man died suddenly at the age of twenty-three.[52] De la Guerra's younger sons nonetheless followed in their brother's footsteps by receiving a formal education in Mexico City and also later visiting Europe.

Before beginning their travels Pablo and his brother Joaquín, along with their Hartnell nephews, had become the first pupils at their uncle's school. While studying in Monterey the boys learned to write poetry and other flowery verses. The school provided an atmosphere where a boy or girl could express poetically the honest affection that existed between the young. The literary flair of Hartnell's pupils matched that learned by most children in the province. A poem written later in life and dedicated by Pablo to his young niece, Amelia Hartnell, reflected his earlier schoolboy training.[53] He described her as "pure as a diamond, of graceful and proud form, wide ivory-colored forehead, delicate scarlet mouth, mischievous and lazy eyes." A true beauty who could doubtless conquer the unwary heart of a youth by her charms alone.[54] But Pablo's academic excellence was restricted to poetry at this point for he did not match this fervor in other subjects. Apparently his youthful distractions and familiarity with tutors at age fourteen prevented him from completely immersing himself in serious study.[55]

CALIFORNIA GIRLS

A formal education was generally unavailable for most young girls in the Spanish and Mexican periods. Opportunities were limited to tutoring or private schooling if affordable for upper class females. Similar educational disadvantages were shared by the poor. Frontier isolation of northern Mexico from the rest of the country provided California with meager public instructional facilities. The few schools in the province usually stayed open for only short periods at a time. Nor were they sufficient enough to meet the needs of the populace.[56]

As a consequence, self-motivation served as an educational incentive for upper class women. Some of the wealthy maintained family libraries which afforded young girls like Angustias de la Guerra the unique opportunity to educate themselves.[57] However, girls received at best a rudimentary education commensurate with their future role as wives and mothers. In many upper class homes girls learned and acquired skills in home management, drawn work, music, and dance.[58] The frontier society of the Mexican era considered domestic and social refinement a valuable asset

and more practical than formal learning for girls of all classes. But emphasis on domestic skills never precluded the possibility or necessity of socializing young girls to the rigors of frontier living.

The observations of an astonished Anglo-American male who visited California in the early American era illustrates the success of socializing young girls and women to handle the rigors of the frontier. He was clearly vexed and surprised by what he saw on one occasion.

> Well, I washed my clothes, a job I positively hate—I would rather climb a three-thousand-foot mountain—and to make matters more aggravating, as I was in the midst of it, along came two women, one young and quite pretty, who were assisting as *vaqueros*. A rodeo took place near camp, and several thousand head of cattle were assembled, wild almost as deer. Of course it takes many vaqueros to manage them, all mounted, and with lassos. A rodeo is a great event on a ranch, and these women, the wife and daughter of a ranchero came out to assist in getting in the cattle. Well mounted, they managed their horses superbly, and just as I was up to my elbows in soapsuds, along they came, with a herd of several hundred cattle, back from the hills. I straightened my aching backing, drew a long breath, and must have blushed [if a man can blush when tanned the color of smoked bacon] and reflected on the doctrine of woman's rights—I, a stout man, washing my shirt, and those ladies practicing the art of *vaqueros*.[59]

Others became superb horsewomen, traveling "sixty or seventy miles in a day" without complaining.[60] Some travelers praised the skills of young Mexican girls, comparing them favorably to women in the United States. Remarked one traveler, "I never saw ladies in the East who could approach the poorest of the Spanish ladies whom I have yet seen ride."[61]

By the advent of United States control of California, socialization of young girls remained basically unaltered. But the benefits of more formal education as well were now available to upper class daughters and granddaughters. Some wealthy and affluent families sent their granddaughters to convents in northern California.[62] However, among the poorer segment of the populace, both male and female, illiteracy remained the rule. At best most were able to sign their names. Nonetheless, as deficient as systematic educational opportunities might have been, a majority of Hispano-Mexican youth achieved a healthy and mature outlook regarding societal values by middle adolescence. Girls had acquired a realistic conscious understanding of expected role-playing for married life and modeled their aspirations accordingly. Most young males established similar role expectations by late adolescence. The adulthood cycle that followed usually led to marriage which in turn gave birth to a new generation of California children. As parents, young couples initiated the socialization process and ritual anew.

Notes

1 For example, see William Garner, *Letters from California, 1846–1847*, edited by Donald M. Craig (Berkeley: University of California Press, 1970), p. 92, who remarked that "I have no doubt, on the whole, that all women who have been married within the last twenty years in California would average each the birth of a child every fifteen months." Garner could not have possibly had such intimate knowledge of all Hispano-Mexicans. See also Edwin Bryant, *What I Saw In California* (Minneapolis: Ross & Haines, Inc., 1967), p. 261 and Walter Colton, *The California Diary* (Oakland: Biobooks, 1948), p. 9.

2 The *gente de razon* populace of California and northern New Spain included all Christian subjects regardless of race: Spaniards, mixed-bloods, and baptized non-mission Indians.

3 The largest family at San Francisco included fourteen children. Monterey's largest had six children and San José's biggest family included seven children. See 1790 Provincial Census of California, Thomas Workman Temple Collection (xerox of originals in Chancery Archives, Los Angeles), Santa Barbara Mission Archives hereafter cited SBMA.

4 1834 Santa Barbara Census, Temple Collection.

5 *1836 Mexican Census of Los Angeles and Orange County Area.* Family sizes in Los Angeles remained static over the next decade with the average households in 1844 comprised of 3.9 children. See Richard Griswold del Castillo, "La Raza Hispano-Americana: The Emergence of an Urban Culture among the Spanish-Speaking of Los Angeles, 1850–1880" (Doctoral Dissertation, University of California, Los Angeles, 1974), p. 181, note 41.

6 The next most numerous family had eleven children. Four had nine progeny, while twelve couples had eight and seven children respectively. Sixteen couples had six, and twenty-two had five; twelve had four children; eighteen listed three children; thirteen listed two offspring and twenty-three only one.

7 At Los Angeles one couple had eleven children and four listed ten offspring. Two had nine; eight had eight and ten families were comprised of seven children while seventeen couples had six progeny. Twenty-three couples had five children with twenty-seven reporting four youngsters. Twenty-six listed three children with twenty-eight couples claiming only two offspring. Thirty families had only one child.

8 Marie Northrop, "Las Familias de California," *Historical Society of Southern California Quarterly,* XLII (March 1960), p. 89.

9 Thomas B. Dibblee, *Family Notes* (Santa Barbara: By the Author, 1822), pp. 20–21, Folder 1100, De la Guerra Collection, SBMA.

10 Maynard Geiger, O.F.M., *Mission Santa Barbara, 1782–1965* (Santa Barbara, 1965), p. 22.

11 Joseph W. Revere, *Naval Duty in California* (Oakland: Biobooks, 1947), p. 146.

12 Statistical data for the Spanish period indicates that fertile women generally became mothers on the average at seventeen or eighteen.

13 Angustias de la Guerra Jimeno, Journal, September 17, 1846, Folder 725, De la Guerra Collection. Oranges were consumed in large quantities by Josefa Romero Valle of Baja California. See Josefa to José Maria Valle, October, 1843, Del Valle Collection, Los Angeles County Natural History Museum.

14 Domingo Carrillo to José de la Guerra, July 1, 1835, Santa Barbara, Folder 141,, De la Guerra Collection.

15 José de la Guerra to Pablo de la Guerra, October 10, 1849, Santa Barbara, Folder 478, De la Guerra Collection.

16 Manuela Carrillo de Jones to José de la Guerra, June 2, 1840, Santa Barbara, Folder 567, De la Guerra Collection.

17 María Estebanez de Cota to María Antonia Carrillo de la Guerra, June 6, 1831, Lima, Peru, Folder 206, De la Guerra Collection.

18 Josefa Romero Valle to Jose Maria Valle, January 31, 1844, Tepic, Number 1916, Del Valle Collection; Susanna B. Dakin, *The Lives of William Hartnell* (Stanford: Stanford University Press, 1949), p. 165.

19 Colton, *California Diary*, p. 9 Bryant, *What I Saw In California*, p. 261.

20 María a Estebanez de Cota to María a Antonia de la Guerra, June 6, 1831, Lima, Peru, Folder 206; Manuela Carrillo de Jones to José de la Guerra, June 2, 1840, Santa Barbara, Folder 567, De la Guerra Collection.

21 "Alphabetical and Chronological Burial Register of Non-Indians, Santa Barbara, 1782–1848," SBMA, lists a female infant dying within two months of birth in 1782 with a male child dying after receiving baptism in 1784. That same year another male child died at two years of age. For both periods a total 172 adults and 272 infants and young children died.

22 In the Spanish period sixty male children and fifty-one females died. In the Mexican era eighty-eight male and seventy-three female children died.

23 A total of 103 adult deaths were reported for the Spanish period with an additional 171 listed for the Mexican era.

24 José Raimundo Carrillo to Governor José Juan Arrillaga, December 31, 1803, Santa Barbara. Archives of California. Provincial State Papers. (Benicia) Military, Volume 16, Transcripts, May 10, 1805. Informes y Correspondencia, 1802–1822. Archivo de la mision de Santa Barbara, Volume 9, BL.

25 José M. Bonilla, "Documentos para la Historia de California," Ms., BL.

26 Maynard Geiger, O.F.M., "Selected Letters of Pablo de la Guerra to his Wife, Josefa Moreno, 1851–1872," *Noticias*, XX (Fall 1974), p. 10.

27 Hubert H. Bancroft, *California Pastoral* (San Francisco: The History Company, Publishers, 1888), p. 613.

28 "Baptismal Register of Non-Indians, Santa Barbara, 1782–1861," SBMA.

29 The illegitimate set of twins was born to a widow with the father's identity listed as unknown. They were born on December 9, 1844, Numbers 1642 and 1643 in the Santa Barbara Baptismal Register. A mother died giving birth to two female twins on April 2, 1822. See Numbers 612 and 613 in the Baptismal Register. A male stillborn twin died July 21, 1812. See No. 410 in the register.

30 See Numbers 460, 664, and 674 in the Santa Barbara Baptismal Register.

31 Geiger, *Mission Santa Barbara* p. 22.

32 Angustias de la Guerra Jimeno, Journal, November 5, 1846, De la Guerra Collection, predicted that she was going to have a daughter and if correct, she would name her Carolina in honor of the second mission founded in California, San Carlos. At the time Angustias was approximately eight months pregnant.

33 José Señan, O.F.M. to José de la Guerra, March 15, 1819, San Buenaventura, Folder 904, De la Guerra Collection. The missionary sent the military commandant of Santa Barbara a birthday greeting on the feast day of Saint Joseph.

34 Geiger, *Mission Santa Barbara*, p. 19; Colton, *California Diary*, p. 57; Craig, *Garner Letters from California*, p. 109.

35 *El Chato* meant flatnosed. María a Antonia's nickname, however, remains obscure in its meaning. Angustias de la Guerra Jimeno, Journal, August, 1846, Folder 725, De la Guerra Collection; Joseph Thompson, O.F.M., *El Gran Capitan Jose de la Guerra (Los Angeles: Cabrera & Sons, 1961), p. 6;* Hubert Howe Bancroft, *Register of Pioneer Inhabitants of California, 1542–1848* (Los Angeles: Dawson's Book Shop, 1964), p. 174.

36 *El Obispo* means the bishop while *bebeleche* means milk drinker. *Cuchichito's* meaning is unknown. William Hartnell to José de la Guerra, March 23, 1834, Monterey, Folder 492, De la

Guerra Collection; Dakin, *Lives of William Hartnell*, p. 112; Geiger, "Selected Letters of Pablo de la Guerra to his Wife, Josefa Moreno," PP. 12, 22 *note*, 44; Geiger, *The Letters of Alfred Robinson to the De la Guerra Family of Santa Barbara, 1834–1873* (Los Angeles: Zamorano Club, 1972), pp. 27, 61, note 113.

37 Geiger, "Selected Letters of Pablo de la Guerra to his Wife, Josefa Moreno," p. 21, note 17. The Nahuatl *coatl* is the root word for the Mexican Spanish term *cuate* and *cuata*.

38 Craig, *Garner Letters from California*, p. 110; Colton, *California Diary*, p. 57.

39 Erwin G. Gudde, trans. and ed., *Edward Vischer's First Visit to California* (San Francisco: California Historical Society, 1940), p. 13.

40 Alexander Forbes, *California: A History of Upper and Lower California* (San Francisco: John Henry Nash, Printer, 1937), p. 171.

41 Theodore H. Hittell, *History of California* (4 vols.; San Francisco: N.J. Stone & Company, 1897), II: 490.

42 Almost all accounts on the gente de razon contain information on the social graces of the populace. Apart from the memoirs of the native-born, foreign residents and travelers also commented on this aspect of family life. For example, see William Heath Davis, *Seventy-Five Years in California* (San Francisco: John Howell, 1929), pp. 61, 68.

43 José Arnaz, "Memoirs of a Merchant," *Touring Topics*, XX (September–October 1928), p. 18.

44 William Hartnell to José de la Guerra, June 12, 1834, Monterey, Folder 492, De la Guerra Collection.

45 *Ibid.* Hartnell to De la Guerra, June 12, 1834. Hartnell also informed his father-in-law that Pablo had made progress in his studies and if he applied himself he would improve more than he had up to that point. Commenting on his own son, Nathaniel, Hartnell proudly boasted that "el obispo" was a good boy with an excellent mind, utilizing his capabilities more so than his older brother.

46 Davis, *Seventy-Five Years in California*, p. 240

47 *Ibid.*

48 Mariano G. Vallejo, "Ranch and Mission Days in Alta California," *Century Magazine*, XLI (November 1890–April 1891), p. 191; Davis, *Seventy-Five Years in California*, p. 61.

49 Dakin, *Lives of William Hartnell*, p. 159.

50 Juan José entered the Jesuit institution, Stonyhurst College, in 1828. See Dakin, *Lives of William Hartnell*, p. 166.

51 Juan José de la Guerra to William Hartnell, November 24, 1826, Liverpool, England, Folder 386, de la Guerra Collection.

52 Dakin, *Lives of William Hartnell*, p. 171.

53 Personal Papers of Pablo de la Guerra, Folder 1093, De la Guerra Collection.

54 *Ibid.*

55 William Hartnell to José de la Guerra, March 23, 1834, Monterey, Folder 492, De la Guerra Collection. According to Pablo's tutor, Father Patrick Short, he was doing poorly in algebra.

56 Bancroft, *History of California* (7 vols.; San Francisco: A.L. Bancroft & Company, Publishers, 1884), II: 680 and *California Pastoral*, p. 496, describes the sporadic and meager educational facilities in Santa Barbara. The first private school was established in 1784 and lasted about three years. A public school followed in 1795. During the 1820's sixty-seven students were reportedly attending school in the community with Marcos Bonilla listed as the Schoolmaster in 1835. For a dated but general study of education in California before 1846 see J. Andrew Ewing, "Education in California During the Pre-Statehood Period," *Historical Society of Southern California Annual Publications*, XI (1918), 51–59.

57 Joseph Thompson, O.F.M., "Casa de la Guerra," Ms., p. 3, De la Guerra Collection; Dakin, *Lives of William Hartnell*, pp. 168–169.

58 Thompson, "Casa de la Guerra," p. 6.

59 Francis P. Farquahar, ed., *Up and Down California in 1860–1864: The Journal of William H. Brewer* (New Haven: Yale University Press, 1930), pp. 285–286.

60 *Ibid.*, pp. 160–161.

61 *Ibid.*, p. 75.

62 Thompson, "Casa de la Guerra," p. 6; Bishop Alemany to Angustias de la Guerra Jimeno, July 21, 1856, San Francisco, Folder 19, De la Guerra Collection. Angustias sent her daughters to a nun's school in Benicia to receive formal education.

## CHAPTER 7

PSYCHOHISTORY AND JOHN CHARLES FRÉMONT

EDITOR'S INTRODUCTION

Of all the "new directions" in contemporary American historiography, perhaps none has been pursued with greater enthusiasm than psychohistory. Responding with equal fervor, critics of the new discipline have denied its claims to legitimacy.

Psychohistorians use a systematic psychology—most notably psychoanalysis—to explain the motivation of historical figures. The psychohistorians are provocative because they turn much of traditional historical analysis on its head. Rather than investigating how public events affect private lives, psychohistorians seek to show how private fantasies are acted out on the public stage. Rather than focusing on the activities of adult men's lives, they analyze how history is first determined by women and children, as well as men, and how early childhood experiences are later reflected in adult public activities. The main drama in psychohistory is not the struggle between classes or nations or races, but between Freud's tripartite divisions of the mind, the id, the ego, and the superego.

The importance of early childhood experiences for this type of analysis is suggested by the unofficial slogan of the *Journal of Psychohistory,* "no childhood, no psychohistory." Many psychohistorians subscribe to the "psychogenic theory of history," in which the basis for understanding human motivation is not economic or social class but "*psycho*class"—shared childrearing modes. Thus the primary motivating force for men and women is a lifelong search for *relation,* rather than a drive for money or power.[1]

Critics have leveled the charge of reductionism at the psychohistorians, complaining that they have reduced history to a study of merely personal motives.[2]

---

[1]Lloyd deMause, *Foundations of Psychohistory* (New York, 1982), ii–iii, v.

[2]For a discussion of the charge of reductionism, see Saul Friedlander, *History and Psychoanalysis: An Inquiry into the Possibilities and Limits of Psychohistory,* trans, Susan Suleiman (New York, 1978), 32–34.

The psychohistorians respond that all motives are personal, and that by identifying and cataloging these motives they are simply doing what all social scientists attempt to do: to render seemingly complex and disparate phenomena into simpler and more basic laws or principles. It is the writers of traditional narrative history, the psycho-historians assert, who are the true reductionists. The narrative historians, with their naive antitheoretical empiricism, themselves reduce history to an assemblage of "facts" bereft of meaning or significance.

The leading advocate of the use of psychohistory in California studies is Andrew Rolle. In the following selection, Rolle analyzes John Charles Frémont and offers an intriguing explanation of the motives of this perplexing figure. Heretofore treated as both a hero and scoundrel, Frémont has long stirred passionate debate among historians.[3] Rolle moves this debate into a new arena. What were Frémont's true motivations? How can psychohistory help us to unravel the contradictions and often self-destructive behavior of Frémont? In answering these questions, Rolle emphasizes Frémont's early childhood experiences, his illegitimacy, the early death of his father, and his marriage to Jessie Benton Frémont as major factors in determining the course of Frémont's adult career.

Andrew Rolle is Cleland Professor of History at Occidental College. He is the author of more than a dozen books, including *California: A History* (1987). He received his training in psychoanalysis and psychiatry at the Southern California Psychoanalytic Institute and at the Cedars-Sinai Medical Center in Los Angeles.

---

[3]The classic defense of Frémont is Allan Nevins, *Frémont: The West's Greatest Adventurer*, 2 vols. (New York, 1928); the sharpest critique appears in Bernard DeVoto, *The Year of Decision: 1846* (Boston, 1961). See also Cardinal Goodwin, *John Charles Frémont: An Exploration of his Career* (1930) and Ferol Egan, *Frémont: Explorer for a Restless Nation* (New York, 1977).

Psychohistory and John Charles Frémont

Andrew Rolle

For several generations John Charles Frémont has perplexed historians. We have called him "a man unafraid," "the West's greatest adventurer," "the pathfinder," and, less generously, the follower of other men's trails. In 1890, the year of Frémont's death, the American philosopher Josiah Royce wrote that "an analysis of the very peculiar qualities that marked the late General Frémont would doubtless be a charming task for the student of psychology." Royce considered "our hero" to be an "enigma," who had been "profoundly mysterious" about his "nebulous past."[1] In the light of new techniques, it would now seem possible to clear up at least some of the conflict and confusion about Frémont's long, enigmatic career.

Frémont's life pattern, torn by controversy and filled with unpredictable acts, commingled inconsistency with what lay persons usually call arrogance and vanity. But the ambition and guile, which ultimately tarnished and stained his record, had deep roots. The "new psychohistory" seeks to uncover those buried impulses that make such a person's activities clearer. Historians trained in psychiatry and psychoanalysis need to explore with compassion a leader's emotional structure, though his motives may, on the surface, seem countervailing and ambivalent. We must somehow learn how to interpret unconscious feeling—including id (drives), ego (selfhood), and superego (conscience) factors. These emotional subtleties function as important causal determinants in history. To neglect the role of feeling and unconscious motivation in the life of a Frémont

amounts to a form of denial, of indeed the ultimate "reductionism." Thus this essay shall review key episodes in Frémont's life and then attempt various alternative psychohistorical analyses of his behavioral patterns.

Frémont was the illegitimate son of an *émigré*, Charles Frémon (no "t") and of a Virginia woman of upperclass origins, Anne Pryor. In 1813, when John Charles was born, his mother was still technically, but unhappily, married to an elderly Revolutionary War veteran, Major John Pryor. A dozen years after their wedding, Anne met Frémon, a teacher of French to young women, and a painter of frescoes who did occasional upholstering. Frémon later became, if only briefly, a "French professor" in a "female academy." Frémon, also referred to as a "dancing master," conducted language classes at various Richmond residences. By June 1810 he had intruded himself into the Pryor household. When the major learned that he had been cuckolded, he seems to have vowed retribution. Anne wrote to a brother-in-law that Pryor had turned her "out of doors at night and in an approaching storm" and that he threatened her with "the most cruel and violent treatment."[2] In Richmond society scandal was difficult to hide. A petition of December 7, 1811, speaks of "criminal intercourse" between Frémon and Anne. The last one sees in print about the infuriated Major Pryor is a newspaper notice, published in 1811, to the effect that his wife had abandoned his home and run off with Frémon.

In 1818, five years after the birth of John Charles, his father died, leaving Frémont's mother with three children to rear in straitened circumstances. While such a loss is often resented by small children, Frémont was to deny any early influences upon his later life. In all his

Adapted from "Exploring an Explorer: Psychohistory and John Charles Frémont," by Andrew Rolle. Copyright © 1982 by the American Historical Association, Pacific Coast Branch. Reprinted from *Pacific Historical Review*, Vol. LI, No. 2, pp. 135–164, by permission of the Association.

writings he does not once mention his father. He rationalizes his early behavior and minimizes all of his setbacks and disappointments. Although his childhood frustrations did sink out of sight (like an underground stream below the prairies he was to traverse), later they reappeared in different forms. To chart the course of Frémont's unconscious emotions, which surfaced as waywardness, is not easy. For, in his defense of selfhood, he utilized two illusive psychoanalytic mechanisms—repression and transference.

The young boy grew up in Charleston, South Carolina, where he was befriended by prominent persons. He is described as "spoiled" as well as "wanting in discipline," as possessing a love of pleasure and excitement.[3] Like his refugee father, Frémont became a wanderer—from an early age roving restlessly from place to place. He remained in love with the out-of-doors. His widowed mother found it hard to control so high-spirited a lad, yet a close attachment to her developed:

> We were only two, my mother and I. We had lost my sister. My brother was away....I was unwilling to leave my mother. Circumstances had more than usually endeared us to each other and I knew that her life would be solitary without me....[4]

During these years Frémont was lean, wiry, and was said to be as handsome as Lord Byron and as mysterious as Sir Richard Burton. He attracted the attention of Joel Poinsett, prominent in South Carolina politics, who secured an appointment for him in 1833, at age twenty, as a teacher of mathematics aboard a naval sloop-of-war, the *Natchez,* for a cruise along the South American coast. In 1838 Frémont began service as an officer in the topographical engineers of the United States Army; he surveyed future railroad sites and mapped unexplored territory throughout the Middle and Far West.

New and prominent sponsors, in addition to Poinsett (who became Secretary of War), appeared. These allies included the explorer Jean

Nicholas Nicollet and the expansionist Senator Thomas Benton. The young Lieutenant John Charles married Benton's sixteen-year-old daughter, Jessie, in 1841. Frémont was then twenty-seven. The ceremony was in secret because the Bentons did not wish their daughter to marry an unknown and penniless young officer over ten years older than she. By eloping with her, Frémont went against the authority of his most powerful new friend and mentor.

Benton was in a powerful position to sponsor his son-in-law in a series of expeditions designed to open up the American West. Frontier explorations and the influence of Benton rapidly made Frémont one of the best known men of his time. Jessie's reminiscences assert that the War Department was actually run from the Benton library in Saint Louis and from her father's Washington committee room. She called her father (who for twenty years was chairman of the Senate Military Committee) "practically the Secretary of War in all those years, for he was a fixture while a Secretary is only a political accident...."[5]

ESCAPADES

We must now consider a series of escapades that resemble Ian Fleming's character James Bond. How many controversies and personal difficulties in which Frémont proceeded to embroil himself! (I shall not dwell at length upon all these quarrels and precipitate acts but shall seek in this essay to examine the reasons behind half a dozen key events.) They occurred during various expeditions.

The first of these was in mid-1842. That year Frémont left his young wife six months pregnant and headed northwest from Saint Louis to chart the Platte River and the South Pass route toward Oregon. On the return trip he found the Platte swollen and difficult to cross. Accompanied by the cartographer Charles Preuss, Frémont decided to save his party the trouble of unloading their baggage by shooting the rapids of the flooded Platte River in a collapsible rubber boat. When it capsized, the guns, ammunition, various journals, the sextant, telescope, and food were lost. This impetuous risk-taking "might have destroyed completely the records of his expedition."[6]

In 1843–1844 Frémont's second government exploring expedition produced further instances of rash and opportunist judgments involving people and events. On that occasion he took along a (later overly celebrated) twelve-pound cannon which was to cast doubt upon the peaceful intent of his thirty-nine man contingent. After he left home, when the party was camped but four miles away, Jessie Frémont received a dispatch from Washington requesting that her husband explain why he was taking such a weapon on a nonmilitary trip. Jessie was a senator's daughter. She knew that this query might delay if not cancel the expedition. She held the letter back. Only upon Frémont's return did he learn of this correspondence. From the start one notes a connivance between John Charles and Jessie.[7]

Following the Platte again, the explorer made a wide circle through much of present-day Oregon after surveying the Columbia River Basin. In what is today western Nevada, Frémont suddenly decided to cross the Sierra Nevada into California. There were few passes and, obviously, no maps. Peaks soared to the 14,000 foot level and no white man had ever crossed the range from east to west in winter. Frémont's men were tired and footsore as well as anxious to return eastward to Saint Louis. After an arduous struggle with both weather and terrain (during which the small cannon was cached), the party emerged near today's community of Woodfords. His men suffered from snow blindness and resembled a band of skeletons. Only two years later the celebrated Donner Party was decimated while attempting the same foolhardy exploit.

Frémont may have reached a previous understanding with Benton to reconnoiter the strength of the Mexican forces in the province. Nevertheless, this departure from his schedule and mid-winter crossing of the Sierra, never before attempted, endangered the lives of his men. He was to do so again on his fourth expedition, and that time with tragic results.

The next year, 1845, at age thirty-two, Frémont left Saint Louis on a third expedition in the company of the frontier scout Kit Carson. They explored the Salt Lake Basin, and reentered California in December of that year. He took a band of sixty-eight men, including six Delaware Indians, to Monterey in order to confer with United States Consul Thomas Oliver Larkin. Suddenly he and his men appeared, menacingly, in the hills outside Monterey. General José Tiburcio Castro, prefect of California's capital district, notified Frémont that he would have to leave the province. The explorer ignored this message and led his party to the summit of Gavilan Peak. Despite the advice of the embarrassed Larkin, Frémont built a log and earth fort. Only "slowly and growlingly," as he later described it, did he take his group (still ostensibly an exploring party) northward toward today's Oregon border.

Overtaken at Klamath Lake by Marine Lieutenant Archibald H. Gillespie—the "messenger of destiny"—with letters and dispatches, Frémont swung back toward California. Approaching the Marysville Buttes, sixty miles north of Sutter's Fort, he met a band of dissident Americans bearing rumors of impending war between Mexico and the United States. In June these settlers captured a band of horses being driven to the Santa Clara Valley by the Californios, and took them to Frémont. On the fourteenth of June, these "Bear Flaggers" also raided the northern town of Sonoma, hoisted a Bear Flag, and captured General Mariano Guadalupe Vallejo, commander of the northern frontier zone of California. This official was actually quite friendly toward Americans. Frémont, allowing himself to be drawn into this affray, gave the unofficial revolt his tacit support. The uprising could have become California's Alamo disaster had Commodore John Sloat not captured Monterey soon thereafter. Frémont later claimed he had received authorization from the United States government. We have no solid evidence to verify his justification.[8] "The Bear Flag Revolution," according to John Hawgood, "would undoubtedly not have bulked so large in history...but for the attempts to tamper with the record by John C. Frémont...and by his gifted wife...."[9]

Next, Frémont became the center of a power fight that involved two branches of the military in California: Commodore Robert F. Stockton (who replaced Sloat) and the crusty Brigadier General Stephen Watts Kearny. Stockton appointed Frémont commander of a new military force, the California Battalion, composed of American volunteers and the members of his original exploring group. Meanwhile, General Kearny and a party of three hundred dragoons headed west, arriving at San Diego on December 12, 1846, after suffering an embarrassing defeat at nearby San Pasqual. Frémont added to Kearny's insult by recovering howitzers captured from Kearny's troops.

Early in January 1847 the resentful Kearny, as well as Stockton and Frémont, converged upon Los Angeles. There Andrés Pico, brother of California's governor, surrendered the town (occupied by Stockton and Kearny) not to the general or to the commodore but to Frémont, who had been made a major by Stockton. He was later commissioned (on June 25, 1846) a lieutenant colonel by President Polk. Stockton's promotion, bestowed upon Frémont by a navy man, was most irritating to General Kearny. The Cahuenga Capitulation of January 13, which Frémont signed with Pico, was furthermore a lenient document, also resented by Kearny.

Commodore Stockton, who had gone out to sea on January 16, left Kearny and Frémont to settle their differences. At issue were two matters: Kearny's anger over the surrender of Los Angeles to Frémont, and the question of who

should be the military governor of California. Although clearly outranked, Frémont disregarded Kearny's wishes. Kearny withdrew to the capital, Monterey, while Frémont remained in Los Angeles. The general repeatedly ordered Frémont to report to him. Instead, the younger man acted as though he were the military governor for a period of two months.

Most young officers only thirty-four years old would never have engaged in a foolish jurisdictional controversy with a senior officer newly promoted to general. Frémont not only ignored the repeated summons of Kearny but challenged the general's subordinate, Colonel Richard B. Mason (himself later military governor of California), to a duel with double-barreled shotguns. After Frémont's repeated disobedience, Kearny established his own authority as the chief military officer in California. He seems vindictively not to have informed Frémont of new instructions from Washington appointing him governor. Kearny possibly "strung out" Frémont to produce grounds for a future court-martial. Eventually Kearny took Frémont eastward under arrest. At Washington he charged the upstart with mutiny, disobeying the commands of his superiors, and conduct prejudicial to good order and military discipline.

Although a pattern of erratic and impulsive behavior had by then already emerged, Frémont never recognized this in himself. His *Memoirs* virtually ignore his conflict with General Kearny with this bland statement:

I close the page because my path of life led out from among the grand and lovely features of nature, and its pure and wholesome air, into the poisoned atmosphere and jarring circumstances of conflict among men, made subtle and malignant by clashing interests.[10]

Indeed, Frémont stopped his *Memoirs* at the very point where he was held up in life itself by the court-martial. He mentioned neither his trial nor Kearny beyond the description in his narrative when he accepted the capitulation of the

Californians at Los Angeles. Frémont preferred, instead, to speak in terms of "an unreflecting life among chosen companions," of "an unrestrained life in the open air," of being able to enjoy each day "as it came, without thought for the morrow."[11]

During Frémont's court-martial trial there is evidence that the verdict might have been more favorable if he had stopped his cross-examination of General Kearny earlier. By persisting in counterattacking Kearny's charges of disobedience to his orders, he and Benton made Kearny a sort of underdog instead of the villain. The military jury sentenced Frémont to be dismissed from the army. The Benton clan saw the judgment as most unfair, yet President James K. Polk reluctantly approved this verdict, except as to mutiny, and remitted the penalty. Instead of accepting Polk's pardon, Frémont haughtily resigned his army commission on February 19, 1849.[12]

Frémont was known as a man who did not look back, lose courage, or express regrets, even about reprimands from two Presidents of the United States (Polk and, later, Abraham Lincoln). On the contrary, after his court-martial he seemingly "became more determined than ever to win laurels as an explorer." He also grew "more aloof...and sensitive about his own honor and less sensitive about the welfare of the men who joined his expeditions." If anything, the court martial added to Frémont's national reputation—fortifying the fantasy that "he had played a daring role in the acquisition of California."[13]

ANALYSIS

The formative periods of our childhood and youth remain in deepest shadow. Yet it need not surprise us if, at an early stage, Frémont found it necessary to wall himself off from powerful feelings of sorrow over the loss of his father and his own illegitimacy. In the nineteenth century his bastard status was considered much more scandalous than now. What emerged was a life pattern of a restless, driving, often unfulfilled person. He reminds one of the cliché: "The enemy is within us." To what extent did the illegitimate child fester inside Frémont? Was he one of those rebels who seek to destroy authority because they wish to restore a lost security? He lived as though he could, through repeated adventures, prove himself—as though his exploits would make him a legitimate child.

In all his writings Frémont never mentioned his father, nor did he acknowledge that he was illegitimate, or that his father died when the boy was only five years old. Yet all of one's life is linked together, especially by traumatic events around us.

Frémont also had an interior life. We know that illegitimate one-parent children often feel abandoned. To offset their sense of aloneness they may resort to dramatic (if self-defeating) means. Frémont's adventurous and dangerous roles allowed superficial feelings of victory to transcend the original sadness over the loss of his father.[14] Also, small boys may take satisfaction in supplanting their fathers when they leave or die. We do not really know what Frémont's relations with his father were like and must attempt to reconstruct the probabilities, based upon similar cases. What we do know is that, before he met Senator Benton, Frémont seems to have related well to men. In his early maturity these included the already mentioned Poinsett and Nicollet as well as Captain W. G. Williams, Lieutenant David Farragut, and Dr. John Robertson. However, a series of emotional storms with antagonists were masked by the seeking of publicity and renown. On occasion Frémont's conduct resembled that adolescent excess designed to anger one's parents or superiors. People either loved or hated his flamboyance, usually mixed with irresponsibility.

There was something almost obsessive about Frémont's refusal to set limits for himself.[15] A childlike determination could have stemmed from the absence of a father's discipline. Frémont's later clashes with authority figures, including generals, high civilian officials, and even two Presidents of the United States, resembled an unconscious plea for the restraint he probably never experienced as a child. In these struggles he seemed almost to be battling the father he never knew. A child deprived of Freud's classical Oedipal struggle can develop a compulsion to act out repeatedly the testing of his father that never occurred earlier. Frémont reminds one of Alexander Hamilton (also a bastard), who seemed driven to establish his "rightful place" in the world, perhaps to make up for early deficit and loss. Both leaders openly flouted authority at the expense of others.

Frémont, rebellious and quixotic, does not emerge as a mercurial figure. Superficially, he was described as "bland and gentlemanly" as well as "quiet, well bred, and retiring," yet observers saw in him "something which showed contempt of danger and proclaimed him a man to be obeyed under all circumstances."[16] On two expeditions, he placed his men in grave jeopardy. Other leaders in history have endangered (indeed, sacrificed) the lives of their followers in a vain attempt to enhance their self-image. Excessive narcissism is apparent in Frémont's attempt to cross the Sierra in midwinter, or in driving his men into the treacherous mountain snows of New Mexico. To what extent did such risk-taking and bravura involve a mocking of authority? At times Frémont's conduct was like that of a gambler snatching triumph from disaster. Just as he challenged mountains, he defied order. Allan Nevins saw two disabilities in Frémont—impetuousness and bad judgment, expecially in choosing subordinates. It may have been impossible for this explorer-businessman-military leader-politician to allow those around him to function as "successfully" as he did.

Another important determinant in Frémont's life was the role of his driving wife, Jessie, and of her father, Senator Benton. At one level

Frémont certainly resented intimidation by such an awesome political figure. Yet he could not openly show his anger against so powerful a male authority. Benton remained his major sponsor, and we discern ambivalence on both sides. Although Frémont found a new center in the senator's household, his marriage into such an influential family did not provide him with a new identity. His old conflicts lived on within him unresolved. These were further exacerbated by Jessie's continuing admiration and ill-disguised preference for her father, for which there is considerable evidence.

Frémont cast himself in a glamorous role. But this idealized self-image remained vulnerable. Quarrels, even within the Benton menage, left him not only unrepentant but defiant. He seems never to have expressed regrets. Despite so many outward successes, Frémont did not seem to achieve that real self-sufficiency and adult integration clinically described by Erik Erikson. His self-esteem needed constant reinforcement. Craving glory and fame, he even sought the pinnacle of the presidency.

Jessie, whom historians and biographers have portrayed as a supporting, consistent mate, expressed many of her father's forceful characteristics toward her husband. Kenneth M. Johnson sees Frémont's family dilemma as follows: "After reading a great deal by and about John Charles and Jessie, I reach the opinion that during the earlier part of his career Frémont was caught between a powerful, domineering father-in-law and a wife with a will of iron who could carry a grudge for years."[17] In 1848, even when General Kearny lay dying and requested her to visit him, Jessie refused. She believed that the death of her first son, Benton, was caused by the anxieties during her pregnancy which she had undergone during Frémont's court-martial trial. She stated in her memoirs: "There was a little grave between us I could not cross."[18]

Both Frémont and his wife were enormously ambitious for public acclaim. They formed a symbiosis (or dyad) which, carried along by the Benton name, put them at the very center of national life. Jessie provided Frémont with an image of cohesion and integration. In the nineteenth century she was the type of lady sometimes called a "virago," a masculinized woman. Lincoln, though normally mild and unrebuking, was quoted as saying to Jessie: "You are quite a female politician."[19] Jessie worked indefatigably to give Frémont a national reputation. Her graceful literary style made his field reports popular reading. With her at his side, he probably deceived himself as well as others.

Although an explorer whose mapmaking had a widespread impact, he convincingly exaggerated his role in the conquest of California and in the opening up of the West. It has been charged that Frémont's cartography retraced the work of other expeditions. His fellow officers in the Army Corps of Topographical Engineers had a right to be enraged over the publicity which Frémont engendered. Although they were West Point graduates and he was not, John Williams Gunnison, James W. Abert, and the latter's father John J. Abert (actually first commander of the corps and Frémont's chief) received nowhere near the publicity which this son-in-law of Senator Benton generated, with the help of Jessie.[20] It is as though she participated in a sort of connivance to make Frémont's exploits seem utterly unique. In psychoanalytic terms, did not Frémont's wife, thus, help to bolster his masculine ego?

The roots of Frémont's strong dependency upon his wife are suggested by the early loss of his father. He did, however, have a caring mother who constantly appears in his correspondence and that of Jessie. What he lacked was a father role model to provide nurturing strength.

By marrying Jessie, Frémont may have sought in Benton (perhaps metaphorically via Jessie) that parental substitute for the direction which an absent father had never offered. His mother, too, could also have described Frémont's father as a romantic adventurer who had audaciously torn her away from a respectable marriage and who earlier was a minor military hero captured by the British and imprisoned in the West Indies. This fantasized portrayal was dashingly foreign, but it provided no adult modeling which stressed a need to set goals or to complete projects without acrimony. Instead, Frémont was, as we have noted, a "one-parent child." Lucille Iremonger's *Fiery Chariot, a Study of British Prime Ministers and the Search for Love* (1973) indicates that an unusual number of British leaders lost one parent in childhood. The title refers to Phaeton, a Greek mythological figure who expressed his anxieties by driving a fiery chariot through the skies. Among notable American leaders, George Washington's father died when he was eleven and Thomas Jefferson's when he was fourteen years old.

Lincoln himself observed that Frémont's "cardinal mistake is that he isolates himself and allows nobody to see him...by which he does not know what is going on in the very matter he is dealing with."[21] Frémont did more than isolate physically. He seems also to have walled himself off emotionally. Repression of emotions can accompany physical isolation. Although Frémont was described by contemporaries as a bland and mild person, by means of repression he seems to have combatted hidden aggressive impulses. Anna Freud has described the use of isolation as a mechanism for the defense of ego. Each such defense "is first evolved in order to master some specific instinctual urge and so is associated with a particular phase of infantile development."[22]

More recent studies of patients with acting-out disorders indicate how emotional impoverishment relates to irrational behavior. A damming up of psychic energy can lead to channeling one's anxiety into self-destructive pursuits. In Frémont this came out as impetuousness and fool-hardy conduct. The acting-out patient is accustomed to *act* rather than to feel or to think, to *do* rather than "to be." An inability to tolerate frustration without movement and action is characteristic of such persons. They cannot see the destructiveness of their manipulation of events and persons outside themselves. Self-deception takes the place of accepting responsibility for one's own conduct. Poor impulse control and disastrous object-choices may mark their behavior.[23]

Such individuals may also engage in fantasies of omnipotence that are a continuation of unfulfilled childhood wishes. Frémont partook of a virtual frontier psychodrama, featuring the North American wilderness, which challenged everyone's unresolved anxieties. Dangerous Indians, barren mountain peaks, wild beasts, and forbidding deserts provided him with a backdrop of constant danger.

The explorer seemed at his best while riding at the head of his Indian scouts, hunting buffalo and deer, sketching Indian ritual celebrations, gathering fauna and flora, trading with the Klamaths for salmon, resembling an adventurer out of one of James Fenimore Cooper's novels. Eventually, Frémont's acted-out fantasies seemed to overtake his sense of reality. He grew to live in a world of headlines, not footnotes, despite the scholarly reports that came out over his name.

Thirty years ago Harold Lasswell began to examine how political figures displace private motives onto public objects, how they rationalize these personal aims in the name of impersonal interests. Lasswell found political power-seekers who pursued authority as a compensation for past deprivations. Their disabilities included bad parenting by dominant or absent fathers. Frequently, the mother was submissive, at least on the surface. Perhaps (like her) repression became an early defense mechanism for the child. From the nursery and the bedroom come fantasies which form a rich source for the understanding of a leader's inner life.[24]

THE MISSING FATHER

To what degree did Frémont seek to make reparations and to overcome the fact that he was a bastard son of a quixotic and unsuccessful foreigner who had disappeared by death? The English psychoanalyst John Bowlby has found such early losses crucial among patients who later suffer separation anxiety and sometimes a breakdown. In Frémont's case there may have been little overt attachment to the father in his first five years of life, perhaps too little to produce depression. Did he postpone or actually suffer that early and intense anxiety usually associated with the loss of a father? Clinical studies indicate that some children who lose a parent before puberty are unable to mourn. Others permanently lose their affectual capacities. More importantly, children (and later even some adults) do not really understand death, especially at the age of five. They frequently see it as an abandonment. Frémont's cordial relations with most men, until he met Benton, may suggest that he had experienced a relatively good rapport with his father. Angered by such a loss, however, he (like modern patients) could well have felt let down by the absent dominant parent who was not there to guide or to sustain him.[25]

Frémont's loss almost certainly occurred prior to that Oedipal struggle which Freud called universal. Sorrow over the father's death was probably never fully experienced. But unresolved emotional damage seemingly required a continuing battle with authority figures. It also necessitated suppression of painful memories. How did Frémont feel his loss? The psychoanalyst Martha Wolfenstein would probably say that he glossed over the loss because he was unable to feel it. She and Bowlby believe, that a surviving child may remain emotionally arrested within the time frame in which the original loss occurred. Wolfenstein and other psychiatrists have found that patients may stay "in their development at the stage in which they were at the parent's death. If the parent, or parents, had been lost when the patient was an adolescent, the patient was still, years later, living emotionally like an adolescent." In addition, Wolfenstein and Helene Deutsch maintain that ambivalence marks the reaction to the loss of a parent or sibling—an indecisiveness which may well continue throughout a person's life. To complicate matters further, some individuals may project these duplicitous or ambivalent feelings toward authority (substitute parental) figures who cross their path. In short, according to Wolfenstein: "The child needs the continuing relation with the parent in order to advance in his development."[26]

Without the nurturing of both parents some children do not develop essential emotional parts of themselves. Frémont's lifelong vacillations and lack of concentration resembled preadolescent behavior similar to the childishness of a five-year-old. Jessie probably filled the place of his absent male parent in a curious masculine way; her "son" and surrogate husband trowelled over his anxieties by means of erratic and stormy adventures which made him into a national hero. He could thereby project outward his inner loss in an ongoing quest for potency that provided a defense against helplessness, a desire for mastery.

Although human actions do have antecedents, not all of these flow from inner forces alone. External factors helped Frémont along in his meteoric rise to fame. The spirit of an age, the needs of a nation, making the most of one's contacts—all play a part in any leader's unfolding of character. Frémont's spectacular career is, thus, partly explainable by such external factors, especially the astonishing support of powerful patrons and the national need to open up and map the mysterious American West. Yet he was also propelled by his own needs to enter this wilderness, not so much to explore it, but to fill it with his being. Frémont's contemporaries were either puzzled or embittered by his sudden shifts of mood and contradictory deci-

sions. They could not have guessed that his projection of tension may have been necessary to achieve control over both environment and superiors.

The Kern brothers, who accompanied Frémont on several expeditions, stated that he required constant flattery in order to keep his spirits up. "He loves to be told of his greatness," E. M. Kern wrote. The Kerns became embittered following the fourth expedition in which Frémont lost a third of his men. They were chagrined that he insisted upon regarding the expedition a success. This apparent pattern of narcissism also included depreciation of others. Many years after Frémont had been aided and befriended by Thomas Oliver Larkin (American consul at Monterey during the conquest of California in 1846) he denigrated Larkin, as he had so many others who crossed his path.[27]

Frémont's narcissism was not necessarily "abnormal," although it was probably based upon low self-esteem. Heinz Kohut believes that one's maintenance of a "grandiose self" becomes an important compensatory gesture of bravura. One thereby substitutes fears of inadequacy and incompleteness by an "acting out" pattern featuring fantasies of omnipotence. These relieve contemptuous internal feelings. It seemed necessary for Frémont to lash out against older authority figures, as if the Oedipal struggle with his father had not been satisfactorily resolved.

Were Frémont's victories and successes, then, the attempt of an abandoned son to force a metaphorical apology from his father? He does seem to have tried to disengage himself from the dead parent. Striking out toward freedom may have been his way to move away from sadness and mourning, that denial which we have already mentioned. He sought thereby to create his own meaning of life. Perhaps unable to face abandonment, he "left" each of his male superiors first. It is as if the child within him were saying: "I will abandon you before you leave me." Frémont defiantly refused to give both enemies or friends what they demanded. The Dutch analyst Pieter C. Kuiper writes: "Revenge feelings for the frustration experienced in the oral phase of development can lead to reluctance to give something to others."[28]

Rage may also grow out of other phases of emotional development in which frustration has occurred. Anal obstinacy, for example, is a well-described obsessional phenomenon. Later in life those individuals who do not make a healthy identification with their fathers may unconsciously act out in stubborn ways their hostility and anger. A person caught in a "rageful" position is, however, in a deprived resentful state as regards maturing toward full emotional adulthood. He is also capable of hurting those around him as he lashes out in childish ways.

Probably Frémont's most important chance for growth, emotionally as well as materially, occurred when he met Senator Benton. Great opportunities loomed as he also gained a beautiful and talented wife. He did so, however, only by wresting her away from the potent senator, a man who thought himself more powerful than the President himself. From that time onward Frémont seemed to be at war with older men. These could, paradoxically, have provided the young and ambitious officer a harmonious model with which to identify as he matured. Instead, Frémont's way of resolving a healthy Oedipal struggle with his missing father was to challenge authority figures, as if to gain self-worth. Each time that he was squelched there certainly occurred injury to selfhood. The 1848 courtmartial alone must have been a crushing blow. Such searing psychic wounds often create a rage that is repressed, for it cannot easily be discharged without punishment.

Frémont's superiors unknowingly forced him to leak out his anxieties and anger bit by bit. Psychiatrists call this pathology "passive aggressive." Frémont could thereby appear as outwardly affable and courteous while he disguised his rages. . . .

Only in a limited way could Jessie and her powerful father, Senator Benton, buoy up Frémont's defenses. His search for integration still depended upon the small child in him who had never fully matured. He could be no one's dutiful son. Frémont, like Alexander Hamilton, waged a lifelong battle for self-validation. In the former a major battle, fought almost subliminally, was with his father-in-law. Both Frémont and Hamilton refused to dwell in their writings upon their early past. Instead, each sought to further his career without compromising. To yield would be intolerable—weakness itself. For Frémont, this behavior stirred the nation he served but it could not quiet his roving and tempestuous soul.[29]

Notes

Parts of this paper were presented to an NEH seminar convened by W. Eugene Hollon at the Huntington Library, San Marino, California, on July 18, 1978. Another version was read at the American Historical Association meeting in New York City on December 27, 1979. Thanks are expressed also to the Southern California Psychoanalytic Institute and to the Cedars-Sinai Medical Center, Los Angeles, where the author received his training in psychoanalysis and psychiatry.

1 Josiah Royce, "Frémont," *Atlantic Monthly,* LXVI (Oct. 1890), 548. Royce had carried on an acrimonious relationship with Frémont, reflected in his book *California, from the Conquest of 1846 to the Second Vigilance Committee in San Francisco: A Study of American Character* (1886; New York, 1948). For a digest of Frémont's life pattern, see Andrew Rolle, *Encyclopedia Americana,* IX (1967), 862–863.

2 John Bigelow, *Memoir of the Life and Public Service of John C. Frémont* (New York, 1856), 20; also see "Professional Biography of Moncure Robinson," *William and Mary Quarterly,* I (Second Series, 1921), 238; *Tyler's Quarterly Historical and Genealogical Magazine,* XII (1930–1931), 261; Donald Jackson and Mary

Lee Spence, eds., *The Expeditions of John Charles Frémont* (Urbana, Ill., 1970), I, xxii. See also Richmond *Enquirer,* July 12, 1811; "Richmond During the War of 1812," *Virginia Magazine of History and Biography,* VII (1900), 412; "The Randolph Manuscript," *ibid.,* XVII (1910), 358.

3 Frémont, *Memoirs of My Life* (Chicago, 1887), 18–20; Allan Nevins, *Frémont, Pathmarker of the West* (New York, 1939), 1–8. Unfailingly supportive, and frequently uncritical of his biographers, Nevins's adulative portrait of Frémont features success over failures.

4 Frémont, *Memoirs,* 21–22.

5 Jessie Benton Frémont, *Souvenirs of My Time* (Boston, 1887), 145.

6 Nevins, *Frémont,* 109. Frémont became an excellent topographer, skilled in describing fauna, flora, as well as soil and water resources. During this expedition a rare barometer was smashed accidentally against a rock. With only a powderhorn scraped to translucency and glue made from Buffalo tendons, Frémont resourcefully restored the instrument to working condition.

7 On the cannon episode, see Donald Jackson, "The Myth of the Frémont Howitzer," *Bulletin of the Missouri Historical Society,* XXII (1967), 205–215. Frémont's California expeditions are summarized in Rolle, *California: A History* (3rd ed., Arlington Heights, Ill., 1978), 167–169, 178–189. See Nevins's edition of Frémont's reports, *Narratives of Exploration and Adventure* (New York, 1956). Nevins also wrote two biographies, the latest being *Frémont: Pathmaker of the West* (New York, 1939). An early but untrustworthy biography is John Bigelow's *Frémont: Memoir of Life and Public Services* (New York, 1856). Cardinal L. Goodwin's *John Charles Frémont: An Exploration of His Career* (Stanford, 1930) strongly disagrees with Nevin's adulatory judgments. The most recent biography is Ferol Egan's *Frémont, Explorer for a Restless Nation* (New York, 1975).

8 Frémont's activities in California have been much debated. Consult William H. Ellison, "San Juan to Cahuenga: The Experiences of Frémont's Battalion," *Pacific Historical Review,* XXVII (1958), 245–261, and George Tays, "Frémont Had No Secret Instructions," *ibid.,* IX (1940), 159–171.

See also John A. Hawgood, "John C. Frémont and the Bear Flag Revolution. A Reappraisal," *Southern California Quarterly,* XLIV (1962), 67–96, and Richard R. Stenberg, "Polk and Frémont, 1845–1846," *Pacific Historical Review,* VII (1938), 211–227. Jessie Benton Frémont's *Souvenirs of My Time* (Boston, 1887) and *Far West Sketches* (Boston, 1890) are unreliable as to events of the conquest era. She, like her husband in his "The Conquest of California," *Century Magazine,* XLI (April 1890), 917–928, and *Memoirs of My Life* (New York, 1887), argues *ex post facto,* justifying his conduct. Thomas Hart Benton, *Thirty Years View* (2 vols., Boston, 1854–1856), is by Frémont's noted father-in-law.

9 Hawgood, "Frémont and the Bear Flag Revolution," 68–69.

10 Frémont, *Memoirs,* 602.

11 *Ibid.*

12 The dispute with General Kearny is treated in an anti-Frémont way by Dwight L. Clarke, *Stephen Watts Kearny, Soldier of the West* (Norman, 1961). Details of the California conquest embroglio are cited in *Proceedings of the Court Martial in the Trial of (J.C.) Frémont* (Washington, D.C., 1848); see also Kenneth M. Johnson, *The Frémont Court Martial* (Los Angeles, 1968). The entire proceedings are reproduced from the 1848 government document in Jackson and Spence, *The Expeditions,* II, *passim.*

13 Quotes are from Jackson and Spence, *The Expeditions,* II, xv–xvi.

14 Consult Peter Neubauer, "The One-Parent Child and His Oedipal Development," *Psychoanalytic Study of the Child,* XV (1960), 186–309.

15 Impulse neuroses are discussed in Otto Fenichel, *The Psychoanalytic Theory of Neurosis* (New York, 1972), 324–386.

16 Alfred S. Waugh, *Travels in Search of the Elephant,* edited by John F. McDermott (Saint Louis, 1951), 15.

17 Johnson, *Frémont Court Martial,* 78–79.

18 Nevins, *Frémont,* 342; Spence and Jackson, *The Expeditions,* II, xliv.

19 Quotes are from Carl Sandburg, *Abraham Lincoln: The War Years* (4 vols., New York, 1939), I, 344, 350. The strident phrase "phallic woman" is sometimes employed too loosely as a description of a female with masculine attributes who, in

fantasy only, is endowed with a penis. Metaphorically, these women are also spoken of as "castrating." Some analysts maintain, again symbolically, that such persons mentally keep the phallus received in coitus inside their bodies. See J. Laplanche and J. B. Pontalis, *The Language of Psychoanalysis* (New York, 1974), 311.

20 Suggestive sources for exploration of the early activities of Frémont's fellow officer are Nolie Mumey, *John Williams Gunnison, the Last of the Western Explorers* (Denver, 1955); John J. Abert, *Report of Col. John J. Abert and Col. James Kearney* (Washington, D.C., 1831); and James William Abert, *Notes of a Military Reconaissance* (Washington, D.C., 1848).

21 Quoted in J.G. Randall, *Lincoln the President* (New York, 1946), II, 24.

22 Anna Freud, *The Ego and the Mechanisms of Defense* (Rev. Ed., New York, 1966), 51.

23 John F. Borriello, "Patients with Acting-out Character Disorders," *American Journal of Psychotherapy,* XXVII (1973), 4–14; see also P. C. Kuiper, *The Neuroses* (New York, 1972), 88–89.

24 Consult Lasswell's *Psychopathology and Politics* (Rev. ed., Chicago, 1977).

25 Consult John Bowlby, *Attachment and Loss* (New York, 1969).

26 Martha Wolfenstein, "How Is Mourning Possible?" *Psychoanalytic Study of the Child,* XXI (1966), 107–108, 112; see also Helene Deutsch, "Absence of Grief," in *Neuroses and Character Types* (New York, 1965), 226–236; J. Fleming and S. Altschul, "Activation of Mourning and Growth through Psychoanalysis," *International Journal of Psychoanalysis,* XXIV (1969), 419–431; and Wolfenstein, "Loss, Rage, and Repetition," *Psychoanalytic Study of the Child,* XXIV (1969), 433.

27 Consult William Joseph Heffernan, *Edward M. Kern, Artist-Explorer* (Bakersfield, Calif., 1953), 57–58; and Robert V. Hine, *Edward Kern and American Expansion* (New Haven, 1962), 64. Both Heffernan and Hine quote from a long and revealing letter from E. M. Kern to his sister Mary, Feb. 1849. See also John A. Hawgood, *First and Last Consul: Thomas Oliver Larkin and the Americanization of California* (San Marino, 1961), *passim.*

28 Pieter C. Kuiper, *The Neuroses* (New York, 1972), 155.

29 The similarities in the lives of Frémont and Hamilton are startling. I am grateful to professor Jacob Cooke of Lafayette College for insights about such parallels. They will be incorporated into the larger biography of Frémont which I am preparing.

CAUSES OF THE MEXICAN WAR

EDITOR'S INTRODUCTION

The Mexican War was one of the most profitable wars ever fought by the United States. Under terms of the Treaty of Guadalupe Hidalgo, Mexico ceded to the United States more than 525,000 square miles, a vast area rich in mineral wealth and agricultural potential. From the Mexican Cession would come all or parts of the future states of California, Nevada, Utah, Arizona, New Mexico, Colorado, and Wyoming.

For all its profitability, the Mexican War has not been universally acclaimed. As Norman A. Graebner points out in the following selection, debate has swirled around the war ever since it was fought. The contemporary political division between Democrats, who largely supported the war, and Whigs, who opposed it, has continued to the present. The supporters of the war agreed with President James K. Polk that the war was caused by Mexico; the war's opponents placed the burden of responsibility on the aggressive designs of Polk and his administration.

While historians continue to debate the causes of the Mexican War, much of the most recent scholarship has transcended the old Whig-Democratic dialectic and adopted a more evenhanded approach.[1] K. Jack Bauer, for instance, in *The Mexican War: 1846–1848* (1974), argues that both sides in the conflict bear responsibility. Both Mexico and the United States made mistakes and consistently misread the intentions of the other. In a critique that might well apply to more recent American diplomatic relations, Bauer charges that the Polk administration mishandled the impending crisis because it did not understand Mexico and the character of the Mexican people.

---

[1]The best survey is Thomas Benjamin, "Recent Historiography of the Origins of the Mexican War," *New Mexico Historical Review*, 54 (July 1979), pp. 169–181. A useful collection is Ward McAfee and J. Cordell Robinson, *Origins of the Mexican War: A Documentary Source Book*, 2 vols. (Salisbury, N.C., 1982).

Mexico could not accede to American demands for territorial concessions in California and Texas because Mexican sensibilities were too inflamed.

This view is largely confirmed by Gene M. Brack's *Mexico views Manifest Destiny, 1821–1846: An Essay on the Origins of the Mexican War* (1975). Brack argues that many Mexicans lived in fear of the United States because of American racism and expansionism.[2] The people of Mexico in the 1840s felt their national existence was at stake; thus they were unwilling to concede territories to the "colossus of the North." American cupidity coupled with Mexican intransigence made war inevitable.

The best single volume on the coming of the war is David M. Pletcher's *The Diplomacy of Annexation: Texas, Oregon, and the Mexican War* (1973). Pletcher also adopts a balanced view of the origins of the war, but is especially critical of the inept and chauvinistic diplomacy of the Polk administration. Polk's foreign policy, in Pletcher's view, was one of overstatement and bluster. The president did not seek a general war with Mexico, but he was willing to use the threat of war or even a limited war to accomplish his goals. His attempt at bluffing Mexico into accepting his territorial demands backfired, and war resulted.

In the selection that follows, Norman A. Graebner tackles once again the question of causation. More than thirty years ago, in his *Empire on the Pacific* (1955), Graebner argued that commercial interests in the Northeast were responsible for the Mexican War. American merchants, desiring ports on the Pacific coast, dictated an aggressive foreign policy. In the present selection, Graebner draws upon the most recent scholarship and reexamines developments in both the United States and Mexico. He also carries the inquiry to a higher level of analysis by seeking to identify the "universal causes of war which transcend individual conflicts." In the text and notes of his article, Graebner draws parallels between American actions during the crisis with Mexico and actions taken prior to the Civil War, the Spanish-American War, World War I, World War II, and the Vietnam War. His conclusions are clearly intended to apply to wars past, present, and future.

Norman A. Graebner is Stettinius Professor of Modern American History at the University of Virginia.

---

[2]For a complementary study of American attitudes toward Mexico and the war, see Robert W. Johannsen, *To the Halls of Montezuma: The Mexican War in the American Imagination* (Oxford, 1985).

Causes of the Mexican War

Norman A. Graebner

On May 11, 1846, President James K. Polk presented his war message to Congress. After reviewing the skirmish between General Zachary Taylor's dragoons and a body of Mexican soldiers along the Rio Grande, the President asserted that Mexico "has passed the boundary of the United States, has invaded our territory and shed American blood upon the American soil.... [W]ar exists, and, notwithstanding all our efforts to avoid it, exists by act of Mexico...." No country could have had a superior case for war. Democrats in large numbers (for it was largely a partisan matter) responded with the patriotic fervor which Polk expected of them. "Our government has permitted itself to be insulted long enough," wrote one Georgian. "The blood of her citizens has been spilt on her own soil. It appeals to us for vengeance." Still, some members of Congress, recalling more accurately than the President the circumstances of the conflict, soon rendered the Mexican War the most reviled in American history—at least until the Vietnam war of the 1960s. One outraged Whig termed the war "illegal, unrighteous, and damnable." Whigs questioned both Polk's honesty and his sense of geography. Congressman Joshua Giddings of Ohio accused the President of "planting the standard of the United States on foreign soil, and using the military forces of the United States to violate every principle of international law and of moral justice." To vote for the war, admitted Senator John C. Calhoun, was "to plunge a

dagger into his own heart, and more so." Some critics in Congress openly wished the Mexicans well.

For well over a century such profound differences in perception have pervaded American writings on the Mexican War. Even in the past decade, historians have reached conclusions on the question of war guilt as disparate as those which separated Polk from his wartime conservative and abolitionist critics. Justin H. Smith's *The War with Mexico* stands at the core of the perennial debate. Few books of American history have such impressive scholarly credentials; the footnotes and bibliography alone seem worthy of the Pulitzer Prize which the book received in 1920. According to Smith, the war was "deliberately precipitated by the will and act of Mexico."[1] For the past half century every judgment of the Mexican War has begun with the acceptance or rejection of that verdict. Bernard DeVoto, in *The Year of Decision*, wondered how Smith could accept conclusions which denied the very facts he presented. "If there is a more consistently wrongheaded book in our history, or one which so freely cites facts in support of judgments which those facts controvert," wrote DeVoto, "I have not encountered it."[2] Similarly Glenn W. Price, in his *Origins of the War with Mexico*, concluded that "Smith's work, in all its argument that pertained to the origins of the War, was simply preposterous as history...."[3] Yet as recently as 1971 Seymour V. Connor and Odie B. Faulk, in their *North America Divided: The Mexican War, 1846–1848*, while acknowledging that they did not follow Smith "slavishly," concluded that Smith's study "remains today a monument of historical scholarship."[4] Although nationalistic biases will color the judgments of those who study war, it seems strange that historical

Adapted from "The Mexican War: A Study in Causation," by Norman A. Graebner. Copyright © 1980 by the American Historical Association, Pacific Coast Branch. Reprinted from *Pacific Historical Review*, Vol. LXIX, No. 3, pp. 405–426, by permission of the Association.

agreement on a subject as remote and as well documented as the Mexican War should be that elusive. President Polk's diary, published in 1910, remains the last major addition to the historic record on the origins of that war.

In some measure the diversity of judgment on the Mexican War, as on other wars, is understandable. By basing their analyses on official rationalizations, historians often ignore the more universal causes of war which transcend individual conflicts and which can establish the bases for greater consensus. Neither the officials in Washington nor those in Mexico City ever acknowledged any alternatives to the actions which they took. But governments generally have more choices in any controversy than they are prepared to admit. Circumstances determine their extent. The more powerful a nation, the more remote its dangers, the greater its options between action and inaction. Often for the weak, unfortunately, the alternative is capitulation or war. Certainly the choices available to Franklin D. Roosevelt and Cordell Hull in their relations with Japan in 1941 were far greater than either would acknowledge. Similarly, as James C. Thomson has noted so well, the John F. Kennedy administration vigorously eliminated a multitude of available alternatives when it bound itself to a single course of action in Vietnam.[5] Polk and his advisers developed their Mexican policies on the dual assumption that Mexico was weak and that the acquisition of certain Mexican territories would satisfy admirably the long-range interests of the United States. Within that context, Polk's policies were direct, timely, and successful. But Polk had choices. Mexico, whatever its internal condition, was no direct threat to the United States. Polk, had he so desired, could have avoided war; indeed, he could have ignored Mexico in 1845 with absolute impunity.

In explaining the Mexican War historians have dwelled on the causes of friction in American-Mexican relations. In part these lay in the disparate qualities of the two populations,

in part in the vast discrepancies between the two countries in energy, efficiency, power, and national wealth. Through two decades of independence Mexico had experienced a continuous rise and fall of governments; by the 1840s survival had become the primary concern of every regime. Conscious of their weakness, the successive governments in Mexico City resented the superior power and effectiveness of the United States and feared American notions of destiny that anticipated the annexation of Mexico's northern provinces.[6] Having failed to prevent the formation of the Texas Republic, Mexico reacted to Andrew Jackson's recognition of Texan independence, in March 1837, with deep indignation. Thereafter the Mexican raids into Texas, such as the one on San Antonio in 1842, aggravated the bitterness of Texans toward Mexico, for such forays had no purpose beyond terrorizing the frontier settlements.

But such mutual animosities, extensive as they were, do not account for the Mexican War. Governments as divided and chaotic as the Mexican regimes of the 1840s usually have difficulty in maintaining positive and profitable relations with their neighbors; their behavior often produces annoyance, but seldom armed conflict. Belligerence toward other countries had flowed through United States history like a torrent without, in itself, setting off a war. Nations do not fight over cultural differences or verbal recriminations; they fight over perceived threats to their interests created by the ambitions or demands of others.

What increased the animosity between Mexico City and Washington was a series of specific issues over which the two countries perennially quarreled—claims, boundaries, and the future of Texas.

THE TEXAS ISSUE

Congress's joint resolution for Texas annexation in February 1845 raised the spectre of war among Mexican editors and politicians alike. As early as 1843 the Mexican government had warned the American minister in Mexico City that annexation would render war inevitable; Mexican officials in Washington repeated that warning. To Mexico, therefore, the move to annex Texas was an unbearable affront. Within a month after Polk's inauguration on March 4, General Juan Almonte, the Mexican minister in Washington, boarded a packet in New York and sailed for Vera Cruz to sever his country's diplomatic relations with the United States. Even before the Texas Convention could meet on July 4 to vote annexation, rumors of a possible Mexican invasion of Texas prompted Polk to advance General Zachary Taylor's forces from Fort Jesup in Louisiana down the Texas coast. Polk instructed Taylor to extend his protection to the Rio Grande but to avoid any areas to the north of that river occupied by Mexican troops.[7] Simultaneously the President reinforced the American squadron in the Gulf of Mexico. "The threatened invasion of Texas by a large Mexican army," Polk informed Andrew J. Donelson, the American chargé in Texas, on June 15, "is well calculated to excite great interest here and increases our solicitude concerning the final action by the Congress and the Convention of Texas...."[8] Polk assured Donelson that he intended to defend Texas to the limit of his constitutional power. Donelson resisted the pressure of those Texans who wanted Taylor to advance to the Rio Grande; instead, he placed Taylor at Corpus Christi on the Nueces. Taylor agreed that the line from the mouth of the Nueces to San Antonio covered the Texas settlements and afforded a favorable base from which to defend the Texas frontier.[9]

Polk insisted that the administration's show of force in Texas would prevent rather than provoke war. "I do not anticipate that Mexico will be mad enough to declare war," he wrote in July, but "I think she would have done so but for the appearance of a strong naval force in the Gulf and our army moving in the direction of her frontier on land." Polk restated this judgment on July 28 in a letter to General Robert Armstrong, the United States consul at Liverpool: "I think there need be but little apprehension of war with Mexico. If however she shall be mad enough to make war we are prepared to meet her." The President assured Senator William H. Haywood of North Carolina that the American forces in Texas would never aggress against Mexico; they would, however, prevent any Mexican forces from crossing the Rio Grande. In conversation with Senator William S. Archer of Virginia, on September 1, the President added confidently that "the appearance of our land and naval forces on the borders of Mexico & in the Gulf would probably deter and prevent Mexico from either declaring war or invading Texas."[10] Polk's continuing conviction that Mexico would not attack suggests that his deployment of United States land and naval forces along Mexico's periphery was designed less to protect Texas than to support an aggressive diplomacy which might extract a satisfactory treaty from Mexico without war.

United States policy toward Mexico during 1845 achieved the broad national purpose of Texas annexation. Beyond that it brought U.S. power to bear on Mexico in a manner calculated to further the processes of negotiation.[11] Whether the burgeoning tension would lead to a negotiated boundary settlement or to war hinged on two factors: the nature of Polk's demands and Mexico's response to them. The President announced his objectives to Mexico's troubled officialdom through his instructions to John Slidell, his special emissary who departed for Mexico in November 1845 with the assurance that the government in Mexico City was prepared to re-establish formal diplomatic relations with the United States and negotiate a territorial settlement.

CALIFORNIA

Mexico's troubles were not limited to the Rio Grande frontier. During July 1845 California had become the major topic of concern in the Mexican capital.[12] Informed Mexicans could recall that President Andrew Jackson had attempted to purchase the Bay of San Francisco in 1835. Only a year later Mexico accused Americans of supporting a revolution in California which ousted the governor. José María Tornel, the Mexican minister of war, predicted in 1837 that the loss of Texas, if accepted by Mexico, "will inevitably result in the loss of New Mexico and the Californias."[13] What disturbed Mexican leaders more profoundly was Commodore Thomas ap Catesby Jones's seizure of Monterey in 1842. Jones, as commander of the United States Naval Squadron in the Pacific, had acted under the rumor that the United States and Mexico were at war.

When Californians launched a second revolution in 1844 to overthrow the Mexican regime, officials in Mexico City assumed that Americans were attempting to repeat the Texas drama in California. Captain John C. Frémont's defiance of local authorities at Monterey prompted Tornel to repeat his earlier warning:

> The passion of the Anglo-American people, their pronounced desire to acquire new lands, is a dynamic power which is enhanced and nourished by their own industry. An ill-defined line, the source of a yet unknown river, scientific explorations with the pretext of establishing monuments that shall *mark with perfect accuracy* the limits of both nations, all these have given a golden opportunity to the combined efforts of the people and government to promote their plans to acquire what belongs to their neighbors.

"California is entirely at the mercy of the North Americans," lamented *El Amigo del Pueblo* (Mexico City) in August 1845. "In regard to the United States," echoed *El Patriota Mexicano* (Mexico City) in November, "its designs [on California] are no longer a mystery." For *El Siglo Diez y Nueve* (Mexico City) the strongest evidence of American ambition was the "irritating insolence" which the newspapers of the United States displayed in advocating emigration and the annexation of California.[14]

Confronted with the loss of its borderlands, Mexico reached out to Britain for help. Earlier, Mexican officials warned the British minister in Mexico City, Charles Bankhead, that without British guarantees an independent Texas would not protect Mexico's northern border. Now they offered Britain a protectorate in California; some suggested that Britain purchase the province. In September 1845 a distraught Mexico again sought a British commitment to the defense of is frontiers. But British diplomacy was not prepared to underwrite the Mexican cause. British Foreign Secretary Aberdeen, hoping to keep California out of American hands, suggested that Mexico concentrate all its military power in California. Bankhead admitted that Mexico, standing alone, had little chance of success in its mounting crisis with the United States, but he refused to draw his country into the quarrel. He acknowledged a British interest in Mexico's welfare, nothing more.[15]

Unable to offer British support, Bankhead could only advise the Mexicans to show greater restraint in their relations with the United States. Mexican writings, he complained, were too inflammatory; moreover, they created objectives which no Mexican government could achieve. Politicians and journalists aggravated the Mexican spirit of defiance by insisting that the United States was militarily weak, was divided over slavery and the justice of Polk's demands, and therefore would not fight. Mexico, they added, would benefit from the advantages that accrue to defensive power. Yet among Mexico's leaders there was always a sharp contrast between their public expressions of confidence and their private admissions of dread. Mexico, they knew, stood no chance in a war with the United States. If Mexico was too weak to fight, Bankhead warned, it had no choice but to negotiate. He advised Mexican President José Herrera's government in Mexico City to deal directly with Washington rather than risk a drift toward war. Yet that regime, even as it toppled in December 1845, denounced the United States to counter the appeals of its political opposition to Mexican nationalism. Such behavior distressed Bankhead. "The self conceit and weakness of the government here," he complained to Aberdeen, "preclude the possibility of my giving them any advice...."[16] Bankhead recognized Herrera's vulnerability. Mariano Paredes, he reported as early as August, could overthrow him whenever he chose. Yet Paredes, Bankhead believed, would be an improvement over Herrera's Federalists. As the leader of the Centralists, Paredes appeared better able to give Mexico the strong, central administration that it required. Despite his deep disillusionment with Mexican politics, Bankhead believed Slidell's arrival unwisely premature, for it seemed no less than an American effort to impose an immediate boundary settlement on a chaotic Mexico under the threat of force.[17]

Actually, Slidell's presence in Mexico inaugurated a diplomatic crisis not unlike those which precede most wars. Fundamentally the Polk administration, in dispatching Slidell, gave the Mexicans the same two choices that the dominant power in any confrontation gives to the weaker—the acceptance of a body of concrete diplomatic demands or eventual war.[18] Slidell's instructions described United States territorial objectives with considerable clarity. If Mexico knew little of Polk's growing acquisitiveness toward California during the autumn of 1845, Slidell proclaimed the President's intentions with his proposals to purchase varying portions of California for as much as $25 million. Other countries such as England and Spain had consigned important areas of the New World through peaceful negotiations, but the United States, except in its Mexican relations, had never asked any country to part with a portion of its own territory. Yet Polk could not understand why Mexico should reveal any special reluctance to part with Texas, the Rio Grande, New Mexico, or California. What made the terms of Slidell's instructions appear fair to him was Mexico's military and financial helplessness. Polk's defenders noted that California was not a *sine qua non* of any settlement—that Polk offered to settle the immediate controversy over the acquisition of the Rio Grande boundary alone in exchange for the cancellation of claims. Unfortunately, amid the passions of December 1845, such distinctions were lost. Furthermore, a settlement of the Texas boundary would not have resolved the California question at all.[19]

THE WAR CRISIS

Throughout the crisis months of 1845 and 1846, spokesmen of the Polk administration warned the Mexican government repeatedly that its choices were limited. In June 1845, Polk's mouthpiece, the Washington *Union*, observed characteristically that if Mexico resisted Washington's demands, "A corps of properly organized volunteers...would invade, overrun, and occupy Mexico. They would enable us not only to take California, but to keep it." American officials, in their contempt for Mexico, spoke privately of the need to chastise that country for its annoyances and insults. Confidential agent William S. Parrott wrote to Secretary of State James Buchanan in October that he wished "to see this people well flogged by Uncle Sam's boys, ere we enter upon negotiations....I know [the Mexicans] better, perhaps, than any other American citizen and I am fully persuaded, they can never love or respect us, as we should be loved and respected by them, until we shall have given them a positive proof of our superiority." Mexico's pretensions would continue, wrote Slidell in late December, "until the Mexican people shall be convinced by hostile demonstrations, that our differences must be settled promptly, either by negotiation or the sword." In January 1846 the *Union* publicly threatened Mexico with war if it rejected the just demands of the United States. "The result of such a course on her part," it declared, "may compel us to resort to more decisive measures...to obtain the settlement of our legitimate claims." As Slidell prepared to leave Mexico in March 1846, he again reminded the administration: "Depend upon it, we can never get along well with them, until we have given them a good drubbing."[20] In Washington on May 8, Slidell advised the President "to take the redress of the wrongs and injuries which we had so long borne from Mexico into our own hands, and to act with promptness and energy."[21]

Mexico responded to Polk's challenge with an outward display of belligerence and an inward dread of war. Mexicans feared above all that the United States intended to overrun their country and seize much of their territory. Polk and his advisers assumed that Mexico, to avoid an American invasion, would give up its provinces peacefully. Obviously Mexico faced growing diplomatic and military pressures to negotiate away its territories; it faced no moral obligation to do so. Herrera and Paredes had the sovereign right to protect their regimes by avoiding any formal recognition of Slidell and by rejecting any of the boundary proposals embodied in his instructions, provided that in the process they did not endanger any legitimate interests of the American people. At least to some Mexicans, Slidell's terms demanded nothing less than Mexico's capitulation. By what standard was $2 million a proper payment for the Rio Grande boundary, or $25 million a fair price for California? No government would have accepted such terms. Having rejected negotiation in the face of superior force, Mexico would meet the challenge with a final gesture of defiance. In either case Mexico was destined to lose, but historically nations have preferred to fight than to give away territory under diplomatic pressure alone. Gene M. Brack, in his long study of Mexico's deep-seated fear and resentment of the United States, explained Mexico's ultimate behavior in such terms:

President Polk knew that Mexico could offer but feeble resistance militarily, and he knew that Mexico needed money. No proper American would exchange territory and the national honor for cash, but President Polk mistakenly believed that the application of military pressure would convince Mexicans to do so. They did not respond logically, but patriotically. Left with the choice of war or territorial concessions, the former course, however dim the prospects of success, could be the only one.[22]

Mexico, in its resistance, gave Polk the three choices which every nation gives another in an uncompromisable confrontation: to withdraw his demands and permit the issues to drift, unresolved; to reduce his goals in the interest of an immediate settlement; or to escalate the pressures in the hope of securing an eventual settlement on his own terms. Normally when the internal conditions of a country undermine its relations with others, a diplomatic corps simply removes itself from the hostile environment and awaits a better day. Mexico, despite its animosity, did not endanger the security interests of the United States; it had not invaded Texas and did not contemplate doing so. Mexico had refused to pay the claims, but those claims were not equal to the price of a one-week war. Whether Mexico negotiated a boundary for Texas in 1846 mattered little. The United States had lived with unsettled boundaries for decades without considering war. Settlers, in time, would have forced a settlement, but in 1846 the region between the Nueces and the Rio Grande was a vast, generally unoccupied wilderness. Thus there was nothing, other than Polk's ambitions, to prevent the United States from withdrawing its diplomats from Mexico City and permitting its relations with Mexico to drift. But Polk, whatever the language of his instructions, did not send Slidell to Mexico to normalize relations with the Mexican government. He expected Slidell to negotiate an immediate boundary settlement favorably to the United States, nothing less.

Recognizing no need to reduce his demands on Mexico, Polk, without hesitation, took the third course which Mexico offered. Congress bound the President to the annexation of Texas; thereafter the Polk administration was free to formulate its own policies toward Mexico. With the Slidell mission Polk embarked on a program of gradual coercion to achieve a settlement, hopefully without war. That program led logically from his dispatching of an army to Texas and his denunciation of Mexico in his annual message of December 1845 to his new instructions of January 1846, which ordered Taylor to the Rio Grande. Colonel Atocha, spokesman for the deposed Mexican leader, Santa Anna, encouraged Polk to pursue his policy of escalation. Polk recorded Atocha's advice:

> He said our army should be marched at once from Corpus Christi to the Del Norte, and a strong Naval force assembled at Vera Cruz, that Mr. Slidell, the U.S. Minister, should withdraw from Jalappa, and go on board one of our ships of War at Vera Cruz, and in that position should demand the payment of [the] amount due our citizens; that it was well known the Mexican Government was unable to pay in money, and that when they saw a strong force ready to strike on their coasts and border, they would, he had no doubt, feel their danger and agree to the boundary suggested. He said that Paredes, Almonte, & Gen'l Santa Anna were all willing for such an arrangement, but that they dare not make it until it was made apparent to the Archbishop of Mexico & the people generally that it was necessary to save their country from a war with the U. States.[23]

Thereafter Polk never questioned the efficacy of coercion. He asserted at a cabinet meeting on February 17 that "it would be necessary to take strong measures towards Mexico before our difficulties with that Government could be settled...." Similarly on April 18 Polk instructed Calhoun that "our relations with Mexico had reached a point where we could not stand still but must treat all nations whether weak or strong alike, and that I saw no alternative but

strong measures towards Mexico." A week later the President again brought the Mexican question before the cabinet. "I expressed my opinion," he noted in his diary, "that we must take redress for the injuries done us into our own hands, that we had attempted to conciliate Mexico in vain, and had forborne until forbearance was no longer either a virtue or patriotic...."[24] Convinced that Paredes needed money, Polk suggested to leading Senators that Congress appropriate a million dollars both to encourage Paredes to negotiate and to sustain him in power until the United States could ratify the treaty. The President failed to secure Calhoun's required support.[25]

CAUSATION

Polk's persistence led him and the country to war. Like all escalations in the exertion of force, his decisions responded less to unwanted and unanticipated resistance than to the requirements of the clearly perceived and inflexible purposes which guided the administration.[26] What perpetuated Polk's escalation to the point of war was his determination to pursue goals to the end whose achievement lay outside the possibilities of successful negotiations.[27] Senator Thomas Hart Benton of Missouri saw this situation when he wrote: "It is impossible to conceive of an administration less warlike, or more intriguing, than that of Mr. Polk. They were *men of peace, with objects to be accomplished by means of war;* so that war was a necessity and an indispensability to their purpose...."[28]

Polk understood fully the state of Mexican opinion. In placing Taylor on the Rio Grande he revealed again his contempt for Mexico. Under no national obligation to expose the country's armed forces, he would not have advanced Taylor in the face of a superior military force. Mexico had been undiplomatic; its denunciations of the United States were insulting and provocative. But if Mexico's behavior antagonized Polk, it did not antagonize the Whigs, the abolitionists, or even much of the Democratic Party. Such groups did not regard Mexico as a threat; they warned the administration repeatedly that Taylor's presence on the Rio Grande would provoke war. But in the balance against peace was the pressure of American expansionism. Much of the Democratic and expansionist press, having accepted without restraint both the purposes of the Polk administration and its charges of Mexican perfidy, urged the President on to more vigorous action.[29]

During March 1846 Taylor established his headquarters on the northern bank of the Rio Grande, opposite the Mexican village of Matamoros. He assured citizens of the Mexican community that the United States, in placing an army on the Rio Grande, harbored no hostility toward Mexico and would not disturb the Mexicans residing north of the river. His army, he added, would not, in any case, go beyond the river unless the Mexicans themselves commenced hostilities. Still Mexican officials reacted violently. "The civilized world," proclaimed the Mexican commandant at Matamoros, "has already recognized in [the annexation of Texas] all the marks of injustice, iniquity and the most scandalous violation of the law of nations.... The cabinet of the United States does not, however, stop in its career of usurpation. Not only does it aspire to the possession of the department of Texas, but it covets also the regions on the left bank of the Rio Grande." What hope was there of treating with an enemy, continued the proclamation, that sent an army into territory which was not an issue in the pending negotiations? "The flame of patriotism which burns in our hearts," warned the statement, "will receive new fuel from the odious presence of these invaders for conquest...."[30] On April 11, General Pedro Ampudia, backed by 3,000 Mexican troops, arrived at Matamoros and immediately ordered Taylor to return to Corpus Christi. Taylor refused to move, declaring that he had taken

positions along the Rio Grande under presidential orders. He warned Ampudia that the side which fired the first shot would bear responsibility for the war.

Facing the certainty of a clash along the Rio Grande, Polk made no effort to avoid war. On May 5 the cabinet discussed the status of the American army on the Rio Grande and the possibility of a brush with Mexican forces. On the following day the President noted in his diary that he had received dispatches from Taylor dated as late as April 15. "No actual collision had taken place," he wrote, "though the probabilities are that hostilities might take place soon." On May 9 the cabinet agreed that any Mexican attack on Taylor's forces would require an immediate message to Congress requesting a declaration of war.[31] Polk, in this crisis, wanted war with Mexico precisely as Franklin D. Roosevelt wanted war with Germany amid his private operations in the Atlantic during the summer and autumn of 1941. There would be no war until Mexico committed the necessary act of open hostility; thereafter, that country would bear the responsibility alone. The United States, dealing from strength, could afford to wait. The Mexicans, facing a symbolic threat at the Rio Grande to their entire military and diplomatic position, revealed the impatience of those who find their strength disintegrating.

Faced with the prospect of further decline which they could neither accept nor prevent, they lashed out with the intention of protecting their self-esteem and compelling the United States, if it was determined to have the Rio Grande, New Mexico, and California, to pay for its prizes with something other than money.[32] On April 23, Paredes issued a proclamation declaring a defensive war against the United States. Predictably, one day later the Mexicans fired on a detachment of U.S. dragoons. Taylor's report of the attack reached Polk on Saturday evening, May 9. On Sunday the President drafted his war message and delivered it to Congress on the following day. Had Polk avoided the crisis, he might have gained the time required to permit the emigrants of 1845 and 1846 to settle the California issue without war.

What clouds the issue of the Mexican War's justification was the acquisition of New Mexico and California, for contemporaries and historians could not logically condemn the war and laud the Polk administration for its territorial achievements. Perhaps it is true that time would have permitted American pioneers to transform California into another Texas. But even then California's acquisition by the United States would have emanated from the use of force, for the elimination of Mexican sovereignty, whether through revolution or war, demanded the successful use of power. If the power employed in revolution would have been less obtrusive than that exerted in war, its role would have been no less essential. There simply was no way that the United States could acquire California peacefully. If the distraught Mexico of 1845 would not sell the distant province, no regime thereafter would have done so. Without forceful destruction of Mexico's sovereign power, California would have entered the twentieth century as an increasingly important region of another country.

Thus the Mexican War poses the dilemma of all international relations. Nations whose geographical and political status fails to coincide with their ambition and power can balance the two sets of factors in only one manner: through the employment of force. They succeed or fail according to circumstances; and for the United States, the conditions for achieving its empire in the Southwest and its desired frontage on the Pacific were so ideal that later generations could refer to the process as the mere fulfillment of destiny. "The Mexican Republic," lamented a Mexican writer in 1848, "...had among other misfortunes of less account, the great one of being in the vicinity of a strong and energetic people."[33] What the Mexican War

revealed in equal measure is the simple fact that only those countries which have achieved their destiny, whatever that may be, can afford to extol the virtues of peaceful change.

Notes

1 Justin H. Smith, *The War with Mexico* (New York, 1919), I, 155.

2 Bernard DeVoto, *The Year of Decision: 1846* (Boston, 1943), 510.

3 Glenn W. Price, *Origins of the War with Mexico: The Polk-Stockton Intrigue* (Austin, Tex., 1967), 103.

4 Seymour V. Connor and Odie B. Faulk, *North America Divided: The Mexican War 1846–1848* (New York, 1971), 192–193.

5 For James C. Thomson's analysis of the efforts of the Kennedy administration to eliminate all alternatives to its single course of action, see "How Could Vietnam Happen? *An Autopsy." The Atlantic,* CCXXI (April 1968), 47–53.

6 For an excellent review of Mexican attitudes toward the United States, see Gene M. Brack *Mexico Views Manifest Destiny 1821–1846* (Albuquerque, N.M., 1975).

7 For Taylor's instructions, see George Bancroft to Taylor, June 15, 1845, *House Ex. Doc. 60,* 30th Cong., 1st sess., 81; William L. Marcy to Taylor, July 30, 1845, *Senate Ex. Doc. 18,* 30th Cong., 1st sess., 9.

8 Polk to Donelson, June 15, 1845, Polk Papers, Manuscripts Division, Library of Congress.

9 Taylor to Donelson, July 30, 1845, Donelson Papers, Manuscripts Division, Library of Congress.

10 Polk to A. O. J. Nicholson, July 28, 1845; Polk to General Robert Armstrong, July 28, 1845; Polk to William H. Haywood, Aug. 9, 1845, Polk Papers; John Milton Quaife, *The Diary of James K. Polk* (Chicago, 1910), I, 13.

11 For Polk's preference for peaceful negotiations see James Buchanan to John Black, Sept. 17, 1845, *House Ex. Doc. 60,* 30th Cong., 1st sess., 12. Others agreed with Polk that the mere presence of American forces in Texas would compel the Mexicans to negotiate. For example, the St. Louis *Missouri Reporter* declared on July 29, 1845: "By displaying a competent military and

naval force, we shall command respect, and secure the objects we have in view without delay. The Administration should, in the meantime, be looking forward to what may be accomplished by negotiation.''

12 Aberdeen to Bankhead, Oct. 1 and Dec. 31, 1844, Foreign Office, 50, vols. 172, 183; Bankhead to Aberdeen, June 29, 1844, and July 30, 1845, Foreign Office, 50, vols. 174, 186.

13 Carlos E. Castaneda, trans. and ed., *The Mexican Side of the Texas Revolution by the Chief Mexican Participants* (Dallas, 1928), 368, 370; quoted in Frank A. Knapp. Jr., "Mexican Fear of Manifest Destiny in California," in Thomas E. Cotner, ed., *Essays in Mexican History* (Austin, Tex., 1958), 195.

14 *Ibid.*, 196, 200, 203.

15 Bankhead to Aberdeen, Jan. 29 and July 30, 1845, Foreign Office, 50, vols. 184, 186.

16 Bankhead to Aberdeen, Sept. 29 and Nov. 29, 1845, Foreign Office, 50, vols. 186, 187.

17 Bankhead to Aberdeen, Aug. 29, Sept. 29, and Nov. 29, 1845, Foreign Office, 50, vols. 186, 187.

18 The issues were different—the desire for California as opposed to the demand for an independent Cuba, the preference for a British victory, or the defense of China's integrity—but the limited choices which the United States gave its opponents in 1846, 1898, 1917, and 1941 were similar in quality and had the same effect.

19 Historians who regard Polk's proposals fair have scant respect for Mexico's belligerent rejection of them. Dwelling on Mexican behavior which followed Congress's completion of annexation and the arrival of Polk's emissary, Slidell, in Mexico during December 1845, Connor and Faulk have rebuilt the classic case against Mexico. For them, Mexico's responsibility for the coming of war was unmistakable: the Mexicans simply translated their inexcusable animosity toward the United States into preparations for war and the final decision of April 1846 to attack. "Perhaps it was all foreordained," they wrote, "for there can be no question but that the annexation of Texas precipitated a reaction among patriotic zealots in Mexico which produced war—California, Polk, Manifest Destiny, claims, Nueces boundary notwithstanding." Connor and Faulk argue logically that California was no issue in the coming of the war. That province, they noted, "was peripheral to the main issue—the arousing of Mexican nationalism (by Herera's opponents) over the annexation of Texas. By the time of Slidell's appointment in November 1845 Herrera's overthrow was imminent and war was virtually inevitable. It really matters little whether Polk was interested in California or not." Connor and Faulk, *North America Divided,* 22, 27, 28, 32.

20 Parrott to Buchanan, Oct. 11, 1845, Slidell to Buchanan, Dec. 27, 1845, and Slidell to Buchanan, March 18, 1846, all in William R. Manning, ed., *Diplomatic Correspondence of the United States: Inter-American Affairs 1831–1860* (Washington, D.C., 1937), VIII, 760, 803, 832. Slidell again revealed his lack of respect for Mexico and its power when he wrote on April 2, 1846: "The best security for the inaction of Paredes is his utter inability, to concentrate on the frontier, a sufficient force to cope with General Taylor, he cannot at present by any effort untie six thousand men for that object, and from what I have seen of the Mexican troops, I should have no apprehension of the result of any attack with that number." Slidell to Buchanan, April 2, 1846, *ibid.,* 839.

21 Quaife, *Diary of James K. Polk,* I, 382.

22 Brack, *Mexico Views Manifest Destiny,* 179.

23 Quaife, *Diary of James K. Polk,* I, 228–229.

24 *Ibid.,* 233, 337, 354.

25 *Ibid.,* 306–312, 317.

26 During the spring of 1846 Polk made clear in his diary that the settlement he sought would include no less than the Rio Grande border and the transfer of the Bay of San Francisco to the United States. See *ibid.,* 307.

27 Such inflexibility of purpose underwrote the most classic of all escalations in U.S. history—that in Vietnam between 1965 and 1968.

28 Thomas Hart Benton, *Thirty Years' View* (New York, 1856), II, 680. Italics are those of the writer.

29 See Norman A. Graebner, *Empire on the Pacific: A Study in American Continental Expansion* (New York, 1955), 151–153.

30 For Taylor's communications, see the notes in the Trist Papers, XXXIII, Manuscripts Division, Library of Congress.

31 Quaife, *Diary of James K. Polk,* I, 379, 380, 384.

32 Mexico's behavior was symbolically identical to that of the South when it attacked Fort Sumter in 1861, to that of Spain in its resistance to American demands in 1898 (a variant because Spain did not order the destruction of the *Maine* although the effect of the destruction was the same), to that of Germany when it launched unrestricted submarine warfare in 1917, and to that of Japan when it attacked Pearl Harbor in 1941. In each case, the United States, as the more powerful antagonist and with its interests not directly engaged, could rest easily behind its uncompromising demands, while the weaker power, conscious of its slipping position and with its interests directly engaged, made the decision for war in the hope of salvaging what it could from an immediately threatening and ultimately hopeless situation. It is well to recall that Admiral Tojo, in explaining the Japanese decision for war in 1941, remarked that "sometimes a man has to jump with his eyes closed, from the temple of Kiyomizu into the ravine below." The Mexican-American confrontation of 1846 presented a pattern of challenge and response not unlike those which brought the United States into most of its wars.

33 Quoted in Brack, *Mexico Views Manifest Destiny,* 1.

CHAPTER 9

ARGONAUTS ON THE OVERLAND TRAIL

EDITOR'S INTRODUCTION

The gold rush has probably attracted more attention from historians than any other topic in California history. It is an epic story, filled with high drama and adventure. Some of the great classics in California historiography—such as Rodman Paul's *California Gold* (1947), John Caughey's *Gold is the Cornerstone* (1948), and George R. Stewart's *The California Trail* (1962)—are devoted to its telling.

Likewise, historians have edited and published hundreds of gold rush diaries, firsthand accounts of the nation's westering. The standard formula for editing such diaries is to write a brief introduction and include in the notes a few comparative descriptions from journals of other argonauts. One of the best of these is David M. Potter's *Trail to California: The Overland Journal of Vincent Geiger and Wakeman Bryarly* (1945). In his search for comparative descriptions, Potter consulted thirty-three other forty-niner diaries. Even more ambitious is J. S. Holliday's recent editing of the diary of argonaut William Swain. In preparing *The World Rushed In: The California Gold Rush Experience* (1981), Holliday attempted to consult every available gold-rush diary from the period 1849 and 1850.

In spite of the extensive research devoted to the subject, few systematic attempts have been made to analyze the experience of the argonauts on the overland trail.[1] John Mack Faragher significantly raised the level of sophistication of western historiography with the publication of his *Women and Men on the Overland Trail* (1979). Borrowing the technique of content analysis from literary criticism, Faragher evaluated twenty-two men's and twenty-eight women's diaries according to a list of

[1]The most thorough account is John D. Unruh, *The Plains Across: The Overland Emigrants and the Trans-Mississippi West, 1840–1860* (Urbana, 1979).

fifty-three predetermined values. Faragher's purpose was to assess the importance of gender in the perception and reality of the overland trail experience.

David Rich Lewis, in the following selection, makes a similar analysis of forty-four diaries and journals. Unlike Faragher, however, Lewis is particularly interested in the experiences of the young single men who took to the trail for California. Lewis demonstrates that the experiences and values of this group were similar to those of the larger overland migration. He divides their experiences into a half-dozen or more main categories and describes each category in turn.

Especially important is Lewis' discussion of aggression and conflict on the overland trail. In recent years several historians have challenged the notion that lawlessness and violent conflict were widespread during the gold rush.[2] John Phillip Reid, for example, found a remarkable persistence of law-abiding habits among those who were heading west. Shared values and past experiences kept the trail orderly and safe.[3] Mary McDougall Gordon, likewise, discovered that even when serious dissension broke out, violence was rare and old traditions tended to prevail.[4] Even in the mining camps, Roger D. McGrath recently concluded, criminal and lawless behavior affected only a few specialized groups.[5] David Rich Lewis, however, finds that aggression and social conflict were part of the core experience of the argonauts. He analyzes the sources of tension and conflict on the trail and concludes that the trail "communities" were little more than unstable compromises between individual self-interest and the common good.

David Rich Lewis, a Ph.D. candidate at the University of Wisconsin, Madison, received the 1984 Bert M. Fireman Prize from the Western History Association for an earlier version of the article reprinted here.

[2]See, however, Richard Maxwell Brown, *Strain of Violence: Historical Studies of American Violence and Vigilantism* (New York, 1975).

[3]John Philip Reid, *Law for the Elephant: Property and Social Behavior on the Overland Trail* (San Marino, 1980).

[4]Mary McDougall Gordon, ed., *Overland to California with the Pioneer Line: The Gold Rush Diary of Bernard J. Reid* (Stanford, 1983).

[5]Roger D. McGrath, *Gunfighters, Highwaymen and Vigilantes: Violence on the Frontier* (Berkeley, 1984).

READING 9

Argonauts on the Overland Trail

David Rich Lewis

In the spring of 1849 John Evans Brown and his young companions from North Carolina set off on the adventure of their lives—to cross the continent by horse and wagon and find gold in the new El Dorado of California. In the exuberance of youth, Brown recorded his hopes and fears before passing out of "civilization" and into the "wilds": "All is work and excitement and proving ourselves men, leaving family and friend to go amongst the wilds. Who can tell which or how many will fall by disease, an Indian arrow or the several dangers that will beset our path, but to the West we have set our faces, and to the West we go."[1] Determined to face whatever hardships the trail had to offer and make his place in adult society, Brown set out to "see the Elephant." He observed the pachyderm well before he reached the goldfields of California—the hardship, difficulty, and struggle to survive so often described by other overlanders as the real "Elephant" of the gold rush.

The struggle, triumph, failure, and tears of argonauts during the gold rush years of 1849 to 1853 have been well covered in history and have worked their way into the pantheon of American myth.[2] The purpose of this study is not to add to the extensive catalogue of overland experiences, but rather to suggest a more systematic method and larger cultural perspective. As a method, content analysis helps uncover and arrange the important experiences and cultural values recorded in a set of overland trail diaries. From these values and experiences two themes emerge: (1) the continuity of larger cultural norms and values, and (2) the applica-

bility of theoretical models of social organization, community interaction, and conflict to mobile trail communities. What this article suggests is a starting point for further synthesis.

In recent years several important studies have treated the overland experience of women and men through contemporary journal and diary accounts. John Faragher, Lillian Schlissel, Howard Lamar, and Glenda Riley have all contributed to our knowledge. While their methods, focus, and findings differ considerably, they find agreement in excluding from their surveys the predominantly young and single male gold rusher, for very practical reasons—these men do not represent the migration of stable family units in which the relationships between men and women can be studied. Acknowledgments are made to this segment of the trail population, but they are treated as an aberrant appendage of the larger migration process, somehow representing different experiences and expressing different values.[3] My reading of primary and secondary accounts leads me to suggest that these male gold rushers' expressed concerns and trail experiences were more similar to the experiences and cultural values of the larger overland migration than has been previously recognized. Underlying this suggestion is the notion implicit in the theory and method of value-analysis—that there is a core of sameness, an "all-pervasive character of the value-system of our own culture," commonly and widely held, which can be empirically studied.[4] By applying value-analysis to sampled diaries of male argonauts and gathering the rhetorical and behavioral expression of common cultural values contained therein, similar experiences, expressions, and behaviors emerge. Differences do exist, but when viewed in terms of common cultural values and social norms, the experiences of these lone male argonauts blend with the larger trail community experience as recognized and described by Faragher and other scholars.

The findings of this study in value-analysis and a collective ranking of the top seven value areas expressed are listed in Table 1.[5]

The analysis indicates that the bulk of the gold rushers' concerns fall into three general areas: the practical and economic aspects of the trip; physiological factors such as rest, health, safety, and comfort; and expressions of the natural beauty of their changing environment. The fourth value area revolves around the notion of the new experience of westward movement and day-to-day trail occurrences. The fifth area captures the argonauts' concern for friendship and family connections—a significant point considering that these predominantly single males traveling in masculine companies lacked an immediate family setting. The sixth expressed value concerns food and its presence or absence, and the seventh notes the prominence and nature of aggression and conflict, both on the trail and within the trail community—a

TABLE 1 TABULATED RESULTS OF VALUE-ANALYSIS: PERCENTAGE DISTRIBUTION OF MEASURED THEMATIC CONTENT

Category	Argonauts*	Total percentages†
Practical (a)	30.0	24.3
Physiological (b)	26.4	21.4
Beauty	10.1	8.1
New Experience (c)	9.2	7.4
Friendship/Family (d)	8.8	7.2
Food	6.7	5.4
Aggression (e)	1.8	1.5
Others	7.0	24.7
Total	100%	100%

*Tabulation from the top seven values of all diaries. Use this column for comparison with John Faragher's value analysis percentages. N = 8,697.

†Tabulation of *total* value responses recorded. N = 10,739.
(a) value categories = Work and Economic Value; (b) value categories = Rest, Health, Comfort, Safety, and Activity; (c) value categories = New Experience and Excitement; (d) value categories = Friendship, Family Home, Family Affection, Companionship, and Community; (e) value categories = Aggression and Dominance.

point that will be noted with particular attention to models of community consensus and conflict.[6]

But first, the picture sketched here with numbers needs to be filled in. Just as the bleached bones of dead draft animals were repugnant to the overland emigrant of the 1840s and 1850s, so is the bare-boned quantitative explanation of a historical problem to the narrative-oriented historian of the present. The overland trail experience represents a broad range of activities that changed over time and space and that cannot be fully understood and treated in article length. Nevertheless, value-analysis provides a tool for organizing cultural themes of overland trail life as perceived by the participants themselves, and hopefully will serve as a suggestive model for more comprehensive comparative studies.

PRACTICAL MATTERS

There were many practical aspects of the overland journey. Overland diaries contain the everyday experiences and progress of an individual, or group of individuals, moving across a vast expanse of land. Recording this experience day by day for as long as six months, the argonaut passes onto us the notion of daily trail life in all its facets—monotony, excitement, hope, fear, and especially of back-breaking work. The circadian rhythms of work fell into four time sequences: breaking camp, driving and the work of the trail, setting up camp again, and the night guard. In the morning, stock had to be rounded up and harnessed, wagons repacked, and cold food washed down with coffee before departure. The day varied depending on weather and environment, but the monotonous chores of walking, herding, gathering fuel, driving and repairing wagons, and hitching and unhitching stock at the "nooning" remained constant. On other days hunting was added, or the tasks of ferrying wagons across rivers or lowering them down steep hills by rope, and of doubling teams to pull wagons out of mudholes or back up the steep hills again. Evening found the argonauts setting up camp, unhitching stock, pitching tents, unpacking wagons, and cooking food for their evening and next day's meal. The evening held odd jobs to be done by fading sunlight or candlelight and finally night guard. Work seldom ended and frequently spilled over to days of rest. So routine and constant was the work that most diarists merely noted their activities and exertions without particular comment. Some, like David Staples, scribbled impatiently, "It is the most vexing life man ever led."[7]

Yet for the California argonaut traveling in predominantly male companies, the nature and extent of his work was compounded by the absence of women. When traveling in family settings, men worked at their peak while the wagons were rolling and then could relax somewhat and let the women take over in camp. But in male companies, separate spheres of work broke down, and men faced cooking, mending, washing, gathering fuel, arranging the tent and wagon, hauling water, and other activities considered to be "woman's work."[8] Men attempted to ameliorate this killing workload and diffuse the potentially serious conflict that arose from this breakdown in the traditional sexual division of labor by distributing the chores among various members in each "mess." Often chores were rotated within the mess in the same manner that night guard duty was throughout the entire company—each taking a specific assignment each day or week so that no one had to drive or herd or cook all the time.[9]

When it came to cooking—a particularly female skill—some men were eager to pay for others to do it. Joseph C. Kiser was not alone in his sentiments when he wrote home from Fort Kearny that he and his nine companions had hired another man to do their cooking all the way to California for ten dollars, "which I think was very cheap...for I Would Not Wash the Dishes for Twice That Amount."[10] Even

though cooking duties were generally shared, or "intrusted to the most skillful," and some men were undoubtedly proficient at cooking some items, it was not a chore relished by the diarists. Walter Pigman gives us a picturesque account of preparing supper while "sitting upon a buffalo's head, cooking buffalo on a fire made of buffalo chips," but others like Edward Kitchell complained more realistically of battling the elements, the smoke and fire, insects, and the cavil of messmates "sick of my corn bread."[11]

Washing was another low-priority chore usually recognized as "woman's work," and was done, or mentioned, infrequently among the male argonauts. It was not until reaching Fort Laramie that Henry Tappan first "tried my hand in the art of washing dirty clothes." Young George Kellogg found it easier to systematically discard dirty clothes than to wash them. George Brown spoke for male and female alike when he deemed washing "the most disagreeable part of the trip."[12]

If "work" was the common denominator of trail life and the single most noted value among male argonauts, practical economic values underlying their rush to California during the "golden" years were not far behind. Given the cost of preparing for the trail, the expectations for finding instant wealth, and the recognition among some that their economic futures were potentially less secure than those of stay-behinds, it is little wonder that economic considerations ranked high in the gold rush mentality. Money was both the vehicle enabling them to go and their reason for going. Like their farm family counterparts, virtually every male gold rusher noted the cost of equipment and supplies at home and along the trail, the outrageous as well as the just cost of ferries along the route, and the economic trade-offs made in order to achieve their goals.

Perhaps the most common expression of economic concern came in the record of items discarded along the trail and the treatment of expensive animals and equipment. Not one of the sampled gold rushers failed to take notice of, or lament, the piles of abandoned tools, accessories, clothing, foodstuffs, and jaded animals that cost so much at the "jumping-off place." The amount of waste staggered them, yet most contributed at one time or another to it. Having reached the base of the Sierra Nevada, H. Merrill spoke in retrospect of the overland trail: "From Fort Laramie to this place, the road is lined with dead cattle, wagons, and fragments of wagons. Log chains in any number, trunks and clothing are scattered all along the route, and bacon and flour we passed in piles and piles—Such a destruction of property, such a vast amoant [sic] of valuables thrown away to rot and mould, can scarce be dreamed of at home."[13]

But the most important items lost or abandoned on the trail were draft animals. Dependent upon them, Benjamin Clark noted that there was "considerable alarm manifest & long faces [were] very common" as stock began to fail. Actual loss occasioned even more anxious words. Carcasses of dead animals lined the trail from Fort Laramie to the Sierra Nevada, an unpleasant obstacle and a warning to those who followed. Argonauts noted hundreds or thousands of dead and abandoned animals, some with "about enough life to turn up their heads to look at us as we passed." Such sights provoked serious reflection on the nature and practical realities of their venture.[14]

These were the practical expressions—notions of work and economic value—that fill the pencil-written diaries of men off to see the "Elephant." Like their family-centered counterparts, they used the pages of their diaries to record the practical matters uppermost in their minds. It made little difference whether they were on the trail to California or the agricultural frontier.

THE PHYSIOLOGY OF WESTERING

Physiological concerns were with the argonauts every day. The nature of life on the trail led to abundant expressions of concern for health, safety, and comfort. If gold rushers lacked original family-centered organization and relationships, they nevertheless spent a good portion of their time noting the physiological realities of their own, and their group's, experience.

Rest was a rare and valued commodity. Within gold rush companies the push to reach destinations was a compound of economic motivation and fear of being trapped by early snows. Given this situation, total rest was seldom possible. Baking, washing, and repairs, often put off for lack of time, filled the days when a company stopped to recruit men and animals. Generally the argonauts simply noted that they "laid by today" or "stayed in camp." Other times they articulated their appreciation of opportunities to rest, particularly after passing difficult stretches of road. George Washington Short expressed constant dismay that his companions broke the Sabbath. On a Sunday morning in July he noted that "the Devil is to work again as usual to get the company to travel to-day; took a vote on it, a majority for laying by...I am truly thankful for the chance of resting myself both in body and mind."[15]

Health and safety were equally important aspects of this physical world. In a period and culture in which sickness and death had not been removed from the family sphere, their occurrence was a natural and important concern, aggravated somewhat by trail life and mobile communities. Good health meant faster and more comfortable travel; sickness slowed progress and threatened survival; and death often signaled epidemics, more death, and possible failure.

It is estimated that between 4 and 6 percent of those who started the overland emigration between 1842 and 1859 died on the trail. The death rate would have been around 2.5 percent had they remained at home. Of the trail deaths, as many as 90 percent were disease related, with cholera heading the list.[16] Comments on cholera deaths were generally brief and to the point: "We passed many wagons which had camped on account of the Cholera. Many were sick, some dying, and others dead."[17] Physicians on the road, like John Dalton and Joseph Bradway, were in great demand to treat cholera and the other common trail diseases: dysentery, mountain fever, and scurvy. But their heroic medical techniques—kill-or-cure prescriptions and drugs—proved largely inadequate. Called to another train halted by cholera, Dr. Dalton noted that "[I] did all I could for Capt. W[hite] but after reviving a little, he sunk very fast, and died in about two hours."[18]

Next to diseases, accidents were the major threat to the health and safety of all overlanders. Virtually every diary records accidental drownings. Others record accidental gunshot wounds and deaths from careless treatment or stowage of the numerous loaded weapons brought on the trip to defend against Indians and to procure game. Andrew Orvis, who shot himself in the hip with his revolver early in the trip, recorded another such incident at South Pass and reflected that "there has been several kiled and wounded on the road in the same way by just being carless with their fire arms." John Brown "felt persuaded that more danger is to be apprehended from the carelessness of arms among fellow emigrants, than from the hostile Indian."[19]

Threats to safety more subtly acknowledged than river crossings, hazardous road passages, stampedes, and sickness or injuries were argonaut fears of the Indian that were conditioned by the widespread image of the Indian as "Savage." Stories of Indian depredations abound in the diary accounts, but the majority of stock thefts and violence actually occurring was restricted to one area—the Great Basin region. Also, the diarists recount more attacks on other companies than upon their own, secondhand accounts, which may have been enlarged in the telling from group to group or were used to explain stock losses that actually occurred from

neglect. Conflict with Indians did occur and animals were lost to theft or well-placed arrows, but the perceived threat to safety weighed more heavily on argonaut minds than the actual losses.[20]

Rounding out the common expression of physiological values were those dealing with activity outside the sphere of daily work and with comfort, or more typically the lack of it. Given the amount of work, the push for speed, and the lack of women and children who often initiated it, there was little outside socializing. Physical comfort was noted as frequently as was health, but diarists usually referred to its scarcity. They faced "dust flying like snow in winter—Hot days and cold nights," sudden prairie storms and mountain snowstorms, mosquitoes "ready to take poscesion of us and all we poscesed," and "blistered and sadly galled feet." Constantly at work, with little or no female companionship or family to ease the stress of trail life, the argonauts noted little comfort in their physical experiences, aside from the occasional smooth road, full stomach, or stretch of pleasant weather.[21]

BEAUTIES TO BEHOLD

In the category of beauty, gold rushers frequently took time out to record appreciation of the land through which they passed. Recognition of grandeur and beauty seems universal to all overland emigrants. Never before had most of them seen the plains or mountains to match the Rockies and the Sierra Nevada; nor had they ever sensed the relief provoked by a sparkling cold stream or verdant fields after passing miles of forbidding alkaline waste. Even in extremely difficult situations, overland emigrants noticed and found some release in the picturesque, and they innocently expressed their delight. Notations appear on almost every page, and even the most inveterate "trail-loggers" were sometimes prompted to break their monotonous account of miles made, road and water conditions, and camping spots. Grand sights led to the greatest instances of self-expression and literary attempt. Sitting on a hillside at dusk, David Brainard characterized the plain below him: "A more beautiful sight I never saw. The moon, as she sailed majestically over the plain, gave it the appearance of a vast body of water, and the undulations looked like the white-caps of the ocean. Our wagons were small row-boats, tossing on the foaming billows. My thoughts dwelt for a moment upon the grand scenery around me, reverted to former and less romantic scenes of my native land."[22]

In Nebraska, Court House Rock, Chimney Rock, and Scott's Bluff all elicited some notice or description. Argonaut and emigrant alike wondered at the singularity of these features, seeing in them the ruins of prehistoric castles and cathedrals. "Every place scemes [sic] like a fairy vision," wrote Thomas Woodward. "All starts into Being with a Boldness and architectural Beauty That is astonishingly grand But it is no use me Trying to describe Them for Language cannot do it." Further along the trail, mountains, and particularly Laramie Peak, caught their attention, and as H. E. Foster noted, "struck me with wonder surely."[23] The natural beauty of the Sweetwater rushing through Devil's Gate in Wyoming, the shimmering appearance of the Salt Lake valley, the unearthly jumble of the City of Rocks in Idaho, and the jagged mountains and lush valleys of the Sierra Nevada were indelibly imprinted in their minds and diaries. Passing through the most beautiful and most desolate of countries, these gold rushers recorded both the large and small wonders of nature as an important part of their cultural and trail experience.

NEW EXPERIENCES

The overland journey to California was both a new and an exciting experience. Many were leaving parents, friends, and families for the first time and striking off on the unprecedented adventure that would take them across the continent to El Dorado. From the first discovery of gold, restless imaginations soared and adventurers willing to face the uncertainties of a new experience took to the trails. At least fifty (71 percent) of the argonauts surveyed had a history of interstate or international mobility prior to their departure, yet few were immune to the new sights and sensations awaiting them on the trail.

While many new attractions caught their attention, the first and most universally noted was their encounter with buffalo. The sighting, chase, kill, and first meal combined to make a grand occasion. David Brainard enthusiastically scribbled, "This was the first one most of us had ever seen, and such an excitement I never saw. If we had found a gold mine there could not have been a greater commotion." William Kilgore wrote in honest amazement, "I see more Buffalo this afternoon than I had any Idea of Seeing on the whole trip."

Many other new experiences elicited comment. While many had seen Indians of some sort previously, they were able to visit and comment on Indian villages along the trail, see their customs and life-styles firsthand, and even experience fear and frustration as a result of depredations or by the very proximity of Indians. Gold rushers and emigrants alike had the opportunity to experience a culture different from their own. Some, like George Davidson, stopped to appreciate it; others passed by in preconceived fear and disgust. Other new experiences ranged from the physical nature of the western environment and roads to the appearances of mirages and the visual distortion of distances, from prairie dog cities to the appearance of "toads with horns," which "excited considerable wonder." Cooking with "bois de vache" in the treeless plains also drew considerable attention, as did the hot springs of Idaho and Nevada. Even in the measured monotony of daily trail activities, these men found time for hunting or exploring side trips and eagerly recorded their individual adventures and experiences away from the group in the unfamiliar western environment. New scenery, new companions, new problems, conflicts, and solutions confronted them daily as the environment shifted. Some regretted their trip. Others like Lucius Fairchild "would not take $10,000 for what I have learned."[24]

FRIENDSHIP AND FAMILY

Although California argonauts traveled overland in masculine companies, they nevertheless placed a good deal of value on trail friendships and on the friendship and family connections of a home they planned to return to after amassing their "pile." In the absence of extensive family or kinship bonds (only thirteen, or 19 percent, of those surveyed traveled with any discernable relative), they established surrogate family units around the mess and placed limited community values in the fragile company. These argonauts, like their family counterparts, traveled mainly with wagons until necessity dictated otherwise. As one historian has noted, "The wagon was plainly a community vehicle," requiring a group effort to haul it across rivers, out of bogs, and up steep hills. At night it served to define the community compound and provided group and individual shelter.[25] Brought together by the practical necessities and immediate pressures of the trail and by the desire to maintain order and a semblance of middle-class Protestant morality, these men formed companies with constitutions and laws to replicate family and social institutions left behind. Nearly all of the men studied describe some form of company organization, law, and instances of democratic decision making or justice. Whether or not they were effective is another question.[26] Frequently based on prior acquaintance and mutual trust, the trail mess of friends, neighbors, and even relatives provided a renewed social contract and a comfortable blanket of familiarity—similar in some ways to

that provided by the family. Yet this sense of trail "family" or "community" did not spill over into the settlement phase, particularly among the gold rushers. If the mess had not dissolved in conflict or disagreement along the trail before reaching California, members were quick to go their separate ways after arrival. Bound together for the trip by a sense of mutual interest, security, and efficiency, broader group values were largely missing. These ephemeral "families" devolved rapidly to the level of individual interest and economic concern once they reached California.[27]

Even enroute, expressions of home friendships and kinships extended beyond the messes and the trail communities. California argonauts, whether young and single or middle-aged family men, spent a good deal of time writing home, thinking of parents, wives, children, and friends, and contemplating prospects of seeing them again. Joseph Bradway reflected that he left "home, friends, all that I hold dear save life, health, and virtue, behind....Cannot make it seem that I am leaving home for so long a time as 2 years at least." Under a starry Nebraska sky, Edward Kitchell dreamt of "happy days gone by," of his parents and siblings in Illinois, and "could let my mind go whether it willed but my body staid with the oxen, wrapped up in a blanket." Married argonauts expressed frequent concern for the welfare of their wives and children. Younger men with strong family ties experienced bouts of homesickness.

While gold rushers and family men on the overland trail may have expressed less concern for family, friendship, and home in their diaries than women did, their written thoughts return again and again to those relationships and ties. One historian suggests that a shared awareness of the absence of family among the forty-niners resulted in "a new consciousness of the practical and emotional roles women and families played in their lives"—their psychological importance making them "shadow members" of every California argonaut company.[28] Argonauts were quick to note their encounters with women and children, or the civilized appearance of Salt Lake City. Far from home and longing for its sights and sounds, Elisha Lewis and his company pulled into a campsite of 200 wagons along the Humboldt River. Even in such an inhospitable environment, Lewis noted that "the ringing of cowbells the cries of children and the beating of the drum reminded us of a land of Civiliseation"—it reminded them of home.[29]

Food and provisions were also given careful consideration as argonauts and emigrants prepared for their overland adventure. Trail guide books provided estimates of goods needed, and diarists often detailed the extent and variety of their provisions. While everyday meals were rarely mentioned by the argonauts sampled, occasions of fresh meat or fish, special celebration meals and imported delicacies, oddities like "prairie dog stew," or especially the severe lack of food for man and beast at crucial times drew special comment.[30] Overland argonauts were warned by several books against depending on the hunt for food because of its uncertainty, consumption of time, inherent dangers, and the strain it placed on "horse flesh." But preserved foodstuffs, particularly among male argonauts who were admittedly more proficient at eating than cooking, proved exceedingly tiresome. Almost every trail diary notes with relish the procurement of fresh meat, whether buffalo, sage hen, antelope, duck, or trout.

Besides comments on the fresh meat obtained, these argonauts were equally quick to recognize the lack of food as they trailed into Nevada. Along the trail, many argonauts sold or dumped their surplus provisions. But as supplies dwindled and game and fresh water became scarce, they record an increasing preoccupation with this threatening situation. Most diarists echo John Grindell's observation that "there is a vast number of teams now on the road and nearly all out of provisions." Elijah Farnham described a day's meal as "one or two crackers a handful of beans and a couple swallows of water," while others were forced to eat the stringy flesh of dead draft animals.[31] The price of food and water soared in the Nevada deserts, and provisioners from the Carson and Truckee rivers both saved emigrants and profited from the situation. Aware of both the cultural norms and physiological necessities of food, these California gold rushers recorded the culinary highlights and sufferings of their migration, but rarely the mundane and day-to-day meals that fueled their activities.

AGGRESSION AND CONFLICT

It is not surprising that expressions of aggression and conflict rank among the top value categories in argonaut diaries. Encounters with hostile Indians and accounts of murders and retributions dot many journals. But generally, aggression and conflict were directed toward the internal organization of trail companies, between companies, and most important, between individuals within companies or messes. The expressions are manifest in both verbal and behavioral terms and include the most noted phenomena of the trail experience—quarreling, fighting, individual and group dissension, and organizational dissolution. These colorful incidents are recounted by historians interested in defining legal and social behavior on the overland trail, yet few have carried this analysis through to test theories of social organization and community development. While previous discussion of social theory has centered on the sedentary community, mobile communities of the overland trail provide a unique opportunity to extend this analysis to the virtual limits of frontier communities "in the process of becoming."[32]

In the years since Frederick Jackson Turner verbalized the popular notion of frontier behavior, settlement, and the development of a uniquely American society, three distinct theoretical models of social development in nineteenth-century frontier communities have emerged. The first, advanced by Stanley Elkins and Eric McKitrick, sought to reconfirm the basic premises of Turner's thesis. Briefly, Elkins and McKitrick argue a consensual interpretation based on samples from scattered county histories and on Robert Merton's sociological study of two twentieth-century communities. They maintain that the physical and political problems faced by a young, homogeneous population, without an established leadership structure resulted in extensive social cooperation and interaction in voluntary association to solve these problems in the short run and continued to be a positive community force well after the original difficulties had been overcome. Elaborated by Daniel Boorstin in terms of communal cooperation and town boosterism, this theory reinforced ideas of the environmental impact of the frontier in determining the development of American democracy.[33]

In response to the optimism of consensus history and its weakly rooted evidence, Allan G. Bogue proposed a more realistic theory of social organization. Unlike the "neo-Turnerian" interpretation of cooperative democracy, Bogue suggests that new communities existed in an atmosphere of conflict, instability, and economic insecurity and self-interest and that these new communities were culturally and socially diverse, highly mobile, and experienced difficulty in defining social norms and leadership. Informal cooperation was prevalent in the face of a difficult economic environment (providing conflict was absent), yet the lack of well-established institutions and social customs during the settlement period involved individuals in a "greater number of conflict situations than before migration." Bogue's model is substantiated most explicitly in Robert R. Dykstra's study of Kansas cattle towns, which stresses the political and social conflict in new community organization and development, and the "harmonious image"

created by town promoters and accepted all too readily by historians.[34]

Finally, Don Harrison Doyle refined these models in his study of Jacksonville, Illinois, as he searched for the things that held frontier communities together. Acknowledging in the Bogue model that "conflict was an integral and permanent aspect of a pluralistic community in which no single hierarchy of authority and values could instill consensus," Doyle divides conflict into different levels suggestive of the sophistication of social organization: interpersonal violence, factional cliques, and conflict between formal organizations. In the latter, consisting of churches, political parties, and voluntary associations, Doyle finds the institutionalization and control of community conflict. In turn, these voluntary associations ordered conflict in the maturing community by defining status and leadership, integrating various groups and factions into the community, and insuring the ascendency of native, middle-class values and social control. Their success is the story of Jacksonville, and as Doyle argues, other frontier communities as well.[35]

At first glance, the overland experience would appear to be a vindication of the neo-Turnerian interpretation of spontaneous democratic social organization and cooperation. Companies formed along democratic lines, elected leaders, and drew up constitutions, rules, and duties. Men and women worked together in a cooperative effort to move across the country with a maximum of efficiency and security. Yet the norms and laws they adopted were not a response to the new environment but were an application of existing institutional forms to new situations.[36] Company formation was an early voluntary response to the perceived practicality and necessity of community cooperation in meeting the unknowns of geographic mobility, but one that faded quickly with actual experience, particularly on the crowded trails of the gold rush years.

Of the California argonauts in this value-analysis sample, 88 percent mentioned formal company organizations or constitutions. Of these, well over half explicitly noted that the organization was ignored or ineffective in ordering the group by the time it reached South Pass. Fully 75 percent of the companies effected divisions and recombinations along the trail, with 62 percent citing anger, quarreling, or personal violence explicitly or implicitly as reasons for (or closely accompanying) the split. Explanations for such individual and company dissension ranged from disputes over the rate of advance, food, leaders, and group decisions, to jobs and trail responsibilities, personal quarrels, and vendettas, to sheer boredom. Fistfights, brawls, and spontaneous assaults with knife or gun occurred in both emigrant and argonaut companies but were not as typical as the constant verbal wranglings. Such social behaviors are not surprising given living conditions and work that drained men physically and wore on nerves and tempers. While every diarist noted such incidents, Charles Gray recognized the expression, the motivations behind it, and the nature of humans living in social community everywhere when he wrote, "Nearly everybody in camp for the past few days have been constantly wrangling & contending—the reason, phylosophikically I should say, because we get tired to death with our monotonous course of life & a quarrel or two or three or ten of them makes some excitement! Such is man! quiet, restless, satisfied, dis-satisfied; But such is life here as else where."[37]

Practical logistical problems were also a source of tension and potential conflict within argonaut companies. Large companies were slow and awkward. Size increased their problems of coordinating activities and of finding adequate campsites, feed, fuel, and water. Walter Pigman noted this common problem of large companies: "Among all the well organized trains on the route we have seen none that remain together, the scarcity of grass and dis-satisfaction from other causes is sure to cause them to break to pieces. Small companies, say three waggons, find it much better traveling together than in large trains. The only advantage which can possibly be realized from large trains is to form a more safe and formidable front or defense from an attack of Indians." Bryon McKinstry denied even this necessity for larger groups and decried the military "flummery" of company organization, while Charles Smith blamed large companies for the frequent difficulty and "hesitation on the plains, which invariably results in disagreement."[38]

While practical reasons for company divisions undoubtedly were a part of many company splits, such decisions were reinforced by the social conflict generated between individuals and groups of individuals within the trail community.[39] Like emerging communities of the nineteenth century, the trail community was a compromise between the ideals of unrestrained individualism and individual self-interest and the native middle-class ideals of social and communal good. Although organized under supposedly binding constitutions, laws, and financial arrangements, the trail community was little more than a "community of limited liability"—one in which individuals promoted their common interests with only limited social and psychological investment in the whole. Larger social rules and cultural values persisted, but because the trail community itself was a voluntary association, one of "limited liability," and already in motion, mobility in and out of the group was even more fluid, and ephemeral group values tended to become lost in the shuffle. Allowing easy withdrawal when the community failed to meet the individual's needs and perceived investment or when open conflict erupted, the majority of overland companies disintegrated and recombined on the trail. In a process of social sifting, dissatisfied individuals or messes organized into smaller, more compatible companies for mutual support and companionship—once again joining or forming a new trail "community" to help realize their immediate goals.[40]

Aggression and social conflict were part of the core experience of these mobile communities. Yet social cooperation, instances of group unity, and larger group consciousness found expression at the outset of the trip and during times of universal need and mutual suffering on the trail. Still, this awareness was soon evanesced by experience and individual motivations, and "rarely was ongoing collective action the outgrowth of the Overland Trail."[41] Lacking motivation for prolonged communal affinity, durable institutional structures, and the continuity of associated membership, little prevented the escalation of conflict and pursuit of self-interest within the trail community. Although exacerbated by the mobile reality of the trail, these communities are suggestive of the broader cyclical pattern of frontier community organization, integration, disenchantment, and sifting that took place throughout the early "urban" frontier West.

"The California Gold Rush was not an aberration in nineteenth-century American history," according to Ralph Mann, "nor were the forty-niners alienated from the values of their time."[42] They were part and parcel of an expansive and mobile age, seeking wealth and adventure and experimenting in socially acceptable ways. Like their family-oriented counterparts, they traveled west in search of economic betterment and carried with them a belief in similar social institutions and cultural norms. They moved through the same environment, witnessed the beauties and terror of nature, faced many of the same hardships, and counted the many personal and economic costs. Although they lacked the nuclear or extended framework of the family, with its social, psychological, and physical benefits and its gender-role division of labor, these argonauts attempted to recreate similar structures within the mess. They formed trail communities in the image of those communities left behind and witnessed conflict, dissolution, social sifting, and the formation of new trail communities over time and geographic space. Their values varied only slightly from the prevailing social and cultural norms, and their experiences become less exceptional when viewed in this context. While obvious differences in the purpose for migration and in its physical makeup exist, the overland trail experience of gold-rushing argonauts blends into the larger mosaic of overland migration, reaffirming the continuity of cultural values and echoing the experience of early social organization and community development in the American West.

Notes

1 John Evans Brown, "Memoirs of an American Gold Seeker," *Journal of American History,* 2 (no. 1, 1908), 132. Throughout this paper passages taken from diaries and letters are reproduced as they appear in the original text.

2 Among the most important for this article are John D. Unruh, Jr., *The Plains Across: The Overland Emigrants and the Trans-Mississippi West, 1840–1860* (Urbana, 1979); Merrill J. Mattes, *The Great Platte River Road: The Covered Wagon Mainline via Fort Kearny to Fort Laramie* (Lincoln, 1969); John Mack Faragher, *Women and Men on the Overland Trail* (New Haven, 1979); David M. Potter, ed., *Trail to California: The Overland Journal of Vincent Geiger and Wakeman Bryarly* (New Haven, 1945); and Howard R. Lamar, "Rites of Passage: Young Men and Their Families in the Overland Trails Experience, 1843–69," in *"Soul-Butter and Hogwash" and Other Essays on the American West,* ed. Thomas G. Alexander (Provo, 1978), 33–67.

3 Faragher, *Women and Men;* Lillian Schlissel, *Women's Diaries of the Westward Journey* (New York, 1982); Lamar, "Rites of Passage"; and Glenda Riley, "The Frontier in Process: Iowa's Trail Women as a Paradigm," *Annals of Iowa,* 3d. ser., 46 (Winter 1982), 167–197. While I am indebted to Faragher for his insights and methodology and agree with much of his analysis, his work contains several flaws. Yet methodologically, his work stands well above the others in the

sophistication of analysis. Schlissel in particular wrestles with this problem, yet loses her direction in emphasizing the unusual, dark, and morbid within women's diaries. Grave counting and powerlessness, as she uses them, are not representative of the larger experience. See Marilyn Coffey, "A Solemn Thing," *Journal of the West,* XXII (October 1983), 82–83. For further critiques of both Faragher and Schlissel, see Sandra Myres, "Women in the West," in *Historians and the American West,* ed. Michael P. Malone (Lincoln, 1983), 369–386. Both Howard Lamar and Glenda Riley present more balanced pictures, and I am indebted to them for several insights.

4 Ralph K. White, *Value-Analysis: The Nature and Use of the Method* (Glen Gardner, NJ, 1951), 1. White's systematic method of content analysis is particularly applicable to historical first-person narratives. According to White, "Any kind of verbal data...can be described quantitatively, with a maximum of objectivity and at the same time with a maximum of relevance to the underlying emotional dynamics." By developing a list of predetermined values (see Faragher, *Women and Men,* 202, and White, *Value-Analysis,* 12, 22–39) and measuring every sentence against that list, given values are noted each time the writer expresses one, verbally or behaviorally. By tallying the final score sheet, areas of importance expressed by the *writer* are systematically ranked, not those expressions interposed by the historian looking for the "quotable quote" or fascinated by a particularly well-articulated statement. When applied to a collection of related documents, the collective thematic content, or cultural "values," of the sample can be determined in a more systematic manner and ranked for further study or agenda setting. This methodology has its own problems and limitations, yet its strengths in gathering evidence from multiple sources for analysis and generalization outweigh its weaknesses. See also Klaus Krippendorff, *Content Analysis: An Introduction to Its Methodology* (Beverly Hills, CA, 1980). The definition of *value* used in this paper is described by White as a two-fold concept: "A value is...any goal [that can be selfishly enjoyed] or standard of judgement [criteria for judging persons or situations] which in any given culture is ordinarily referred to as if it were self-evidently desirable (or undesirable)," White, *Value-Analysis,* 12–13. See also Clyde Kluckhohn, "The Study of Values," in *Values in America,* ed. Donald N. Barrett (Notre Dame, 1961), 17–24; and Robert F. Berkhofer, Jr., *A Behavioral Approach to Historical Analysis* (New York, 1969), 100–108, 121–129, 142, 194.

5 This study is based on a value-analysis of forty-four diaries and journals written by men on the overland trail to California between 1849 and 1853. Also, twenty-eight published diaries, reminiscences, and letter collections were read in order to provide additional statistical and narrative detail. These sources are not included in the value-analysis tabulation of the diaries because of their temporal and emotional removal from the situations and events they describe. All of the diarists are white males, the majority (65 percent) between 16 and 30 years old, New England or Northcentral "Yankees" by birth or childhood residence. At the time of departure, 79 percent of the sampled group (71 percent of the total group) resided in the Midwest, and 66 percent were unmarried. As with any sample based on written and preserved sources, there is inherent bias. This sample is socially top-heavy and largely midwestern in makeup, reinforcing the general notion that diary writers are, by the very action of writing and preserving their diaries, atypical in nineteenth-century America in general and in the overland trail experience in particular. Overall, all overland diarists comprise a small portion (about 0.3 to 0.4 percent) of the estimated 200,000 California, or 300,000, total western emigrants between 1840 and 1860. As with any extrapolation from such sample data to the larger population, the following findings must remain suggestive.

6 While 34 percent of those surveyed were married men traveling without their families, there appears to be little significant variation in the basic thematic expressions between single and married argonauts. Within that framework, older married men were more likely to express concerns for "Health," while younger single men were more enraptured with the prospects of the "New Experience." Much of what turned up in this analysis corresponds closely to Faragher's findings for men and women traveling as family groups.

While differences do exist, it is significant to note the close similarities. Faragher's tabulation is as follows: Practical: (M)en 28%, (W)omen 24%; Physiological: (M) 26%, (W) 27%; Aesthetic (Beauty): (M) 21%, (W) 23%; Amiable (Friendship): (M) 6%, (W) 15%; Aggression: (M) 15%, (W) 7%; Other: (M) 4%, (W) 4%. My analysis indicates more expressions of the "New Experience" and less "Aggression"—something that will be elaborated later. "Food" was a category Faragher excluded as a physical necessity without gender significance. See Faragher, *Women and Men,* 198–203.

7 Harold F. Taggert, ed., "The Journal of David Jackson Staples," *California Historical Society Quarterly,* XXII (June 1943), 126.

8 See Faragher, *Women and Men,* 68–87, for working schedules and spheres of work. See also Schlissel, *Women's Diaries,* 35–36, 102; Sandra L. Myres, *Westering Women and the Frontier Experience, 1800–1915* (Albuquerque, 1982), 98–140; Glenda Riley, *Frontierswomen: The Iowa Experience* (Ames, IA, 1981), 20–26; and Julie Roy Jeffrey, *Frontier Women: The Trans-Mississippi West, 1840–1880* (New York, 1979), 59–61.

9 John E. Dalton, "Overland Trail Diary of John E. Dalton," August 9, 1852, 31–32; Winslow Blake, "Journal of a Trip to California, 1852," June 11, 1852, 34; and Edward Kitchell, "A Trip across the Plains: Diaries of Edward Kitchell, 1852," May 23, 1852, p. 8, all in State Historical Society of Wisconsin (SHSW), Madison. Most of the diaries discuss these arrangements in one form or another.

10 Joseph C. Kiser to [?], May 27, 1850, Joseph C. Kiser Papers, 1840–1902, SHSW.

11 Brown, "Memoirs," 130; Ulla S. Fawkes, ed., *The Journal of Walter Griffith Pigman* (Mexico, MO, 1942), 23–24; and Kitchell, "Diaries," May 26, 1852, SHSW, 10.

12 Everett Walters and George B. Strother, eds., "The Gold Rush Diary of Henry Tappan," *Annals of Wyoming,* 25 (July 1953), 125; George J. Kellogg, "California Diaries," 2 vols., June 24, 1849, George J. Kellogg Papers, 1842–1918, SHSW, v. 1:74; and Brown, "Memoirs," 148. These expressions of displeasure and the difficulty of washing and cooking are echoed by westering women as well. See Myres, *Westering Women,* 106, 123–124.

13 H. Merrill, "Journal of the Overland Route to California," *Milwaukee Daily Wisconsin,* February 5, 1850.

14 Ralph P. Bieber, ed., "Diary of a Journey from Missouri to California in 1849," *Missouri Historical Review,* XXIII (October 1928), 17; Merrill J. Mattes and Elsey J. Kirk, eds., "From Ohio to California in 1849: The Gold Rush Journal of Elijah Bryan Farnham," *Indiana Magazine of History,* XLVI (December 1950), 414; and Aaron W. Harlan, "Journal of A. W. Harlan While Crossing the Plains in 1850," *Annals of Iowa,* 3d. ser., XI (April 1913), 45.

15 George Washington Short, "Diary of George Washington Short, March 29, 1852, to Nov. 7, 1853, Covering His Trip to and From California," July 11, 1852, SHSW, 5.

16 Unruh, *Plains Across,* 408–409. See also Georgia W. Read, "Diseases, Drugs, and Doctors on the Oregon-California Trail in the Gold Rush Years," *Missouri Historical Review,* XXXVIII (April 1944), 260–276; Charles Rosenberg, *The Cholera Years: The United States in 1832, 1849, and 1866* (Chicago, 1962); and Ramon Powers and Gene Younger, "Cholera on the Overland Trails, 1832–1869," *Kansas Quarterly,* 5 (Spring 1973), 32–49. Of the gold rushers surveyed, one died of cholera on the trail, several were afflicted but lived to tell about it, and at least two died after reaching California from the plagues raging there.

17 David Brainard, "Journal of the Walworth County Mutual Mining Company," May 23, 1849, SHSW, 12.

18 Dalton, "Diary," May 15–30 and June 4, 1852, SHSW, 6–8, 10–11. Treatments of large doses of calomel, laudanum, bleeding, tobacco smoke enemas, and the like were common practice, but could lead to massive dehydration, mercury poisoning, and even death. See Rosenberg, *Cholera Years,* 2–3, 66–67, 115, 152–153.

19 Andrew M. Orvis, "California Trail Diary, Reminiscences, and Letters of Andrew Orvis, 1849–1850," May 29, June 28, 1849, Beinecke Library, Yale University, New Haven, 5, 12; and Brown, "Memoirs," 140.

20 Mabelle E. Martin, ed., "From Texas to California in 1849: Diary of C. C. Cox," *Southwestern*

Historical Quarterly, XXIX (July 1925), 43, 137. See also Potter, ed., *Trail to California,* 93; Merrill J. Mattes, ed., "Alexander Ramsay's Gold Rush Diary of 1849," *Pacific Historical Review,* XVIII (November 1949), 460; Glenda Riley, "Frontierswomen's Changing View of Indians in the Trans-Mississippi West," *Montana the Magazine of Western History,* 34 (Winter 1984), 23–24; and Glenda Riley, "The Specter of a Savage: Rumors and Alarmism on the Overland Trail," *Western Historical Quarterly,* XV (October 1984), 427–444. See also Unruh, *Plains Across,* 408, 156–200. Unruh estimates that only 4 percent of trail deaths were Indian related, and he discusses the impact of the Indian on the emigrant in greater detail than can be done here.

21 Dalton, "Diary," August 10, 1852, 33; and Elisha Lewis, "Diary, Overland Trip to California in 1849," June 11, 1849, 20, all in SHSW. See also Sawyer, *Way Sketches,* 96–97.

22 Brainard, "Journal," September 28, 1849, SHSW, 40. See also Faragher, *Women and Men,* 14. In his value-analysis of women and men, Faragher found "Beauty" to be the singlemost expressed value, while I found it to be the second-most expressed.

23 Woodward, "Diary," May 27, 1850, 11; and H. E. Foster to his father, December 25, 1852, all in SHSW. For a fascinating discussion of Americans, nineteenth-century romanticism, the "cult of the wilderness," and descriptive conventions of natural beauty, see Roderick Nash, *Wilderness and the American Mind* (New Haven, 3d. ed., 1982).

24 Joseph Schafer, ed., *California Letters of Lucius Fairchild,* vol. XXXI of Wisconsin Historical Publications *Collections* (Madison, 1931), 38.

25 Daniel J. Boorstin, *The Americans: The National Experience* (New York, 1965), 56, 51–57.

26 Robert V. Hine, *Community on the American Frontier: Separate But Not Alone* (Norman, 1980), 49–69; Lamar, "Rites of Passage," 35–39; John Phillip Reid, *Law for the Elephant: Property and Social Behavior on the Overland Trail* (San Marino, CA, 1980); and David J. Langum, "Pioneer Justice on the Overland Trails," *Western Historical Quarterly,* V (October 1974), 421–439.

27 Lamar, "Rites of Passage," 35–37, 49; and Hine, *Community,* 68–69. This breakdown of messes and companies formed to cross the continent *and*

settle as mining companies is evident in Brainard's "Journal of the Walworth County Mutual Mining Company," SHSW.

28 Faragher, *Women and Men,* 201, found that women expressed more than double the percentage of this category than men did. My findings suggest a slightly higher expression of this category among argonauts than Faragher's family men (see Table 1 and n. 6). It is not surprising that these argonauts would express friendship and family values in equal or greater proportions than men who were moving westward within their family spheres. It is natural to reflect on things left behind and to take the things on hand more for granted. Andrew J. Rotter, "'Matilda for Gods Sake Write': Women and Families on the Argonaut Mind," *California History,* LVIII (Summer 1979), 129, 139, tends to overdraw the psychological dependence of these men on women, at least while on the trail. In the gold camps his analysis might ring true, but men on the trail appear to have been more practical and stoic about the situation. See Johnny Faragher and Christine Stansell, "Women and Their Families on the Overland Trail to California and Oregon, 1842–1867," *Feminist Studies,* 2 (nos. 2–3, 1975), 153.

29 Lewis, "Diary," September 3, 1849, SHSW, 53.

30 I chose to evaluate "Food" as a category separate from the physiological because of its frequent expression. One problem identified by Clyde Kluckhohn, "Study of Values," 20, is the necessity of separating "needs" such as food and water (biological givens) from "values." This becomes difficult in as much as food takes on important cultural and social meanings at certain times.

31 John Grindell, "Diary of a Trip from Platteville, Wisconsin, to California in 1850," July 13, 1850, 24; and Brainard, "Journal," November 27, 1849, 55, all in SHSW. See also Mattes and Kirk, eds., "From Ohio to California," 414.

32 Riley, "The Frontier in Process," 168. See also Faragher, *Women and Men,* 14, 201. Faragher exaggerates the occurrence and focus of aggression by including hunting in his definition. This questionable and presentist definition ignores both the norms and values of food and the strict definitions of value categories as defined by White, *Value-Analysis,* 27.

33 Frederick Jackson Turner, "The Significance of the Frontier in American History," *Report of the American Historical Association* (Washington,

DC, 1894), 199–227; Stanley Elkins and Erik McKitrick, "A Meaning for Turner's Frontier," *Political Science Quarterly,* LXIX (September 1954), 321–353, 565–602; and Boorstin, *The Americans,* 113–68.

34 Allan G. Bogue, "Social Theory and the Pioneer," *Agricultural History,* XXXIV (January 1960), 21–34; and Robert R. Dykstra, *The Cattle Towns* (New York, 1968), 371–383.

35 Don Harrison Doyle, *The Social Order of a Frontier Community: Jacksonville, Illinois, 1825–70* (Urbana, 1978), 11–15, 61; and Don Harrison Doyle, "Social Theory and New Communities in Nineteenth-Century America," *Western Historical Quarterly,* VIII (April 1977), 151–165. While this model begs the question of developmental conflict prior to the establishment of such formal institutions (the period Bogue is most concerned with), its incorporation of the concept of "community of limited liability" is valuable. For the concept, see Morris Janowitz, *The Community Press in an Urban Setting: The Social Elements of Urbanism* (Chicago, 2d. ed., 1967), 210–213. For an overview of these models tested on a mining frontier, see Ralph Mann, *After the Gold Rush: Society in Grass Valley and Nevada City, California, 1849–1870* (Stanford, 1982), 204–220.

36 Earl Pomeroy, "Toward a Reorientation of Western History: Continuity and Environment," *Mississippi Valley Historical Review,* XLI (March 1955), 579–600; Mann, *After the Gold Rush,* 3–5, 22, 196; and Reid, *Law for the Elephant,* 9–15, 147, 335.

37 Thomas D. Clark, ed., *Off at Sunrise: The Overland Journal of Charles Glass Gray* (San Marino, CA, 1976), 15.

38 Fawkes, ed., *Journal of Walter Griffith Pigman,* 25; Bruce L. McKinstry, ed., *The California Gold Rush Overland Diary of Bryan N. McKinstry, 1850–1851* (Glendale, 1975), 104; and R. W. G. Vail, ed., *Journal of a Trip to California* (New York, 1920), 52.

39 P. A. M. Taylor, "Emigrants' Problems in Crossing the West, 1830–70," *Birmingham University Historical Journal,* V (no. 1, 1955), 83–102, argues the consensus insight of group division for purely practical reasons, based largely on the Mormon experience.

40 Doyle, "Social Theory," 165; and Janowitz, *Community Press,* 210–213. In this argument I am referring mainly to the argonaut companies that divided much more frequently on a crowded trail than earlier Oregon-bound or Mormon companies. Yet the argument is applicable to all companies that divided on the trail. One problem not dealt with here because of space is the role of "core" populations and mobile peripheral "joiners" in community organization and control. Both are difficult to define in the mobile atmosphere of the trail.

41 Hine, *Community,* 68. The value-analysis of argonaut diaries bears out this point. Positive expressions of "Community" and "Group Unity" appear with regularity in most diaries during the period of group formation, but tend to become negative or disappear over time and geographic space. Such expressions barely exceed 1 percent of the total responses—a figure somewhat inflated by expressions of "mess" solidarity in the face of an impending company division.

42 Mann, *After the Gold Rush,* 1.

CHAPTER

AFTER THE GOLD RUSH

EDITOR'S INTRODUCTION

During the past two decades historians have adopted from the social sciences several new methods of analyzing quantitative data. Historians are now able to amass enormous bodies of data drawn from manuscript censuses, tax lists, town directories, and probate records. From these data, historians extract information about the age, sex, ethnic origin, occupation, family size, and wealth of the residents of a particular town or community. Aided by sophisticated computer programs, scholars thus are able to assess social and geographical mobility, spatial and ethnic distribution, and patterns of work and consumption.

Following the lead of Stephan Thernstrom's seminal study of working-class Boston, practitioners of the new social history are particularly interested in questions of social mobility.[1] How frequently have American workers been able to get better jobs, accumulate wealth, purchase homes, and pass these gains on to their sons and daughters? Most "mobility studies" have concluded that few individuals were able to rise from the bottom to the top of society, but a substantial minority of workers experienced modest gains in status. More common than upward mobility has been geographical mobility. Indeed, the workers who were least successful in improving their social status were generally the ones most likely to change their place of residence.

While most of the new social historians have focused their research on the cities of the northeast, a growing number of scholars have begun to analyze conditions on the frontier. Here the question of mobility is particularly intriguing because of the long-held belief that the west symbolized opportunity. While the findings are not conclusive,

[1]Stephan Thernstrom, *The Other Bostonians: Poverty and Progress in the American Metropolis, 1880–1970* (Cambridge, Mass., 1973). But see also James A. Henretta, "The Study of Social Mobility: Ideological Assumptions and Conceptual Bias," *Labor History,* XVIII (1977), 165–178.

116

many studies have found that opportunities on the western frontier were less then imagined and perhaps even less than in the older, more established areas of the country.[2]

In the following selection Ralph Mann brings the new social history to two mining camps on the California frontier, Grass Valley and Nevada City. His interest lies chiefly in the changing social structure of the towns. On the central question of mobility, Mann finds that the miners' prospects for instant wealth were quite dim. The heady days of placer mining *seemed* to represent a great chance for making a fortune, but actually it was only after industrialization had ended frontier conditions that most miners were solvent. And the miners most likely to succeed were the highly skilled hard rock miners who labored for a steady wage, not the ever-hopeful amateurs who worked the placers.

The high level of failure in the diggings was given literary expression at the time in such bitter accounts as William Shaw's *Golden Dreams and Waking Realities* (1851), George Payson's *Golden Dreams and Leaden Realities* (1853), and the acerbic Hinton Rowan Helper's *Land of Gold: Reality Versus Fiction* (1855). A common motif in this literature is the frustrated miner's abandonment of his claim, his stake in California, and his dreams of instant wealth. Ralph Mann underscores these accounts with his finding that only about 5 percent of the miners who were in the camps in 1850 were still there six years later.

Among Mann's other conclusions are that ethnic and occupational diversity increased during the 1850s, and that by the end of the decade a family-based, propertied middle class had emerged in the camps. Mann observes that having a family in the camps tended to be an indicator of class; just as Gloria E. Miranda noted in an earlier selection that family size in Hispanic California was regarded as a symbol of rank.

Ralph Mann obtained his Ph.D. from Stanford University in 1970 and is currently an Associate Professor of History at the University of Colorado, Boulder. He is the author of *After the Gold Rush: Society in Grass Valley and Nevada City, California, 1849–1870* (1982).

---

[2]Ralph Mann, ''Frontier Opportunity and the New Social History,'' *Pacific Historical Review*, LIII (November, 1984), 463–491.

READING 10

After the Gold Rush

Ralph Mann

At a time when gold mining dominated California's economy, Grass Valley and Nevada City were the two richest, most productive gold camps in the state. The two towns lie four miles apart in the lower foothills of the Sierra Nevada, approximately seventy miles northeast of Sacramento. Both began as placer mining camps, but achieved their greatest importance as centers of the quartz mining industry. Because the first gold excitement in the area was at Nevada City, that community was able to become the county seat and establish itself as the commercial focus for camps which developed later. When its placers declined in value, Nevada City was able to maintain itself through its political, legal, and business importance until rich hydraulic and quartz mining interests could be developed. Grass Valley, with poorer placer deposits, initially grew more slowly, but when mining technology advanced to the point where its extensive quartz gold deposits could be effectively exploited it quickly eclipsed its neighbor and all other camps in California. The mineral wealth of these towns allowed them to thrive long after most camps had disappeared. Although reduced in size and no longer producing gold, they still survive.

This paper investigates elements of the social structure of these two camps during their first decade. Social conditions during the gold rush have received much attention from historians, while social structures have not; and neither has been closely examined in the period after the flush times. The standard accounts of Cali-

fornia mining and miners after the gold rush have put only slight emphasis on such matters as ethnicity, family life, and living patterns. The contemporary work of John S. Hittell and the more recent work of Rodman Paul give the rough outlines of society in the mines, but there has been little detailed research into the structure of individual communities. By using statistics and a computer, and analyzing the important mining towns of Grass Valley and Nevada City, I shall attempt to draw a more detailed picture of mining society. Since the two towns developed at different speeds and in slightly different directions, comparisons of structures can show the social results of differing economies.

The heart of this study's data was drawn from the manuscript censuses of the two towns for the years 1850 and 1860. These censuses give the name, age, sex, birthplace, and occupation of each inhabitant. Town directories listed occupations and residences for certain intermediate years, and an almost complete newspaper file starting in 1851 supplied additional information. Unfortunately, the sources are not free of bias. The city directories were less careful about including miners and laborers than about professionals. Consequently, study of persistence which relies only on these directories exaggerates to a small degree the differences between occupational groups. The census-takers may also have been slightly less accurate with the poor, especially among miners in the first census when miners were extremely mobile.

The data collected from these sources was collated by individual subjects, coded, and entered on IBM cards. Correlations within this body of data were done by the use of an IBM 360/67 computer and a "packaged" program,

Adapted from "The Decade after the Gold Rush: Social Structure in Grass Valley and Nevada City, California, 1850–1860;" by Ralph Mann. Copyright © 1972 by the American Historical Association, Pacific Coast Branch. Reprinted from *Pacific Historical Review*, Vol. XLVI, No. 4, pp. 484–504, by permission of the Association.

the Statistical Package for the Social Sciences, developed in 1968 by Norman H. Nie, Dale H. Bent, and C. Hadlai Hull for the department of political science, Stanford University. It permits the cross-tabulation of many variables, and allows for nearly unlimited numbers of controls. The use of the computer made possible the accurate correlation of data drawn from the entire populations of the two towns. The expense of computer time and the prohibitive time involved in collection forced the use of a twenty percent sample of the miners in both towns in 1860, and the use of a twenty-five percent sample of the total population of Nevada City in 1850. The uniformity of data collected indicates that no validity was lost through the use of these samples.

TRANSIENCE AND HOMOGENEITY

In their first years, the most pronounced characteristic of Grass Valley and Nevada City was the transience of their physical and social structures. By the end of 1850, Nevada City had already experienced two distinct mining excitements, the first focused on the rich placers of Deer Creek and its tributaries, and the second centered in the gravel deposits in the hills above the camp. In Grass Valley, the first discovery of veins of quartz gold attracted large numbers of miners, but as yet it was a much smaller town then Nevada City. In both camps the days of simple placer mining were passing, giving way to more sophisticated techniques.

Nevada City had developed a well defined mercantile area with stores, saloons, and professional services concentrated along two streets. The dwellings of the miners were apart from this area and scattered along the ravines and hills, placed strictly for convenient access to the owners' mining claims. Interspersed with the miners were a few artisans and traders, whose small stocks of salt pork, flour, and whiskey could serve the miners' everyday needs. Grass Valley had a smaller and more rudimentary commercial district, but otherwise duplicated the pattern of Nevada City, residents living where their claims were.[1]

Grass Valley and Nevada City had physical characteristics typical of most mining camps. Board cabins and timber-framed, cloth-walled "calico shirt" houses were the usual quarters. The contents were crude and simple; the furniture consisted of trunks and boxes, a few dishes and cooking utensils, and a fireplace made of mud, sticks, and stones. Business establishments were as insubstantial as the miners' homes, although built on a larger scale.[2] The buildings were seldom painted, and the mud streets were littered with the detritus of mining life: empty barrels, boxes and bottles, worn out equipment, clothing, and garbage. The hills and ravines around the camp had a ravaged look—stream banks undermined, pits dug, hillsides washed, and timber stripped, all in the search for gold. The whole physical ambient of the miners suggested that they expected to race in, grab their share of gold, and then immediately return home to enjoy their wealth. Since the camp was only a stopping place in the quest for riches, there was little reason to build it to last, and a few physical discomforts could be borne if a fortune awaited.

The society that existed in the two camps appeared to be just as transitory and unstable as the canvas-walled houses. By any standards of a conventionally structured community, Grass Valley and Nevada City should have collapsed quickly into chaos. In 1850 the population of the two towns was almost wholly male. As would be expected in a society founded on the search for riches through physical exertion, the men were young. Over 60 percent were between twenty and thirty years of age, and an additional 30 percent were between thirty and forty. There were virtually no men in either town who had had long experience in leadership or in a profession. (See Tables I and II.)

Nothing seemed more to reflect the transience of the mining camp than what passed for home life. The most common living arrangement in the two towns was a cabin shared by two to five inhabitants. Only about three men out of a hundred had their families with them, and very few men lived alone. The composition of a household was largely determined by personal contacts made before the gold rush, rather than by any expectation of building a new community; a very high percentage of the houses contained men with common origins. In a sample of fifty dwellings in Grass Valley, sixteen contained men related to each other, usually brothers; thirty-five had two or more inhabitants born in the same state, and twenty-five had men born in adjoining states, especially states along the route of westward migration. A similar pattern prevailed in Nevada City. (See Table III.) A typical combination would be two brothers, one born in Tennessee and the other in Missouri, and three others, from Missouri, Tennessee, and Kentucky. Only twelve dwellings contained men who were born in a different region from the majority of the inhabitants, and these men were often foreigners who had possibly immigrated first to the home state of the other man. Very probably the composition of a living group reflected the continuance of at least part of a group that had traveled to the mines together. Despite the fact that almost all the grandiose companies organized in the East to come to California disintegrated on the trail, small units of them retained cohesion and regional identification. At a time when immigration from Europe to the United States was at a peak, and the foreign born constituted a substantial percentage of the population, Grass Valley and Nevada City inhabitants were overwhelmingly native born. The Sonorans, who had dominated camps to the south, had not penetrated this far north in any numbers, partly because force was used to prevent their coming to compete for gold. The Californios had never settled this far into the mountains and, being ranked by the Anglos with Sonorans, were also driven out of the camps. The native Maidu

Indians were ignored by the census takers.[3] Despite the excitement created in Europe over the gold discovery, only a handful of English, French, and Germans were in the two camps. (See Table IV.) Those immigrants, like the Irish refugees from the Potato Famine, who had arrived in America just prior to the discovery of gold, were usually too poor to undertake the expensive journey to California. California was a free state, so southerners could not bring slaves to assist in the digging, and free Negroes were also too poor to finance the trip, so there were only a very few Negroes in the two camps.

The populations of the two towns were as homogeneous in occupation as they were in age, sex, and national origin. In Nevada City, eight out of every ten men were miners, and in Grass Valley, seven of ten. Grass Valley had proportionately more artisans, traders, and unskilled laborers because it did not have as highly productive mines as Nevada City. In places where the mines were paying well, most men dug for gold; where mining was uncertain, men tended to adopt other occupations.

In both camps the numbers of artisans and unskilled laborers were low, even though shortages of them kept wages very high. A surprising number of men "came to mine the miners"; in Nevada City there was one man trying to sell provisions for every nine miners. In Grass Valley the ratio was nearly one to four. Most of the men were traders with small stocks and small incomes. These men frequently turned from trading to mining and back again, and were indistinguishable from the miners in status. Neither camp had much of an occupational elite, except for a few professional men and large merchants. In both towns, approximately three percent of the population were professionals, mostly doctors and lawyers. The preponderance of miners was so great that newspapers used the term "honest miner" to denote a typical solid citizen. (See Tables V and VI.)

TECHNOLOGY AND TRADE

The development during the 1850s of Grass Valley's quartz mines and Nevada City's success in establishing itself as an important trading center meant that the two camps would enjoy some permanence. The sophisticated technology and large-scale capital investment necessary for profitable quartz and hydraulic mining also produced extensive changes in the society of the two towns. A managerial and ownership class established itself, as did an important commercial group. For the majority of the towns' inhabitants, the life of a gold miner had completely changed in nature. Instead of being independent or a member of a small cooperative group, the miner was more likely to be a salaried employee. The hopes for instant wealth had become dimmer each year and with each technological change in mining. With the advent of corporate mining, they were completely gone. The common man in both camps was now engaged in a form of hard manual labor completely devoid of romance.[4]

The new type of mining might have caused problems of adjustment for the miners. How would a man respond to working for someone else after he had been expecting to make a fortune on his own? For Grass Valley and Nevada City this question is both unanswerable and irrelevant. As Table VII indicates, almost none of the men who had enjoyed the two camps' flush times were still there by the time large-scale industrial mining became dominant; they did not have to adjust, at least not there. Of the populations of both camps in 1850, only about five out of every hundred can be located in these towns in 1856. It is a commonplace that miners were always moving on for better prospects, but a turnover of this magnitude in camps as rich as Grass Valley and Nevada City is startling.

It is impossible to determine with any accuracy where they went; some may have faced the new kind of mining life in another town, while others probably went on to help man the subsequent mining rushes to other parts of the West. The majority probably did what they had expected to do when they came to California, that is, they went home after trying mining for a time. Once a man had spent a few years in the towns, he seems to have put down roots. There was not a great decline between the years 1856 and 1860 in the numbers of miners who remained, even though the great rush to the Comstock Lode during this period threatened to depopulate both cities.

The professional and artisan classes were less transient than miners and unskilled laborers, and the most stable element within the two towns consisted of the merchants, attorneys, and craftsmen of Nevada City. These men were able to get in on the ground floor of Nevada City's growing commercial and political importance and build relatively permanent careers. But, as Table VIII indicates, even among these men, four out of five there in 1850 were gone by 1856.

Despite the change in the towns' mining and commercial economies, the occupational structures in both communities in 1860 resemble those of 1850. Miners, although slightly less dominant than they had been before, continued to demonstrate by their numbers that gold was the foundation of both towns. Being more dependent on mining, Grass Valley naturally had a greater proportion of miners, almost eight out of ten, but even in Nevada City, two out of three men were miners. The reversal of proportions of miners between the towns since 1850 was to be expected, because Grass Valley had become the more important mining center. (See Tables V and VI.)

The proportion of professionals to the rest of the population did not change in either city between 1850 and 1860, continuing at only three or four percent. Nevada City, the county seat, had a slight advantage in the number of professionals, because politics attracted attorneys and newspapermen. Merchandising underwent a striking change during the fifties, as the commercial development of the town meant the virtual eliminaton of the small traders. The percentage engaged in selling goods declined, while the numbers of large, established merchants grew, especially in Nevada City. (See Tables V and VI.)

As the communities developed a more stable economic base, there arose a growing demand for both artisans and unskilled labor. In Grass Valley, with its dominant mining interests, the proportion of artisans did not change greatly, while, in the more commercially oriented Nevada City, artisans, except for miners, became the largest element in the population. Unskilled laborers, who did the non-mining manual labor in the camps, also increased greatly in numbers, until in both towns nearly one in ten was a common laborer or followed some other non-skilled trade. (See Tables V and VI.)

DIVERSITY AND CONFLICT

The growth in large-scale merchandising and in technologically advanced mining meant that, although both towns were still occupationally dominated by miners, the former homogeneity in status was gone. Besides the miners, there were appreciable numbers of men with large business interests, and others who were marginally employed, doing whatever manual labor was available. Most importantly, instead of "honest miners," now there were mine owners and mine employees. In addition, the different ways in which Grass Valley and Nevada City grew caused a different social structure to develop in each city. Because of Nevada City's more diversified economy, it became more of a middle-class community, with 9 percent of its population merchants and professionals, and 13 percent skilled craftsmen. In Grass Valley, the artisans, merchants, and professionals made up only 14 percent of the population. (See Tables IV and V.)

The differences in the economies of Grass Valley and Nevada City attracted different ethnic groups, which in turn widened the social divergences of the neighbors. The large quartz mines of Grass Valley created opportunities for Irish laborers, who would gladly work for wages that were higher than in the East. By 1853 there were enough Irish to support a Catholic church.[5] As the mines became more and more technically sophisticated, they attracted experienced Cornish miners, who had been driven out of their mines by a continuing depression. The Cornish were perhaps the best hard rock miners in the world, and their skills accelerated the development of Grass Valley mining. The Cornish picnic and games, featuring wrestling matches, which became an annual affair in Grass Valley, were first held in 1859. The size and organization of these gatherings signaled the importance of the Cornish group in the community.[6] By 1860 the Irish were 22 percent of the population and the British 20 percent. The next largest group of foreign born were the Chinese, who, as semi-serfs to one or another of the Cantonese companies, had begun arriving in numbers in 1851 to rework the mine tailings and undertake various kinds of unskilled labor.[7] Smaller groups of Germans, Frenchmen, and men of other nationalities were present, making over half the adult male population of Grass Valley foreign born by 1860. In Nevada City, where mining was neither as booming nor as technologically sophisticated as in Grass Valley, the Chinese, who did not figure largely in quartz mining, but who could find placer gold where others had given up, constituted the largest ethnic group, over 17 percent of the total population. British, Irish, and a large group of Germans followed, bringing the total foreign-born population to 46 percent of all male residents. (See Table IV.)

The arrival of the foreign born in towns populated previously almost totally by the native born did not proceed without friction. In 1851 Grass Valley had a riot over a disputed election that centered on rivalry between American and foreign miners. The next year, claiming that the foreigners obeyed neither civil nor mining laws, the Americans petitioned the California legislature to bar them from the town.[8] Inevitably, ethnic strife entered into politics, and as in many parts of the country the election of 1855 resulted in a sweeping victory in Nevada County for the Know-Nothings and their anti-Catholic, anti-Chinese platform. Whig and Know-Nothing newspapers considered the Irish stupid, bellicose slaves of the Pope, while the *Nevada Democrat* defended them and attacked the Chinese. The Chinese were editorially represented as chicken thieves, and were described as ignorant, degraded, cowardly, and, most importantly, like the Irish, threats to the jobs of Americans.[9] The arrival of other ethnic groups did not result in such an outcry, in part because the largest group among them, the Cornish, possessed skills needed for the general prosperity of the mines and towns. Also, they did not have to combat adverse stereotypes as did the Irish and Chinese. The Cornish, however, aroused resentment for their clannishness and for the ease with which they found mining work. Brawls occurred between them and both the Irish and the native born.[10]

A superficial study of the society of the towns would suggest a class structure based on ethnicity with the foreign born concentrated in the lower echelons of society and the native born dominating the upper reaches, and with ethnic and religious differences widening social gaps. But this is too simplistic a picture. The majority of the foreign born in Grass Valley and Nevada City, like the Americans, were engaged in mining, where they were a slightly higher proportion of the work forces than of the total populations. The proportion of unskilled men in the American sector of the labor force, however, was as great as in the foreign-born sector, and Americans held only a slight advantage in mercantile and professional occupations. (See Table IX.)

The Germans, a good many of whom were Jewish, and the British were not prevented from entering in large numbers into high prestige positions. The German-Jews played an important role in the commercial life of both towns, and especially in the large businesses of Nevada City. They also dominated clerking and bookkeeping, so that the percentage of Germans in professional, merchant, and artisan roles was higher in proportion to their total numbers than that of any other national group, including the native born. As is illustrated by Table IX, several men born in Great Britain held positions of high prestige. The most important of these were mine officers and engineers, who in Grass Valley especially, dominated these fields. The British also were important in mine-related crafts and were, in sum, vital to the economic well-being of the mines. The only professions that the British and Germans did not penetrate in significant numbers were newspaper work and the law, which remained the preserve of Americans.

The occupational status of the Irish and the Chinese does suggest that in part the social structure of the communities was based on ethnicity. The two groups which aroused the most antipathy upon arrival remained in inferior positions. The Irish occupied, on the whole, more low-prestige positions in proportion to their numbers than did the native born, British or Germans. They were concentrated in the ranks of wage earning miners, and had a slightly lower proportion of artisans and professionals among them. Table IX reveals that the Chinese were at the bottom of the social ladder, and were barred from any kind of occupational prestige. They had, of course, a status structure of their own dominated by merchants and representatives of the Cantonese companies who, while not recognized by the rest of the town, might well be able to command more financial resources than any other merchants. The growing percentage of foreign born raises the question of whether, as nativists claimed, foreigners drove out American residents by taking away their jobs. In some cases and some occupations this was true; Chinese unskilled labor was cheaper than American unskilled labor. In other instances, immigrants simply could do the job better, as in the case of the expert Cornish miners.[11] There is a more important factor than job competition in explaining the decline in the proportion of native born. Because of the high population turnover, a slowdown in migration from any one source would quickly show in the ethnic composition of the towns. In the eyes of many Americans, California was less attractive in 1860 than it had been in 1850. The hysteria of the gold rush had disappeared; those who wanted to follow the old dream of instant riches would go to newer mining districts like the Fraser River or the Comstock. Technically sophisticated industrial mining did not present the opportunities for most Americans that it did for skilled British miners, nor were the native born as likely to go West for the wages of manual labor as were the Irish.

FAMILIES AND NEIGHBORHOODS

As the towns stabilized economically, they also matured physically, with well developed business districts boasting "fire-proof" brick stores, hotels, banks, and solidly built residences. By 1860, the crudest forms of dwellings, except for those of the Chinese, had been superseded. However, constant expansion, abetted by the fires that ravaged both communities wth monotonous regularity, continued to give the towns a raw aspect; the streets were still alternately mud and dust, and excavations and ruins gave evidence of abandoned mining ventures.[12]

More importantly, many features of mining society in 1850 had not changed during the decade. The men were young, mostly in their twenties and thirties, although somewhat older on the whole than the men of 1850 had been. (See Table II.) Most residents of both towns still lived in an all-male society. Fewer than ten men in a hundred were married and living with their families. Families demanded a stability and an economic position out of the reach of most of the inhabitants. Therefore, having a family tended to be an indicator of class. In Grass Valley, professionals who made up around 6 percent of the population had 24 percent of the families, while miners, who constituted nearly 80 percent of the town, had just over 40 percent of the families. Of every six professionals, one lived with a wife and family; of every thirty-three miners, one did so. Nevada City had slightly higher proportions of married men, both in the general population and among miners as a group. (See Table I.)

Having a family was generally determined by occupational class, not ethnic origin. Except for the Chinese, a member of any foreign group was likelier to be married than a native. Even the Irish, who were concentrated in lower status jobs, were married in greater proportion than the Americans. There were almost no Chinese women in the camps, and, if the census takers can be believed, almost no Chinese family groups. (See Table X.)

While many men of the merchant and professional class lived in their places of business or boarded at hotels, the increase in the number of middle-class families led to the development of definite family neighborhoods. They were very small in relation to the total population of the towns, and they were not exclusive in composition; shops and miners' cabins often were interspersed with bankers' homes. However, they developed a definite identity early in each town's history and maintained it. One such area in Nevada City, Aristocracy Hill, received its name in derision of the pretensions of its inhabitants, but the name came to have real meaning, as did the appellation of its later developed neighbor, Nabob Hill. These areas can be easily defined by using the Nevada City town directory of 1856 to compare the occupations of the inhabitants with their addresses. The results show a concentration of merchants and professionals living on the upper reaches of two of the town's main streets. Another neighborhood, Piety Hill, had developed a strong middle-class character by 1860. Because of the lack of a comparable city directory for Grass Valley, it is difficult to determine whether similar areas emerged there during the early days. By 1860, however, Grass Valley had a definite middle class concentration along two streets north of the main commercial street.[13]

The towns' newspapers, frequently calling for the establishment of stable families, which along with solid businesses would insure the permanence of the camps, delighted in these neighborhoods. The middle class areas were by no means the norm in the two towns, and their stability was not transmitted to the poorer areas. As in 1850, most of the adult male population of both Grass Valley and Nevada City lived as small groups in cabins which were only a slight improvement over the calico shirt houses of the rush. While the earlier cabins had been located near the owners' claims, the cabins in 1860 were clustered around producing, corporate mines. As before, large areas of thirty or more residences might contain no men who were not miners or mine laborers and no women at all.[14] Many of the men in a house continued to share a common regional or ethnic identification, although to a lesser extent than had the men of 1850. As the possibility of quick wealth faded, these men's ties with home weakened, and there was much more mixing of men from different regions and countries. (See Table III.) There was only a slight tendency for whole districts to have a definite ethnic dominance, the extreme case being the Allison Ranch district of Grass Valley, which was a mining center discovered and developed by Irishmen, and largely peopled by them. As a rule, the native born, British, Irish, and Germans had only a slight tendency toward ethnically defined settlement areas. This included the middle class neighborhoods, where foreign-born as well as

American professionals lived. The Chinese and the small number of Negroes were definitely segregated; racial differences created a spatial differentiation that national, religious, and even economic differences did not produce.[15]

CONCLUSIONS

In the ten years after Grass Valley and Nevada City first attracted large numbers of gold miners, each town developed a stable economy, important commercial interests, a definite leadership class, and permanent family-oriented neighborhoods. As mining camps went, they were paragons of stability and wealth. In his account of California mining life after the gold rush, John S. Hittell pointed out the persistence of crude living conditions, the scarcity of families among miners, the continuation of migratory habits, and the heavy influx of foreigners, especially Chinese, into the mines. Rodman Paul, drawing on Hittell and corroborating his findings with other contemporary sources, paints the same picture.[16] The census statistics from Grass Valley and Nevada City confirm their observations on mining towns.

I believe, however, that the early emergence of large-scale industrial mining in these towns brought with it more complex society. A middle class, defined by families and neighborhoods, both appeared earlier and had more importance in these towns than most accounts of mining life would suggest. Industrial mining not only created a middle class, it attracted at the same time a large foreign-born population ranging from expert Cornish miners to poverty-stricken Chinese. Mineral wealth and technical innovation placed these two towns ahead of most other camps in developing mining economies; as a result, they also developed this social and ethnic structure earlier and more permanently than their rivals.

The comparison of the two camps shows how differences in economic bases and levels of industrial development could create difference-sin the social structures within mining communities. Nevada City, the political and commercial center, had a larger stable, family-oriented middle class than its neighbor. The nature of its gold deposits also attracted a larger number of the poorest element within the mining population, the Chinese. The corporate mining that made Grass Valley the most productive camp in California created a larger working class population and resulted in fewer men at each extreme of society. Despite these differences, the experience of the average man was the same in both camps. In 1860, as in 1850, he was a miner, living in rough surroundings in a transient male society. The greatest difference was in what he expected from Grass Valley or Nevada City; instead of instant riches, he now hoped for steady wages.

TABLE I MARRIAGE BY OCCUPATION

		% Married	% of all married men	% of population
Grass Valley 1850				
Professional and merchant	6	6%	46%	20%*
Artisan	1	4%	8%	6%
Miner and unskilled	6	2%	46%	75%
Total married	13	3%		
Nevada City 1850				
Professional and merchant	10	9%	68%	13%*
Artisan	2	5%	10%	3%
Miner and unskilled	4	1%	21%	83%
Total married	19	2%		
Grass Valley 1860				
Professional and merchant	51	28%	24%	6%
Artisan	54	30%	25%	8%
Miner and unskilled	110	3%	51%	86%
Total married	217	6%		
Nevada City 1860				
Professional and merchant	85	34%	27%	9%
Artisan	87	24%	27%	13%
Miner and unskilled	149	7%	47%	75%
Total married	321	12%		

Note: All statistics dealing with Nevada City in 1850 are based on a sample representing 25% of the population.
*Includes large numbers of small traders; the census takers did not differentiate by size or permanence.
Sources: *Population Schedules of the Seventh Census of the United States, 1850,* National Archives Microfilm Publications, microcopy 432, roll 36, California, Yuba County, pp. 547–610, 619–630; *Population Schedules of the Eighth Census of the United States, 1860,* National Archives Microfilm Publications, microcopy 653, roll 61, California, vol. 4, Napa and Nevada counties, pp. 143–330.

TABLE II AGE OF WORKING MALES

	1850		1860	
		Nevada City		
Born before 1790	0	0%	3	0%
Born 1790 through 1800	5	1%	18	2%
Born 1801 through 1810	41	4%	17	2%
Born 1811 through 1820	280	31%	119	11%
Born 1821 through 1830	576	63%	463	42%
Born 1831 through 1840	9	1%	447	41%
Born 1841 through 1850	0	0%	21	2%
		Grass Valley		
	1850		1860	
Born before 1790	2	1%	0	0%
Born 1790 through 1800	7	2%	7	1%
Born 1801 through 1810	23	6%	10	1%
Born 1811 through 1820	84	22%	74	6%
Born 1821 through 1830	245	64%	495	42%
Born 1831 through 1840	20	5%	575	48%
Born 1841 through 1850	0	0%	24	2%

Source: Same as Table I.

TABLE III CABIN RESIDENTS BY BIRTHPLACE

Relatives	Same state	Adjacent states	Same foreign country	Different sections of U.S. or different countries
		Grass Valley 1850		
16	35	25	—	12
		Nevada City 1850		
4	37	26	—	19
		Grass Valley 1860		
10	17	7	10	33
		Nevada City 1860		
7	12	4	16	34

Note: All statistics based on a sample of 50 dwellings. Figures represent the number of dwellings out of the sample which contain two or more residents in the category indicated, i.e., blood relations, men who were born in the same state or foreign country, etc.
Source: Same as Table I.

TABLE IV   ORIGINS OF TOTAL MALE WORKING POPULATION

	1850		1860	
		Nevada City		
United States	905	95%	1492	54%
Great Britain	13	2%	321	12%
Ireland	13	2%	197	7%
Germany and Scandinavia	12	2%	198	7%
France and Italy	3	0%	59	2%
Canada	3	0%	18	1%
Latin America	3	0%	1	0%
China	0	0%	459	17%
	952		2745	
		Grass Valley		
United States	379	95%	1408	43%
Great Britain	5	1%	685	20%
Ireland	4	1%	749	22%
Germany and Scandinavia	6	1%	112	3%
France and Italy	2	1%	91	3%
Canada	5	1%	9	0%
Latin America	0	0%	1	0%
China	0	0%	304	9%
	401		3359	

Note: Differences in total population figures between tables are caused by lack of complete information on some individuals.
Source: Same as Table I.

TABLE V   GRASS VALLEY OCCUPATIONS

	1850	1860
Doctor	5	13
Teacher, preacher	1	6
Lumberman	0	7
Attorney	3	10
Merchant	70*	93
Mine officer	1	14
Hotel keeper	0	20
Manufacturer	0	11
Newspaperman	0	4
Multiple investments	0	4
Farmer	5	20
Carpenter	12	47
Butcher	0	17
Blacksmith	2	21
Clerk	0	47
Engineer	1	21
Amalgamator	1	4
Other artisan	3	65

TABLE V (*Continued*)

	1850	1860
Saloon keeper	0†	15
Miner	288	2580
Teamster	9	47
Unskilled mine job	1	2
Laborer	2	196
Other unskilled	2	74
Servant	0	2
Gentleman	0	3
	406	3343
Professionals	3%	3%
Merchants	17%	3%
Artisans	6%	8%
Miners	71%	77%
Unskilled	4%	10%

*Mostly small traders.
†In 1850 liquor was sold by the small traders, who are listed under merchant.
Source: Same as Table I.

TABLE VI NEVADA CITY OCCUPATIONS

	1850	1860
Doctor	9	12
Teacher, preacher	3	5
Lumberman	1	8
Attorney	10	23
Merchant	87 *	134
Mine officer	1	9
Manufacturer	0	13
Newspaperman	4	10
Multiple investments	5	13
Farmer	22	26
Carpenter	8	75
Butcher	7	14
Blacksmith	2	26
Clerk	2	62
Engineer	0	10
Amalgamator	0	0
Other artisan	8	124
Saloon keeper	3†	23
Miner	755	1864
Teamster	8	48
Unskilled mine job	0	0
Woodchopper	0	3
Laborer	1	148

(*Continued*)

TABLE VI *(Continued)*

	1850	1860
Other unskilled	0	51
Servant	1	6
Gentleman	0	2
Mariner	0	1
	919	2731
Professionals	4%	4%
Merchants	9%	5%
Artisans	3%	13%
Miners	82%	68%
Unskilled	1%	9%

*Mostly small traders.
†In 1850 liquor was sold by the small traders, who are listed under merchant.
Source: Same as Table I.

TABLE VII PERSISTENCE

	Grass Valley		Nevada City	
Total population, 1850 census*	404		920	
# who appear only in the 1850 census	385	95%	867	94%
# who appear also in 1856	19	5%	53	6%
# who appear also in 1860	15	4%	45	5%

*Nevada City statistics in 1850 are based on a sample representing 25 percent of the population; Grass Valley figures represent the total population.
Sources: Same as Table I, plus Nat P. Brown and John Dallison, *Brown and Dallison's Nevada, Grass Valley, and Rough and Ready Directory* (San Francisco, 1856), 47–116: *Grass Valley Telegraph*, 1853–1855; *Nevada Democrat*, 1853–1863: *Nevada Journal*, 1851–1861.

TABLE VIII PERSISTENCE BY OCCUPATION

	Professionals		Artisans		Miners and unskilled	
	Grass Valley					
Total 1850 work force	84		26		294	
# who appear only in the 1850 census	77	92%	24	92%	284	96%
# who appear also in 1856	7	8%	2	8%	10	4%
# who appear also in 1860	4	6%	2	8%	9	4%
	Nevada City					
Total 1850 work force*	123		33		773	
# who appear only in the 1850 census	96	78%	23	67%	748	97%
# who appear also in 1856	27	22%	10	33%	25	3%
# who appear also in 1860	25	20%	10	33%	21	3%

*Nevada City statistics in 1850 are based on a sample representing 25 percent of the population; Grass Valley figures represent the total population.
Source: Same as Table VII.

TABLE IX   OCCUPATION BY ORIGIN

Nevada City 1860

	United States		Great Britain		Ireland			
Professionals & merchants	146	10%	15	4%	4	2%		
Artisans	222	15%	39	12%	25	14%		
Miners	970	65%	235	73%	130	65%		
Unskilled	154	10%	32	10%	38	19%		
	1492		321		197			
	Ger. & Scand.		Fr. & Itl.		Brit. Am.		China	
Professional & Merchants	52	26%	16	27%	1	6%	14	3%
Artisans	58	29%	12	20%	5	28%	4	1%
Miners	70	35%	25	42%	10	56%	425	93%
Unskilled	18	9%	6	10%	2	11%	16	3%
	198		59		18		459	

Grass Valley 1860

	United States		Great Britain		Ireland			
Professional & merchants	79	6%	40	6%	21	3%		
Artisans	148	10%	40	6%	31	4%		
Miners	1005	71%	565	83%	640	85%		
Unskilled	178	13%	40	6%	57	8%		
	1028		685		749			
	Ger. & Scand.		Fr. & Itl.		Brit. Am.		China	
Professional & merchants	30	27%	5	5%	0		4	1%
Artisans	32	29%	5	5%	1	11%	0	
Miners	40	36%	55	60%	5	56%	270	89%
Unskilled	10	9%	26	29%	3	34%	30	10%
	112		91		9		304	

Source: *Eighth Census microfilm, microcopy 653, roll 61 pp. 143–330.*

TABLE X   MARRIED MEN BY ORIGIN 1960

	Total Population	Married Men	Percent
	Grass Valley		
United States	1408	90	6%
Great Britain	685	57	8%
Ireland	749	51	7%
Ger. & Scand.	112	17	15%
France & Italy	91	2	2%
Brit. Am.	9	0	0%
China	304	0	0%
Total	3358	217	6%

(Continued)

TABLE X   *(Continued)*

	Nevada City		
United States	1492	191	13%
Great Britain	321	43	13%
Ireland	197	33	17%
Ger. & Scand.	198	35	18%
France & Italy	59	19	32%
Brit. Am	18	0	0%
China	459	0	0%
Total	2744	321	12%

Source: Same as Table IX.

Notes

1 Edwin F. Bean, *Bean's History and Directory of Nevada County, California* (Nevada City, 1867), 77–81; Nat P. Brown and John Dallison, *Brown and Dallison's Nevada, Grass Valley, and Rough and Ready Directory* (San Francisco, 1856), 11–12, 22–23; John S. Hittell, *Mining in the Pacific States of North America* (San Francisco, 1861), 22, 61–62.

2 *Bean's History,* 76–79; Louise A. K. Clappe, *The Shirley Letters* (New York, 1949), 30–31.

3 Leonard Pitt, *The Decline of the Californios* (Berkeley and Los Angeles, 1966), 52–59; Rodman W. Paul, *California Gold* (Cambridge, Mass., 1947), 110–112.

4 Paul, *California Gold,* 117, 171.

5 *Ibid.,* 120–121; *Brown and Dallison's Directory,* 40–41.

6 Arthur C. Todd, *The Cornish Miner in America* (Glendale, 1967), 20–21, 62–63; Harry L. Wells, *History of Nevada County, California* (Oakland, 1880), 151.

7 Gunther Barth, *Bitter Strength* (Cambridge, Mass., 1964), 3, 51, 67; Howard L. Scamehorn, ed. *The Buckeye Rovers in the Gold Rush* (Athens, Ohio, 1965), 161.

8 *Bean's History,* 128.

9 *Nevada Journal,* July 6, 1855, 1:1, May 8, 1856, 2:1, Nov. 7, 1856, 2:6, March 5, 1858, 3:1, Feb. 11, 1859, 2:1, *Nevada Democrat,* March 22, 1854, 2: 1–2, Nov. 19, 1856, 1: 4–5.

10 Todd, *Cornish Miner,* 22; Scamehorn, *Buckeye Rovers,* 161.

11 S. W. Kung, *Chinese in American Life* (Seattle, 1962), 67; Todd, *Cornish Miner,* 21–22, 62.

12 *Bean's History,* 88–89; Wells, *Nevada County,* 82–83.

13 *Brown and Dallison's Directory,* 46–117; Hugh B. Thompson, *Directory of the City of Nevada and Grass Valley* (San Francisco, 1861), 21–58, 99–126.

14 Since the census lists were compiled by going from door to door, this male living-pattern can be seen by scanning the manuscript census. See, for example, *Population Schedules of the United States,* 1860, National Archives Microfilm Publications, microcopy 653, roll 61, California, Vol. 4, Napa and Nevada counties, 183, 190, 197.

15 *Eighth Census,* 183, 190, 220–221, 225, 227–231, 269–270, 299–303.

16 Hittell, *Mining,* 211; John S. Hittell, *The Resources of California* (San Francisco, 1863), 359, 364, 440–441; Paul, *California Gold,* 317–320.

PROSTITUTES IN SAN FRANCISCO

EDITOR'S INTRODUCTION

The history of women in California and the west remains largely unwritten. Women are invisible in most accounts; their contributions often deemed unimportant.[1]

When attention has been paid to the role of women, historians have tended to portray them in stereotyped images. Joan M. Jensen and Darlis A. Miller recently assembled these images into four major categories: *gentle tamers, helpmates, hell-raisers,* and *bad women.* The gentle-tamer category includes all those imagined women who carried westward the trappings of civilization, and who assumed the major responsibility for reestablishing the social and cultural values of their former homes. The helpmates were the long-suffering women who not only performed traditional chores but who also helped by doing "men's work" during times of need. More masculine women were the hell-raisers, the Calamity Janes who acted more like men than women. Bad women, quite simply, were the prostitutes. Jensen and Miller challenge historians to move beyond these stereotypes, to ask new questions, and to apply more sophisticated methods of analysis. What is most needed, they conclude, are studies of how women fit into the economic structure of the west through their labor.[2]

Jacqueline Baker Barnhart, as if in response to the call of Jensen and Miller, reexamines one of the most common stereotypical roles of western women in *The Fair but Frail: Prostitution in San Francisco, 1849–1900* (1986). Barnhart analyzes the prostitutes of San Francisco, not as deviants or victims, but as a group of professional workers.[3] She places them within the tradition of gold-rush

---

[1]See, however, Joan M. Jensen and Gloria Ricci Lothrop, *California Women: A History* (San Francisco, 1987).

[2]Joan M. Jensen and Darlis A. Miller, "The Gentle Tamers Revisited: New Approaches to the History of Women in the American West," *Pacific Historical Review,* XLIX (May 1980), 209.

[3]For a more traditional view see Curt Gentry, *The Madams of San Francisco* (Garden City, 1964); and Ronald Dean Miller, *Shady Ladies of the West* (Los Angeles, 1964).

entrepreneurship, noting that most prostitutes came to California seeking economic opportunity and that many were willing to leave lucrative jobs working for others to open businesses of their own.[4]

Barnhart pays special attention to the changing economic structure of prostitution. In the early years, prostitutes in San Francisco were relatively undifferentiated. Most were of the entrepreneurial elite known as parlor-house prostitutes. In a society over 90 percent male, the market was clearly in their favor and the prostitutes' ability to take advantage of this unique opportunity determined their economic success and social freedom. As market conditions changed, other categories of prostitutes appeared and competition increased.

A major contribution of Barnhart's work is her analysis of the relationship of prostitution to the larger society. In the period 1849 to 1870 prostitutes were at first admired, then tolerated, and finally ostracized. The changing status of the prostitutes was reflected in the terms used to describe them. Between 1849 and 1851 prostitutes were known by a variety of euphemisms. The coarse and abusive term *whore,* according to Barnhart, was never used. Twenty years later the term was commonly used, and prostitution was no longer tolerated. With the arrival of families—gentle tamers included—San Francisco "fell under the influence of the Victorians" and prostitution was seen as a threat to public respectability.

Like Ralph Mann in the previous selection, Barnhart is also interested in the question of social mobility. She describes the causes of upward and downward mobility, but leaves unanswered the question of whether San Francisco prostitutes enjoyed greater or lesser mobility than their counterparts back east.

Jacqueline Baker Barnhart received her Ph.D. from the University of California, Santa Cruz, in 1976 and is currently a Professor of History at California State University, Chico.

---

[4]A similar conclusion is reached in Marion S. Goldman, *Gold Diggers and Silver Miners: Prostitutes and Social Life on the Comstock Lode* (Ann Arbor, 1981).

READING 11

Prostitutes in San Francisco

Jacqueline Baker Barnhart

Prostitutes coming to San Francisco in the first decade following the gold rush were professionals. Since the definition of a professional is one who follows an occupation as a profession and raises one's trade to the dignity of a profession, the requirements for a professional prostitute include full-time commitment to her occupation and a conscious effort to maintain or improve her place in the institution. In 1849 and 1850 the city's lack of standard social mores gave each the opportunity to be as entrepreneurial as she chose.

Between 1851 and 1856, however, prostitution in San Francisco was divided into the four categories found in most major cities in the nineteenth century: parlor-house residents, brothel prostitutes, dance-hall harlots, and streetwalkers. Before that, only parlor-house prostitution could be clearly observed. Given the opportunities of the frontier, the fact that the elite segment of the profession was the first to secure its position was not surprising.

PARLOR-HOUSE RESIDENTS

Professional prostitutes who traveled on their own to California were coming to improve their position. The primary goal was to acquire a fortune, but the opportunity to upgrade their social or business standing was also available. In more established cities, the parlor house offered greater earnings from higher fees as well as an atmosphere of comfort and elegance. Those who recognized that the unique position they held at the moment was due to the less-restrictive lifestyle of the western frontier sought to secure a place in the elite sector of the profession. Common business sense dictated this ambition, for from London to New Orleans the parlor house was traditionally the most desirable place to work, requiring, as it did, the highest standards of professionalism.

In San Francisco, as elsewhere, the parlor-house resident had to be not only beautiful but accomplished. A visit to a perfectly managed parlor house was much like a visit to a private home, and the prostitutes in residence resembled, in decorum and dress, the daughters of the house. Some writers wittily argued that the only difference, in fact, was that the prostitute was more attractive, more intelligent, and more accomplished than the young society lady.[1]

Visitors, usually "influential gentlemen of the city," would be conducted to a parlor by the madam or a maid. If the customer was not calling on a specific woman, one was chosen by the madam and sent to join him. In the reception room, he would generally find other businessmen and acquaintances being entertained by equally lovely and decorous young women. Witty and intelligent conversation was required of the prostitute, and when necessary the madam would school her in behavior and repartee. Occasionally one of the residents would play the piano, or there might be games of chance for the amusement of the visitor. A supper with all the delicacies San Francisco could offer was served to the guest free, but a charge of ten dollars was added to the customer's bill for every bottle of wine or champagne that he could be induced to purchase. In the very best houses everything was "conducted with the utmost propriety," and any hint of commercialism was kept to a minimum. When the customer was eventually conducted to an elegantly furnished bedroom by the prostitute of his choice, it was usually the madam or a maid who collected the fees, in order to maintain the social distinction between parlor house and commercial brothel, where the prostitute had to collect her own fee.[2]

The very term *parlor house* was to remain an apt description until the Red-light Abatement Act was put into effect in 1914, and houses of prostitution of all descriptions were systematically closed down throughout the city. Until then, the inhabitants of the parlor house appeared to be "ladies," and their place of business appeared to be the same as the other homes in the residential areas where they were found. During the first ten years or so, these other residences were usually boarding houses, which tended to make the parlor houses even less visible than they would be toward the end of the century. The true parlor house was never found in a well-known red-light district, such as the notorious Barbary Coast, because to locate there would have been a contradiction of the image of elegant and refined "respectability."[3]

The interior decor of a typical parlor house usually surpassed the other homes in the neighborhood for luxury. White lace curtains and damask drapes covered the windows. The fixtures and furniture were plush and opulent, in the early 1850s few people other than the parlor-house madam had the inclination or the incentive to spend time and money on a residential dwelling. But in order to attract a wealthy and influential clientele, it was as necessary for the madam to supply refined elegance in the surroundings as in the women she hired.[4]

To maintain the necessary image, run a house inhabited by ten to twenty young women, and attract sufficient customers to assure profits for both the house and the prostitutes took considerable skill and executive ability. Not all madams were successful. The successful madam seldom worked as a prostitute herself, because to do so would have placed her in competition with her employees, possibly causing dissent among them.

In some houses, the residents paid the madam a flat fee for rooms and additional charges for maid and laundry services, medical treatment, and bribes to the police to assure protection from arrest during periods when vice was the target of municipal reform. In other houses, the madam took care of all financial transactions and kept a percentage of the prostitutes' income. In both cases, considerable bookkeeping skill was required to keep the accounts balanced and avoid conflicts. In some instances, madams might own or run more than one house, which demanded even more managerial ability. They also had to deal with dressmakers to make sure their employees were stylish and well dressed, to bargain with food and wine merchants to guarantee their standards of excellence were met, and to bring in new faces regularly to replace those whose popularity had declined.[5]

In addition to all of these necessary functions, it was the madam's responsibility to attract customers within the bounds of decorum and good taste required of the parlor-house image. One acceptable method of advertising, which became a successful parlor-house custom throughout the century, was the soiree. The first of these functions on record in San Francisco took place in 1849. Elisha Crosby (assigned to set up the judicial branch of government in the new state) recorded in his memoirs that a noted courtesan of the city, called the Countess, maintained a two-story frame house on Washington Street across from the Plaza. Her method of advertising was to send out engraved invitations to the "most prominent men in San Francisco." According to Crosby, when the men arrived they somehow understood that "a gratuity was to be left with the bookkeeper—not less than an ounce ($16) and as much as the liberality of the guest might suggest." Because the Countess had only six or eight young ladies in her employ, she invited others "from the few demimonde houses then in operation." The reception was "very correct, nothing rude, everything refined and elegant, and it was astonishing to see the class of men who gathered there—executive, legislative, judicial, commercial, ministerial, all of what are commonly considered the upper class of society."[6]

At a soiree the best suppers were served and the best wines sold at 500 percent profit. The entire evening often cost the madam a thousand dollars (she was usually able to recoup this expense by the sale of wine or from the customers who chose to spend the night), but it was a necessary expense to advertise her house and a convenient method of introducing a newly hired prostitute to regular customers who might otherwise switch their patronage to another house for variety's sake.[7]

Another successful means of advertising was the daily promenade. As San Francisco became an established city with wooden or brick sidewalks and streets, there were fashionable promenades where ladies could be seen strolling or driving past in carriages. In San Francisco, many of the ladies were part of the demimonde, using the fashionable hour of the promenade to advertise their presence.[8]

Visibility was a necessary aspect in all segments of the trade, and since they had entree to public entertainments, the prostitutes attended the few social events available outside the gambling halls. Since there were very few families in San Francisco and even fewer homes, private parties were rare (even in the late 1850s gatherings in private homes or apartments where a hostess was present were so scarce that they called for special mention in letters and journals); but public lectures, plays, concerts, and balls were favorite San Francisco pastimes. Virtually the only "society" articles in the newspapers before 1852 were reports of attendance at these public affairs, especially dances and balls at new hotels such as the Parker House, or social events sponsored by groups like the Monumental Fire Company. According to the *Alta California*, May 24, 1849, such affairs were attended by "the staid matron and quiet maid" as well as "beauteous gazelle-eyed maidens of Alta California." The public balls attracted both the fair and the frail of the female population, and there was very little condemnation of manners and decorum. The masked balls, on the other hand, led many writers to warn against the dangers that anonymity might lead to. It was feared masks might make some women feel liberated from moral restraints.[9]

As the numbers of women in San Francisco increased, the grand ball gradually became restricted until ladies were admitted only by an invitation card.[10] But the masked or masquerade balls remained open to all, and the *Alta California* reported that they were "recherché affairs."

> By the private entrance come the maskers, male and female. The Spanish bandit, with his high tapering hat, ornamented with ribbons; the gipsy, with her basket and cards; the Bloomer, bountiful in short skirts and satin-covered extremities; the ardent young militaire...the flaunting Cyprian, not veiled by domino or mask; and the curious, but respectable lady, hidden by cloak and false visage. There is the Frenchman in a fantastical dress; and Gallic count imitating the Yankee; the Yankee affecting "Aunty Vermont"; and men already feeling the force of their libations affecting sobriety....
>
> Away they whirl through the waltz, or dash along the mazourka, or crash away promiscuously in the gallapade. Where there are no masks exercise brings no new rose tint or crimson to the soft cheek—the rouge or carmine is too thick for that. The music draws to a close and ends with a grand flourish. Off to the bar and coffee stand go the maskers, the gentlemen to treat, the others to be treated.[11]

With drink came violent encounters among men and women. "Jealousy's eyes take a greener tinge from the bottle imp, and woman, forgetting her last prerogative—gentleness—joins the ring and gives point and effect to feminine oaths by the use of feminine nails.''[12]

Recherché or not, such functions remained a popular pastime in San Francisco, and the high attendance by ''flaunting Cyprians'' was probably surpassed only by their numbers at the Prostitutes Ball sponsored by the proprietor of the Music Hall.[13]

A CHANGE IN STATUS

The very fact that the event was advertised as a prostitutes ball is an indication of the change taking place in the demimonde of San Francisco by 1856. In the first year or two of the decade, euphemisms for prostitutes were the *fair but frail* or *ladies in full bloom*. By 1853, however, more derogatory terms like *prostitute, cyprian, harlot,* and even *whore* were used more frequently. There are two obvious explanations for the change in status. First, wives and families were arriving in San Francisco in sufficient numbers to insist on exclusive rights to respectability. Second, the number of prostitutes in San Francisco had grown sufficiently (some estimate there were two thousand by 1853) to make it impossible for all to be able to maintain the more admired status of courtesan. There were, in fact, cyprians, bawds, and even whores among the professional prostitutes.[14]

As members of the profession began to separate into more traditional categories within the institution, so did their places of employment and the range of their economic opportunities.[15] The parlor-house resident offered illusion along with sex in order to attract her wealthy clientele; her income, accordingly, was at the top of the scale. The brothel prostitutes, for the most part, dispensed with lavish elegance, and although they could not command the same fees as the parlor-house resident, their expenses for accommodations and wardrobe were less. A few brothels were nearly as elegant as a parlor

house, the only difference being lower fees, a poorer quality of wine, and a madam whose requirements for decorum and appearance were less stringent. Most were cheap boarding houses, rented exclusively to prostitutes and run by a landlord or landlady.

The dance-hall harlot, on the other hand, had to rely on quantity rather than quality to assure her income. She met her customers in dance halls (sometimes a synonym for cheap gambling saloons or barrooms), and if the hall did not provide cubicles or back rooms for her use, she often used her own room in a hotel or boarding house or rented a room in one of the ''large and flimsily built houses called 'cribs,''' built exclusively for prostitution, ''consisting of many small rooms'' opening onto a street or alley, where the prostitute could solicit customers as they passed.[16] The *WASP,* a San Francisco weekly newspaper, described the scene on September 20, 1876: ''God-forsaken women are permitted to stand in their doors and windows dressed, or 'undressed,' in the most shameful manner, inviting men and boys to enter their vile dens.'' Cribs contained anywhere from 15 to 160 rooms; some were run like hotels, where the women simply rented the rooms by the night to conduct their business; others had managers who recruited prostitutes.

Brothels between these two extremes appeared to be simple boarding houses. The structures were not distinctive and were often found next door to a private residence. In a two-block area of the sixth ward, for example, there were ten brothels housing thirty-four prostitutes. In the midst of this bevy of sexual industry lived a steel contractor and his family and a minister of the Reformed Church and his wife. The landlady or landlord of these brothels was a cross between a madam and a crib manager and was usually an employee (as was the crib manager) rather than the owner. The owners were often small groups of businessmen or municipal officials who could afford to buy city property at the inflated prices of the 1850s and 1860s. One brothel on Jackson Street was actually called the Municipal Crib, because both patrons and owners were the politicians and officials of the city. As competition increased, brothel prostitutes had less choice in their place of employment and therefore less opportunity to improve their position in the hierarchy.[17]

Cheap brothels and cribs were usually found in the Barbary Coast, a nine-block area bounded by Montgomery Street on the east, Stockton Street on the west, Broadway on the north, and Washington Street on the south. It grew up around the nucleus of Sydney Town and Little Chile at the foot of Telegraph Hill but did not become a notorious red-light district until after 1865. The heart of the Barbary Coast was Pacific Street, the most notorious street was Kearny, and the Chinese district was on Dupont (Grant Street). Bars, dance halls, cribs, and dives crowded the area, and every conceivable source of crime, vice, and entertainment was to be found.

Because private accommodations in San Francico remained scarce in and out of the Barbary Coast through the 1870s, many boarding houses and hotels rented to both prostitutes and nonprostitutes. The St. Francis Hotel, for example, listed a number of prostitutes as residents, along with the typical transient clientele. Boarding houses throughout the fourth, sixth, and eighth wards (roughly the central area of the city) housed anywhere from two to ten prostitutes as well as laborers, bartenders, gamblers, and the like. The brothel run by Eli and Kate Calli in the fourth ward also rented rooms to three machinists. Women unable to find a place in a brothel or crib worked out of their own rooms, which they might share with their children, husband or mother. Brothel keepers, as opposed to parlor-house madams, usually lived with their families in the brothel. The problem of finding a permanent place in a brothel or desirable accommodation of any kind increased with each decade, particularly for the dance-hall harlot.[18]

Dance-hall work after 1856 was actually an extension of gambling-saloon work and barroom work, which was what most prostitutes did in 1849–1850. Gambling itself was becoming less visible, although in the clubs that continued to flourish women were still hired as waiter girls to serve drinks and food, some to dance or sing on stage, and, in the dives or beer joints, to dance with customers for twenty-five cents a dance. In clubs like the Bella Union, the Olympic, and Gilbert's Melodeon, all in the heart of the Barbary Coast, gambling was available, stage shows added to the festivities, and on a mezzanine, in private boxes that could be curtained off, waiter girls would provide sex as well as food and drink. At Hell's Kitchen and the Opera Comique there was less luxury in the surroundings, but the second floor was divided into cubicles for the convenience of customers and the forty "pretty waiter-girls" hired to serve them.[19]

The dance-hall harlot who had to provide her own room very often did not receive a salary for her presence in the dive where she found customers. She was, in fact, San Francisco's version of a streetwalker or whore. Until the Red-light Abatement Act closed houses of prostitution in every category, streetwalkers were few in number and were clearly the worst paid and least professional members of the institution. During the Barbary Coast era (1865–1914) the streetwalkers did most of their soliciting in the dives and cheap barrooms that did not hire their own harlots. It was women in this category who occasionally showed up on police arrest records as common prostitutes, while brothel and crib prostitutes, when arrested, were charged with the misdemeanor of "soliciting for a house of ill-fame." There were also occasional arrests for keeping a house of ill fame and for being an inmate of a house of ill fame, but these were associated with the lower-class brothels and cribs. Although the parlor-house residents and their madams were among the best-known women in the city, they were almost never arrested.[20]

Well-known madams of San Francisco appear in memoirs and records throughout the nineteenth century. One apparent favorite of the 1890s was Tessie Wall. Many anecdotes have been told about Tessie, but the one which best reflects a madam's business abilities and class consciousness is the one about Gump's Jade and Oriental Art Emporium. Tessie's parlor house on O'Farrell Street was furnished with the traditional elegance of such establishments, so it was not unusual for her to order a thousand-dollar painting from this exclusive store. When one of the younger Gump sons delivered the painting, he and Tessie celebrated with a bottle of champagne. When he returned to the store, however, he carried only $990. Tessie deducted $10 for the wine from the sale price of the painting![21]

Another regular customer of Gump's was May Stuart, also a well-known madam. When her bill at the store reached $500, one of the Gump sons visited her and politely requested payment. May readily acknowledged her debt, promised to pay as quickly as possible, and as collateral showed him the sleeping form of the "scion of one of the old families." She paid her bill in full the following day.[22]

Tessie and May's place in San Francisco society seemed reasonably safe and accepted, because they did not flaunt their occupation. Generally, only the open vice of the Barbary Coast aroused outcries from religious and reform groups. At the beginning of the period—the early 1850s—two other famous madams did flaunt their lifestyle, and the usually tolerant frontier society rose up against them. No women so clearly depict the changing status of the prostitute in the first decade after the gold rush as do Irene McCready and Belle Cora.

Irene arrived in San Francisco in April 1849 with her lover and business partner, James McCabe. McCabe had been a successful businessman in the East, and he was able to in-

crease his wealth in San Francisco. He was co-owner of the El Dorado and apparently helped his mistress set up one of the earliest bagnios in the city. He also helped her to rebuild it in keeping with the ideal of the parlor house after the fire of December 1849 destroyed both the house and the El Dorado.[23]

During her first year in San Francisco, Irene and the other women in her occupation were in effect the *haut ton* of female society. As one forty-niner later claimed, "the commonest proverb in the street was that the only aristocracy we had here at the time were the gamblers and prostitutes; and it was true too."[24] But Irene was, perhaps, not astute enough to realize that her position was the result of unique circumstances. Consequently, it must have come as a distinct and unwelcome surprise to learn that the men who bowed to her in the street or paid her elaborate compliments when they visited her house would ask her to leave a gathering that included their wives.

The incident involving Irene and the few "respectable" ladies of the town occurred sometime in 1850 and was perhaps the first time the security of the prostitute's status was tested. A dozen or so ladies from four churches in the city, including Sara Royce (who left us an account of the incident), had organized a benevolent society and held an "entertainment" to raise funds for their charitable work. In the midst of the tea-party-like atmosphere "a man [McCabe], prominent for wealth and business-power," entered with his mistress, Irene. She was, Royce explained, "a splendidly dressed woman, well known in the city as the disreputable companion of her wealthy escort." At their wives' insistence, a delegation of men asked McCabe to leave with the famous madam, because the ladies refused to associate with her or have her introduced to their daughters.[25] The confrontation was undoubtedly a result of Irene's inflated self-confidence. Nevertheless, the incident does reflect the view some prostitutes had developed of their position in San Francisco society.

THE CASE OF BELLE CORA

It was another five years before the presence of the demimonde society was challenged at a public function. If Irene displayed her presence because of unrealistic self-confidence in her acceptability, Belle Cora flaunted her position fully conscious of the reaction she would create. She made the challenge and expected to win. Bancroft, who treated prostitutes sympathetically in his writings though he deplored the institution, described her thus:

> Like Cleopatra, she was very beautiful, and beside the power that comes of beauty, rich; but oh, so foul. Flaunting her beauty and wealth on the gayest thoroughfares, and on every gay occasion, with senator, judge, and citizen at her beck and call, and being a woman as proud as she was beautiful and rich, she not infrequently flung back upon her stainless sisters the looks of loathed contempt with which they so often favored her.[26]

Like Irene and many of the other early prostitutes and madams, Belle was the mistress of a gambler. She had accompanied Charles Cora to San Francisco in 1849, and during 1850 and probably 1851, they spent most of their time in the mining towns of Sacramento, Sonora, and Marysville. Charles gambled, with apparently mixed success; Belle opened at least one bagnio in Sonora and was as successful as she was to be with all the houses she owned. In 1852 they were back in San Francisco, and Belle started her career as the city's most successful madam by opening a parlor house on Dupont Street. By 1855 she had at least two houses, the second being a two-story brick structure on Waverly Place. It was in November of 1855, while she and Charles were enjoying the economic rewards of their respective professions, that Belle confronted "respectable" society. Unlike Irene, Belle won her battle, but Charles paid the price at the end of a vigilante rope.[27]

As they had done many times before, Belle and Charles attended a play at the American Theater. Seated directly in front of them were United States Marshal W. H. Richardson and his wife. When Mrs. Richardson realized who was behind her, she insisted her husband tell them to leave. The Coras refused. Richardson called the manager of the theater, demanding the Coras be evicted. The manager also refused to comply. In the end it was the Richardsons who left the theater, while Belle kept her seat in triumph. But two days later, Cora and Richardson confronted each other in a saloon, quarrelled (presumably over the theater incident), and before witnesses could be sure of the actual course of events, Cora had shot the marshal. He was very quickly arrested for murder.[28]

Belle might conceivably have regretted her victory over the virtuously outraged Mrs. Richardson but, unlike that lady, she did not succumb to vapors and tears. Her first action was to use a substantial portion of her wealth to hire the best criminal defense lawyers in San Francisco. There was sufficient evidence to suggest that Cora had shot Richardson in self-defense. But Belle was a realist: Charles might be convicted because he was a gambler with a notorious madam as his mistress and because Richardson was a United States marshal. Unwilling to take chances, Belle used additional funds to bribe various witnesses and some members of the jury. Such practices were not unusual in San Francisco, but unfortunately for Cora the bribes were discovered. The prosecution and the press had a field day with this "proof of guilt." Nevertheless, Colonel Edward Baker, Cora's lawyer, managed to convince at least some of the jury that self-defense was a possibility, and when they were unable to reach a unanimous verdict, Cora was held over for a second trial.

Because of Belle's attempted bribes, Baker was forced to defend her actions, and his remarks to the jury might be read as the first legal testimony to the existence of the prostitute with a heart of gold. Belle Cora, Baker told the jury, might have been misguided in her bribery attempts but she was only trying to help her friend. "It is a woman of base profession, of more than easy virtue, of malign fame, of a degraded caste—it is one poor, weak, feeble, and, if you like it, wicked woman—to her alone he owes his ability to employ counsel to present his defense." Charles and Belle might not have conformed to the standards of society or been sanctioned by the church, but "they were bound together by a tie which angels might not blush to approve. A bad woman may lose her virtue; it would be infinitely worse to lose her faith according to her own standards....If any of you have it in your heart to condemn, and say 'Stand back! I am holier than thou,' remember Magdalene."[29]

Baker's eloquence was sufficient to save Cora from a legal hanging, but on May 23, 1856, the second vigilance committee took him from the jail, gave him a second "trial," and hanged him. Always punctilious on the etiquette governing a prisoner's last request, the committee allowed Cora, a Catholic, the services of a priest. And when Archbishop Allemany "refused to grant him absolution, unless he first married the woman he had been living with so long as his wife," the committee brought Belle from Waverly Place, and she was legally united with the man whose name she used for so long.[30]

Belle had not bowed to defeat when Charles was arrested, nor did she do so when she became his widow. On the contrary, true to the description Bancroft wrote of her later, she continued to flaunt herself before her "stainless sisters," promenading on the city's thoroughfares and maintaining her luxurious parlor house on Waverly Place until her death in 1862. Even Irene, though she had to retire from the presence of "respectability," continued her successful career for many years. But the life of a madam, though requiring a keen business sense, was physically less taxing than that of the majority of women in the profession.

MOBILITY

Very simply, for women in any category of prostitution to move upward in the profession required beauty, financing, the desire and ability to maintain professional standards, and self-discipline. Downward mobility resulted from the failure to maintain any one of these requirements. Beauty is, of course, not something that can be controlled, especially in a profession that requires late hours that are physically taxing. Also, if a woman was not sufficiently professional to maintain self-discipline, she very often used alcohol or drugs to sustain herself. The result was usually the decline of her status in the hierarchy.[31]

There were other causes for downward mobility, not the least of which was venereal disease and unwanted pregnancies, constant dangers in the profession. There are not statistics on pregnancy among prostitutes, but in reform literature and benevolent society tracts the problem of abandoned and unwanted children was a continuing subject for debate and the object of charitable works. How much birth control was known or practiced among prostitutes is also unknown, but police and court reports show occasional arrests of abortionists throughout the nineteenth century.[32]

Losing one's place in a brothel because of pregnancy, however, did not mean retiring from the profession. In the 1870 census, which lists prostitution as an occupation, many women on the rolls had their child or children living with them. In some cases they worked as entrepreneurial prostitutes in their own home; in other cases, they rented rooms in a brothel and left the child with a sitter or relative. Pregnancy did not automatically mean downward mobility or setting up on one's own, but very few brothels or parlor houses would hold the place of an employee who could not work. Furthermore, in all kinds of houses, the constant need for new faces made for little job security.

The easiest method to move up in the profession was through a sponsor. If a brothel prostitute or dance-hall harlot could attract the interest of a wealthy or influential man, he could very often use his influence to establish her in his favorite parlor house or in one of the better brothels. Judge McGowan, a notorious character even for San Francisco, not only kept his favorite prostitute in his favorite house but occasionally even lived there with her. Since madams were usually willing to humor their regular customers, the price was probably no more than a new wardrobe for the favorite, one more in keeping with her new surroundings. Whether she kept her new position when her sponsor's interest diminished depended on the vagaries of customer demand, and her age, beauty, and ability to adapt to her new status.[33]

The length of a prostitute's professional life is difficult to estimate. In 1850, one courtesan retired after making $50 thousand in one year. At the other end of the scale is the information in an 1895 almshouse report about a ninety-three-year-old woman who had apparently been a regular inmate of the almshouse, off and on, for a number of years. Her habits were still listed as intemperance and prostitution! Obviously the average prostitute fit neither of these extremes. The census reports list women from their teens to their fifties as working prostitutes. There were mothers and daughters practicing the profession at the same time, but evidence on the length of their career is sketchy and inconclusive. As there was no penicillin to fight syphilis, many died from this occupational disease or from bungled abortions. Some left the profession to take jobs in other occupations open to women in the nineteenth century, such as clerks or domestic workers. The more frugal among them, according to some observers, opened their own dress or hat shops. And still others gave up the profession for marriage.[34] Beyond that point we can only speculate, but it is clear that though the halcyon days for prostitutes in early San Francisco did not continue long, their position in society was never quite as far beyond the pale as it was in the East. Once the day-to-day hardships of building a city were past, the early pioneers romanticized their city, and the demimonde was just as much a part of that romance as the anecdotes of empire building, of overnight millionaires, and of a city that could be raised six times from the ashes like a phoenix.

Notes

1 Frank Soulé, John H. Gihon, and James Nisbet, *The Annals of San Francisco* (1855; reprint, 1966), pp. 668–669.

2 Elisha Oscar Crosby, Bancroft Collection, "Events in California" (c. 1878); Soulé, Gihon, and Nisbet, *Annals;* Benjamin E. Lloyd, *Lights and Shades in San Francisco* (1876); and Hubert Howe Bancroft, *The Works of Hubert Howe Bancroft* (1886–1888) remark on the decorous conduct of the prostitutes and the respectability of their customers. But these writers are men who claim never to have been customers in the "gilded palaces" (parlor houses) and who seem to feel it necessary to seem slightly shocked by the vice hiding itself in "staid dignity." Their suggestion was that the "poor fallen creature" in this setting was grateful to be able to "act and appear as a lady" once more. Had they suggested that the prostitute was pleased to be *treated* as a lady, it would not be difficult to accept this analysis. Given the situation in frontier San Francisco, however, the suggestion that the parlor-house prostitute was envious of other women around her is questionable. She was treated with respect, she was making more money and living in more comfortable surroundings than any other woman in the city. She was also a businesswoman, and she acted and appeared in whatever manner would bring her the most business. The attitude of the writers mentioned above was typical of the nineteenth-century view of prostitutes; it was seldom if ever suggested that any woman voluntarily entered the profession. Even in frontier literature, where prostitutes were generally given more liberal treatment, writers were careful to qualify their complimentary statements by reminding the reader that such women were fall-

en, lewd, and outcasts of society. The contradiction between description and analysis makes it difficult to present an accurate picture.

3 The Barbary Coast developed after 1865.

4 Soulé, Gihon, and Nisbet, *Annals*, p. 668.

5 These conclusions are drawn from a variety of references throughout the nineteenth century. In addition to sources already cited, see accounts in the daily newspapers of the time: *California Courier*, July 6, 1850; *San Francisco Evening News and Picayune*, November 1, 1853; *Evening Bulletin*, November 18, 1855; *Sunday Varieties*, January 23, 1859; *California Police Gazette*, November 18, 1865, and many others. These sources and various police reports refer to police bribes, the existence of "houses" in residential neighborhoods, and the shrewdness of individual madams.

6 Crosby, Bancroft Collections, pp. 121–123. Curt Gentry's very entertaining journalistic history, *Madams of San Francisco (1964)*, discounts the existence of the Countess. Gentry's skepticism is based primarily on his belief that she did not "appear in *any* account until the 1930s." She did in fact appear in Crosby's dictation to Bancroft, (Collections), in which he reminisced about events in California in 1849. One of Gentry's arguments against her existence is based on the fact that the El Dorado, the most lavish establishment in San Francisco, was still housed in a tent in December of 1849, and it is therefore unlikely, he insists, that the Countess presided in better surroundings. Crosby, however, does not claim her house was lavish, merely that it was "a large frame house two stories high." Henry Williams, a builder and carpenter from Virginia, arrived in San Francisco in February 1849, when "the town consisted of a few houses about the plaza," and immediately he had more work than he could handle (or hire men for) in constructing frame buildings (Bancroft Collections). By September, he related, prefabricated houses were arriving from the East, and in October he built a brick storehouse three stories high. The gambling saloons may have been the most lavish and usually the first to become permanent structures; this was generally the case, though not without exception. Other statements by Gentry are equally arguable, but as he bases his conclusions on the

1930s account rather than on the original, it is not necessary to include them here.

7 Soulé, Gihon, and Nisbet, *Annals*, p. 668.

8 Ibid., p. 259; Lloyd, *Lights and Shades*, p. 83; Bancroft, *Works*, vol. 23, p. 234.

9 *Alta California*, February 2, 1850; Soulé, Gihon, and Nisbet, *Annals*, p. 355. The Monumental was the first organized firefighting company in the city.

10 *Daily Town Talk*, 1857, ads and announcements of balls.

11 Soulé, Gihon, and Nisbet, *Annals*, pp. 666–668.

12 Ibid. Similar descriptions can be found for different periods throughout the century in Lloyd, *Lights and Shades*, p. 512; Bancroft, *Works*, vol. 24, p. 243; and in the newspapers.

13 *Sunday Varieties*, September 7, 1856. The Prostitutes Ball was apparently a regular event at the Music Hall beginning in 1855; how long it continued is unclear.

14 Such terms are, of course, arbitrary, and it is unlikely that when they were coined it was a prostitute who chose them. They are, however, familiar terms that indicate the "class" of the prostitute—or by my definition, her degree of professionalism. If prostitution was simply viewed as an occupation, they would coincide with such job descriptions as executive, white-collar worker, blue-collar worker, semiskilled laborer, and unskilled laborer.

15 There is no reliable information on a common fee for any category of prostitution. According to Benard de Russailh, *Last Adventure*, and Soulé, Gihon, and Nisbet, *Annals*, a courtesan made from $95 to $400 for one night, depending on whether the year was 1849–1850 or beyond. Apparently the prices graduated downward to a dollar a trick for a dance-hall harlot.

16 Lloyd, *Lights and Shades*, p. 82. See also Edward O. Janney, M.D., *The White Slave Traffic* (1911), pp. 41–44. In Monterey and Salinas, relics of these structures are preserved and open to the public.

17 Eliza W. Farnham, *California In-Doors and Out* (1856), p. 274; Janney, *White Slave Traffic*, p. 44; Herbert Asbury, *The Barbary Coast* (1949), p. 260.

18 U.S. census, 1860 and 1870.

19 See *California Police Gazette*, September 14, 1867; Lloyd, *Lights and Shades*, p. 82; see H. S.

Drago, *Notorious Ladies of the Frontier* (1969), for descriptions of dance halls by name and location.

20 *Municipal Records.* The number of arrests for common prostitution in 1859 were fourteen; 1861, two; and 1863, none. This pattern continued until the 1870s, when a combination of events brought at least a minimal attempt to "prohibit and suppress...all houses of ill-fame" and prostitution. The board of supervisors had the power to enforce the prohibition granted to them by the state legislature as early as 1863, but it was not until Chief of Police Cockrill took office in 1874 that there was any significant change in the arrest pattern (one arrest for being an inmate of a house of ill fame in 1862; 89 for the same misdemeanor in 1874). The largest number arrested for soliciting was 547 in 1880, but even that is an insignificant number when it is remembered that there were an estimated three thousand prostitutes working in the Barbary Coast district during this period. Also, the arrests were for misdemeanors, and even when the woman was convicted, only a small fine of $10–$25 was charged, with the woman able to return to her occupation the following day. It is also highly probable that a large percentage of these arrests were against Chinese prostitutes—though the figures are not broken down by ethnic origin—because Chinese women as well as men were victims of anti-Chinese agitation among officials and citizens in San Francisco during the 1870s and 1880s.

21 Carol Wilson, *Gump's Treasure Trade* (1949) p. 34.

22 Ibid., p. 34.

23 Sarah Royce, *Frontier Lady* (1932) p. 114.

24 Caleb Fay, "Statement of Historical Facts on California" (1878), Bancroft Dictations, p. 10.

25 Royce, *Frontier Lady,* p. 114.

26 Bancroft, *Works,* vol. 2, p. 240.

27 Ibid., pp. 29, 240.

28 Ibid., p. 31; *Evening Bulletin,* November 21, 1855. Following this incident, James King of William, editor of the *Bulletin,* began one of his periodic campaigns against vice, crime, and municipal corruption in the city.

29 E. D. Baker, *Eloquence of the Far West* (1899), pp. 311–315.

30 William Watkins, "Statement on Vigilance Committee" (1878), Bancroft Collections. Watkins, a member of the 1856 Vigilance Committee, was part of the delegation sent to bring Belle to the place where Charles was confined.

31 Lloyd, *Lights and Shades,* pp. 84–85; Mary Grace Edholm, *Traffic in Girls and Work of the Rescue Mission* (1900), "Seduction and Marriage."

32 Lloyd, *Lights and Shades,* p. 85. It was Lloyd's contention that the working life of a prostitute was four to five months. Since his goal to discourage recruitment into the trade, it is safe to assume this is an exaggeration. Nevertheless, all of the factors listed above limited the working years of prostitutes and supports the theory of some writers that the elite sector of the profession moved regularly among the red-light districts of major cities.

33 Bancroft, *Works,* vol. 2, p. 334.

34 U.S. census, 1870.

VIGILANTES AND HISTORIANS

EDITOR'S INTRODUCTION

The vigilantes of San Francisco have long been a subject of controversy in California historiography. The traditional, once standard interpretation was generally sympathetic to the vigilance committees. According to this view, the vigilantes were forced into action by the corruption and crime which plagued gold-rush San Francisco. The vigilantes were a selfless lot, motivated by the simple desire to protect lives and property. The dissenting, more critical interpretation denounced the vigilantes for setting a dangerous precedent of extralegal action. The vigilantes were a group of self-promoters who trampled on the civil liberties of their victims.

Scholarship on the vigilantes has now entered what Robert M. Senkewicz, S.J., calls the "phase of analysis." During this phase, historians have concluded that the vigilantes were businessmen motivated by a complex set of ethnic, political, and class interests. The latest work of analysis is Senkewicz's own *Vigilantes in Gold Rush San Francisco* (1985). Central to his interpretation of vigilantism is a portrait of San Francisco in the 1850s as a city of failed hopes and faded dreams. Among the city's most frustrated residents were its large importers and commission merchants. Their problem was a chronic oversupply of goods. With too many goods chasing too few consumers, prices and profits were in decline during the 1850s. The merchants tried their best to remedy the problem, but nothing seemed to work. In their frustration they turned to scapegoats. During the doldrums of the summer of 1851, the merchants formed San Francisco's first Committee of Vigilance. Their scapegoats: Australian immigrants. Then, in 1856, the merchants formed the second committee and attacked a new set of scapegoats, Irish Catholics and Democratic politicians.

The failings of the San Francisco mercantile class were symptomatic of the frustrations of gold-rush Californians generally. As we know from the new social history, opportunities on the frontier for upward mobility were often far less than what was anticipated. Frustration and disappointment apparently led not only to increased geographical mobility but to vigilantism as well.

Senkewicz systematically examines the stated rationales for the formation of the committees of vigilance and he rejects each one in turn. San Francisco politics, he avers, were not remarkably corrupt; charges of fraud and violence were "greatly exaggerated." Nor was crime the great problem that the vigilantes claimed. While acknowledging the difficulty of getting accurate crime statistics, Senkewicz argues that it is unlikely that San Francisco experienced any increase in crime prior to the formation of the committees. What was increasing, rather, was the *fear* of crime.

The vigilantes discovered in their role as public defenders a kind of success and status denied them as businessmen. "The proudest time of their lives," Senkewicz speculates, "the only time that served to redeem the failure of their dream, was a time of collective and impersonal action: those brief periods in the summers of 1851 and 1856 when each of them had been known, not by name, but by rank and serial number." Here is an important insight, a valuable clue which helps us to understand the enthusiasm which the vigilantes brought to their work. Vigilantism provided the members of the committees with something otherwise denied them, a sense of purpose and accomplishment.

In the following selection, Robert M. Senkewicz offers an interpretive survey of the historiography of vigilantism. Of particular interest is his discussion of Roger Lotchin's account of the rise of the 1856 committee. Lotchin's emphasis on the role of wives and their opposition to prostitution in the city parallels the analysis of Jacqueline Baker Barnhart in the previous selection.

Robert M. Senkewicz received his Ph.D. from Stanford University in 1974. Currently he is an Assistant Professor of History and Vice President for Student Services at Santa Clara University.

READING 12

Vigilantes and Historians

Robert M. Senkewicz, S.J.

Because they were connected with such dramatic and public events, the vigilance committees of San Francisco served as the focus around which much of the history of the gold rush port was written. History is a collective enterprise, as each writer tries to build on the insights of predecessors. The historiography of early San Francisco has consisted of two broad phases. The first, the phase of imitation, began shortly after the 1856 committee disbanded, and it lasted for about a century. The second, the phase of analysis, began in the 1960's and has continued until the present.

A remark by a close observer serves to delineate the contours of the imitative phase of scholarship. Of the more than 50,000 residents of San Francisco during the 1850's, the man who was to become the best-known national figure in later nineteenth-century America opposed the formation of the committee of vigilance in 1856. William Tecumseh Sherman had been a banker in the gold rush city, and when he came to write his *Memoirs* a quarter-century after his California sojourn, he said of the vigilantes, "As they controlled the press, they wrote their own history." His largely accurate comment serves to underscore the close relationship throughout the first phase of historiography between what gold rush San Franciscans said about the vigilantes ("the press") and what later writers recorded ("history"). In fact, for almost a century, many historians of gold rush San Francisco seemed intent on standing Santayana's celebrated axiom on its head: the more

they studied the past, the more they tended to repeat it.[1]

The imitative phase involved three movements, and, by the time it was over, it had come full circle. First, from the 1860's to the 1920's, during the period of California historiography that Gerald D. Nash has labeled the pioneer era (1850–90) and the romantic era (1890–1920), many early historians of the city sought to justify the vigilantes. Some actually seemed to be taking up residence in the vigilante headquarters, Fort Gunnybags, and establishing themselves as head cheerleaders for Judge Lynch. For the most part, their commentaries echoed what the pro-vigilance *Chronicle* and its allies had thundered in 1856, "This community must be purged from its dregs, the creatures, whoever they are, who have poisoned the fountains of society and made the place as loathsome as a charnel house." These historians outdid one another in describing how terrible life had been in the gold rush port, how the sober citizens took it for as long as they could, and how, when all other remedies had been exhausted, they finally came to the difficult conclusion that they had to take the law into their own hands if the city were to be saved. Second, around 1920, beginning the historiographical period that Nash termed the age of realism (1920–45), the hurrahs began to be toned down. Following the lead of people like Sherman, historians increasingly began to question the long-range utility of casting aside the law even for allegedly noble purposes. Finally, around 1950, the actions of the committee became increasingly condemned. The remarks of the anti-vigilance *Herald* came into vogue: "We rest now beneath the shadow of a vast and ominous tyranny. We have had extended over us, in time of profound peace, an unquestioned military tyranny.'' And so the circle closed, with the men of the committee more humbled than exalted.[2]

LUCKINGHAM AND BROWN

This second phase, which I am calling the phase of analysis, began in 1968 with a dissertation at the University of California, Davis. In "Associational Life on the Urban Frontier: San Francisco, 1848–1856,'' Bradford Luckingham viewed the 1856 vigilance committee as one instance of the myriad voluntary associations that were so pronounced a feature of antebellum life throughout the United States. Luckingham impressively catalogued the existence of scores of voluntary associations—cultural, educational, religious, social—in the first decade of the history of San Francisco.

Although Luckingham's approach was to some degree imitative in that he tended to accept the crime and corruption model of the justification historians, he also called attention to the highly organized structure of the vigilance committee. He insisted that the committee should be looked at not just as a reaction to corruption but as the culmination of the very manifest urban tendency of associational activity. Speaking of the leaders of the committee, Luckingham says, ''Unable to envision violent mob action, and unable to rely on corrupt city officials, they met the problem in the only way they knew how: they formed an association.'' Luckingham's impressive catalogue of voluntary associations in gold rush San Francisco and his insistence that the vigilance committee should be examined in this context invited historians to look beyond fragmentary crime statistics and occasional political brawling for clues to the impetus for extralegal organization.[3]

In the next year Richard Maxwell Brown, in two important essays, offered a new interpretation of the 1856 committee.[4] Brown placed San Francisco vigilantism in a comparative and na-tional context. Drawing on his study of the 326 known vigilante movements in American history, he generalized that ''the main thrust of vigilantism was to establish in each newly settled area the conservative values of life and property, law and order.'' For Brown, Josiah Royce's phrase ''Business Man's Revolution'' described more than just San Francisco vigilantism: ''Vigilante movements were usually led by the frontier elite. This was true of the greatest American vigilante movement—the San Francisco Vigilance Committee of 1856—which was dominated lock, stock and barrel by the leading merchants of the city.'' Brown argued that the typical American community in the nineteenth century was marked by a threefold social structure. On top was the local elite of successful businessmen, eminent professionals, affluent farmers, and so on. In the middle were the average farmers, traders, and craftsmen, and on the third level were the honest poor. Below this third level were the ''lower people,'' the ''ne'er-do-well, shiftless poor whites,'' who were ''not outlaws, but often tended to lawlessness and identified more with the outlaw element than the law-abiding members of the community.'' According to Brown, the local elite provided the vigilante leadership, the middle level filled the vigilante rank and file, and the lower people served as vigilante targets. Brown also called attention to what he called an ''ideology of vigilantism'' widespread in nineteenth-century America. This ideology included a pervasive doctrine of ''vigilance'' in all things and a philosophy that was compounded of the right of self-protection, the right of revolution, and the notion of popular sovereignty. The final element in the ideology was an economic rationale that emphasized that vigilante justice tended to be cheaper than regular justice. Brown also distinguished vigilantism in situations in which the regular system of law and order was absent and in which it was functioning effectively. Following John Caughey, he placed the 1856 committee in the latter category, calling it "vigilantism as a parallel structure."[5]

When he turned his attention specifically to San Francisco, Brown joined William Tecumseh Sherman and others in claiming that there was no "crime wave" in 1856. He stated, "A survey of the police news column in the *Bulletin* and *Town Talk* [both of which supported the committee] during the fall, winter, and spring of 1855–1856 has convinced me that the San Francisco crime problem was under control." So he looked elsewhere and presented an ethnic explanation for the formation of the committee. A close analysis of some 2,500 applications for membership in the committee that survive at the Huntington Library enabled Brown to form a more precise picture of the composition of the committee than any previous writer. He reported that the vigilance committee was "composed of young men in their twenties and thirties." These men were of virtually every ethnic strain, but the bulk of the American membership was "from the northeastern United States from Maine to Maryland"; in other words, they tended to be old-stock Yankees. Brown further noted that there were few Irishmen in the committee. He reported that "the vigilantes came largely from the ranks of the city's merchants, tradesmen, craftsmen, or their young employees." On the basis of these findings, he attempted to relate the vigilance committee to "tensions" in the city between "upper and middle class, old American, Protestant merchants" and "a political faction based on Irish Catholic lower class laborers." He agreed with Henry Gray and James O'Meara that the basic goal of the committee had been the destruction of the Democratic political organization led by David C. Broderick, and he offered a novel explanation for the existence of this goal. He related the formation of the committee to a mercantile desire for "fiscal reform at the municipal level." In this view:

The mercantile complexion of the vigilance committee is the key to its behavior. The merchants of San Francisco were dependent on Eastern connections for their credit. Like most businessmen, the San Francisco merchants had a consuming interest in their own credit ratings and the local tax rate. In the eyes of Eastern businessmen, San Francisco's economic stability was being jeopardized by the soaring municipal debt, rising taxes, and approaching bankruptcy under the Broderick machine. The spectre of municipal bankruptcy made Eastern creditors fearful that the city was on the verge of economic chaos. The restoration of confidence in San Francisco's municipal and financial stability was a *sine qua non*. It had to be accomplished—and in such a way that would let Easterners know that conservative, right-thinking men had definitely gained control. Fiscal reform at the municipal level was thus basic to the vigilante movement. But in order to bring about fiscal reform it was first necessary to smash David C. Broderick's machine.[6]

According to Brown, the precision of the committee's attacks, directed almost exclusively against Irish Catholic henchmen of Broderick (this had already been noted by James O'Meara), made the 1856 vigilance committee a "pivot" between "old" and "new" styles of American vigilantism. The old vigilantism was directed "mainly at horsethieves, counterfeiters, outlaws, bad men, and lower people." The new vigilantism, which became important at the end of the nineteenth century, "found its chief victims among Catholics, Jews, immigrants, Negroes, laboring men and labor leaders, political radicals, and proponents of civil liberties." Brown's judgment was that the 1856 committee "represented a blending of the methods of the old vigilantism with the victims of the new."[7]

Brown's major contributions to the study of San Francisco vigilantism were his insistence on looking at the city as a whole, his detailed research on the composition of the committee, and his attempt to work the ethnic and political aspects of the committee's work, already noted by others, into a coherent framework. His was the most sophisticated account to date of the 1856 committee.

WILLIAMS, OLMSTED, AND STARR

In the same year in which Brown's important essays appeared (1969), David A. Williams published a biography of Democratic politician David C. Broderick. Following O'Meara, Williams emphasized the political nature of the committee's work. "In effect," he said, "the committee became a 'political engine' which was utilized by some of its members to strike at Broderick and his associates." Where Brown had attacked the "crime wave" justification of the committee, Williams went after the "political corruption" charge. Not only were many members of the committee old political enemies of Broderick but also the committee failed to produce any hard evidence of political fraud against Broderick or most of his cronies. He concluded: "The failure reflected the paucity of evidence, for much of what the committee's investigators assembled was faulty, insignificant, or not related to Broderick."[8]

In 1970 Roger Olmsted also took up the question of vigilantism, noting, with a mixture of truth and exaggeration, that the committees "have never been vigilantly examined by western historians in terms of their social context." Following John S. Hittell and Josiah Royce, Olmsted argued that the economic slump after 1854 was related to vigilantism, and he added a twist that sought to make that relationship more precise: "When everyone is getting rich, municipal corruption is often the object of a kind of rueful civic pride. Such was the general attitude of the citizens of San Francisco until the bubble burst. Then suddenly the unmerited affluence of fraudulently elected officials became an affront increasingly hard to put up with." In other words, the depression did not so much reveal corruption, as Royce had argued; rather it made political corruption an object of distaste and jealousy on the part of the city's hard-pressed businessmen. In terms that were also reminiscent of Royce, Olmsted argued that "the deep-rooted corruption of San Francisco politics was more a function of popular psychology than individual depravity" and that the committee's "exposure" of this corruption was its chief work. Though it shared much with the justifying writings of the imitative phase, Olmsted's account demonstrated the effect that the analytical phase was having on the literature. Even a writer who generally approved of the committee could no longer accept the vigilantes' own self-estimate without serious qualification.[9]

Kevin Starr, in his wide-ranging *Americans and the California Dream,* discussed the 1856 committee only briefly, but in an interesting way, in a chapter entitled "City on a Hill" that dealt with the New England ministers who arrived in California with the intention of transforming Eldorado into a "Puritan commonwealth." The ministers fought slavery, gambling, prostitution, and lack of observance of the Sabbath, and they were very prominent in the establishment of San Francisco's public school system. Their efforts eventually failed, because, among other things, "the Roman Catholic presence was too strong." Echoing John Nugent, Starr saw a connection between the Know-Nothing activity in San Francisco in 1854–55 and the vigilance committee in 1856. In Starr's view, they were both accounted for by "anti-foreign reformism on the part of outraged businessmen." Since the design of his work took him elsewhere, Starr did not attempt to describe the practical effects of "the Catholic presence" or the components of "reformism." But his introduction, albeit brief, of religion so centrally into the picture was entirely new and highly imaginative.[10]

ROGER LOTCHIN

In 1974, San Francisco historiography took an enormous step forward with the appearance of

Roger Lotchin's detailed and comprehensive study of the early city, *San Francisco, 1846–1856: From Hamlet to City*. Topical in organization, Lotchin's study is a generally successful attempt to insert the early history of San Francisco into the mainstream of American urban history. For example, an early contest between San Francisco and Benicia over which would become the bay's major port occurs in a chapter entitled "Urban Rivalries," thereby putting it in the context of other commercial rivalries between sets of American cities. Schools are treated in a chapter entitled "Urban Institutions," and there are also chapters on government, labor, politics, and so on. Lotchin's book is undoubtedly the best account of the early American period.

Lotchin deals with the 1856 committee in a chapter entitled "The Revolution of 1856." He does not accept what he calls the "deterioration-tyranny" thesis that the city was in the grip of crime and corruption. With John S. Hittell, he points to the enactment of the Consolidation Act and to the fact that the confused real estate titles were being straightened out by the courts as indications that things were looking up in the city at the beginning of 1856. He makes the point that electoral violence was on the wane and that Broderick's political power was tenuous at best, and concludes that there was simply no insoluble crisis that explained the formation of the vigilance committee.

He suggests three main causes leading to the organization of the committee: "spouses, spatial relationships, and spurious sensationalism." The sensationalism was that of San Francisco *Bulletin* editor James King of William, whom Lotchin regards as having "ignited a class struggle of sorts, though not of the European variety involving the classic duality of working class and middle class." Rather, King appealed to those who regarded themselves as "an all-embracing alliance of worthy citizens that cut across the categories of upper, middle, and lower orders." In this light, Lotchin maintains, "The upheaval of 1856 was pre-eminently a revolution of the legitimates." The spouses, according to Lotchin, were the ones who were responsible for the "moral fervor" of the vigilance struggle (and not, as Walton Bean had suggested, guilt feelings). King, in championing "family and home interests in the metropolis against gamblers, prostitutes, and their allies," gave voice to female concerns. And the spatial relationships in the city, Lotchin says, gave these concerns their intensity and guaranteed the continuing urgency of the values King was defending. Relying on his own detailed study of the residential and commercial patterns of land use in the early city, Lotchin argues that the period under investigation witnessed "a decentralization of economic and residential patterns...considerable specialization of land use...and greater concentration of the various categories within each." While the business section of the city remained downtown, "the middle classes moved west and the separation of places of home and work unfolded." As a result:

> Men worked downtown and lived on the heights; but in between these two areas and to an extent mixed in with them was a large concentration of sin, especially along Dupont and cross streets between there and Stockton. Many middle-class people still lived on Dupont; and even those who did not were thrown into proximity with this vice street, whose inhabitants were entrenched upon the access routes to downtown. A trip to the dentist, the doctor, the milliner, the husband's office, and sometimes even to church kept the situation explosive by renewing the contact between the housewives and harlots.

The shooting of King sparked "institutional form to these frustrations," namely the vigilance committee, which, Lotchin says, was "a species of urban revolution against the Gold Rush status quo": "The colorful, lawless metropolis had often been exciting, and many would remember it affectionately. Yet contemporaries had seen enough of it.'' As a result of the activities of the vigilance committee an ''ideology of community,'' which stressed the importance of local issues and the malevolence of politicians, crystallized.

For the most part, Lotchin downplays the more traditional foci of discussion, but where he does touch on them, he tends to side with the opponents of the committee. He joins Stephen P. Webb and others in excoriating public apathy, and remarks that in pre-vigilante San Francisco it was not so much that democracy failed as that it was never tried. He denies with William Henry Ellison and John Caughey that any ''regeneration or purification'' resulted from the vigilante action: ''San Francisco in 1857 did not differ markedly from what it had been in 1855.'' He agrees with David A. Williams that there was little specific evidence for contending that ''fraud carried the day in San Francisco elections.''[11]

DECKER AND BURCHELL

In 1978 extensive quantification finally appeared in the historiography of San Francisco with the publication of Peter R. Decker's *Fortunes and Failures: White Collar Mobility in Nineteenth Century San Francisco,* which covers the years 1848–80. Decker culled his data on occupational mobility from the State Census of 1852, the city directories, and the credit reports of R. G. Dun and Co. Too frequently in American quantification history, insight and argument are lost in impenetrable prose, but Decker's findings are a happy exception, and he presents his sophisticated findings on San Francisco in clear, readable, and disarming fashion.

Decker's main argument is that in the gold rush city there were ''distinct gradations within the merchant occupation.'' At the summit were ''commission merchants, importers, wholesalers (including those who combined wholesaling

and retailing), and jobbers''; at the next level were ''general retail merchants''; and ''petty merchants: the retail shopkeepers, dealers, traders, grocers, and peddlers'' were ''lowest on the occupational scale.'' He makes the point that the gold rush economy, like most American economies, was cyclical: ''By 1858, San Francisco had experienced four major business cycles, all quite independent of the national economy: June 1848–January 1850—boom; February 1850–April 1852—recession; May 1852–December 1853—boom; January 1854–January 1858—depression.'' He follows John S. Hittell in arguing that ''the oversupply of goods in the San Francisco market was the single most important factor that fueled the excessive business cycles.'' While some groups, such as German Jewish merchants, fared better than most, during the 1850 decade ''the rate of failure was probably somewhere between half and two-thirds of all merchants.'' All in all, the 1850's were ''a decade of economic loss rather than profit.'' In particular, ''The high status merchants, those who owned the commission houses, wholesale outlets, and import firms, found it difficult…to maintain their occupational status.'' By 1860, Decker says, less than half of this group had managed to stay at the level at which they had begun their mercantile careers in San Francisco.

Like Hittell, Royce, and others, Decker attempts to relate the 1856 vigilance committee to this context of business uncertainty. With a few reservations, he generally adopts Brown's interpretation that the businessmen wanted to ''protect both their individual credit ratings and the general fiscal reputation of the city.'' The merchants, according to him, attempted by vigilance ''to halt the corrosive effects of economic recession'' that was affecting them so adversely. Though the vigilance committee may not have done very much for the city as a whole, it did benefit the merchants who organized it: ''Taking all committee members who held either civil or military executive positions in the vigilance committee, 70 percent of whom were either high status general merchants, importers-wholesalers, bankers, brokers, manufacturers, or professionals, over 80 percent either maintained or improved their occupational status. They did, in fact, outperform the merchants and general population of the city in the years 1852–1860.''[12]

R. A. Burchell's *The San Francisco Irish, 1848–1880,* which appeared in 1980, was the first work to deal exclusively with the urban Irish during the gold rush period. It revolves around what the author terms ''two themes'': the major theme is ''the local circumstances that produced...feelings of satisfaction'' on the part of the city's Irish; the minor theme involves ''the host culture's at best ambivalence, at worst hostility, to the immigrant presence.'' Most of the book centers on the major theme, and Burchell argues that the San Francisco Irish fared rather well during the period he investigated. He argues this major theme so strenuously, in fact, that he occasionally has to interrupt the presentation and caution the reader not to get the wrong idea—as in this comment that occurs at the beginning of one chapter: ''It may appear, though it is not its purpose to do so, that this study argues in some rightly suspicious and peculiar way that all members of the Irish were satisfied with their lives in San Francisco. This was hardly the case.'' But the thrust of the book revolves so definitely around the major theme of a favorable environment for the Irish in San Francisco that Burchell, in the last paragraph, feels it necessary to add ''a final caution'': ''It is not argued that the Irish performed as well as the native stock in San Francisco. The point is that, given the time, the mid-to-late nineteenth century; the place, the United States; and the group, the Irish, their history in San Francisco was, by contrast with that elsewhere, comparatively successful and fortunate.''

Burchell attempted to do for the San Francisco Irish what other historians during the 1970's had done for the blacks and other minority groups: to present them not only as historical victims but as historical actors. And in that task he was eminently successful. Following Luckingham, he presents a very complete account of the host of voluntary associations which the Irish formed and directed. He argues that the Irish family in the city was more stable than the native stock family, that ''the occupational status of the Irish-born males improved slowly but surely until after 1870,'' and that the second-generation Irish were ''marginally in front of the total community'' in job status. Although the vigilance committee and the Civil War, in weakening the Democratic party, did diminish Irish political power in the city, he says, the weakening was temporary and did not consign the Irish to a ''permanently secondary role in San Francisco politics.''

Burchell's discussion of the 1856 vigilance committee tends, like Decker's, to follow the broad outline of Brown's argument. He agrees with David A. Williams and Brown that the committee attacked Broderick men, and he terms the committee's acts ''a very neat surgical operation on the body politic.'' But since his focus is almost exclusively on the Irish, he does not speculate at any length on the reasons for the formation of the committee or on the functions of nativism in the city.[13]

In my study, I have tried to combine the two phases that I have outlined above. On the one hand, I think that the writers of the imitative phase were correct when they accorded vigilantism a central place in their histories of the gold rush period. On the other hand, the analytical writers have brought great sophistication to the study of the early city, and I have availed myself of some of their insights, for I agree with the thrust of their writings. Some of the analytical writers who treat vigilantism as an aspect of a larger process such as urbanization or social mobility tend to remove themselves a bit too much from the texture of life as it was lived in the 1850's. San Franciscans of that period did not think of themselves as urbanizers or the like, but they *did* think of themselves as vigilantes or law and order people. I have attempted to be critical and yet to tell their story in terms that they would have understood, for history involves entering worlds in which we might feel as strangers or out of place.

On the other hand, the analytical writers have brought great sophistication to the study of the early city, and I have availed myself of some of their insights. For I agree, as the present study makes clear, with the thrust of their writings.

Notes

1 William T. Sherman, *Memoirs of General William T. Sherman,* 1: 159. I should note that I am not attempting an exhaustive bibliography of the literature dealing with the 1856 committee. I am rather concentrating on the works that, in my judgment, are important for the development of the historiography. The most complete bibliography up to 1971 is Doyce Nunis, ed., *San Francisco Vigilance Committee of 1856,* pp. 170–176.

2 *Chronicle,* May 16, 1856; Gerald D. Nash, "California and Its Historians: An Appraisal of the Histories of the State," *Pacific Historical Review* 50 (1981): 387–413; *Herald,* May 22, 1856.

3 Bradford Luckingham, "Associational Life on Urban Frontier: San Francisco, 1848–1856," p. 153.

4 See Richard Maxwell Brown, "The American Vigilante Tradition," in Hugh Davis Graham and Ted Robert Gurr, eds., *Violence in America: Historical and Comparative Perspectives* (New York: Bantam Books, 1969); and Richard Maxwell Brown, "Pivot of American Vigilantism: The San Francisco Vigilance Committee of 1856," in John A. Carroll, ed., *Reflections of Western Historians* (Tucson: University of Arizona Press, 1969). Both essays are conveniently reprinted in Brown, *Strain of Violence: Historical Studies of American Violence and Vigilantism,* pp. 95–143.

5 For the interpretations of Josiah Royce and John Caughey, see Royce, *California, From the Conquest in 1846 to the Second Vigilance Committee in San Francisco: A Study of the American Character* (1886; rpt. Santa Barbara and Salt Lake City: Peregrine, 1970), pp. 328–366; Earl Pomeroy, "Josiah Royce: Historian in Search of Community, *Pacific Historical Review* 40 (1971):

1–20; Caughey, "Their Majesties the Mob," *Pacific Historical Review* 26 (1957): 221–31; and Caughey, *Their Majesties the Mob* (Chicago: University of Chicago Press, 1960).

6 Brown, *Strain of Violence,* pp. 137–138. The interpretations of Henry Gray and James O'Meara are found in Gray, *Judges and Criminals. Shadows of the Past. History of the Vigilance Committee of San Francisco, Cal., with the Names of Its Officers* (San Francisco: printed for the author, 1858); and O'Meara, in Nunis, ed., *San Francisco Vigilance Committee of 1856,* pp. 8–9, 12, 24, 43, 46.

7 Brown, *Strain of Violence,* p. 134.

8 David A. Williams, *David C. Broderick: A Political Portrait* (San Marino: The Huntington Library, 1969), pp. 125, 129, 143. Warren A. Beck and David A. Williams, *California: A History of the Golden State* (Garden City: Doubleday, 1972), pp. 178–79, argues along the same lines.

9 Roger Olmsted, "San Francisco and the Vigilante Style," *American West* 7, no. 1 (1970): 6–10, 63–64; no. 2:20–27, 60–62. The material is also in T. H. Watkins and R. R. Olmsted, *Mirror of the Dream: An Illustrated History of San Francisco* (San Francisco: Scrimshaw Press, 1976), pp. 55–94.

10 Kevin Starr, *Americans and the California Dream* (New York: Oxford University Press, 1973), pp. 85–87, 93–94.

11 Roger Lotchin, *San Francisco, 1846–1856: From Hamlet to City* (Lincoln: The University of Nebraska Press, 1979), pp. 17, 245–58, 268, 275, 381, 384. For the views of Walton Bean, Stephen P. Webb, and William Henry Ellison, see Bean, *California: An Interpretive History* (New York: McGraw-Hill, 1968), pp. 137, 148; Webb, "A Sketch of the Causes, Operations, and Results of the San Francisco Vigilance Committee of 1856," *Essex Institute Historical Collection* 84, no. 2 (1948): 100, 130; and Ellison, *A Self-Governing Dominion: California, 1849–1860* (Berkeley and Los Angeles: University of California Press, 1950), pp. 247, 263, 266–267.

12 Peter R. Decker, *Fortunes and Failures: White-Collar Mobility in Nineteenth Century San Francisco* (Cambridge: Harvard University Press, 1978), pp. 34, 37, 61–63, 72–73, 81, 85, 92, 129, 140.

13 R. A. Burchell *The San Francisco Irish, 1848–1880* (Berkeley: University of California Press, 1980), pp. 14, 52, 54, 123, 129, 184.

MARRIAGE AND DIVORCE IN VICTORIAN CALIFORNIA

EDITOR'S INTRODUCTION

One of the most fruitful areas of new research in the history of women is the critical analysis of prevailing stereotypes. Scholars have subjected traditional images of women to literary criticism and have tested the images against empirical evidence. Through careful quantitative and archival research, the validity of the stereotypes are measured, and new, more accurate images of women are crafted. A common approach in such studies is to analyze a large number of documents for a limited geographical area.

To some extent this is the approach of Jacqueline Baker Barnhart in her study of the prostitutes of San Francisco. She reexamines the traditional image of the "bad woman," and recasts the prostitute as an entrepreneur and professional.

The most pervasive of all stereotypes of American women in the late nineteenth century was that of the Victorian housewife. Virtuous and submissive, the housewife was revered and suffocated by a male-dominated society. The proper role of women was outlined in a mountain of prescriptive literature, and historians have written a good deal about this literature. Only recently, however, have historians begun to evaluate the extent to which the Victorian image fit the reality of women's lives.

In the following selection, Robert L. Griswold uses the methodology of the new social history to analyze the status and relationships of women in San Mateo and Santa Clara counties between 1850 and 1890. His sources are typical of the new social historians: manuscript censuses, county directories, and local annals. Griswold adds to this mix of evidence the divorce records from county courthouses. As Elaine Tyler May, Nancy Cott, and Linda Kerber have shown elsewhere, divorce records are of vital importance for historians interested in the history of women and the family.[1]

---

[1]See, for instance, Elaine Tyler May, *Great Expectations: Marriage and Divorce in Post-Victorian America* (Chicago, 1980); and Nancy Cott, "Eighteenth-Century Family and Social Life

The records contain letters, sworn testimonies, and depositions which provide unique and intimate details about married life. By cross-tabulating such data, Griswold is able to draw a remarkable portrait of nineteenth-century California women.

Among the major findings of Griswold's study is a shift toward a companionate ideal of marriage and away from harsh, patriarchal male-dominated relationships. Increasingly, women were willing to initiate divorce proceedings, and the courts were willing to recognize women's complaints based on ideals of mutuality, the necessity of men to respect their wives, and the domestic power of women. Likewise, Griswold demonstrates that women were more likely to desert bad marriages than were men, suggesting that a vision of female independence was growing in acceptance.

Newly independent women had a variety of options for support, the most important of which was employment. Griswold finds that nearly half of all working women in his study were employed as domestics. Here is another rejoinder to popular stereotypes of women of the period. As T. A. Larson discovered in his analysis of women workers in the west, while women most commonly were employed as domestics they were almost never portrayed as such in western literature.[2] Griswold's most startling conclusions are on the sexual independence of California women. The variance between the Victorian image of the sexless woman and the reality of sexual liberation is considerable.

Robert L. Griswold received his Ph.D. from Stanford University in 1979 and is currently an Associate Professor of History at the University of Oklahoma. He is the author of *Family and Divorce in California, 1850–1890: Victorian Illusions and Everyday Realities* (1982).

Revealed in Massachusetts Divorce Records,'' *Journal of Social History,* X (1976), 20–43.

[2]T. A. Larson, ''Women's Role in the American West,'' *Montana: The Magazine of Western History,* XXIV (Summer 1974), 3–11.

READING 13

Marriage and Divorce in Victorian California

Robert L. Griswold

The popular image of victorian housewives is not a flattering one: the tableau usually includes husbands commanding obedience from all members of the family and wives busying themselves in the front parlor or fluttering about the nursery. Women, according to this view, are sentimental, maternal, and above all dependent upon and submissive to their unemotional, rational, and austere husbands. This popular image is not without historical foundation. Nineteenth-century moralists urged upon women a set of values known collectively as the "cult of true womanhood" and with unremitting persistence they advised women to center their lives around piety, purity, submissiveness, and domesticity.[1] This cult, so historians and social critics have argued, condemned women to the private world of home and family and cut them off from the social world inhabited by their husbands. Nineteenth-century wives were praised as angels, but treated like China dolls; cheered for their domesticity, but banned from public life; honored for their nurturing, but saddled with child care. The vacuous praise, the argument goes, merely covered the real oppression women experienced.

But did the cult of true womanhood strip wives of their independence and leave them captives in the home? The answer lies in finding evidence that reveals the actual marital situation of nineteenth-century women, evidence that goes beyond the exhortations of moralists and offers clues as to the real options open to women. This study draws upon such evidence—divorce records—to explore the family life of nineteenth-century wives in San Mateo and Santa Clara counties of California between 1850 and 1890.[2] An analysis of 401 cases offers both statistical evidence and personal testimony suggesting that married women were not without options and that, through their own initiative or the help of friends and relatives, they could and did take action independent of their husbands.

DIVORCE AND DESERTION

Simply filing for a divorce is, of course, an independent action, and as Nancy Cott revealed in her study of the relationship between divorce and the status of women in eighteenth-century Massachusetts, an increasingly large number of women were exercising such an option. She also argued persuasively that the disproportionate growth in women's divorce petitions "suggests that they, even more than men, had rising expectations in marriage" and that women's increased success in gaining favorable decrees meant that the status of women improved during that century. Cott found that between 1692 and 1774, only 49 percent of the wives bringing suit received favorable decrees, but that between 1775 and 1786, 70 percent were successful petitioners; moreover, in that revolutionary decade, 62 percent of the petitioners were women, in contrast to earlier decades when the proportion of husbands bringing suit was either equal to or higher than that of wives.[3] The divorce evidence from California shows that this trend extended into the nineteenth century and that the divorce court had become an effective means by which wives could gain independence from their husbands. In the 1850s and 1860s, women brought 75

Adapted from "Apart but Not Adrift: Wives, Divorce, and Independence in California 1850–1890," by Robert L. Griswold. Copyright © 1980 by the American Historical Association, Pacific Coast Branch. Reprinted from *Pacific Historical Review*, vol. XLIX, No. 2, pp. 265–283, by permission of the Association.

percent of the suits; in the 1870s, 74 percent; and in the 1880s, 65 percent. When the analysis shifts to actual decrees of divorce, the data reveal that women in approximately 90 percent of the cases either won the case or had it dismissed; thus, for all the emphasis placed on the sanctity of women's place in the nineteenth-century home, judges were by no means reluctant to grant divorces. Table 1 shows by decade the percentage of female plaintiffs who either received a divorce or dismissed their own complaints.

Far from being hostile to women's desires, the divorce court, as the figures in Table 1 reveal, was an effective institution enabling women to start new lives. Community and family pressure certainly kept many women from filing for divorce, but when they finally summoned the courage to face economic uncertainty and social stigma, wives could expect a favorable disposition by the court.

But despite the increasing number of women in divorce court and the success they encountered there, many women chose a more direct and cheaper way to gain independence from their husbands. Perhaps the boldest display of independence from a wife came when she simply deserted her husband and made no attempt to obtain a divorce. Desertion was by far the most common complaint levied against women, and women were also more likely to be charged with and found guilty of desertion than were men; women were charged with desertion in 64

percent of the cases brought by men, but men were so charged in just 37.7 percent of the actions brought by women. The bases of divorce judgments showed a similar pattern; a finding of desertion appeared in 40 percent of the judgments against husbands and in 64 percent of the judgments against wives. Tables 2 and 3 compare both the incidence of different legal complaints brought against men and women and the bases of divorce judgments by sex.[4]

These tables suggest that desertion was the major way in which women escaped an intolerable situation in which husbands had the preponderance of physical and economic power. While husbands might turn to cruelty, drink, or general indolence to vent their frustrations, women more often simply abandoned the home when marriage soured.

Significantly, women from all class backgrounds were willing to incur the risks that came with desertion.[5] The percentage of women found guilty of desertion, as Table 4 reveals, showed no dramatic skewing at either end of the social scale. But one difference among classes and women's mobility appears when the location of the service of summons is examined by class: women from upper-class backgrounds were more likely to live far from their estranged husbands than were women from other classes. Table 5 compares by class

TABLE 1 DIVORCE AWARDS AND DISMISSALS FOR WOMEN PLAINTIFFS BY DECADES

	I		II		I+II
Decade of complaint	Plaintiffs receiving divorces		Cases dismissed by plaintiff		
	%	(N)	%	(N)	%
1850s and 1860s	73.1	(19)	11.5	(3)	84.6
1870s	89.2	(66)	9.5	(7)	98.7
1880s	80.6	(108)	16.4	(22)	97.0

TABLE 2 DIVORCE COMPLAINTS AGAINST MEN AND WOMEN

Type of complaint	Brought by husbands against wives (total N=125)		Brought by wives against husbands (total N=276)	
	%	(N)	%	(N)
Desertion	64	(80)	37.7	(104)
Intemperance	9.6	(12)	21.4	(59)
Adultery	20.8	(26)	10.9	(30)
Nonsupport	0.0	(0)	48.2	(133)
Felony conviction	0.0	(0)	.4	(1)
Cruelty	20.8	(26)	45.7	(126)

TABLE 3 DIVORCE JUDGMENTS AGAINST MEN AND WOMEN

Basis of judgment	Against wives (total N=75) %	(N)	Against husbands (total N=197) %	(N)
Desertion	64	(48)	40	(78)
Intemperance	5	(4)	20	(39)
Adultery	28	(21)	9	(18)
Nonsupport	1	(1)	45	(88)
Felony conviction	0	(0)	1	(1)
Cruelty	13	(10)	34	(66)

TABLE 4 DESERTION JUDGMENTS AGAINST WOMEN, BY CLASS

Social class of wife	% of women in each class found guilty of desertion (total N)	
Upper class	50.0	(16)
Middle class	44.4	(9)
Farmers	37.5	(8)
High trades	18.2	(11)
Low trades	50.0	(6)
Laborers	40.0	(5)

the percentage of locally served summonses with summonses either published or served out of state.[6]

Two explanations for this sharp contrast seem reasonable. First, upper-class women's

TABLE 5 LOCATION OF THE SERVICE OF SUMMONS, BY CLASS

		I Served in same country as divorce filing (%)	II Served in California but outside county (%)	I+II (%)	Served outside state or published (%)
Social class of wife	(N)				
Upper class	(13)	7.7	15.4	23.1	76.9
Middle class	(7)	42.9	28.6	71.5	28.5
Farmers	(7)	57.1	14.3	71.4	28.6
High trades	(8)	62.5	12.5	75.0	25.0
Low trades	(6)	66.7	16.7	83.4	16.6
Laborers	(5)	60.0	20.0	80.0	20.0

access to money may have enabled them to leave California or to refuse to go there with their husbands, either action making them liable for a charge of desertion. Second, upper-class women, who were (in this study) for the most part the wives of lawyers, doctors, and merchants, may have felt particularly sensitive to social respectability and have fled the area rather than stay and face their neighbors once they were sued for divorce.

WORKING WOMEN

Women without their husbands encountered a hostile economic environment, but many women, nevertheless, were up to the challenge. The economic situation of wives who deserted their husbands is unknown—in these cases it is the husbands, not the wives, who appear in the divorce records—but the economic situation of wives deserted by their husbands or wives forced to leave cruel, intemperate, or financially nonsupporting husbands can be analyzed. Either situation required a woman to support herself or to turn to the community for help. The jobs held by the wives in this study are shown in Table 6.[7]

Menial occupations comprised 81 percent (65/80) of the work mentioned in the records, and nonmenial work made up the other 19 percent (15/80). The high percentage of women doing menial work paradoxically reveals both the narrowness of job opportunities for wives

TABLE 6 OCCUPATION OF WIVES

Nonmenial	(N)	Menial	(N)
Actress	(1)	Domestic	(37)
Bookkeeper	(1)	Seamstress	(17)
Clerk	(1)	Prostitutes (alleged)	(7)
Hotelkeeper	(1)		
Doctor	(1)	Cooks/servants	(4)
Storekeeper	(2)		—
Nurse	(2)		(65)
Teacher	(6)		
	—		
	(15)		

and the fact that jobs did exist that enabled them to use their domestic skills. The menial-jobs clearly kept women in a domestic setting. Domestics, seamstresses, cooks, and servants spent their days not in the hurly-burly of the marketplace but in the protective confines of the home. Even among the nonmenial workers, the two nurses and six teachers worked in jobs thought particularly appropriate for women. For the great majority of these wives, then, self-support entailed no severe displacement from one sphere to another but merely a transfer of skills within a familiar setting. While such narrow job opportunities surely discouraged some wives from supporting themselves, the fact that women could use their domestic skills to earn an income must have encouraged others.

Specific cases reveal the determination and self-confidence of wives despite the economic obstacles they faced. J. W. Landon twice overheard William Hendrickson urge his wife to return home, but on both occasions she adamantly refused, telling him "to take care of himself and that she would look out for herself."[8] Annie Parker showed similar determination and self-confidence. When her husband deserted her in Linden, California, Annie testified: "I came to San Francisco to find employment and better my condition." By her own labor and with the help of friends, she succeeded.[9] Susan Battey and Mary Gray did the same. When Battey discovered that her husband expected her to live in a decrepit flophouse, she became a laundress and secured decent quarters. Gray, who left her husband because of his cruelty, worked so profitably as a dressmaker that she bought property in Redwood City.[10] Elaika Mattson, a miner's wife, possessed similar determination. She endured a year of wifebeating and then, at the age of nineteen, escaped the cruelty and earned her own living. After five years on her own, she filed for divorce. When asked why she had waited so long to bring suit, she replied that she had to save enough money to bring a case. Her

diligence was rewarded in 1881 when she received a divorce.[11]

An estranged wife's economic situation did not depend solely on her ability to support herself. Wives left in financial straits by indolent or departed husbands could turn to neighbors, friends, or relatives for help. Table 7 summarizes the sources of such aid for those women who provided this information in the divorce proceedings. (The total percentage is greater than 100 because women often received support from more than one source.) The table reveals that women depended primarily on themselves for support.[12] Despite the poor job opportunities, three-fourths of the wives earned at least part of their own livelihood. The other sources of help were split almost evenly between kin (parents, children, siblings, and other relatives) and friends or neighbors.

Unfortunately, the records do not indicate the size of the contributions so the absolute numbers may be deceiving. Parental help, for example, was probably more substantial and of longer duration than neighborly aid. Nevertheless, the number of wives receiving community charity is striking. Women who "failed" in marriage were obviously not social pariahs avoided by their friends.

However, this community support was not automatic but usually came only after the wife's innocence or guilt had been established in the

TABLE 7 SOURCES OF SUPPORT FOR WIVES

Source of support	Women who mentioned receiving such support (total N=172)	
	%	(N)
Supported by Self	75.0	(129)
Supported by Friends/Neighbors	37.8	(65)
Supported by Parents	15.6	(27)
Supported by Relatives	15.1	(26)
Supported by Children	6.4	(11)
Supported by Siblings	5.2	(9)

eyes of the community. When income sources for female plaintiffs (the innocent party) are compared with sources for female defendants (the accused party), sharp differences emerge, particularly in the support offered by friends and neighbors. Wives bringing suit received help from the community in 46.0 percent of the cases (total N = 134); but the same figure for women accused of destroying the marriage was a mere 7.9 percent (total N = 38). Community assistance was an accurate barometer of wifely morals; it was high when her actions were judged morally correct and almost nonexistent when her character was in question.[13]

For Victorian wives, life without a husband was hard but not impossible. Friends and relatives were willing to help, and their aid, coupled with the wife's own labor, meant that a husband's desertion or nonsupport was not catastrophic. Certainly the transition from domestic duties to work outside the home was eased by the domestic nature of much of the work, but the high percentage of women who supported themselves speaks well for their ability, when necessary, to move beyond dependence on their husbands.[14]

THE WORLD OF LOVE AND RITUAL

Economic support from relatives and friends was not the only kind of assistance wives received. Women also relied on other women for moral and sororal support. The "female world of love and ritual," so perceptively analyzed by Carroll Smith-Rosenberg, was a world of intense, life-long, and special friendships which could be called upon in times of crisis.[15] This is dramatically revealed in the case of Samantha Hughes, a farmer's wife, who was accused of desertion by her husband in 1863. Sometime earlier Elisha Hughes had written her a letter asking her to return and suggesting that she must be miserable now that they no longer lived together. Her reply appears in the divorce records. "You are very much mistaken," she told him. "I *am not* sad and lonely. I am only in

bad health." She then thanked him for his offer of assistance but quickly added, "I do not neede [*sic*] anything. I am as happy as any one can be who is in bad health. I have a good home with Julia and plenty of good kinde [*sic*] friends." Samantha's language became even bolder and more resolute: "I would beg, starve, and die rather than live with you againe [*sic*]. I do not want a husband. All I want is a good home and that I have with Julia and will have as longe [*sic*] as she lives....I never will live with you againe [*sic*]. Do you understand, never NEVER."[16]

Such sororal assistance threatened men who feared an independent wife. In 1882 Edwin Parker, an unemployed school teacher, was accused of cruelty and failure to support his wife. He attributed his wife's charges to her association with a group of women in San Francisco whom he disparaged as a "batch of low bred scandal loving women...who kneel at the shrine of a religion which teaches its devotees that they ought to leave their *undeveloped husbands* and seek their affinity elsewhere." Chief among the "low bred" and the woman responsible for convincing his wife to search for a rich husband (in contrast to an "undeveloped" one) was a "medium, Mrs. Wilson, No. 675 Mission Street, [who] received a communication from some one purporting to be her first husband that she ought to leave that undeveloped man." Edwin, often unemployed and anything but wealthy, saw a cabal of women—led by a mystic who communicated with her dead husband—luring his wife to the pursuit of a rich husband. He concluded a rather bizarre letter to his wife by revealing just how threatened he was by her new-found independence: "So you have secured the pound of flesh and...now as I assume the role of a mind reader for the time being, I can see you as you fly away on the wings of fancy to some drawing room, yourself the central figure reposing as a boudoir flower, all troubles at an end."[17] Certainly his wife's association with these women—whatever the merits of their beliefs—gave her a degree of support and independence that left her husband angry, threatened, and slightly dumbfounded.

If women drew strength and support from other women, they drew them as well from relatives. Disputes on moving to California offer evidence that wives were not powerless when husbands made unilateral decisions to head West. In the following cases, the women either refused to leave or returned to the state in which they were married. If we assume marriage occurred at the bride's home, then these women chose their families of birth over their families of marriage. While this choice may seem like no great show of independence, it does suggest that women were not without options and that families were flexible and forgiving when daughters made choices that contravened the female role.

Jennie Denson, for example, refused to accompany her new husband to Galveston, Texas, soon after her marriage in 1876, but she did agree to move to New Orleans because it was closer to her home in Tennessee. To the detriment of his business, Richard Denson moved to Louisiana where his wife joined him, but in a few days she announced her refusal to live "in any other city or place in the world except at her home among her folks at or in the immediate neighborhood of Moscow, Tennessee." Denson refused to "sacrifice all his business affairs," and she refused to budge from Tennessee. The marriage ended with Jennie at home and Richard in California.[18]

Parental security also provided Zilpha Plumb with the confidence to remain apart from her husband when, after going bankrupt, he decided to recoup his fortunes in the West. She refused to follow him. "We had been living in Boston, Massachusetts and I failed in business," he explained to the divorce court. "My wife left and went to her mother's home in Orleans County, New York, since which time we have never lived together." His wife's stubbornness—coupled with economic support from her mother—enabled her to defy her hus-

band's intentions: "She refused to return then, and repeatedly since that time....She has refused all and every offer I have made to her for reconciliation."[19] Addie Gray was another who refused to leave her relatives behind. Her stepdaughter overheard Addie tell her husband that she would not leave Illinois, and Addie personally informed her stepdaughter "that she would not under any consideration reside in the state of California."[20]

The experiences of other wives reveal that unilateral decisions by husbands to move were often fraught with danger when women had alternatives at their disposal. Park Henshaw convinced his wife to leave Missouri, but he failed to keep her in California after they reached Chico in 1877. Soon after arriving, she told a friend that she "did not like California," "regretted that she had come," "would not live in California and wanted to return to Missouri." When her two children died, Ella returned to her home in Missouri, later came back to California for one month, then returned again to Missouri, this time permanently, even though "Mr. Henshaw had gone to considerable expense in fitting up a house for them to live in."[21]

The love of kin and community also persuaded Emma Waterbury, Mary King, Jane Keith, and Emily Merrill to remain in their home state rather than make the trip to California. Like others, William Waterbury came to California in 1869 to "better my condition." A year later he sent for his wife because he "was anxious to have her with me." The feeling was far from reciprocated; she would neither leave her home in Virginia nor respond to his letters, and in 1883 William received a divorce on grounds of desertion.[22] Mary King and her husband married in Wisconsin and lived there for eight years before her husband was transferred to California. She refused to accompany him, an act of independence that resulted in a successful desertion suit against her.[23] For ten years, Jane Keith adamantly refused to leave Illinois to join her husband in California. Twice he sent his brother to Illinois to fetch her, and both times she refused to leave. Joseph Keith finally sued for divorce in 1865.[24] Brave words accompanied Emily Merrill's decision to stay in Maine when, five months after marriage, her husband announced they were moving to California. He could go where he pleased, she told him, but "she was capable of taking care of herself and intended to do so...." Three years later, Emily was still in Maine, reputedly living in bigamy with farmer James Miller.[25]

SEXUAL INDEPENDENCE

Another important area of female independence is virtually inaccessible to historical inquiry. Much to the dismay of their husbands, some wives refused to suppress their extramarital sexual desires, a refusal suggesting that the Victorian woman's alleged lack of interest in sex stemmed more from the fervent hopes of moralists than from reality. Women were not sexless, passionless creatures hopelessly locked in a suffocating domestic world. Nineteenth-century moralists might insist on sexual fidelity in marriage, they might insist that all women, regardless of social class, subscribe to the tenets of Victorian sexual morality, but dissatisfied women could establish a new sexual relationship if the opportunity arose and their sense of independence overcame the pull of contemporary morality.[26] Ann Stevens was such a woman.

Five years after marriage, Lew Stevens suspected his wife had committed adultery, and in late 1883, he brought a divorce suit against her. As part of the evidence, he included two letters his wife had written her lover, and though it was unclear how the letters made their way into court, they left no doubt that Ann was an independent woman enthusiastic about sexual activity. She was also quite clever. Ann wrote parts of the letters, specifically some of the sections dealing with sex, in an ingenious code comprised of number substitutes for letters—the strange mix of "f38d th2 wly 5p y457 t94ws29s" became "find the way up your trowsers" when decoded. Moreover, she was not one to be put off by community pressure. When a friend disparagingly remarked that Ann apparently thought "a good deal" of Walter Knight, her lover, Ann defended her sentiments: "I told him I certainly did. I never should deny that at all. I told him I had a perfect right to think a good deal of you." Never mind she was a married woman living in a small California town. Ann also described to Walter how she planned to increase the friction within her marriage: "There is going to be a picnic here in Woodside next Sunday and I am going just to plague Lew. I am going everywhere I can [and] nothing will make him mad so quick as that." She hoped by such behavior to drive her husband away so that she and Walter could get together. "He thinks I do not care anything for him. That is just what I want—I hope I can act so that he will go to Colorado and if he once goes I will take good care he never comes back."[27]

Until Lew left, Ann could only fantasize about the future, but her letters gave her lover a vivid sense of the sexual enjoyments to come. Ann Stevens—and certainly many other Victorian women as well—bore little resemblance to the "typical" Victorian woman described by William Acton as "not very much troubled with sexual feelings of any kind."[28] After lamenting her loneliness, Ann excitedly wrote that she might soon visit Chico, Walter's town: "Then there would be some tall diddling done and a little hugging thrown in....And when I see you again, perhaps I might find the way up your trowsers leg. At the same time, if I could see you a few minutes, I should sit down on you a few times."[29] In a letter written several weeks later, Ann even more directly stated her sexual desires: "I wish you was here tonight. I am upstairs in my room where you slept—and if you was here, I suppose we should do some tall fucking." Ann ended this second letter on a bittersweet note as she reaffirmed her sexual desires yet bemoaned her separation from Walter: "Oh how I wish you was round so I could get hold of you now and then. I just feel like having a racket with you once in awhile and there *you* are and *here* I am. I hope we won't always be so far apart. I can be near enough to them I care nothing for."[30]

The behavior of Julia Grosjean, like that of Ann Stevens, exhibited a lusty independence not generally associated with Victorian womanhood. Camille Grosjean, a successful grocer, described the disgrace he incurred due to his wife's behavior. "Whenever I took her into society she would act like a woman of loose character, and finally she was shunned by the best people in town." Her impropriety consisted of "flirting with everyone she met, and making love to married men with whom she was thrown into contact, until her name had become a byword for extreme levity of character if nothing worse...." Camille worried that she would "ruin and disgrace me," a fear that suggests the close relationship between female sexual propriety and social standing among the middle class.[31] He then offered an explanation for her behavior that was restrained but firmly anchored in Victorian morality: "I can only say this. She could have no other reason than she could not be satisfied with the restraint of a virtuous life. She loved and coveted the admiration of other men, and in that respect she was unfit for the duties and responsibilities of wifehood and motherhood. I do not desire to speak stronger than this in regard to one that bears the station of wife to me." Grosjean had offered a classic Victorian indictment of his wife. She lacked restraint and virtue, her dedication to her husband was grossly suspect, and her general character meant she was ill-equipped for that most womanly of tasks—motherhood. Camille concluded by sadly noting the strength of the public's association of a husband with his wife, an association that gave Julia a negative but powerful influence over her husband: "Af-

ter she left, I remained some time intending to brave it out, but the disgrace of her conduct made it impossible for me to continue business [any] longer in Houston."[32] The moral weight of polite society was too great to bear; like others, Camille went West to get a fresh start.

While Lew Stevens and Camille Grosjean could not control their wives' extramarital affairs, Cornelius Paddock had a problem of a different sort. In 1877, the teamster complained that his wife repeatedly embarrassed him despite his patient efforts to curb her indelicacies. She sang lewd songs in front of friends and, on one occasion, had allegedly exposed herself to others at their home in Woodside by "lifting up her clothes and undergarments to her waist, having no drawers on and exposing her person." He also stated she caused him great anguish when she would tip back in her chair, "open her limbs, and indecently expose her person."[33] To prove his wife's intractableness, Cornelius obtained the testimony of a former lodger, Charles Peterson, who at one time had shared the same bedroom with Cornelius and his wife. "She sat down in a chair," recalled Peterson, "and told Ida, her daughter, to wash her feet and [then] she pulled her clothes up over her knees. She had drawers on as far as I noticed. She pulled her clothes up above her knees....She lay back in the chair and screamed something. I went outside." The court asked if Peterson considered her exposure indecent: "Yes, if a man had a good view of her." On other occasions, the lodger "saw her sit down in chairs and pull her clothes up and put her feet upon the stove." He also remembered a lewd song that the irrepressible Ann Paddock had insisted on singing. "She sung a song in 1876. The song was beef steak, mutton chop and a little old hat. Mr. Paddock told her if she wanted to sing such a song to go outside and sing it." Peterson was slightly uncertain about the lyrics but quite sure that a true lady had no business singing them: "The meaning so far as I understand must be a fast house song. It means if you get hold of a woman, you want a little from her."[34] Peterson, it should be noted, was no sensitive shrinking violet. At the time he testified, the laborer was a prisoner at San Quentin penitentiary.

The disposition of the Paddock case revealed a judge less concerned with household propriety than with a rising divorce rate. After Cornelius had presented his evidence, the judge dismissed the case: "The acts proven are only a little peevishness and some little jealousy," he declared, "but in my opinion are not such acts as are by the statutes considered good grounds for a divorce." They "do not endanger life or render matrimonial intercourse unsafe, and ought not even to render it unpleasant to a man of philosophic turn of mind."[35] Apparently Cornelius lacked—and the judge possessed—that turn of mind that might find something oddly refreshing in Ann's eccentric independence. Moreover, the judge believed that divorces "are becoming too common in this country and courts should in all cases require *full* statutory proof before dissolving so sacred a relation as that which should exist between husband and wife."[36] In light of the rising divorce rate, the judge reasoned that nineteenth-century marriage had ample room for female independence even if the wife's actions directly annoyed the husband's sensibilities.

If nineteenth-century American society restricted a wife's economic opportunities and the cult of true womanhood relegated her to the home, she nonetheless could find alternatives to a life of constant submission and obedience. While many of the women in this study were perhaps more courageous than most in their willingness to test or break what people agreed was a sacred bond, the kinds of options and support available to them were open to other women as well. Self-support or assistance from friends and relatives helped wives overcome financial dependency on their husbands; a community of kin and friends protected wives against unilateral decisions made by husbands; and close friendships with other women provided emotional support in the difficult process of ending a marriage.

Notes

The author thanks Professors Carl Degler and Terrence McDonald for their helpful suggestions and criticisms and the Center for Research on Women at Stanford University for providing financial assistance during the early research on this project.

1 On the cult of true womanhood, see Barbara Welter, "The Cult of True Womanhood: 1820–1860," *American Quarterly*, XVIII (1966), 151–174. The analysis of this domestic ideology has been refined by Nancy Cott, *The Bonds of Womanhood: "Woman's Sphere" in New England, 1780–1835* (New Haven, 1977), 8, 22, 63–100; and Kathryn Kish Sklar, *Catherine Beecher: A Study in American Domesticity* (New Haven, 1973), 158–167.

2 The divorce cases are from the Divorce Records of District and Superior Courts, 1864–1890, San Mateo County Hall of Justice and Records, Redwood City, California; and Divorce Records of District and Superior Courts, 1850–1890, Santa Clara County Superior Court House, San Jose, California. Throughout the period 1850 to 1890, these two San Francisco Bay Area counties were rural communities with an economy dominated by farms and small shops. Santa Clara had a population of slightly less than 50,000 by 1890 and San Mateo barely rose over 10,000. The divorce cases start with a Santa Clara case in December 1850 (San Mateo's first case came fourteen years later in 1864) and end with cases tried in December 1889 in both counties. The first date in the title is that of the earliest case on record and the second date marks that point where written testimony appeared infrequently and the cases provided less valuable evidence for historical analysis. The San Mateo evidence includes every case during these years, a total of 197 suits; in Santa Clara County, the larger population necessitated a systematic sample of every fifth case, a procedure that yielded 204 cases. Thus the total number in the study is 401 cases involving 276

female plaintiffs (68.8 percent) and 125 male plaintiffs (31.2 percent). Of these 401 cases, 272 (68 percent) ended in a divorce for one party or the other. All data unless otherwise noted are taken from this sample.

These 401 families represented part of a growing nationwide trend. For whatever reasons, Californians along with other Americans would not tolerate behavior that their parents and grandparents had accepted as a normal part of marriage. In the United States from 1870 to 1880, the population rose 30.1 percent but the divorce rate jumped by 79.4 percent; in the next decade the population increased by 25.5 percent and the divorce rate 70.2 percent. The rate of divorce increased even faster in the two California counties; for example, in the 1880s, the counties' population increased 33 percent but the divorce rate went up by 101 percent. For the national figures, see U. S. Bureau of the Census, *Special Reports: Marriage and Divorce, 1867–1906* (Washington, D.C., 1909), Part 1, 12.

3 Nancy Cott, "Divorce and the Changing Status of Women in Eighteenth-Century Massachusetts," *William and Mary Quarterly,* XXXIII (1976), 586–614; see also her article, "Eighteenth-Century Family and Social Life Revealed in Massachusetts Divorce Records," *Journal of Social History,* X (1976), 20–43.

4 From the start, California law provided wideranging grounds for divorce. By an act of 1851, a man or woman who had established residence for six months could sue for divorce on the following grounds: natural impotency, adultery, extreme cruelty, willful desertion or neglect, habitual intemperance, fraud, and conviction for a felony. From 1851 to 1872, various legislative acts reduced the period required for a spouse to demonstrate intemperance, desertion, and neglect from three years to a year; after 1872, the divorce statutes remained relatively unchanged, and the six grounds available to the plaintiff—adultery, cruelty, desertion, neglect, intemperance, and conviction for a felony—provided ample legal opportunity for unhappy California husbands and wives to escape from their bonds. See *Statutes of California: Second Session, 1851,* pp. 186–187; *Statutes of California: Eighteenth Session, 1869–1870,* p. 291; *West's Annotated California Codes: Civil Code, Sections 1 to 192* (St. Paul, 1954), 337. In Tables 2 and 3, the complaints are arranged according to several categories. Many individuals were sued on more than one ground, and rather than list the permutations, I have organized the complaints (and the grounds of judgment) as shown in the tables. For this reason, the numbers in the columns add up to more than the "total N" listed in the column headings.

5 From the divorce records, county directories, manuscript censuses, and county histories, the occupations of more than half the sample were found, and these occupations were then grouped into six classes based roughly upon the same scheme employed by Michael Katz in his study of Hamilton, Ontario. (See Katz, *The People of Hamilton, Canada West: Family and Class in a Mid-Nineteenth Century City* [Cambridge, Mass., 1975], passim.) Those classes consist of the following: 1) the upper class—businessmen, merchants, lawyers, and ranchers; 2) the middle class—bookkeepers, dentists, druggists, and storekeepers; 3) farmers; 4) high trades—such skilled tradesmen as bakers, carpenters, cooks, and tailors; 5) low trade—miners, teamsters, millworkers, and other unskilled tradesmen; and 6) laborers—those men who identified themselves as such or were so identified by others; their ranks included both town and rural laborers as well as men described as "unemployed" who were clearly not tradesmen, farmers, or members of the upper class. Of the 203 heads of families whose occupations were identified, 17 percent were classified as upper class, 17 percent as middle class, 14 percent as farmers, 19 percent as skilled workers, 9 percent as unskilled artisans, and 24 percent as laborers. Of course, unless the full occupational structure of the two counties is known, we cannot tell whether one class or another was over- or underrepresented. But even without this detailed analysis—an analysis that could be done with the manuscript census but is beyond the scope of this essay—the high number of working-class people is nevertheless surprising.

6 Table 5 includes all women defendants whose class background was identified and for whom summons information was available; that is, this

table includes women sued for divorce on all grounds, not just those sued for desertion.

7 Nationally, over 95 percent of white married women did not work outside the home in the nineteenth century. The sizeable percentage of working wives in this study stemmed from the fact that most of these California women worked because their husbands either refused to support them or because their husbands had deserted them. On the figures for working women, see Daniel Scott Smith, "Family Limitation, Sexual Control, and Domestic Feminism in Victorian America," *Feminist Studies,* I (Winter-Spring, 1973), 42–43.

8 *William* v. *Sophia Hendrickson,* Case 382, San Mateo County, 1882 (testimony of J. W. Landon). This form of citation will be used throughout the essay. The date (1882) refers to the year in which the plaintiff's divorce complaint was filed. The information in parentheses refers to the specific source of the information. The cases are without pagination.

9 *Annie* v. *Edwin Parker,* Case 403, San Mateo County, 1882 (testimony of Annie Parker).

10 *Walter* v. *Susan Battey,* Case 1404, Santa Clara County, 1860 (defendant's answer); *Mary* v. *James Gray,* Case 635, San Mateo County, 1885 (formal complaint).

11 *Elaika* v. *Marlin Mattson,* Case 214, San Mateo County, 1880 (testimony of Elaika Mattson).

12 The records generally indicate that most women supported themselves and, in addition, received help from various people. The evidence does not, however, reveal the pattern of support. Thus, for example, it is impossible to determine whether women who supported themselves received steady additional aid from their parents or friends or received such help only in times of crisis. Nor can it be determined if children volunteered support or were requested to do so by their mother or her concerned friends. For 229 cases, there was no information whatsoever on the wife's economic situation.

13 These figures came only from those cases which included information about the woman's source(s) of support, regardless of whether she was the plaintiff or the defendant. Not surprisingly, most cases in which females were defendants contained no information about their economic

situations, but these cases were not included in the comparison above.

14 On the purposeful, instrumental nature of wives' domestic labor, see Cott, *The Bonds of Womanhood,* 42 ff., 54–58, 63–100; and Sklar, *Catherine Beecher,* 151–167. Also, see my "The Character of the Family in Rural California, 1850–1890" (Ph.D. dissertation, Stanford University, 1979), 61–69.

15 Carroll Smith-Rosenberg, "The Female World of Love and Ritual," *Signs: A Journal of Women in Culture and Society,* I (1975), 1–30.

16 *Elisha* v. *Samantha Hughes,* Case 1810, Santa Clara County, 1863 (letter of Samantha Hughes to Elisha Hughes). Emphasis in original. Samantha's friend, Arena Gardner, also testified that Samantha had no intention of living with her husband: "I have heard her say she never would live with him. Had heard her say so frequently. We had several conversations about it. She told me she would starve before she would live with him."

17 *Annie* v. *Edwin Parker,* Case 403, San Mateo County, 1882 (letters of Edwin Parker to his wife and to the superior court judge). On the importance of mediums in many women's lives in the nineteenth century, see R. Laurence Moore, *In Search of White Crows: Spiritualism, Parapsychology and American Culture* (New York, 1977).

18 *Richard* v. *Jennie Denson,* Case 1268, San Mateo County, 1878 (formal complaint).

19 *Mills* v. *Zilpha Plumb,* Case 364, San Mateo County, 1882 (testimony of Mills Plumb).

20 *William* v. *Addie Gray,* Case 480, San Mateo County, 1883 (testimony of Carrie Gray).

21 *Park* v. *Ella Henshaw,* Case 837, San Mateo County, 1887 (testimony of Cora Kennedy). Ella was married in Missouri.

22 *William* v. *Emma Waterbury,* Case 419, San Mateo County, 1882 (testimony of William Waterbury).

23 *Will* v. *Mary King,* Case 375, San Mateo County, 1882 (formal complaint).

24 *Joseph* v. *Jane Keith,* Case 385, San Mateo County, 1865 (testimony of Elisha Keith).

25 *Ruell* v. *Emily Merrill,* Case 895, San Mateo County, 1873 (formal complaint). For other cases of wives preferring to live in the state where they married, see *Joseph* v. *Helen Gilpatrick,* Case

633, San Mateo County, 1869 (formal complaint); *John* v. *Annie Bradbury,* Case 461, San Mateo County, 1883 (formal complaint); *Charles* v. *Kate Leszynsky,* Case 228, San Mateo County, 1881 (formal complaint).

26 Although the cult of feminine purity is generally associated with middle-class women, Carl Degler is surely correct in arguing that middle-class women—and hence middle-class values—"undoubtedly set the tone and provided the models for most women." See Degler, "What Ought to Be and What Was: Women's Sexuality in the Nineteenth Century," *American Historical Review,* LXXIX (1974), 1469. The divorce records also reveal that women from all social classes were expected to follow middle-class ideas about sexual propriety. See my "The Character of the Family in Rural California, 1850–1890," 98–109.

27 *Lew* v. *Ann Stevens,* Case 517, San Mateo County, 1883 (letter of May 4, 1882, from Ann Stevens to Walter Knight).

28 Action is quoted in Degler, "What Ought to Be and What Was," 1467.

29 *Lew* v. *Ann Stevens,* Case 517, San Mateo County, 1883 (letter of May 4, 1882, from Ann Stevens to Walter Knight).

30 Ibid. (letter of May 23, 1882, from Ann Stevens to Walter Knight).

31 *Camille* v. *Julia Grosjean,* Case 345, San Mateo County, 1882 (testimony of Camille Grosjean). "Making love" here apparently refers to flirting and not sexual intercourse; adultery was not charged against Julia.

32 Ibid. (testimony of Camille Grosjean).

33 *Cornelius* v. *Ann Paddock,* Case 1276, San Mateo County, 1877 (amended complaint). This case provides good evidence that middle-class ideas about sexual propriety infused working class values as well. The point of this testimony is to reveal that Ann—a teamster's wife—did not adhere to proper notions of female decorum despite social expectations that she do so.

34 Ibid. (testimony of Charles Peterson).

35 Ibid. (judge's order dismissing the case).

36 Ibid.

CHAPTER

CHINESE LIVELIHOOD

EDITOR'S INTRODUCTION

Most students of California history are familiar with the story of the Chinese. They know that Chinese immigrants were victims of prejudice and discrimination, and that eventually the Chinese were barred from further entry into the United States. Historians who have studied the Chinese in America have devoted much of their attention to the causes and consequences of this anti-Chinese movement.[1] It is hardly surprising, therefore, that general knowledge of Chinese-American history is often centered on those who opposed the Chinese rather than on the immigrants themselves.

The few studies we have of Chinese immigrant communities are focused on various Chinatowns, and on San Francisco's Chinatown in particular. Earlier studies portrayed the more lurid or exotic aspects of the Chinatowns, while recent accounts have examined their social and institutional structure. Yet the majority of the Chinese in California (and the United States) never lived in a Chinatown. The largest proportion of nineteenth-century Chinese immigrants lived in the rural counties of California, at first in mining areas and later in agricultural regions.[2]

Sucheng Chan's *This Bittersweet Soil: The Chinese in California Agriculture, 1860–1910* (1986) is the first major study of the Chinese experience in rural America. As Chan points out, scholars have been slow to study the rural Chinese because of the paucity of primary sources. Newspaper accounts are fragmentary; travelers' accounts, often unreliable.

[1]See, for instance, Elmer Sandmeyer, *The Anti-Chinese Movement in California* (Urbana, 1939); and Alexander Saxton, *The Indispensable Enemy: Labor and the Anti-Chinese Movement in California* (Berkeley, 1971).
[2]Sucheng Chan, "Chinese Livelihood in Rural California: The Impact of Economic Change, 1860–1880," *Pacific Historical Review*, LIII (August 1984), 276.

Chan's sources are the manuscript schedules of the United States census. She cautions, however, that even these sources are problematical. Many Chinese avoided being counted by census takers, fearful that any public notice might lead to persecution. Chan also suggests that inaccuracies crept into the record simply because of the language barrier. Further problems are presented by the physical deterioration of the manuscript schedules—many are faded, torn, or incomplete. Nevertheless, Chan concludes, the manuscript censuses are an indispensable source for any serious student of Chinese-American history.

In the following selection, Sucheng Chan surveys the structure of Chinese livelihood or occupation in California. Her analysis is complex. She compares conditions in mining regions, agricultural counties, and San Francisco as those conditions evolved through four distinct stages between 1850 and 1900. She demonstrates that while many Chinese experienced upward mobility, the overall pattern is one of decline. As Ralph Mann pointed out in a previous selection, although class and ethnic lines in California were not identical, whites consigned the Chinese as a group to the lowest status.

Several scholars have recently warned that much of the new social history fails to place matters in their proper context.[3] One of the great strengths of Chan's analysis, in fact, is her integration of the Chinese experience into the larger political and economic history of the state. She does not deal with the Chinese in isolation; rather, she demonstrates the ways that the Chinese both contributed to and were shaped by larger forces in late nineteenth-century California.

Sucheng Chan received her Ph.D. from the University of California, Berkeley, in 1973, and won the Theodore Saloutos Award for the best book in American agricultural history in 1986. Currently she is a Professor of History and Provost at Oakes College, University of California, Santa Cruz.

---

[3]See Elizabeth Fox-Genovese and Eugene Genovese, "The Political Crisis of Social History: A Marxian Perspective," *Journal of Social History*, X (Winter 1976), 205–219; Laurence Veysey, "The 'New' Social History in the Context of American Historical Writing," *Reviews in American History*, VII (March 1979), 1–12.; and Gertrude Himmelfarb, *The New History and the Old* (Cambridge, Mass., 1987).

Chinese Livelihood

Sucheng Chan

The development of the Chinese occupational pattern in nineteenth-century California may be divided into four stages: an initial period from 1850 to 1865, when the Chinese worked mainly as miners and traders; a period of growth and development from 1865 to the late 1870s, when they branched into agriculture, light manufacturing, and common labor; a period of consolidation from the late 1870s to the late 1880s, when they competed successfully with others in a wide variety of occupations; and a period of decline from the late 1880s to the turn of the century, when they were forced to abandon many occupations. Data tallied from the manuscript schedules of the 1860 census of population provide a glimpse into the first period, data from the 1870 census show the pattern in the years of development, data from the 1880 census give a picture of the period of consolidation, whereas the years of decline are difficult to document because the manuscript schedules of the 1890 census were lost in a fire, so that there is a twenty-year gap between the 1880 and 1900 data.

The occupational pattern of the Chinese differed considerably among the mining regions, the city of San Francisco, and the agricultural counties, reflecting differences in the structure of the three sectors of the California economy—mining, manufacturing, and agriculture—and how Chinese fitted into them. Overall, in the 1850–80 period, mining occupied more Chinese than any other economic activity. Even more important, the presence or absence of mining in an area strongly affected what other occupations the Chinese entered because there was an inverse relationship between the percentage of the Chinese population who mined and those who earned a living as laborers or providers of personal services. Where mining was available, few became laborers or providers of personal services, but as mining waned from the 1860s onward, an increasing number of Chinese became laundrymen, laborers, servants, and cooks. Where mining was not available, the first Chinese to enter those areas had to take menial jobs from the beginning. The proletarianization of the Chinese population was partially arrested in the early 1870s when many Chinese became independent entrepreneurs in light manufacturing and agriculture. While the Chinese engaged in light manufacturing (primarily in San Francisco) for only about a quarter of a century, they farmed all over California for six or seven decades. Therefore, agriculture succeeded mining in providing an economic foundation for Chinese communities in rural California. However, agriculture never dominated the livelihood of rural Chinese in quite the same way that mining had done.

BEGINNINGS

As is shown in Table 1, a large proportion of the Chinese in the three mining regions in 1860 were miners: seven-eighths of those in the Southern Mines, more than four-fifths of those in the Northern Mines, and seven-eighths of the ones in the Klamath/Trinity mining region. In California as a whole, miners constituted over 70 percent of all gainfully employed Chinese above age fifteen; this concentration was more than double the 32 percent found among the non-Chinese population in 1860. Chinese miners were strung out along rivers and streams, since most of them engaged only in placer mining. Few Chinese worked in hardrock areas.

Adapted from *This Bittersweet Soil: The Chinese in California Agriculture, 1860–1910,* by Sucheng Chan, pp. 57–78. Copyright © 1986 by The Regents of the University of California.

All other occupations were subsidiary to and were sustained by the income from mining. In the major mining camps a small number of Chinese merchants, grocers, truck gardeners, cooks, servants, laundrymen, barbers, herbalists, prostitutes, professional gamblers, and even a fortune-teller or two served the subsistence and recreational needs of their fellow countrymen. In each of the three mining regions, professionals made up about 1 percent of the Chinese population, while merchants ranged form 1.5 percent of the Chinese population in the mining camps of the remote Klamath/Trinity mountains to 3.0 percent in the prosperous Southern Mines. In these mining camps and mountain towns, Chinatown took up a few blocks or part of a block in the central district; here, Chinese grocery and general merchandise stores and recreational facilities were clustered. The owners of these enterprises usually lived in the back or the upstairs of their establishments.

The Chinese miners in 1860 were men who had survived a decade of sporadic violence against them. In the 1850s, Chinese had been frequently robbed, beaten, driven away from their diggings, or even killed.[1] As early as 1849, before the arrival of large numbers of Chinese miners, white miners in Tuolumne County were already paranoid enough to pass a resolution to prohibit Chinese from working claims.[2] Chinese had little recourse to justice because an 1850 law that barred Indian and Negro testimony in court was extended to apply to them in 1854.[3] Once in a while, however, some white men out of a sense of fair play defended the Chinese. For example, the *Shasta Republican* reported in late 1856 that Francis Blair was the first white man to be hanged for murdering Chinese.[4] Also, though Chinese miners were expelled from many localities, there were some spots where they managed to work in relative peace for many years consecutively.[5] Chinese miners had also persisted despite a discriminatory Foreign Miners' Tax, first set at twenty dollars a

month but later reduced to either three or four dollars. Originally intended to drive Mexican and Chileno miners away, it soon came to be collected only from Chinese miners. The tax was reduced because too large an amount drove even the Chinese away, and their departure deprived merchants of trade, and county governments of their chief source of revenue. Ping Chiu has calculated that the receipts from this tax provided over half of the total revenue for the mining counties in the 1850s.[6]

From the beginning of Chinese immigration, the Chinese in San Francisco developed an occupational pattern that was quite distinct from that found in the mining regions.[7] Though many of the Chinese counted in the San Francisco census were transients, there was a stable core of people in the city who handled the immigration traffic, San Francisco being the chief port of entry for Chinese immigrants to America. Merchants had already established themselves as representatives of the Chinese community by 1852 when large numbers of aspiring miners came. They had built or rented buildings to house the new arrivals, and soon made money by provisioning them and finding them employment. Even more lucrative were the establishments that served the miners' recreational needs. By 1860 over 10 percent of San Francisco's gainfully employed Chinese males worked in one of several branches of the vice industry: gambling, the sale of opium, and prostitution. In addition, 23.4 percent of the city's Chinese were prostitutes. (Only nonagricultural laborers rivaled the prostitutes in number.) Thus, fully one-third of the gainfully employed Chinese in the city were engaged in providing recreational vices—an unfortunate fact which gave rise to strong negative images of the Chinese. Another notable occupation that San Francisco Chinese engaged in was fishing—an industry that the Chinese dominated in those days—which provided a living for 15 percent of the Chinese population in the county.[8] Merchants not engaged in the vice industry and laundrymen each made up about 5 percent of the city's Chinese population. Most of the merchants and professionals served their fellow countrymen, whereas servants, cooks, laundrymen, laborers, and some prostitutes served whites.

In the late 1860s and early 1870s, the employment of Chinese workers by the Central Pacific Railroad, the decline of placer mining, and the development of manufacturing and agriculture helped to change the occupational distribution of the Chinese in California. The employment of approximately 10,000 Chinese workers by the Central Pacific Railroad confirmed the belief of many Americans that Chinese could be employed in gangs to carry out large construction projects. After the transcontinental railroad was completed, several hundred Chinese were kept on by the Central Pacific for maintaining the right of way and to build branch lines. Thousands more, however, were discharged, and many sought work as common laborers in agriculture and various construction projects, while others became cooks, servants, and laundrymen. This development served to harden the lines of division in California's racial hierarchy, which eventually relegated all Chinese—regardless of their standing within the Chinese immigrant community—to a position well below the lowest class of whites.

GROWTH AND DEVELOPMENT

Data compiled from the manuscript schedules of the 1870 census reveal the changes taking place in this period of change and development.[9] As Table 2 reveals, overall, mining still dominated Chinese livelihood. In the Southern, Northern, and Klamath/Trinity mines, 75.4, 50, and 87.1 percent of the Chinese, respectively, still mined for a living. The 16,000 or so remaining Chinese miners constituted about 35 percent of the gainfully employed Chinese in the state, whereas only about 11 percent of non-Chinese still mined for a

living. More interesting than the Chinese persistence in mining, however, was the fact that developments in the Southern Mines differed from those in the Northern Mines, while the situation in the remote Klamath/Trinity mountains remained more or less the same. The Southern Mines had lost more than half of its Chinese population in the 1860–70 decade as placer mining in that region gave out and other avenues of employment did not open up. In contrast, in the Northern Mines where the Chinese population remained about the same as ten years earlier, half remained as miners while the other half managed to find other means of livelihood, primarily as nonagricultural laborers, whose ranks had swelled from 418 in 1860 to 2,205 in 1870. Providers of various personal services more than doubled from 639 in 1860 to 1,368 in 1870. Such work was available because the western portions of four of the counties in the Northern Mines lay in the Sacramento Valley—an area that provided employment opportunities other than mining.

Though Chinese managed to make a living, from both their own point of view as well as that of white Americans, working as common laborers, servants, and cooks represented a considerable descent in social status from that of independent miners. While they cannot be called an industrial proletariat, these laborers and providers of personal services did constitute an emergent Chinese working class in rural California. Meanwhile, a small number of Chinese had begun to work in factories, woolen mills, and sawmills in the more prosperous mining counties—Placer, El Dorado, and Mariposa. Such individuals were the forerunners of what might have become a true Chinese industrialized proletariat in California. (No such development ever materialized, because of Chinese exclusion.) Finally, as both the absolute number and the percentage of merchants in all three mining regions increased, they began to consolidate their position as the socioeconomic elite in Chinese communities in rural California, just as they had in San Francisco.

Considerable changes had also occurred in San Francisco, which was blossoming into a manufacturing, trade, and service center for Chinese as well as white Californians.[10] Fully 22 percent of the some 12,000 Chinese in the city in 1870 worked in factories, making cigars, shoes and boots, woolen textiles, and clothing. The Civil War had boosted manufacturing in California because it had disrupted the importation of goods from the East Coast. After the war ended, importation resumed, and the lower-priced eastern goods threatened the survival of California's nascent industries. Only those establishments that had low enough production costs to compete against eastern imports managed to survive, and Chinese sweatshops were among them.[11]

As was true of white-owned manufacturing enterprises during this transitional period of industrial development, Chinese production took two forms: artisans, working alone or with a small number of partners and assistants, made most of the manufactured items, but in selected industries, factory production employing wage workers had also begun. For example, shoemakers produced shoes, slippers, and boots in tiny workshops, but boot and shoe factories had also come into being. Similarly, cigar makers worked either in small storefronts or in larger establishments. Tailors and seamstresses had their own shops, but there was also an increasing number of garment workers making underwear, shirts, pants, and overalls in Chinese-owned sewing factories. Thus, from census data alone, it is difficult to determine how many of these individuals can be regarded as wage workers and how many as independent producers.

In addition to these factory workers and independent producers, there were over 1,000 Chinese professionals, artisans, and merchants in the city, along with over 1,300 laundrymen and laundresses. The growth of manufacturing, trade, and services thus greatly enlarged the economic base of San Francisco's Chinatown,

diversifying it, and moving it well beyond its former role as a provider of imported goods and recreational vices.

The other Bay Area counties, though close to San Francisco, did not share in its industrial development. The small valleys they contained were becoming productive agricultural areas, which offered work in farming and fishing to about 30 percent of the Chinese there. Santa Clara County had over 250 Chinese strawberry-growers and over 100 truck gardeners, and Alameda County had over 100 truck gardeners. Chinese had also begun to work as seasonal farm laborers in these counties: Marin, Solano, and Santa Clara counties each had over 100 farm laborers, San Mateo County had almost 200, and Alameda County had over 300. The bulk of the other Chinese found work as laundrymen (9.3 percent), cooks (8.2 percent), servants (6 percent), and common laborers (32.4 percent). Factory workers included 49 who made bags in Alameda County, 64 who made shoes in San Mateo County, and 24 who made woolen textiles in Santa Clara County. The 165 professionals, artisans, and merchants together made up only a little over 3 percent of the Chinese population, and there were virtually no prostitutes, gamblers, or opium dealers—perhaps a reflection of the fact that Chinese in these areas preferred to go to the much better stocked Chinatown in San Francisco for their shopping and recreational needs.

The occupational distribution pattern in the Sacramento Valley—another prime agricultural region—was very similar to that in the Bay Area counties, except for the 887 miners found in the Sierra Nevada foothills. Farmers, truck gardeners, and poultry raisers made up 2.7 percent of the Chinese population, another 17.6 percent worked as farm laborers, and 0.1 percent fished, bringing the total in agriculture and fishing to 20.4 percent. Just over 30 percent earned a living as nonagricultural laborers, while laundrymen, cooks, and servants made up 8.1, 7.1, and 4.6 percent of the Chinese population, respectively. The number of merchants, professionals, and artisans was similarly small, with the cities of Sacramento and Marysville containing the largest clusters. The 100-plus truck gardeners were distributed among all the counties of the valley, but the 32 farmers were concentrated in the Sacramento Delta, where Chinese had helped to reclaim the land and had begun to lease it for farming. Though Chinese had engaged in truck gardening almost from the beginning of their immigration into California, their entry into larger-scale farming was a phenomenon associated with these transitional years.

CONSOLIDATION

The period from the mid-1870s to the end of the following decade saw a consolidation of the patterns that had begun to emerge in the preceding period.[12] In 1880, even though mining itself was on the decline except for quartz mining in Nevada and Amador counties, there were still about 15,000 Chinese miners, one-fifth of the Chinese population in the state. In comparison, only about 7 percent of the gainfully employed non-Chinese still mined for a living. As is shown in Table 3, though the Chinese population in the Southern Mines had decreased by some 2,000, there were still over 3,500 Chinese miners there, forming 71 percent of the Chinese population. In the Northern Mines, where the Chinese population had increased by over 2,000 since 1870, over 6,700 of the 13,000-plus Chinese, or 51.6 percent, were miners. The number of Chinese miners in this region, therefore, had increased by almost 1,200 over that of ten years earlier, reflecting the general prosperity brought about by the boom in hardrock mining in Nevada County in the late 1870s. In the Klamath/Trinity region, 3,700, or 70.7 percent, of the over 5,000 Chinese dug gold for a living. Over a thousand additional Chinese miners were found outside of the major mining regions, mostly in Sacra-

mento County. So far as the Chinese were concerned, the gold rush was not yet over.

The differences noted in the occupational distribution of Chinese in the three mining regions in 1870 were even more prominent in 1880. The Northern Mines, which had a more diversified economic base, were able to continue to sustain a sizable Chinese population because nonmining work was available. Almost 1,300 provided personal services, while some 2,100 earned a living as common laborers. These individuals were no doubt disappointed miners forced to accept menial jobs for survival. Similar work was apparently not available in the Southern Mines or the Klamath/Trinity region. The larger population in the Northern Mines also enabled a larger absolute number and percentage of Chinese to flourish as merchants, professionals, and artisans.

In San Francisco the most notable change was an increase in the number as well as the variety of Chinese factory workers who were now employed in broom, candle, cigar, coffee, collar, cotton, fuse, gum, match, pen, sack, sewing, shoe, soap, and sugar factories; flour, jute, paper, saw, and woolen mills; electrical, powder (ammunition), and salt works, as well as tanneries and packing houses. The inconsistent manner in which occupations were listed in the manuscript census makes it difficult to state exactly how many Chinese were factory workers and how many were independent producers. While all those listed as working in a factory were counted as factory workers, there were also others, listed as "makers" of cigars, shoes, slippers, boots, candles, or matches, who might have worked in factories, but who could also have been independent artisans. Moreover, it is not certain whether persons listed as "manufacturers" were owners of factories or workers in them. Only those specifically listed as "proprietors" of factories can be considered owners, but these were few in number. If all persons listed as working in factories, all manufacturers, and all makers of goods amenable to factory production are included, then over 6,000—some 30 percent of San Francisco's gainfully employed Chinese, or 28 percent of its total Chinese population—were engaged in manufacturing.

The 2,230 merchants and their 331 employees made up 11.8 percent of the Chinese in the city, while an additional 95 individuals ran brothels, gambling halls, and opium joints. The 2,148 laundrymen constituted 10 percent of the Chinese population. San Francisco's Chinatown was not only a thriving center of Chinese-owned and operated factories and sweatshops but also the home of many independent skilled craftsmen, 1,614 of whom engaged in a wide array of crafts, including shoemaking, tailoring, carpentry, and the making of beds, bricks, brooms, cages, candles, chairs, coffins, fishnets, harnesses, ivory carvings, lace, lanterns, locks, roofs, ropes, silverware, tents, umbrellas, watches, and whiplashes. There were also Chinese printers, machinists, painters, brick and stone masons, as well as bakers, candy makers, bean-cake makers, and butchers. No doubt a great deal of the Chinese-manufactured goods was sold to the general public, but many trades in this city obviously specialized in the production of items intended for the Chinese ethnic market. Professionals in the city included actors and musicians, herbalists and physicians, linguists and interpreters, teachers, priests and missionaries, fortune-tellers, and even artists, photographers, letter writers, lawyers, newspapermen, nurses, and secretaries. The status of San Francisco as the metropolis of Chinese America is best gleaned from the fact that professionals, artisans, entrepreneurs of various sorts, and their assistants made up 56.9 percent of the city's total Chinese population.

Providers of personal services, including barbers, cooks, dishwashers, drivers, errand boys, janitors, porters, prostitutes, servants, waiters, and night watchmen, made up 23.1 percent, while nonagricultural laborers formed another 10.8 percent of the city's Chinese population. There were dozens of sailors, steamer stewards, mess boys, coal heavers, and firemen among the nonagricultural laborers, San Francisco being a port for both ocean liners and river steamers. A small number of Chinese also worked as ragpickers and scavengers.

Finally, the city and county had 371 Chinese fishermen, 37 truck gardeners, 2 farmers, 7 poultry raisers, 66 woodchoppers, 56 miners, and 121 farm laborers—the last two groups obviously transients visiting the city.

The other Bay Area counties continued to grow as agricultural areas providing employment for few Chinese farmers but for more than twice as many farm laborers as a decade earlier. In the Santa Clara and Sonoma valleys, four-fifths of the Chinese earned a living in agriculture while in the Vaca Valley of Solano County, about three-fifths worked in various agricultural pursuits. Individuals providing personal services and nonagricultural laborers each increased two and a half times in number, the former growing from 883 in 1870 to 2,192 in 1880, the latter jumping from 1,645 to 4,147 in the same decade. The Bay Area outside of San Francisco thus had the largest proportion of working-class Chinese of any of the regions under consideration.

Between 1870 and 1880, the number of Chinese earning a living in agriculture had increased in the Central Valley. The almost 1,000 Chinese farm laborers and woodchoppers in the Sacramento Valley made up 11.4 percent of the Chinese population, the bulk of whom, over 500, were in Sacramento County. Unlike the Sacramento Valley, where rainfall and water from streams provided sufficient water to grow a wide variety of crops without irrigation, the more arid San Joaquin Valley was still devoted to ranching and wheat growing, the sole exceptions being that portion of San Joaquin County which forms part of the San Joaquin Delta, and an area in Tulare County around the fans of the Kings and Kaweah rivers. Though ranching and wheat growing were less labor-intensive, nonetheless, 741 Chinese farm laborers were found in the San Joaquin Valley in 1880, forming 15.3 percent of the Chinese population, the largest number being in San Joaquin County.

The inverse relationship between mining and menial labor can most clearly be seen by comparing the occupational distribution of Chinese in the mining regions with those in the agricultural ones. In the mining regions, the percentage of nonagricultural laborers in the total Chinese population varied from 2.8 percent in Shasta County, where 82 percent of the Chinese were miners, to 27 percent in Butte County, where only 46 percent of the Chinese were miners. Nonagricultural laborers were more numerous in the Sacramento and San Joaquin valleys, which had mining only in the eastern flanks of a few of their counties: here, laborers constituted 26.4 and 24.4 percent of the Chinese population, respectively. Not only were there more of them, but the work Chinese laborers did was also more diverse, with hundreds of brick makers, soap-root diggers, woodchoppers, lumber sawyers and pilers, as well as many engaged in other forms of semiskilled labor.

Similarly, the percentage of Chinese who worked as cooks in the various regions of rural California also varied inversely with the percentage who were miners. Only about 3 percent of the Chinese in the Southern and Klamath/Trinity mines, which still had a high percentage of miners in 1880, were cooks, while almost 8 percent of the Chinese in the Northern Mines were. In the Sacramento and San Joaquin valleys, 11.8 and 14.9 percent of the Chinese, respectively, earned a living as cooks. Among these, at least one-third were farm cooks who resided in the households of farmers, and many more may have been, but there is no way to ascertain the exact number because a large proportion of the cooks listed in the manuscript schedules of the census lived in their own households. The percentage of Chinese servants in different regions also varied inversely

with the number of miners. These statistics indicate clearly that as Chinese left mining, the more enterprising ones became manufacturers or merchants in the urban areas and farmers or truck gardeners in the rural and suburban areas, while the less fortunate everywhere became laborers, cooks, and servants.

DECLINE

The 1880–90 decade brought many important changes for Chinese communities in the United States because the 1882 Chinese Exclusion Law not only cut off the major source of addition to the Chinese population but made it quite clear to the Chinese who chose to remain that they were a despised and unwanted minority. Unfortunately, since the 1890 published census provided no information on the occupations of the Chinese population, and the manuscript schedules are no longer available, almost nothing can be said about the immediate effects of these legal restrictions on the kind of work the Chinese did.

It has been noted that an increasing number of Chinese moved to other sections of the country after the passage of the Chinese Exclusion Act in 1882. What needs to be added is that the ratio of urban to rural Chinese in California as well as the nation increased substantially during the last two decades of the nineteenth century. This urbanizing population, however, had fewer and fewer means of livelihood open to its members because Chinese were being driven out of manufacturing from the mid-1880s onward. Boycotts of Chinese-made goods by white consumers reduced the number of Chinese factory owners and workers in San Francisco from 1,023 and 4,264, respectively, in 1880 to only 84 and 1,694, respectively, in 1900. By 1920 there were virtually no Chinese cigar or shoe and boot makers left. At the same time, it must be remembered that manufacturing in the United States had long left its artisanal stage behind, so that only those with large amounts of capital could afford to engage in manufacturing industries. Thus, even had there been no discrimination, it is not certain how many Chinese could have remained in manufacturing by the early twentieth century.

In 1900 there were barely any Chinese left in the Southern and Klamath/Trinity mining regions of California, but of the 3,547 counted in the Northern Mines, over a thousand were still doggedly mining.[13] As Table 4 shows, the other Chinese in the latter region were more or less evenly distributed as agriculturalists and agricultural laborers, entrepreneurs, providers of personal services, and nonagricultural laborers. In San Francisco, although the percentage in business and manufacturing was still high (38.1 percent), the most notable change between 1880 and 1900 was the increase in the percentage engaged in common labor. Agriculture absorbed an ever larger percentage of the Chinese population in the Bay Area counties outside of San Francisco and in the Sacramento and San Joaquin valleys. In particular, not only the percentage but the absolute number in farming increased in the San Joaquin Valley.

Chinese farmers, farmworkers, fruit packers, and commission merchants were most concentrated in the Sacramento–San Joaquin Delta, where some 95 percent of the Chinese population earned a living in agriculture at the turn of the century. The percentage of those who survived through farming and farm work was almost as high in other major agricultural areas, such as the Sonoma and Vaca valleys and the foothills of Placer County. Elsewhere in California, from one-quarter to over one-half of the Chinese depended on agriculture for a living. Rather than having been driven out of rural California, as some writers have alleged, Chinese agriculturalists in fact flourished during these decades when the Chinese population as a whole, paradoxically, was experiencing a general demographic and economic decline.

Sizable numbers continued in farming until the end of World War I. Except for the Sacra-

mento–San Joaquin Delta, where a settled Chinese community persisted, the Chinese exodus from agriculture finally took place in the late 1910s and 1920s. They left because they were growing old, their children preferred other work, they could not compete against the more aggressive Japanese immigrants who now greatly outnumbered them, and a great drop in agricultural commodity prices in the mid-1920s caused a farm recession, which made it hard for farmers to make ends meet.

Throughout the nation wherever Chinese had settled, more and more retreated to urban centers to earn a living in trade and common labor during the early decades of the twentieth century. By 1920 fully 48 percent of all the Chinese in the United States were in small businesses, while 27 percent provided personal services. Only 11 percent were in agricultural occupations, 9 percent in factory work and the skilled crafts, 2 percent in transportation, 1 percent in the professions, and 2 percent in white-collar work. There were only 151 Chinese miners left in the United States, but it is not known where they were located.[14]

The extraordinary increase in the number of merchants and small shopkeepers resulted partly from the implementation of the various Chinese exclusion laws. After the initial 1882 law came into effect, additional laws were enacted in the following two decades which not only made it impossible for all but a handful of Chinese to enter legally, but caused those who were already here great hardship. Merchants, belonging to one of the "exempted" classes, became the main source of new blood in Chinese American communities. Since few Chinese women were in the United States at the time exclusion was imposed, and even fewer came in the ensuing six decades, the Chinese population was unable to replenish itself easily through natural increase. The only addition to the community, therefore, came from immigration. Although many of the immigrants probably were not merchants originally, they very likely bought shares in existing businesses in order to qualify for entry as merchants. Those who were not fortunate enough to become businessmen eked out a living as cooks, servants, and laborers. Seven decades of rapid economic change, anti-Chinese discrimination, and finally Chinese exclusion—rather than any inherent racial or cultural characteristics—had made the Chinese in the United States into an urban mercantile and servile population by the early twentieth century.

TABLE 1 THE OCCUPATIONAL DISTRIBUTION OF THE CHINESE IN CALIFORNIA BY ECONOMIC SECTOR AND BY REGION, 1860

	Southern Mines[a]		Northern Mines[b]		Klamath/Trinity Mines[c]		San Francisco	
	Number	Percent	Number	Percent	Number	Percent	Number	Percent
Primary producers and extractors	13,062	88.7	9,195	83.8	3,027	88.1	470	17.3
Agriculturalists	161	1.1	126	1.1	12	0.3	31	1.1
Agric. laborers	3	0	6	0.1	0	0	13	0.5
Fishermen	0	0	2	0	0	0	418	15.4
Miners	12,898	87.6	9,061	82.6	3,015	87.7	8	0.3
Professionals and skilled artisans	174	1.2	96	0.9	27	0.8	197	7.2
Enterpreneurs and their assistants	614	4.2	554	5.0	76	2.2	575	21.1
Merchants	447	3.0	270	2.5	49	1.4	147	5.4
Clerks and shop assistants	53	0.4	50	0.5	7	0.2	10	0.4
Owners of recreational vices	28	0.2	20	0.2	1	0	274	10.1
Laundrymen/women	86	0.6	214	2.0	19	0.6	144	5.3
Factory owners	0	0	0	0	0	0	0	0
Factory workers	0	0	0	0	0	0	0	0
Providers of personal services	640	4.3	639	5.8	107	3.1	723	26.6
Cooks	153	1.0	261	2.4	48	1.4	67	2.5
Servants	29	0.2	73	0.7	12	0.3	11	0.4
Prostitutes (listed)	139	0.9	58	0.5	40	1.2	0	0
Prostitutes (probable)	291	2.0	199	1.8	5	0.1	636	23.4
Others	28	0.2	48	0.4	2	0.1	9	0.3
Nonagricultural laborers	112	0.8	418	3.8	43	1.3	650	23.9
Miscellaneous and no occupation	126	0.9	71	0.6	157	4.6	104	3.8
Total	14,728	100.0	10,973	100.0	3,437	100.0	2,719	99.9
(Published total)	(14,792)		(11,104)		(3,439)		(2,719)	

Source: My tally from U.S. National Archives, Record Group 29, "Census of U.S. Population" (manuscript), 1860.
[a]Includes El Dorado, Amador, Calaveras, Tuolumne, and Mariposa counties.
[b]Includes Plumas, Butte, Sierra, Yuba, Nevada, and Placer counties.
[c]Includes Del Norte, Siskiyou, Shasta, Trinity, and Klamath counties.

TABLE 2 THE OCCUPATIONAL DISTRIBUTION OF THE CHINESE IN CALIFORNIA BY ECONOMIC SECTOR AND BY REGION, 1870

	Southern Mines[a]		Northern Mines[b]		Klamath/Trinity Mines[c]		San Francisco[d]		Other Bay Area[e]		Sacramento Valley[f]	
	Number	Percent	Number	Percent	Number	Percent	Number	Percent	Number	Percent	Number	Percent
Primary producers and extractors	5,593	77.1	6,076	54.5	3,420	88.5	547	4.9	1,502	29.5	2,015	36.4
Agriculturalists	56	0.8	253	2.3	34	0.9	6	0	417	8.2	150	2.7
Agric. laborers	66	0.9	240	2.2	21	0.5	53	0.5	934	18.4	971	17.6
Fishermen	0	0	6	0	0	0	145	1.3	135	2.7	7	0.1
Miners	5,471	75.4	5,577	50.0	3,365	87.1	343	3.1	16	0.3	887	16.0
Professionals and skilled artisans	43	0.6	287	2.6	32	0.8	565	5.1	81	1.6	125	2.3
Enterpreneurs and their assistants	414	5.7	972	8.7	117	3.0	4,394	39.5	708	13.9	679	12.3
Merchants	149	2.1	374	3.4	45	1.2	518	4.7	84	1.6	101	1.8
Clerks and shop assistants	36	0.5	41	0.4	13	0.3	97	0.9	0	0	25	0.5
Owners of recreational vices	132	1.8	171	1.5	30	0.8	—[h]	—	1	0	50	0.9
Laundrymen/women	18	0.2	292	2.6	28	0.7	1,333	12.0	471	9.3	450	8.1
Factory owners	0	0	3	0	0	0	—[h]	—	2	0	35	0.6
Factory workers	79	1.1	91	0.8	1	0	2,446	22.0	150	3.0	18	0.3
Providers of personal services	364	5.0	1,366	12.3	187	4.8	2,414	21.7	883	17.4	924	16.7
Cooks	162	2.2	873	7.8	114	3.0	—[h]	—	415	8.2	395	7.1
Servants	23	0.3	101	0.9	20	0.5	1,256	11.3	305	6.0	252	4.6
Prostitutes (listed)	148	2.0	306	2.7	44	1.1	—[h]	—	91	1.8	60	1.1
Prostitutes (probable)	16	0.2	11	0.1	2	0.1	1,000[g]	9.0[g]	15	0.3	175	3.2
Others	15	0.2	75	0.7	7	0.2	158	1.4	57	1.1	42	0.8
Nonagricultural laborers	474	6.5	2,205	19.8	35	0.9	2,210	19.9	1,645	32.4	1,665	30.1
Miscellaneous and no occupation	370	5.1	239	2.1	73	1.9	1,000[g]	9.0[g]	264	5.2	122	2.2
Total	7,258	100.0	11,145	100.0	3,864	99.9	11,130	100.0	5,083	100.0	5,530	100.0
(Published total)	(7,236)		(11,177)		(3,872)		(12,022)		(5,240)		(5,683)	

Source: My tally from U.S. National Archives, Record Group 29, "Census of U.S. Population" (manuscript), 1870

a Includes El Dorado, Amador, Calaveras, Tuolumne, and Mariposa counties.
b Includes Plumas, Butte, Sierra, Yuba, Nevada, and Placer counties.
c Includes Del Norte, Siskiyou, Shasta, Trinity, and Klamath counties.
d The figures in this column come from U.S. Bureau of the Census, *Census of U.S. Population, 1870*, p. 799, Table XXXII, and not from my tally of the manuscript schedules. (The given figures are for the city only; figures have been rearranged from the published table.)
e Includes Sonoma, Napa, Marin, Contra Costa, Alameda, Santa Clara, and San Mateo counties; *excludes* San Francisco.
f Includes Tehama, Colusa, Sutter, Sacramento, Yolo, and Solano counties.
g Estimate.
h Not given in published table.

TABLE 3 THE OCCUPATIONAL DISTRIBUTION OF THE CHINESE IN CALIFORNIA BY ECONOMIC SECTOR AND BY REGION, 1880

	Southern Mines[a]		Northern Mines[b]		Klamath/Trinity[c]		San Francisco		Other Bay Area[d]		Sacramento Valley[e]		San Joaquin Valley[f]	
	Number	Percent	Number	Percent	Number	Percent	Number	Percent	Number	Percent	Number	Percent	Number	Percent
Primary producers and extractors	3,795	4.4	7,954	61.0	3,799	72.6	660	3.1	3,009	26.6	3,035	35.1	1,417	29.3
Agriculturalists	87	1.7	436	3.3	77	1.5	46	0.2	286	2.5	956	11.1	332	6.9
Agric. laborers	82	1.6	784	6.0	22	0.4	187	0.9	1,975	17.4	982	11.4	741	15.3
Fishermen	1	0	1	0	0	0	371	1.7	670	5.9	15	0.2	95	2.0
Miners	3,625	71.1	6,733	51.6	3,700	70.7	56	0.3	78	0.7	1,082	12.5	249	5.2
Professionals and skilled artisans	63	1.2	215	1.6	48	0.9	2,186	10.1	188	1.7	182	2.1	116	2.4
Enterpreneurs and their assistants	305	6.0	1,020	7.8	190	3.6	10,091	46.8	1,505	13.3	1,241	14.4	649	13.4
Merchants	151	3.0	337	2.6	91	1.7	2,230	10.3	306	2.7	276	3.2	139	2.9
Clerks and shop assistants	38	0.7	76	0.6	14	0.3	331	1.5	7	0.1	3	0	46	1.0
Owners of recreational vices	66	1.3	178	1.4	51	1.0	95	0.4	12	0.1	16	0.2	30	0.6
Laundrymen/women	49	1.0	367	2.8	28	0.5	2,148	10.0	1,036	9.1	722	8.4	335	6.9
Factory owners	1	0	4	0	1	0	1,023	4.7	4	0	35	0.4	1	0
Factory workers	0	0	58	0.4	5	0.1	4,264	19.8	140	1.2	189	2.2	98	2.0
Providers of personal services	328	6.4	1,298	10.0	313	6.0	4,986	23.1	2,192	19.4	1,490	17.2	1,076	22.3
Cooks	157	3.1	1,014	7.8	182	3.5	857	4.0	958	8.5	1,019	11.8	721	14.9
Servants	26	0.5	48	0.4	25	0.5	2,443	11.3	1,104	9.7	376	4.4	191	4.0
Prostitutes (listed)	84	1.6	108	0.8	38	0.7	432	2.0	16	0.1	10	0.1	78	1.6
Prostitutes (prob)	22	0.4	29	0.2	38	0.7	600	2.8	27	0.2	12	0.1	43	0.9
Others	39	0.8	99	0.8	30	0.6	654	3.0	87	0.8	73	0.8	43	0.9
Nonagricultural laborers	322	6.3	2,136	16.4	790	15.1	2,336	10.8	4,147	36.6	2,280	26.4	1,179	24.4
Miscellaneous and no occupation	285	5.6	420	3.2	93	1.8	1,289	6.0	285	2.5	412	4.8	396	8.2
Total	5,098	99.9	13,043	100.0	5,233	100.0	21,548	99.9	11,326	100.1	8,640	100.0	4,833	100.0
(Published total)	(5,120)		(13,255)		(5,289)		(21,745)		(11,445)		(8,503)		(4,869)	

Source: My tally from U.S. National Archives, Record Group 29, "Census of U.S. Population" (manuscript), 1880.

[a]Includes El Dorado, Amador, Calaveras, Tuolumne, and Mariposa counties.

[b]Includes Plumas, Butte, Sierra, Yuba, Nevada, and Placer counties.

[c]Includes Del Norte, Siskiyou, Shasta, Trinity, and Klamath counties. (Klamath County was dissolved in 1874 and its territory was divided up between Siskiyou and Humboldt counties)

[d]Includes Sonoma, Napa, Marin, Contra Costa, Alameda, Santa Clara, and San Mateo counties; *excludes* San Francisco.

[e]Includes Tehama, Colusa, Sutter, Sacramento, Yolo, and Solano counties.

[f]Includes San Joaquin, Stanislaus, Merced, Fresno, Tulare, and Kern counties.

TABLE 4 THE OCCUPATIONAL DISTRIBUTION OF THE CHINESE IN CALIFORNIA BY ECONOMIC SECTOR AND BY REGION, 1900

	Northern Mines[a]		San Francisco		Other Bay Area[b]		Sacramento Valley[c]		San Joaquin Valley[d]	
	Number	Percent	Number	Percent	Number	Percent	Number	Percent	Number	Percent
Primary producers and extractors	1,698	47.9	286	2.0	1,704	31.2	2,353	43.5	2,295	40.6
Agriculturalists	203	5.7	61	0.4	302	5.5	502	9.3	338	6.0
Agric. laborers	489	13.8	165	1.2	1,135	20.8	1,815	33.5	1,942	34.3
Fishermen	0	0	38	0.3	158	2.9	1	0	0	0
Miners	1,006	28.4	22	0.2	109	2.0	35	0.6	15	0.3
Professionals and skilled artisans	56	1.6	1,669	11.7	38	0.7	170	3.1	133	2.4
Enterpreneurs and their assistants	541	15.3	5,455	38.1	1,471	27.0	806	14.9	765	13.5
Merchants	344	9.7	1,440	10.1	268	4.9	316	5.8	436	7.7
Clerks and shop assistants	36	1.0	259	1.8	8	0.1	51	0.9	32	0.6
Owners of recreational vices	6	0.2	54	0.4	1	0	1	0	0	0
Laundrymen/women	155	4.4	1,924	13.4	821	15.1	346	6.4	294	5.2
Factory owners	0	0	84	0.6	1	0	0	0	1	0
Factory workers	0	0	1,694	11.8	372	6.8	92	1.7	2	0
Providers of personal services	479	13.5	2,603	18.2	1,173	21.5	1,015	18.7	1,222	21.6
Cooks	357	10.1	1,197	8.4	815	14.9	666	12.3	905	16.0
Servants	18	0.5	659	4.6	263	4.8	174	3.2	43	0.8
Prostitutes (listed)	5	0.1	269	1.9	0	0	14	0.3	5	0.1
Prostitutes (probable)	76	2.1	0	0	38	0.7	97	1.8	180	3.2
Others	23	0.6	478	3.3	57	1.0	64	1.2	89	1.6
Nonagricultural laborers	669	18.9	3,534	24.7	754	13.8	933	17.2	1,001	17.7
Miscellaneous and no occupation	104	2.9	771	5.4	314	5.8	138	2.5	238	4.2
Total	3,547	100.1	14,318	100.1	5,454	100.0	5,415	99.9	5,654	100.2
(Published total)	(3,614)		(13,954)		(6,511)		(5,959)		(6,165)	

Source: My tally from U.S. National Archives, Record Group 29, "Census of U.S. Population" (manuscript), 1900.

[a]See note [b] in table 3.
[b]See note [d] in table 3.
[c]See note [e] in table 3.
[d]See note [f] in table 3.

Notes

1 The *San Francisco Bulletin* reprinted an item from the *Auburn Placer Press* of May 19, 1857, which described how Chinese miners had been robbed by men with double barreled guns, who then hanged three of the Chinese witnesses.

2 Mary Roberts Coolidge, *Chinese Immigration* (New York, 1909), p.32.

3 This decision was rendered by the California Supreme Court in the case of *The People v. George W. Hall, 4 Cal.* 399 (1854).

4 The article from the *Shasta Republican* was reprinted in the *San Francisco Bulletin* of December 18, 1856, and stated that "hundreds of Chinese" had been "slaughtered in cold blood during the last five years by 'desperados.'" Though the papers were hardly pro-Chinese, the reporter sounded as though he thought it was proper and just to hang a white man for murdering Chinese.

5 Sucheng Chan, "Chinese Livelihood in Rural California: The Impact of Economic Change, 1860–1880," *Pacific Historical Review,* 53 (1984), pp. 282–283.

6 Ping Chiu, *Chinese Labor in California, 1850–1880* (Madison, 1963), p. 23.

7 The best analysis of the Chinese in the San Francisco labor market is Paul M. Ong, "Chinese Labor in Early San Francisco: Racial Segmentation and Industrial Expansion," *Amerasia Journal,* 8 (1981), pp. 69–92.

8 For the Chinese in fishing, see Arthur F. McEvoy, "In Places Men Reject: Chinese Fishermen at San Diego, 1870–1893," *Journal of San Diego History,* 23 (1977), pp. 12–24; and Eve Armentrout-Ma, "Chinese in California's Fishing Industry, 1850–1914," *California History,* 60 (1981), pp. 141–157.

9 The following account is based on my tally, computation, and analysis of data on Chinese individuals listed in the manuscript schedules of the 1870 U.S. census of population as summarized in table 2. In these tables, I have grouped individual occupations into categories differently from the way the U.S. Bureau of the Census did. The Bureau of the Census used the following broad categories: Agriculture; Professional and Personal Services; Trade and Transportation; Manufacturing and Mining. Thus, the Bureau of the Census lumped together barbers and servants with physicians and surgeons under "Professionals and Personal Services," and placed miners, fishermen, blacksmiths, clerks, factory owners, and tailors under "Manufacturing and Mining." I have separated the professionals (defined as persons with skills acquired through higher education) from the providers of more menial personal services (such as barbers, cooks, waiters, dishwashers, and servants). Instead, I have placed skilled artisans (defined as persons who acquire specialized skills through apprenticeships to become journeymen) together with professionals. Furthermore, instead of separating those in agriculture from those in fishing and mining, I have grouped farmers, truck gardeners, fishermen, and miners together as primary producers and extractors (i.e., persons who earn a living by working with the natural resources of the earth).

10 The figures for San Francisco are not from my own tally but have been culled from U.S. Bureau of the Census, *Ninth Census of the United States: Population, 1870* (Washington, D.C.: Government Printing Office, 1872), p. 799, table XXXII. The figures in the published table refer only to the city of San Francisco. Certain occupations that were important for the Chinese population were not listed, so these have been estimated in table 2.

11 Chiu, *Chinese Labor,* pp. 55–61 and 89–128.

12 The following account is based on my tally, computation, and analysis of data on Chinese individuals listed in the manuscript schedules of the 1880 U.S. census of population as summarized in table 3.

13 See table 4.

14 U.S. Bureau of the Census, *Fourteenth Census of the United States: Population, 1920* (Washington, D.C.: Government Printing Office, 1921–22), vol. 4, pp. 342–359.

CHAPTER

15

BLACK NEIGHBORS

EDITOR'S INTRODUCTION

The history of Afro-Americans in California stretches back to the time of the state's earliest settlement. About half of the founding adults of the pueblo of Los Angeles were all or partly black. Spanish-speaking blacks or mulattoes served as soldiers at the presidios and missions, while others rose to positions of prominence in the colonial administration. Blacks, both free and slave, came to California during the gold rush. San Francisco attracted a substantial number of black residents and as early as the 1850s they had established their own newspaper, churches, political organization, library, and debating society.

Douglas Henry Daniels' groundbreaking study, *Pioneer Urbanites: A Social and Cultural History of Black San Francisco* (1980), attempts to recreate the quality of life and urban identity of the black residents of the San Francisco Bay Area from 1850 to World War II. While Daniels uses sources typical of the new social historians—including manuscript censuses and city directories—he is interested in different sorts of questions. In the book's preface, Daniels warns (or reassures) the reader that this is not an examination of social mobility, social class, or working-class culture. "Nor is this a quantitative history," Daniels explains, "but rather a qualitative one. I am more concerned with what should be counted than with the actual enumeration."

Daniels' implied critique of the social historians' fascination with quantification is similar to the comments of David Rich Lewis, in a previous selection, that "bare-boned" quantifying is as repugnant to many narrative historians as the bleached bones of dead draft animals were to the argonauts on the overland trail. To put added flesh on the bones of his study, Daniels conducted in-depth interviews with informants whose families were among the early black settlers of the Bay Area.

In the following selection, Daniels analyzes the residential pattern of the black pioneers. He effectively demonstrates that during the pioneer era, which lasted for blacks until World War II, there were no ghettos in San Francisco. Blacks were dispersed throughout the Bay Area. Many lived near their places of employment along the waterfront or near popular "entertainment districts." Others lived in ethnic enclaves among Chinese and Latin Americans.

Daniels compares favorably the status of Bay Area blacks to that of the Chinese and other immigrants. He argues that "racism as a rule was not as rigidly imposed on Afro-Americans as it was on Chinese in California," and as a consequence blacks had greater residential options. Yet Daniels also makes clear that racism and discrimination were constant factors in restricting the employment opportunities for blacks. In the maritime industry blacks generally were relegated to the lowest ranks; on shore they remained concentrated in service, food, and menial occupations.[1] Throughout most of the period of Daniels' study, job opportunities for blacks remained unchanged. While Sucheng Chan, in the previous selection, found that the occupational structure of the Chinese underwent major changes in the nineteenth century, such was not the case for blacks.

Because their opportunities for occupational advancement were limited, Daniels concludes, the black pioneers devoted great attention to improvements in the private world of family, home, and neighborhood. For contemporary Californians, black and white, Daniels offers a fascinating look at the pre-ghetto days of these pioneer urbanites.

Douglas Henry Daniels received his Ph.D. from the University of California, Berkeley, in 1975. He currently is an Associate Professor and Chair of the Department of Black Studies at the University of California, Santa Barbara.

---

[1]See also Rudolph Lapp, *Afro-Americans in California* (San Francisco, 1979), 25.

READING 15

Black Neighbors

Douglas Henry Daniels

The day I was born...I heard all these different women, different names—like in those days you weren't born in the hospital, you were born at home, and I heard them speak about Mrs. Moriah, Mrs. Tracy, Mrs. O'Brien, Mrs. Silva, Mrs. Riposa, and Mrs. Filotta, all those different names, I said, "Doctor, hey, doc, what kind of a place is there where all these people of different nationalities come to help this old Black woman with her baby?"

And he said, "This is West Oakland."

And I said, "Well, jeez, West Oakland really must be a heaven on earth. It must be a really fine place."

Royal E. Towns

The black pioneers of San Francisco were neighbors of many national, ethnic, and racial groups; scattered throughout the city, they knew nothing of a ghetto. In fact, ghettos were nonexistent in all Pacific slope cities until World War I, and, in San Francisco, Oakland, and Berkeley, even beyond that date. This was also true in southern cities, as well as in Boston, New York, Chicago, Minneapolis–St. Paul, Cleveland, and Cincinnati. Thus we must revise the popular notion that the ghetto is the usual physical setting of Black urbanites.[1] In San Francisco, the different neighborhoods mirrored the social and cultural complexities of the pioneers. As the city grew, and specific sections like the waterfront and the entertainment district appeared, complex residential locations became the pattern for Afro-Americans. These areas were located in different neighborhoods and, later, in East Bay municipalities as well. Their distribution indicates that Blacks were thoroughly familiar with the entire Bay Area.

Early San Franciscans lived near their workplaces, within walking distance of the original settlement, Yerba Buena, in the midst of the business blocks. As the population rapidly increased, the city spread south of Pine Street, beyond Market Street, west to Nob Hill, and across the bay to Berkeley, Oakland, and Alameda. Real estate developers filled the swampy terrain at the bay's edge, leveled hills, extended streets, and erected buildings.

Initially, San Franciscans found accommodations along the waterfront that stretched from south of Market Street around the tip of the peninsula and west almost to Fort Mason. If not on the urban perimeter, near the foot of Broadway, they dwelled in central business blocks along Montgomery, Kearny, and Dupont (later known as Grant). Some resided on Market Street, the city's widest boulevard, which ran diagonally southwest from the northeast tip of the peninsula. They dwelled on east-west streets like Pacific, Washington, and Clay, and later on the routes south of Pine, and on secluded back lanes like Hinkley, Pinkney, Scott, and Stone, in houses and flats, above shops, and in rooms for boarders.[2]

Throughout its history, the city's many hills have been "barometers of wealth and position." Beginning in the seventies, silver kings and railroad barons built palaces atop Nob Hill. Below the summit dwelled the moderately well-to-do. Still lower, businessmen, tourists, transients, and various citizens found situations in the downtown hotels, in lodging houses, and in ethnic enclaves. After 1906, affluent San Franciscans occupied the expensive hotels and apartments on Nob and Russian Hills, and the less fortunate inhabited the slopes.

Even with the development of the flatlands south of Market and Pine in the 1860s, and the advent of cable cars in the following decade, San Franciscans remained neighbors within walking distance of each other. They preferred living in a tightly packed cluster in the midst of businesses, shops, and offices, remaining between Van Ness and the waterfront until the earthquake and fire.

Blacks also inhabited the walking district of nineteenth-century San Francisco. Some lived near the waterfront, especially in the 1850s. Others resided in the entertainment districts, such as the Barbary Coast and along lower Broadway. A few lived in Spanish-speaking enclaves near Kearny Street and Broadway. Most stayed around the residential area at Broadway and Powell (Fourth Ward) and, after 1870, in the artisans' and workingmen's districts south of Market near Third Street. Table 1 gives their residential patterns and distribution in 1870. The difficulties of

Table 1 U.S. AND SAN FRANCISCO ENUMERATIONS, BY COLOR AND BY WARD, 1870

	White		Black	
Ward	U.S.	S.F.	U.S.	S.F.
1	10,385	10,426	77	77
2	11,359	11,368	145	137
3	2,400	2,509	13	6
4	10,282	10,672	621	389
5	2,758	2,790	3	3
6	6,139	6,250	216	220
7	10,228	10,189	16	12
8	16,006	16,188	88	89
9	10,420	10,564	49	49
10	21,985	22,099	48	46
11	21,825	22,003	43	45
12	12,270	12,343	22	21
Total	136,057*	137,401	1,341	1,094

*Total is incorrectly given as 136,059 in the *Directory*.
Source: Henry G. Langley, comp., *The San Francisco Directory, 1872*, p. 13.

enumeration in a large city were particularly apparent in Ward Four, where residences, businesses, churches, government offices, and Chinatown were all jammed together.[3] Unlike the Blacks, the Chinese, considered by contemporaries to be the most foreign of foreigners, lived in a few square blocks in the eastern part of Ward Four. But as late as 1940, the Black San Franciscans maintained their dispersal, spreading out with the city's population to new areas of the metropolis.

The changing waterfront reflected San Francisco's development in shipping and transportation; its growth marked the formation of a metropolitan area. More and larger piers and wharves penetrated its waters as the city expanded, and its waterfront was lined by a variety of ocean-going vessels, river steamers, ferries, and smaller craft, crowded with a hodgepodge of wheeled vehicles on shore, and populated by tourists, adventurers, hackmen, and seamen. The piers, which extended the city into the bay, and the variety of people highlighted San Francisco's interdependence with the far west and the world. In the twentieth century, the waterfront functioned even more as a zone of transition for the metropolitan area. Oakland possessed a substantial waterfront of its own, where oceanic vessels docked and local ferries landed. It was a familiar sight for East Bay-bound urbanites, commuting workers, and East Bay residents out for a night in San Francisco.[4]

Black sailors inhabited this, one of the roughest, most notorious waterfronts in the United States, from pioneer days. In 1860, 16 percent of San Francisco's Afro-Americans lived there, often because of connections with sea travel, along with newcomers and other residents. Boarding-house keepers maintained accommodations, and also provided banking and employment services. Colored sea rovers, cooks, and waiters resided in these establishments, some of which were run by Afro-Americans.

The Golden Gate Boarding House, probably at Broadway near Sansom, accommodated thirty Blacks, mostly mariners and cooks, in 1860. At the foot of Broadway, Abraham Cox, a seaborne waiter, ran the Pioneer Seamen's Boarding and Lodging House. In 1866, John Callender, another former seaman, assumed control of the establishment. Callender, his family, two Black sailors, and thirteen lodgers from Europe and the United States lived there in 1880. As the seasons changed, so did his customers. When the whaling fleet arrived in one autumn, a newspaper reported: "Colored gentlemen of every shade frequent his hostelry, and there remain until their hard-earned dollars have finished."[5] This milieu was as harsh and violent for the ordinary seaman as his conditions of work, particularly in the nineteenth century. Mariners, who had few rights until the twentieth century, probably suffered more if they were Afro-American, as that group could not rise through the ranks and become officers until well into the twentieth century. They remained ordinary seamen, just as Negroes on shore were destined to occupy menial positions all their lives.[6]

When they came ashore, the Black seamen were prey for avaricious boarding-house keepers and were likely to be shanghaied. In 1873 Edward J. Scott, a ship's steward, was drugged and robbed after one beer in a resort appropriately named Hell's Kitchen. Aurelious Alberga recalled a saloon, The Last Chance, where a trap door was used to kidnap unwary sailors. Hoodlums or "footpads" waited outside the "blind tigers" (illegal saloons without liquor licenses), dance halls, dives, and underground melodeons.[7]

These conditions changed somewhat as seamen's unions emerged and after reforms in working conditions, beginning in the late nineteenth century. Equally important, the waterfront's role changed. An urban transportation revolution led to more warehouses, wharves, and factories, and fewer accommodations on the waterfront. Thousands of rush-hour commuters passed through these sites every morning and late afternoon.[8]

In the twentieth century, fewer Blacks inhabited the waterfront, but transients and seamen still spent time there. When trains supplanted passenger ships, Blacks worked as redcaps, cooks, waiters, and porters, while others became newspaper vendors, bootblacks, and lodging-house operators. They congregated near the transbay terminal, at the railroad depot on Third and Townsend, and across the bay on Seventh Street and near the Oakland Mole, where the trains crossed the bay to San Francisco.[9] At such active spots, Afro-Americans learned of distant places and gauged the variety of citizens of the metropolis. When William E. Towns, an early settler who worked on the trains at the turn of the century, took his youngest son, Royal, to the Ferry Building, he explained the workings of the metropolis, pointed out a clamshell dredge, and, as Royal recalled, informed him that the vessels had names for identification.[10] Like William Towns, the Black inhabitants and workers of this zone served as bridgeheads to the distant world for isolated Afro-Americans on the Pacific slope. They taught Negro urbanites of the faraway places whose vessels, products, and citizenry made San Francisco a worldly spot.

ENTERTAINMENT DISTRICTS

The famous entertainment districts were another dimension of city life. The Barbary Coast and the Tenderloin housed both permanent inhabitants and tourists and transients. The oldest entertainment area, the Barbary Coast, matched in notoriety New Orleans's Storyville. It was linked with the waterfront by resorts on Pacific and Broadway streets and was bounded by Stockton, Kearny, Broadway, and Washington. In its heyday the Coast possessed "a few dives...patronized by negroes and drunken sailors, and where white and colored women of city, San Franciscans lacked a common cause or background. The communities distributed through the downtown blocks represented both the residents' diverse interests and their heterogeneous backgrounds. The singularity of the metropolis, particularly before the earthquake and fire, lay in its polyglot character, established several decades before the "new" immigration to and the rise of foreign-born ghettos in eastern cities.[22] Living in these enclaves shaped the lives of some Blacks and attracted others. Some pioneers lived among ethnic groups with common cultural and linguistic ties. Blacks with Spanish surnames and Central and Latin American origins occasionally lived with Mexicans, Panamanians, Peruvians, and Portuguese.

Infinite combinations of heritage and culture resulted in a region newly colonized by varied ethnic and national groups, where individuals associated with one another according to their inclinations. Fifteen Afro-San Franciscans resided with Mexican and Spanish-surnamed urbanites near Kearny and Broadway in 1880. A foreign-born Black was apt to be of African descent and Central American background, or a dark-skinned Iberian, or not Black at all, but a Hispanicized Indian, whose dark complexion confused the census taker. Determining a resident's background and racial heritage is difficult, if not impossible, for the contemporary scholar, just as it was for the federal census enumerator.[23]

The area around the 500 block of Broadway reflected the mix of nationalities and the way their neighborhoods overlapped. Although part of the Barbary Coast, and situated on the edge of Chinatown, the area housed a number of Central Americans, Latin Americans, and Italians on Kearny, Hinkley, and Pinkney streets. It also had a governmental character, as the county jail was located in the 500 block. The dwelling at 522 Broadway represented in microcosm San Francisco's mix of nationalities, races, and linguistic groups. A Black cook from Peru named José Seminario, his Panamanian wife, their four children (all but one born in Panama), and a Mexican boarder (designated "mulatto") lived at this address. A Black Panamanian with the family name of Cajar and two Mexican Black women with Spanish surnames shared the site. In the various apartments Chileans, European-born Irish, Italians, and Germans, and United States citizens mingled. The same pattern was found offshore. The U.S.S. *Pensacola,* which was anchored in the bay, was home for several foreign-born Blacks, principally from the West Indies and the Canary Islands.

Black residents had a number of options on where to live in the city, one of which was to stay with the Chinese. Described as a "coal black" Spaniard, Ong Fung Yu lived with the Chinese for nearly three decades. Born in Spain and named Montoya, he went to sea, was shipwrecked off the Chinese mainland, and spent twenty-seven years in servitude in China. When his master emigrated to San Francisco in 1881, Ong Fung Yu accompanied him and then gained his freedom. Interviewed in the mining country, he explained in Spanish that he preferred to associate with his adopted countrymen, to wear their clothes, and to speak what had become as much his language as theirs. In the twentieth century, as well, Blacks lived with Chinese for various reasons.[24] Jean Ng, "a well-known character of San Francisco's demimonde," resided at 520 Pacific (formerly Lester Mapp's Olympia and before that Purcell's), where the Coast and Chinatown met. Born in Kansas of Afro-American parents, she seems to have abandoned her ties to marry a Chinese rooming-house operator and underworld figure. When she died shortly after her husband, her adopted people claimed the body, prepared it for the funeral, and interred it in their cemetery in 1934.[25]

Few Afro-Americans went that far, but some associated with or, if necessary, claimed to be foreigners. Occasionally traveling musicians roomed with Chinese to avoid white discrimination. "There used to be a hotel next to the Orpheum on O'Farrell Street," Ethel Terrell, a bandleader and pianist, recalled. "That's where I stayed. And then as now people would come in San Francisco and didn't know where to stay, you stayed in Chinatown because they would always receive you. The Chinese would always let you stay anyplace where other people would not accept you." At least one informant, drawing upon her Panamanian background, assumed a Spanish identity to find accommodations for her large family in San Francisco.[26]

More typical were the Black individuals and families living on secondary streets or back lanes near Broadway and Powell and behind the Palace Hotel on Market Street. Prosperous Blacks resided on Sacramento and Washington Streets in the Fourth and Sixth Wards. In the 1870s newcomers inhabited the long narrow streets of Minna, Tehama, and Natoma, a few Black families to a city block. A total of four Afro-American families lived in the 1100 and 1200 blocks of Clay Street among German- and American-born residents in 1880. Similarly, the 100 block of Tehama housed ninety-seven whites, eight Chinese, and eight Afro-Americans.[27]

The largest contingent of Black pioneers (nearly 33 percent) inhabited the Fourth Ward (between Chinatown and Russian Hill) in 1880, but they were nonetheless widely dispersed. On Auburn Street fourteen Afro-Americans lived among 103 urbanites, including Irish, West Indians, Germans, Mexicans, and Italians. Even on Stone Steet, off Washington and Powell, the high percentage of Negroes (thirty-four of fifty-three citizens) resulted from two Black boarding houses located in this narrow lane. More commonly, Blacks lived in frame buildings next door to whites, sometimes sharing homes with them.[28]

A number of Afro-American gathering places, including the three Black churches, sat on the east slope of Russian Hill west of Chinatown. The two Methodist churches were on Stockton near Sacramento and on Powell near Jackson. The Baptist Church was also on Powell, between Bush and Sutter. Young Men's Hall, Prince Hall Masonic rooms, and billiard parlors were found on Broadway or on Pacific near Powell. The traditionally Black-operated boarding houses, one at 28 Stone Street and another at 1109 Stockton Street, were nearby. While the twentieth century brought important new developments in Black residential patterns, the Afro-American pioneers remained scattered over the metropolitan area.[29]

Across the Bay in West Oakland, Berkeley, and Alameda, Negroes similarly lived among native and foreign-born whites. John T. Callender, Ezekiel Cooper, and Jeremiah B. Sanderson lived in the East Bay in the late nineteenth century. Other Black pioneers soon followed, most of them living near the railroad terminals and the harbor west of downtown Oakland. The West Indian sea captain, William Shorey, and his family resided at 1774 Division Street. Their neighbors included an actor, a marine engineer, and their families (at 1778); a Swedish-born boilermaker (at 1770); an English railroad car repairman and three lodgers (at 1768); and an English railroad foreman and his family. All were white.

Near Brush Street, just south of the railroad tracks that ran down Seventh Street (where the elevated Bay Area Rapid Transit runs today), lived a number of Afro-Americans. A cook from British Guiana and his family inhabited a one-story frame house at 804 Brush. Across the street at 805 lived a carpenter, his wife, and their in-laws. A little way up, in two attached flats, were another Black couple and three boarders and lodgers (one white). A white Irish domestic probably owned these dwellings at 812. Further along lived a day laborer, his wife, grown children, and their spouses (860). Two Blacks families shared a two-story dwelling around the corner on Fifth Street (721), and on

Sixth Street Afro-American families occupied one, one-and-a half, and two-story frame structures (713, 721, 758, 760, 765).[30]

INTERPRETATION

These Black living trends call for an explanation, particularly in the older urban area. In a city famed for its ethnic neighborhoods and heterogeneous population, no "Negro quarter" existed. The *Chronicle* observed this in 1904, pointing out that San Francisco's Blacks were the prosperous descendants of pioneer servants and businessmen. According to J. S. Francis, the editor of the *Western Outlook,* the reasons for this were simple. Colored citizens were "allowed to rent in most parts of the city" as "no strong color line [was] drawn in this city." Their singular status, he claimed, resulted from the fact that "influential members of the race" actually discouraged "the undesirable element" from coming to the city and aided only those "negroes of education and general eligibility." The article is the only mention of a Black district, or the absence of one, in San Francisco until 1944.[31]

In a study of Bay Area Negroes during World War II, Charles S. Johnson, the noted Black sociologist, observed that until the 1940s "no rigidly segregated Negro community existed in the city." Unlike eastern cities, "Negro inhabitants were to some degree lost in the city's population complex." Even as, in the 1930s, they congregated along Fillmore Street, one site of today's ghetto, they lived among Japanese, Chinese, Filipinos, and "sizeable groups of whites."[32]

Because before the 1940s Blacks migrated as individuals and over a long period of time, they scattered over a wide area. They found accommodations as single family units and as individuals, not as a large contingent of newcomers. On the other hand, we know that when thousands of Blacks suddenly entered a city, as in the east during World War I and in the Bay

Area during World War II, the familiar ghetto resulted. (The same institution emerged when masses of foreign-born whites occupied American cities.) Discrimination, profit-seeking real estate agents, and housing shortages promoted ghettos more than did any desire of Blacks to live together. Varying occupations and specific preferences among Negro San Franciscans also accounted for their scattered locations.

The presence of dark-skinned inhabitants from southern Europe, Latin America, Oceania, and Asia, and traditions of cosmopolitanism enabled Blacks to enjoy uncommonly numerous options in terms of neighborhood locations. Black culture also assumed an important role in permitting their distribution in the city. American customs, institutions, and language were the heritage of the vast majority of pioneer urbanites, and, when merit and ability were the sole criteria, they found easy access to different sections of society. But merit and ability were not the only standards, and discrimination barred entry to some places. Yet to an extent their color also worked in their favor, permitting entrance to certain circles as servants and menials, jobs which would have been denied them if they were considered equals.

With their knowledge of the language and customs of the United States and San Francisco, the pioneers acquired job skills, a degree of literacy, and a variety of social contacts out of the reach of recently arrived European and Asian immigrants. Such foreign-born residents needed years, if not generations, to acquire vital language and job skills and to adjust to the American urban scene, unless they possessed wealth, high social station, or professional training when they came to the U.S.

San Francisco and Oakland Blacks learned the accents, intonations, jokes, and vocabularies of their foreign neighbors. Royal E. Towns maintained that his association with a variety of urban dwellers allowed him to learn many distinctive speech patterns and idioms. He said that a uniquely cosmopolitan atmosphere existed in West Oakland (and the Bay Area) because so many national and ethnic groups shared a tradition of neighborliness, cooperation, and goodwill. To illustrate what a Black child might learn, he recited incidents and jokes in first an Irish and then a Jewish accent.

Towns told of visiting his son on a ship in Brooklyn Harbor in New York in the 1940s. Stopped by an Irish policeman, Towns explained that he was in the merchant marine, but the Irishman, "with all the flannel on his tongue that he could possibly have, he said, 'No yuz don't,' he says, 'nobody goes down to the ship, and arders is arders.'" Towns then showed him his identification, indicating he was a lieutenant in the Oakland Fire Department and had a port pass for San Francisco. "'I don't give a damn who you are, you just don't go down to the ship,' he says, and 'arders is arders.'" Towns replied, "'You know something, you are the first Irishman that ever believed me. When was you born—in the year of the black potatoes or the year of the big wind?' And he said, 'Where did you get the blarney?' I said, 'Out where I live.' He said, 'Many Irishmen out there?' I said, 'Ha! I was born in old man O'Brian's house right next to Mr. Tracy's,' and I said, 'There's O'Boyle, O'Hallihan, McAllister,...' and jeez, I started naming a whole gang of micks, you know, and he said 'Wait a minute, wait a minute!' He said, 'Hey, Pat, come here and take this Irishman down to the boat.' (Laughter.) It's all in knowing the language or the vernacular of the particular ethnic group that you live with....This has happened in many instances in my life where I have utilized some of the things I learned from those kids down there [in West Oakland]."[33]

By contrast, Asian and European migrants sometimes balked at learning English, and often retained an accent or manner of speaking that evinced their origins. The accents and dialects, not to mention the languages, that characterized San Francisco were evidence of the recent arrival and distant origins of many of its inhab-itants. While foreign newcomers attempted to preserve their traditions, Afro-American culture was not only American, but had been American for several generations. If it served their ends, Blacks learned the languages of the newcomers, thus acquiring a European and Asian veneer.

Asian and European immigrants, in fact, preserved their original cultures while learning American ways in San Francisco, re-creating their homelands in their ethnic enclaves. Newcomers imported countrymen, foods, and goods to surround themselves with familiar remnants of home. Afro-Americans, on the contrary, felt little desire to bring anything but a bit of New Orleans, Philadelphia, or New York City to the far western metropolis. They were at home any place in the American city where prejudice did not make conditions intolerable; the variety of their neighborhood locations, and their eventual shift from the city center highlighted their familiarity with the urban scene much as their speech evidenced a native acquaintance with American culture. The dispersal of pioneer urbanites, and their shifting locations accompanying the city's expansion, contradict those who desire to see all Black urban life in the ghetto environment.[34]

DISPERSAL AND SUBURBANIZATION

In 1906, the earthquake and fire all but destroyed downtown San Francisco. Residents moved temporarily to the lightly settled Western Addition beyond Van Ness Avenue and to the growing East Bay, Oakland in particular. The city was quickly rebuilt, but large business blocks and expensive hotels rose where businesses and residences had been mixed. The well-to-do and the Chinese built stores and accommodations in the downtown districts. The growing metropolis penetrated the residential Western Addition and enveloped suburbs which were sometimes cities in their own right. The typical Black San Franciscan located in these expanding regions, inhabiting the row-houses and flats along Bush, Pine, Sutter, and Post Streets, rooms above stores on Divisadero and Fillmore, or the larger homes of Oakland. East Bay residents, who depended on trolleys, trains, and ferries to travel to the city center, had overcome their inclination to dwell more than walking distance from downtown.[35]

By World War I the Bay Area's residential patterns had crystallized. This was partly due to the growth of industry in the East Bay, but transportation changes were also crucial to both the city's expansion and the new living patterns of Blacks. The introduction of cable cars in the 1870s accelerated the city's growth and settlement of the steep hills. Eventually electric trolleys and rapid trains enabled San Franciscans to live some distance from their workplaces in the city center, while an efficient ferry system hastened the growth of Oakland and Berkeley. The ferries traveled at regular intervals, and in 1912 carried 15,000 transbay commuters during each rush hour. The advent of the automobile and consolidation of the city's transportation system around World War I spurred suburban development. Construction of the Bay and Golden Gate bridges in the 1930s facilitated the movement of trains, trucks, automobiles, and commuters. As distinct commercial and residential neighborhoods appeared, the new mobility of commuters complicated matters. Swiftly moving motorized transportation (public and private) obliterated distinctions between the city proper and its surrounding regions, whether suburbs, countryside, or seaside resorts.[36]

Bay Area Blacks took advantage of the residential shift and adopted the new life style, embracing suburban ways more readily than other urbanites. After 1906 a few relocated on Russian Hill, in the city center, and in the Western Addition, but by 1910 most Bay Area Afro-Americans lived in Oakland. In the 1920s, when San Francisco's total population outnumbered Oakland's by more than two to one,

almost twice as many Blacks lived in Oakland as in San Francisco. Usually viewed as members of American society's rear guard, Blacks had adopted a life style that would not become the norm until the mid-twentieth century.[37]

In the nineteenth century, Blacks who lived in the city center for convenience's sake often used the pastoral East Bay for excursions and picnics. As early as 1880 nearly six hundred Afro-Americans lived in Oakland, constituting the second-largest group of Black city dwellers in the state. Oakland's rustic character disappeared during the economic boom of the 1890s, but the city retained a decidedly suburban atmosphere and, characteristically, a lower population density than San Francisco. The East Bay's proximity, suburban character, expanding economy, cheaper rents, and larger homes accounted for the more than 8,000 Afro-Americans in Oakland and more than 3,000 in Berkeley by World War II.[38] The Black migration to the East Bay in the 1890s also followed the rise of the white labor unions that excluded Blacks from their traditional positions. Afro-Americans found jobs quite readily on the trains which terminated in Oakland; as these positions were reserved for Blacks, discrimination forced them to adapt to new trends while whites stayed in San Francisco.[39]

The East Bay's cheap and available housing also caused many pioneer families to relocate. Though as a rule racism was not as rigidly imposed on Afro-Americans as it was on Chinese in California, it eventually affected Negroes' housing choices. There are no complaints about housing discrimination in the remaining copies of the nineteenth-century Black newspapers; probably San Francisco life was initially so rich that when discrimination occurred, it hardly mattered. Perhaps city folk were too busy seeking wealth to exclude Blacks from neighborhoods or even from households. At any rate the problem of discrimination in housing was first mentioned in a white newspaper in 1889.[40] Richard C. O. Benjamin, author, newspaperman, and political organizer, argued that San Francisco was as prejudiced as the south. "Right here in San Francisco," he exclaimed, "it is impossible for respectable negro families to rent homes except in certain communities." Eighteen years later, the Oakland *Sunshine* echoed this sentiment. "To live in either of the [Bay] cities, it is almost necessary for you to own your own home; rents are high and real estate agents do not care to rent to Negroes." One advantage of suburban living was that homes could be purchased "at the price of a monthly rental." In the 1920s, an informant said, discrimination made it all but impossible to obtain anything but "rundown" accommodations in San Francisco.[41] In 1930 Black householders in San Francisco paid an average of five dollars per month more than their counterparts in Oakland, usually for less space. The East Bay's lots were wider than San Francisco's, making possible commodious houses, yards, and gardens, and room for children.[42]

A conscious choice of alternatives was evident in the move to Oakland. Rather than flee the metropolis because of job discrimination, expensive housing, and increasing racism, devotees of the Bay Area moved to new residential sections. Faced with limited opportunities, the Black urban dwellers devoted their time and energy to improving their immediate home environment, buying spacious houses in the East Bay or comfortable Victorian dwellings in San Francisco's Western Addition. The less expensive East Bay homes freed portions of householders' budgets to buy furnishings, plant flowers, and devote space to their children's play activities. The new suburban residential districts provided a quieter setting that contrasted with the expensive, crowded, noisy, downtown districts.

It is impossible to ascertain how many Blacks moved to the East Bay at the turn of the century. What is significant is that adoption of the suburban life style, based on motor transport, entailing residency in a neighborhood far from downtown, and implying an affinity for trees, flower gardens, and more space, distinguished the pioneers from the average American and from many San Franciscans. The pioneers embraced the new pattern more quickly than most Americans, white or Black, because they were flexible and willing to seek new opportunities to better their lives. They chose to enrich their home lives because other forms of advancement were not readily available. In the late nineteenth century, as working conditions worsened due to labor competition and chances for wealth dwindled, home and family became the new means of expressing ideals.

For newcomers to the Bay Area, the East Bay offered both jobs and an attractive physical locale that especially appealed to migrants from southern small towns and crowded, dirty eastern cities. Noisy, expensive, and exclusive, San Francisco repelled all but the most cosmopolitan and skilled newcomers; the high cost of living there also discouraged migrants with families. When single Black San Franciscans married, they moved to the East Bay for the welfare of their families. Most of the informants' parents left San Francisco to live in Oakland or Berkeley by 1900, and the informants themselves often purchased homes in the East Bay for good prices during the Depression.

CONCLUSIONS

The pioneers and their unique urban ways went relatively unnoticed by contemporary observers and, perhaps as a consequence, have been neglected by scholars. They merit attention because they contrast with both the contemporary ghetto dweller and the average white urbanite of the late nineteenth and early twentieth centuries; analysis of these pioneer suburbanites might shed light on the problems of metropolitan life in the late twentieth century. At the very least, study of their conversion to suburban living furthers our understanding of the historical origins of that way of life and its implications for whites as well as for Blacks.

Emphasis on the "problems" of Black and white urban life results not so much from careful analysis of the history of different ethnic groups, but from scholars' concern with social policy, crime, and health. The experiences of pioneer urbanites in the Bay Area show that the availability of different neighborhood locations can improve those aspects of urban life—given the right setting. While contemporary residents enjoy emphasizing the Bay Area's liberal, multi-racial, and multi-ethnic heritage, the region's history indicates a more complicated picture. Perhaps the city did accommodate versatile and literate Afro-Americans in the nineteenth century, but it was not so generous with Chinese of that era or with the Japanese in the twentieth century. And when large numbers of Black southerners arrived during World War II, the Bay Area cities finally faced the problems that had plagued eastern cities since World War I. Black ghettos formed at Hunters Point, along Fillmore Street, and around Seventh Street in Oakland. The "Negro problem" emerged full-blown, and the area's singularity and belief in its non-racial ways disappeared. All the characteristics of ghetto life—high mortality rates, inadequate housing, and crime—heralded a new phase for San Franciscans. Comparison of the two different urban patterns—those of pioneers and those of ghetto dwellers—should illuminate our understanding of each.[43]

The pioneer experience forces us to modify the usual portrait of Negro urban life and to take into account differences between cities and between regions. Analyzing Black San Franciscans' neighborhood locations shows the complexity of city life. Negro urbanites learned of the city's complicated functions and of the larger world outside it by living in or working on the waterfront. The entertainment and ethnic districts lent a bohemian, if not a licentious,

quality and a degree of ethnic sophistication to Black life. From their neighbors, the pioneer Blacks learned to be sophisticated urbanites who valued lasting friendships based on childhood experiences and individual preferences, rather than on ethnic background. In many ways this freed them from some of the effects of racial oppression.

Such living conditions may have been the prevailing pattern on the Pacific slope, although much research needs to be done on this subject. Edward J. "Buster" Johnson, who worked on the trains along the Pacific coast, said that there was little variation in Black life from city to city. "Up and down the coast,...Seattle, Portland, San Francisco, Los Angeles—it was all the same...Negroes lived the same as they did here all the way up and down the coast." There was also considerable freedom. On public transportation, for example, "you paid your fare and sat down and rode and you didn't have to ride at the back of the bus or somewhere else, just wherever you could find a seat. We didn't have none of that funny stuff like they had in the south."[44] Despite Jim Crow restrictions, Blacks seem to have been well dispersed in many nineteenth-century U.S. cities. The relationship between this living pattern and racial prejudice needs to be explored in order to compare the quality of Black urban life from region to region.

The Bay Area pioneers shared another characteristic with Negro urbanites outside the far west. While Black urbanites are frequently viewed as laggards behind the nation, they were in the vanguard in San Francisco and Boston. Starting in the late nineteenth century, Black Bostonians moved to the "streetcar suburbs" because of lower rents, lower home purchase prices, more pleasant physical surroundings, and less antipathy for their group. Boston and San Francisco Blacks moved to the suburbs at comparable rates, if only at the outset: "So far as increasing residence in the more open and healthful outlying districts is concerned, the

Negroes have in the main fared better than the rest of the population.''[45]

The benefits of urban life seem to have counterbalanced discrimination in employment, or so many Black San Franciscans believed— and their opinions must be weighed when we assess the effects of racism and the quality of their lives. If their childhood memories minimized racial strife and were a bit nostalgic for the cosmopolitan pre-ghetto era, their segregated social life reminds us of the restrictions they faced.

Notes

1 On northern residential patterns in the nineteenth century, see James Weldon Johnson, *Black Manhattan* (New York, 1968 ed.), pp. 58–59; and W. E. B. Du Bois, *The Philadelphia Negro* (New York, [1969 ed.]). On New York at the turn of the century, see Mary White Ovington, *Half A Man: The Status of the Negro in New York* (New York, 1911), pp. 18–26. On the midwest, see: Allan H. Spear, *Black Chicago: The Making of a Negro Ghetto 1890–1920* (Chicago, 1967); David Vassar Taylor, "Pilgrim's Progress: Black St. Paul and the Making of an Urban Ghetto, 1870–1930" (Ph.D. diss., University of Minnesota, 1977); and David M. Katzman, *Before the Ghetto: Black Detroit in the Nineteenth Century* (Urbana, Ill., 1973). Kenneth L. Kusmer argues: "It seems doubtful that anything even remotely resembling a real black ghetto existed in American cities north or south, prior to the 1890s," *A Ghetto Takes Shape: Black Cleveland, 1870–1930* (Urbana, Ill., 1976), p. 12. See also Paul J. Lammermeir, "Cincinnati's Black Community: The Origins of a Ghetto, 1870–1880," in John H. Bracey, August Meier, and Elliot Rudwick, eds., *The Rise of the Ghetto* (Belmont, Calif., 1971). Historians of the south concur; for example, see: John W. Blassingame, *Black New Orleans: 1860–1880* (Chicago, 1973), p. 16; Ira Berlin, *Slaves Without Masters: The Free Negro in the Antebellum South* (New York, 1974), p. 253.

2 For the city's growth, see: John P. Young, *San Francisco: A History of the Pacific Coast Metropolis*, 2 vols. (San Francisco, [1912]); Roger

W. Lotchin, *San Francisco, 1845–1856: From Hamlet to City* (New York, 1974), pp. 3–30; Bion J. Arnold, *Report on the Improvement and Development of the Transportation Facilities of San Francisco* (San Francisco, 1913); Frank Soulé, John H. Gihon, and James Nisbet, *The Annals of San Francisco* (New York, 1855), map opposite p. 22; Margaret G. King, "The Growth of San Francisco, Illustrated by Shifts in the Density of Population" (M.A. thesis, University of California, Berkeley, 1928); and Martyn J. Bowden, "Dynamics of City Growth: An Historical Geography of the San Francisco Central District, 1850–1921" (Ph.D. diss., University of California, Berkeley, 1967).

3 Locations of Black residents were determined with the United States Census, beginning with the Eighth, in its published and manuscript versions. Henry G. Langley, comp., *The San Francisco Directory* (hereafter referred to, with the appropriate year, as *City Directory*) also gives addresses of Blacks and locations of institutions and businesses.

4 Richard H. Dillon, *Shanghaiing Days* (New York, [1961]); Benjamin Lloyd, *Lights and Shades of San Francisco* (San Francisco, 1876); William F. Rae, *Westward by Rail: The New Route to the East* (New York, 1871), p. 260; San Francisco *Chronicle,* March 17, 1889, p. 8, Feb. 7, 1904, p. 7; Herbert Asbury, *The Barbary Coast: An Informal History of the San Francisco Underworld* (New York, 1933), pp. 198–231; William M. Camp, *San Francisco, Port of Gold* (Garden City, N.Y., 1947), pp. 197–388; Young, *San Francisco,* II: 660–61; Andrew S. Hallidie, "Manufacturing in San Francisco," *The Overland Monthly* XI (June 1888), 637. Two useful views of the cityscape are: George H. Goddard, "Bird's Eye View of the City of San Francisco" (1868); and William R. Wheaton, "Index Map of the City of San Francisco" (1867); both are in the Bancroft Library, University of California, Berkeley.

5 [United States Census Bureau], Original Schedule of the Eighth Census, 1860, San Francisco, California (hereafter cited as Manuscript Census, with the appropriate year). *City Directory, 1860* gives the address of the Golden Gate Boarding House; San Francisco *Elevator,* June 30, 1865, p.

3; Delilah L. Beasley, *Negro Trail Blazers of California* (New York, [1969] ed.), p. 122; on Callender's boarders, Manuscript Census, 1880, and *Elevator*, March 17, 1877, p. 2; on Callender's career, San Francisco *Examiner*, June 16, 1889, p. 10; for problems of an old Black seaman, *Elevator*, Oct. 25, 1873, p. 2. San Francisco *Daily Alta California*, Nov. 29, 1889, p. 1.

6 San Francisco *Call*, Nov. 8, 1897, p. 32; Soulé, Gihon, and Nisbet, *Annals*, p. 472; Harold Langley, "The Negro in the Navy and the Merchant Marine," *Journal of Negro History* LII (Oct. 1967), 273–86; and Frederick Harrod, *Manning the New Navy* (Westport, Conn., 1978) discuss Blacks in the late nineteenth-century U.S. Navy. Asbury, *Barbary Coast*, pp. 104–5; for a romantic depiction of this environment in the 1920s, see the tale of the Jazz King in Oakland *Western Outlook*, Feb. 25, 1927, p. 7; Charles Keeler, *San Francisco and Thereabout* (San Francisco, 1902), pp. 14–15 gives a similar portrait.

7 Dillon, *Shanghaiing Days*, p. 180; *Daily Alta California*, Nov. 29, 1888, p. 1, Dec. 15, 1886, p. 1; Young, *San Francisco*, II: 623; Edwin S. Morby, trans. and ed., *San Francisco in the Seventies: The City As Viewed by a Mexican Political Exile*, by Guillermo Prieto (San Francisco, 1938), p. 75; Walton Bean, *California: An Interpretive History* (San Francisco, [1968]), pp. 287–88. Interview, Aurelious Alberga, July 27, 1976.

8 Bean, *California*, pp. 287–88; Arnold, *Report*, p. xvii.

9 Horace R. Cayton, *Long Old Road* (Seattle, [1967]), pp. 124–26. Aurelious P. Alberga, J. C. Rivers and John Taylor ran bootblack stands near the terminal building; San Francisco *Western Appeal*, April 1, 1927, p. 3; *City Directory, 1900; Western Appeal*, May 3, 1922, p. 1.

10 Interview, Royal Towns, Aug. 30, 1973.

11 *Call*, Nov. 8, 1897, p. 32; Soulé Gihon, and Nisbet, *Annals*, p. 472; Asbury, *Barbary Coast*, pp. 104–5; Workers of the Writers' Program of the Works Project Administration in Northern California, *San Francisco: The Bay and its Cities* (New York, 1947), pp. 214–16.

12 San Francisco *Vindicator*, March 16, 1887, p. 1, June 11, 1887, p. 2; *Call*, July 10, 1900, p. 12, April 7, 1900. p. 7.

13 *Vidicator*, May 16, 1887, p. 1; Workers of the Writers' Program, *San Francisco*, pp. 106–7; Clifton Rather, *Here's How: An Autobiography* (Oakland, 1968–70), pp. 21–23; Asbury, *Barbary Coast*, pp. 105, 130, 235, 255; Sally Stanford, *The Lady of the House: The Autobiography of Sally Stanford* (New York, 1966), pp. 46–47, 66–69; *Western Appeal*, Jan. 13, 1928, p. 8, tells of the dispersal of resorts after the closing of vice districts. Elizabeth Anne Brown, "The Enforcement of Prohibition in San Francisco, California" (M.A. thesis, University of California, Berkeley, 1948), pp. 20, 22, 31–39; San Francisco *Spokesman*, Sept. 23, 1932, p. 1 tells of a Black social "club" in the Western Addition.

14 Manuscript Census, 1880.

15 Asbury, *Barbary Coast*, p. 130; *Alta California*, Jan. 30, 1873, p. 1; San Francisco *Evening Bulletin*, Jan. 30, 1873, p. 3; *Chronicle*, Jan. 30, 1873, p. 3, Oct. 22, 1875, p. 3. (*Daily Alta California*, Jan. 31, 1873, p. 1 gives details of Tuers's trials.) Contrast this case with that reported in the *Daily Alta California*, Sept. 6, 1888, p. 2.

16 *Elevator*, Dec. 29, 1865, p. 2, Jan. 7, 1874, p. 3, Oct. 24, 1874, p. 2.

17 San Francisco *Pacific Appeal*, March 5, 1864, p. 4, Jan. 7, 1871, p. 2; *City Directory, 1860*, p. 152; *Elevator*, Oct. 18, 1871, p. 2.

18 *Elevator*, June 11, 1898, p. 3, Oct 18, 1890, p. 3, June 16, 1892, p. 3.

19 Ibid., June 11, 1898, p. 3; *City Directory, 1900 and 1970;* Marshall and Jean Stearns, *Jazz Dance: The Story of American Vernacular Dance* (New York, [1968]), p. 128; *Western Appeal*, Oct. 19, 1921; Oakland *Pacific Times*, July 19, 1912, p. 2; Samuel Dickson, *San Francisco Kaleidoscope* (Stanford, Calif., 1949), pp. 254–55; *Examiner*, Dec. 26, 1921, p. 1.

20 This world is depicted in: Ann Charters, *Nobody: The Story of "Bert" Williams* (London, [1970]); Rudi Blesh and Harriet Janis, *They All Played Ragtime* (New York, 1971 ed.); Alan Lomax, *Mister Jelly Roll: The Fortunes of Jelly Roll Morton, New Orleans Creole and "Inventor of Jazz"* (New York, [1950]): James Weldon Johnson, *Along This Way* (New York, [1961] ed.), and Johnson, *Black Manhattan*.

21 Quote is from Oscar Lewis, ed., *This Was San Francisco* (New York, 1962), pp. 174–75.

Bowden, *Dynamics,* p. 57; Samuel Williams, "The City of the Golden Gate," *Scribners' Monthly* X (July 1875), 270; the Manuscript Censuses of 1880 and 1900 were helpful for analyzing locations of different citizens and groups because they give street addresses. Lloyd, *Lights and Shades,* p. 79, and the account of Chinatown, is valuable; on the Latin Quarter, see *Call,* March 6, 1895, p. 4.

22 Lotchin, *San Francisco,* pp. 100–135 is a good discussion of ethnicity in San Francisco.

23 Manuscript Census, 1880.

24 Ibid. Cloverdale *Reveille,* April 8, 1882, p. 2; Roberto Daughters brought this article to my attention.

25 *Spokeman,* Sept. 20, 1934, p. 1; James Abajian informed me of Jean Ng. Also ibid., Jan. 20, 1933, p. 1.

26 Interviews, Ethel Terrell, April 20, 1973, Claudia Cheltenham, April 17, 1973. Mrs. Cheltenham could give no reason for being presumed Spanish; her granddaughter, Jewel Cooper, pointed out that it would have been easy for her to assume a Spanish identity, as the aged informant spent several years in Panama as a young girl and knew Spanish.

27 Manuscript Census, 1880.

28 Sanborn Fire Insurance Maps, Department of Geography, California State University, Northridge, Calfornia.

29 *City Directory, 1865,* p. 599; *City directory, 1872,* pp. 870, 875–76. *Elevator,* March 18, 1870, p. 2, Nov. 29, 1873, p. 2, Dec. 27, 1863, p. 2, May 2, 1885, p. 3, June 18, 1892, p. 3, June 11, 1898, p. 3; San Francisco *Pacific Coast Appeal,* May 3, 1902, p. 8. See King, "Growth of San Francisco"; Bowden, "Dynamics"; Arnold, *Report;* and Judd Lewis Kahn, "Imperial San Francisco: History of a Vision" (Ph.D. diss., University of California, 1971) on the rebuilding of the metropolis. Charles S. Johnson, *The Negro War Worker in San Francisco: A Local Self-Survey* (San Francisco, 1944), p. 3.

30 Manuscript Census.

31 *Chronicle,* Feb. 7, 1904, p. 7.

32 Johnson, *Negro War Worker,* p. 3; *Spokesman,* July 6, 1933, p. 6; Maya Angelou, *I Know Why the Caged Bird Sings* (New York, 1971 ed.) describes the city in the 1940s (Patricia Myers Davidson informed me of this); *Chronicle,* Sept. 19, 1945, p. 13. The *City Directory, 1860* and *1870,* the Manuscript Censuses of 1880 and 1900, and Charles F. Tilghman, comp., *Colored Directory of the Leading Cities of Northern California, 1916–1917* (Oakland, 1916) all indicated widespread distribution of Afro-Americans in San Francisco and the East Bay.

33 Interview, Royal Towns, Aug. 30, 1973. Town's father spoke Spanish and some Chinese.

34 Gunther Barth, "Metropolism and Urban Elites in the Far West," in Frederic Cople Jaher, ed., *The Age of Industrialism in America: Essays in Social Structure and Cultural Values* (New York, 1968), pp. 158–87; Gilbert Osofsky, "The Enduring Ghetto," *Journal of American History* LV (Sept. 1968), 243; Allan Spear, "The Origins of the Urban Ghetto, 1870–1915," in Nathan I. Huggins, et al., eds., *Key Issues in the Afro-American Experience,* 2 vols. (New York, [1971]), II: 153–56.

35 Young, *San Francisco,* II: 618 (on the growth of Oakland) and II: 939 (on its manufacturing increase). Arnold, *Report,* pp. xvii, 13; Young, *San Francisco,* II: 575–76; Edgar M. Kahn, *Cable Car Days in San Francisco* (Stanford, Calif., [1944]), pp. 27–70.

36 Young, *San Francisco,* II: 862, 864; Arnold, *Report,* table 3 and plate 5 for data on the shift of the San Francisco population; also King, "Growth of San Francisco," pp. 119–23, 142–45.

37 United States Census Office, *Fifteenth Census, 1930: Population* (Washington, D. C., 1931), I: 165, II: 72 for the number of Blacks in Oakland in 1930 and in previous decades; *Fourteenth Census, 1920: Population,* III: 127 indicates the move of Black folk to the Western Addition and shows that few lived in the city center.

38 Young, *San Francisco,* II: 618; *Tenth Census, 1880: Population* (Washington, D. C., 1883), I: 416; *Fifteenth Census,* II: 72; *Sixteenth Census, 1940: Population* (Washington, D. C., 1943), part 1, pp. 599, 637, 657. Arnold, *Report,* plate 5.

39 In *Chronicle,* June 6, 1894, p. 5, a Black minister mentions union discrimination. Beasley, *Negro Trail Blazers,* p. 159.

40 *Chronicle,* June 16, 1947, p. 10.

41 *Daily Alta California,* Oct. 21, 1889, p. 8; *Spokesman,* March 19, 1932, p. 3; Oakland *Sunshine,*

Dec. 21, 1907, p. 2; interview, Claudia Cheltenham, April 17, 1973.

42 *Fifteenth Census,* VI: 61; higher rents were charged
in San Francisco after 1906; see Young, *San
Francisco,* II: 864; *Chronicle,* Feb. 7, 1904, p. 3;
on Black Oaklanders, see "A Successful Business
Venture," *The Colored American Magazine* XIII
(Dec. 1907), 269–72. See the pictures of Bay Area
homes throughout Tilghman, *Directory.*

43 *Chronicle,* Nov. 17, 1947, p. 24, June 16, 1947, p.
10. See also ibid., Sept. 19, 1945, p. 13, in which
a National Urban League spokesman compares
San Francisco's Black district of the 1940s to
Harlem a generation earlier: "San Francisco's
Negro district is today right where the New York
and Chicago districts were forty years ago."
Thomas Lee Philpott, *The Slum and the Ghetto:
Neighborhood Deterioration and Middle-class
Reform, Chicago, 1880–1930* (New York, 1978) is

an excellent comparative analysis of the neighborhoods and housing of Blacks and white ethnic
groups.

44 Interview, Ed Johnson, Aug. 14, 1973. See also
Cayton, *Long Old Road,* pp. 1–40, for an account
of his childhood in the Pacific Northwest; and
Elmer R. Rusco, *"Good Time Coming?": Black
Nevadans in the Nineteenth Century* (Westport,
Conn., [1975]). Los Angeles's Black population
was also distributed before the 1920s; see Lawr-
ence B. de Graaf, "The City of Black Angels:
Emergence of the Los Angeles Ghetto,
1890–1930," *Pacific Historical Review* XXXIX
(Aug. 1970), 333.

45 John Daniels, *In Freedom's Birthplace: A Study
of the Boston Negroes* (Boston, 1914), pp. 150,
459–60. Sam B. Warner, Jr., *Streetcar Suburbs:
The Process of Growth in Boston, 1870–1900*
(New York, 1971).

A MYTH FOR SOUTHERN CALIFORNIA

EDITOR'S INTRODUCTION

The 1880s were a boom time in southern California. Images of a land of sunshine and citrus, healthfulness and romance proved irresistible to thousands of Americans who flocked to the southland. The population of Los Angeles swelled from 11,000 to 50,000 in a single decade. It was also in the 1880s that southern California consolidated its own mythic regional identity. Central to this identity was a reincarnation of the California missions.

For a generation after the American conquest, the missions had been all but forgotten. Californians growing up among the scattered ruins viewed them with a disinterest bordering on contempt. "Looked at with the cold eye of one indifferent to material," wrote a native Californian, "it is doubtful if there is any structure on earth colder, barer, uglier, dirtier, less picturesque, less romantic, than a California mission."[1] Many of the surviving mission buildings suffered from a malign neglect, their adobe walls allowed to melt into rain-soaked piles of mud. Others were converted into saloons and dance halls, silos and sheep sheds.

This conspicuous decay of the missions fulfilled an important ideological need for the generation of the conquest. The mission ruins became a symbol of the righteousness of the American action in seizing California. They were a convincing demonstration of the superiority of the New Order in California, a sign of the fulfillment of the nation's Manifest Destiny. The star of the American present could shine ever more brightly as it was contrasted with the black hole of the Hispanic past, an era only dimly recalled by these miserable piles of rotting adobe.

[1] Gertrude Atherton, "A Native on the California Missions," *The Critic*, IX (1888), 271. Atherton would later contribute to the romanticization of the missions. See her *Before the Gringo Came* (1894) and *The Californians* (1898).

Then, beginning in the 1880s, a curious thing happened. The missions came roaring back to public attention as part of a loving legendry about the Old Spanish Days. The missions were celebrated as places of happiness and contentment, beautiful leisure, song and laughter. The mission era was envisioned as a time when noble Franciscans were revered with mystical adoration by their humble Indian neophytes. Charles Fletcher Lummis, a key player in this emerging mission myth, described the missions as "staunchest survivors of the old regime of restfulness and romance...noble monuments to the noblest of missionaries."[2]

One of the first visible results of the renewed interest in the missions was a movement to preserve and restore them. Starting in 1884, with the construction of a new shingle roof over the ruins at Carmel, mission after mission underwent rehabilitation. From the 1880s through the early twentieth century the tiles, gables, and towers of the missions were copied and mimicked in thousands of Mission Revival houses, hotels, schools, and train stations. The missions became the subject of dozens of pageants, plays, and celebrations, serving as the favorite locale for a whole generation of California local colorists. The missions also had a powerful, and as yet unstudied, impact on public education. They entered the curriculum at the fourth grade level and there they have remained.

This great enthusiasm for the missions is difficult to explain. Part of the explanation lies simply in the passage of time. By the 1880s, the image of the mission-as-ruin was bereft of any ideological significance. There was now a new generation of Californians upon the land with other, more pressing needs to be fulfilled. Kevin Starr, in the following selection, identifies these needs and shows how the mission myth was able to meet them. He explains why it was that southern Californians were so insistent in their evocation of a romantic past. His analysis centers on the work of Helen Hunt Jackson, whose novel *Ramona* (1884) stands as the point of origin for the mission myth.

Kevin Starr is the author of a monumental undertaking, a multivolume cultural history of California. His special interest is in the process by which works of the imagination transform "the materials of experience into the building blocks of identity." Starr received his Ph.D. from Harvard University in 1969, and currently is Professor of Communication Arts at the University of San Francisco.

---

[2]Charles Fletcher Lummis, "The Old Missions," *Drake's Magazine*, VII (1889), 191. See also the discussion in James D. Hart, *American Images of Spanish California* (Berkeley, 1960).

READING 16

A Myth for Southern California

Kevin Starr

In the 1880s emerges a consolidated myth of Southern California. Its two most important elements are health and romantic nostalgia. Southern California was a healthy place, it was felt, because of the climate. Nineteenth-century medicine had great faith in the curative powers of climate, most obviously in the case of tuberculosis and other pulmonary disorders. In his now classic *Climatology of the United States* (1857), Lorin Blodget gave the climate of California the equivalent of three Michelin stars. He compared it to the climates of Italy, Spain, and Portugal. Linking climate with healthfulness, Blodget claimed that Southern Californians seemed especially free from lung disease. During the decades 1860 to 1880 Blodget's judgment ticked away like a time bomb, tinkered with by others but never broadly acted upon because Southern California was so remote. The arrival of the railroads, however, together with the ensuing drastic reduction of fares, precipitated a health rush. Consumptives flocked to the region, hoping (often against hope) for a cure. Sanitariums and boardinghouses catering to consumptives sprang up, and a diverse literature promoting Southern California as a health resort found its way into print.

The promise, of course, outran the reality. Some found restoration, but many more coughed away what little life remained, alone and lonely in a faraway land, mocked by the sunshine they thought would save them. The effect on Southern California's developing culture of so many desperate Americans fleeing there only to die is easy to imagine. A paradoxical morbidity, an anger against defeated expectations of healthfulness and other hopes, subtly pervaded the civilization of the Southland. In Los Angeles during these years, death seemed everywhere, and a mood of death, strange and sinister, like flowers rotting from too much sunshine, remained with the city.

HELEN HUNT JACKSON

This amalgam of death and sunshine, morbidity and romance, went into the making of Helen Hunt Jackson's best-selling novel *Ramona* (1884). No other act of symbolic expression affected the imagination of nineteenth-century Southern California so forcibly. This tale of star-crossed Indian lovers and Spanish ranch life as it lingered on into the 1870s cast a spell on Southern Californians. They appropriated the characters, mood, and plot of *Ramona* as the basis of a public myth which conferred romance upon a new American region.

First of all, Southern California in the 1880s was more than ready for nostalgia. Subdivision and the growth of cities had shifted the emphasis of society away from the ranchos. Psychologically, the urban immigrant, caught in the throes of a rapidly expanding American present, wanted some emotional and imaginative connection to the Southern Californian past. The gargantuan annals issued throughout the 1880s by the Bancroft Company in San Francisco answered one aspect of this need, chronicling the story of California with a narrative breadth and a massiveness of detail which attested to the need in Californians to shore up a sense of present identity by searching out a usable historical myth. Attitudes toward the missions began to change. Once the neglected vestiges of a justly displaced theocracy, they became the objects first of scrutiny, then of romantic veneration.

Helen Hunt Jackson came to Southern California in 1881 as an investigative reporter for *Century* magazine. By background and temperament she was an ideal mythmaker. She and Southern California had a confluence of needs.

First of all, Southern California needed promotion as a region of beauty, peace, and healthfulness. No one sought such values of place with greater appetite than Helen Hunt Jackson. Ever since her first husband, an army engineer, was killed in an ordnance accident during the Civil War, she had wandered the world in search of a place where she could feel at home. Even when she remarried, she spent long periods of time away from her second husband. Sudden voyages to Europe, dashes by train across the United States, movement from city to city at home or abroad, and—once she finally chose a city—removals from hotels to lodging houses to private rooms to the homes of friends: Helen Hunt Jackson's search for a place to be at peace with herself was an obsession—and also an income, for she supported herself as a travel writer. She was neurotic and difficult to be around. Orphaned as a teenager, widowed as a young woman after losing two children, she fell frequently into despondency. Periods of overwork alternated with periods of physical and emotional collapse.

Southern California calmed her. She did not get along with everyone there, but her quarrels were fewer. Traveling about in a hired open carriage, she gathered data for an article on the outdoor industries of Southern California. Bees, sheep, citrus, olives: the sunny Mediterraneanism of it all soothed her ever restless nerves. She was especially impressed by the Rancho Camulos in the Santa Clara Valley of Ventura County, forty-five miles northwest of Los Angeles. Here, under the watchful supervision of Doña Ysabel del Valle, the widowed mistress of the estate, the old ways held on as fact and as recoverable poetry. Fountain, patio, orange grove, winery, the private chapel near an arbor smothered in grapevines, the excite-

ment of sheep-shearing time, the retinue of relatives and retainers: the observant Mrs. Jackson stored up the details.

She made her living by the picturesque, yet here, at Rancho Camulos and a few other places—Mission Santa Barbara and the home of Don Antonio de Coronel in Los Angeles, for instance—she felt the presence of something more compelling than mere prettiness. She felt a connection with the Latin Catholic past of Southern California. By the early 1880s relics of this Spanish past—a past not yet intensified by romantic myth—were few indeed. Of twenty-one missions, only Mission Santa Barbara remained in Franciscan hands. Many of the rest—their roofs collapsed, their protective cover of lime plaster long since flaked away—were being washed back into the adobe hills from which they first came by the swift, devastating rains of Southern California. In the course of two Southern California visits Mrs. Jackson managed to visit most of the California missions. At the Bancroft Library in San Francisco she did her own sort of haphazard, intuitive research into the mission era. At Mission Santa Barbara in January 1882, charmed by its mood of monastic tranquillity and by the beauty of its site overlooking the sea, she browsed in the library and chatted with the friars. One old padre, Francisco de Jesús Sánchez, especially intrigued her. Born in Mexico in 1813, Padre Sánchez had been in California since 1841. Pious, benevolent, rotund—the old friar seemed to Mrs. Jackson the last of his kind, the last to experience that peculiar blend of energies, religious and secular, which had brought the Spanish north from Mexico.

In Los Angeles, Bishop Francisco Mora of the Roman Catholic Diocese of Los Angeles, to whom she had a letter of introduction, referred Mrs. Jackson to Don Antonio de Coronel and his young wife Mariana. The Coronels lived in an adobe just outside Los Angeles, where the family had resided since 1834. Brought to Southern California as a teenager in 1834, Don

Antonio, in semi-retirement when Mrs. Jackson met him, had had a varied career in both Mexican and American California. In 1846, during the resistance, he had been commissioned by the embattled Californian government to ride to Mexico City with American flags captured in battle. In the new regime, Don Antonio served as mayor of Los Angeles in 1853 and state treasurer in 1867. Turning to antiquarianism in middle life, he filled his home with the artifacts of Old California. Dressed in Mexican costume, he and Mariana (decades younger than Don Antonio, and a very handsome woman) would perform the old dances and sing the old Spanish songs. It was Don Antonio de Coronel who suggested that Mrs. Jackson visit Rancho Camulos to see how Californians had lived in times gone by, and it was he who most imbued her with a feel for the flavor and physical texture of the Spanish past.

All this proved a heady wine. The daughter of a Calvinist theologian teaching at Amherst, Mrs. Jackson had grown up with a derogatory view of Mediterranean Catholic culture. Her earlier printed remarks regarding the Church of Rome ran in the Whore of Babylon vein, the staple expression of Yankee Protestant distaste. As a travel writer she reported on Italy with caustic scorn, preferring Bavaria. The New England culture, however, of which she was a protagonist (Emerson went out of his way to praise her now forgotten poetry) had been for some decades effecting a rapprochement—on the level of the imagination, at least—with the Latin Catholic South. The monumental histories of Ticknor and Prescott, the scholarship and poetry of Longfellow, the marvelous landscapes of Hawthorne's fiction: the pre-Civil War phases of this meditation had resulted in an energetic harvest of Mediterranean thoughts, symbols, feelings, and heroic figures (Dante, above all others) into the granaries of New England culture, then dangerously depleted by a constriction of sympathy and association endemic to a self-obsessed people for too long

feeding on what their forefathers had planted and gathered. The dialogue had religious dimensions. An assortment of New Englanders—George Ripley, Orestes Brownson, Isaac Hecker, for instance, veterans of transcendentalism and Brook Farm—left the stony ground of unbelief for the lush meadows of Rome or Canterbury. Hawthorne's daughter Rose founded an order of Catholic nursing nuns dedicated to the care of terminally ill patients.

Helen Hunt Jackson's developing interest in things Catholic lacked such depth and magnitude. She knew, however, that she despised the orthodox Calvinism of her youth. For a while, in a period of near insane grief after the death of her husband and son, she, along with so many others in the late 1860s and 1870s, had turned to spiritualism, but only as a desperate flirtation. Spiritualism was a form of therapy, only half believed in. It could never take the place of a mature creed. A feeling of baffled religious longing pervaded many of her poems, a hunger for some act of assent that might assuage her existential loneliness. Such faith never came, but in Southern California she felt warmed vicariously by its banked fires. Her long essay, "Father Junípero [Serra] and His Work," published in the May and June 1883 issues of *Century* magazine, shows a total sympathy with the context and purposes of Spanish Catholicism. Already for her—and because of her, eventually for all of Southern California—the days of the padres shimmered in a golden haze of mingled myth and memory, free of fanaticism and injustice, their cruelty and pain forgotten.

No matter that the mission system itself was founded on ambiguity: the enforced enclosure of the Indians. No matter that the Spanish soldiers hunted them in the hills like so much prey and drove them down into the mission compounds like so much cattle. There, in churchly captivity, the majority of them declined—from the syphilis the soldiers gave their women, from the alien work the padres made them do, from the trauma of having their way of life and their tribal places so cruelly taken away. In Helen Hunt Jackson's version of it all (and by the 1890s it was official myth), grateful Indians, happy as peasants in an Italian opera, knelt dutifully before the Franciscans to receive the baptism of a superior culture, while in the background the angelus tolled from a swallow-guarded campanile and a choir of friars intoned the *Te Deum*.

Strangely enough, although she accepted the myth in its historical dimensions, she had no illusions regarding the present plight of the Mission Indians. *Ramona*, in fact, was intended as an act not of romance but of social protest. Among her set in Boston after the Civil War, the crusade for Indian rights had replaced abolitionism as a fashionable concern. Mrs. Jackson herself devoted the last six years of her life to Indian philanthropy (she died of cancer in San Francisco on 12 August 1885). After extensive research in the Astor Library of New York, she assembled what was in effect a massive legal brief regarding violated Indian rights, *A Century of Dishonor* (1881), and sent it at her own expense to government officials and members of Congress. So well known was Mrs. Jackson as an expert on Indian affairs that in 1883, while she was in Southern California, she received a commission from the Department of the Interior to investigate the condition of the Mission Indians.

Accompanied by Abbot Kinney (about whom more later) and a driver, she toured the Indian villages of the southern counties in an open trap. Temecula, Agua Caliente, Saboba, Cahuilla Valley, Santa Ysabel: everywhere, Mrs. Jackson wrote in the August 1883 issue of *Century* magazine and in the official *Report* (1883) she and Kinney filed in Washington, everywhere Mission Indians were in grave decline. The Spanish had kidnapped and then abandoned them. The Americans completed the process of destruction, exploiting their labor, bullying them, removing them from what little land they possessed.

Two incidents stood in Mrs. Jackson's mind as representative of the entire tragedy. Near San Jacinto, she heard how in 1877 Sam Temple, a drunken, wife-beating teamster, frequently afoul of the law, had shot and killed a Cahuilla Indian, Juan Diego, allegedly in self-defense. Juan Diego, the story ran, was given to periods of partial insanity. During the last of these, he took a horse belonging to Temple and hitched it before his own hut, where he lived with his wife. As a piece of theft, it was so obvious that it underscored Juan Diego's insanity. Temple, nevertheless, rode over to Diego's hut in a state of rage. He later told the court (which acquitted him) that Juan Diego attacked him with a knife. Others said that Temple had summarily executed the unarmed, half-crazed Indian on the spot, leaving the bullet-ridden corpse in the arms of Juan Diego's Indian wife.

From Don Antonio de Coronel and from Father Anthony Ubach—a tall, bearded diocesan priest in San Diego, devoted to the Mission Indians (as well as to snipe hunting, buttermilk, and doughnuts)—Mrs. Jackson heard how in 1869 a sheriff's posse had, under orders from the district court, physically removed an entire Indian village, Temecula in San Diego County, from lands which the Indians thought the government had granted them but which whites had won in a legal action. They and their belongings were carted off to an inferior site nearby, Temecula remaining (Mrs. Jackson visited it in 1883) nothing but an abandoned burial ground.

Out of all this, then—the impressions of her Southern California sojourn, her frustration at having the recommendations of her and Kinney's *Report* ignored (they called for a survey of Indian lands, the removal of white squatters, a program of medical and educational assistance)—Mrs. Jackson, back in New York City, resolved to write an *Uncle Tom's Cabin* for the Mission Indian, which she did, in her rooms at the Berkeley Hotel: *Ramona*, first appearing as a serial in the *Christian Union* on 15 May 1884.

THE RAMONA SAGA

It was a tale of love and death, race and religion, the passing of a social order, and the spirit of time and place. On the Moreno ranch, founded by the late General Moreno in the 1820s, the ways and values of Old California are jealously preserved into the late 1860s by his widow and son, despite the loss of many acres to the Yankee courts. Among the dependents of Señora Gonzaga Moreno is Ramona Ortegna, nineteen, a half-breed orphan raised to think of herself as Spanish. Falling in love with Alessandro Assis, an Indian, captain of the sheep-shearing band from Temecula, Ramona rediscovers her suppressed Indianhood. Señora Moreno opposes the match, and so the couple flee to San Diego, where they are married. They cannot settle in Temecula because the Indian lands have been confiscated by the American courts. After a year and a half of struggle, Alessandro manages to establish himself as a small farmer near San Pasqual, where a colony of Temecula refugees scratch meager livings from the arid soil. In desperation over his infant daughter's illness, he enrolls his name with the Indian Agency as a dependent, hoping for medical assistance. The white doctor, however, refuses to make a crucial house call. Their daughter dies. The government orders all agency Indians removed to a reservation. Once again Ramona and Alessandro take flight, settling this time in the back-country near Mount San Jacinto, where another daughter, Majella, is born.

Alessandro, however, loses his mental balance. He becomes obsessed with Americans, who by now have taken two farms from him. He suffers lapses of memory, and his will to begin again is feeble. In a dispute over a horse he is gunned down by a white, Jim Farrar, and dies in Ramona's arms. Felipe Moreno, heir to the Moreno ranch now that Señora Moreno is dead, seeks out Ramona and her daughter Majella. They are eventually married but decide to live in Old Mexico, because for both Indian and Spaniard Southern California is now an alien place.

Attempting a parable, Helen Hunt Jackson offered a symbolic anatomy of the Southern California experience as she encountered it in the early 1880s. Every character and detail of *Ramona* was based on fact, or composites of facts. The Moreno estate was based upon Rancho Camulos in Ventura County. Into the delineation of Ramona and Alessandro went a number of observed or heard-of people. Juan Diego, the Cahuilla Indian shot by Sam Temple in 1877, and Juan's widow Ramona Lubo (who lived until 1924) provided the factual beginnings of her central characters, their histories augmented by elements from the lives of Rojerio Rocha, another Indian, skilled like Alessandro in the church music of the missions; Blanca Yndart, a Spanish orphan raised on Rancho Camulos; and Guadalupe, daughter of a Piru chief, also part of the crowded Camulos retinue. Señora Moreno can be traced to Doña Ysabel del Valle, the widowed owner of Camulos, and Felipe to her son Reginald. Father Salvierderra, the saintly Franciscan who takes a special interest in Ramona's education and who represents the finest possibilities of the mission protectorate, is Padre Francisco de Jesús Sánchez, the old Mexican missionary who so impressed Mrs. Jackson when she visited Mission Santa Barbara. Father Ubach, the secular priest who championed the cause of the Temecula Indians, became Father Gaspara, the parish priest who marries Ramona and Alessandro.

The source of *Ramona's* popular appeal, however—why it ranks with Harold Bell Wright's *The Winning of Barbara Worth* (1911) and Margaret Mitchell's *Gone with the Wind* (1936) as one of American's persistent best-sellers—is not that it translates fact into fiction, but that it translates fact into romantic myth. Despite its exaggerated, sometimes shrill sentimentalism, its awkward character development and occasional hysteria, *Ramona* spoke to Southern California with the direct and compelling power of culture-defining romance. Gathering to herself the scattered, fragile, inert materials of the Southern Californian experience, Helen Hunt Jackson enlivened them, as best she could (she had a minor but lively talent), with the repairing touch of significant associations: religion, the twilight days of a race, the spirit of time and place, and the yearning for present possession of a healing past.

In *Ramona* Helen Hunt Jackson collapsed American Southern California back onto the Spanish past. There, she suggested, in the days of the Franciscan missions, Southern California could find spiritual foundations with which to upgrade the crass vacuity of the present. The protagonists of *Ramona* defy the Americans by their piety. Each religious observance is part of a continuing act of self-definition in which they remind themselves who they are as a people. Señora Moreno, who dresses in black like a nun, veiled and with a rosary around her waist, goes so far as to have high wooden crosses erected on the hills of the Moreno estate so as to remind Americans that they are passing through Old California, whose occupants yet remember their religion and their past. The yearly arrival of Father Salvierderra at shearing time brings even closer the feel of the old days. Based in Mission Santa Barbara, Father Salvierderra walks El Camino Real as three generations of Franciscans have trod it before him. Pushing his way through the blooming mustard fields outside the Moreno ranch, he chants the Canticle of the Sun by Saint Francis of Assisi. At the ranch, the sacred vessels, smuggled out of Mission San Luis Rey by the sacristan during the Conquest to prevent them from falling into Yankee hands, are brought from their cases, and the old Franciscan celebrates mass for the household in the estate's private chapel.

None of this is to suggest that *Ramona* sustains any significant spiritual drama or offers much in the way of theological reflection. What does occur, however—and this is why the Ramona myth took such hold of the popular imagination in Southern California—is that through literature a representative Protestant sensibility, Mrs. Jackson's, deracinated from place and dogma, feels the comforts of a local Catholic tradition. *Ramona* was a Pacific Coast extension of the larger process of the New England mind Mediterraneanizing. Amherst and Calvinism she had abandoned, but here in Southern California, in mid-middle age, Helen Hunt Jackson experienced and expressed lingering, comforting traces of faith and place. Through *Ramona,* in turn, Americans of Mrs. Jackson's time, fearful about themselves and what they had wrought in Southern California, took some warmth from the banked fires of the culture they had displaced.

A paradox, obviously, was involved in turning into a founding fable a story whose central characters either hated or were being destroyed by Americans—unless, of course, the fable was being appropriated partly as a corrective. *Ramona* made some atonement to Spanish California by acknowledging what had been done; meanwhile, it availed itself of the Spanish past for its own purposes. Henceforth the mission era was part of American history.

Social protest, Mrs. Jackson's original intent, was suppressed in the savoring of *Ramona's* celebration of Southern California as a sunny Arcadia. On the Moreno rancho the myth of Southern California attained a local habitation and a name. *Ramona* exudes enchantment. Here indeed, Mrs. Jackson suggested, was the poetry and the color of this new American region and the arcadia which had once obtained—and might again, when American energies were properly directed: the arroyos, lined with willow and sycamore, so mysterious by evening, in whose chiaroscuro of shadow and moonlight the Indian lovers met for stolen moments; the long, low hacienda of whitewashed adobe and red tile, bulwarked on its eastern side by a veranda where ancient Juanita, now senile, earned her keep by shelling beans in the midmorning sun, where Anita and Mary, twins born on the ranch forty years previously, gossiped at noon, and where Juan Capito, the head shepherd, cajoled more food from Marda the cook; sheep-shearing time, when the Indians came in from the villages, organized into competing bands; the work of the ranch in feeding so many; the sanctuary light burning in the chapel; the great oaken furniture in the thick-walled, cool rooms within the main house; the patio garden planted in cactus, carnations, geraniums, and musk; the finches, the swallows; the days of quiet content; the orange grove; the orchards fragrant with the springtime blossoms of almond, peach, apricot, and pear.

It was, obviously, a mythical time and place, a garden of earthly delight which in truth had never existed with such sensuous and imaginative fullness, although its inspiration, Rancho Camulos, was among the most beautiful places in Southern California. As a myth, however, *Ramona's* ideal Southland gave expression to a yearning that Southern California be a land of beauty and memory and sunny afternoons. The pastel ideality of *Ramona's* locale was a way of suggesting that the frontier was over, that aesthetic self-consciousness had come to *California del Sur*. From now on—from the 1880s on, that is—Southern California would pay attention to more than getting and spending.

Contemporary critics made the point that, while Mrs. Jackson idealized her subject, she had captured the spirit of the Southland taken at its best. Well into the 1930s the *Ramona* myth remained one of the essential elements by which Southern California identified itself, to itself and to others. For years a massive public pageant based on Helen Hunt Jackson's novel was produced annually at Hemet, in a natural amphitheater at the base of Mount San Jacinto, where much of *Ramona's* story takes place. Garnet Holme, who had written and produced a number of pageants in the Greek Theater in Berkeley, directed a cast of nearly two hundred players, most of them volunteers from nearby towns. The Ramona Pageant was compared to the Passion Play at Oberammergau. Mrs. Jackson herself became something of a cult figure. Nearly every hour of her Southern California sojourn was the object of painstaking scrutiny and hagiological documentation. She had, after all, coaxed Southern California along toward self-consciousness. She had given it a myth by which to know itself.

Notes

Glenn Dumke's *Boom of the Eighties in Southern California* (1944) documents the frenzy of the 1880s. Theodore Strong Van Dyke's *Millionaires of a Day* (1890) is a good contemporary account, while Frederick R. Sanford's *Bursting of a Boom* (1889) is a weak but sometimes informative novel. Earl S. Pomeroy illuminates some aspects of the rush to Southern California in *In Search of the Golden West: The Tourist in Western America* (1957). John Packard's "The Role of the Tourist Hotel in California Development to 1900," M.A. thesis, University of Southern California (1953) should have been published years ago. The Bancroft Library has a number of publicity pamphlets from the Hotel Del Coronado, 1890–1900. See also J. Harold Peterson, *The Coronado Story* (1954).

John E. Baur's *The Health Seekers of Southern California, 1870–1900* (1959) commands the topic. For contemporary claims, see L. M. Holt, *The Great Interior Fruit Belt and Sanitarium of Southern California: San Bernardino County...* (1885); Peter Charles Remondino, *The Mediterranean Shores of America* (1892); William A. Edwards and Beatrice Harraden, *Two Health-Seekers in Southern California* (1897); and F. C. S. Sanders, *California as a Health Resort* (1916). See also Oscar O. Winther, "The Use of Climate as a Means of Promoting Migration to Southern California," *Mississippi Valley Historical Review 33* (1946): 411–424.

Ramona appeared in 1884. Helen Hunt Jackson's other Southern California sketches are available in *Glimpses of Three Coasts* (1886). *Helen Hunt Jackson* by Ruth Odell (1939) is complete and well-written. The development of the Ramona myth can be traced through Charles Fletcher Lummis, *The Home of Ramona* (n.d.); Adam Clark Vroman and

T. F. Barnes, *The Genesis of the Story of Ramona* (1899); George Wharton James, *Through Ramona's Country* (1908); and Carlyle Channing Davis, *The True Story of Ramona* (ca. 1914). The Bancroft Library has a file of articles, pamphlets, and other ephemera relating to the Ramona Pageant Play by Garnet Holme. In 1906 the Los Angeles Chamber of Commerce issued a catalogue of *Ramona*-related material, the *Antonio F. Coronel Collection*.

THE EMERGING CORPORATE STATE

California government and politics in the late nineteenth century were dominated by a great debate over the role of the Southern Pacific Railroad. Critics charged that local, state, and even federal officeholders were little more than hired hands of the railroad monopoly. Even the courts were not immune from railroad influence; corrupt jurists acted as the company's defensive shield against hostile litigation. Big city bosses and small town politicos were all part of a vast political machine.[1] As San Francisco's James D. Phelan observed, the Southern Pacific had created a government within a government.

Historians generally have agreed that the power of the railroad was both pervasive and corrupt. George E. Mowry, for instance, began his history of the California progressives with a chapter titled "The Southern Pacific's California." In a classic formulation of the antirailroad view, Mowry wrote: "California, like so many of her sister commonwealths at the turn of the century, had only the shadow of representative government, while the real substance of power resided largely in the Southern Pacific Railroad Company. To a degree perhaps unparalleled in the nation, the Southern Pacific and a web of associated interests ruled the state."[2]

In recent years several scholars have attempted to reassess the Southern Pacific's role in California history. They have concluded that the railroad was neither as powerful nor as evil as its contemporary critics alleged. R. Hal Williams, a Professor of History at Yale University, argues that while Californians in the late nineteenth century commonly believed that the Southern Pacific ruled an invisible government, "research has revealed little to sustain this view." Railroad domination of California

---

[1]An excellent summary of the antirailroad position appears in Ward McAfee, *California's Railroad Era, 1850–1922* (San Marino, 1973), 211 ff.

[2]George E. Mowry, *The California Progressives* (Berkeley, 1951), 9.

politics, Williams concludes, has been so exaggerated that it has become "a legend."[3] Likewise, historian Richard J. Orsi complains that scholars have too often accepted the rhetoric of the railroad's critics and have focused their research on conflicts between the Southern Pacific and the public interest. While Orsi acknowledges the "essential truth" of many traditional accounts of the railroad's power, he calls for historians to move beyond the study of conflict and identify ways in which the railroad's interests paralleled those of the public. Orsi argues that in fact the railroad did much to strengthen California's economy, stabilize its chaotic society, and further the welfare of its citizens.[4] A more strident defense of the railroad appears in the work of Don L. Hofsommer, who dismisses the charges against the railroad as a part of "western folklore" and claims that they have been "repeated by succeeding generations of writers and others who invented history to satisfy strangely perverse needs."[5] The nature of the perversity Hofsommer has in mind is not specified.

In the following selection, Spencer C. Olin cogently restates the traditional view that the Southern Pacific was the greatest single influence in California politics from about 1870 until 1910. Olin is careful to point out, however, that the railroad was not always able to dictate public policy and that it was divided from within by dissension. Furthermore, Olin argues, the railroad was only *one* of several powerful influences in state government. It was corporate monopolies generally, not just the Southern Pacific, that dominated California politics. California emerged in the late nineteenth century as a "corporate state," while the forces arrayed in opposition produced what Olin calls "the politics of antimonopoly."

Spencer C. Olin, Professor of History at the University of California, Irvine, is the author, coauthor, or editor of five books, including *California's Prodigal Sons: Hiram Johnson and the California Progressives, 1911–1917* (1968).

[3]R. Hal Williams, *The Democratic Party and California Politics, 1880–1896* (Stanford, 1973), vii, 206–232.

[4]Richard J. Orsi, "The Octopus Reconsidered: The Southern Pacific and Agricultural Modernization in California, 1865–1915," *California Historical Quarterly,* LIV (Fall 1975), 197–220.

[5]Don L. Hofsommer, *The Southern Pacific, 1901–1985* (College Station, Texas, 1986), 7, 314.

READING 17

The Emerging Corporate State

Spencer C. Olin, Jr.

In the 1880s public antipathy toward railroad domination became the basic element of California politics. Such antipathy grew in the years after the adoption of the second constitution in 1879 as the Southern Pacific increased its political activity, concentrating its manipulative efforts on state legislators and engaging in countless legal battles over taxation sections of the state constitution. One contemporary political analyst asserted that the constitution of 1879 "gave the railroad the choice of going into politics or going into bankruptcy."[1]

So pervasive did the Southern Pacific's power become that within a few years it was attempting to name and control virtually every candidate for every political office from the governorship on down. In 1884 the railroad spent more than $600,000 influencing legislation. Of special concern that year was the Barry bill, introduced by a San Francisco assemblyman and designed to prevent the railroad from eliminating all seagoing competition by granting generous rebates to those shippers who agreed to send all freight by rail. As was the customary pattern, the Barry bill was killed in the senate, where railroad spokesmen successfully emasculated its major provisions. Other antirailroad bills submitted that year met the same fate. The railroad's lobbying efforts were not restricted to California, as its agents also distributed money as far away as Kentucky, where the legislature was considering a charter for "the Southern Pacific Company," a new holding company for all the subsidiary railroads controlled by the Big Four. In these and other ways, the railroad sought to ensure its own continued prosperity and its freedom from effective state regulation,

while striving to prevent rate reductions and other incursions into corporate privilege.

Though the railroad was not effectively regulated until the early twentieth century, it experienced difficulty in achieving its goals even during the later years of the nineteenth. Not only was it confronted with economic competition from rival railroads and several potent political challenges to its extensive power, but it also had to deal with its own internal dissension. To be sure, the Big Four did not always act as a cohesive unit. In 1885, for example, Collis Huntington opposed Leland Stanford's senatorial ambitions, and thereby let his deep and festering resentment of his partner's public acclaim and of his own more menial managerial role in railroad affairs become known. In 1890, Huntington would reluctantly pledge his support for Stanford's reelection as senator only if Stanford stepped down as president of the railroad (a position he had held for thirty years) so that he, Huntington, could assume the office. An agreement to this effect was reached between the now-estranged business partners, whereupon Huntington as president publicly announced his refusal to "use this great corporation to advance my personal ambition at the expense of its owners, or put my hands in the treasury to defeat the people's choice, and thereby put myself into positions that should be filled by others."[2]

Such a striking remonstrance of his predecessor's activities reinforced the hostile judgment of the railroad long shared by many Californians. These evidences of internal factionalism, moreover, did not alter the common perception of railroad corruption, excessive economic power, and unwarranted political influence. Nor did it erase memories of such incidents as the Mussel Slough massacre of

1880. Occurring near Hanford, in Kings County, farmers battled agents of the railroad assisted by county officials, and seven homesteaders lost their lives. The issue was the legality of land titles. More than any other single event, the killings at Mussel Slough had mobilized public antagonism against large landholders and the railroad.[3] Such popular resentment was sustained with varying degrees of intensity throughout the 1880s, and resulted in making the railroad the focus of political agitation and a reference point for social activists.

In the early 1890s, William F. Herrin, a well-known and skilled attorney, became general counsel for the Southern Pacific. Undeterred by widespread antirailroad sentiment, he boldly created the Political Bureau, an integral part of the railroad's legal department and a lobbying force in its own right. Using the Political Bureau to increase the Espee's political visibility, he strengthened the existing working alliance with San Francisco's "city bosses," such as Christopher Buckley (who was indicted by the grand jury in 1891 and later fled California to avoid prosecution) and Dan Burns (whom Herrin attempted to make United States senator). These city bosses, who controlled large blocs of legislators and delegates, served as a conduit between politically ambitious corporate leaders and the political system. Because of their immense usefulness, therefore, Herrin also established important contacts with bosses, particularly in Sacramento, Stockton, and San Jose.[4]

THE POLITICS OF ANTIMONOPOLY

The Southern Pacific Railroad was undeniably the greatest single influence on California politics from roughly 1870 until 1910, but it is important to understand that it was not the *only* such influence. By no means was California politics in the late nineteenth century limited to controversies surrounding railroad machinations. Some vigorous reform movements also arose during this period. A few focused specifically on the Southern Pacific, but all expressed a common opposition to serious power imbalances introduced by the emergence of corporations. Such opposition was most effectively mobilized in the 1880s and 1890s by the California Democratic Party, which was once again in the ascendant after reaching its nadir at the end of the 1870s. Recovering slowly from the wounds earlier inflicted by intense internal debates over slavery, secession, and the Civil War, and from a decimation of its ranks by former Democrats who had gravitated into the Workingmen's Party, Democratic leaders were faced with a major rebuilding task. In this process of reconstruction, antimonopolists took the lead. They assumed control of local Democratic organizations across the state and won the election of 1882. In capturing nearly every state office, all positions on the Railroad Commission, six congressional seats, and a vast majority of the state legislative seats, the Democratic Party in California demonstrated a vital resurgence as a political force as well as the broad popularity of its antimonopoly stance.[5]

By the mid-1880s, however, antimonopolists in both the Democratic *and* Republican parties faced some deeply engrained public attitudes which ran counter to their plans. Among these were concerns about the sanctity of private property and the extent to which government should interfere in economic matters. As well, there were many who had come to appreciate the contributions of the Southern Pacific and the Santa Fe in the return of prosperity. In fact, perhaps the most important factor in improving public conceptions of the railroad was the alleged benefits of competition between the Espee and its new rival, the Santa Fe. This competition initially drove railroad rates down sharply, producing increased immigration which in turn led to a real estate boom in southern California. Most viewed the operation of such "natural laws" of competition as much more desirable than government activism and regulatory legislation. As a consequence, popular support began to wane for antimonopolists such as Barclay Henley, William D. English, and Stephen Mallory White (who worked as a Southern Pacific attorney in the late 1880s while also serving as a state senator). (This loss of public confidence proved to be momentary. When depression returned to California in the 1890s and when the public recognized that competition between the Southern Pacific and the Santa Fe had not eliminated the problem of monopoly, Californians once again pressed for antirailroad legislation.)

More favorable attitudes toward the railroads even affected the decisions of the Railroad Commissioners, who reported in 1888: "A better understanding and feeling now exists between the railroad companies and their customers than has ever before existed in this State."[6] To the chagrin of stalwart reformers, Democratic members of the commission interpreted their mission conservatively. They refused to use the full powers of their commission because it seemed to them that regulatory power was similar to the bureaucratic systems of European monarchs, and they praised rather than criticized the railroads.

In the mid-1880s, as has been suggested, California's economy finally recovered from its prolonged depression. This economic revival was accompanied by a rapid growth in population of more than 340,000 during the 1880s. These newcomers, primarily midwesterners from Illinois, Iowa, Ohio, and Indiana, brought the state's total population to some 1,200,000 by 1890. Even though San Francisco was by this date the eighth largest city in the United States, with a population of 300,000, the major growth occurred in southern California, where once languishing "cow counties" were transformed into thriving commercial centers. Such economic development was accelerated by the extension of the Santa Fe railroad line into southern California in 1885, leading to an unprecedented rivalry with the Southern Pacific and resulting in a rate war of immediate benefit to passengers and shippers alike.

In political terms, southern California gained enormous leverage from this immigration because the size of its delegations to conventions and to the legislature increased greatly. Furthermore, its new status was acknowledged by the selection of Los Angeles as the site of both the 1886 Republican and the 1888 Democratic state conventions. Such developments fanned a smoldering sectional rivalry between the northern and southern parts of the state. Finally, marked increases in the numbers of Republicans both threatened the hegemony of the Democratic Party and pointed up certain social changes then occurring.

Not until the mid-1890s, when economic depression returned and when competition among railroad giants had lessened, did antirailroad politics emerge once again as a vital force. The movement directed against the railroads was even more intense and popular than either the agitation by the Grange and Workingmen's parties in the 1870s or the antirailroad sentiment that permeated both the Democratic and Republican parties in the 1880s.

The most notable political manifestation of this social discontent was Populism, which originated in southern California among followers of the utopian reformer Edward Bellamy and then joined its mainstream counterparts in campaigning vociferously against the Southern Pacific. California Populism derived in large part from Nationalism, a movement which had grown rapidly in the state after Bellamy's utopian novel, *Looking Backward*, was published in 1888. Bellamy struck a responsive chord for many dissatisfied Californians in advocating a nationalized, cooperative state where public control over the economy supplanted private ownership of the means of production. Given Californians' antirailroad attitudes, such a program was well received by many segments of the population. Indeed, by 1890 there were sixty-two Nationalist clubs and some thirty-five hundred members, representing more than a third of the national total. Nationalist strength was primarily in Los Angeles, where Clara Folts, Anna Ferry Smith, and Arthur Vinette, and Socialist Herbert Guy Wilshire were active organizers, and in San Francisco. There the eccentric anarcho-syndicalist and communitarian Burnette Haskell was prominent in labor and radical movements, including Nationalism, from the early 1880s until the end of the century.

In 1890 the Nationalists held their only state convention, during which a bitter dispute arose between those advocating immediate nationalization and a more moderate faction that favored antitrust legislation and currency inflation. Failure to win broad public support in the 1890 election hastened the movement's decline, as many Nationalists turned their energies to a new movement called the Farmers' Alliance and the People's Party of California. In fact, in many rural sections of southern California, former Bellamy clubs were converted into local units of the Farmers' Alliance.

The most prominent leader of this new California Populist movement of the 1890s was Thomas V. Cator, who perhaps best represents the smooth transition from Nationalism to Populism. Arriving in San Francisco in 1887 at the age of thirty-six, after a political career in New Jersey, Cator immediately dedicated himself to "the great fight against plutocracy." Before long he had established himself as a major spokesman for those Californians who wished either to defy or reform the two major parties.

With converts like Cator, the Farmers' Alliance grew most rapidly in southern California, especially in economically depressed areas. Encouraged by these early successes, Alliance representatives from thirteen counties met in San Jose in November 1890 to create a statewide Farmers' Alliance and Industrial Union. Its platform was typically antimonopoly, lashing out at Wall Street and at the "abject subserviency" of United States politicians to "the narrow and selfish demands of a purse-proud oligarchy."[7]

Resisting the temptation to form a third party, Alliance leaders initially favored endorsements of candidates supportive of their goals. By 1892, however, Alliance membership had risen to thirty thousand members in more than five hundred units, an increase that encouraged delegates at a statewide convention to adopt a bold political strategy. They would create a new party in California, the People's Party, and a platform which they hoped would be attractive to the masses. In this way, California followed the pattern established in much of the nation, as the agrarian revolt moved into its political phase throughout the South (especially in Georgia, Alabama, and Texas) and the Midwest (where farmers in Kansas, the Dakotas, and Nebraska responded favorably to its program).

At its first formal convention in October 1891, the People's Party called for government ownership of communication and transportation, women's suffrage, and the eight-hour day on all public works. In their attempt to find platform support, the party's leaders faced serious obstacles. In the first place, as the 1892 election results would demonstrate, the People's Party, whose major strength was in traditionally Republican areas, could not attract urban workers away from the Democratic Party. Secondly, where the Farmers' Alliance was strongest, in the southern and interior regions, the Democratic leadership cleverly appealed to those voters who favored Populism. Finally, Republicans, not content to sit idly by, launched a vigorous campaign against Populism, charging that the movement was dangerously radical and ought therefore to be renounced by all Californians.

Populist candidates in the 1892 election managed to attract more votes from disenchanted Republicans, who believed their party had become too "plutocratic," than from Democrats. Because the party was predominantly a rural movement, it never attracted a large following in the cities. It failed, moreover, to win a single senatorial seat in the state legislature, even though it did elect eight assemblymen. At the local level, the Populists' presidential candidate, James B. Weaver of Iowa, received only 2,500 votes in San Francisco, less than five percent of the city's total. In Tulare County, the Populists garnered no more than twenty-one percent of the vote in any of the towns, while in rural precincts the response to their candidates ranged from thirty-eight percent to seventy-five percent.

As a consequence of their uneven showing in the 1892 elections, California Populists made every effort during 1893 and 1894 to broaden their support. In particular, party leaders organized a greatly expanded and more effective campaign to attract labor votes. "I have fears," declared one party leader to Thomas Cator, "that we have a great task to win a large mass of those city laborers but we must hold out the olive branch and do the best we can for them."[8] In the 1894 election, where all contending parties focused on essentially the same issues—especially free silver and antirailroad measures—the Populists markedly improved their previous showing, doubling their votes of two years earlier. In drawing votes away from Democratic candidates, they helped ensure massive Republican victories in Congress, the state legislature, and the entire executive slate from the lieutenant governor down. One Democrat, the prominent antirailroad figure James H. Budd, waged an aggressive campaign against the Southern Pacific and resisted the Republican tide by winning the governorship by a narrow margin. The Democrats also managed to elect a majority of the Railroad Commission. But in general the election belonged to the Republicans, with the Populists also making impressive gains. In 1896, however, the Populists were less successful, as the party disintegrated in the face of dissatisfaction over its fusionist strategy and defections among its members to the new Socialist Party of Eugene Debs.

Historians have disagreed about the meaning of Populism. Some view it as a reactionary, fundamentalist rebellion against a modernizing, industrializing society, and others claim that its primary constituency (impoverished farmers) endorsed a harshly radical critique of the American economic system and an enlightened program for constructive change. Those who view Populism in such positive terms would tend to agree with C. Vann Woodward's judgment that Populism "constituted the largest and most powerful movement attempting the structural reform of the American economic and political system in the nineteenth century."[9] Others more skeptical of Populism's alleged accomplishments would likely favor the assessment of Lawrence Jelinek, commenting on the California experience:

> The achievements of late nineteenth century farmer discontent were marginal. In neither economic, constitutional, nor political terms were small farmers able to restructure California agriculture, much less the major transportation, banking, and commercial interests that controlled so much of agriculture from within and without. Reform of this magnitude required a faith in party politics built on farmer-worker cooperation more than upon the decentralized tools of direct democracy. It was and has remained an improbable chemistry.[10]

This complex scholarly debate cannot be resolved here, but California Populism was undoubtedly less influential than its counterparts in the Great Plains and the South. Also, the California variant was rather different, being less attractive to foreign immigrants and possessing a more urban and middle-class composition than elsewhere. Even so, Populism appealed most directly to, and received greater support from, Californians in rural districts. What is peculiar to California is the nonfarm support received by the Populist Party and the ability of Populists to incorporate some urban, working-class discontents. Though California Populists did not achieve the political successes enjoyed by their members in other parts of the country, they nonetheless were an important catalyst in raising issues of principle and in forcing the major parties to address leading issues forthrightly. Moreover, in emphasizing the significance of citizen control of government (as opposed to control by party bosses and party conventions), the Populists stimulated public interest in such "direct democracy" measures as the primary, the initiative, the referendum, and the recall. Finally, their antirailroad stand was consistent with that of the major parties, thus demonstrating that the issue of railroad domination continued to serve as a rallying point for Californians from across the political spectrum.

Many Californians in the 1890s were particularly aroused by the railroads' blatant attempts to escape payment of the debt owed to the federal government for grants received under the Railway acts of 1862 and 1864. In the case of the Central Pacific, most activists pushed for foreclosure of its mortgage, figuring that such a stringent measure would enhance chances for increased railroad competition and would inflict a damaging wound to Huntington's railroad empire. Others saw in the potential demise of the Central Pacific through foreclosure and sale a perfect opportunity for government ownership. Groups as disparate as the San Francisco Chamber of Commerce and the California Farmers' Alliance joined with the state's major political parties and its leading newspapers (including the conservative *Los Angeles Times*) to advocate government ownership. Such unanimity of opinion led Collis Huntington, who observed the entire scene from his New York headquarters, to back away from his attempt to obtain complete debt exoneration, choosing instead to amortize that debt over a long period of time. Final resolution of the problem came in early 1897, when the House of Representatives soundly defeated a bill that would have allowed the Central Pacific to pay its debt through the issuance of bonds, with repayment to extend over *eighty* years. Instead, the House later

approved a bill which was much less favorable to the railroad and required full payment within ten years.

This victory, while by no means complete, nevertheless emboldened the antirailroad Californians who gathered in common cause a remarkably diverse group of organizations and interests. In the late 1890s this diverse opposition to the railroad was nowhere more clearly demonstrated than in the bitter fight over a modern, deep-water harbor for Los Angeles. In this instance, Collis Huntington had long pressed for such a harbor to be built at Santa Monica (because of Southern Pacific ownership of land there), thereby reversing Leland Stanford's previous policy favoring its location at San Pedro. The very real possibility that their harbor might be operated under Southern Pacific control, as had San Francisco's for more than forty years, stirred Los Angeles residents to action. Joining forces in a coalition against Huntington were people of widely different political persuasions, such as Democratic United States senator Stephen M. White, editor-owner Harrison Gray Otis of the *Los Angeles Times,* and several St. Louis finance capitalists involved in the San Pedro harbor project. Huntington ultimately lost the battle, as a board of engineers recommended San Pedro over Santa Monica, and construction was at last begun there in April 1899.[11] Thus the state was set for an even more dramatic confrontation between the railroad and its opponents in the early twentieth century.

CONCLUSION

To reiterate the view expressed earlier, full understanding of the railroad's role in state politics during the late nineteenth century requires acknowledgment of both its major impact *and* its own internal divisions and periodic defeats. From 1898 on, for example, the Democratic Party placed at least one antirailroad candidate on the ticket in every gubernatorial election. In 1898 such a candidate, James G. Maguire, made a good run against the Southern Pacific's choice, Republican Henry T. Gage, an attorney who had represented the railroad for many years and whose subsequent administration would be marked by strife and scandal. In 1902 Democrat Franklin K. Lane (with 143,743 votes) almost defeated George C. Pardee (with 146,322 votes), who owed his nomination to the railroad machine. In 1906 Democrat Theodore A. Bell (who would run again in 1910 against reformer Hiram Johnson) was narrowly defeated for the governorship by James N. Gillett, who had received Southern Pacific backing.

Even within the Republican Party there was an effective, if loosely organized, reform element. Prominent among these independently minded Republicans was conservative Thomas Robert Bard of Ventura County. Bard, who had been active in local politics from the time he came to California in 1865, was primarily involved in land development, banking, grain, shipping, sheep-raising, and petroleum (he was a founder and first president of the Union Oil Company of California). In 1899 Bard and a few others became convinced that Governor Henry T. Gage was a tool of the Southern Pacific and unworthy of further support. Their subsequent political activities, and Bard's ultimate election to the United States Senate in 1900 on an antirailroad platform, marked the first major break between "regular" and "antirailroad" Republicans and constituted another effective challenge to Southern Pacific control.

These various elections provide additional evidence of growing opposition to machine-dominated politics in California. Furthermore, the Southern Pacific's commercial supremacy in the state was eroded in the late nineteenth and early twentieth centuries by business enterprises, including two competing railroads, the Santa Fe and the Western Pacific. Nor could the Southern Pacific's Political Bureau confidently rely upon its strength in the state's metropolitan centers, as local leaders in in-creasing numbers refused any longer to mortgage the future of their cities in order to promote railroad development.

By the turn of the century California had thus departed markedly from the original vision embodied in the constitution of 1849, namely, an open, democratic society with a pluralistic political system and an economy characterized by free competition among small, independent entrepreneurs. Instead, as powerful business interests captured the major political parties in California, other less advantaged segments of the population acquired less and less representation in government. Also, the small entrepreneurs who had previously been the mainstay of the state's market economy had been largely supplanted in importance by corporate capitalists, such as the Big Four in railroad construction and operation, Alvinza Hayward in mining, Peter Donahue in iron manufacturing, and Isaias Hellman in banking. Under such conditions of restricted opportunity it was unlikely that the status quo would remain unchallenged.

Notes

1 See John P. Irish, "California and the Railroad," *Overland Monthly,* XXV (1895), 677.

2 As quoted in Walton Bean, *California: An Interpretive History* (3rd ed., New York: McGraw-Hill, 1978), 255.

3 See William Clyde McKinney, "The Mussel Slough Episode: A Chapter in the Settlement of the San Joaquin Valley, 1865–1880" (M.A. thesis, University of California, Berkeley, 1948); and James L. Brown, *The Mussel Slough Tragedy* (n.p., 1958).

4 See William A. Bullough, *The Blind Boss and His City: Christopher Augustine Buckley and Nineteenth-Century San Francisco* (Berkeley and Los Angeles: University of California Press, 1980).

5 For an excellent account of the Democratic Party in the late nineteenth century, see R. Hal Williams, *The Democratic Party and California Politics, 1880–1896* (Stanford, Calif.: Stanford University Press, 1973).

6 Quoted in ibid., 92.

7 *San Francisco Examiner,* November 21–23, 1890. Much of my account of Nationalism and Populism is based upon Williams, *Democratic Party and California Politics,* esp. 134–139.

8 J. L. Gilbert to Thomas Cator, November 18, 1893, Cator Papers, as cited in Williams, *Democratic Party and California Politics,* 163.

9 C. Vann Woodward, "The Promise of Populism," review of Lawrence Goodwyn's *Democratic Promise: The Populist Moment in America* (New York: Oxford University Press, 1976), in *New York Review of Books,* October 28, 1976, 28.

10 Lawrence J. Jelinek, *Harvest Empire: A History of California Agriculture* (San Francisco: Boyd & Fraser, 1979), 46.

11 See Richard W. Barsness, "Railroads and Los Angeles: The Quest for a Deep-Water Port," *Southern California Quarterly,* XLVII (1965), 379–391.

ORGANIZED LABOR AND POLITICS

EDITOR'S INTRODUCTION

The history of organized labor in California stretches back to the gold-rush era when the first unions were organized in San Francisco. The state's earliest unions were short-lived affairs and their efforts to obtain higher wages and better working conditions were sporadic. It was not until the 1880s that stable, effective working-class organizations appeared in California. Ever since, organized labor has played a major role in the state's economic, social, and political history.

As Michael Kazin points out in the following selection, scholars in recent years have produced a wealth of new studies of California labor. These studies constitute the building blocks for a comprehensive labor history of the state, a history that is yet to be written. Kazin's article stands as a prospectus for this history, offering both an interpretation of the outstanding characteristics of California labor as well as a periodization for the years 1870 to 1940.

The first period in the state's labor history, from 1870 to 1898, was a time of ideological and organizational experimentation. The Workingmen's Party of California (WPC) emerged during these years as the first in a series of labor-oriented political parties. The WPC, led by sandlot orator Denis Kearney, was virulently anti-Chinese and antimonopoly. Kazin views the WPC as a legitimate white working-class organization, styling it an "invaluable bridge" to later unionization. During the 1880s and 1890s urban trade councils and powerful craft unions, some of which were under radical leadership, formed in San Francisco. By the turn of the century, labor was firmly entrenched in what came to be called "the first closed-shop city in the United States."

The second period of California labor history extended from 1898 to 1922, and was an era of consolidation of labor's strength. Kazin demonstrates that during this period labor again turned to political action with the formation of the Union Labor Party in San Francisco. Asian immigration continued to be an important issue and many of the state's labor leaders actively supported the anti-Japanese movement. Kazin also demonstrates that in the early twentieth century California's mainstream union leaders cooperated openly with socialists and anarchists. Labor's relationship with the middle-class progressives was more problematical. While the progressives and the leaders of organized labor shared many goals, they also found themselves competitors for political support.

Organized labor waned during the 1920s as the forces of conservatism gained strength. Then, in the midst of the depression of the 1930s, labor again went on the offensive. The depression-era resurgence of union strength marks the third period of California labor history. As in earlier periods, radicals played an important role in labor's revitalization and labor leaders once again were politically active. Labor supported the candidacies of former Socialist Upton Sinclair for governor in 1934 and of liberal Democrat Culbert Olson four years later.

Kazin begins his overview of the state's labor history by quoting Carey McWilliams's classic study, *California: The Great Exception* (1949). Although Kazin disagrees with many of McWilliams's conclusions, he affirms that in several respects the labor history of California does represent an exception to the national experience. Central labor councils, for instance, remained a major force in California's cities long after they had diminished in strength elsewhere in the nation. Labor leaders in California also cooperated with radicals more openly—and co-opted their rhetoric more boldly—than did American unionists generally. And whereas American labor in general rejected the idea of forming a political party of its own, California labor consistently engaged in independent political action.

Michael Kazin received his Ph.D. from Stanford University in 1983 and is the author of *Barons of Labor: The San Francisco Building Trades and Union Power in the Progressive Era* (1987). He is currently an Assistant Professor of History at American University.

READING 18

Organized Labor and Politics

Michael Kazin

In 1949, Carey McWilliams summarized, with one phrase, the character of organized labor in his adopted state: "It has been the *total engagement* of labor in California that has, from the beginning, given the California labor movement its distinctive character." He continued, "The labor struggle in the state has not been partial and limited but total and indivisible; all of labor pitted against all of capital." McWilliams's saga featured a cast of radicalized workers whose frequent and often violent confrontations with management contributed significantly to what he termed the state's "marked political instability."[1] By focusing on dramatic strikes and colorful personalities, McWilliams evoked the ubiquity of "total engagement" and then moved on to sketch the many other ways in which California diverged from the general American pattern.

Since the publication of *California: The Great Exception,* American labor history has blossomed into an empirically rich and conceptually acute field. As in other fields of social history, regional and local studies have proliferated. A widening stream of recent books and dissertations on California has greatly augmented knowledge of various sectors of the state's work force in different periods of its history. The majority of these monographs focus on patterns of work and residence, but their authors also share a fascination with the subject of working-class consciousness—what it means and how it develops out of specific occupations and cultural traditions. These studies provide

the seeds from which a serious history of California workers is growing. None of them, however, offers a broad political perspective which emulates that which Carey McWilliams offered in one short chapter written almost forty years ago.[2]

From 1870 to 1940, California left its glorious isolation on the fringe of European settlement and became both an economic giant and a significant political region from which firebrands like Denis Kearney, Hiram Johnson, and Upton Sinclair emerged to shake the nation. The years from 1870 to 1940 also saw the California labor movement grow to maturity. During the Gilded Age, skilled workers organized themselves into trade unions which withstood the blows of open-shop employers and two severe depressions. In the Progressive era, the labor movement attained great influence for a time before being humbled in the aftermath of World War I. During the 1930s, unions regained strength, albeit with a loss of political independence, and tripled their membership in less than a decade.

Three major characteristics emerge from the labor history of this period. First, with little opposition, urban federations of skilled craftsmen dominated the labor movement until the 1930s. White women, agricultural workers of all races, and menial laborers in the cities sometimes acted on their own, but the objectives and accomplishments of their isolated struggles were limited in almost every case by the ideological and institutional hegemony of craft unionists. Key to this supremacy was the sustained influence of strong, citywide central labor federations in both San Francisco and Los Angeles. The attraction of such organizations went beyond their economic utility. "City centrals" sponsored and financed whatever labor

Adapted from "The Great Exception Revisited: Organized Labor and Politics in San Francisco and Los Angeles, 1870-1940," by Michael Kazin. Copyright © 1986 by the Pacific Coast Branch, American Historical Association. Reprinted from *Pacific Historical Review*, Vol 55, No. 3, pp. 371–402, by permission of the Association.

newspapers existed, and because of their inclusive, representative nature, they could forcefully bring working-class demands to the attention of state and municipal officials.

Second, these dominant groups incorporated much of the critique and rhetoric of the political left rather than opposing it as did the national AFL leadership. Carey McWilliams's description of a "more or less indigenous radicalism which has always gone hand-in-hand with the labor movement" can be explained by labor's ability to adapt the ideas of Marxists and egalitarian utopians like Henry George to its own trade unionist ends.[3] The most successful unionists routinely spoke to workers and the general public in a language filled with allusions to "class struggle" and "monopoly rule." Yet only a small minority had a desire, much less a strategy, for overthrowing the capitalist system. Their aim instead was to increase the power of trade unions in every area of society as a counterweight to organized corporate might. In this effort, radical ideas and radical activists were tremendously useful: the former provided a vision attractive to many Californians; the latter organized with almost incorruptible dedication. However, control of labor's offensive always lay with those working-class leaders whose only loyalty was to their unions and not to any left organization that may have been involved.

Third, the California labor movement pursued its aims as much through political activity as by exerting its muscle at the workplace. Unionists unstintingly yoked their fortunes to candidates, parties, and legal reforms that promised to make the government more responsive to working-class concerns. In fact, it is difficult to identify any significant figure in the history of California unionism who subscribed to the national AFL's vaunted policy of "voluntarism"—the notion that electoral partisanship and labor legislation would only restrict the freedom of unions and embroil them in endless factional disputes.[4] Moreover, until World War

I white workers in California's urban centers often had a "labor party" for which to vote. From the scanty evidence collected thus far, it seems they gave that party at least a plurality of their votes, although none of the chosen vehicles was a frequent winner or dedicated itself to social change once in office.[5] When they could not mount an independent ticket, most union leaders aligned themselves with one of the major parties and, in return, received nominations, and appointments for themselves, and legislation to benefit their members. Political involvement flowed naturally from the labor movement's claim to be the representative of all *white* working-class Californians. That the campaign for Asian exclusion required continuous pressure on office-holders in both Sacramento and Washington, D.C., contributed to this self-image, but it was not the sole influence. Craft unionists regularly also participated in municipal campaigns in which the issue of Chinese and Japanese immigration played only a minor role.

Thus, the most salient feature of California urban labor was not, as Carey McWilliams believed, its radical ideology or militant tactics, but the ability of existing unions to direct working-class discontent to their own ends. The most influential labor leaders proved themselves to be both ecumenical towards political factions within their own ranks and fierce opponents of management at times of industrial conflict. This combination allowed California unionists to avoid bitter internal quarrels that, in other parts of the nation, often split the movement into irreconcilable parts. California's north-south differences did hinder the *success* of statewide organizing efforts, but the basic *character* of unionism was essentially similar above and below the Tehachapi Mountains. The labor movement encompassed more than just unions, but affiliates of the AFL and CIO skillfully harnessed to their wagons most radical parties, working-class ethnic associations, and single-issue labor reform groups.

The history of urban labor in California from 1870 to 1940 can be separated into three eras— each of which represents a stage in labor's ongoing engagement with political ideas and political power. Despite the different fortunes of the movement in Los Angeles and San Francisco, the aims of working-class activists and the associations formed to achieve them remained essentially the same in both cities throughout the entire period.

GILDED AGE BEGINNINGS

From 1870 to 1898, the ideological and organizational contours of the labor movement were established. Workers experimented with a wide range of collective forms—independent parties, radical sects, producer cooperatives, union federations, and craft-based locals—before settling upon a durable amalgam of "business unionism" infused with prodigious political ambitions.

The era opened with what Isaac Kalloch, a Baptist preacher who became a controversial mayor of San Francisco in 1879, called the "terrible Seventies."[6] The effects of a nationwide depression—exacerbated by a severe drought and the arrival of cheap eastern goods on the new transcontinental railroad—and the failure of either major party to halt Chinese immigration persuaded many wage-earners to break with their old political loyalties. The Workingmen's party of California (WPC) captured the labor vote in the late 1870s and then self-destructed, leaving an assortment of radical groups to pick up the pieces.

The WPC also filled a vacuum left by the collapse of craft unions that had been created in the 1860s, and it sparked a labor revival. For all the attention paid to Denis Kearney's demagogic oratory and the controversies that swirled around the party's role in writing the new state constitution of 1879, the WPC's functional role is often neglected. The party served as an invaluable bridge to more stable and popular unions.[7] Its sweeping victory in San Francisco and Los Angeles municipal elections demonstrated the appeal to white workers of a platform that attacked both Chinese immigration and a monopolized economy. Members of the WPC also had to pay an initiation fee and regular dues, practices soon adopted by trade unions. The party's major shortcoming, in the view of labor activists, was its domination by opportunists like Kearney and those animated by racial hatred alone. Shorn of those failings, it provided an excellent model for those who wanted to fuse political mobilization with a spirited call for the redress of economic grievances.[8] During the 1880s, skilled workers in California's urban centers reestablished their unions, most of which are still operating, on this broad new basis.

Under the tutelage of Gilded Age leaders like Frank Roney, these unions were far from autonomous bodies of conservative artisans, ever-jealous of their privileged status. For example, Roney advocated the formation of trade councils linking together all crafts in the same industry, thus creating the functional equivalent of an industrial union. In 1886, when the San Francisco Iron Trades Council won a closed shop in the city's iron mills, it sparked the Pacific Coast's first Labor Day parade. Grand Marshall Frank Roney led the orderly procession of 10,000 union men and a few women. Symbolic of labor's political influence, Democratic Governor George Stoneman rode behind Roney in an event that contrasted sharply with the contemporaneous bloodshed in Chicago's Haymarket Square.[9]

Gilded Age unionists shared a political mission as well as a penchant for organizations that bridged craft boundaries. At any given time in the late nineteenth century, a remarkable variety of ideas and proposals circulated through working-class communities in California. Individuals readily moved from the Workingmen's party to insurrectionist anarchism, the Socialist Labor party, utopian land colonies, producer cooperatives, groups espousing the creeds of Henry George and Edward Bellamy, and various factions within the two major parties. As Alexander Saxton has written, "Everything in the house of labor in those days was interpermeable; ideas overlapped; personnel swapped places."[10]

Yet there *was* a common thread in this dense variety of projects for the melioration and/or replacement of the capitalist order. White workers were articulating a desire for full participation in the economic realm which they already possessed in the political sphere. They sought democratic control of and fair compensation from their society, not its destruction. For example, Henry George's proposal for a confiscatory "single tax" on all unimproved land attracted immense popular support in the state because it seemed a rational way to level income while avoiding the class violence which had recently broken out in Pittsburgh, Chicago, and other industrial cities.[11] Politics of a more conventional type involved the majority of working-class activists. All over the state, union men ran for office on a program that included the eight-hour day, public ownership of utilities, police neutrality during strikes, and the permanent exclusion of Chinese labor.

Unarguably, California labor's most successful political campaign during the Gilded Age was the one waged against the Chinese, culminating in the federal Exclusion Act of 1882. Using boycotts, union labels, and the unifying agency of "city centrals," white workers and the politicians whom they championed developed a sense of mastery that endured into the next century. "Much of the present strength of the California labor movement is due to the sense of common interests and the habit of united action which were acquired in this great campaign," wrote prounion economist Lucile Eaves in 1910.[12] In one of the cruelest ironies of California's past, unions increased their membership and social power at the expense of workers from another race.

CONSOLIDATION OF POWER

Union power was consolidated and extended during the quarter-century from 1898 to 1922, which began with the economic boom touched off by the Spanish-American war and ended in the recession-wracked aftermath of World War I. During this period, San Francisco emerged as the quintessential union town: the closed shop prevailed in construction, transportation, and the bulk of manufacturing industries as well as an array of service trades, such as white-owned steam laundries and most restaurants and bars.[13] Los Angeles provided a contrasting study in weakness. Except for a flurry of organizing in 1910 and 1911, unions in the southern metropolis made little headway against the disciplined and well-financed juggernaut of the Merchants and Manufacturers Association headed by Harrison Gray Otis and F. J. Zeehandelaar. Even though Los Angeles was rapidly overtaking its fire-charred and peninsula-bound rival in wealth and population, its unionists of necessity still looked to San Francisco as their citadel. The major institutions that thrived within the Bay City were simply more mature versions of the central federations first created during the 1880s and 1890s. The San Francisco Labor Council (SFLC) contained over a hundred affiliates that ran the gamut from Michael Casey's Teamsters and Andrew Furuseth's Sailor's Union of the Pacific, which held a potential stranglehold over the distributive arteries of the West Coast, to small, predominately female unions like the Glove Workers and Bottle Canners, which barely survived on the margins of the city's economy.[14]

A frequent rival of the SFLC for the allegiance of local workers was the Building Trades Council of San Francisco, perhaps the most powerful local section of the AFL anywhere in the nation during the Progressive era. The BTC acted, in almost every respect, like an industrial union. Its leadership—headed by ex-carpenter

Patrick H. McCarthy and Norwegian radical (and erstwhile cement mason) Olaf Tveitmoe—ruled on all strikes, jurisdictional disputes, and requests for higher wages and lower hours that arose from any of its fifty-three affiliated locals, which ranged from "aristocratic" bricklayers to poorly paid street laborers.[15] The BTC also organized its San Francisco locals into a political machine which boosted union men to seats on the Board of Supervisors and the state legislature. In 1909, BTC officials took control of the Union Labor Party, which had recently been weakened by a series of trials in which many of its officeholders had confessed to taking graft from utility companies. Two years later, building tradesmen and their allies convinced San Francisco voters to elect Patrick McCarthy mayor. The Irish immigrant was the first labor leader ever chosen to run a major American city. "Labor is now fighting with both fists—politically and industrially," wrote Olaf Tveitmoe in 1911. "And in the language of the 'pug,' it 'carries a knockout blow in each mit.'"[16]

San Francisco served as the model for what California unionists could accomplish politically. Labor parties sprouted up in San Jose and Eureka, and some activists even dreamed of a unified organization capable of capturing the state government. Los Angeles union men tried hardest to imitate the success of their northern brethren. The Los Angeles Central Labor Council coordinated drives for new membership, and the Los Angeles Building Trades Council synchronized strikes among the various construction crafts. But Angeleno unionists were not able to sustain their organizing campaigns despite frequent infusions of money and personnel from San Francisco and the national AFL. Before World War I, both Los Angeles central federations together never included more than 6,000 affiliated members, only a tenth the membership of the San Francisco Labor Council and BTC at their zenith.[17]

During the Progressive era, white workers in California took as prominent a part in the anti-Japanese campaign of their time as had their predecessors to whom Chinese were the major villain. This time, however, union officials initiated the campaign, and no freelance orator-politicians emerged to challenge their control. "Sandlot agitation is a thing of the past," P. H. McCarthy wrote in 1900, referring to the site near San Francisco's City Hall where Denis Kearney had once whipped up the crowds.[18] McCarthy and his counterparts in other unions managed the anti-Japanese campaign as they did strikes and boycotts against employers—as one of several priorities that had to be balanced to further the ends of organized labor as a whole. In 1913, Olaf Tveitmoe, in his capacity as president of the labor-financed Asiatic Exclusion League, even called for a temporary halt to anti-Japanese activities, lest they jeopardize the success of the upcoming Panama-Pacific International Exposition that had hired thousands of union construction workers.[19]

This pragmatic stance also characterized the relationship of mainstream unionists towards the organized left, specifically the Industrial Workers of the World and the Socialist party. Both groups had significant numbers of supporters in the state. In 1914, the IWW boasted some forty locals and 5,000 members and was the only organization that seriously tried to organize farm laborers of all races against the abysmal regime under which they lived and worked.[20] At its height from 1910 to 1913, the California Socialist party claimed over 6,000 members (including 2,000 in Los Angeles County alone), support inside many unions (especially the carpenters, painters, culinary trades, and machinists) and among woman suffragists, and was able to elect two state assemblymen and the mayors of Berkeley and Daly City.[21]

AFL leaders in the state generally regarded leftists as allies who, in a dogmatic and clumsy fashion, were pursuing the same goals and attracting the same enemies as they did. For example, when thousands of IWW sympathizers suffered injury and incarceration during the 1912 San Diego Free Speech Campaign, Olaf Tveitmoe and California Labor Federation official Paul Scharrenberg visited that city and reported that their "sympathizers and their acts are part of the workers' struggle for better conditions and brighter lives." Such tolerance was possible because the IWW did not compete with established California unions in their urban bases. Except for free speech fights, which left few traces after the jails emptied, IWW organizers focused on the farms of the Central Valley where their agitation won only transitory victories.[22]

Moreover, the AFL sometimes stole the syndicalists' thunder. The IWW's messianic creed was color-blind and thus appealed to a number of Mexican revolutionaries turned labor organizers in Los Angeles and the surrounding citrus-growing region. But it was Job Harriman, a socialist lawyer associated with the Los Angeles Central Labor Council (CLC), who in 1908 defended Ricardo Flores Magón, champion of the Mexican left, against charges that he had violated the federal Neutrality Act. And it was CLC functionary Fred Wheeler, a moderate socialist like Harriman, who won the council's backing for a 1903 strike by Japanese and Mexican beet workers in Oxnard that the national AFL had spurned for candidly racist reasons.[23]

Harriman and Wheeler embodied the close relationship that existed between their majority, reformist wing of the Socialist party and the mainstream of the California labor movement. Members of this faction sought fusion with municipal labor parties in San Francisco and Los Angeles in the vain hope that a pragmatic electoral strategy would advance the cooperative commonwealth more than would the preservation of ideological purity. The "right" had its base in Los Angeles, but worked comfortably with ambitious union leaders throughout the state, all of whom needed the votes of radical workers and professionals to win public office.[24]

The rival "revolutionary" wing of the Socialist party was strongest in the Bay Area where its most prominent figures were unremittingly hostile to the entrenched leaders of the San Francisco AFL whom they condemned as "class collaborationists." Yet unwilling to ally with the established labor movement and unable to build an alternative to it, the revolutionaries left only a small impression on California workers. It is telling that Tom Mooney, who made numerous attempts to organize nonunion employees of Bay Area utility companies, drew little notice until 1916 when he was arrested for the gruesome Preparedness Day bombing, an act he did not commit.[25]

A major reason why revolutionary socialism had so little success among trade unionists is that AFL leaders in California co-opted some of its visionary content. Labor officials endorsed an array of reformist and utopian schemes in their quest for a larger share of power for the movement and the people it represented. Two decades after Henry George's death in 1897, the "single tax" remained on the political agenda of the State Building Trades Council and the California Federation of Labor. In 1914, when Job Harriman grew disillusioned with the struggle for municipal socialism and started the cooperative Llano del Rio colony in the Antelope Valley north of Los Angeles, the State Building Trades Council vigorously defended the experiment and added, "the unions ought to have a tract of land where every striker could put in his labor in support of himself and his family."[26] Such sentiments allowed AFL leaders to present the labor movement as the capable vanguard of a better world that socialists could only proclaim.

Besides potential competitors on their left, California unionists also had to confront the far more serious challenge of progressivism. Every union in the state supported measures, such as the public ownership of utilities and initiative, referendum, and recall, which were also dear to the hearts of Hiram Johnson and his associates in the Lincoln-Roosevelt League. But working-class activists, in addition, advocated state-financed health insurance and a strict anti-injunction law, both of which made all but the most radical progressives recoil.[27] During the legislative sessions of 1911 and 1913, union lobbyists worked closely with Johnson's "insurgent" majority to pass the state's first effective workmen's compensation act, an eight-hour law for women and children, and a number of other bills. In gratitude, working-class voters swung decisively to progressive Republicans in elections for the rest of the decade. At the state level, the AFL became a valued ally in Johnson's battles with conservatives in his own party.[28]

However, back in the cities, the relationship of organized labor to elite reformers was more contentious. Within the local environment, labor had something to lose—the promise and sometimes the reality of urban rule. In San Francisco, the Union Labor party was twice toppled from power by associations of wealthy progressives: first, in 1906–1907, by the graft prosecution that Rudolph Spreckles and James D. Phelan financed; and second, in 1911, by James Rolph, Jr., a genial politician who had the support of every banker and major employer in the city. That same year in Los Angeles, after the McNamara brothers, James and John, confessed to bombing the *Times* building, socialist-labor candidate Job Harriman lost his race for mayor to progressive incumbent George Alexander.[29] As Democrats across the country had defeated the local workingmen's parties of the 1830s and 1880s by adopting some of their demands and recruiting their ablest candidates, so progressive Republicans rescued the cities of California in the 1910s from the spectre of what they termed "class rule."[30]

The forced retreat from city government cost labor dearly in the immediate aftermath of World War I. The Mooney-Billings case, the massive strike wave, and a turn toward radical-ism inside many unions frightened San Francisco employers into mounting a broad, well-financed offensive against centers of labor strength among longshoremen, sailors, and the building trades. With no intervention by the Rolph administration, the "best union town" in the nation became, by the end of 1921, an open-shop stronghold. In Los Angeles, employers used injunctions to break a number of major strikes, effectively puncturing the brief optimism of AFL organizers who, during the war, had built the Central Labor Council to an unprecedented membership of 40,000 affiliated workers.[31]

The political climate was no more favorable in Sacramento. The state Criminal Syndicalism Act, passed in 1919, was aimed specifically at the IWW and members of the infant Communist Labor party. However, Governor William Stephens made clear that the act, which banned the *advocacy* of violence "as a means of accomplishing a change in industrial ownership or control or effecting any political change," could be used against rebellious unionists, regardless of their political views. Thus, the state AFL, no hotbed of radicalism in the 1920s, lobbied throughout the decade to overturn the law.[32] In San Francisco and Los Angeles, an ideologically splintered labor movement tried to rally working-class precincts to back pro-union candidates. But the conservative tide either defeated their favorites or, once in office, persuaded them to move swiftly to the right.[33] Disheartened, unionists returned to the political margins from which they had escaped a half-century before.

LABOR ON THE OFFENSIVE

The decade of the 1930s is remembered as a time when millions of workers, with the aid of the federal government, challenged the major industrial corporations in the nation and won recognition for their unions. This upsurge was nowhere as impressive as in California. Longshoremen, warehousemen, farm laborers, retail clerks, and the mélange of trades in the motion picture industry led the way with well-publicized organizing campaigns and massive strikes that inspired other wage-earners to follow their example.[34] Radicals, especially members of the Communist party, played a critical role as motivators, educators, and handlers of detail. By the time the United States entered World War II, San Francisco had regained its reputation as a union town, and Los Angeles had finally shed its image as a paradise for open-shop employers. Almost 200,000 workers, including men and women of *all* races, joined freshly minted affiliates of either the AFL or the CIO.[35] Of the state's major industries, only agriculture and banking were still able to operate free from organized workers and union contracts.

The rank-and-file movement of the 1930s, which was the engine of labor's California revival, severed organizational connections that had endured for a half century, but it marked less of a *political* departure than most observers realized at the time. The San Francisco general strike of 1934, which grew out of a walkout by maritime workers up and down the West Coast, did touch off a whirlwind of activity, affecting practically every manual occupation in the state. Harry Bridges, who advanced in three years from spokesman of a radical faction on the San Francisco waterfront to head of the International Longshoremen's and Warehousemen's Union (ILWU) and director of the California CIO, symbolized to supporters and enemies alike a "syndicalist renaissance" that seemed to threaten the perpetuation of the social order.[36] However, once the initial flush of organizing fervor had cooled, the new industrial unionists revealed goals no different from those which previous workers had espoused: higher pay, better treatment from supervisors, and control over the hiring process.

In 1934, the California AFL endorsed Socialist-turned-Democrat Upton Sinclair for

governor the day after his fall campaign platform was published. The radical author pleased unionists by praising the striking maritime trades and promising good jobs for the unemployed and freedom for Tom Mooney. However, the labor federation was cool towards Sinclair's EPIC (End Poverty in California) plan for the cooperative ownership of excess land and industry, a concrete elaboration of ideas that Henry George had first made popular. In fact, the state AFL had preferred George Creel, a Roosevelt ally whom Sinclair defeated in the Democratic primary. The aging officials of the state labor federation were anxious about the fate of trade unions inside future EPIC enterprises where, Sinclair guaranteed, no one would toil more than two hours a day.[37]

After Sinclair lost the general election, the California AFL and the infant unions attached to the CIO both took a more active role in state politics. Their common aim was to place in Sacramento a Democratic administration that would safeguard and extend the power the labor movement was rapidly gaining at the workplace. In 1938, these efforts climaxed with the victory of Culbert Olson, a left-wing New Dealer who courted labor more assiduously than had Sinclair.[38] When Olson, a week after taking office, pardoned Tom Mooney, California unionists rejoiced that their status as political outsiders had ended. "It was a big day for the working class," remembered San Francisco ILWU leader Henry Schmidt about the tumultuous San Francisco crowd that celebrated Mooney's release from San Quentin. "They don't come very often."[39]

CONCLUSION

Thus, from 1870 to 1940, California labor had evolved from a lily-white social movement composed of struggling craft unions, leftist sects, and working-class reform groups into a multi-racial formation dominated by large industrial unions. Organized labor had won a legitimate place in the state's political and economic life, one that all but isolated devotees of the far right accepted.

But ironically, the broadening of labor's constituency was accompanied by a narrowing of its political aspirations. The growth of unionism in the 1930s also brought an end to the tradition of craft-centered radicalism which had animated the movement since the gold rush. Even left-wing activists in the CIO did not seriously propose victorious workers' parties, collectively owned plots of land, or plans for sweeping tax reform that had been popular among the Western European immigrants and native-born whites who established labor's presence during the Gilded Age. Once they won legal protection through the Wagner Act and a number of other New Deal measures, most unionists welcomed integration into the Democratic coalition headed by Franklin Roosevelt nationally and Culbert Olson in Sacramento. In triumph, statist liberalism occupied the ideological ground that the labor movement had once reserved to itself. With the coming of World War II, the federally financed boom in the steel, aircraft, shipbuilding, and petroleum industries bound organized labor even more tightly to its friends in high places, which by the mid-1940s included liberal Republican Governor Earl Warren.[40] A big day for the working class has not come again.

By the 1960s, the California left, except for a few remnants of Communist party influence in the ILWU and a handful of smaller unions, became synonymous with the deeds and slogans of activists from the college-educated middle class and Third World communities like Watts, East Los Angeles, and San Francisco's Chinatown where unions have always led a sporadic existence. Meanwhile, the dominance of service and clerical occupations in the state has made increasingly archaic old definitions of "the working class" and "class consciousness" that were based on the historical experience of blue-collar wage-earners. To its

shrinking membership, the ILWU may be a scrupulously democratic union with a glorious past, but that image means little to a young Chinese woman who commutes from the suburb of Daly City to a data processing job at Bank of America in downtown San Francisco.

Workers who are active in their unions still, without being aware of it, routinely follow the seventy-five-year-old advice of Olaf Tveitmoe to "fight with both fists" when they canvass and raise funds for liberal Democrats. But the society in which that phrase once had radical implications no longer exists.

Notes

An earlier version of this essay was read at the annual meeting of the American Historical Association in San Francisco on December 29, 1983. I would like to thank Bruce Dancis for allowing me to use his collection on the history of the California left.

1 McWilliams, *California: The Great Exception* (New York, 1949), 127, 149. My book, *Barons of Labor: The San Francisco Building Trades and Union Power in the Progressive Era* (Urbana, Ill., 1987) discusses the California labor movement (especially the AFL) and state and local politics at greater length.

2 Recent monographs include Luis L. Arroyo, "Industrial Unionism and the Los Angeles Furniture Industry, 1918–1954" (Ph.D. dissertation, University of California, Los Angeles, 1979); Pedro G. Castillo, "The Making of a Mexican Barrio: Los Angeles, 1890–1920" (Ph.D. dissertation, University of California, Santa Barbara, 1979); Frederic C. Chiles, "War on the Waterfront: The Struggles of the San Francisco Longshoremen, 1851–1934" (Ph.D. dissertation, University of California, Santa Barbara, 1981); Dino Cinel, *From Italy to San Francisco: The Immigrant Experience* (Stanford, Calif., 1982); Daniel Cornford, "Lumber, Labor, and Community in Humboldt County, California, 1850–1920" (Ph.D. dissertation, University of California, Santa Barbara, 1983); Cletus Daniel, *Bitter Harvest: A History of California Farmworkers, 1870–1941* (Ithaca, N.Y., 1981); Joel Franks, "Boot and

Shoemakers in 19th-Century San Francisco: A Study in Class, Culture, Ethnicity, and Popular Protest in an Industrializing Community'' (Ph.D. dissertation, University of California, Irvine, 1983); James N. Gregory, ''The Dust Bowl Migration and the Emergence of an Okie Subculture in California, 1930–1950'' (Ph.D. dissertation, University of California, Berkeley, 1983); Michael Kazin, ''Barons of Labor: The San Francisco Building Trades, 1896–1922'' (Ph.D. dissertation, Stanford University, 1983); John Alan Lawrence, ''Behind the Palaces: The Working Class and the Labor Movement in San Francisco, 1877–1901'' (Ph.D. dissertation, University of California, Berkeley, 1979); Douglas Monroy, ''Mexicans in Los Angeles, 1930–1941: An Ethnic Group in Relation to Class Forces'' (Ph.D. dissertation, University of California, Los Angeles, 1978); Joseph Bruce Nelson, ''Maritime Unionism and Working-Class Consciousness in the 1930s'' (Ph.D. dissertation, University of California, Berkeley, 1982); Ricardo Romo, *East Los Angeles: History of a Barrio* (Austin, Tex., 1983); Vicki L. Ruiz, ''UCAPAWA, Chicanas, and the California Food Processing Industry'' (Ph.D. dissertation, Stanford University, 1982); Alexander Saxton, *The Indispensable Enemy: Labor and the Anti-Chinese Movement in California* (Berkeley, 1971); Harvey Schwartz, *The March Inland: Origins of the ILWU Warehouse Division, 1934–1938* (Los Angeles, 1978); Neil Shumsky, ''Tar Flat and Nob Hill: A Social History of Industrial San Francisco During the 1870s'' (Ph.D. dissertation, University of California, Berkeley, 1972); Jules Tygiel, ''Workingmen in San Francisco, 1880–1901'' (Ph.D. dissertation, University of California, Los Angeles, 1977).

Valuable institutional studies are Ira Cross, *A History of the Labor Movement in California* (Berkeley, 1935); Robert E. L. Knight, *Industrial Relations in the San Francisco Bay Area* (Berkeley, 1960); Louis B. and Richard S. Perry, *A History of the Los Angeles Labor Movement, 1911–1941* (Berkeley, 1963); Frederick L. Ryan, *A History of the San Diego Labor Movement* (San Diego, 1959); David F. Selvin, *A Place in the Sun: A History of California Labor* (San Francisco, 1981); Grace H. Stimson, *Rise of the Labor Movement in Los Angeles* (Berkeley, 1955).

3 McWilliams, *California,* 129.

4 This was also the case in many other states. See Gary M. Fink, ''The Rejection of Voluntarism,'' *Industrial and Labor Relations Review,* XXVI (1973), 805–819. For the policy itself, see Michael Rogin, ''Voluntarism: The Political Functions of an Apolitical Doctrine,'' ibid., XV (1962), 521–535.

5 The only statistical studies of this focus on San Francisco. See Jules Tygiel, '' 'Where Unionism Holds Undisputed Sway'—A Reappraisal of San Francisco's Union Labor Party,'' *California History,* LXII (1983), 196–215; Steven Philip Erie, ''The Development of Class and Ethnic Politics in San Francisco, 1870–1910: A Critique of the Pluralist Interpretation'' (Ph.D. dissertation, University of California, Los Angeles, 1975). However, during the Progressive era, the Los Angeles press reported that working-class areas in the city gave Union Labor, Public Ownership, and Socialist candidates the bulk of the votes they received.

6 Lawrence, ''Behind the Palaces,'' 28.

7 On the collapse of unions in the 1870s, see *San Francisco Evening Post,* July 23, 1877; Cross, *History of the Labor Movement,* 13, 49, 52, 58. See also Michael Kazin, ''Prelude to Kearneyism: The July Days in San Francisco, 1877,'' *New Labor Review,* no. 3 (1980), 5–47; Stimson, *Rise of Labor Movement,* 5–6. On the rise and fall of the WPC, see Saxton, *Indispensable Enemy,* 115–156.

8 Stimson, *Rise of Labor Movement,* 23–24; Frank Roney, *An Autobiography,* edited by Ira B. Cross (Berkeley, 1931), 261–313.

9 Roney, *Autobiography,* 233–237; Marian Dixon, ''The History of the Los Angeles Central Labor Council'' (M.A. thesis, University of California, Berkeley, 1929), 7–9; Kazin, ''Barons of Labor,'' 73–80; Stimson, *Rise of Labor Movement,* 89; Ira B. Cross, ''Labor Day Parades in the Metropolis,'' *Labor Clarion* (organ of the San Francisco Labor Council), Sept. 2, 1910.

10 Saxton, *Indispensable Enemy,* 165.

11 Charles A. Barker, ''Henry George and the California Background of Progress and Poverty,'' *California Historical Society Quarterly,* XXIV, (1945), 105. The utopian colonies which flourished in this period—often with union support—were also attempts to return to an artisanal

"golden age." See Robert V. Hine, *California's Utopian Communities* (San Marino, 1953), 163.

12 Lucile Eaves, "Labor Day in San Francisco and How Attained," *Labor Clarion,* Sept. 2, 1910.

13 Unions represented roughly a third of the wage-labor force and benefited from the small-scale, regional nature of most San Francisco businesses. Knight, *Industrial Relations,* 375–378.

14 Paul S. Taylor, *The Sailors' Union of the Pacific* (New York, 1923). In 1908, University of California professor Jessica B. Peixotto estimated that only three to four percent of female workers in the state were members of unions, almost all of them in San Francisco, "Women of California as Trade-Unionists," *Publications of the Association of Collegiate Alumnae,* Series III, no. 18 (1908), 40–49. Also, see Lillian Ruth Matthews, *Women in Trade Unions in San Francisco* (Berkeley, 1913).

15 On the history of the BTC in this period, see Frederick L. Ryan, *Industrial Relations in the San Francisco Building Trades* (Norman, 1935); Kazin, "Barons of Labor."

16 *Organized Labor* (weekly newspaper of the California State Building Trades Council, edited by Tveitmoe from its founding in 1900 to 1919), Sept. 9, 1911. On the graft trials, see Walton Bean, *Boss Ruef's San Francisco: The Story of the Union Labor Party, Big Business, and the Graft Prosecution* (Berkeley, 1952).

17 Kazin, "Barons of Labor," 423–434; Stimson, *Rise of Labor,* 242–244, 292.

18 *Organized Labor,* April 14, 1900.

19 Roger Daniels, *The Politics of Prejudice: The Anti-Japanese Movement in California and the Struggle for Japanese Exclusion* (Berkeley, 1962), 51–52. Thus, Carey McWilliams was wrong to write that "From 1900 to 1910 a union charter in California was, in some respects, primarily significant as an authorization to engage in anti-Japanese agitation." *California,* 140–141. Unions began to grow again in the late 1890s, several years *before* Japanese were widely perceived as a threat, and they always had a political agenda far broader than Asian exclusion. On Los Angeles labor and the Japanese, see John Modell, *The Economics and Politics of Racial Accommodation: The Japanese of Los Angeles, 1900–1942* (Urbana, Ill., 1977), 32–36.

20 David Brody, *Workers in Industrial America: Essays on the Twentieth Century Struggle* (New York, 1980), 37; Daniel, *Bitter Harvest,* 81–87; Hyman Weintraub, "The Industrial Workers of the World in California, 1905–1931" (M.A. thesis, University of California, Los Angeles, 1947).

21 The fullest accounts of the California Socialist party are by Ralph E. Shaffer, "A History of the Socialist Party of California" (M.A. thesis, University of California, Berkeley, 1955); and Shaffer, "Radicalism in California, 1869–1929" (Ph.D. dissertation, University of California, Berkeley, 1962). The membership total is from "Radicalism in California," p. 166. For the influence of socialists in the woman suffrage movement, see Bruce Dancis, "The Socialist Women's Movement in the United States, 1901–1917" (Senior thesis, University of California, Santa Cruz, 1973), 202–233; Mari Jo Buhle, *Women and American Socialism, 1870–1920* (Urbana, Ill., 1981), 118–120.

22 San Francisco Labor Council, Special Investigating Committee, "San Diego Free Speech Controversy, Report Submitted, April 25, 1912," p. 12, copy in Doe Library, University of California, Berkeley. In 1915, state AFL leaders also came to the defense of Blackie Ford and Herman Suhr, two Wobblies convicted of murder after the famous episode (often inaccurately termed a "riot") at a Wheatland, California, hop farm. See Cletus E. Daniel, "In Defense of the Wheatland Wobblies: A Critical Analysis of the IWW in California," *Labor History,* XIX (1978), 499–500.

23 On Harriman's role, see Juan Gómez-Quiñones, *Sembradores, Ricardo Flores Magón y el Partido Liberal Mexicano: A Eulogy and Critique* (Los Angeles, 1973), 33; on Los Angeles labor's support for Magón and his two codefendants, see Stimson, *Rise of Labor Movement,* 321–332; on Wheeler, see Juan Gómez-Quiñones, "The First Steps: Chicano Labor Conflict and Organizing, 1900–1920," *Aztlán,* III (1972), 25; and Tómas Almaguer, "Racial Domination and Class Conflict in Capitalist Agriculture: The Oxnard Sugar Beet Workers' Strike of 1903," *Labor History,* XXV (1984), 325–350.

24 Useful documents of the California "moderate" socialists include Gaylord Wilshire, *Socialism Inevitable* (New York, 1907); Stanley Wilson,

The Gospel of Socialism (Los Angeles, 1913) (Wilson was, for a long time, editor of the official Los Angeles Central Labor Council Newspaper, *The Citizen,* as well as a popular Christian socialist orator); J. Stitt Wilson, *How I became a Socialist and Other Papers* (Berkeley, 1912). California was also home to one of the leading black socialists of the pre-World War I period, Reverend George Woodbey of Los Angeles. See Philip S. Foner, ed., *Black Socialist Preacher: The Teachings of Reverend George Washington Woodbey and his Disciple, Reverend G. W. Slater, Jr.,* (San Francisco, 1983); and Foner, "Reverend George Washington Woodbey: Early Twentieth Century California Black Socialist," *Journal of Negro History,* LXI (1976), 136–157.

25 On the left wing of California's Socialist party, see Miriam A. DeFord, *Uphill All the Way: The Life of Maynard Shipley* (Yellow Springs, Ohio, 1956); Richard H. Frost, *The Mooney Case* (Stanford, Calif., 1968), 1–70; Austin Lewis, *The Rise of the American Proletarian* (Chicago, 1907); and Lewis, *The Militant Proletariat* (Chicago, 1911).

26 Arthur Young, *The Single Tax Movement in the United States* (Princeton, N.J., 1916), 163–167; *Organized Labor,* April 27, 1912; Commonwealth Club of California, *Transactions,* XI (1916); Franklin Hichborn, "California Politics, 1891–1939," III, 1805, bound typescript in Stanford University Library; *Organized Labor,* July 9, 1910, Jan. 29 and Feb. 19, 1916.

27 Lucille Eaves, *A History of California Labor Legislation with an Introductory Sketch of the San Francisco Labor Movement* (Berkeley, 1910), 440–441; Philip Taft, *Labor Politics American Style: The California State Federation of Labor* (Cambridge, Mass., 1968), 56; *Organized Labor,* April 6, 1918. In 1918, many articles advocating state health insurance appeared in the California union press.

28 Michael P. Rogin and John L. Shover, *Political Change in California: Critical Elections and Social Movements, 1890–1966* (Westport, Conn.), 35–89. The most complete account of the reform legislation appears in Crockett, "History of California Labor Legislation," passim.

29 Kazin, "Barons of Labor," passim; Fogelson, *Fragmented Metropolis,* 214–217.

30 Fink, *Workingmen's Democracy,* passim; Edward Pessen, *Jacksonian America; Society, Personality, and Politics* (Homewood, Ill., 1978), 270–279.

31 On San Francisco, see Cross, *History of the Labor Movement,* 250–254; Ryan, *Industrial Relations,* 134–166; and Nelson, "Maritime Unionism," 104–118. On Los Angeles, see Perry and Perry, *History of the Los Angeles Labor Movement,* 106–162.

32 Howard A. DeWitt, *Images of Ethnic and Radical Violence in California Politics, 1917–1930: A Survey* (San Francisco, 1975), 7–8; Earl C. Crockett, "The History of California Labor Legislation, 1910–1930" (Ph.D. dissertation, University of California, Berkeley, 1931), 288–289; George W. Kirchwey, "A Survey of the Workings of the Criminal Syndicalism Law of California" (California Committee, American Civil Liberties Union, 1926), copy in Bancroft Library, Berkeley.

33 In 1919, the Los Angeles CLC set up an elaborate precinct organization to mobilize union members for boycotts and elections. However, Meredith Snyder, the victorious candidate whom the CLC supported in that year's mayoral election, refused to take labor's side in a street railway strike. This prompted all three union appointees in his administration to resign from their city jobs. Perry and Perry, *History of the Los Angeles Labor Movement,* 121.

34 Elements of this upsurge are discussed in many works, including those cited in footnote 2 above by Cletus Daniels, Douglas Monroy, Joseph Bruce Nelson, Harvey Schwartz, Vicki Ruiz, and Luis L. Arroyo. Carey McWilliams evoked the period well in *The Education of Carey McWilliams* (New York, 1979), 64–97. During the 1920s in Los Angeles, organizing successes in the film, garment, and furniture industries (the latter two with a heavily Mexican American workforce) provided a springboard for gains made in the next decade. See Murray Ross, *Stars and Strikes: Unionization of Hollywood* (New York, 1941); Arroyo, "Industrial Unionism," 23–25; Perry and Perry, *History of the Los Angeles Labor Movement,* 221–222.

35 In 1938, there were 300,000 union members in the state, three times the total in 1933. Schwartz, *March Inland,* ix. Almost half the state's 1,222

union locals in 1939 had been chartered for less than a decade, Calif. Dept. of Industrial Relations, *Labor in California: Bienniel Statistical Report, 1939–1940* (Sacramento, 1940), 48.

36 The phrase is borrowed from Nelson, "Maritime Unionism," 12.

37 Clarence F. McIntosh, "Upton Sinclair and the EPIC Movement, 1933–1936" (Ph.D. dissertation, Stanford University, 1955), 15, 213–214, 218–226, 244–245, 304–305; Perry and Perry, *A History of the Los Angeles Labor Movement,* 288, 306.

38 Robert E. Burke, *Olson's New Deal for California* (Berkeley, 1953), 14–34.

39 Henry Schmidt, "Secondary Leadership in the ILWU, 1933–1936" (1983), 277, transcript of interview, Bancroft Library, Berkeley.

40 On the prolabor position of state Republican officeholders in the 1940s and 1950s, see J. David Greenstone, *Labor in American Politics* (New York, 1969), 151.

A STATESWOMAN IN THE AGE OF REFORM

EDITOR'S INTRODUCTION

One of the major changes in California society during the Progressive era was the expanding role of women. Increasingly, middle-class women found themselves freed from the drudgery of traditional household responsibilities by technological improvements and by their own affluence. At the same time, new educational opportunities provided them with increased career choices and the possibilities of greater public service. The cause of reform owed much to the efforts of a remarkable group of articulate, well-educated, middle-class California women.

By the late nineteenth century, California already was known for the efforts of its crusading women reformers. Kate Douglas Wiggin was heralded for her work in establishing a free public kindergarten in San Francisco, the first in the United States. The San Francisco school was an important social experiment, intended to ameliorate the life of poor and working-class families in the city. Wiggin was the wife of a successful Boston attorney and she was able to attract the support of many wealthy benefactors. The Golden Gate Kindergarten Association was underwritten by such California heiresses as Mary Crocker, Jane Lanthrop Stanford, Miranda Lux, and Phoebe Apperson Hearst. By 1895 the association was operating forty free kindergartens that enrolled more than 3,500 children.[1]

Early in the twentieth century upper- and middle-class women in San Francisco and Los Angeles formed clubs to agitate for social reform. They were successful in elevating several humanitarian issues to the level of compelling public questions. The most vital of these issues was women's suffrage. California clubwomen organized a statewide organization, the California Equal Suffrage League,

[1]See the discussion in Kevin Starr, *Inventing the Dream: California Through the Progressive Era* (New York, 1985), 221–224, 258–259

and conducted an effective lobbying campaign. Typical of the activists in the league was Elisabeth Thacker Kent, member of a wealthy and politically prominent family in Marin County.

The California suffragists in 1910 formed a coalition with the Republican progressives, promising their support in the election of Hiram Johnson in return for a constitutional amendment giving women the vote. The coalition was a natural one. The leaders of the progressive and suffrage movements had much in common: Both were drawn from the same social class and both were committed to reform. Following the election of Hiram Johnson, the suffragists were disappointed in his failure to endorse publicly their cause. Nevertheless, the voters in 1911 approved (by a narrow margin) the suffrage amendment and California thus became the sixth state to grant women the right to vote.

The most important woman reformer of the Progressive era was Katherine Philips Edson, a leader of the Los Angeles clubwomen and a prime mover in the campaign for women's suffrage. Edson is typical in many ways of the middle-class reformers of the period, sharing not only their social conscience but also their class and racial prejudices. The following selection by Jacqueline R. Braitman provides a brief overview of Edson's public career. As Braitman notes in her opening remarks, Edson's activism represented a challenge to prevailing notions of femininity. Here one is reminded of Robert L. Griswold's discussion, in a previous selection, of the "cult of true womanhood" in which women were praised for their domesticity but banned from public life.

Braitman surveys Edson's career from its beginnings in the Los Angeles pure milk campaign, through her work on behalf of women's suffrage and the protection of women in the workforce, and on to her service in the cause of disarmament and world peace. Braitman demonstrates that once enfranchised, women were no more in agreement than men in their politics. Edson remained loyal to the Republican party while many of her fellow progressives rallied behind the candidacy of Democrat Woodrow Wilson. Braitman also notes the toll which Edson's activism took on her personal life.

Jacqueline R. Braitman has conducted extensive interviews with the surviving members of the Edson family. She is currently completing her doctoral dissertation on Katherine Philips Edson at the University of California, Los Angeles, under the direction of professors Norris Hundley, Kathryn Kish Sklar, and Eric Monkkonen.

A Stateswoman in the Age of Reform

Jacqueline R. Braitman

In a public career which challenged nineteenth- and early twentieth-century notions of femininity, Katherine Philips Edson (1870–1933) helped transform California into a leading Progressive state. As an important figure in California's Progressive party, Edson was instrumental in bringing about major industrial and social reforms affecting women as workers and consumers. She also campaigned tirelessly and effectively for the right of women to participate meaningfully in electoral politics, asserting that in a modern, industrial society women could not attend to their traditional domestic concerns unless they were able to affect the policies that determined the conditions of home life. This theme was to carry her in a logical progression from fighting for the regulation of milk production for the Los Angeles market to protect babies from disease all the way to participation in the International Conference for the Limitation of Armaments in Washington. Yet her consistent pursuit of women's rights also led to pragmatic political alliances which brought her together in the national arena with Charles Evans Hughes at a time when many of her Progressive colleagues supported Woodrow Wilson and later with Warren Harding. In a tragic irony, Edson's competence and energy on behalf of the rights of women in the public sphere also contributed at least in part to the deterioration and eventual dissolution of her marriage.

Katherine Philips Edson grew up in a reform-minded family in Kenton, Ohio. Her father, a medical doctor who specialized in women's health problems, was active in state politics,

often on behalf of equal rights for women. Edson's own early interests, however, were in the realm of the artistic. After graduating from the Glendale Female Seminary in Ohio, she studied operatic singing at a Chicago conservatory, where at the age of twenty she met a kindred spirit in music teacher Charles Farwell Edson. They married and planned a European trip to study grand opera. To finance their project, the young couple borrowed money from Charles's wealthy relatives and invested it in an almond orchard and ranch in southern California's Antelope Valley. In 1891 they moved to the property.

Charles, Katherine, and his parents managed the Chinese workers on the ranch for nine years. Perhaps to combat the boredom and isolation of ranch life, and to compensate for the failed dream of European travel, Katherine began an informal series of what she called "female roundups," gathering the women of the region to share experiences, knowledge, and skills such as setting a hen, teaching a calf to drink, kneading bread, and the fundamentals of nutrition. In her mind, she was carrying on her mother's tradition of community neighborliness.[1]

The couple found farm life increasingly frustrating, however, particularly after undertaking a series of unprofitable irrigation schemes. Soon after the birth of their second child, Philips Josiah, Charles and Katherine decided in 1899 to give up ranching for what they hoped would be a more lucrative and creative life style in Los Angeles. They brought baby Philips along but left four-year-old Katharane with Charles's parents until they could establish a secure financial base.

By the time Charles sent for his daughter and his parents five years later, the Edsons had made a central place for themselves in the

Adapted from "A California Stateswoman: The Public Career of Katherine Philips Edson," by Jacqueline R. Braitman. Copyright © 1986 by the California Historical Society. Reprinted from *California History*, Vol. LXV, No. 2, pp. 82–95.

cultural life of the growing city. According to one observer, Charles's workshop studio "filled with souvenirs of pioneer days,"[2] was not only for business but "was also a delightful rendezvous for lovers of the artistic, and for Bohemians."[3] Kate and Charles regularly held European-style salons in their comfortably furnished home, where members of the political and arts communities would come for dinner and sparkling conversation.

Despite such pleasures, there was also bitterness. Katharane and her grandparents had difficulty adjusting to the family's new situation, and the long separation between Katharane and her mother created a schism almost impossible to repair. Both strong and willful, they were often at odds with each other. Meanwhile, the marriage was strained by continuing financial dependence on Charles's mother, Maria Louise Farwell.[4] When Philips Josiah contracted polio in about 1902 or 1903, Katherine responded with an all-consuming concern that distanced her from her husband. Over the years, Charles and Katherine would grow further apart from each other as she became involved in crusades outside the home and Charles's career failed to provide economic security.

In the early years, however, Charles encouraged his wife's ambition. He also published articles and poetry championing liberal causes in the *California Outlook*. His own family's legacy was one of dedicated public service in the tradition of the nineteenth century social gospel. During the California women's suffrage campaign of 1896, while Katherine was pregnant with Philips Josiah, Charles took over his wife's campaigning. In 1913 the press touted them as an example of a modern couple who were able to establish a mutually supportive and stable partnership in their marriage.[5]

ACTIVIST

By the time Charles Farwell, Jr., was born in 1905, Katherine Edson had gained a reputation

as an effective organizer and soon held a variety of local leadership posts. She served first as secretary of the prestigious Los Angeles Friday Morning club, and then, between 1908 and 1911, as the club's vice president. In this early period her most significant contributions came during her term as chairman of the club's Committee on Public Health from 1911 to 1913 and the Committee on Industrial and Social Conditions from 1913 to 1915. These committees, along with her continuing work on behalf of suffrage, were the stepping-stones for Edson to become one of California's leading pioneers in social and labor reform. Under her guidance, according to the *Pacific Empire Express Reporter,* "the Friday Morning Club became the most powerful civic body in Los Angeles."[6] She played a major role in the club's evolution from an organization devoted to cultural and philanthropic affairs to one advocating reform of municipal and state agencies, political rights, conservation, public health, labor legislation, consumer consciousness, and a host of other issues. As one of many local affiliates of the California State Federation of Women's Clubs, the Friday Morning Club allowed women to participate in civic affairs within the Los Angeles community while also linking them to the General Federation of Women's Clubs, a nationwide organization which by 1910 had a membership of perhaps one million.[7]

Among Edson's earliest campaigns was her fight for pure milk legislation, in which she orchestrated an alliance of women's groups against business leaders and municipal authorities who were reluctant to take action that she deemed essential. The campaign provided Edson with her first opportunity to articulate publicly her ideas about the challenges facing women in a modern society. The demand for enforceable sanitation standards in milk production and distribution arose from alarm over the high rate of infant death in major American cities. One report concluded that "vital statistics showed that mortality among infants fed cow's milk was much higher than among breast-fed infants. Digestive disorders and diarrheal diseases of infants are thought to be due to impure food, especially milk."[8]

Between 1890 and 1910 most states and larger cities in the United States enacted regulatory milk laws. Edson led the pure milk movement in Los Angeles. Beginning in late 1909 as a private citizen representing the Friday Morning Club, she investigated production techniques in southern California dairies. The producers came to dread Edson since she frequently surprised them with her visits. In the course of her nine-month investigation, she gained an appointment as the only non-medically licensed member of the Los Angeles County Medical Milk Commission.[9] Already considered an expert on the pure milk issue, she now had the force of authority behind her.

When Edson presented her findings to the Friday Morning Club in June, 1910, the *Los Angeles Record* announced "Club Women Can Start Campaign for Pure Milk!"[10] "The improvement of the milk situation," declared Edson, "rests with the legislative committee of the city council."[11] At present, the "city health officer can do nothing, for he has no authority. The health department needs a thorough overhauling. The health officer can neither appoint nor dismiss his subordinates. This is done by the Board of Health." According to Edson, "our milk ordinances are excellent, and if we had an adequate force of veterinarians and inspectors to enforce them rigidly we would not now be starting a crusade against tubercular cows." Edson's findings indicated that at least ten percent of the cows providing milk to the city were carriers of bovine tuberculosis.[12]

The City Council endorsed Edson's recommendations for more veterinarians and inspectors, and they applauded the role of the women's clubs in the investigation, but they failed to provide the necessary funds. From Mayor George Alexander came even less support. He defended the Board of Health's record and suggested that the women's clubs target the state legislature for the needed money since the issue was far from a local problem.[13] In the latter respect the mayor was correct. Los Angeles received milk from some 1,500 dairies scattered throughout central and southern California.[14] The city had no jurisdiction over the production or the quality of the imported milk.

Edson countered that the city's Board of Health had "cumbersome and archaic" regulations. By mid-June, 1910, she had obtained a seat on the Los Angeles charter revision committee, which enabled her to help "revamp" the municipal code.[15] The new charter allowed for two additional milk inspectors and a veterinarian, and it placed milk inspection in the forefront of city services.[16] Edson also recognized the need to alter existing state regulations, and in 1912 persuaded the annual convention of the Federation of Women's Clubs to pass a resolution endorsing state and federal action to "stamp out bovine tuberculosis in dairy herds."[17] Dairy producers—sometimes concerned about milk quality but more worried about higher costs—opposed congressional and state regulation. Several bills calling for more rigid processing standards were presented to the 1913 legislature, one of which finally received Governor Hiram Johnson's signature. The new law empowered the state to regulate the production and sale of certified milk, cream, ice cream, butter and cheese.[18]

Edson was delighted, but by this time she was fighting battles on other fronts. She had campaigned for Hiram Johnson in his 1910 gubernatorial election and then had played a major role in the campaign for women's suffrage in California. Both the suffrage campaign and the battle for pure milk had introduced her to the world of practical politics and reaffirmed her conviction that women had a special role to play in government. Edson wrote to a friend what she had often said in public:

If the milk supply is in the hands of politicians, how can a woman who wants to do the right thing by her babies stay at home and keep quiet while they drink impure milk? If your water supply is bad, are you going to keep quiet or are you going to demand pure water? And have you ever demanded anything that comes under politics and got it if you didn't have some force behind you? Do you get full measure when you buy, and are weights and measures properly regulated and really inspected? We didn't need the ballot when we all lived in small communities and when we had control of all these things. Control of them has passed into the hands of the community, and it is perfectly senseless to suppose that the men are going to look after them, now. They never have and they never will![19]

As the official organizer for the Political Equality League of Los Angeles, it was Edson, according to one California historian, who "induced the Lincoln-Roosevelt League at its first meeting (in 1907) to endorse woman suffrage."[20] The League later gained control of the machinery of the Republican party, and in 1910, due to Edson's efforts, a suffrage plank was included in the state Republican platform. In 1911, after Johnson's successful campaign and during the state drive for women's suffrage, Edson was chosen as the League's representative to lobby at Sacramento.[21] She was the only woman from southern California until the last week of the session and, as one paper reported, she "hung on the flank of the first Progressive legislature until it drafted a suffrage amendment."[22]

Edson believed that the ballot would place the demands of the home, the family, and childrearing on firmer ground in the competition for society's limited resources. The ballot, she explained, would provide "the power to make the demand of the home and school as effective as harbor control, good roads and power and light development. All are equally essential to a great city, a great state and nation, a harmonious state where the best of man and woman is reflected in the government."[23] No longer confined to local affairs, women could play a larger part in "social uplift" and "upkeep" as well as realize their power as individuals and citizens. She was particularly jubilant at future prospects for women of her generation. "The whole world," she wrote, "seems to be opened up to us...and we are going to be one of the very important forces in politics."[24]

Governor Johnson recognized Edson's energy and skill, and, perhaps because of the influence she possessed among his constituents, he appointed her as a deputy inspector in the state Bureau of Labor Statistics in 1912. This post allowed her to study the industrial working conditions of women and children throughout California. What she discovered, especially about conditions in the canning industries, gave her a new set of issues. The fruit, fish, and vegetable canneries employed approximately 22,000 women during the canning season. This was more women than were employed in any other industry. Almost three-quarters of them were foreign born; most were from Italy and Portugal. Edson angrily noted the defects in equipment and the miserable conditions under which most of these women labored. They stood knee deep in waste products and fish residue, breathing poorly ventilated air, and often in pain because of the ten, twelve, or more hours per day they had to stand in postures which deformed young and older women alike. Her inquiries into hours and payrolls revealed to her "for the first time the horrors of trying to live on an inadequate wage."[25] Edson now began to see women not only as mothers but also as a class of workers who were discriminated against and unable to help themselves, and she set out to alleviate the most despicable aspects of factory labor.

Her strategy included exposing other middle-class clubwomen to the lives of women less fortunate than themselves, and she noted approvingly the "humbling" process that her peers experienced as they learned about the misery just outside their immediate environs. But she also used her new information to impress upon the governor the need for immediate state intervention. Johnson encouraged her to draft a bill for the 1913 legislature. After studying similar legislative measures in other states and countries, Edson led the successful fight for California's 1913 minimum-wage law for women and children. To assure the constitutionality of the measure, the same legislature submitted for ratification by the voters an amendment to the state constitution which allowed the lawmakers to establish a minimum wage for women and minors and to provide "for the comfort, health, safety, and general welfare of any and all employees." This amendment was carried by a majority of 84,000 in 1914.[26] The 1913 law authorized the governor to create an Industrial Welfare Commission (IWC) which would set and enforce wages, hours, and working conditions for women and children. Required by statute to appoint at least one woman to the five-member commission, Johnson named Edson.

COMMISSIONER

The IWC was part of a concept of state administration popularized by reformers who believed that government agencies could help balance the competing interests within a capitalistic democracy. These agencies or commissions were to be staffed by politically neutral experts, who would consider the needs of different interests and utilize the new insights of scientifically rationalized management to make policy. Cooperation and compromise were expected to characterize negotiations and policies, but frequently co-optation and impotence resulted. Nevertheless, the commission form of government represented a major victory for reformers and provided important opportunities for women like Edson. Thirteen women were among Johnson's appointees to the commissions created during his administration. Significantly, seven of them were members of the California Federation of Women's Clubs.

Edson was straightforward about the philosophy that she took to her new post. As she saw it, minimum-wage legislation was based on the economic theory "that the basis of competition must be fixed, and it must not go below the weakest members of society, and they are the women and children. It fixes a basis for competition, so that under it none can go; and therefore women and children are protected from exploitation by society."[27] As progenitors of the race, women were believed to be fragile creatures in need of special care in the work force. Reformers felt that the state had a responsibility to provide that care because trade unionists had failed to organize women and give them the protection of the collective bargaining process. Most unionists looked upon unskilled women workers as an unstable element within the work force. They also feared that if the state legislated the minimum wage for women, the women would be less inclined to join the unions that did welcome them. Moreover, such a precedent might encourage future legislation designating the maximum wage that workers could earn. Such opposition reflected a deep distrust of state interference. Yet labor heralded state intervention when it put limits on employers' practices. Although Edson believed that collective bargaining was a fundamentally correct means of giving women workers a share in the control of conditions of employment, she believed that the immediate possibility of getting women to organize was remote.[28]

For Edson the IWC was more than a regulatory agency. She believed that the commission reflected a substantial shift in capitalist ideology. The most important achievement of the IWC, she argued, would be to bring to "big business throughout the state the realization that private business is no longer private business but public business." The state would no longer sanction the idea that "any man's method of conducting his own business, as it touches the lives of others, is his own affair."[29] Edson's notion about the state's responsibility to its citizenry, which challenged traditional laissez-faire attitudes, paralleled her belief that women's roles could no longer be determined by nineteenth-century proscriptions that allowed only men to be active in the public sphere while relegating women to the private domestic sphere.

Although Edson also promoted legislation on behalf of child labor, her main concerns focused on adult female workers. At first the women most affected by the IWC were those in the canning industries. Cost-of-living studies made in 1914 showed that $9.63 a week was the minimum required for what was then deemed a "proper" living for an independent woman. Payroll inspections showed that more than half of the working women in the major industries received less than this weekly wage. The IWC accordingly established a $10 minimum wage in 1917 and 1918 in the mercantile, laundry, fish canning, fruit-and-vegetable canning, and packing and manufacturing industries in general, as well as in professional offices and in the unskilled and unclassified occupations. Over the years Edson guided studies which resulted in higher wage rates. In 1919 the minimum wage was set at $13.50, and in 1920 at $16.00. She also administered policies regulating workers' hours in the fruit-and-vegetable canning industry, in which the basic day was reduced to nine hours in 1917 and to eight hours in 1918.[30] The IWC's regulations were difficult to enforce in its early, underfunded years, but after 1916 state funding was increased and the commission acquired new confidence and power. In 1922 its jurisdiction was expanded to include the hotel and restaurant industries; the motion picture industry was added in 1926.

Edson's vigorous efforts to improve the lot of working women contrasted sharply with the attitudes toward Asian laborers that she shared with most Californians in and out of the Progressive party. She kept a lower profile than many on the issue, however. While Governor Johnson backed the efforts of the exclusionists, and the California Federation of Women's Clubs belonged to the Japanese Exclusion League, Edson did not publicly (or privately in her correspondence) espouse support of California's 1913 Alien Land Act, which denied Asians ineligible to citizenship the right to own land. Furthermore, as a member of the 1915 San Francisco Panama-Pacific International Exhibition Committee, she opposed measures that would have interfered with Japanese participation in the event. She did not take a public position on the Asian immigration issue until after the second alien land law was passed in 1920. That legislation was designed to plug loopholes in the 1913 measure.[31] In 1921, after a year of public debate on the issue, Edson published an article entitled "California's Japanese Problem." Believing that the press had focused attention only on what she called the "Japanese side" of the issue, Edson felt an obligation to set out "California's side" by defining the interests of American Californians.[32] Despite the anti-Oriental attitudes common among most Progressives, Edson's opposition to Asian landownership was couched in economic terms. Racial prejudice is implicit in the tone of her inveighment against the "old problem of Orientalization" and her fear of the "Oriental tide." Opposition to the Japanese was not confined merely to the "ignorant rabble," she asserted, and it was "false to assume that only intelligent, broad-minded people of the state are pro-Japanese."[33] "Naturally labor, and especially organized labor" she wrote, "was the first to take a stand against this new influx and demand that it be stopped, for the Japanese immigrants were all laborers." And as more Japanese came, they drove "white labor out and then forced orchardists and farmers first to lease and then to sell to them, setting up vegetable stands and little shops and driving out small white merchants..."[34] Further research will be necessary to determine whether or not Edson's feelings about this issue affected IWC policies.

The confidence and constitutionality of the IWC were badly shaken in 1923. On April 9, 1923, the United States Supreme Court declared unconstitutional the minimum-wage law of Washington, D.C. Despite the adverse decision, the enforcement of minimum-wage regulations in California continued with cooperation from employers until July. At that time, according to an IWC report, the "ancient and always active enemy of industrial legislation, John R. Millar of the California Cotton Mills and President of the California Manufacturer's Association, challenged the constitutionality of the California law." Later in 1923, state Senator T.C. West sought an injunction against the IWC in the name of Helen Gainer. The commission, he argued, had prevented Gainer from securing employment in a candy factory at $6.00 per week because the IWC had set her minimum apprenticeship rate at a higher level. When the lower court refused to grant the injunction, the case was appealed to the California Supreme Court where briefs were filed in support of the minimum wage by the IWC, the National Consumers' League, the California Federation of Women's Clubs, the California League of Women Voters, the Los Angeles local of the United Garment Workers' Unions of America, the Los Angeles local of the Waitresses and Cafeteria Workers' Union, and the Women's Christian Temperance Unions of both southern and northern California. Gainer petitioned to cancel the complaint on January 26, 1926, on the grounds that she was being used and was ignorant of the case.[35] The next day the case was dismissed. The IWC continued to enforce the minimum-wage law.

Edson remained on the Industrial Welfare Commission until 1931, serving as the chief of the Division of Industrial Welfare of the State Department of Industrial Relations for the last thirteen of these years. Throughout her service, as she became synonymous in the public's eye with the IWC, she continued to expand her knowledge of industrial issues and her influence among women voters. Her influence also derived from the considerable time that she spent lobbying the state legislature.

LOBBYIST AND CAMPAIGNER

To Edson, the "third house" was absolutely necessary in a democracy, especially in California, where "the difference between the present system of government and the past is that in the past we didn't have to have lobbyists, because when you wanted something...all you had to do was to go to the Southern Pacific boss." Women, she believed, had a special place in the informal aspects of the legislative process, for "no woman...was lobbying for any personal interest or property interest. Most women lobbyists were representing some humanitarian interest and were there on behalf of some class of people."[36] According to a *Los Angeles Examiner* reporter, "there is woe and wailing and gnashing of teeth among the lobbyists...but not by one Mrs. Charles Farwell Edson of Los Angeles, who comes near being the most energetic of the lobby flock." When an order was issued to clear the chamber of lobbyists, Edson was stopped at the door. The doorkeeper told her she could not go in. She replied, "why of course I can go in. I am a state officer. I am a deputy of the labor commission." The *Examiner* summed up the situation, "now her work is easier than ever, for she has the lobby to herself."[37]

Edson's influence among both men and women also increased as she traveled extensively as one of the most sought-after speakers for California women's clubs as well as for agricultural, labor, business, municipal, and state organizations. Frequently she traveled along back roads to speak before unorganized and isolated rural folk, meeting the challenges of sometimes rowdy crowds who were skeptical toward a solitary city woman addressing anonymous faces from a stump. Often giving two or three speeches a day, and frequently winding up in bed for a week or more to regain her strength, she became Governor Johnson's leading defender and "information broker" to thousands throughout the state and particularly in the "cow counties" of southern California. Edson also traveled widely outside of California to study procedures of industrial oversight.

Gradually Edson forged links with northeastern and midwestern women's political, labor, and social reform associations and kept in touch by lengthy and frequent correspondence with prominent individuals such as Florence Kelley of the National Consumers' League, Carrie Chapman Catt of the National American Women's Suffrage Association, and Margaret Drier Robins of the Women's Trade Union League. National campaigns brought many of these reformers together as they attempted to bridge regional and class divisions in the hopes of unifying on gender-related issues. But the alliances centered on gender issues were weaker in the national arena than in the state, and political differences were greater, causing many women activists to come to a parting of the ways. This became cruelly clear to Edson in 1916 when she experienced the pitfalls of a national presidential campaign.

Edson was among the members of California's Progressive party who reluctantly fused with the Republican party in the election of 1916. Incumbent Democrat Woodrow Wilson defeated challenger Charles Evans Hughes in 1916 by the closest margin in any national election up to that time.[38] When Hughes lost California by less than 4,000 votes, he also lost the election.[39] Hughes's less than colorful personality elicited a poor public response in California and elsewhere, but there is evidence that his California defeat was primarily the result of the split between the Progressive and "old guard" factions within the Republican party. Conservative Republicans' dislike for Governor Johnson and opposition to his bid for the U.S. Senate in 1915 caused them to rally behind another candidate and to take control of Hug-

hes's California campaign. During his stay in California, Hughes failed to acknowledge Johnson, who, unbeknownst to him and old-line Republicans, still commanded a large loyal following.

Before the snub became public, Edson and some other leading women reformers were campaigning for Hughes. Among reformers they were a minority, since most Progressives supported Wilson because of his accomplishments during the last two years. Edson believed that her programs would find more support from Hughes than from Wilson, partly because of Hughes's progressive record in New York. But the campaign for Hughes was a frustrating experience, especially for those who participated in Hughes's Women's Auxiliary Alliance.

Edson and other representatives of the Women's Auxiliary joined Hughes's "National Campaign Train," called the "Golden Special" by some of its detractors. Humorous as well as serious problems arose along the route. The campaign literally got off on the wrong track. Arriving in St. Paul, the engineer brought the train in on a different track from the one scheduled. "The welcoming committee of about fifteen women," noted a reporter, "had run a distance to catch the train and had only just straightened their hats and tucked in the strands of their hair loosened by the run, when the engineer backed the train out to the yards and shunted down the right track and the whole band of indignant women had to take another run."[40]

The Democratic opposition met the train at every stop, and newspapers throughout the country reported the mishaps experienced by the passengers on their speaking tour. Edson was among these targeted for trouble. When she tried to speak before a large crowd in Portland, Oregon, she was greeted by a rowdy group of women representing the Industrial Workers of the World, which had come out in favor of Wilson. Front-page headlines announced "Mrs. Edson in Political Riot!"[41] She was escorted to safety by police, rioters were arrested, and her speech was delivered later at an undisclosed location. Edson had been heckled before, but never with such ferocity.

Following Hughes's loss of the election, Edson looked forward to returning to her work with the IWC. Her disappointment at women's failure to unite behind Hughes soon turned to bitterness, as former allies turned against her and other women who had supported him. The breakup of the Women's Auxiliary Alliance for Hughes exposed the weaknesses in Republican efforts to organize women for national political activity. Edson reasoned that women's experience in national politics reflected their historical divisiveness, for they had never learned to identify with each other. "As you know," she wrote to Carrie Chapman Catt, "solidarity is about the last development in human nature," and she passed on a sentiment expressed by another friend: "women and dogs have been trained for eons to be loyal to men and disloyal to each other, so six months of campaigning could not have overcome the training of generations."[42]

There were more successful and fulfilling years ahead, however. As a mediator between workers and employers she turned many of those who had previously been hostile to government intervention into supporters of her wage measures. She "succeeded so well that other governmental agencies called upon her services."[43] Her reputation extended beyond California's borders and brought her new responsibilities, including appointment as an arbitrator for navy defense contracts and enforcement of industrial standards during World War I.[44]

Early in 1918 Felix Frankfurter, then chairman of the War Labor Policies Board, offered Edson a position with the War Labor Administration. She was to be assigned to a nationwide speaking and educational campaign aimed at developing "a concrete practicable program for engaging women in the war effort." Frankfurter

appealed to the IWC to relieve her of her duties for a few months, since she is "the only person for the work because of her adaptability, experience and personality."[45] A. B. C. Dohrmann, chairman of the IWC, agreed to the request but insisted that Edson could not leave until December because of pending wartime wage legislation. By then the war was over and an appointment unnecessary.[46]

During and after the war Edson continued her efforts on behalf of a national suffrage amendment. When it gained approval in 1920 she represented southern California women at the 1921 St. Louis Convention of the National American Suffrage Association. Inspired by the events of the convention, she returned home and created the California branch of the League of Women Voters. She remained a life-long member and served a short term as the state chairman of the Committee on Women in Industry.

In addition to her efforts on behalf of the nonpartisan League of Women Voters, Edson remained a loyal Republican. As a member of the Los Angeles "Johnson for President" committee in 1920, she was one of five women elected as Hiram Johnson delegates to the Republican National Convention. There she seconded Johnson's nomination for President. Before she and six other women delivered nominating speeches at the convention, only Jane Addams had done so.[47] Johnson lost the nomination to Warren G. Harding, to whom Edson at first gave only lukewarm support. Later, when she met Harding personally during the visit of a women's delegation to his home town of Marion, Ohio, she changed her mind. On problems involving women and labor, she found him to be "entirely sincere."

Edson enthusiastically hit the campaign trail for Harding, whom she called "gravy vest Harding" because he often had mishaps at the dinner table.[48] In this campaign she stopped in her home town of Kenton, Ohio, to make a speech on "Why She Is a Republican." She gave as reasons the Democrats' economic policies, and especially that party's stand on suffrage. "Of the thirty-six states which ratified the national suffrage amendment," she announced, "twenty-nine were Republican dominated states and only seven were Democratic states." Harding's election, Edson told her audience, would mean "influence in getting the legislation and the measures we believe in." "Republicans Freed Women!" read the headline of the local newspaper.[49]

Harding's election paid off for Edson in a most unexpected way. The new President selected her as one of four women to serve on the American advisory delegation to the International Conference for the Limitation of Armaments, which convened in Washington, D.C., in 1921.[50] Her fellow delegates included such luminaries as John L. Lewis of the C.I.O., Samuel Gompers of the A.F. of L., General John J. Pershing, Assistant Secretary of the Navy Theodore Roosevelt, Jr., Under-Secretary of State Henry B. Fletcher, Secretary of Commerce Herbert C. Hoover, and Louisiana Governor John M. Parker. The other female delegates were Anna Child Bird, chairman of the State Republican Club of Massachusetts and a member of the National League of Women Voters; Eleanor Franklin Egan, a magazine writer specializing in Far Eastern affairs; and Alice A. Winter, president of the General Federation of Women's Clubs of Minneapolis.[51] The conference had been convened largely at the prodding of women's groups and religious and teachers' organizations. Edson had not been a prominent member of the peace movement, although other well-known Progressives were. Her selection grew out of her work during the war as a member of the national Board of Directors of the National League for Women's Service and chairman of The California State Council of National Defense.[52] The appointment also reflected her loyalty to the Progressive-Republican cause and her leadership in the West.

At the conference Edson assumed the role of lobbyist, interpreting public opinion to those in attendance and communicating information about the conference to Californians. Although she and the other advisory members could not vote on the resolutions introduced by the delegates, she approved of and actively participated in committee deliberations, formulating recommendations, such as the abolition of chemical warfare and the limitation of naval armament. As a West Coast resident, Edson believed that the elimination of the British-Japanese pact was, after the Four Power Treaty, the next greatest accomplishment of the conference.[53] The conference was a milestone for women as well, for their representatives on the advisory delegation served "as citizens and had the same relation to the work as the men had. They did not form a separate committee as seemed to be believed by so many people."[54] But Edson felt that women did bring their special vision and experience to the conference. Women had more confidence and were "less fearful than men, they have more faith that permanent peace can be accomplished than men, more faith in humanity and in open diplomacy."[55]

Edson used the conference as a forum for bringing her views on the minimum wage to an international audience. She saw the minimum wage as a fundamental ingredient of a lasting peace. "A life-sustaining wage," she explained, "is more vital to world peace than battleships," for ultimately "disarmament of suspicion, cleansing of minds of men and women who toil for a pittance, raising the hope and aims of the toiler, will do more to bring peace on earth and goodwill toward men than scrapping every battleship afloat!"[56]

When the conference ended, Edson returned to California and settled into familiar and routine patterns. Her public career continued for another ten years, but at a pace often hard for her to maintain and frequently at great personal cost. In 1924 after an earlier surgery, a second tumor under her left arm appeared. Her activities were curtailed and she served only as a delegate at large for the 1924 Johnson presidential campaign.[57]

THE PRIVATE AND PUBLIC SPHERES

Edson's family life had deteriorated as well as her health. Her lengthy jaunts throughout the state had kept her away from home so much that she rented an apartment in San Francisco around 1916 to be near IWC headquarters. The already withered relationship with Charles could no longer remain hidden behind a façade of domestic harmony. In 1925, the thirty-five year marriage ended officially in divorce after nine years of increased periods of separation.[58] During the disarmament conference in 1922, the *Los Angeles Times* had noted that while Edson was off solving problems of worldwide importance, "sitting with the great potent International Disarmament Conference nabobs of the world," Charles, "local basso, and bon-vivant literateur, is exhibiting his collection of autographed photographs at the Collector's Club."[59]

Perhaps one reason for the failure of the marriage was that Charles, unlike his wife, was more visionary than practical. It was rumored that he had been inspired by the acoustics of a nearby canyon and initiated the creation of the famed Hollywood Bowl. According to his daughter, he heard his echo while singing in the Cahuenga Pass and persuaded others of the potential there for musical concerts. Though his role in establishing the Hollywood Bowl is unclear, Charles was in fact among the charter members of the initial but aborted attempt to develop it.[60] Charles also had distinct ideas about how to spread "culture" to the growing population of Los Angeles. He developed and conducted the temporarily successful and publicly supported Peoples' Orchestra as an alternative to the high prices of the Friday evening concerts of the Los Angeles Philharmonic. Hoping to make "high" culture affordable and convenient to the "masses," the orchestra sur-

vived several seasons. It folded about the time that Charles's pupils stopped coming to his studio on Toberman Street. Charles's story remains to be told. Although he failed to provide a steady income for his family, his creative contribution to his adopted city was real. He was clearly an innovator and a cultural iconoclast in Los Angeles during the Progressive era, but his wife's legacy currently overshadows his own.

Katherine Edson continued her work for the California Federation of Women's Clubs and League of Women Voters. During the Pan Pacific Women's Conferences held in Honolulu in 1928 and 1930, she served as chairman for the mainland and leader of the discussions on labor. Speculation has it that she was among those considered for President Franklin Delano Roosevelt's Department of Labor, but her own choice was Frances Perkins, whom Roosevelt finally named to the post. Health problems caused her to curtail and cancel many engagements in 1933 before she finally died in August of that year. A redwood grove in Humboldt Redwoods State Park was dedicated in her honor by the California League of Women Voters.

California's reforms in the first decades of the twentieth century owe much to the efforts of Edson and the few women like her. Her promotion of the ideals of progressive feminism, improved public health facilities, and the rights of women and workers helped bring about significant political and social change in California. Her contemporaries recognized and applauded her achievements. For historians, Edson's hopes, successes and disappointments reflect women's ambiguous position in the political sphere, where her work stands as a milestone in the movement to raise women from their subordinate position in the labor force and in public life.

Notes

The author would like to thank professors Eric Monkkonen, Kathryn Kish Sklar, and, in particular,

Norris Hundley for their assistance in the preparation of this article.

1 The title of this article is taken from Peter MacFarlane's article of a similar name, 'Katherine Philips Edson, A California Stateslady." *Collier's,* 52, no. 7 (Nov. 1, 1913): 7.

2 "R. Hay Chapman's Tribute to Charles Farwell Edson," clipping from *California Outlook,* box 13, folder 3, Katherine Philips Edson Collection, UCLA (hereafter cited as Edson papers).

3 Ibid.

4 Maria Louise Farwell was the sister of Senator Banjamin Farwell and John Villiars Farwell. John V. was one of Chicago's wealthiest developers. She and her relatively impoverished husband apparently received a stipend.

5 *Collier's,* p. 6.

6 *Pacific Empire Express Reporter,* 1913, p. 8.

7 Mrs. Finlay Cook, ed. *California Federation of Women's Clubs Directory, 1921–1922,* (Berkeley: California Federation of Women's Clubs, n.d.), cover page. Also, William O'Neill, *The Woman Movement* (London: George Allen and Unwin Ltd. Pub., 1969), p. 48.

8 Roland W. Bartlett, *The Milk Industry* (New York: The Ronald Press Co., 1946), p. 252.

9 Unidentified newspaper clipping. Scrapbook, Edson papers.

10 *Los Angeles Record,* June 17, 1910, p. 1.

11 *Los Angeles Herald,* June 18, 1910, Edson Collection, UCLA.

12 *Los Angeles Record,* June 17, 1910.

13 *Los Angeles Record,* June 18, 1910, p. 1.

14 *Los Angeles Record,* June 7, 1910, p. 1.

15 *Los Angeles Herald,* June 18, 1910, p. 1.

16 "Los Angeles City and County," 25th Edition, *The Women's Bulletin,* Los Angeles City of Commerce, 1912; USC Los Angeles Political Equality League Collection.

17 *California Federation Handbook,* Cook., ibid., p. 195.

18 *Final Calendar of Legislative Business, 1913,* Friend Wm. Richardson, Superintendent of State Printing, Sac. Ca., 1913, p. 683.

19 Katherine Philips Edson to Mrs. Bryan Thomas, January 23, 1914, box 1, folder 2, Edson papers.

20 Walton Bean, *California: An Interpretive History,* 3rd ed. (New York: McGraw-Hill Inc., 1978), p. 282.

21 "Well Known Clubwoman Boosts 'Hi' Johnson As Suffrage Getter," unidentified newspaper clipping, box 5, folder 2, Edson papers. Also typed manuscript in box 5, folder 2.

22 *The Santa Ana Blade,* October 30, 1913, box 4, folder 9, Edson papers.

23 Ada G. De Nyes, "An Appreciation," *California Federation News,* 13, no. 6 (April 1934): 6, GFWC Collection, McHenry Library UC Santa Cruz.

24 *California Outlook,* June 14, 1913.

25 *Colliers,* p. 29, and quote from biography in private Nordman collection. (Edson's granddaughter)

26 Norris Hundley, "Katherine Philips Edson and the Fight for the California Minimum Wage Law, 1912–1923," *Pacific Historical Review,* 29 (1960), pp. 271–285.

27 Katherine Philips Edson, "Woman's Influence on State Legislation," *California Outlook,* June 14, 1913, p. 8.

28 *Bulletin, National League of Women Voters,* 1, no. 4 (March 1924): 3 National League of Women Voters papers, Library of Congress.

29 Unidentified newspaper clipping, c. Feb. 24?, "Making Employers Realize Private Business is Public Business—This is the Job of the State Welfare Commission," box 4, folder 9, Edson papers.

30 "What California Has Done to Protect the Women Workers," CIWC, May 1927, p. 5.

31 Roger Daniels, *The Politics of Prejudice* (New York: Atheneum Press, 1968), p. 88.

32 Katherine Philips Edson, "California's Japanese Problem," *The Woman Citizen,* Nov. 5, 1921, p. 9; box 5, folder 7, Edson papers.

33 First draft of above article, p. 2, box 5, folder 7, Edson papers. This statement is not in the published version.

34 "California's Japanese Problem," p. 9.

35 CIWC Report, May 1927, p. 8

36 Katherine Philips Edson, "Women's Influence on State Legislation," p. 7.

37 *Los Angeles Examiner,* May 7, 1913.

38 S. D. Lovell, *The Presidential Election of 1916* (Carbondale: Southern Illinois University Press, 1980), p. viii; Spencer Olin, "Hiram Johnson, the California Progressives, and the Hughes Campaign of 1916," *Pacific Historical Review,* 31 (November 1962), pp. 403–412.

39 Spencer Olin, *California's Prodigal Sons* (Berkeley: University of California Press, 1968), p. 407.

40 *New York Times,* October 8, 1916.

41 *The Los Angeles Record,* October 14, 1916, p. 1; Edson papers.

42 Katherine Philips Edson to Florence Kelley, November 18, 1916, box 1, folder 4, Edson papers.

43 Norris C. Hundley, Jr. *Notable American Women, 1607–1950* (Cambridge: Belknap Publications of Harvard University Press, 1971), pp. 562–564.

44 De Nyse Memorial, *Federation News,* p. 6.

45 Government Night Letter: Felix Frankfurter to KP Edson, October 17, 1918; box 2, folder 15, Edson papers.

46 Night Letter from A. B. C. Dohrmann to Felix Frankfurter, box 2, folder 13, Edson papers.

47 Unidentified newspaper clipping, box 14, Scrapbook, Edson papers: Josephine Good, *History of Women in Republican National Conventions* (Washington: Republican National Committee 1960–64, Women's Division, 1963).

48 Unpublished interview with Edson's daughter, Katharine Mershon, June 1984. To be published in June 1986 by the UCLA Oral History Program.

49 *The News Republican,* Kenton, Ohio, September 15, 1920, p. 1.

50 *Conference on the Limitation of Armaments; Address of the President of the United States;* Document no. 125 (Washington: Government Printing Office, 1922), p. 5.

51 C. Leonard Hoag, *Preface to Preparedness; The Washington Disarmament Conference and Public Opinion* (Washington, D.C.: Council on Public Affairs, 1941), p. 90.

52 *New York Times,* Nov. 2, 1921, p. 2.

53 *Los Angeles Evening Express,* January 6, 1922, box 4, envelope 6, Edson papers.

54 Unidentified newspaper, January 18, 1922, box 4, envelope 3, Edson papers.

55 Unidentified newspaper, box 4, envelope 3, Edson papers.

56 *Stockton Record,* Nov. 4, 1921, box 4, envelope 6, Edson papers.

57 Katherine Philips Edson to Maud Wood Park, February 21, 1924, Series 1, box 6, National League of Women Voters Papers, Library of Congress.

58 *Los Angeles Times,* August 30, 1925, box 4, envelope 6, Edson papers.

59 Alma Whittaker, "The Last Word." in *Times,* city unknown, probably Los Angeles, box 4, envelope 6, Edson papers.

60 Grace A. Koopal, *Miracle of Music, The History of the Hollywood Bowl,* Golden Jubilee Edition, 1972, p. 1.

FROM THE FAMILY FARM TO AGRIBUSINESS

EDITOR'S INTRODUCTION

The pattern of large-scale landownership in California is sometimes imagined to be a tradition stretching unbroken from the days of the missions to the present. We think of the vast ranchos of the Mexican period, the huge land grants of the Southern Pacific Railroad, and the modern landholdings of such agribusiness giants as the J. G. Boswell Corporation and the Shaler Land Company.

There was a time, however, when small family farms played a major role in California agriculture. In his comprehensive study, *From the Family Farm to Agribusiness: The Irrigation Crusade in California and the West* (1984), Donald J. Pisani divides California's agricultural history into three distinct stages: the pastoral and wheat boom era (1850–1890), the small-farm phase (1880–1920), and the era of consolidation, in which the state's farms were transformed into "factories in the fields" (1920s–present).[1]

Pisani demonstrates that, during the first of these stages, when large units of land were held by absentee wheat and cattle barons, Californians were concerned about the relative absence of family farms in their state. "Nineteenth-century California bore little resemblance to the older agricultural states of New England and the Midwest," Pisani observes, "and the social critics worried deeply about the Golden State's future." Reformers seized upon irrigation as a means of promoting agricultural diversification and the expansion of the number of family farms. "Irrigation became a tool by which the arid West could be made to conform to the familiar traditional patterns of land tenure 'back home.'"

As irrigation districts were established in the late nineteenth and early twentieth centuries, the number of small family farms increased. Irrigation reformers, for a time,

[1]For a convenient summary see Richard S. Kirkendall, "Agrarianism and Modernization in History and Historians," *Reviews in American History*, XIV (March 1986), 97–103.

were encouraged. Yet at the heart of Pisani's study is a great irony. The long-term effects of irrigation were precisely the opposite of those intended. The goal of the irrigationists was to break the hold of "land monopoly" on the state, yet irrigation eventually strengthened the grip of agribusiness. Irrigation districts levied assessments for the construction and operation of their water delivery systems. The districts operated according to the doctrine that the costs of irrigation should be borne by the primary beneficiaries, the farmers themselves. Small family farmers soon found it difficult to pay the costs of increasingly ambitious irrigation projects. The wealthy farmers who could afford to pay acquired more water and more land.[2]

In the early twentieth century the reformers hoped that the doctrine of "multiple use" would reverse this trend. Other sources of revenue, such as the generation of hydroelectric power, were expected to defray the costs of irrigation. The reform-minded irrigationists were foiled again, however, as the mammoth state and federal water projects provided disproportionate benefits to large-scale users.

By the 1920s, according to Pisani's analysis, the water reformers had largely given up their struggle to restore the family farm as the dominant entity in California agriculture. Agribusiness was triumphant. In the following selection, Pisani describes the final attempt by the reformers to reestablish the yeoman farmer. A short-lived and largely unsuccessful scheme of "scientific colonization" was promoted during the progressive administration of Governor Hiram Johnson. As Pisani observes, the colonization plan proved to be both anachronistic and impractical.

Donald J. Pisani received his Ph.D. from the University of California, Davis, in 1975. He is the author of numerous scholarly articles and is currently an Associate Professor of History at Texas A&M University.

[2]See also Lawrence J. Jelinek, *Harvest Empire: A History of California Agriculture* (San Francisco, 1979), 61–94.

READING 20

From the Family Farm to Agribusiness

Donald J. Pisani

All of American history reflects conflict between rural and urban values, between an often idealized life close to the earth and the impersonal, complicated social and economic relationships intrinsic to a commercial and by the late nineteenth and twentieth centuries, industrial nation. Californians were both more and less nostalgic than other Americans. Since statehood, their lives had been dominated by "the city," San Francisco, so they never witnessed at close hand the waning influence of the country vis-à-vis the metropolis. Nevertheless, the absence of strong rural traditions made those traditions all the more attractive. From the 1870s to the 1920s, leaders of the irrigation movement in California agreed that the state's cities were overcrowded and growing much too fast; that large farms created a wide range of problems from tenantry to an inadequate rural transportation system; that more had to be done to make country life attractive; and that the family farm was the foundation of a stable society and the wellspring of republican virtues. They saw irrigation as a way to return to a more homogeneous, virtuous, middle-class society, but also as a way to make farming more efficient and profitable. Irrigation promised to promote the cultivation of high value fruits, nuts, and vegetables; reduce the size of farms; stimulate community life; arrest the migration from country to city; and attract new immigrants from outside the state.

The year 1931 represents a convenient dividing line. By that time most Californians acknowledged, though not always directly, that the health of their economy and society did not

Adapted from *From the Family Farm to Agribusiness: The Irrigation Crusade in California and the West, 1850–1931,* by Donald J. Pisani, pp. 440–456. Copyright © 1984 by the Regents of the University of California.

depend on the existence, perpetuation, or proliferation of the family farm. They might exhibit a sentimental attachment to "small town America," if not farming itself, but they also recognized that the values represented by the small freehold—widespread property ownership, high wages, and economic independence, to name a few—were anachronistic, however attractive. Californians had begun to see their state as "the great exception," and even to revel in its exceptional qualities, rather than try to recapture the institutions and life-style that had prevailed in the Midwest or "back East." By the 1930s, and especially after World War II, irrigation entered a new phase. It was no longer an agent to transform society, but an ally of the agricultural establishment.

During World War I, the crusade for the family farm enjoyed a renaissance in many parts of the United States, but nowhere more than in California. A special California commission on land colonization reported in 1916:

Within the last five years questions of land tenure and land settlement have assumed a hitherto unthought of importance in the United States. The causes for this are the disappearance of free, fertile public land; the rising prices of privately-owned lands; the increase in tenant farming and a clearer recognition of its dangers; and the increasing attractions of city life which threaten the social impairment of rural communities by causing young people to leave the farms.... In [some] countries the state has taken an active part in subdividing large estates and in creating conditions which will enable farm laborers and farmers of small capital to own their homes. They have adopted this policy because experience has shown that nonresident ownership and tenant farming are politically dangerous and socially undesirable; that ignorant and nomadic farm labor is bad; and that the balance between the growth of city and country can be maintained only through creating rural conditions which will make the farm as attractive as the office or factory for men and women of character and intelligence.

The problem of land monopoly and nonresident ownership was particularly acute in California where 310 property owners held over 4,000,000 acres of prime farmland suited to intensive cultivation, land capable of providing 100,000 40-acre farms and sustaining 500,000 additional rural residents. The Southern Pacific Railroad owned over 500,000 acres; four Kern County land companies owned over 1,000,000 acres, or more than half the county's privately owned land; and in Merced County, Miller and Lux owned 245,000 acres. Most midwestern states had relatively homogeneous populations, few very large or very small farms, few nonresident owners, and few very rich or very poor farmers. However, in many parts of California, rural society was characterized by wealthy, nonresident land barons and migratory farm laborers or tenants who had no allegiance to place or sense of civic responsibility. The commission on land colonization argued that land monopoly undermined democratic values and political stability just as it retarded the state's agricultural development.[1]

The interest in restoring the family farm also grew out of a deep fear of the "yellow peril." By 1920, the Japanese, who had begun to migrate to California in great numbers in the 1890s to replace the excluded Chinese as field hands, had acquired over 500,000 acres of land, most of it reclaimed swamps in the Central Valley. They dominated the production of rice and tomatoes, and their success raised the prospect that they would one day displace the white farmer. Given the prevailing belief in white supremacy, many Californians assumed that democracy was possible only in a homogeneous society. They favored measures to restrict Japanese immigration, segregate Japanese schoolchildren, and prohibit alien landowner-

ship. They also hoped to lure more white farmers onto the land.[2]

Aside from the problem of land monopoly and the "yellow peril," Californians shared the assumption of many other Americans that a massive economic slump, if not depression, would follow hard upon the end of World War I. Helping returning soldiers acquire a farm could soften the economic impact of demobilization, reward faithful service to the nation, and reverse the migration from country to city. "Nothing short of ownership of the land one toils over," Elwood Mead remarked, "will suffice to overcome the lure of the city." Federal reclamation had tried, but failed, to turn the tide. The United States population increased from 76,000,000 to 106,000,000 from 1900 to 1920, but the Reclamation Bureau had managed to provide rural homes for only about 1 percent of these new people. To make matters worse, easier living conditions in the cities and high wages, especially during World War I, led to dramatic increases in tenant farming and the abandonment of many farms in the older agricultural regions. Michigan alone contained 19,000 idle farms in 1920.[3]

In California, one of the prime obstacles to taking up a farm was the high price of land and water. The average price of unimproved farmland increased from $27.63 an acre in 1900 to $116.84 in 1920. The value of the average farm tripled in the same period, and the price of improved land increased even faster. By 1920, most irrigated land sold for $100 to $500 an acre. And the cost of setting up a new farm, including the price of livestock, machinery, barns, and fences, made farming even more expensive.[4]

"SCIENTIFIC COLONIZATION"

In 1915, the California legislature created a Commission on Land Colonization and Rural Credits; Hiram Johnson appointed Elwood Mead chairman. The irrigation engineer had just returned from Australia where from 1907 to 1914 he served as chairman of the Victoria Rivers and Water Supply Commission overseeing arid land reclamation and colonization in that province. After a survey of thirty-two California land settlement schemes in 1916, which demonstrated the lack of planning in rural settlement, the commission concluded that the state was ripe for a "demonstration in scientific colonization" based on the Australian experience. Irrigation was a vital part of the "demonstration" because small farms could not be created without it. The Commonwealth Club of California drafted a bill containing most of Mead's recommendations, and the legislature passed it in 1917 with a $250,000 appropriation to launch the program. The lawmakers expected this money to be repaid, along with 5 percent interest, within fifty years.[5]

As the home of the first colony, Mead and the California Land Settlement Board selected a 6,239-acre tract at Durham, in the middle of the Sacramento Valley just south of Chico. The land cost an average $88 an acre. Durham represented a sharp break with the policies of the Reclamation Bureau and private land development companies. The site had been chosen over thirty-nine others for its relatively low price, soil quality, ease of preparation for irrigation, and access to transportation (rather than for the political reasons that too often influenced the choice of sites for federal reclamation projects). The land had been tested and graded according to its productive capacity by soil scientists from the University of California and priced from $48 to $225 an acre. Instead of the uniform-sized farms found on federal projects, the 110 units at Durham varied in size from 8 to 300 acres, depending on whether the land was best suited for raising forage or fruit. There were also 26 two-acre farm laborer plots. When the first settlers arrived in 1918, they found roads, irrigation ditches, barns, houses, and fences ready. In fact much of the land had already been seeded to pasture.

The average cost of reclamation at Durham ran $80 an acre, including $25 to $83 an acre simply to level the land and prepare it for irrigation. This was, as Mead freely acknowledged, more than the price of improved acreage in the East or South. However, the farmer had twenty years to repay the cost of the land (5% down and 5% per year at 5% interest). To protect against land speculation, which contributed to the problems experienced on federal reclamation projects, settlers had six months to move onto their farms and were required to reside there for at least eight months a year for the first ten years. For the first five years, they could not mortgage, transfer, or sublet any part of their land without approval from the board. The state also provided a range of ready-made house plans drafted by architects in the state engineer's office. Settlers decided on the size and floor plan when they filed for their farm, left construction to the land board, and found farmhouses ready for occupancy when they moved onto the land. The state loaned up to 60 percent of the cost and up to $3,000 for other improvements, equipment, and supplies.

Mead often commented that federal reclamation had been too concerned with constructing dams and canals, but little interested in the farmers it served. The settlement of government projects had been random and haphazard, with little attention to community life or cooperative institutions. Durham, by contrast, was settled systematically, created as an irrigation community rather than a loose collection of individuals. The land settlement board carefully sifted through 1,000 applications for the 100 farms and 150 applications for the 26 two-acre farm laborer plots. Those accepted were required to have some agricultural experience (except the laborers), an ability to work hard, and a minimum of $1,500 capital. Married men with families and former tenant farmers received preference. The board turned to landscape architects at the University of California for a townsite plan, which contained plenty of room for schools and public buildings on a twenty-two acre "commons" in the middle of the settlement, just as it relied on the Office of Good Roads and Rural Engineering of the U.S.D.A. to furnish plans and supervise construction of the irrigation and drainage systems. The board helped organize cooperative marketing associations that sold poultry and dairy products; provided heavy farm machinery; bought barbed wire, cement, pipe, lumber, and other supplies in wholesale lots to reduce the cost to Durham residents; provided a superintendent to advise farmers on crops to plant and help solve agricultural problems, and even established a mosquito abatement district to reduce the danger of malaria. In short, the land settlement board anticipated and provided for nearly every need.[6]

One of the many early writers who visited Durham provided an idyllic picture for *Collier's* readers in 1925:

> Here some 150 families have been making a prosperous living and having a bully time in the very same hard-boiled period when a million people in a single year left our farms, starved off. Nobody wants to leave Durham....Then what's the secret? No pioneering. Cooperation. Expert advice. Available capital. And no isolation. Unless you are naturally a crab you won't be dull in Durham. Farmers don't live miles apart but in a close-knit, pretty township covering 6,000 acres, laid out logically for business and pleasure. No tiring trips after chores to go to a dance, see the school movie, hear a radio, drop in at the club, take a dip in the swimming hole in Butte Creek, join a picnic, or attend the fair.

Durham, the writer gushes, was "the seed of a new land policy for the United States."[7]

The early success at Durham was not matched by a second colony established in Merced County in the San Joaquin Valley in 1920. The 4,800-acre Delhi Colony, built on land acquired from the Turlock Irrigation District, suffered crippling problems from the start. After grading and the installation of irrigation

pipe, the farms cost an average of $230 an acre, substantially more than at Durham. Moreover, much of the soil was poor and required frequent, heavy doses of fertilizers. It was so sandy that some of the first alfalfa crops literally blew away. The project opened just as the agricultural boom of World War I ended. With inadequate capital and falling crop prices, more than 90 percent of the settlers fell behind in their payments to the state. By 1925, only about 57 percent of the land at Delhi was under cultivation, and 38 percent of the farms had returned no income at all.[8]

California voters turned down a $3,000,000 bond issue to aid settlement in 1922, and Governor Friend Richardson strongly opposed any new colonies. In 1925, he charged that "the sandy wastes at Delhi was [sic] purchased by the projectors of this amazing scheme [the land settlement board] at much more than its worth; settlers without experience and without funds were lured to the colony by glowing advertisements; advice regarding crop planting by alleged experts proved worthless, and money was squandered on railroad switches, town site and other unnecessary dreams. The result has been disastrous to the settlers. For two years we have been trying to salvage this wreck left as a legacy from the Delhi projectors."[9] Elwood Mead, who had resigned from the board at the end of 1923, engaged in a running dispute with the governor. Richardson, he claimed, had encouraged the complaints of Delhi residents and replaced Mead with a real estate agent who opposed state-sponsored colonization on principle. In Mead's words, Delhi "would have succeeded if it had been supported by Governor Richardson as the Durham settlement was supported by his predecessor."[10] Nevertheless, the legislature shared the governor's concerns. The lawmakers investigated conditions at Delhi in 1923, 1925, and 1927, and extended relief to the Delhi settlers by writing off much of their debt. Subsequently, farmers at Durham demanded the same concessions. In 1929, the state worked out a schedule reducing the cost of farms on the two projects from inflated World War I prices to the prices prevailing in the late 1920s, and in the following year turned management of the projects over to the farmers themselves. The *Washington Post* characterized both schemes as failures, even though Mead stalwartly insisted that Durham had been a success. The newspaper blamed their failure not just on the high price of land during the war, but also in "incompetent [soil] surveys," inadequate screening of prospective settlers, and general "mismanagement." The *Post* story ended with a comment that must have stung Mead. Mead, as Commissioner of Reclamation after 1924, had tried to introduce many features of his California program into the federal projects. "The experience of California," the newspaper concluded, "is similar to that of the Federal Government on some of its ill-chosen reclamation projects."[11]

During World War I, Mead predicted that the land settlement ideas he had worked out in Australia would ultimately result in the investment of $300,000,000 in planned colonies and the addition of 250,000 farmers and their families to California's rural population. He had hoped that Durham and Delhi would serve as a model to private land developers. "State settlements should...be considered as an educational agency, as examples of correct methods and policies and as places where records can be kept of costs and results," he wrote in 1923. "The greater part of the area to be developed must be developed by private enterprise or by a different type of organization."[12]

Mead believed that the day of the land speculator and unplanned development had passed, that land colonization was the wave of the future. But his attempt to reconstitute rural America using irrigation was anachronistic and impractical. Private colonization had worked well on the Kings River near Fresno in the 1870s, and in southern California in the 1880s. It promoted intensive farming, the subdivision of

large estates, a population boom, a dramatic increase in property values, and relatively homogeneous communities of small freeholders. But conditions had changed by the mid-1920s. From 1909 to 1919, an average of 28,000 acres of trees and vines were added to California's horticultural productivity each year. Then, from 1919 to 1925, an average of 112,000 acres were planted each year. At the same time, the value of most fruits dropped sharply. From 1919 to 1923, the price of oranges fell by 35 percent, almonds and apples by 50 percent, raisins and peaches by about 70 percent, and apricots by nearly 80 percent. The value of land planted to fruit declined by half during the same years, and these figures were adjusted for postwar inflation. Frank T. Swett, president of California's Pear Growers' Association, commented in 1925: "The fruit industry, ultimately, will get over its present troubles, if the Bullfornia unscrupulous land peddlers, boomers, and poets and painters of rainbows will let it alone for a while." Such observers became prime critics of the expansion of irrigation.[13]

In 1925, Frank Adams noted that more than 400,000 acres under ditch within the state's irrigation districts remained to be settled and perhaps 1,000,000 acres in the state as a whole. Adams agreed with Mead that the $5,000 or more needed to buy and develop a 40-acre irrigated farm exceeded the resources of most prospective settlers. He concluded that "obtaining settlers is the most urgent need and not bringing more land under irrigation projects."[14] Nevertheless, Adams believed that the state's agricultural problems resulted as much from underconsumption or lack of adequate transportation as from over-production. He did not worry about the irrigation projects planned for the San Joaquin Valley; they would take years to complete and the nation's rapid increase in population would provide new markets in the future. California's population increased by 44 percent during the second decade of the twentieth century, and in 1923 the Division of Engineering and Irrigation predicted that by 1940 the demand for California farm products would triple. Moreover, even during the early 1920s, demand for vegetables increased—demonstrating that not all crops suffered uniformly—and irrigated land sold briskly in many parts of the state. The Commonwealth Club's Section on Irrigation observed that only 75 percent of the state's readily irrigable land was under ditch opposed to 87 percent in Colorado and more than 80 percent in both Utah and Idaho.[15]

Since they faced distinct competitive disadvantages, the question of whether California *needed* more irrigated family farms was largely academic anyway. For example, as California farmers tapped national and international markets, they recognized the value of flexibility, of being able to raise different crops from year to year to anticipate gluts. But different crops usually required new harvesting machines, which dramatically increased the cost of farming. Similarly, as the San Joaquin Valley's water table fell during the 1920s, the powerful pumps needed to draw water to the surface became more expensive to buy and operate. William L. Preston has shown that in Tulare County irrigation contributed to a substantial increase in ten- to forty-acre farms from 1895 to 1925, especially during the boom years of World War I. But, he concludes, "by 1926, fluctuating prices, increasingly expensive irrigation water, migrant-labor unrest, rising land taxes, and the growing profitability of machine harvested crops had tipped the scales in favor of large farmers once again." Small farmers usually held heavily mortgaged land which, in the words of another historian, "made for the eventual consolidation of farming lands in the hands of a few absentee landlords and receiverships like Trans-America Company of the Bank of America, who coordinated the bankrupt but productive farms, both large and small, into systems that have been aptly characterized as 'factories in the fields.'"[16]

Tulare County farms shrank in size from an average 460 acres in 1900 to 242 in 1910 to 159 in 1925 as irrigation agriculture supplanted dry farmed wheat and made land too valuable for free grazing. But by 1945, as intensively cultivated farms were consolidated, the trend reversed and the average farm size rose to 213 acres. Nor was the Tulare County experience unique. Statewide, the average farm decreased from 397 acres in 1900 to 250 acres in 1920 to 224 acres in 1930. But by 1950 the average stood at 267 acres. The number and size of farms larger than 1,000 acres increased dramatically from 1920 to 1945. In 1920, the state contained 4,906 farms in this category covering 17,638,199 acres. By 1945, the number had increased to 5,939 farms encompassing 24,663,631 acres.[17]

THE LOST DREAM

The 1920s represented a turning point in the history of California agriculture. By then, few of the state's army of boosters spoke of using irrigation to restore the dominance of the yeoman farmer, provide homes for jobless city dwellers, or reinforce traditional American values. The West had entered a new era. Little public land remained, successful farming required much more knowledge as well as equipment, and the city offered new opportunities as well as temptations. The economic hard times of the 1920s and 1930s increased the gulf between landownership and the act of tilling the soil—a gulf symbolized by the plight of migrant farm workers. Both the Central Valley Project and State Water Project contributed to the growth of agriculture as a business and the disappearance of farming as a way of life. The C.V.P. allowed large farmers to strengthen their hold on the countryside in several ways. It provided interest-free loans under the Reclamation Act of 1902. Power sales, sales of water to towns and cities, and direct federal appropriations subsidized the cost of massive dams and canals. Until the late 1950s, little effort was made to enforce the 160-acre limitation on cheap federal irrigation water. Even then, this restriction could often be evaded. Most important, both the Central Valley Project and State Water Project of the 1960s and 1970s represented a shift away from local control as water bureaucracies in Washington and Sacramento assumed vast new powers. Local water agencies, including irrigation, storage, and water conservation districts, survived but lost much of their autonomy. And as more and more decisions concerning water resource development were made in Washington and Sacramento, those water users who were well organized and wealthy—able to maintain armies of lobbyists and mold public opinion—virtually dictated state and national water policies. The rise of agribusiness coincided not just with the decline of the family farm ideal, but also with the virtual disappearance of the hope that California agriculture could be built on relatively autonomous, middle-class rural communities.

Of course, demographic shifts also contributed to the rise of agribusiness and the decline of "rural California." In 1900, 47.7 percent of the state's population resided in communities of 2,500 or fewer. This number decreased to 38.2 percent in 1910, 32.1 percent in 1920, and 26.7 percent in 1930. Though the state's rural population increased from 708,233 in 1900 to 1,099,902 in 1920, migration from out of state accounted for less than half the increase. Put in a broader perspective, California's urban population grew by 89 percent from 1900 to 1910 while the rural population increased by only 28.4 percent. In the next decade, the growth rate was 58.5 percent urban and 21 percent rural. During the 1920s, the rate was 78.8 percent to 37.9 percent. In the same three decades, some farm states, including Illinois and Iowa, suffered *absolute* declines in rural population. But both these states had a proportionately larger farm population than California, which had always been far more urban than other western or midwestern states.[18]

California had contributed much to western economic development since statehood. It served as a laboratory where the engineers, publicists, and promoters of irrigation, such as William Ellsworth Smythe, George H. Maxwell and Elwood Mead, tested their ideas. For better or worse, it provided a system of water law, the "California Doctrine," followed by many other states. It had introduced the multiple-use concept of water planning on the Sacramento River long before that idea found expression in the great western water projects of 1928 and after. And it provided the West with the irrigation district, an institution responsible for much of the region's agricultural growth in the early decades of the century. But urbanization, farm mechanization, the soaring price of land and water, and other trends could not be reversed. After 1930, irrigation became one of the foundation blocks of agribusiness. The dream of using it to reform California society was all but forgotten.

Notes

1 "Report of the Commission on Land Colonization and Rural Credits of the State of California, November 29, 1916," *JCSA*, 42d sess. (Sacramento, 1917), Appendix, 2: 5, 8.

2 Roger Daniels, *The Politics of Prejudice: The Anti-Japanese Movement in California and the Struggle for Japanese Exclusion* (Berkeley, 1962); Lloyd Fisher and Ralph L. Nielson, *The Japanese in California Agriculture* (Berkeley, 1942); Masakazu Iwata, "The Japanese Immigrants in California Agriculture," *Agricultural History* 36 (January 1962): 25–37; Adon Poli and W. M. Engstrand, "Japanese Agriculture on the Pacific Coast," *Journal of Land and Public Utility Economics* 21 (November 1945): 355–364.

3 Elwood Mead, *Helping Men Own Farms* (New York, 1920), 10; "How California is Helping People Own Farms and Rural Homes, August, 1920," University of California, College of Agriculture, Experiment Stations Circular no. 221, Bureau of Reclamation Records; "(512) Correspondence re Plans and Methods Employed by States in Colonizing and Settling Lands—Thru

1924," RG 115, National Archives, Washington, D.C.; and the comments of J. C. Forkner, chairman of the board of consultants to the State Department of Engineering and Irrigation, in the transcript of the board's meeting, November 4, 1922, file entitled "Water Resources Investigation: Transcripts and Minutes of Meetings, 1922," microfilm reel 1029, DWR Archives.

4 Frank Beach, "The Economic Transformation of California, 1900–1920: The Effects of the Westward Movement on California's Growth and Development in the Progressive Period" (Ph.D. diss., University of California, Berkeley, 1963), 106.

5 For general discussions of the Mead colonization scheme in California see James R. Kluger, "Ellwood Mead: Irrigation Engineer and Social Planner" (Ph.D. diss., University of Arizona, 1970), 105–134; Gerald D. Nash, *State Government and Economic Development: A History of Administrative Policies in California, 1849–1933* (Berkeley, 1964), 344–347; F. L. Tomlinson, "Land Reclamation and Settlement in the United States," *International Review of Agricultural Economics* 4 (1926): 255–272; and Roy J. Smith, "The California Land Settlement Board at Durham and Delhi," *Hilgardia* 4 (1943): 399–492.

6 Elwood Mead, "The Relation of Land Settlement to Irrigation Development," January or February, 1923; "(516) General Correspondence re Soldier Settlement Plans and Methods thru 1925," RG 115; Mike Commons to Mead, May 3, 1924, in "(512) Correspondence re Plans and Methods Employed by States in Colonizing and Settling Lands—thru 1924."

7 Gertrude Matthews Shelby, "Nobody Wants to Leave this Town," *Collier's* 75 (May 30, 1925): 26, 34. For other laudatory articles on the Durham settlement, see "The Most Helpful Experiment in the Settlement of Irrigated Lands," *Engineering News-Record* 81 (December 5, 1918): 1013; "Developing Irrigated Land with Selected Settlers," 1014–1018; Elwood Mead, "Farm Settlement on a New Plan," *American Review of Reviews* 59 (March 1919): 270–277; H. A. Crafts, "Back to the Land: California Pioneers the State Land Settlement Plan," *Scientific American* 121 (August 23, 1919): 185; "The State and the Farmer: Successful Development of the California Land Settlement Scheme" 123 (November 13, 1920): 494, 507–508; W. V. Woehke, "Food First: Work of the California Land Settlement Board," *Sunset* 45 (October 1920): 35–38; "California's Farm Colonies," *The American Review of Reviews* 64 (October 1921): 397–404.

8 Robert Welles Ritchie, "The Rural Democracy at Delhi," *Country Gentleman* 85 (November 27, 1920): 8, 36; Nathan A. Bowers, "California's Land Settlement at Delhi," *Engineering News-Record* 88 (July 23, 1925): 143–145.

9 *San Francisco Chronicle,* April 11, 1925.

10 *Orland Register,* May 29, 1925. In a letter to E. F. Benson, March 13, 1926, "(516) General Correspondence re Soldier Settlement Plans & Methods 1926 & 1927," RG 115, Mead wrote: "One has to know how personally vindictive he [Richardson] is to understand his attitude on settlement....His personal animosities govern his public acts. He is an enemy of land settlement as he has been of all the state's social and economic activities."

11 *Washington Post,* March 26, 1929.

12 Mead, "The Relation of Land Settlement to Irrigation Development."

13 "Irrigation and Agriculture," *Transactions of the Commonwealth Club* (hereafter TCC), 20 (November 24, 1925): 346, chart on 348, 351. The Swett quote is from p. 351.

14 Frank Adams to John Gabbert, October 22, 1925, Frank Adams Collection, California Water Resources Archives. California's irrigated land increased from 1,466,000 acres in 1900, to 2,664,000 acres in 1910, to 4,219,000 acres in 1920. However, during the 1920s the increase was a more modest 528,000 acres, and in the following decade only 323,000 acres were added to the total. Then, from 1940 to 1950, the total mushroomed from 5,070,000 to 6,599,000 acres, as Shasta Dam and other units in the Central Valley Project began to operate.

15 Frank Adams, "Are We Developing Our Irrigated Areas Too Rapidly?" *TCC* 20 (November 24, 1925): 375–388, 397–399; *Water Resources of California: A Report to the Legislature of 1923,* Department of Public Works, Division of Engineering and Irrigation Bulletin no. 4 (Sacramento, 1923), 17, 39, 45, 55.

16 William L. Preston, *Vanishing Landscapes: Land and Life in the Tulare Lake Basin* (Berkeley, 1981), 199; Beach, "The Transformation of California, 1900–1920," 127.

17 Preston, *Vanishing Landscapes,* 170, 200; *United States Census of Agriculture: 1935,* vol. 1 (Washington D.C., 1936), 944–947; Lawrence Je-linek, *Harvest Empire: A History of California Agriculture* (San Francisco, 1979), 63.

18 For an excellent overview of California's population patterns from 1850–1950, see Warren S. Thompson, *Growth and Changes in California's Population* (Los Angeles, 1955). The statistics cited are from pp. 11, 13, and 277.

CHAPTER 21

WORK AND RESTLESSNESS IN EAST LOS ANGELES

EDITOR'S INTRODUCTION

Hispanics are by far the largest ethnic minority in California. The 1990 census is expected to find that nearly a quarter of the state's population is of "Spanish origin," most of whom are Mexican Americans. Demographers project that in forty years the number of Hispanics will nearly equal the number of Anglos.

As the state's Hispanic population has grown in size and importance, so too has the field of Chicano studies. Within the past decade several young Hispanic scholars have completed ambitious research projects on the history of Mexican Americans in California. Often employing the methods of the new social history, Chicano historians have been particularly interested in questions of occupational structure and mobility, class and race. Their research, according to Tomás Almaguer and Albert Camarillo, points to one major finding: "Mexicans were in the lowest levels of an occupational structure which was divided along racial lines."[1] Race was a barrier to upward mobility not only for the Chinese in rural California, as we learned from Sucheng Chan in an earlier selection, and for blacks in San Francisco, as Douglas Henry Daniels concluded, but also for Mexicans in southern California.

Two of the most important contributions to the field of Chicano studies have described the status of Hispanics in southern California during the nineteenth century. Richard Griswold del Castillo has found that while some of the surviving *ranchero* families experienced a temporary prosperity following the American conquest, nearly all Hispanics soon found themselves locked in a stagnant occupational structure. What few gains were made in upward mobility occurred before the great influx of

[1]In Armando Valdez, Albert Camarillo, and Tomás Almaguer, eds., *The State of Chicano Research in Family, Labor and Migration Studies: Proceedings of the First Stanford Symposium on Chicano Research and Public Policy* (Stanford, 1983), 6.

Anglos in the 1860s.[2] Albert Camarillo has chronicled a similar pattern of stagnation among the Hispanics in Santa Barbara and throughout southern California. Mexican Americans were routinely excluded from high-status jobs and were thus subordinated as a class of semiskilled or unskilled workers.[3] Both Griswold del Castillo and Camarillo have found that Hispanic Californians experienced very limited occupational mobility and high rates of spatial mobility. Their findings confirm what the new social historians have observed in cities across the country: Workers who were least successful in achieving upward mobility were the ones most likely to move.

Ricardo Romo's *East Los Angeles: History of a Barrio* (1983) is one of the first books to recount the history of Mexican Americans in southern California during the twentieth century.[4] Romo's major focus is on the period from World War I to the late 1920s, and he considers a broad range of topics including the demographic expansion of the barrio, race relations, and social and voluntary organizations. In the following selection Romo analyzes the occupational and spatial mobility of Mexican workers. Just as Robert L. Griswold, in an earlier selection, demonstrated the importance of divorce records for the social historian, Romo shows that new insights can also be gained from using marriage records. Romo's findings for the twentieth century are remarkably similar to what we know of the nineteenth. Opportunities for upward mobility were rare, while rates of geographical mobility were unusually high. The California Dream of opportunity and prosperity, Romo concludes, was seldom fulfilled in the barrio of East Los Angeles.

Ricardo Romo received his Ph.D. from the University of California, Los Angeles, in 1975, and is currently an Associate Professor of History at the University of Texas at Austin. He is the co-editor of *The Mexican American Experience: An Interdisciplinary Anthology* (1984).

---

[2]Richard Griswold del Castillo, *The Los Angeles Barrio, 1850–1890: A Social History* (Berkeley, 1979), 7–11, 31–49, 54–61.

[3]Albert Camarillo, *Chicanos in a Changing Society: From Mexican Pueblos to American Barrios in Santa Barbara and Southern California, 1848–1930* (Cambridge, 1979), 29, 32, 47–51, 89–90, 126–129.

[4]See also Rudolfo F. Acuña, *A Community under Siege: A Chronicle of Chicanos East of the Los Angeles River, 1945–1975* (Berkeley, 1985).

Work and Restlessness in East Los Angeles

Ricardo Romo

Despite the nativism of the World War I period, as Los Angeles grew, industrialists welcomed Mexican labor and, in many cases, actively recruited workers south of the border. The city's proximity to Mexico provided it with a pool of common labor not available to other industrial regions of the United States. In addition, a large number of migrants of Mexican descent, drawn by job opportunities in industry and agriculture, came to Los Angeles from nearby southwestern states. This chapter summarizes findings concerning occupational and spatial mobility of Mexican workers in Los Angeles between 1918 and 1928.[1]

Like most urban working-class groups, Mexican laborers did not record everyday experiences, and little is known about their adjustment to industrial urban centers such as Los Angeles. Compared to other workers in Los Angeles and Boston, Mexicanos in the Los Angeles work force experienced unusually low occupational mobility. Mexican workers with expectations of entering high blue-collar or white-collar professions during the years 1918 to 1928 were sorely disappointed. Moreover, Mexicanos in Los Angeles changed their place of residence or left the city with far greater frequency than other groups in five other cities over a similar period of time.

Los Angeles marriage records and city directories provided the major sources of data for this chapter. From the 1917 and 1918 city marriage license applications, which furnished the age, occupation, nativity, and religious affiliation of the groom, every man of Mexican ancestry, either born in Mexico or Spanish surnamed, was selected for the sample group.[2] Information about an individual's occupation and residence derived from these records was checked or traced in the 1917, 1918, and 1928 city directories to determine changes in occupational or spatial status of the sample. The information about the nativity of the groom made it possible to determine the occupation status of first-, second-, and third-generation Mexicanos.[3]

The selection of the years 1918–1928 for the analysis of Mexican occupational and spatial mobility in this chapter required special consideration. Most twentieth-century studies on mobility have been based on ten-year periods. Studies of Atlanta, San Antonio, and Boston used the first year of a new decade, such as 1890, 1900, or 1910, and 1920, as the starting point for each period.[4] The year 1910 was unacceptable as an initial date for the study of Mexican workers because few Mexicanos lived in Los Angeles at that time. Moreover, that date would necessitate terminating the study in 1920, which would omit the twenties, an era of tremendous industrial activity in the city as well as the decade of the greatest immigration from Mexico in American history. Thus the time period 1918–1928 was selected because it included the twenties, and still excluded the era of the Great Depression, which had an unusual effect on Mexican laborers. Also in 1929 and several years thereafter, thousands of Mexicans were repatriated to Mexico through the efforts of city and county officials,[5] and such unnatural population losses in the Mexican community would have biased the sample.

Adapted from *East Los Angeles: History of a Barrio,* by Ricardo Romo, pp. 112–128, with permission of the publishers, University of Texas Press. Copyright © 1983 by University of Texas Press. An earlier version was published in *Pacific Historical Review,* Vol. 46, no. 2 (May 1977).

MEXICAN LABOR

Writers popularized the image of California as the "land of Golden Promise."[6] To hundreds of thousands of immigrants and native midwesterners and easterners, California came to symbolize opportunity and wealth. Southern California businessmen conducted extensive advertising and publicity campaigns designed to lure newcomers to their region. Between the years 1918 and 1930, boosters promoted California as a "Garden of Eden" and a worker's paradise. California was a land "with a climate of semitropical friendliness that robs the mere business of sustaining life of its rigors and leaves human energy free for whatever other tasks the spirit may conceive."[7] No city in California worked harder at attracting migrants, immigrants, and new industries than Los Angeles. Blessed with a year-round pleasant climate and expanding trade due to the opening of the Panama Canal, Los Angeles appealed to both business leaders and workers. Some promoters went so far as to say that climate enhanced employment and social mobility. "The climate is the poor man's benison as well as the rich man's luxury. There is no other place in America where social stratification is so little marked, where all classes do so nearly the same thing at the same time."[8]

Southern California boosterism, which officially began in the late 1880s with the founding of the Los Angeles Chamber of Commerce,[9] reached new proportions after World War I. In Los Angeles, Bruce Bliven wrote in the *New Republic* in 1927, "the first comers, if they can just get their fingers on a little property, are sure to grow rich with unearned increment."[10] Following the recession of 1921, Los Angeles became one of the first industrial centers in the United States to achieve full economic recovery. Industrial output climbed from $800 million in 1921 to $1.2 billion by 1923, and more than 2,400 new industries were established in Los Angeles in the years between 1920 and 1924.[11] For those seeking a new start during the lean months of 1921, James A. B. Scherer recommended Los Angeles, where "every newcomer who's willing to work gets his chance, and gets

wholesome sympathy and respect. Climate takes care of the rest."[12]

Promotional campaigns met with striking success as the population of Los Angeles grew from 319,000 to 1,238,000 in the period from 1920 to 1930.[13] The Mexican population in the city also grew in prodigious proportions after 1910. Between 1910 and 1920, the United States census reported that the Mexican population in the city increased from 5,611 to 31,172. By 1930, the Mexican population had more than tripled. Within the city limits of Los Angeles, the Mexican population numbered 97,116, while an additional 70,000 Mexicans resided in Los Angeles County.[14]

Since 1900, Mexicans had worked in agriculture, railroad construction, and mining in the border regions. After the outbreak of World War I, they began to move farther north, filling labor needs created by the war.[15] In 1929, Robert N. McLean, a religious leader in Los Angeles, acknowledged, "In Los Angeles and, indeed, in many communities, it is the Mexican[s] who do the common labor. In fact, we have imported them for that very purpose."[16] Several Los Angeles industrialists explained their preference for Mexican laborers over other workers. For example, A. C. Hardison argued, "There is a certain type of work that the Mexican will do and our experience is that Americans will not do. The American is physically unfitted for certain classes of menial labor that must be done if we are going to preserve our economic position in the world."[17]

Constantly under fire for employing Mexican workers over Anglo workers, industrialists took their case to the public. A. Bent, a Los Angeles contractor, asserted, "I am a construction man, and if we have got a job in the Imperial Valley, for instance, to construct water works in those hot regions, I am compelled to use Mexicans. We cannot get our own men to go there to perform that work."[18] Another Californian from the Imperial Valley representing agribusiness put the issue of using Mexican menial labor in this manner: "Mexicans are much preferred to whites. Once fixed, they are permanent and reliable. I do not think that they are good for other types of labor."[19]

Few studies of the period 1900–1930 have closely examined the participation of Mexican immigrants in the Los Angeles labor market. Early publications of Emory S. Bogardus, Jay S. Stowell, and Robert N. McLean briefly discussed urban employment patterns of Mexicans and described the general social and economic experiences of Mexicans in the United States.[20] G. Bromley Oxnam and Charles S. Johnson both utilized sample surveys to estimate the occupational structure of the Mexican community during the 1920s, but, like much other research of that era, Oxnam's and Johnson's studies provide limited data. Using information from jail record files, Oxnam estimated that 72 percent of the Mexicanos in Los Angeles were employed as laborers and another 14 percent held skilled positions.[21] Johnson, who conducted one of the best studies of Blacks in Los Angeles during the 1920s, sampled only a few industries in which Mexicans worked, primarily transportation, building trades, and automobile manufacturing.[22] Very few of those industries, Johnson reported, employed Mexicans, and he found no Mexicans working in the railroad industries. Actually, however, the railroad companies and agricultural groups were among the most active recruiters of Mexican workers, sending their labor agents to numerous border towns in search of laborers. Studies by the United States Department of Labor and data from the United States census indicate that some eleven thousand Mexicanos were employed by the railroad companies in California,[23] and a large percentage of those laborers worked in the numerous railroad yards and camps of Los Angeles.[24]

The major attractions for the Mexican immigrants who settled in the Los Angeles area were economic opportunities in transportation, manufacturing, and agriculture.[25] Most migrants, however, remained in Los Angeles only for a short time. Low wages, a high cost of living, discrimination, and excessive competition for jobs often made life difficult for Mexican laborers and accounted for their exceedingly high turnover.

Industrial establishments with a hundred or more workers on their payrolls employed the majority of Mexican laborers in nonagricultural work in California.[26] Paul Taylor and Emory Bogardus both reported increasing movement of Mexicanos into industrial centers during the 1920s,[27] as did J. B. Gwin, who wrote: "They [Mexicans] have moved into the cities to engage in all kinds of common labor. They replace other laborers, partly because they are working for less wages and partly because they have shown more endurance and strength. They are also more dependable."[28] Governor Clement C. Young's Fact-Finding Committee estimated that the stone, clay, and cement industries employed 40 percent of all the Mexican workers in California during the 1920s.[29] Mexicans were regarded as being among the best tile workers and cement finishers in southern California. The rise in popularity of "Spanish" homes in California during the 1920s created a demand for workers familiar with the construction of tile roofs and floors like those common in Mexico. Metal, wood, food, and clothing industries and public utilities followed the stone and cement industries as the largest employers of Mexicanos in the state between the years 1917 and 1930.[30] New textile factories opened in Los Angeles during the 1920s and employed hundreds of Mexican women and a fair number of Mexican men. The Los Angeles gas company alone employed more than 1,200 Mexican laborers by the mid-1920s.[31] "Los Angeles," wrote Elizabeth Fuller in 1920, "so far has considered the Mexican immigrant chiefly as an industrial asset."[32]

Table 1 indicates that male Mexican workers in Los Angeles in 1917–1918 were much more concentrated in a limited number of industries (most were in blue-collar unskilled positions) than male workers in Boston or native White male workers in Los Angeles. Several thousand Mexican workers in Los Angeles were employed in bakeries, slaughter and packing houses, textile factories, paper and printing establishments, and laundries. Industries employing the majority of Mexican women in Los Angeles were the textile industry, laundries, hotels, wholesale and retail trade establishments, and bakeries.[33] "The secondary recruiters of Mexican labor," wrote Robert McLean, "are the factories and foundries, and construction projects in the great cities.... A Mexican, for example, drifts to Los Angeles when the labor demand is at its lowest ebb. He finds employment on a construction gang, and hesitates to leave when the crop which recruited him originally is again calling."[34]

OPPORTUNITIES

Most social scientists agree that one's social position is closely correlated to one's occupation. Peter M. Blau and Otis D. Duncan discussed this relationship in their study, *The American Occupational Structure*. "The occupational structure in modern industrial society," they stated, "not only constitutes an important foundation for the main dimensions of social stratification but also serves as the connecting link between different institutions and spheres of social life, and therein lies its greatest significance."[35] In Los Angeles, the occupational structure during the 1920s was closely related to race and ethnic background. Native Whites had positions in the occupational structure substantially higher than even second- and third-generation Mexicanos. As the last column in Table 1 indicates, less than 1 percent of the Mexican men (first-, second-, and third-generations combined) belonged to the professional class. Only 6.7 percent of them held white-collar occupations, as contrasted to 47.0 percent of the native White men. Sixty-eight

percent of the male Mexican workers in Los Angeles labored in the unskilled ranks, compared to only 10 percent of the male workers in Boston and 6 percent of the native White male workers in Los Angeles.

As can be seen in Table 3, occupational opportunities for Mexicanos in high blue-collar and all white-collar positions did indeed prove elusive not only for recent immigrants, but for second-and third-generation Mexicanos as well. Among first-generation Mexican men, for instance, nearly 92 percent were employed in blue-collar occupations (unskilled, semiskilled, and skilled workers). Compared to the immigrants, the sons of American-born Mexicanos fared much better in securing semiskilled, skilled, and low white-collar jobs, such as clerical work. Still, few second- and third-generation Mexicanos entered the professional and proprietor classes. As Table 3 indicates, only 6.6 percent of the first generation and 4.5 percent of the second-generation Mexican men held white-collar jobs, although 32 percent of the Boston men (Table 1) held similar positions.

In a survey conducted in 1920 by the Interchurch World Movement in Los Angeles, investigators found that 72 percent of the Mexicans in the city were employed as common laborers, a figure which was amazingly close to the figure of 71.6 percent computed in this study for first-generation unskilled workers (Table 3).[36] Whereas the Interchurch study reported that 7 percent of the Mexicanos were employed in the professions, my findings (see Table 3) indicate that among first-, second-, and third-generation Mexican men, some 6.7 percent worked in white-collar professions, a figure again remarkably close to the earlier estimate. The Interchurch study, unfortunately, did not give a breakdown of the occupational structure of the Mexicanos, nor did it separate American-born Mexicans from recent immigrants. In my study, evidence showed, most of the white-collar workers were employed in clerical positions and few held jobs in the proprietary, semiprofessional, or professional ranks (Table 3).

The data computed here indicate that second-generation Mexicanos fared only slightly better in employment opportunities than the first generation. Ninety-five percent of the second-generation Mexican men held blue-collar jobs, but a smaller percentage, as compared to those in the first generation, were in unskilled work. In 1929, in the only previous study of second-generation Mexicans in Los Angeles, Emory Bogardus may have shed some light on the reasons for the limited occupational opportunities of Mexicans during the 1920s: "In the occupational field, the second generation Mexicans are beginning to aspire to higher levels. They are seeking entrance into the skilled trades and the professions, but are meeting with rebuffs. Often classed with mulattos, they have few opportunities and soon grow discouraged and bolshevistic. Their color is one of the main handicaps."[37]

Only a small percentage of the first-, second-, and third-generation Mexicanos found opportunities in the skilled trades and professions. Most surprising of the results of the study was the high participation of third-generation Mexicanos in blue-collar jobs in 1917 and 1918; nearly 90 percent of third-generation Mexicanos were employed as blue-collar workers in Los Angeles during this period (Table 3). Marked differences existed, however, in the numbers of Mexicanos involved in skilled occupations among the first- and third-generation groups. Of the third-generation group, over 29 percent worked in skilled occupations, while no more than 13 percent of the first-generation group held similar positions. Only 47.7 percent of third-generation laborers were unskilled laborers, as compared to 71 percent of the first generation. In comparison, 69.0 percent of non-Mexican men who married Mexican women during the same two-year period worked in blue-collar occupations, a situation similar to the percentage of blue-collar positions held by Boston workers in 1920 (see Tables 4 and 1). These non-Mexican men held significantly more high blue- and white-collar positions than Mexican men. Among these non-Mexicans, mostly Anglo-Americans, 28.9 percent held white-collar positions, generally low-paying clerical and sales jobs. Most of the non-Mexicans were skilled and semiskilled workers, with only 20.6 percent earning their living as unskilled laborers. Only 3.1 percent of this group could be classified in the professional ranks.

A CLOSED SOCIETY?

In their study *Social Mobility in Industrial Society*, Seymour Martin Lipset and Reinhard Bendix theorized that mobility, "as measured by movement across the manual–non-manual dividing line, has been considerable in many countries of Western Europe as well as in the United States." They concluded that "no known complex society may be correctly described as 'closed or static.'"[38] In agreement with this definition of an "open" society are both Stephan Thernstrom and Michael Hanson, who found that in the period 1910–1920 White workers moved freely from low blue-collar and high blue-collar to white-collar positions.[39] Mexicans in Los Angeles during the 1920s, however, encountered a far more "closed" society; their movements from manual to nonmanual employment categories were almost nonexistent. (See Table 5.)

Among first-, second-, and third-generation semiskilled and unskilled male Mexican laborers in Los Angeles, not a single individual moved upward to a white-collar position during the ten years between 1918 and 1928 (See Table 5).[40] Michael Hanson, in a study of all male Los Angeles workers, noted that during the decade 1910–1920, 20 percent of the unskilled workers moved up to white-collar positions. In a similar study of Boston, Stephen Thernstrom found that 18 percent of the city's unskilled (male) workers moved up to white-collar ranks in the decade 1910–1920. At this time, no occupational-spatial mobility studies are available for the 1920s, and Mexican occupational mobility during the ten-year period 1918–1928 must be compared with studies of other groups reflecting the earlier period, 1910–1920. Although comparisons must be made between different decades, it is doubtful that Mexicans would have had a higher rate of mobility ten years earlier.

The number of white-collar workers among Mexican men in Los Angeles was extremely small, and therefore no generalizations can be made from statistics about this handful of individuals. Only eight Mexicans out of a total of ninety-two, or 8.5 percent, held white-collar positions in 1917–1918.

Mexican skilled workers suffered an unusual downward mobility compared to White workers in both Boston and Los Angeles. Only 2 percent of the skilled workers in Hanson's Los Angeles survey slipped into unskilled positions between 1910 and 1920, whereas among Mexican workers, 32 percent of the 1917–1918 skilled workers held unskilled jobs in 1928. In Boston, Thernstrom found that only 1 percent of the skilled workers in 1910 moved downward to unskilled jobs by 1920. Among semiskilled workers in Boston, 20 percent moved up into low white-collar positions, while 3 percent moved into high white-collar occupations. Similarly, Hanson reported that in Los Angeles 21 percent of the semiskilled workers gained lower white-collar positions, but none reached high white-collar status. In contrast, Mexicans in semiskilled occupations in Los Angeles registered no movement at all into either low white-collar or high white-collar positions between 1917–1918 and 1928; in fact, 37.5 percent moved downward.

MOBILITY

The working-class populations of Boston and Los Angeles between 1910 and 1930 were re-

markably mobile geographically. In a comparison of six different cities (Boston; Los Angeles; Omaha; Norristown, Pennsylvania; Waltham, Massachusetts; and San Francisco) between the years 1880 and 1968, Thernstrom found a striking consistency in persistence rates of workers (50–60 percent) in all the cities.[41] Unfortunately, since none of the data pertained to persistence rates of ethnic groups at the lower income level, one can only compare the spatial mobility of Mexicanos to that of the overall population in Thernstrom's study. In Los Angeles, as Table 6 demonstrates, first-, second-, and third-generation Mexicanos had comparatively high degrees of spatial mobility, especially among unskilled and semiskilled workers. In Boston, for example, 35 percent of the low blue-collar workers in 1910 could still be found in the city a decade later (Table 6), whereas in Los Angeles, only 15.2 percent of the low blue-collar Mexican workers in 1917–1918 were still in the city a decade later. Hanson found that 58 percent of the low white-collar (clerical and petty proprietor class) workers in 1910 were still in Los Angeles ten years later. Among Mexican low white-collar workers in 1917–1918, only 38.8 percent could still be traced a decade later. Among high white-collar workers (semiprofessional and professional classes) in 1910, Hanson discovered that 72 percent could still be located in Los Angeles a decade later, but among Mexican high white-collar workers in 1917–1918, only 42.6 percent remained in the city for a period of ten years.

Mexicanos seem to have been more spatially mobile than native and foreign Whites for several reasons. No doubt the proximity of Los Angeles to the Mexican border was one of the most important factors. The border was close enough that Mexicanos employed in California could maintain a home in Mexico by working part-time in the United States. Many preferred to live in Mexico and crossed the border to work only out of economic necessity. Improvements in railroad and highway connections between Los Angeles and Mexico after 1900 added another incentive for Mexicanos to travel back and forth across the border on a regular basis.[42] With little expense and trouble, they traveled to Los Angeles for a season of work and then returned to their homeland. In many instances, barrio residents relocated to other communities within the expansive eastside sector. The eastside neighborhoods appeared to be in a constant state of flux, although, as demographic data indicate, these small sections of the barrio all registered significant growth.[43]

In addition, the nature and location of Los Angeles in relation to the rest of California contributed to high rates of spatial mobility for Mexican workers there during the 1920s. Throughout the period 1910–1930, Los Angeles served as one of the three great clearing centers for Mexican workers. Los Angeles, like San Antonio and El Paso, functioned as a depot or "stepping stone" for Mexican immigrants recruited to work in the Midwest and other areas of the Southwest. Agriculture and railroad industries came to Los Angeles in search of workers for the San Joaquín and Imperial valleys. Helen Walker, a Los Angeles social worker, wrote of the movement of Mexican laborers to other parts of the state: "At certain times in the year when the ranchers of Southern California must have many laborers for a short season to harvest their crops, the employment bureaus are anxious to send out great crews of men to do this work." Mexican labor in southern California, she noted, "migrates up and down the length of the state year around, following the grapes in Fresno; the Valencia oranges, nuts, beets, beans, in Orange County; the naval oranges in Riverside County; the cotton, lettuce, melons, grapefruit in the Imperial Valley; ...and so on and on."[44]

The unusually high proportion of Mexican laborers who moved in and out of Los Angeles may also be attributed to the fact that high wages were paid in agriculture and railroad construction. These jobs, however, were fre-

quently found outside the city. Jay Stowell reported that some Mexican industrial laborers in Los Angeles actually earned as little as $1.25 per day for a ten- to twelve-hour day.[45] John McDowell of the Home Mission Council in southern California stated that transportation, street paving, and cement companies paid workers "two or three dollars per day."[46] Those industries required day laborers who frequently worked less than six months of the year. Oxnam calculated that in 1920 Mexican workers in Los Angeles earned $2.00 to $3.00 a day and averaged $18.00 per week.[47] For thousands of Mexican workers, the disadvantages of industrial work were the higher costs of housing and food in the city and the ever pressing problem of finding work for younger members of the family.

In agriculture, Mexican workers commonly gained the advantage of combining the earnings of other family members for a more adequate family income. Ethel M. Morrison estimated that during the months of April, July, and October, California agriculture paid an average of $22.50 per week without board, and in other months, a few dollars less per month.[48] Nevertheless, few persons other than agricultural employers have ever suggested that working and living conditions in rural areas were better than those found in the cities, and the latter most frequently were extremely harsh. Reviewing the plight of Mexican workers in the cities during the 1920s, Carleton Beals remarked, "The Mexican workers in our country are more ruthlessly exploited than are other foreigners. They are not absorbed rapidly into autonomous unions in industrial centers and so cannot escape the pitiless exploitation that the 'greener' [immigrant] almost invariably suffers."[49]

Similarly, the presence of negative stereotypes and prejudice stifled the Mexicano's opportunity for upward mobility. During the 1920s, employers stereotyped Mexicanos as menial workers incapable of doing work that required skill or intelligence. Summarizing findings of a 1914 survey, the sociologist William W. McEuen explained the social problems of the Mexican by characterizing him as "a spend-thrift and a born gambler, a happy-go-lucky, careless merry person who seems to have no higher ambition than to live as easily as possible."[50] Los Angeles employers expressed the opinion that "in lines of employment calling for individual judgment and initiative, the Mexican is much inferior to the white."[51] Ernesto Galarza, an economist who only a few years earlier had worked among Mexican laborers in agricultural fields, wrote about the exploitation of Mexicanos in the United States. The Mexican, Galarza stated in 1929, "still feels the burden of old prejudices. Only when there are threats to limit immigration from Mexico is it that a few in America sing the praises of the peon....At other times the sentiments which seem deeply rooted in the American mind are that he is unclean, improvident, indolent, and innately dull."[52]

Finally, in most efforts to improve their socioeconomic status, Mexicanos found that the barriers of overt bigotry were prodigious and steadfast. William McEuen observed racial prejudices in discussions with members of the Los Angeles community. "All other races," he noted, "meet the Mexican[s] with an attitude of contempt and scorn," and generally regard them "as the most degraded race in the city." In the opinion of Emory Bogardus, "color" barred second-generation Mexicanos from the better jobs. In sum, as Ernesto Galarza stressed, in the 1920s the racial prejudice of California employers was to blame for the plight of Mexican families in the United States.[53]

CONCLUSIONS

The findings of this study lend little credence to the myth that California was a land of golden opportunity for all. Judging from the low occupational status and limited upward mobility of Mexican workers in Los Angeles, Mexicanos would have been surprised to learn that the 1920s in California was often called the era of the "second gold rush." Data also suggest that the upward mobility of Mexicans in Los Angeles, when compared to that of workers in Los Angeles and Boston, measured unusually low. This low rate of upward mobility among Mexicans may partially explain their high spatial mobility. Mexican laborers who found it difficult to advance in employment status had excellent incentive to leave the area to seek better opportunities. The spatial mobility of low blue-collar Mexican workers was 20 percent higher than that of eastern United States workers during a similar period. The greater geographic mobility of Mexicans in Los Angeles further suggests that they did not remain "trapped" in barrios or slums like the Italians in the East as portrayed by some historians.[54] The barrios of Los Angeles attracted new Mexican immigrants daily, most of whom were common laborers, and the Mexican colonies served as a base for many Mexicans who worked in areas outside of Los Angeles or frequently crossed back into Mexico. Throughout the period 1900–1930, Los Angeles served as a regional distribution center for Mexican workers. Although many of these workers came to Los Angeles on their way to other jobs or as casual laborers, enough of them eventually established their roots in East Los Angeles to make it the "Mexican Capital" of the United States.

TABLE 1   OCCUPATIONAL DISTRIBUTION OF MALE LABOR FORCE IN BOSTON AND LOS ANGELES

Occupation	Boston: Overall population, 1920 (%)	Los Angeles: Native Whites, 1920 (%)	Los Angeles: Mexicanos, 1917–1918 (%)
White-collar	32	47.0	6.7
Professional	5	3.9	0.6
Other white-collar	27	43.1	6.1
Blue-collar	68	53.0	91.5
Skilled	27	28.3	15.4
Semiskilled	31	18.7	8.1
Unskilled	10	6.0	68.0

Sources: Thernstrom, *The Other Bostonians: Poverty and Progress in the American Metropolis, 1880–1970* (Cambridge, Mass., 1973), p. 50; U.S. Bureau of the Census, *Fourteenth Census of the United States Taken in the Year 1920*, vol. 4, *Population; Occupations* (Washington, D.C., 1923), pp. 168–172; Data Obtained from 1917 and 1918 Los Angeles marriage records.

TABLE 2   OCCUPATIONAL STRUCTURE OF MEXICAN MEN IN CALIFORNIA, 1930

Occupation	Number employed	Percentage employed	Percentage of total Mexican workers
Agriculture	41,455	100.0	37.0
Laborers	40,052	96.6	
Mining	1,660	100.0	1.5
Operatives	1,628	98.1	
Manufacturing	34,858	100.0	31.1
Apprentices	520	1.5	
Carpenters	924	2.7	
Machinists	515	1.5	
Mechanics	861	2.5	
Molders	411	1.2	
Painters	948	2.7	
Plaster-cement	493	1.4	
Tailors	366	1.0	
Clay-glass	431	1.2	
Operatives			
Food	721	2.1	
Iron-steel	858	2.5	
Lumber	357	1.0	
Laborers			
Building	11,698	33.5	
Chemical	1,275	3.7	
Clay-glass	3,192	9.2	
Food	1,520	4.4	
Iron-steel	2,530	7.3	
Lumber	990	2.8	
Transportation	18,878	100.0	16.8
Drivers	1,662	8.8	
Road-street labor	3,362	17.8	
Railroad laborers	11,677	61.9	
Clerks-stores	360	1.9	

TABLE 2 *(Continued)*

Occupation	Number employed	Percentage employed	Percentage of total Mexican workers
Laborers-porters	1,052	17.3	
Helpers			
Retail	1,391	22.9	
Sales	1,267	20.8	
Public service	856	100.0	0.8
Laborers	641	74.9	
Professional service	1,748	100.0	1.6
Musicians	335	19.2	
Attendants-helpers	451	25.8	
Domestic personnel	5,194	100.0	4.6
Service			
Barbers	504	9.7	
Janitors	534	10.3	
Labor	314	6.0	
Laundry	512	9.9	
Servants	2,080	40.0	
Clerical	980	100.0	0.9
Clerks	627	64.0	
Total males over ten years old: 143,925			
Total number employed: 112,119			
Percentage employed: 77.9			

Source: Computed from the U.S. Bureau of the Census, *Fifteenth Census of the United States: 1930,* vol. 4, *Population: Occupation* (Washington, D.C., 1932), pp. 86–90. The census lists more than 100 different occupations in which Mexicanos were employed. This table records only the job classifications where 300 or more Mexican workers were employed.

TABLE 3 OCCUPATIONAL STRUCTURE OF FIRST-, SECOND-, AND THIRD-GENERATION MEXICANO MEN IN LOS ANGELES, 1917–1918

Occupation	First-generation (%)	Second-generation (%)	Third-generation (%)	Number	Percentage of total
White-collar	6.6	4.5	9.1	24	6.7
Blue-collar	91.8	95.5	89.0	326	91.6
Student	0.3	0	0	1	0.3
Unknown	1.4	0	2.3	5	1.4
Total				356	100.0
White-collar					
Clerical	3.8	0	9.1	15	4.2
Proprietor	1.4	0	0	4	1.1
Semiprofessional	1.1	0	0	3	0.8
Professional	0.3	4.5	0	2	0.6
Blue-collar					
Unskilled	71.6	59.1	47.7	242	68.0
Semiskilled	7.2	13.7	11.7	29	8.1
Skilled	13.0	22.7	29.6	55	15.4

Source: Data computed from 1917 and 1918 marriage records.

TABLE 4 OCCUPATIONAL STRUCTURE OF NON-MEXICAN MEN WITH MEXICAN WIVES, 1917–1918

Occupation	Non-Mexican men (%)	(N)
Blue-collar		
Unskilled	20.6	20
Semiskilled	24.7	24
Skilled	23.7	23
Total	69.1	67
White-collar		
Clerical	18.6	18
Proprietor	6.2	6
Semiprofessional	1.0	1
Professional	3.1	3
Total	28.9	28
Student	1.0	1
Unknown	1.0	1
Total		97

Source: Data computed from 1917 and 1918 marriage records. Significantly, the marriage files indicate that for these two years, at least, the number of Mexican women marrying non-Mexicans was greater than the number of Mexican men marrying outside of their own group.

TABLE 5 COMPARISON OF MALE OCCUPATIONAL MOBILITY IN LOS ANGELES AND BOSTON

	Los Angeles (overall population)					
	Occupation in 1920					
Occupation in 1910	HWC (%)	LWC (%)	S (%)	SS (%)	US (%)	Number
High white-collar (HWC)	88	8	4	0	0	25
Low white-collar (LWC)	7	78	11	3	1	129
Skilled (S)	0	13	79	7	2	61
Semiskilled (SS)	0	21	12	67	0	24
Unskilled (US)	0	20	10	30	40	10

	Boston (overall population)					
	Occupation in 1920					
Occupation in 1910	HWC (%)	LWC (%)	S (%)	SS (%)	US (%)	Number
High white-collar	90	7	0	3	0	31
Low white-collar	10	79	2	7	3	134
Skilled	2	21	66	10	1	103
Semiskilled	3	20	5	65	8	106
Unskilled	0	18	8	36	39	39

TABLE 5   *(Continued)*

Occupation in 1917–1918	Los Angeles (first-, second-, third-generation Mexicanos)						
			Occupation in 1928				
	HWC (%)	LWC (%)	S (%)	SS (%)	US (%)	Unknown (%)	Number
High white-collar	50.0	0	0	0	0	50.0	2
Low white-collar	0	66.6	0	16.6	16.6	0	6
Skilled	4.0	4.0	48.0	12.0	32.0	0	25
Semiskilled	0	0	0	50.0	37.5	12.5	8
Unskilled	0	0	17.6	15.7	64.7	0	51

Sources: Michael Hanson, "Occupational Mobility and Persistence in Los Angeles, 1910–1930" (unpublished paper, University of California, Los Angeles, June 1, 1970); Thernstrom, *The Other Bostonians,* p. 238; data computed from 1917 and 1918 Los Angeles marriage record files and the 1928 city directory.

TABLE 6   PERSISTENCE RATES FOR BOSTON AND LOS ANGELES

Occupation in 1910	Boston, 1910–1920	Still in city in 1920 (%)
High white-collar		58.0
Low white-collar		50.0
High blue-collar		36.0
Low blue-collar		35.0
Total		41.0

Occupation in 1910	Los Angeles, 1910–1920	Still in city In 1920 (%)
	Number	
High white-collar	36	72.0
Low white-collar	229	58.0
High blue-collar	137	45.0
Low blue-collar	118	29.0
All white-collar	265	60.0
All blue-collar	255	38.0
Total	520	49.0

Occupation in 1917–1918	First-, second-, and third-generation Mexicanos in Los Angeles, 1917–1918 to 1928	Still in city in 1928 (%)
	Number	
High white-collar	7	42.6
Low white-collar	18	38.8
High blue-collar	71	35.2
Low blue-collar	322	15.2
All white-collar	25	40.0
All blue-collar	393	18.8
Total	418	29.4

Sources: Data compiled by tracing the names in the 1928 city directory of all the Mexican men who applied for marriage licenses in 1917 and 1918; Thernstrom, *The Other Bostonians,* p. 230; Hanson, "Occupational Mobility and Persistence in Los Angeles."

Notes

1 Recently, historians have applied quantitative techniques to the study of the urban working class, but for the most part, these studies—which make use of city directories, birth, marriage, and death records, and census data—have been limited to eastern and midwestern cities and have provided little information about non-European immigrants. This chapter attempts to do for Mexican immigrants in Los Angeles what earlier studies have done for European immigrants in the East and Midwest.

2 Women were not included because so few worked outside the home that the sample was too small to generalize from. It is also extremely difficult to trace women workers over time when using directories because of name changes and because many of them were never listed, while their husbands usually were. Marriage records obviously exclude men who never married, but as Peter M. Blau and Otis D. Duncan have shown in *The American Occupational Structure* (New York: Wiley, 1967), pp. 337–340, the occupational attainment of married men ranks only slightly higher than that of nonmarried men.

3 A bias often associated with marriage records is that they tend to reflect a rather young population. Sixty-three percent of the Mexicanos sampled for this study were in their thirties. Yet, as T. Wilson Longmore and Homer L. Hitt demonstrate in "A Demographic Analysis of First and Second Generation Mexican Population of the United States: 1930," *Southwestern Social Science Quarterly* 24 (September 1943): 145, the median age of the Mexican population of the United States in 1930 was twenty years, in contrast to twenty-six years for the total U.S. population. Furthermore, the authors found that "the Mexican population contained relatively fewer persons above thirty-four years of age" than the U.S. population as a whole.

4 For Boston, see Howard P. Chudacoff, *Mobile Americans: Residential and Social Mobility in Omaha, 1880–1920* (New York: Oxford Univ. Press, 1972), pp. 216–231. For Atlanta, see Richard J. Hopkins, "Status, Mobility, and the Dimensions of change in a Southern City," in Kenneth T. Jackson and Stanley K. Schultz,

eds., *Cities in American History* (New York: Knopf, 1972). For San Antonio, see Alwyn Barr, "Occupational and Geographic Mobility in San Antonio, 1870–1900," *Social Science Quarterly* 51, no. 2 (September 1970): 398–403.

5 Carey McWilliams, in "Getting Rid of the Mexican," *American Mercury,* 28 (March 1933): 323, estimated that the city repatriated thirty-five thousand Mexicans from Los Angeles in 1932 alone.

6 For a literary study of this phenomenon in an earlier period, see Kevin Starr, *Americans and the California Dream, 1850–1915* (New York: Oxford Univ. Press, 1973).

7 George G. West, "California the Prodigious," *Nation* 125 (October 4, 1922): 325.

8 Bruce Bliven, "Los Angeles: The City That Is Bacchanalian—in a Nice Way," *New Republic* 51 (July 13, 1927): 198.

9 The best treatment of this era is Glenn S. Dumke's *The Boom of the Eighties in Southern California,* 4th ed. (San Marino, Calif.: Huntington Library, 1955). See also W. W. Robinson, *Los Angeles: From the Days of the Pueblo* (San Francisco: California Historical Society, 1959), pp. 80–81.

10 Bliven, "Los Angeles," p. 197.

11 Guy E. Marion, "Statistical Facts about Los Angeles," in *Los Angeles City Directory, 1925,* pp. 7–9.

12 James A. B. Scherer, "What Kind of Pittsburgh Is Los Angeles?" *World Week,* 41 (February 1921): 382.

13 U.S. Bureau of the Census, *Thirteenth Census of the United States Taken in the Year 1910, Abstract of the Census,* p. 602; *Fifteenth Census of the United States: 1930, Population,* vol 1, pp. 18, 19, 131, vol. 2, pp. 266–267.

14 U. S. Bureau of the Census, *Thirteenth Census, 1910,* vol. 1, *Population,* pp. 854–855; *Fourteenth Census of the United States Taken in the Year 1920,* vol. 4, *Population,* pp. 729–731; *Fifteenth Census, 1930, Population,* vol. 1, pp. 248–250.

15 Robert Stout, "A Fence for the Rio Grande," *Independent* 120 (June 2, 1928): 519.

16 Robert N. McLean, "Mexican Workers in the United States," in *National Conference of Social Work, Proceedings* (Chicago, 1929), p. 537.

17 U.S. Congress, Senate Committee on Immigration, *Hearings on Restriction of Western Hemisphere Immigration,* 70th Cong., 1st sess. (1928), p. 47.

18 U.S. Congress, House Committee on Immigration and Naturalization, *Hearings on Western Hemisphere Immigration,* 71st Cong., 2d sess. (1930), p. 81.

19 U.S. Department of Labor, Bureau of Labor Statistics, "Mexican Labor in the Imperial Valley, California," *Monthly Labor Review* 28 (March 1929): 62.

20 Emory S. Bogardus, *The Mexican in the United States* (Los Angeles: Univ. of Southern California Press, 1934); Jay S. Stowell, *The Near Side of the Mexican Question* (New York: Home Missions Council, 1921); and Robert N. McLean, *The Northern Mexican* (New York: Home Missions Council, 1930).

21 G. Bromley Oxnam, *The Mexican in Los Angeles: Los Angeles City Survey* (Los Angeles: Interchurch World Movement of North America, 1920), p. 14.

22 Charles S. Johnson, "Industrial Survey of the Negro Population of Los Angeles, California" (unpublished survey, National Urban League, 1926). Details of this survey were made available to me by the National Urban League office in New York City through Professor Emory Tolbert.

23 Paul S. Taylor, *Mexican Labor in the United States: Chicago and the Calumet Region,* University of California Publications in Economics 7, no. 2 (Berkeley, 1932). See also tables provided in Taylor's "Some Aspects of Mexican Immigration," *Journal of Political Economy* 38 (October 1930): 609–615.

24 As Table 2 demonstrates, some 11,677 Mexicanos in the state were employed in railroad industries in California. Ramón García, a fifty-year resident of Los Angeles and an employee of the Southern Pacific Railroad Company from 1922 to 1965, informed me that all of the laborers in the Southern Pacific yard during the 1920s were of Mexican descent. (Interview with Ramón García, October 15, 1973, Los Angeles).

25 Carl L. May, "Our Anti-Social Mexican Population," *Los Angeles County Employee* 2, (1929): 12.

26 *Mexicans in California: Report of Governor C. C. Young's Fact-Finding Committee* (San Francisco: California Department of Industrial Relations, Agriculture, and Social Welfare, October 1930), p. 82.

27 Paul S. Taylor, "Note on Stream of Mexican Migration," *American Journal of Sociology* 36 (September 1930): 287–288; Emory S. Bogardus, "The Mexican Immigrant and Segregation," *American Journal of Sociology* 36, (July 1930): 74–80.

28 J. B. Gwin, "Social Problems of Our Mexican Population," *National Conference of Social Work, Proceedings* (Chicago, 1926), p. 330.

29 *Mexicans in California,* p. 82.

30 Ibid., pp. 80–81.

31 John McDowell, *A Study of Social and Economic Factors Relating to Spanish-Speaking People in the United States* (Philadelphia: Home Missions Council, 1927), p. 16.

32 Elizabeth Fuller, *The Mexican Housing Problem in Los Angeles,* Studies in Sociology, Sociological Monograph, no. 17, vol. 5 (November 1920), p. 6.

33 *Mexicans in California,* p. 105.

34 McLean, "Mexican Workers in the United States," p. 534.

35 Blau and Duncan, *The American Occupational Structure,* pp. 6–7.

36 Oxnam, *The Mexican in Los Angeles,* p. 14. For occupational rankings, I used a model formulated by Stephan Thernstrom, *The Other Bostonians: Poverty and Progress in the American Metropolis, 1880–1970* (Cambridge, Mass.: Harvard Univ. Press, 1973), pp. 290–292. Examples of the occupations found in each of the categories are (1) High White Collar: architects, lawyers, major proprietors, managers, and officials; (2) Low White Collar: clerks, salespeople, and semiprofessionals such as librarians and photographers; (3) High Blue Collar: carpenters, jewelers, mechanics, factory operatives, and tailors; (4) Low Blue Collar: laborers, porters, gardeners, and lumber workers.

37 Emory Bogardus, "Second Generation Mexicans," *Sociology and Social Research* 13 (January–February 1929): 277–278.

38 Seymour Martin Lipset and Reinhard Bendix, *Social Mobility in Industrial Society* (Berkeley: Univ. of California Press, 1959), pp. 11–12.

39 Thernstrom, *The Other Bostonians,* p. 238; Michael Hanson, "Occupational Mobility and

Persistence in Los Angeles, 1910–1930'' (unpublished paper, Univ. of California, Los Angeles, June 1, 1970).

40 For a more complete analysis of the economic ranking of occupations used here, see Thernstrom, *The Other Bostonians,* pp. 290–292. Thernstrom's Appendix B lists more than 140 different occupations in the categories used in Table 6 of this article (High and Low White Collar and Blue Collar).

41 Thernstrom, *The Other Bostonians,* pp. 222, 226.

42 For a fuller discussion of the immigrants' journey, see Ricardo Romo, "Responses to Mexican Immigration, 1910–1930," *Aztlán: International Journal of Chicano Studies Research* 6 (1975): 173–194; and Leo Grebler, Joan W. Moore, and Ralph C. Guzman, *The Mexican-American People: The Nation's Second Largest Minority* (New York: Fee Press, 1970), p. 62.

43 Computed from U.S. Bureau of the Census, *Fourteenth Census, 1920,* vol. 1, *Population,* p. 125; *Fifteenth Census, 1930, Population,* vol. 2, p. 287.

44 Helen Walker, "Mexican Immigrants as Laborers," *Sociology and Social Research* 13 (September 1923): 58–59.

45 Stowell, *The Near Side,* p. 49.

46 McDowell, *A Study of Social and Economic Factors,* p. 16.

47 G. Bromley Oxnam, "The Mexican in Los Angeles from the Standpoint of the Religious Forces of the City," *Annals of the American Academy of Political and Social Science* 93 (January 1921): 131.

48 Ethel M. Morrison, "A History of Recent Legislative Proposals Concerning Mexican Immigrants" (M.A. thesis, Univ. of Southern California, 1929), pp. 27–28.

49 Carleton Beals, "Mexican Intelligence," *Southwest Review* 11 (October 1925): 24.

50 William W. McEuen, "A Survey of the Mexican in Los Angeles (1910–1914)" (Master's thesis, Univ. of Southern California, 1914), p. 9.

51 Ibid., p. 31. See also Mark S. Reisler, "Always the Laborer, Never the Citizen: Anglo Perceptions of the Mexican Immigrant during the 1920s," *Pacific Historical Review* 45 (1976): 231–254.

52 Ernesto Galarza, "Life in the United States for Mexican People: Out of the Experiences of a Mexican," in *National Conference of Social Work, Proceedings* (Chicago, 1929), p. 402.

53 McEuen, "A Survey of the Mexican in Los Angeles," p. 36; Bogardus, "Second Generation Mexicans," pp. 277–278; Galarza, "Life in the United States," p. 402.

54 See, for example, Alexander DeConde, *Half Bitter, Half Sweet: An Excursion into Italian-American History* (New York: Charles Scribner's Sons, 1971), pp. 14–15. The Italian immigrants, DeConde wrote, "poor and friendless, clung together in slums of eastern cities, fearing to settle in the hostile countryside of rural America."

COUNTRY MUSIC AND THE OKIE SUBCULTURE

The history of California during the Great Depression is marked by several dramatic episodes. None has been of more enduring interest than the coming of hundreds of thousands of migrants from the drought-stricken states of Oklahoma, Texas, Arkansas, and Missouri. The so-called Dust Bowl refugees were seen at the time as emblems of the nation's larger economic collapse. Their experiences in California also challenged popular notions about the Golden State, the land of abundance and opportunity. Just as the Mexican immigrants of East Los Angeles were outsiders to the California Dream during the 1920s, as Ricardo Romo concluded in the previous selection, so too were the interstate migrants who roamed the great Central Valley in the 1930s.

Our knowledge of the Dust Bowl migration comes from many sources. The classic account, of course, is John Steinbeck's *The Grapes of Wrath* (1939). The migrants' vision of the good life in California is powerfully evoked by Steinbeck's novel, and so too are the harsh realities of discrimination and poverty which the Okies encountered. Scholarly study of the migration began during the depression and has continued ever since. One of the best accounts is Walter J. Stein's *California and the Dust Bowl Migration* (1973), which describes the migration and the negative reaction it provoked. Scarcely noticed at first, the migrants eventually were viewed with alarm and near hysteria in some parts of the state.

The account which is definitive in many respects is James N. Gregory's *American Exodus: The Dust Bowl Migration and the Making of California's Okie Subculture* (1988). Gregory divides his book into three parts: a study of the process of migration and resettlement, an exploration of California's troublesome reaction to the migrants, and an analysis of what Gregory calls the "Okie subculture." It is this last part of the book that is most valuable. Here Gregory probes the inner dynamics and institutions of the Okie community in California from the 1930s to the present.

The following selection is a revised version of a paper Gregory delivered at the 1985 meeting of the California American Studies Association at San Jose State University. In it he summarizes his analysis of the role of country music in the Okie subculture. He is primarily concerned with the migrants who congregated in the Central Valley, rather than with those who attempted to assimilate in the major metropolitan areas. His analysis suggests several intriguing comparisons with Douglas Henry Daniels' portrayal, in a previous selection, of the early black migrants in San Francisco. Gregory demonstrates that the Okies were encouraged by their music to retain the folkways of their southwestern roots, rather than to make an accommodation to California society. The Okies' rural values and habits, including their distinctive southwestern accents, were celebrated and reinforced in the subculture. Thus, they retained their separate identities and passed them on to succeeding generations. Daniels, by contrast, suggests that the pioneer urbanites in San Francisco retained little of their old southern folkways. They consciously adopted the habits and accents of their California hosts, looking toward assimilation and acceptance.

Daniels argues that the black pioneers in the Bay Area were able to avoid rigid segregation because they migrated as individuals and over a long period of time. The Okies in the 1930s came in great numbers and in a relatively few years. This suggests, of course, that the more apt comparison for the depression-era Okie migration is the "great migration" of blacks during World War II. The scale of these two migrations and the negative reactions they provoked are strikingly similar.

Both Daniels and Gregory stress the importance of music and entertainment in the lives of their respective groups of Californians. The dance halls and honky-tonks of the Okies fostered positive social interaction and reinforced group identity. The black-owned saloons and nightclubs of San Francisco served a similar purpose for the pioneer blacks. Country music stars, such as Gene Autry and Bob Wills, became important success symbols and sources of group pride for the Okies. Blacks in the Bay Area had similar cultural heroes—musicians Jimmy Launceford, Chick Webb, Count Basie, and a host of others.

James N. Gregory received his Ph.D. from the University of California, Berkeley, in 1983. He is currently an Assistant Professor of History at Berkeley, where he teaches classes in American and California history.

READING 22

Country Music and the Okie Subculture

James N. Gregory

The year was 1935; the place, Republic studios in Hollywood, California. Studio president Herbert Yates had just seen his gamble pay off. Months before he had offered a film contract to a smooth-faced young cowboy singer who had made a name for himself on the National Barn Dance, a radio program syndicated weekly by Chicago's station WLS. Yates knew little about hillbilly music, but he realized that the Hollywood westerns needed something new, and in that age of song and dance perhaps some music would do. So Gene Autry got his chance. And with the release of his first feature film, *Tumbling Tumbleweeds,* Republic studios found its future. For Hollywood, the age of the singing-cowboy had begun. Man, horse, hat, six-gun, and guitar would remain one of filmland's most bankable formulas until the advent of television.[1]

The year 1935 also witnessed another beginning. California discovered its "Okie problem" that year, discovered that it was playing host to a vast new influx of impoverished families from the Western South. The press called them Dust Bowl refugees but few were from the areas actually devastated by dust. They came instead from a broad four state area that had been hit hard by drought and depression. Oklahomans, Texans, Arkansans, and Missourians, many of them farm folk but others from the region's cities, represented a new type of immigrant for California. For one thing, most were poor and desperate for work, and that made the

Depression-battered state uneasy. For another, California was not accustomed to newcomers of southern background, at least not in such numbers. Some 375,000 came during the 1930s and still more during the following decade. By 1950 a million and a quarter Oklahomans, Arkansans, Texans, and Missourians (Southwesterners we will call them) had settled in California, accounting for an eighth of the state's population.[2]

These episodes, seemingly discrete, find their nexus in the early history of what is now called country music. Gene Autry and the Okie migrants together built California's country music industry. More important, the music and early stars like Autry figured in the process of cultural negotiation that has shaped the rather unique role of Southwesterners in California since the 1930s. Southwesterners, or at least some of them, have maintained a more definite sense of regional culture than is customary for white interstate migrants who settle in the Golden State. Fifty years after the celebrated Dust Bowl migration, if one looks in the right places the legacy of that experience is still very much apparent.

Bakersfield, Kern County, the southern San Joaquin Valley are the places to look first. There amidst the cotton and oil fields the Okie migration made its largest impact. Apart from the majestic Sierra in the background, a visitor from western Oklahoma or northern Texas feels right at home. Listen to the voices. Nowadays a little touch of the Southwest can be heard in the speech of almost all San Joaquin Valley whites, and if you visit a blue-collar neighborhood or one of the valley's dusty agricultural towns the accent once described as "not quite the twang of the Midwest nor the drawl of the deep South but a composite of both" is unmistakable.[3]

Examine the menu at a typical coffee shop. Chicken-fried steak, chili, biscuits and gravy, cornbread, okra, barbecue—the Southwestern favorites are all there, including Dr. Pepper which seems to outsell Coke and Pepsi. Count the churches. Bakersfield and surrounding Kern County claim more than 430 of them, most of them Protestant, and mostly representing conservative evangelical denominations. This is Southern Baptist, Assemblies of God, Nazarene, Church of Christ, and Full Gospel territory. It is California's Bible Belt and it carries on religious traditions brought from the Western South.[4]

The Dust Bowl migration legacy is apparent also in the Valley's politics and social values. It comes out in occasional flurries of overt racism and the more constant social and political barriers confronting the area's small black and large Hispanic minorities. And it shows itself as well in the Valley's conservative voting patterns. For decades the area has registered Democrat and voted Republican.[5]

Taken together these data suggest a curious pattern of cultural persistence, or more precisely, subcultural development. The San Joaquin Valley is host to an Okie subculture which in lesser density can also be found in other parts of the state. This is not a customary occurrence for California. Americans from other states generally do not reproduce their regional cultures in such fullness. But Southwesterners have not encountered California on the same terms as most white interstate migrants. Partly because of the special features of their regional heritage and partly because of the confrontation that attended their Depression-era resettlement, some Southwesterners developed the kind of social and cultural coherence that invites the term ethnicity.

The Depression set the terms for much of what followed. It was not a good time to be moving to California. Although opportunities surpassed those available in their home states, most of the job prospects were limited to agri-culture. That is why so many of the 1930s migrants ended up in the San Joaquin and other valleys, and a big reason why their social adjustment was so difficult. Agricultural labor was an economic and social trap. The traditional niche of nonwhites, it offered mostly poverty and disesteem. The majority of Southwestern newcomers did not become entrapped—most in fact settled in Los Angeles or one of the other metropolitan areas. But a very substantial minority, including most who looked for work in the valleys, had little choice. Until the 1940s in some cases, the 1950s or 1960s in others, these Southwesterners would make their living in California's fields.

Economic difficulties begat social ones. Stigmatized in any event through their association with farm labor, Southwesterners toward the end of the 1930s became the targets of one of California's periodic bursts of xenophobia. As the number of newcomers outstripped job opportunities and threatened to swamp state and local relief programs, residents began to demand protection from the "horde of empty bellies from the Southwest who come in answer to the tribal call 'there's food in California.' "[6] Especially in the San Joaquin Valley, where the influx was greatest, worry turned to fear and fear yielded contempt. Derided as "Okies" and "Arkies," the newcomers experienced in some cases the sort of undermining comments and unspoken prejudices normally reserved for foreigners or nonwhites. "Ignorant filthy people," a Valley businessman said of them.[7] "Shiftless trash who live like hogs, no matter how much is done for them," echoed a Madera County doctor who helped lead the unsuccessful campaign to close the state's borders.[8]

Not the sentiments of everyone, these evaluations were nevertheless symptomatic of a wider problem of image and stereotype that would haunt Southwesterners for years to come, and not just those living in the Valley. The label "Okie" marked their special burden. A pejorative concept carrying many of the connotations of "poor white trash," it fell almost as readily on migrants from other states as Oklahomans, especially those identified by accent or poverty.

For the migrants, the attitudes of Californians came as a cruel shock. Accustomed to thinking of themselves as upstanding Americans, most were not prepared for the hostile reception. Responses varied. Some returned home, electing to face whatever financial obstacles had sent them west rather than endure the indignities of California. Others escaped the Okie stigma by fitting in, sometimes shedding accents, cultural traditions, even denying their background in order to feel more at ease among the Californians.

Many chose an opposite course. Rejected by California, they pulled together defensively. That response quickened the development of their separate subculture. Cultural differences which in another context might have carried less weight became significant in this one. Alienated and insecure, some of the newcomers found purpose and pride in the shared reproduction of values, outlooks, and institutions they had known back home.

THE ROLE OF COUNTRY MUSIC

Country music was part of both the heritage and the process, a crucial part. The focus of a great deal of pride and something of an Okie enterprise, the medium has for two generations helped give the group its particular values and outlooks. Anthropologist Sherry Ortner talks of "key symbols" that succinctly convey some of a culture's central values or tensions. Country music has done that for Okies.[9] It "was part of our way of thinking," recalls Ernest Martin, whose parents brought him to California from Oklahoma as a child in the 1930s. Country music, he continues, "was a common type of language that everyone understood."[10] From Gene Autry to Merle Haggard, it has been to them what rock'n'roll was to a generation of

young people in the 1950s and 1960s: the symbol, the medium, the "language" that communicated the essence of their subculture.

Known initially as "hillbilly" or "old-time" music, country music emerged as a commercial medium with the spread of radio in the 1920s. Its precise origins and relation to folk styles are much debated and need not concern us. What can be said is that the genre found an audience of a particular sociological complexion: mostly rural, native-born, and white. The primary market was the South (including the Southwest) with a strong secondary interest among rural Midwesterners. Californians, largely urban and still more urbane, showed but slight initial interest. A few hillbilly and cowboy singers could be heard on the radio, but most Californians regarded the music as rustic and unsophisticated and left it to a marginal audience of senior citizens and newcomers from regions where it was more popular.[11]

That began to change after 1935 when singing-cowboy westerns introduced many Californians (and Americans elsewhere) to the cowboy portion of the hillbilly repertoire and when the Dust Bowl migration brought California a vigorous new audience. The Southwest by the 1930s had become the most fertile section of country music's so-called "fertile crescent." Knowing both cotton and cattle and blending the separate folk-music traditions that went with them, the region was home to the cowboy soloist and western swing styles that were just then achieving national popularity. One of the only growth industries the Southwest could claim during that difficult decade, country music stood out in the affections of a large portion of the region's residents and soon-to-be-former residents.[12]

In California observers quickly noted the music's prominent place in the social activities of the migrants. In the farm labor camps that became the initial stopping place for many, guitars, fiddles, harmonicas, and banjos often appeared, said one investigator, as if "by magic."[13] Shirley Cox remembers the way music brought people together in the labor camps where her family stayed. As a young girl she took special pride in the fact that her mother was often asked to sing the old folk songs to the entire group.[14] In another setting, Woody Guthrie watched as the singing of two young girls transformed a huge squatter encampment inhabited by perhaps two thousand people. "People walked from all over the camp and gathered...as still as daylight while the girls sang:"

> Takes a worried man to sing a worried song
> Takes a worried man to sing a worried song
> Takes a worried man to sing a worried song
> I'm worried nowwww
> But I won't be worried long.

The music was like a tonic, the inimitable Guthrie observed. "It cleared your head up, that's what it done, caused you to fall back and let your draggy bones rest and your muscles go limber like a cat's."[15]

In time, commercial interests began to respond to the migrant's musical tastes. Taverns interested in attracting a Southwestern clientele signalled as much with a western name like the Pioneer Club or the Silver Slipper and with a juke box filled with hillbilly hits.

With Hollywood stirring up still more interest, radio stations began to respond as well. The smaller ones, hungry for listeners, proved most responsive, but by the end of the 1930s many stations offered at least one cowboy music program. From then on country music's popularity continued to grow. Enjoyed by increasing numbers of natives as well as Southwesterners, played on radio stations all over California, country music came into its own in the 1940s, by some estimates matching big-band music in popularity.[16]

OPPORTUNITIES

The music's growing appeal meant opportunities of several kinds for Southwesterners, most

directly for musicians. By the late 1930s the silver screen had attracted a distinguished list of country music stars to California, most of them from Oklahoma and Texas. Texas-born and Oklahoma-raised Gene Autry headed a list of Southwestern filmland cowboys (and occasionally cowgirls) that included Tex Ritter, Stuart Hamblen, Bob Wills, Jimmy Wakely, Bill Boyd, Patsy Montana, Tim Spencer, Spade Cooley, Eddy Dean, and Elton Britt. Roy Rogers, an Ohioan, was a notable exception among film stars.[17]

Many of these performers had made names for themselves before moving West, but the cowboy craze also provided opportunities for some migrants who had initially come to California with different purposes in mind. Arriving in Los Angeles in 1937, Woody Guthrie found his relatives busy planning and practicing, hoping to capitalize on the Gene Autry phenomenon. Cousin Jack Guthrie had outfitted himself in cowboy gear and was trying to talk his way into auditions with local radio stations, while several other cousins, an aunt, and an uncle had formed a hillbilly band and were talking about getting into the movies.[18]

The same sort of aspirations captivated the musically inclined in the San Joaquin Valley. When folklorists Charles Todd and Robert Sonkin visited the Farm Security Administration camps in the summers of 1940 and 1941, they intended to record old ballads traditional to the Southwest. They found some of what they were looking for, but reported that the migrants were often more interested in singing current hillbilly hits. Several were anxious to showcase their talents because they were "goin on the air soon." A few affected stage names. "I'm Homer Pierce, the singin' cowboy from way down in Missouri, and I'd like to do a couple of my tunes for you," one young man introduced himself. Another had acquired all the poses and styles appropriate to a cowboy singer but had not yet learned to play the guitar. He was working on that he assured Todd, confident that a bright musical future lay ahead.[19]

For some migrants music did provide a bright future. Jack Guthrie got his radio show, invited cousin Woody to be his singing partner, and both went on to distinguished careers, one legendary. Oklahoma-born Spade Cooley played with several hillbilly groups on the honky tonk circuit in California and Oregon before settling down with his own band in Los Angeles in the early Forties. By the end of World War II he had appeared in several movies, enjoyed a list of hit records, owned a country music club, and styled himself the "King of Western Swing." Rose Maddox was eleven years old in 1937 when she and her four brothers sang their first audition for a Modesto radio station. The family had come to California four years before, mostly riding boxcars. Although from Alabama, they became Okies in California, absorbed along with many other poor whites into that flexible subculture. Within a few years the Maddox Brothers and Rose would have a recording contract and a nationwide following.[20]

If the growing popularity of country music made it the pathway to fame for a handful of migrants and a career option for others, it meant something as well to the thousands of Okies whose relationship to music was that of listener rather than performer. The music's success gave its migrant audience the chance to bask in the reflected glory of musicians from their home states. What Frank Sinatra was for Italians, and Paul Robeson was for blacks, nationally recognized country music stars like Gene Autry became for Okies.

Bob Wills was the real favorite. Perhaps because he seemed to remain closer to his roots and audience than some of the other Hollywood figures, the Texas-born band leader earned the unparalled affection of transplanted Southwesterners. Future country star Merle Haggard was too young to attend the dances, but when Wills came to Bakersfield in the late 1940s, Haggard

and his friends would stand outside the hall absorbing the excitement. These periodic appearances were events of communal significance for the area's Southwesterners, particularly for the younger generation. "We needed a hero," Haggard recalls, "and Bob was certainly that and more...it was like he brought some of home with him."[21] Oklahoma-born Ken Griffis speaks in similar terms of Wills' effect on Southwesterners living in Los Angeles. Wills, he insists, "was very important to people like myself....He was one of us Okies and Arkies. People would say 'That's old Bob, that's our boy'....We were on that stage with Bob Wills."[22]

This was audience involvement of a special kind. By no means the only fans of country music, many Okies nevertheless took almost proprietorial interest in the medium and its performers. The attention was often reciprocated. Some musicians catered closely to Southwestern audiences, responding either for practical reasons or because of the common background. Wills did so by peppering his performances with references to "all of us Okies" and by playing tunes with lyrics about Oklahoma and Texas. Spade Cooley came up with an even better device for insuring the loyalty of the mobs of defense workers who jammed Venice pier each weekend to hear his band. He nicknamed his three vocalists "Okie," "Arkie," and "Tex," claiming that each hailed from the appropriate Southwestern state. It was not quite true. Tex Williams, later a popular band leader in his own right, was actually a native of Illinois. But contrived or not, the names demonstrate the audience power of Southwesterners and the symbolic rewards it sometimes earned.[23]

THE LANGUAGE OF COUNTRY MUSIC

That much is fairly straightforward. There is, however, another more complex aspect to the migrants' relation to country music, involving meanings conveyed in the songs and performance rituals. This is perhaps what Ernest Martin had in mind when he called it a special "language."

Country music is by nature richly expressive and probably the most overtly didactic of all the major forms of popular music. Country songs, it is often said, tell a story. Where other styles usually emphasize mood or musical features, the country song stresses lyrics, sometimes developing a partial narrative, in other cases sketching a scene instead of a plot, in either event accumulating a wealth of expressive detail. Described in one report as "three minute soap operas," songs usually explore issues of deep personal importance (love, death, loyalty, integrity, honor) in ways that serve as object lessons. The message, in other words, is central. Song lyrics are meant to be heard and pondered.[24]

Moreover, as Patricia Averill and other scholars have shown, the values expressed are, or at least were, relatively consistent. We can argue about the relationship today, but in its early decades country music reflected the general worldview of its strongest audience: rural whites, especially Southerners. The Okie migrants thus found in the songs they listened to a template for many of the values and beliefs they carried to California. White people's music, plain people's music, its outlook, like theirs, turned on a neo-populist view of society and economy and an individualistic, Protestant view of life. The medium would help them sustain those views across the years in California.[25]

The "country" perspective—vaguely anti-urban, decidedly white, and rooted in the everyday concerns of common working people—was at least as clear in the 1930s and 1940s as it is today. In that era of green mountain homes and purple plains, songs mostly focused on simple people who often worried about the loss of simple ways. Cowboys rode the range, singing of sweethearts, open skies, courage, and

death. Hoboes and railroadmen rode the trains, regretting lives gone bad and remembering sweet moments of youth and love. Paeans to the joys of rural life abounded, companions to the tragic tales of broken homes, dying parents, and abandoned lovers. God too was often near, ready to receive the faithful, watching over the "circles" of life and family, keeping them, as the hymn promised, "unbroken."[26]

Bucolic and nostalgic, the songs of the period contain few positive references to the sort of world that California had come to represent. Cities were sinful, alienating places—prisons in the metaphor of a popular Carter Family song. Wealth, ambition, flashy styles and fast living held no favor in country songs, a few of which were overtly critical of the rich and powerful. More commonly lyrics simply upheld the basic values of plain living. "I'm back in the saddle again," Gene Autry sang to open his weekly radio show, "Out where a friend is a friend."[27] Here was the critique in its usual form. Choosing the cleansing open spaces, the dignity of "real" work, the genuineness of friendship and family, and the democracy of rural life, the country song said no to many of the postures and preoccupations of modern, urban existence, hence implicitly to many of the ways of California.[28]

It was a critique that many Okies liked to hear. Contending with stereotypes that labeled them ignorant and backward, they took sustenance from lyrics that lauded their plain, unpretentious way of life and that linked it to the nation's deepest political and moral traditions.

The subculture still today finds meaning in that perspective. It shows up to some extent in matters of lifestyle. The group is now spread across too many generations, localities, and social strata to talk meaningfully about an Okie lifestyle. But it does seem that Southwesterners are rather more prone than other Californians to maintain "down home" styles of self presentation. This is most obvious at working-class levels but even those who have made fortunes for themselves in farming, business, politics, or law sometimes also manifest what might be called a "good old boy" manner, which may include items of dress (string tie, cowboy boots or hat), a style of speech (the Okie accent and country aphorisms), and abundant references to humble origins and the importance of good old-fashioned values.

It shows up more broadly in discussions of what it means to be an Okie. Ask a former migrant or a second generation Okie what it means to them personally and he or she may reply with stories that emphasize courage, determination, toughness, and self-reliance. Okies are survivors and fighters who know how to work and how to "stay alive," says Lester Hair who was born in Arizona as his parents made their way from Texas to California in 1924. It is a common claim—a group myth if you will—and it derives in part from genuine experience. But it is significant that these characterological traits are also central themes of country music, and were particularly important during the medium's cowboy phase.[29]

Like the western film, cowboy songs of the 1930s and 1940s can be read as celebrations and sometimes deep explorations of individualism. As usually rendered in popular media, the cowboy was the embodiment of independence and rugged strength. Courage and determination were his religion, honor and freedom his reward. It was not, however, an uncomplicated portrait. No culture as committed as this one was to matters of family and place could give an unqualified endorsement to such a solitary figure. The song cowboy thus wrestled with contradiction, in one song at peace with his role, in another tormented by guilt or loneliness. Many a bittersweet ballad ("Dying Cowboy," "Cowboy's Lament") found the hero facing a lonely death, while others ("Oh, Bury Me Not on the Lone Prairie," even "Home on the Range") played provocatively with the same themes.[30]

For Okies in California facing their own questions of place and dignity, the mythic im-

ages resonated strongly. The cowboy modeled many of the personal traits they believed essential to good character. Like many other Americans of the period, but perhaps with special enthusiasm born of their close relationship to the country music medium, many Southwesterners took the cowboy figure to heart, displaying their allegiance in styles of dress, posture, and speech.

BACK HOME

Another set of themes may have had a still more noticeable impact on the outlooks of the migrant group. One of the striking differences between Southwesterners and other interstate migrants is the extent to which the former maintained strong feelings of loyalty to old home states and home towns across the years and even across generations. Fifty years after coming to California, quite a few former migrants still talk about Oklahoma, Arkansas, Texas, or Missouri as "home." Many have returned upon retirement, others have sent children to school back there, and large numbers still maintain regular visiting habits. These attachments are first and foremost a feature of strong family ties, but seem also to reflect the commitment to home and tradition expressed so strongly in country music.[31]

Nostalgia remains one of the most powerful themes of country music. In one way or another a very large percentage of country songs manage to celebrate the good old days and good old ways. In the 1930s, this motif was refracted through a vast collection of songs that examined the issue of home and being away from home. Song after song centered on ramblers, hoboes, lonesome cowboys, runaway lovers, outlaws on the lam, and other figures cut off from their roots. Scholars have offered varying interpretations of this preoccupation, most seeing it as a metaphor for uncertainty about general forces of modernization and social change.[32]

That may have been the right level of meaning for other listeners, but to Okies in California, a thousand miles from their homes, no metaphor was needed. A song like Jimmie Rodgers' "Daddy and Home" spoke pure homesickness:[33]

Daddy, dear old daddy,
I'm coming back to you.
You made my boyhood happy,
But still I long to roam;
I've had my way, but now I'll say,
I long for you and for home.

The effect was compounded in the many cowboy ballads that featured references to Southwestern locales. Texas was by far the most common song setting of the period. Compositions like "Deep in the Heart of Texas," "By the Silv'ry Rio Grande," and "Red River Valley" appeared in great profusion. Songs about the other states were fewer but the Oklahomans in particular could take pride in some very popular tunes, including Bob Wills' "Take Me Back to Tulsa" and Woody and Jack Guthrie's "Oklahoma Hills." These songs kept the home fires burning bright. Stuart Hamblen stoked the flames each day when he began his Los Angeles radio show with the song "Texas Plains."[34]

Each night in my dreams, somehow it seems,
That I'm back where I belong;
Just a country hick way back in the sticks,
Back where I was born.
City lights, and city ways,
Are driving me insane;
I want to be alone; I want to be back home,
Back to my Texas Plains.

They might as well have been made to order (and some certainly were) so well did these songs match the moods of the migrants. What they actually did was sharpen feelings and give them social validity. Country music expressed the nostalgia that many Southwesterners were feeling and made it into a recognized group mind set. Homesickness, or at least a kind of unresolved attitude towards life in California, became emblematic of Okies.

Nostalgia, plain living, cowboy courage—these standard country music themes of the 1930s and 1940s reached Okies with special intensity. And as they did, the messages helped Southwesterners, or at least many of them, achieve a particular kind of relationship with California society. Psychologically rooted in their home states, insecure in their new one, the songs encouraged them to maintain the outlooks, standards, and associations that became the basis of their subculture.

OKIE PRIDE

Much has changed for California's Southwestern population in the years since then. The problems of social dissonance disappeared long ago as the migrants and their children advanced economically and gained the acceptance they were at first denied. Culturally, their relationship with California society has also been significantly readjusted. There have been modifications on both sides. All along, it should be remembered, some Southwesterners had chosen to exchange their regional markings for California ones, and as the years passed that choice became more and more automatic, especially for the younger generation. On the other hand, California has picked up some Southwestern traits. Today in the San Joaquin Valley, accent, lifestyle, even religious preference are no longer always accurate clues to regional background.

The renegotiation has also altered the way Southwesterners think about themselves and their position in California. For all the symbolic support they received from musicians and songs in the early decades, few initially felt comfortable with the label Okie or with the cultural separation that the label implies. Nowadays it is different. Forthright expressions of Okie pride are heard regularly from former migrants and the children and grandchildren of former migrants. Country music deserves an important share of the credit for this development, and one country music artist in particular, Merle Haggard changed the syntax of the musical language that has always meant so much to California's Southwestern population, and through that helped change the way they think about and describe themselves.

Born near Bakersfield in 1937, not long after his parents had made the journey from Oklahoma, Merle Haggard grew up in the heart of California's Okie country and in the center of the state's second-generation country music scene. By the time he turned professional in the early 1960s, Bakersfield had already launched the careers of Buck Owens, Glen Campbell, Ferlin Husky, and several other important musicians and was on its way towards claiming its currently much coveted title, "Nashville West."[35]

Haggard's career took off quickly, partly on the strength of songs inspired by his "rough and rowdy" youth and the two years it had earned him in San Quentin prison. By 1968 he was a major star and primed for still bigger conquests. They came with a new set of compositions focused on the social and political complaints of white working-class America. With songs like "I Take a Lot of Pride in What I Am," "Workin' Man's Blues," "Okie From Muskogee," and "The Fightin' Side of Me," he found the patriotic-populist voice that made him, in the words of one reporter, "the poet laureate of the hard hats."[36]

He also began to write songs based loosely on his family background, songs that reach deep into the corners of the Okie experience. Beginning with the 1969 recording of "Hungry Eyes" and continuing with "Cotton Fields," "Tulare Dust," "They're Tearing the Labor Camps Down," and "The Roots of My Raisin' ," he resurrected stories of hardship, prejudice, and poverty that had received little attention in almost a generation. Each of these songs is about struggle and dignity and about

the meaning of the Okies' special heritage. He says this best with the line, "The roots of my raising run deep" from the title song of his 1975 album. The song is about family and tradition, from which he gets "the strength that I need." Okies are not mentioned in that tune, but the point is clear enough to those who share his background. It says we share an inheritance of determination and courage, an inheritance of quiet accomplishment and pride.[37]

That is also the lesson of Haggard's most famous composition, "Okie from Muskogee." Released in 1969, the song is not about California Okies. The setting is Muskogee, Oklahoma, the subject patriotism. Attacking pot-smoking hippies and draft-dodging college students, it quickly became a favorite of President Nixon's "Silent Majority." But it had special meanings for its California namesakes. The song's resounding refrain, "I'm proud to be an Okie from Muskogee," gave them a slogan of powerful, indeed consciousness changing, proportions.[38]

Haggard's songs laid the foundation for the Okie pride movement that has become evident since the 1970s. The movement has several faces. Other musicians have written and recorded similar autobiographical material, Buck Owens, Tommy Collins, and Larry Hosgood the most notable. A literary circle led by writers Gerald Haslam and James Houston, has begun to publish the poetry and fiction of a dozen or so second-generation Okie authors. Newspapers have caught the spirit and commissioned dozens of articles. Colleges, libraries, and city administrations in the San Joaquin Valley have sponsored programs to celebrate or study the Okie experience and one or two public schools have even experimented with Okie Studies programs. All this attends a more far reaching change at a personal level. For the first time it has become acceptable, almost fashionable, to be an Okie, and even people who have spent the better part of their lives hiding from that label now increasingly embrace it.[39]

Haggard, it must be understood, was the catalyst, not really the cause. The source of this transformation rests ultimately in recent changes in the way Americans think about ethnicity and cultural differentiation. Okie pride is closely tied to the new ethnic consciousness that has swept the country in the wake of the Civil Rights and Black Power movements. Haggard's songs reflect the search for roots which blossomed in many corners of America during the 1960s and 1970s.[40]

But the point to be made here is that once again it was country music which served as the central communications medium for Okies in California. All along that industry has played a critical role in their experience. One of the Southwest's most visible contributions to California, country music has also mediated the social life and identity of that region's expatriates. Speaking to them and also speaking for them, the songs and singers of country music have helped at various stages and in profound ways to define the special sort of accommodation that Southwesterners have achieved with California over the last half century.

Notes

1 Douglas B. Green, "The Singing Cowboy: An American Dream," *Journal of Country Music* 7(May 1978), 10–20; Gene Autry with Mickey Herskowitz, *Back in the Saddle Again* (New York, 1978).

2 Recent studies of the Dust Bowl migration include: James N. Gregory, *American Exodus: The Dust Bowl Migration and the Making of California's Okie Subculture* (forthcoming, 1988); Walter J. Stein, *California and the Dust Bowl Migration* (Westport, 1973); and Sheila Goldring Manes, "Depression Pioneers: The Conclusion of an American Odyssey. Oklahoma to California 1930–1950" (Ph.D. dissertation, UCLA, 1982).

3 Katherine Archibald, *Wartime Shipyard: A Study in Social Disunity* (Berkeley, 1947), 44. On the preservation of Southwestern accents in the Valley see Bruce Ray Berryhill, "The Relationship Between Regional and Social Dialects and Lin-

guistic Adaptation" (M.A. thesis, California State University, Fresno, 1976). Several journalists have described persisting cultural patterns: Gerald Haslam, "The Okies: Forty Years Later," *The Nation* 220 (March 15, 1975), 299–302; David Lyon, "Campfires Dotted the Still Nights," *Bakersfield Californian,* May 27, 1979; Michael Fessier Jr., "Grapes of Wrath, 1977," *New West* 2 (July 18, 1977), 24–31; Irwin Speizer, "Dust Bowl's Living Legacy, "*Fresno Bee,* July 6, 1986.

4 Pacific Bell Bakersfield Telephone Directory yellow pages (July 1984), 171–176; Bernard Quinn, et al., *Churches and Church Membership in the United States 1980* (Atlanta, 1982), 45–46.

5 Michael Barone, Grant Ujifusa, and Douglas Matthews, *The Almanac of American Politics 1978* (New York, 1977), 77–83.

6 California Citizens Association, "Statement to Assembly Unemployment Relief Committee" (Bakersfield, Feb. 14, 1939), 5, quoted in Stein, *California and the Dust Bowl Migration,* 99.

7 Quoted in Lawrence Hewes, *Boxcar in the Sand* (New York, 1957), 116.

8 Dr. Lee Alexander Stone quoted in Ben Hibbs, "Footloose Army," *Country Gentleman* (February 1940) reprint in Migrant Labor Collection, Beale Public Library, Bakersfield. Similar prejudicial statements are recorded in Walter Goldschmidt, *As You Sow* (Montclair, N.J., 1947, reprinted in 1978), 61; Lillian Creisler, "'Little Oklahoma' or the Airport Community: A Study of the Social and Economic Adjustment of Self-settled Agricultural Drought and Depression Refugees" (M.A. thesis, University of California, Berkeley, 1940), 63–75, 90–94.

9 Sherry B. Ortner, "On Key Symbols," *American Anthropologist* 75(1973), 1338–1346. Manuel Pena, *The Texas-Mexican Conjunto: History of a Working-Class Music* (Austin, 1985), makes a similar case for that culture.

10 Interview by Judith Gannon, April 5, 1981, California Odyssey Project, California State College, Bakersfield, Library. This is an excellent collection of more than forty interviews with former migrants.

11 Richard A. Peterson and Russell Davis Jr., "The Fertile Crescent of Country Music," *Journal of Country Music* 6(Spring 1975), 19–27; Bill C.

Malone, *Country Music USA: A Fifty Year History* (Austin, 1968), 3–78. The pages of the *John Edwards Memorial Foundation Quarterly* (hereafter *JEMF Quarterly)* provide the best look at California's early country music scene.

12 In addition to those already listed, important sources on the Southwest's musical contribution include: Patricia Ann Averill, "Can the Circle Be Unbroken: A Study of the Modernization of Rural Born Southern Whites Since World War I Using Country Music" (Ph.D. dissertation, University of Pennsylvania, 1975), esp. 362–367; Stephen Ray Tucker, "The Western Image of Country Music" (M.A. thesis, Southern Methodist University, 1976); "Music from the Lone Star State," in Patrick Carr, ed., *Illustrated History of Country Music* (New York, 1980), 102–137.

13 Field Notes to the Charles Todd and Robert Sonkin Migrant Camp Recordings, Archive of Folk Culture, Library of Congress. See also Ray Zeman, "Squatter Army," *Los Angeles Times,* July 21, 1937; Robert S. Hardie and Norman I. Course, "A Brief Presentation of the Problem Presented by California's Migratory Agricultural Workers" (n.p.,n.d.), typescript in Farm Security Administration Collection, University of California, Berkeley, Bancroft Library, carton 7.

14 Interview by author, Bakersfield, September 18, 1979.

15 Woody Guthrie, *Bound For Glory* (New York, 1970), 252–253.

16 Gerald F. Vaughn, "Foreman Phillips: Western Swing's Kingmaker," *JEMF Quarterly,* 15(Spring, 1979), 27; Malone, *Country Music USA,* 196.

17 Background information on these and other country musicians can be found in the *JEMF Quarterly;* Malone, *Country Music U.S.A;* Green, "The Singing Cowboy;" Tucker, "The Western Image of Country Music," 60–68.

18 Joe Klein, *Woody Guthrie: A Life* (New York, 1980) 87–89, 92, 102.

19 Todd-Sonkin field notes and recordings. The two folklorists published some of their observations in "Ballads of the Okies," *New York Times Magazine,* November 17, 1940, 6–7. In addition to the eleven hours of songs and interviews they recorded, the Archive of Folk Culture also houses a smaller collection of camp recordings made by Margaret Valiant in 1938 and 1939.

20 Malone, *Country Music USA,* 210–221; Spade Cooley file in the John Edwards Memorial Foundation Collection, UCLA; Keith Olesen, liner notes, Maddox Brothers and Rose, 1946–1951, Volume 1 (Arhoolie Records 5016). For other career stories see interviews with Buck Owens and Bill Woods by Jana Jae Greif, November 6 and May 12, 1976, Oral History Collection, California State College Bakersfield Library. Also the following articles in *JEMF Quarterly:* Ken Griffis, "I Remember Johnny Bond," 14(August, 1978), 110; Gene Bear and Ken Griffis, "The Porky Freeman Story," 11(Spring, 1975), 33–34; Merle Travis, "Recollections of Merle Travis, 1944–1955," 15(Summer, 1979), 107–114.

21 Merle Haggard with Peggy Russell, *Sing Me Back Home: My Story* (New York, 1981), 108.

22 Interview by author, March 27 and April 1, 1985. On Wills' career see Charles R. Townsend, *San Antonio Rose: The Life and Music of Bob Wills* (Urbana, 1976).

23 Vaughn, "Foreman Phillips: Western Swing's Kingmaker," and Ken Giffis, "The Tex Williams Story," both in *JEMF Quarterly* 15(Spring 1979), 5–6, 28.

24 Paul Di Maggio, Richard A. Peterson and Jack Esco, Jr., "Country Music: Ballad of the Silent Majority," in R. Serge Denisoff and Richard A. Peterson, *The Sounds of Social Change* (Chicago, 1972), 41; Averill, "Can the Circle Be Unbroken," 30–34.

25 Averill's "Can the Circle Be Unbroken" is a remarkable resource for students of country music, containing an analysis of more than 2,000 songs recorded from 1928 to 1968. See also Archie Green, "Hillbilly Music: Source and Symbol," *Journal of American Folklore* 78 (July–Sept., 1965), 204–227; D. K. Wilgus, "Country-Western Music and the Urban Hillbilly," *Journal of American Folklore* 83(April–June, 1970), 157–179; Richard A. Peterson and Paul Di Maggio, "From Region to Class, the Changing Locus of Country Music: A Test of the Massification Hypothesis," *Social Forces* 53(March 1975), 497–506.

26 In addition to sources already cited see Alex S. Freedman, "The Sociology of Country Music," *Southern Humanities Review,* 3(Fall 1969), 358–362.

27 "Back in the Saddle," by Ray Whitley/Gene Autry. Copyright © 1939, renewed 1964 by Western Music Publishing Co., All Rights Reserved. Used by Permission.

28 Ivan M. Tribe, "The Hillbilly Versus the City: Urban Images in Country Music," *JEMF Quarterly* 10(1974), 41–51; Wilgus, "Country-Western Music and the Urban Hillbilly;" Anthony O. Edmonds, "Myths and Migrants: Images of Rural and Urban Life in Country Music," *Indiana Social Studies Quarterly,* 28(Winter 1975–76), 67–72.

29 Interview by author, Reedley, April 31, 1985. These character traits are claimed in many of the interviews conducted by the California Odyssey Project, California State Bakersfield. Also in Gerald Haslam's fictional autobiographical *Okies: Selected Stories* (Santa Barbara, 1975).

30 Thoughts on the cowboy and popular culture are found in John Tuska, *The Filming of the West* (Garden City, 1976). On the origins of cowboy music see Thomas F. Johnson "That Ain't Country: The Distinctiveness of Commercial Western Music," *JEMF Quarterly* 17(1981), 75–84; Tucker, "The Western Image of Country Music;" James White, *Get Along Little Dogies* (Urbana, 1975).

31 This is one of several traits that parallels the experience of Southern whites who settled in Chicago, Detroit, and other Northern cities during the middle decades of the twentieth century. The connection between the Okie and "Hillbilly" migrations is explored in Gregory, *American Exodus.*

32 Averill, "Can the Circle Be Unbroken," 303–304, 337–348; Edmonds, Myths and Migrants," 67–72.

33 Daddy and Home: by Jimmie Rogers and Elsie McWilliams. Copyright © 1929 by Peer International Corporation. Copyright renewed by Peer International Corporation. International copyright secured. ALL RIGHTS RESERVED. Used by Permission.

34 "Texas Plains." WORDS AND MUSIC BY STUART HAMBLEN. © Copyright 1933, 1942 by MUSIC CORPORATION OF AMERICA, INC. Copyright renewed. Rights administered by MCA MUSIC PUBLISHING, a division of MCA, Inc., New York, NY, 10019. USED BY PERMISSION. ALL RIGHTS RESERVED.

35 Glenn Hunter, "The Bakersfield Sound," *Westways* 71(July 1979), 28–32; Jana Jae Greif, "Nashville West: The Musical Heritage of Bakersfield," History 373 paper, Spring 1976, in California State Bakersfield Library. See also her interviews with Buck Owens and Bill Woods at the same location.

36 Quoted in Paul Hemphill's article, "Okie from Muskogee," in *The Good Old Boys* (New York, 1975), 140. Details of Haggard's life can be found in his autobiography, *Sing Me Back Home.*

37 "The Roots of my Raisin' " by Tommy Collins. Copyright © 1970, 1976 by Tree Publishing Co., Inc. All Rights Reserved. Used by Permission.

38 "Okie from Muskogee," by Merle Haggard/Roy Burris. Copyright © 1969 by Tree Publishing Co., Inc. All Rights Reserved. Used by Permission.

39 Samples of the literary production can be found in Gerald W. Haslam and James D. Houston, eds., *California Heartland: Writings from the Great Central Valley* (Santa Barbara, 1978); California Odyssey Project, *Guide to "Roots of My Raising"* (Bakersfield, 1982). On other developments see Lyon, "Campfires Dotted the Still Night;" Don Wegars, "The Okies Take a Place in American History," *San Francisco Chronicle,* October 16, 1978.

40 Stephen Steinberg critiques the new ethnicity in *The Ethnic Myth* (Boston, 1981), 3–74.

WARTIME EXILES AND ÉMIGRÉS

EDITOR'S INTRODUCTION

During World War II, the American west emerged from its traditional status as a colonial society to become a pace-setting region for the nation. The infusion of federal capital into wartime California and the west led to an enormous industrial expansion and a population boom. The war also increased the west's ethnic diversity and boosted its role as a center for scientific research. Before the war, many westerners were pessimistic about the prospects for their region; after the war, they looked to the future with hope and great expectation.

Such are the views of Gerald D. Nash, one of the premier interpreters of the twentieth-century west. Nash first expressed these views more than a decade ago in *The American West in the Twentieth Century* (1973). In this pioneering study Nash argued that the war accelerated changes that had been developing slowly for half a century. The war itself, he conceded, "occasioned few new changes."[1] In his most recent work, *The American West Transformed: The Impact of the Second World War* (1985), Nash's estimation of the importance of the war is far more sweeping: "No other single influence on the region—not the Mexican War, not the Civil War, not World War I, nor even the Great Depression—brought such great and cataclysmic changes to the West."

Nash demonstrates, for example, that the war had a major impact on the status of ethnic minorities in the west. He describes in considerable detail the blatant discrimination which confronted minorities during the war, but chooses to emphasize ways in which the war broke down racial barriers. Wartime confrontations between blacks and whites, Nash argues, were the foundation of the postwar civil rights movement. The wartime experiences of Mexican Americans likewise sped their social

[1]Gerald D. Nash, *The American West in the Twentieth Century* (Englewood Cliffs, N.J., 1973), 195.

and cultural integration into American society. Even the wartime relocation of the Japanese Americans had an "unexpectedly positive impact": It accelerated their movement into the American mainstream.

Given the broad compass of Nash's work, not all of his findings are equally applicable to California. Few Californians, for instance, saw themselves as a colonial society before the war. Indeed, in the nineteenth and early twentieth centuries San Franciscans commonly viewed their city as something of an imperial center in relation to the hinterland of the intermontane west.[2] There can be no doubt, however, that Nash is correct in identifying World War II as a critical watershed in California history.

One of Nash's most valuable contributions is his discussion of the cultural impact of the war. He tells the familiar story of Hollywood's wartime role in producing propaganda films, but he quickly moves on to an analysis of the 10,000 political and religious refugees who came to southern California before and during the war. As Nash points out in the following selection, the émigrés included such luminaries as novelist Thomas Mann, playwright Bertolt Brecht, and composer Arnold Schoenberg. Nash ranks their coming as perhaps the most significant cultural migration ever to occur in the history of the west.

James N. Gregory, in the previous selection, described the contribution of the Okie migration of the 1930s to the creation of a California subculture; here Gerald D. Nash balances the record by looking at the contribution of the wartime European émigrés to the "high culture" of California. As these two selections make plain, the wellsprings of California's cultural history are exceedingly diverse.

Gerald D. Nash, editor of *The Historian,* is Presidential Professor of History at the University of New Mexico.

[2]See Judd L. Kahn, *Imperial San Francisco: Politics and Planning in an American City, 1897–1906* (Lincoln, Neb., 1979)

READING 23

Wartime Exiles and Émigrés

Gerald D. Nash

World War II had a profound influence on Hollywood, transforming it from a somewhat isolated and insulated producer of bland entertainment into the free world's movie capital, charged with a major role in the Allied war effort. That transformation was already becoming apparent early in the war when a contemporary observer in Hollywood noted that "Hitler...drove hundreds of Continental players, directors, writers, and artisans into exile. Hollywood was their palm fringed Siberia. Gradually the expatriates were absorbed, and inevitably, their topics of conversation, their convictions. Thus, the film colony's splendid isolation was, in a sense, Trojan-horsed."[1] The lessening of provincialism in Hollywood was symptomatic of much of the West during wartime. However, the influence of European refugees who hastened this transformation was not restricted to the motion picture industry but had a similar effect on most other spheres of western culture.

Indeed, the increasing importance of Hollywood as an emerging cultural center in the West was one important reason why an increasing flow of European exiles from Hitler's tyranny terminated their trek in that city. And their coming constituted perhaps the most significant cultural migration to the West since the region was first settled. Within a decade after their arrival, they left a profound imprint on cultural life in the West and endowed it with a breadth and sophistication that it had previously lacked. Between their arrival in the 1930s and 1969 the refugees garnered twenty-four Nobel Prizes for the United States! As the cultural historian

Peter Gay has noted, in seeking to place this exodus in historical perspective:

> The exile holds an honored place in the history of Western civilization. Dante and Grotius, Bayle and Rousseau, Heine and Marx did their greatest work in enforced residence on alien soil, looking back with loathing and longing to the country, their own, that had rejected them. The Greek scholars from Byzantium who flooded the Italian city-states early in the fifteenth century and the Huguenot bourgeois who streamed out of France across Western Europe late in the seventeenth century brought with them energy, learning, and scarce, welcome skills; New England was founded by refugees who transformed a savage wilderness into blooming civilization. But these migrations, impressive as they are, cannot compare with the exodus set in motion early in 1933, when the Nazis seized control of Germany; the exiles Hitler made were the greatest collection of transplanted intellect, talent, and scholarship the world has ever seen.[2]

In diverse fields, ranging from literature to art and architecture, from music to psychiatry, to the varied phases of the motion picture industry, to natural science and social science and the humanities, the European émigrés made substantial contributions in the Western communities where they settled. Their story deserves to be told.

Although the majority of the approximately 80,000 refugees who fled from Hitler's Europe to the United States between 1933 and 1941 settled east of the Mississippi River, a contingent of 10,000 to 15,000 traveled westward, establishing an important center in southern California. That region's urban aspect and its pleasant Mediterranean climate were one source of attraction for intellectuals drawn from the capitals of Europe. But of course the job opportunities which Hollywood offered to actors, writers, musicians, artists, and a wide range of other specialties made the southland a magnet as well. Moreover, as a wealthy community with a unique social structure, Hollywood also provided a fertile field for physicians and psychiatrists.[3] While some refugee intellectuals could be found in most western towns and cities, the Los Angeles area came to be their major hub.

In Los Angeles the émigrés conducted an active social life among themselves that centered on European-style salons. One of these crystallized around Thomas Mann, a world-famous novelist and Nobel Prize laureate who opened up his comfortable Pacific Palisades home to the leading literati of the West. Mann, as fellow émigré Ludwig Marcuse commented, played emperor to the émigrés of Southern California, "Everything was expected from him, everything was owed to him, and he was responsible for everything," wrote Marcuse, not entirely without envy.[4] The well-known German novelist, Lion Feuchtwanger, conducted another prominent salon in his pleasant home nearby. Artists and sculptors tended to gather at the apartment of Reinhardt A. Braun, an émigré journalist, who also established a meeting place for displaced European intellectuals. The salons provided havens for the émigrés from which they eventually entered into the mainstream of western American culture.

In Hollywood there were also a number of wealthy individuals who were willing to lend the refugees a helping hand. When Hitler's crushing defeat of France in May of 1940 brought another large wave of displaced persons to the United States, they appealed for help to the film community. The famous German director Ernst Lubitsch had been in Hollywood since 1930 and in 1940 decided to organize motion picture personalities in an aid campaign. Called the European Relief Fund, it was supported by pledges from dozens of Hollywood personalities who agreed to donate 1 percent of their salaries. The fund was to provide temporary maintenance for newly arrived refugees and also to furnish them with sponsors who were necessary to allow them admission on national immigration quotas. In addition, Lubitsch secured the services of Fred Kohner, at the time one of the best-known agents in Hollywood, who had close connections to many of the motion picture industry's leading moguls, to obtain promises of a year of employment for a few well known writers. For example, Kohner approached Jack Warner, Louis Mayer of MGM, and Harry Cohn (Columbia) and secured their sponsorship of Bertolt Brecht, Heinrich Mann, and Alfred Doeblin. After they arrived these highly individualistic writers found that they could not stomach their 9 to 5 schedule in a stable of writers ensconced in small cubicles on movie studio lots. But others adapted—men like Billy Wilder, Walter Reich, Robert Thoeren, Frederick Kohner, and George Froeschel—and within a few years became some of the most prominent film writers in Hollywood. As a group they contributed to raising standards of the American film and attracted a wide array of talent that would not have migrated westward without their presence.[5]

THE LITERATI

Many of the European writers who came and made Los Angeles a new literary center had well-established reputations. Preeminent among them was Thomas Mann, already famous throughout the world for best-selling novels like *Buddenbrooks* and *The Magic Mountain*. Austere and Germanic in his bearing—a staunch Protestant whose love of freedom led him to oppose Hitler's tyranny—Mann adjusted well to southern California. In fact, his daughter felt that he was inspired by the atmosphere.

Let me only hint at my belief that the odd elegance of that distant shore, with its almost intangible beauty...had a great influence on him and his work. It drove him from his own traditions to stylistic daring and gave him the courage for ...linguistic experiments.[6]

Mann himself noted with enthusiasm that "I was enchanted by the light, by the special fragrance of the air, by the blue of the sky, the sun, the exhilarating ocean breeze, the spruceness and cleanness of this Southland...all these paradisical scenes and colors enraptured me."[7] Reflecting on the condition of writers in exile like himself, he mused: "It is our destiny to carry on this battle against our own land and its cause of whose corruptness we are convinced. What an abnormal, morbid condition...for the writer, the bearer of spiritual tradition, when his own country becomes the most hostile, the most sinister foreign land! It is [a] question of whether we intend to take up again our former life in our fatherland after its liberation....If I ask myself I must say: No. The idea of returning to Germany...is far from me. I am now on the point of becoming an American citizen just as my grandchildren who were born here, and are growing up here, and my attachment to this country has already progressed so far that it would be contrary to my sense of gratitude to part from it again."[8] Accustomed to taking a daily afternoon walk with his poodle, he was an incongruous sight—fastidiously dressed in suit and tie, stepping smartly under the warm blue California sky—where most people were casually dressed in sports clothes and rarely walked when they could ride in cars.[9]

On many an evening a galaxy of literary talent gathered in the hospitable atmosphere of Mann's home. Among those present was Erich Maria Remarque, author of *All Quiet on the Western Front,* perhaps the most famous novel to emerge from the First World War. A great success in Europe as well as the United States, the book was transformed into a memorable motion picture in 1930 featuring Erich von Stroheim who a decade later also resided in Hollywood. The film won many prizes and became one of the all-time classics of the cinema. Another prominent member of the émigré writers' circle was Franz Werfel. Already well known in Europe whence he fled on foot, Werfel wrote the best-selling novel *The Song of Bernadette* in 1942, which Hollywood also turned into a successful movie.[10]

Among the big names of the literati was Lion Feuchtwanger, a novelist and short story writer with a worldwide reputation. His house in Pacific Palisades was another of the gathering places where the refugees could discuss their work, after which, one participant recalled, Frau Marta (Mrs. Feuchtwanger) would serve "Italian salad and homemade Apfel Strudel with whipped cream" to enliven the spirits of her guests, and to recreate a "gemuetlichkeit" which, many of them knew, they had left behind. Feuchtwanger presumed to speak for many of his fellow writers and sought to acquaint Americans with their plight when he noted that:

> The author who had lost the reading public of his own land frequently loses at the same time the core of his economic existence. Very many writers of the highest talent, whose products were in great demand in their own countries, find no markets in foreign lands, either because their chief merit lies in the stylistic qualities of their language, and these qualities cannot be translated, or because their choice of subjects does not interest the foreign reader....It is surprising how many authors whose accomplishments the entire world has acclaimed in spite of their most earnest efforts now stand helpless and without means....It is no great inconvenience to be forced to live in a hotel room and to be constantly subject to bureaucratic regulations. But not every writer is capable of composing a comprehensive novel in a hotel room; it tears them down double when he does not know whether he will be able to pay his hotel bill tomorrow [or] when his children beg for food.

But Feuchtwanger saw the constructive inducements as well. "For although banishment is destructive," he said, "and makes the victim small and miserable, it also hardens him and adds to his stature. A vast abundance of new materials and new ideas pours in upon him, he is confronted with a variety of impressions he never would have known at home." And he concluded on an upbeat note. "If we make an effort to take a historical view of our life in exile, it becomes evident even now that almost everything that seemed to hamper our work finally contributed to its welfare."[11]

One of the saddest figures was Heinrich Mann, brother of Thomas, who had been as famous as his brother in Europe, but who remained totally unknown in the United States. After a year of unsuccessfully trying out as a script writer in Hollywood, he retreated bitterly into his own world.[12]

In addition to the older writers with established reputations the refugee exodus also brought a younger group who were to gain prominence in the postwar era, many of them adapted to the teamwork required by the major Hollywood studios of their writers. At the same time they also managed to turn out works of their own. Among those who made a successful transition were Leonhard Frank, Joseph Wechsberg, Alfred Polgar, and Raoul Auernheimer. They wrote about their California experience for European audiences and did much to broaden California's image as a cultural center in the intellectual world of Europe.[13] Some also wrote for American readers. Alfred Neuman's *Look Upon This Man* received critical acclaim when it appeared in 1950 as did Victoria Wolf's *Fabulous City* in 1957. Vicki Baum, the well-known author of *Grand Hotel,* became even better known in the United States than in Europe and enjoyed much success with another novel, *Mustard Seed,* in 1953. Her prominence was in part due to a World War II film, *Hotel Berlin,* Peter Godfrey production, that was directly based on *Grand Hotel.* And that book most probably inspired another best seller, Katherine Anne Porter's *Ship of Fools*

(1964), another offshoot of Vicki Baum's influence, for Katherine Porter had a special sympathy for the émigré writers in southern California.[14]

Not all writers could breach language and cultural barriers, however, and remained obscure. That was true of Alfred Doeblin, author of one of the most successful novels of the Weimar years, *Berlin, Alexanderplatz.* Although he worked as a script writer for MGM for one year, he could never really write in English. He subsisted on charity and a stipend from the European Film Fund. After the war he returned to Europe. His friend, Bruno Frank, also remained unknown outside the émigré circle of southern California.[15] Among the alienated was Bertolt Brecht, who, while living in Hollywood between 1941 and 1947, viewed his experience as justifying his condemnation of capitalism and the United States. Although he was one of the best-paid émigré screen writers of the era, he grew to hate his work. One of his screenplays was Fritz Lang's famous World War II movie, *Hangmen Also Die,* the story of the brutal Nazi Gauleiter of Czechoslovakia who was killed by Czech partisans after mass murders of Czechs by German occupation forces. Brecht deeply resented the changes which the studio made in his work, and later success as a screenwriter hardly mollified him. A performance of his *Galileo* with the help of the famous actor Charles Laughton was not well received. And one of his most famous plays, *The Caucasian Chalk Circle,* which he wrote during these years, did not receive the acclaim with which it was showered in later years.[16]

To say that it was the European émigré writers alone who made Los Angeles a major literary center might be an exaggeration. Already during the 1930s Hollywood had begun to attract a group of distinguished American and English writers: F. Scott Fitzgerald, William Faulkner, Ernest Hemingway, Clifford Odets, Robert Sherwood, and S. J. Perelman, and from England, Aldous Huxley, Christopher Isherwood, Evelyn Waugh, and Somerset Maugham. In a few short years the exiles added an international flavor to Hollywood, making it a literary center with quite a large number of the world's leading writers.[17]

It was rather symbolic, therefore, that in 1943 Los Angeles hosted a national writer's conference. Sponsored by the University of California at Los Angeles and the Hollywood Writers Mobilization, it was chaired by Marc Connelly, a well-known American playwright and film writer. To the conference came not only many leading American writers but those of Allied nations as well as important figures from the world of motion pictures, radio, and other mass media. Their purpose was to discuss the writer's role in furthering the war effort, and to underscore freedom of expression as a fundamental democratic value. President Roosevelt highlighted the symbolic nature of the gathering when he wrote to Connelly:

> I send these greetings to the Writer's Congress with a deep sense of the significance of a gathering of writers in these times. It is a symbol, it seems to me, of our American faith in the Freedom of Expression—of our reliance upon the talents of our writers to present and clarify the issues of our times. Already, the men and women gathered there have rendered great service in elucidating for the nation the issues of this war.[18]

Over 1,200 people came to attend meetings and seminars and to consider the problems faced by various media—books, radio, motion pictures, music—in articulating wartime problems to the public. During its concluding sessions the Writer's Congress of 1943 adopted a variety of resolutions. These included pledges of international cultural cooperation as well as Pan American cultural unity. The Congress also addressed itself to the problem of securing the more efficient mobilization of writers and scholars. In its final action, the Congress developed an American Writer's Credo designed to provide guidelines for practitioners of the written

word. In a manner slightly reminiscent of totalitarian societies like Nazi Germany or the Soviet Union, the Congress unanimously asked American writers to pledge their talents "to the service of the truth...[to] dedicate...skill and talent to the sacred right of free expression [and to] pledge to know the thought and feeling of the American people in their varied tasks.[19] Irrespective of its impact, the Congress served to focus national and international attention on Los Angeles as a burgeoning center for literary activity, and as a national center for cultural expression through the mass media. As Gustav O. Arlt noted at the time: "The West Los Angeles telephone directory looks like an issue of *Kuerschner's Almanac*. The announcements of a concert series in Los Angeles might have been printed in Paris or Vienna or Milan."[20]

THE ART SCENE

The European émigrés also made significant contributions to the maturation of Los Angeles as an art center in the West, and indeed, the nation. A few of the more famous refugees brought their art collections with them. Erich Maria Remarque brought Cézanne oil and water color paintings, a Delacroix, four Degas pastels, drawings by Toulouse-Lautrec, and works by Picasso, Daumier, and Utrillo. But Remarque was living in a succession of apartments and rented houses during these years and had no room to display his treasures. In 1942, therefore, he decided to lend his collection to the Los Angeles County Art Museum for public display.[21] The movie producer Joseph Von Sternberg displayed his striking collection of German paintings at the Los Angeles County Museum in 1943.[22] As some of the refugees demonstrated, owning art works was a reflection of sophistication and status, and at the same time constituted a shrewd investment. The Europeans helped to popularize the ownership of distinctive art objects in Hollywood, for as the émigré movie producer and director

Ernst Lubitsch once commented, "Owning a Utrillo is like having an indoor Cadillac."[23]

Other émigrés contributed to the expansion of art galleries in Los Angeles and provided an impetus to the city's emergence as a major American art center, second only to New York. Starting in a small way, by the 1950s the galleries of Ralph Altman, Paul Kantor, Frank Klaus Perls, and Felix Landau, to name only a few, became important centers in the emerging art trade of the West. As cultivators of taste, the émigrés brought with them not only a deep appreciation of European classical art, but also a pioneering spirit in regard to modern art which gradually proved infectious for Americans. Karl With, for example, originally an expert in Oriental art, became Director of the Modern Art Institute in Los Angeles after the war. Vincent Price, who established and operated his own art gallery during the war years, later recalled that on a single day his clients included Thomas Mann, Aldous Huxley, Sergei Rachmaninoff, and Franz Werfel (in whose movie version of *The Song of Bernadette* Price had acted).[24]

In various capacities, therefore—as collectors, museum curators, art dealers, and academic teachers—the émigrés made a significant contribution to the maturation of the art scene in the West. They provided an expertise in the realm of classical European art that was largely lacking in the West before 1940 and introduced patrons to the Continental tradition. At the same time they brought sensitivity to the newer and avant-garde trends in European art which were still hardly known in the United States, and particularly the West. Perhaps the influence of the émigrés would have been less profound in another age. But their coming on the eve of the Second World War coincided with the increasing maturation of the art scene in the West. It was to this movement that the émigrés gave a decided—and far-reaching—impetus. For, as one art critic noted during the period, in evaluating the Santa Fe Fiesta Exhibit in 1941, Western artists were beginning to move beyond the obvious regionalism of the 1920s and 1930s, beyond "piñon studded mesa and mountain, golden aspens, cloud formations on static blue sky." The depth of the land was creeping into their consciousness.[25] To that broadening consciousness the émigrés made a lasting contribution.

MUSIC

In few fields was the contribution of the émigrés more significant than in the world of music in Hollywood. The famous conductor Bruno Walter felt that the adaptation of émigré musicians was easier in the Los Angeles area than anywhere else in the United States. Hollywood offered more job opportunities than other cities because of the large number of movie studio orchestras. Otto Klemperer and Bruno Walter conducted the Los Angeles Philharmonic in the war years; scores of lesser-known instrumentalists filled the chairs of orchestras in the region. Bronislaw Gimpel, for example, became concertmaster of the Los Angeles Philharmonic, in addition to giving private lessons; Robert Pollack, if not as famous as émigré Jascha Heifetz, became an outstanding violin teacher at the Los Angeles Conservatory of Music. Richard Lert (husband of writer Vicki Baum) did much to raise the professional standards of the Pasadena Civic Orchestra as its conductor. As Walter noted: "Experience has shown me that even the average European [musician] has had little difficulty in building up a new existence in the United States provided he was able from the beginning to see the difference between here and 'over there.'"[26]

A significant number of refugees became prominent film composers. Erich W. Korngold was one of the most talented, garnering two Academy Awards. One of the films for which he wrote a score was *King's Row,* starring a young actor named Ronald Reagan. When Reagan was inaugurated as President in 1981, he chose, as the first piece on the program for the gala Inaugural concert, a suite from Korngold's music for the movie.[27] Friedrich Hollaender, Eugen Zador, and Werner Heyman within a few years made themselves some of the most sought-after composers and arrangers in Hollywood. Others, like Ingolf Dahl, Ernst Toch, Ernest Gold, and Ernst Kanitz, divided their time between writing music for the movies and teaching composition at the University of Southern California. Most of these men at one time or another experienced grave doubts about the time they spent on motion pictures, for they exchanged financial independence for the preoccupation with more serious composition in which they had engaged in Europe. Some felt that their careers had been deflected. And yet one well-known music critic felt that they succeeded in introducing much avant-garde music to a mass audience in America through the medium of the feature film.[28]

Even the major composers of the twentieth century were sometimes drawn to write film music. The eminent French émigré composer Darius Milhaud spent the war years as a professor of music at Mills College in Oakland, California. Although he devoted most of his time to serious composition, he could not resist the lure of Hollywood and went there for a month to compose a score. Los Angeles, he said, "is a city, or rather a vast expanse of country, peopled by a whole *world* of artists, writers and musicians from every country. Some of them have been attracted by the climate [and] by the proximity of the film studios." Milhaud was fascinated by the cultural scene of southern California and made a point of visiting it at least once each year.[29]

One composer who refused to write for the movies was Arnold Schoenberg, one of the giants of modern music. Schoenberg had been invited to join the staff of the Juilliard School in New York City but, suffering from asthma, preferred to live in California. There he became a professor of music at the University of California in Los Angeles. Although several of his students were successful film composers and arrangers (Alfred Newman, Franz Waxman, David Raskin, Eddie Powell), he himself looked upon the medium with disdain. The story was told by Oscar Levant and Mrs. Schoenberg that at one time a representative of the famous producer Irving Thalberg came to Schoenberg to persuade him to write the music for the movie version of Pearl Buck's novel *The Good Earth*. "Think of it!!" said Thalberg's representative to Schoenberg, "A terrific storm is going on; the wheat field is swaying in the wind, and suddenly the earth begins to tremble. In the midst of the earthquake Co-Lan [a character in the film] gives birth to a baby! What an opportunity for music." Whereupon Schoenberg, thoughtful and reflective, replied in his ponderous German accent: "With so much going on, why do you need music?" Instead, Schoenberg devoted himself entirely to teaching and to composing a wide range of works reflecting atonality and counterpoint with which he pioneered new directions for twentieth-century music.[30]

Considering the total number of European immigrants in southern California during the World War II era—no more than 10,000—their contributions to the development of music in the West were astounding. The refugees endowed the musical scene in Los Angeles and other cities in the West with a deeper appreciation of traditional classical musical styles as they had developed in the European continental tradition. At the same time, through composition as well as through performances, they did a great deal to introduce new contemporary music into American repertoire, and so enriched the world of music for millions. And through the medium of motion pictures they did much to raise levels of musical composition for films made in Hollywood. No other group of immigrants to the West had made such substantial contributions to the cultural life of the region as the refugees from Hitler's Europe.

FILM AND THEATRE

Language and cultural barriers made adjustments for actors and theater folk more difficult than for émigré musicians and artists. By one of the ironies of history, however, the very individuals responsible for the persecution of the émigrés, the Nazis, also created new job opportunities for them in exile. As war clouds gathered in Europe, Hollywood turned more of its energies to war-inspired films, creating a burgeoning market for actors with German accents who could portray German generals, spies, concentration camp guards, and the like. Most of the émigrés frankly did not relish their roles as Nazis, but it provided them with rare opportunities for employment in their profession. And so Conrad Veidt played the memorable Major Strasser in *Casablanca* (for which the musical score was composed by the émigré Max Steiner); Eric von Stroheim played the ultimate Prussian militarist in *North Star;* Hans von Twardowski brilliantly impersonated the brutal Nazi General Heydrich in *Hangmen Also Die.* Great actors like Peter Lorre and Albert Basserman secured a variety of parts while Alexander Grenach, Fritz Kortner, and Martin Kosleck portrayed the Nazi leaders.[31]

And if Hollywood movie sets during the war became increasingly more realistic and authentic, that was hardly accidental. Behind the scenes at many Hollywood studios were dozens of European refugees. The set designer Hans Peters became one of the most prominent in Hollywood. Many individuals were anonymous, however: a host of former historians, archivists, and painters who found work as costume designers and fabricators and consultants on studio sets. There they applied their Teutonic penchant for accuracy and precision as well as historical knowledge to their newly developed craft.[32]

With somewhat less influence the émigrés also sought to invigorate theatre in Los Angeles. The world-famous Viennese director Max Reinhardt loved southern California and firmly believed that it would be a new Athens. As he wrote to Erika and Klaus Mann (children of Thomas Mann) from Hollywood with some prescience:

> You simply must stay here. It's going to be a new center of culture. America is going to take over the cultural heritage of Europe, and there is no more hospitable landscape...than the Californian. Here is a still youthful country. European and American scientists will meet to prepare a home for our old culture and for the new one that is coming into being here.

But Reinhardt was ahead of his time, and the West was not yet ready for a man of his genius. His efforts to attract financial support for legitimate theatre in Los Angeles failed, and in 1942 he left dejectedly for New York City. On a more modest scale the young Walter Wicclair, a fledgling theatrical producer from Silesia, organized the *Freie Buehne* in 1940. During the next nine years it produced hundreds of plays in English as well as German at the Coronet Theater in Hollywood where it flourished as one of the finest legitimate playhouses in the region, and expanded the repertoire known to audiences in the United States.[33]

CONCLUSIONS

Generalizations about the contributions of the refugee scholars are difficult in view of their diverse fields and temperaments. American scholars tended to be more rigorously empirical than their European colleagues, who sometimes brought new theoretical perspectives to their special fields. Their influence was particularly significant in the West during the 1940s where various disciplines were not as fully developed as they were in older eastern institutions.[34]

As a group, the contributions of European émigrés to the cultural development of the American West were remarkable. In literature, drama, music, art, science, the humanities, medicine, and psychoanalysis, to name only a few major fields, they had a substantial impact. That is not to say that the West was a cultural desert on the eve of World War II. In fact, cultural life in the West had grown during the 1920s, and with encouragement of New Deal programs had continued to flourish during the 1930s. By the time of World War II the region was ready for a "leap forward," for a significant spurt of growth, just as the spread of Nazi totalitarianism in Europe provoked a mass exodus of intellectuals from the continent. The Europeans brought sophistication and an emphasis on theories and abstractions that well supplemented the proverbial American genius for the practical and concrete. Most of the Europeans tried hard to adapt themselves to the tone of American culture at the same time that Americans, under the impact of war, became more hospitable to foreign ideas and insights. The West provided a major arena for the blending of the cultural traditions of Europe and America, for it was more receptive to new influences than the older and more stratified East. If the extraordinary cultural explosion of the West in the 1950s and 1960s is to be understood in historical perspective, then the significant contributions of the émigrés during the World War II era (and beyond) cannot be ignored.

During World War II Hollywood emerged as a major cultural center in the American West, exerting an influence far beyond its immediate environs. Its importance as the nation's motion picture capital was greatly enhanced by World War II in which the movies became an important tool of mass communications and propaganda. This wartime emphasis on Hollywood's role in the national defense effort added a more serious dimension to the movie capital which it had lacked before 1940 and brought the movie colony into the maelstrom of national politics.

But to view Hollywood merely as an entertainment capital is to ignore the cultural life which it spawned, even in an age of popular mass culture. The world of entertainment came to affect writers, musicians, and artists and stimulated the rapid growth of a wide range of cultural endeavors. And these varied activities drew distinguished figures from all over the world which further enhanced the cultural life of the region. The Second World War, by stimulating a mass exodus of many of Europe's leading intellectuals, made a prime contribution to the acceleration of southern California's development as one of the nation's most prominent centers of cultural activities. As no other single event, the coming of the émigrés to Los Angeles during World War II transformed southern California from a provincial and local cultural center to one of national and international dimensions.

Notes

1 Peter S. Nugent, "Hollywood Faces Reality," *New York Times Magazine,* March 8, 1942, p. 16.
2 Peter Gay, "Weimar Culture: The Outsider as Insider," in Donald Fleming and Bernard Bailyn (eds.), *The Intellectual Migration* (Cambridge, 1969), pp. 11–12; see also Laura Fermi, *Illustrious Immigrants: The Intellectual Migration from Europe 1930–1941* (Chicago, 1971), p. 12.
3 Some aspects of the refugee migration are touched on in Jarrell C. Jackman, "Exiles in Paradise: A Cultural History of German Emigres in Southern California, 1933–1950" (Ph.D. dissertation, University of California, Santa Barbara, 1977), and summarized in Jarrell C. Jackman, "Exiles in Paradise: German Emigres in Southern California, 1933–1950," *Southern California Quarterly,* vol. 61 (Summer, 1979), 183–203; among the many reminiscences consult Salka Viertel, *The Kindness of Strangers* (New York, 1969) and Erich Maria Remarque, *Shadows in Paradise,* translated by Ralph Manheim (New York, 1972); Gerald D. Nash, oral interview with Marta Feuchtwanger, in Pacific Palisades, June 14, 1981.
4 Ludwig Marcuse, *Mein Zwanzigstes Jahrhundert: Auf dem Weg zu Einer Autobiographie* (Munich, 1960), p. 288; Gerald D. Nash, oral interview with Marta Feuchtwanger, Pacific

Palisades, California, June 14, 1981; Jackman, "Exiles," in *Southern California Quarterly,* vol. 61, 196–199; Marta Mierendorff, *Exiltag an der Pazifischen Westkueste* (Los Angeles, 1973), p. 4.

5 Frederick Kohner, *Der Zauberer von Sunset Boulevard* (Munich, 1974), pp. 189–190; Joseph Wechsberg, *The First Time Around: Some Irreverent Recollections* (Boston, 1970), pp. 217–218; Viertel, *Kindness of Strangers,* pp. 241, 248, 250–251,258–259. Remarque, *Shadows in Paradise,* p. 229; Jackman, "Exiles in Paradise," pp. 88–92, 107–108, 186; John Spalek and Joseph Strelka (eds.), *Deutche Exilliteratur seit 1933,* vol. I, *Kalifornien* (Bern, 1976), 715–832 has broad coverage.

6 Monica Mann, *Past and Present* (New York, 1960), p. 132.

7 Thomas Mann, *The Story of a Novel: The Genesis of Dr. Faustus,* translated by Richard and Clara Winston (New York, 1981), pp. 64, 186; see also Thomas Mann, *Letters of Thomas Mann,* translated by Richard and Clara Winston (New York, 1971), pp. 362, 366.

8 Thomas Mann, "The Exiled Writer's Relation to His Homeland," in *Writers' Conference, Los Angeles,* pp. 339–340, 343.

9 *Aufbau,* August 7, 1942, p. 15.

10 Luizi Korngold, *Erich Korngold: Ein Lebensbild* (Vienna, 1967), p. 68; Leonhard Frank, *Heart on the Left,* translated by Cyrus Brooks (London, 1954), p. 164; Marcuse, *Mein Zwanzigstes Jahrundert,* p. 266; on Werfel see Lore B. Foltin (ed.), *Franz Werfel* (Pittsburgh, 1961), and Werner Braselman, *Franz Werfel* (Wuppertal, 1960), Remarque, *Shadows in Paradise,* pp. 228–231.

11 On Feuchtwanger see Lion Feuchtwanger, *Stories from Near and Far* (New York, 1945), passim, and "The Working Problems of the Writer in Exile," in *Writers' Conference, Los Angeles,* pp. 345, 346, 348.

12 Heinrich Mann, *Briefe an Karle Lemke und Klaus Pinkus* (Berlin, n.d.), p. 193; Bertolt Brecht somewhat unfairly criticized Thomas Mann—whose conservative political views he resented, anyhow—for not doing enough for his older brother. See Bertolt Brecht, *Arbeitsjournal,* vol. II (Frankfurt am Main, 1973), 643.

13 See Leonhard Frank, *The Baroness* (London, 1950), and *Heart on the Left* (London, 1954); Raoul Auernheimer, *Das Wirtshaus Zur Verlorenen Zeit: Erlebnisse und Bekenntnisse* (Vienna, 1948); Joseph Wechsberg, *The First Time Around,* (New York, 1964); Alfred Polgar, *Anderseits: Erzaehlungen und Erwaegungen: Standtpunkte* (Amsterdam, 1948), passim.

14 Charles Higham and Joel Greenberg, *Hollywood in the Forties* (New York, 1968), p. 91; Vicki Baum, *It Was All Quite Different: The Memoirs of Vicki Baum* (New York, 1964), p. 218; for Katherine Anne Porter see her remarks at University of California at Los Angeles during the 1943 Writers' Congress, in *Writers' Congress, Los Angeles* (1943), p. 329; a concise contemporary assessment of the impact of foreign writers is by Gustav O. Arlt, "The Cultural Contributions of Exiled Intellectuals to America and the World." in *Writers' Congress Proceedings,* 1943, p. 356.

15 Alfred Doeblin, *Briefe* (Freiburg, 1970), p. 273; Marcuse, *Mein Zwanzigstes Jahrhundert,* p. 276; Jackman, "Exiles," *Southern California Quarterly,* p. 194; Harold von Hofe, "German Literature in Exile: Alfred Doeblin," *German Quarterly,* vol. 17 (January, 1948), 28.

16 An excellent account is James K. Lyon, "Bertold Brecht's Hollywood Years: The Dramatist as Film Writer," *Oxford German Studies,* vol. 6 (1971–72), 145–174; see also Bertolt Brecht, *Arbeitsjournal,* vol. II, 643.

17 A detailed cultural history of Los Angeles has not yet been written. Some perceptive comments can be found in Christopher Rand, *Los Angeles* (New York, 1970), originally written as profiles for the *New Yorker* Magazine.

18 Franklin D. Roosevelt to Marc Connelly, September 8, 1943, *Writers' Congress, Los Angeles,* p. 5; *Los Angeles Times,* October 2, 3, 4, 1943; *New York Times,* October 10, 1943.

19 *Writers' Congress, Los Angeles,* pp. 611–613; text of resolutions can be found on pp. 606–610.

20 Arlt, "The Cultural Contributions of Exiled Intellectuals to America and the World," in *Writers' Congress, Los Angeles,* p. 353. Arlt was a well-known professor of German at the University of California and a staunch advocate of the émigré intellectuals.

21 *Los Angeles Times,* January 14, 1942; *Los Angeles County Museum Newsletter,* November 23, 1942; *Time,* November 8, 1943.

22 *Los Angeles Times,* May 23, 1943.

23 *Beverly Hills Press,* April 22, 1954. See also Carla Higgins, "Art Collecting in the Los Angeles Area, 1910–1960" (Ph.D. dissertation, UCLA, 1963), pp. 238–239.

24 I've checked biographical data in *Who's Who in American Art,* 1980 (New York, 1980), pp. 424, 578 and *Who's Who in Los Angeles County, 1950–51,* ed. by Alice Catt Armstrong (Los Angeles, 1950), pp. 161, 270. Vincent Price, *I like What I Know* (New York, 1959), pp. 177–180, 181–186; Viertel, *Kindness of Strangers,* p. 217.

25 Dorothy B. Hughes in *Art Digest,* vol. 10 (October 1, 1941), 10.

26 Bruno Walter, *Themes and Variation* (London, 1947), p. 375; Otto Klemperer, *Meine Erinnerungen* (Berlin, 1963), passim.

27 Luizi Korngold, *Erich Korngold: Ein Lebensbild,* p. 80; *New York Times,* January 19, 1981; *Baker's Biographical Dictionary of Musicians,* 6th ed., revised by Nicolas Slonimsky (New York, 1978), pp. 914–915, and Stanley Sadie (ed.), *The New Grove Dictionary of Music and Musicians* (20 vols., New York, 1980), vol. 10, pp. 210–211.

28 See comments of Fred W. Sternfeld, "Music and the Feature Films," *Musical Quarterly,* vol. 33 (October 1947), 517, 519–532; Howard Swan, in *Music in the Southwest: A History* (San Marino, 1952), pp. 274–275 also noted that the émigrés were responsible for more performances of contemporary music in Los Angeles than anywhere else in the United States outside New York City. *Baker's Biographical Dictionary of Musicians* has excellent articles about these men and their careers.

29 Darius Milhaud, *Notes Without Music* (New York, 1953), pp. 289–290.

30 The literature on Schoenberg is extensive. The story about Thalberg is recounted in Walter H. Rubsamen, "Schoenberg in America," *The Musical Quarterly,* vol. 37 (October, 1951), 485–486; an intimate memoir by one of his students is Dika Newlin, *Schoenberg Remembered: Diaries and Recollections, 1938–1976* (New York, 1980), pp. 13–81, 89–234, 329–338; on the premiere of one of his last works, "A Survivor at Auschwitz," I have consulted Schoenberg's letters in the Kurt Frederick Manuscripts, Fine Arts Library, University of New Mexico, Albuquerque, N.M. In 1974 the University of Southern California announced plans for establishment of a Schoenberg Institute at the university. See *Los Angeles Times,* January 20 and February 6, 1974.

31 Higham and Greenberg, *Hollywood in the Forties,* pp. 87–92; Fritz Kortner, *Aller Tage Abend* (Munich, 1959), p. 550; Kohner, *Der Zauberer,* p. 208.

32 Higham and Greenberg, *Hollywood in the Forties,* p. 92; Guenther Anders, *Die Schrift an der Wand: Tagebuecher 1951 bis 1955* (Munich, 1967), pp. 1–5. Author Anders worked as a costume cleaner in Hollywood, 1941–1943, then left in disgust for New York, and returned to Germany after the war. See also Jackman, "Exiles in Paradise," pp. 133–135, 183–187.

33 Reinhardt quoted in Erika and Klaus Mann, *Escape to Life* (Boston, 1939), p. 265. See also Gottfried Reinhardt, *Der Liebhaber: Erinnerungen seines Sohnes Gottfried Reinhardt an Max Reinhardt* (Munich, 1973), pp. 269–270; Jackman, "Exiles in Paradise," pp. 172–180.

34 A brief list of émigré scholars is found in Bailyn and Fleming (eds.), *The Intellectual Migration,* pp. 675–718; on Max Delbrueck see Cairns, Stent, and Watson (eds.), *Phages and the Origins of Molecular Biology,* and Watson, *The Double Helix,* and for mathematics James R. Newman (ed.), *The World of Mathematics* (New York, 1956); and Laura Fermi, *Illustrious Immigrants,* pp. 175–214.

FROM RELOCATION TO REDRESS

EDITOR'S INTRODUCTION

Few episodes in California history have stirred such passionate debate as has the relocation of the Japanese Americans during World War II. By the end of 1942, 110,000 persons of Japanese ancestry had been removed from their homes along the Pacific Coast and placed in "relocation centers." The total number of persons incarcerated eventually reached 120,000. Ninety-three thousand Californians were included in this mass evacuation.

The action was justified at the time as a military necessity. Proponents of relocation argued that the Japanese Americans would commit disloyal acts of espionage or sabotage if they were allowed to remain at liberty. President Franklin Roosevelt authorized relocation in 1942 and it was carried out by the military officer in charge of the Western Defense Command. When the issue was brought before the United States Supreme Court in 1943 and 1944, the court upheld the constitutionality of relocation on the grounds of wartime military necessity. Leaders of the Japanese-American community maintained that the West Coast Japanese were loyal Americans who posed no threat to the nation's security. Relocation, they believed, was unnecessary, unconstitutional, and racially motivated.

The lines drawn in the battle over relocation in the 1940s have remained fixed for the past four decades. The defenders of relocation are far less numerous and less vocal today than the critics, but the arguments have changed little.

In a rare display of historical consciousness, the United States Congress in 1980 authorized the formation of a Commission on Wartime Relocation and Internment of Civilians. The commission was charged with establishing, once and for all, whether any wrong was done to those who were relocated during the war. And further, if wrong was done, the commission was asked to recommend how restitution or redress could be provided for the victims of that wrong.

After more than eighteen months of study, the commission issued the first of its two reports in February 1983. A key passage from that report, quoted in the following selection by Roger Daniels, declared that relocation was *not* justified by military necessity. The mass evacuation of the Japanese Americans was caused by ignorance, race prejudice, war hysteria, and by a failure of leadership. Was a wrong committed? The commission was clear on this point: The Japanese Americans had suffered a "grave injustice." The commission was especially critical of the nation's wartime military and political leaders who ignored or suppressed findings by the FBI and the Justice Department that there was no sound basis for mass exclusion. Relocation was carried out, the commission concluded, "despite the fact that not a single documented act of espionage, sabotage, or fifth column activity was committed by an American citizen of Japanese ancestry or by a resident Japanese alien on the West Coast."

The following selection is unlike the others in this anthology. It is not a scholarly article, and yet its author is the leading scholar of the relocation experience. The selection is taken from an address given by Roger Daniels to a conference of Japanese Americans and others in Salt Lake City in March 1983. Daniels offers an informal intellectual history of the relocation issue, noting how perceptions of relocation have changed over the past forty years. His comments are especially valuable as they reveal changing attitudes within the Japanese-American community.

Daniels' address is "dated" in one respect, for when he made his remarks the congressional commission had not yet issued its second report. His speculations on the recommendations of that report, nevertheless, proved to be prescient. In June 1983, the commission recommended to Congress that each of the 60,000 surviving Japanese Americans who had been relocated be paid $20,000.

The reports by the congressional commission have rekindled public debate over relocation. Supporters of redress argue that a substantial monetary payment will help deter similar violations of civil liberties in the future. Opponents fear that redress may lead to demands for similar payments from Indians, blacks, and others who have suffered past discrimination.

Roger Daniels is a Professor of History at the University of Cincinnati. Among his many works are *The Politics of Prejudice: The Anti-Japanese Movement in California and the Struggle for Japanese Exclusion* (1962), and *Concentration Camps, North America: Japanese Americans and Canadians during World War II* (1981).

From Relocation to Redress

Roger Daniels

Although I have spoken about the relocation and its ongoing aftermath many times, it was very difficult for me to decide what to say to this audience. I knew that many here would be individuals who had gone through the whole evacuation-incarceration process and that there would be others present who had studied it at length and in depth. What could I say that would have meaning for these members of the audience and yet still communicate something to those who are less aware of what happened, when it happened, and how it evolved? It occurred to me that in one sense at least this talk was different from all the others that I had given. For the first time I was speaking after the publication of the long-awaited report of the Commission on the Wartime Relocation and Internment of Civilians, *Personal Justice Denied*. Once I had realized this, I decided to try to show how perceptions of the evacuation and the relocation have changed over time and are still changing.

While it is true that what happened, happened, it is also true that at different distances in time our perspective of a given event or a complex of events will change.

I am going to discuss, therefore, the relocation as it has appeared at three specific times in the past: in 1967, as it appears in 1983, and during the Second World War. Then, abandoning the role of historian, I will speculate about the possible course of redress.

Certainly 1967 is the most artificial of my three snapshots in time. It was exactly twenty-five years after the evacuation; but I choose it because that spring Harry Kitano and I, with the help of Robert Conhaim and the staff of

UCLA Extension, organized what we believe was the first academic conference devoted to an analysis of the evacuation and some of its consequences. Among the speakers was Leonard Arrington, who was visiting UCLA that year; and we were fortunate in having one repentant wartime sinner—the always genial and entertaining Judge Robert W. Kenny, who had succeeded Earl Warren as attorney general of California in January 1943—who confessed that he had been wrong about some things and remiss about others. We could not find anyone in southern California who was willing, in 1967, to stand up and say that the evacuation was justified, that relocation had been the proper course for the country to pursue.

The atmosphere at and preceding that conference sixteen years ago was quite different from the atmosphere here in Salt Lake City in March 1983. There had been a good deal of genteel pressure from some of the leadership of the Japanese community in Los Angeles not to have the conference at all. Things were going well, some thought; why stir up old bad feelings. None of us thought that we were saying the last word about the relocation; but no one, I think, dreamed that less than two decades later there would be a mass movement for redress, a mass movement that may get significant support from an organ of the federal government. Our chief concern was the awful question "Can it happen again?" and our major suggestions for remedial legislation concerned the desirability of keeping the Japanese American Claims Act open and the possibility of having the preventive detention section of the Internal Security Act of 1950 repealed, since that legislation sanctioned the procedures modeled directly on those used to incarcerate Japanese Americans in 1942.

Adapted from *Japanese Americans: From Relocation to Redress,* edited by Roger Daniels, et al., pp. 3–10. Copyright © 1986 by University of Utah Press.

It is not surprising, in retrospect, that our horizons were so limited. Great progress had been made by many if not most of the victims of Executive Order 9066. Sociologist William Petersen was already hailing Japanese Americans as "our model minority," as much, I suggest, a way of putting down groups he regarded as disruptive as a way of hailing the undoubted achievements of the Nikkei in recovering from the disasters of World War II. And the progress was real. There had been a Japanese American Claims Act in 1948, although with utterly inadequate funding, and in 1952 racial and ethnic bars were removed from the naturalization statutes—no longer were Issei "aliens ineligible to citizenship"—and a token immigration quota had been awarded to Japan. In 1959 Hawaii had been belatedly admitted to the Union, so from that point on, there were Asian American legislators in Washington. A people who had owned no political "clout" in 1942 were now, in a technical sense, overrepresented, an overrepresentation that would be increased when California began to send Asian Americans, one of them a naturalized citizen, to Washington.

By the 1960s, the socioeconomic gains of the bulk of the Nisei and the Sansei were beginning to push many of them into the middle and upper-middle classes. Figures compiled by the state of California in 1965 showed that persons of Japanese ancestry had, on average, more education than whites, but, somewhat paradoxically, earned significantly less money: Japanese American males over fourteen had a median income of $4,388 as opposed to $5,109 for whites. If we look only at the well-to-do, the gap is even greater. Only 7.7 percent of Japanese American men twenty-five years of age and older earned as much as $10,000, while 12.1 percent of the similar white group did. There are many explanations for this discrepancy, including, of course, a reluctance by some employers to put Asian Americans in positions in which they supervised, hired, and fired whites. A major reason surely stemmed from

the fact that the war years were, for most Americans, years of relative prosperity, years in which old debts were paid and savings and investments increased. But many Japanese Americans were simply financially wiped out, and they and their families would always suffer from being a step or two behind where they would have been if the government had only let them continue to live industrious, productive, law-abiding lives. A quarter of a century after the evacuation and twenty-one years after the last camp had closed, the effects of the wartime incarceration were still present. It was quite clear then, as it is today, that the relocation was and is the central event in Japanese American history, the event from which all other events are dated and compared. "Before the war" and "after camp" are the phrases that provide the essential periodization of Japanese American life.

CONTEMPORARY VIEWS

Now, sixteen years later, some of us are again at a conference, but a conference with a different mood, in a different time, and with a different purpose. Perhaps the greatest single difference is the difference in community attitudes, a difference that was becoming apparent even before the traumatic Commission hearings began. No one has articulated that change better than the Nisei writer, Yoshiko Uchida, in her moving memoir, *Desert Exile*.[1]

Today some of the Nisei, having overcome the traumatizing effects of their incarceration and participated in a wide spectrum of American life with no little success, are approaching retirement. Their Sansei children, who experienced the Vietnam War, with its violent confrontations and protest marches, have asked questions about those early World War II years.

Why did you let it happen? they ask of the evacuation. Why didn't you fight for your civil rights? Why did you go without protest to the concentration camps? They were right to ask these questions, for they made us search for some obscured truths and come to a better understanding of ourselves and of those times. They are the generation who taught us to celebrate our ethnicity and discover our ethnic pride.

It is my generation, however, who lived through the evacuation of 1942. We are their link to the past and we must provide them all we can remember, so they can better understand the history of their own people. As they listen to our voices from the past, however, I ask that they remember they are listening in a totally different time; in a totally changed world.

This generational difference is one of the hallmarks of American immigrant life. Almost half a century ago, the Norwegian American historian, Marcus Lee Hansen, considered the father of immigration history, wrote that the second generation in its eagerness to become as fully Americanized as possible tends to reject the heritage of its fathers and mothers; while the third generation, to a degree, tends to reject the values and experience of their own parents, to embrace some of the cultural values of their grandparents' generation, and begins to try to recapture at least some of the ethnic past. Hansen, in the 1930s, did not have Issei, Nisei, and Sansei in mind; he was generalizing from his own Norwegian American experience. That his generalizations seem to have some relevance to the Japanese American experience testifies both to the relative universality of Hansen's insights and to the essential Americaness of the experience of the Nikkei here.

To anyone at all concerned or connected with the Japanese American community once the drive for redress had begun in the late 1970s, it was clear that the winds of change were blowing. Some of the change was not pretty: animosities and resentments, arising out of intracommunity conflicts in the months after Pearl Harbor, came to the surface after more than three decades of repression. The word "inu," literally "dog," but in this context "in-

former" or, colloquially, "rat fink," began again to be applied to persons, living and dead, for what they allegedly had done or not done in late 1941 and early 1942. Even more common were displays of emotion: Time and time again, at meetings in various communities—Seattle, Cleveland, Philadelphia, Chicago—I saw grown men and women of my own age break down and cry in public as they spoke, or tried to speak, of those events during the war that affected them the most. The instance that sticks most in my mind is the man in Cleveland who couldn't quite finish his story about his military leave just prior to going overseas to fight with the 442nd Regimental Combat Team. His folks were still in camp at Minidoka, Idaho, so he went there. What he remembered most was his mother apologizing profusely because she simply was not able to prepare his favorite foods to give him the kind of meal appropriate for a soldier going off to battle. These, and other experiences, convinced me, even before the Commission was created, that the therapeutic effects of the struggle for redress were important events in the history of the community and would be so even if no Commission were established, even if its report papered over the truth.

That, happily is not the case. On February 24th we got the Commission report, and it was a good one. At other sessions of this conference the report will be examined and discussed at length. I merely want here to read and applaud its major conclusion:[2]

The promulgation of Executive Order 9066 was not justified by military necessity, and the decisions which followed from it...were not driven by analysis of military conditions. The broad historical causes which shaped these decisions were race prejudice, war hysteria, and a failure of political leadership. Widespread ignorance of Japanese Americans contributed to a policy conceived in haste and executed in an atmosphere of fear and anger at Japan. A grave injustice was done to American citizens and resident aliens of Japanese ancestry who, without individual review or any probative evidence against them, were excluded, removed and detained by the United States during World War II.

These uncompromising conclusions—"not justified by military necessity" and shaped by "race prejudice, war hysteria, and a failure of political leadership"—were not new. At the UCLA conference in 1967, all of these points were made; and they have been made by many historians and other writers. What was important about the Commission report, was that it was a report of an official body created by the United States Congress, and that, when coupled with President Gerald R. Ford's 1976 proclamation—"We know now what we should have known then: not only was [the] evacuation wrong, but Japanese-Americans were and are loyal Americans"—two of the three branches of the federal government have disavowed the evacuation. And without in any way denigrating what President Ford did, it is quite clear that the Commission's affirmation is much the more important of the two. It made the front page of the *New York Times* and of most newspapers in the United States and Japan and was highlighted by television networks in both countries. Ford's proclamation, except in the western states, was largely ignored; it was not considered "fit to print" by the editors of the *New York Times,* which published nothing about it until the editors ran a letter from me chiding its lapse. And perhaps, even more tellingly, the Commission's report drew an angry reply from the chief living architect of the relocation, John J. McCloy. McCloy, about whom more later, finds the report an "outrage." He could ignore the work of historians—he has never answered letters of inquiry I have sent him—and he ignored President Ford's proclamation. The Commission's report simply could not be ignored.

That report, most of us here tonight hope, will merely be another step on the road to redress, but even if no more steps are taken the journey will have been worthwhile. In 1983 the relocation is out of the closet. That is not to say that the pain is gone, that the controversies are over; almost certainly they are not. And, when the commissioners make their recommendations about redress more bitterness will surely emerge and a new struggle commence. But, never again, I suspect, will the community be able to return to the collective social amnesia that has marked so many of the years since 1942. This is not said as a form of rebuke, and, it seems to me, there has been more than enough pointing of fingers about who did what to whom within the Japanese American community in 1941–42. This kind of internal examination is not just a Japanese American trait: the American Jewish community, for example, still numbed by the dimensions of the Holocaust, is at this very moment involved in an angry dispute about what American Jewish leaders did and did not do, during the Hitler era, to help rescue Jews of Europe. Listening to some of the polemics, one could get the impression that American Jewish leaders, like Rabbi Stephen S. Wise, were actually operating the gas chambers. Some Japanese Americans, in like fashion, talk as if the JACL promulgated Executive Order 9066. In each instance, it seems to me, the criticism is out of balance. We must remember, as Ms. Uchida reminds us, the critics are talking about "a totally different time…a totally changed world." The real enemy of the Japanese Americans was their own government: we know the names of the leaders, from FDR down, who failed us all, then. To be sure, the Japanese American leadership did not always act wisely, and, even more seriously, I think, has tried very hard to "manage" Japanese American history ever since. No historian, least of all me, would ever suggest that the wartime and postwar actions of community leaders should go unprobed. But those probes should be conducted with balance and should avoid both saccharine self-congratulation and paranoid-style fantasy.

WARTIME RELOCATION

Clearly then, there are both advantages and disadvantages in looking at the events of the relocation from more than four decades away. But we must concentrate on the events of 1941 to 1945. And it is important that we call things by their proper names. George Orwell has taught us that twentieth-century political speech is largely "the defense of the indefensible" and that political language consists "largely of euphemism." This certainly has been true of language used to describe the relocation. From Karl R. Bendetsen's memos, which habitually describe Japanese American citizens as "non aliens," to the congressional statute that created the Commission and beyond, euphemisms have prevailed. Rather than the "Commission on Wartime Relocation and Internment of Civilians," it should have been "incarceration" of civilians. "Internment" is a well-defined legal process by which enemy nationals are placed in confinement in time of war. The roughly 2,000 male Issei leaders who were rounded up in the days immediately after Pearl Harbor were interned. They were, although separated from their families, given better treatment than were most incarcerated Japanese Americans; and, above all, once they were locked up, there was a kind of due process as each internee was entitled to an individual hearing. In short, however unjust, the internment of those enemy aliens did follow the forms of law and did conform, generally, to the terms of the Geneva Convention.

What happened to the rest of the West Coast Japanese was lawless. Citizen and alien, male and female, old and young, all were simply swept up, placed in the holding pens from Santa Anita to Puyallup, and then shipped out to ten desolate camps. The Commission report—and this is one serious difference I have with it— argues, in a footnote, that "to use the phrase 'concentration camps' summons up images and ideas which are inaccurate and unfair" and goes on to argue that the term "concentration camp" is synonymous with "death camp." In wanting to avoid the use of the term "concentration camp," the Commission and John J. McCloy are in agreement. As early as March 16, 1942, before the first group of Bainbridge Islanders had been sent to Manzanar, McCloy is on record as wanting to avoid the use of the term "concentration camp." At that same meeting, Dr. Calvert Dedrick, a specialist from the Census Bureau who was loaned to the army to help in the roundup, suggested that the relocation be called a "residence control program."[3] At the other extreme, Raymond Okamura has recently charged me and other scholars with being part of a "cover-up": "although many authors have used titles like...Concentration Camps, USA...none has systematically replaced euphemistic terminology in their text."[4]

Both of these positions are extreme. It is necessary to differentiate between at least three main types of camps in which Japanese Americans were kept during the war: the assembly centers, such as Tanforan or Portland; the relocation centers, such as Topaz and Heart Mountain; and the internment camps, such as Bismark and Missoula. The first were run by the army, the second by the War Relocation Authority, and the third, eventually, by the Immigration and Naturalization Service. To ignore completely the names used in contemporary documents would be as shortsighted as the Commission's refusal to call the camps what they really were: places to which persons were sent, not for crimes or legal status, but because of race or ethnicity. Such places have been known, since the end of the nineteenth century, as concentration camps. They were first established by the British to pen up Boer civilians in South Africa; and the term "concentration camps" was used by Franklin D. Roosevelt himself, on at least three separate public occasions, to describe the camps run by the War Relocation Authority. These camps were not, thank God, death camps or extermination camps. More people were born in the American concentration camps than died in them. At Topaz, for example, there were 384 births and 139 deaths. Most of those who died in camp did so from disease or just simply old age, although some did commit suicide and a few were actually killed by the government.

One of those latter victims was James Hatsuki Wakasa who had come to the United States in 1903.[5] He had been graduated from Keio College in Tokyo and had studied for two years at the University of Wisconsin. A chef by trade, he had been a civilian instructor of cooking at Camp Dodge, Iowa, during World War I. In World War II he had been rounded up with the other Bay Area Japanese and sent to Topaz. There, half an hour before sunset on Sunday, April 11, 1943, this sixty-three-year-old bachelor was shot to death by one of the soldiers who guarded the camp. According to the story released to the press by the army, Mr. Wakasa was killed "while attempting to crawl through the fence." It is now clear that the story was fabricated and, based on an internal WRA report of the following month, this seems to be what really happened: The shooting took place in a relatively isolated corner of the camp, and apparently no one inside knew about it until about forty-five minutes later when 1st Lt. Henry H. Miller, commander of the Military Police company, informed a WRA staff member that "a Japanese resident had been shot and killed...and that his body had been removed."

Evidence developed later by the WRA indicated that the victim had been inside the fence when shot—the center of a large bloodstain was five feet inside the fence—and a postmortem examination of the body found that there was "a perforating wound point of entry made probably by a bullet which entered the thoracic cage [anterior to posterior at the] 3rd rib 2½ cm left of mid-thoracic line. No powder burn. There is an exit wound measuring 1 cm by 3 cm jagged posteriorly at 6th thoracic vertebra 3 cm right of mid-thoracic line." In other words, Wakasa was

facing the soldier who shot him, which is, of course, incompatible with the story that the army put out. In the meantime the M.P. commander armed his troops with riot weapons, high-powered rifles, and tear gas. An idea of the overreaction by the military police detachment may be gleaned from the following statement made by Eiichi Sato, a social worker for Block 36, who, with four other inmates went to inspect the scene of the crime about 10 o'clock the following morning. As he told it later that day:

> We approached the west-south fence, approximately 35 feet away, when an army "jeep" came speeding from the north on the road beyond the fence and, upon seeing us, came to an abrupt halt. The driver stood up from his seat, turned to his companion, and grabbed the submachine gun from the latter's hand. He jumped off the jeep and came dashing to the fence pointing his gun at us [and saying] "Scatter or you'll get the same thing as the other guy got."

That was Monday morning. By 4 p.m. on Tuesday, Lieutenant Miller, perhaps so ordered by higher authority, lifted his "alert," withdrew what he called "emergency armament," and promised that "the Military Police will not molest, injure or exercise any unusual surveillance upon the evacuees at Topaz Center" and that "orders have been issued that members of the Military Police are not to enter the Project Center except on official business approved by the Commanding Officer who will clear with the Acting Project Director in advance." Two weeks later, on April 28, at Fort Douglas, Utah, the sentry who shot Wakasa stood a general court-martial and was found "not guilty." Thus ended what Russell Bankston, the WRA reports officer on whose account I have drawn, called "the Wakasa Incident."

The death of James Wakasa was but an incident in a global war that destroyed millions of other human beings. Unlike the deaths at Dachau or Auschwitz, it was not a crime planned by higher authority, not part of a final solution. It was, nevertheless, a crime—a war crime if you wish. And the chain of responsibility for that crime goes all the way up the ladder—from the sentry who pulled the trigger; to Lieutenant Miller, who helped to cover it up; on up to those soldiers, bureaucrats, and politicians who planned and executed the relocation and who arranged it so that over a hundred thousand persons were deprived of their liberty and much of their property, if not their lives—ending, finally, in the Oval Office, where Franklin D. Roosevelt okayed it, and on Capitol Hill, where the Congress, without a dissenting vote, ratified the decisions of the executive branch.

Of those still alive today, the most important architect of the relocation is John J. McCloy (b. 1895), who, as Secretary of War Henry L. Stimson's deputy, was the ranking member of the government who dealt with the Japanese Americans on a day-to-day basis. McCloy was also one of the chief architects of the 442nd Regimental Combat Team, whose magnificent fighting record did so much to rehabilitate and improve the image of the Nisei. But he was also the man who, in the crucial days of February 1942, threw his weight behind mass evacuation, telling his co-conspirators that "You are putting a Wall Street lawyer in a helluva box, but if it is a question of the safety of the country [and] the Constitution...why the Constitution is just a scrap of paper to me."[6]

McCloy, who called the Commission's Report an "outrage," had testified earlier that he hoped that the Commission would "conclude ...that under the circumstances...and with the exigencies of wartime security, the action of the President of the United States and the United States Government in regard to our then Japanese population was reasonably undertaken and thoughtfully and humanely conducted."[7] Was James Wakasa treated humanely? Was it thoughtful to brand Japanese Americans as security risks, as not to be trusted by their own

country? And for the Wall Street lawyer to insist, forty-one years later, that what was done was in the national interest is merely to compound the felonies he helped to commit then.

"Military necessity." "The safety of the country." "The exigencies of wartime security." For over four decades these have been the reasoned excuses for the relocation, for depriving almost 70,000 American citizens of their constitutional rights, for treating Japanese Americans differently from German Americans and Italian Americans. Is it just civil libertarian hindsight, mere historical Monday morning quarter-backing, that finds the relocation unnecessary? I think not. The best possible judge of military necessity during World War II was Gen. George C. Marshall, chief of staff of the U.S. Army throughout the war and perhaps our greatest soldier. Marshall and his colleagues at army GHQ had already determined that relocating the Japanese Americans was *not* a rational military precaution when the political leaders of the army, Stimson and McCloy, without consulting him, opted for mass evacuation and got the concurrence of the Commander in Chief. Marshall, the good soldier, obeyed the orders of his lawful superiors. Later, however, he and his protege, Gen. Delos E. Emmons, did forestall the mass evacuation of the Hawaiian Japanese, which some highly placed politicians wanted. The incongruity of the decisions about the West Coast Japanese and the Hawaiian Japanese—why evacuate the one and not the other?—can be explained rather simply. The first was a political decision, the second a military one.

REDRESS

What, then, of the future? What are the chances for some kind of meaningful redress? When Congress, at the end of 1980, established the Commission, it charged it with two tasks. First, to inquire whether any wrong was done to Japanese Americans (and later to Aleuts) under the provisions of Executive Order 9066, and second, if it did so find, to make specific recommendations to the Congress as to how redress could be provided for any such wrong. The Commission has, with its February report, *Personal Justice Denied,* fulfilled its first obligation. The report and its conclusions unambiguously establish that wrong was done to both the Japanese American people and the Aleuts. Some have been disappointed that no recommendations for redress were contained in the report and have been critical of this omission. The omission, of course, was deliberate, and I think that the Commission's strategy was both logical and effective. Had the report contained recommendations—especially recommendations involving monetary redress—public attention would have been diverted from the report's historical conclusions and focused on the proposed remedies. It was important that the Commission's conclusions—that the evacuation was not "justified by military necessity," that its root historical causes were "race prejudice, war hysteria, and a failure of political leadership"—be disseminated as widely as possible. With that accomplished, a predicate has been established for the Commission to perform its second task, to make its recommendations to the Congress by June 30, 1983, at which time it is slated to go out of existence.

What will the Commission recommend? Frankly, I do not know. It is always tempting to try to foretell the future, and, perhaps unwisely, it is a temptation that I will yield to tonight. I ought first to establish my bias in the matter. I spoke before the Commission almost two years ago in favor of monetary redress to individuals. This has been a traditional and long-standing method of providing redress for damages since time out of mind. Since the Commission has established, unambiguously, that grievous wrongs were done to both the Aleut and Japanese American peoples, I cannot believe that it will not follow through. I am convinced that some kind of payment to individuals will be

recommended to the Congress. This opinion is not based on hard evidence; it is, rather, an act of faith, although I have, over the past two years, spoken personally to all but one of the commissioners and have some notion of how some of them feel. I will not, here, speculate about amounts and methods of payment. I would hope that the method is made simple and that legal proceedings be avoided whenever possible.

Records exist of who was incarcerated: A flat payment to every such person still alive should be step one in any meaningful redress procedure. Over and above that, it ought to be possible to reopen the whole question of Japanese American and Aleut property claims, and it has often been suggested that, in addition, some kind of foundation for research into race relations should be established.

Some have suggested that real redress will come only in the courts and some ingenious suits have been initiated recently. Without in any way denigrating the merit or the integrity of any such suits, all have what seems to me a fatal weakness: they depend for their success on a creative, liberal approach by the federal judiciary; and, while there are those on the federal bench who are susceptible to innovation, the last word is held by the nine in Washington whose views, as a group, are anything but innovative. To imagine that a court appointed largely by Richard Nixon and Ronald Reagan will rule favorably on such suits is to ignore fourteen years of largely unhappy judicial history.

The Commission's recommendations, then, will have to be enacted by Congress, and will be political. In a sense, this is appropriate. The relocation, as has been shown, was a political decision: it is entirely appropriate that redress from it be political as well. That a recommendation for monetary redress will face certain difficulties in these recessionary times is axiomatic. Any meaningful redress bill will aggregate at least a billion dollars. I will not, here, attempt to rehearse the arguments against such redress.

They are not, I think, compelling. Yet we should not be surprised if redress, once recommended, is not immediately enacted into law. But, despite the recession, despite the political problems involved, positive congressional action on redress is possible. When Congress, in late 1980, created the Commission, its financial implications were clear, and both houses overwhelmingly passed the bill, appropriated money for the Commission to do its work, and, in December 1982, voted it additional funds. Redress is politically possible although it might take more than one Congress.

The arguments for redress are, it seems to me, implicit in the Commission's report. In addition, redress has, I think, great symbolic value, and, we must remember, as Oliver Wendell Holmes, Jr., liked to point out, "we live by symbols." It is one of our most vaunted boasts that an important argument for our system of government is that "democracy corrects its own mistakes." I am not convinced, as a historian, of the universal validity of that adage, but there are times when we can at least try to rebalance the skewed scales of justice. For many of the victims of Executive Order 9066, like James Wakasa, no redress is possible. For the survivors it has been long delayed, and even if Congress acts expeditiously, many more will die before the first payments are made. No redress can wipe out the wrongs of 1942, wrongs exacerbated by more than four decades of neglect. But redress is important, and not just for the survivors. Meaningful monetary redress, more than anything else now possible, will show that the government now realizes that what the late Morton Grodzins once called "the betrayal of all Americans" can no longer be condoned.

Notes

1 Yoshiko Uchida, *Desert Exile: The Uprooting of a Japanese American Family,* (Seattle: University of Washington Press, 1982), 147.
2 Commission on Wartime Relocation and Internment of Civilians, *Personal Justice Denied* (Washington: Government Printing Office, 1982), p. 18.
3 Report of the Special Meeting of the Federal Advisory Council, San Francisco, March 16, 1942, Record Group 210, National Archives. For Dedrick's role, see Roger Daniels, "The Bureau of the Census and the Relocation of the Japanese Americans: A Note and a Document," *Amerasia Journal* 9(1982): 101–105.
4 Raymond Y. Okamura, "The American Concentration Camps: A Cover-Up Through Euphemistic Terminology," *Journal of Ethnic Studies* 10(1982) 3: 95–109.
5 My account is based on a report, "The Wakasa Incident" done contemporaneously by Russell A. Bankston, who was reports officer for WRA at Topaz at the time. It includes copies of a number of documents. It may be found in a collection called "U.S. War Relocation Authority" in the University of Washington Archives, Seattle.
6 McCloy quoted in Transcript of Telephone Conversation, Allen W. Guillion and Mark W. Clark, February 4, 1942, Record Group 389, National Archives.
7 McCloy's testimony, November 3, 1981, qouted in *Personal Justice Denied,* 383–384. McCloy's reaction in *New York Times,* February 25, 1983, and John J. McCloy, "Repay U.S. Japanese," *New York Times,* "Op Ed" page, April 10, 1983.

ANTICOMMUNISM IN HOLLYWOOD

EDITOR'S INTRODUCTION

Historians have yet to offer a satisfactory explanation of why, in the years following World War II, Americans became consumed with a fear of internal communist subversion. By the early 1950s, this "great fear" had reached the point of near hysteria.

Anticommunism in California manifested itself in a variety of ways: the loyalty oath controversy at Berkeley, the activities of the state legislature's "Fact-Finding Committee on Un-American Activities," the rise of extremist organizations such as the John Birch Society, and the use of anticommunism by aspiring politicians. Perhaps the most spectacular recrudescence of anticommunism was the investigation by the House Un-American Activities Committee (HUAC) of subversive influence in the Hollywood film industry.

In 1947 HUAC came to Hollywood "to expose those elements that are insidiously trying to...poison the minds of your children, distort the history of our country, and discredit Christianity."[1] The committee failed to uncover extensive communist influence in the film industry, and eventually even the committee's supporters conceded that the attempt had proved ludicrous. A parade of witnesses was brought before the committee, and when some refused to testify about their political beliefs they were cited for contempt and sent to prison. Industry leaders then launched their own housecleaning campaign and blacklisted dozens of actors, writers, and directors from future employment.

This story, in its broad outline, is generally well known. Most accounts have focused on the violations of civil liberties by the HUAC inquisitors and the damage

---

[1]Quoted in Leon Litwack et al., *The United States: Becoming a World Power* (Englewood Cliffs, N.J., 1982), 726.

done to the careers of those who were blacklisted.[2] The following selection presents the Hollywood story in an entirely new light. Lary May is interested both in the internal history of the film industry and in the larger cultural significance of Hollywood anticommunism.

Lary May explains that during the postwar period Hollywood was divided between two competing visions for America. One was rooted in the tradition of liberal reform and looked for the coming of the "Century of the Common Man" in which the nation's wealth and power would be fundamentally redistributed. Supporters of this vision included many actors and extras who were organized in the Conference of Studio Unions (CSU) and, for a time at least, in the Screen Actors' Guild (SAG). They were antimonopolists who believed in militant action, including strikes when necessary, to achieve their goals. The other vision was for an "American Century" in which labor and management worked in harmony for the expansion of capitalist production and abundance for all. This more conservative ideal found support among industry leaders and such organizations as the International Alliance of Theatrical Employees (IA) and the Motion Picture Industry Council (MPIC).

May demonstrates that the more conservative forces within Hollywood used anticommunism to destroy their opponents in this ideological dispute. With the arrival of HUAC and the blacklisting campaign, the liberal antimonopolists in the CSU and SAG were discredited as subversive and un-American by the IA and MPIC. Through the efforts of conservative actors such as Ronald Reagan, the SAG was transformed into a bastion of anticommunism.

The larger cultural significance of the victory of anticommunism in Hollywood soon became apparent. Reagan and others promulgated a *Screen Guide for Americans* in which the American Century ideology was stated unequivocally. Films produced in conformity with this "guide" reflected a benevolent corporate consensus in which the virtues of private ownership and production were extolled. The focus was not on issues of social justice but on the private world of consumption. A revitalized home and family, comfortably ensconced in suburbia, was the prescribed antidote to communism. Films and television series reinforced the message in countless ways.

Lary May, an Associate Professor in the Program of American Studies at the University of Minnesota, received his Ph.D. from the University of California, Los Angeles, in 1977. He is the author of *Screening Out the Past: The Birth of Mass Culture and the Motion Picture Industry* (1983).

---

[2]See Carey McWilliams, *Witch Hunt: The Revival of Heresy* (Boston, 1950), 67–81; and Victor S. Navasky, *Naming Names* (New York, 1980).

READING 25

Anticommunism in Hollywood

Lary May

Coming out of the cage of the Army...a series of hard nosed happenings began to change my whole view of American dangers. Most of them tied in directly with my own bailiwick of acting....From being an active (though unconscious) partisan in what now and then turned out to be communist causes, I little by little became disillusioned or perhaps, in my case, I should say reawakened.

Ronald Reagan, former president of the Screen Actors' Guild, 1960.

Really and truly, the triumph of McCarthyism was, in effect, the cutting off of a generalized social movement that began before the war....The picking on the Hollywood people...received a lot of attention because everybody knew who the stars were. What I'm trying to say is that you're not dealing with an isolated event, but the focus of such a national event as it happened in Hollywood.[1]

Abraham Polansky, blacklisted film director, 1970.

Shortly after World War II a remarkable article appeared on the front page of the Screen Actors' Guild magazine, suggesting that a struggle over national identity was at the center of the anti-communist crusade in postwar Hollywood. Written by Eric Johnston, the former head of the U.S. Chamber of Commerce and recently appointed president of the Motion Picture Producers Association, the article was titled "Utopia is Production." Like a Puritan minister, Johnston preached that in the new world Americans had created a unique democracy, free of European exploitation and conflicts. The rise of the corporations at the turn of the century, however, had aroused fears that the frontier was gone. Then, during the Great Depression New Deal politicians had generated the "nightmare" of "class rhetoric." In this weakened condition, the nation was attacked by foreign enemies. Yet, Johnston argued, it was the wartime cooperation of labor and capital that had given birth to a new capi-

talism which would restore the American tradition of peace and prosperity. Johnston believed that Hollywood had a great role to play in this work of rebirth and restoration. "It is no exaggeration," he explained, "to say that the modern picture industry sets the styles for half the world. There is not one of us who isn't aware that the motion picture is the most powerful medium for the influencing of people that man has ever built....We can set new styles of living and the doctrine of production must be made completely popular...."[2]

Johnston's words were not mere platitudes. His views are representative of a group of businessmen and politicians who endorsed Henry Luce's vision of an "American Century." Johnston had argued in earlier books like *America Unlimited* (1943) that the war had accomplished what the "class rhetoric" of New Deal politicians had failed to do. It had produced class collaboration, prosperity, and the military power to protect the country. Looking to escape wars and depressions in the future, he called on businessmen and unions to cooperate, affirm the welfare state, and construct an international order grounded in free trade and hos-

Adapted from "Recasting America: Hollywood, the Screen Actors' Guild, and the Making of Cold War Culture," by Lary May, in the forthcoming *Promise and Peril: Explorations in Postwar American Culture,* edited by Lary May. Copyright © 1988 by The University of Chicago.

tility to the Soviet Union. Johnston's calls, however, occurred at a time when the most militant strike wave in history was erupting in the film capital and across the country. Particularly in Hollywood, the strikers' militancy was fueled by former Vice President Henry Wallace's calls for a "Century of the Common Man" in which the nation's wealth and power would be redistributed and the wartime cooperation with the Soviet Union would continue. Given Johnston's business interests, it was not surprising that he would try to convince Hollywood's film stars to side with the producers against the strikers. Yet given our knowledge of the era, it is surprising that Johnston should envisage their aid as part of a larger strategy to transform postwar politics and popular culture.[3]

Johnston's views are important because they point toward a twofold corrective of our understanding of the events known as the Hollywood Red Scare. First, they suggest that the events in Hollywood were not an isolated or irrational episode but had deep affinities with events occurring across the country. Secondly, they suggest that the struggle in the film capital revolved around control of the symbols and values carried by the mass media and popular culture. To this writer, they provide a framework for answering some of the major questions concerning America after 1945. Anticommunist politics had arisen periodically throughout modern American history, especially after World War I, but previous Red Scares had failed to influence established institutions or have lasting appeal. Nor had they focused on the film industry. Why was the situation just the reverse after 1945?

A QUEST FOR IDENTITY

By the advent of World War II, Hollywood, the stars and industry unions were at the very center of a new quest to find an American identity appropriate for the twentieth century.

The Screen Actors' Guild (SAG) in the New Deal era had drawn upon the élan of popular culture to legitimize urban consumption, ethnicity, actors, and unions as the core of a new and better nation. At the same time, the Guild saw the promise of this new America being realized through an unprecedented alliance of the middle and working classes centered in New Deal reform and an insurgent union movement dedicated to antimonopoly. In many ways this combination of class conflict and cultural reform gained enormous publicity not just because of the stars' involvement, but because it served to make radical reform perhaps more visible in Hollywood than in any industry in the country.

Ironically, however, the cultural side of that promise was not to be realized through New Deal reform but through the ambiguous legacy of World War II. With the coming of the war, the film industry was mobilized into a wartime state. The most popular productions of the war—such as *This Is the Army* featuring the current and future presidents of the Guild, George Murphy and Ronald Reagan—celebrated a rejuvenated America grounded in consumption, ethnicity, and racial harmony. Consistent with the merger of the star's image to real life, Guild members enlisted in the armed services, held premieres that boosted war morale, and toured on bond drives.[4]

Yet at the same time, the politics of domestic mobilization began to alter the reformist legacy of the Guild. That process unfolded as the Guild and other labor leaders joined war industry boards and cooperated with business in enforcing wage and price guidelines. But as labor thus received legitimacy through the apolitical process of defense mobilization, a number of unionists defied their leaders and went out on wildcat strikes. In Hollywood these disruptions occurred as the extras—the unskilled and lower class of the actor's profession—demanded a renegotiation of their contract to raise frozen wages. When Guild leaders refused their demands the extras seceded from the Guild and received a charter from the Conference of Studio Unions (CSU). The CSU, led by an ex-boxer named Herbert Sorrell, was an organization of the industry's unskilled laborers, craftsmen, and white-collar office workers. Experiencing the shattering of the alliance between the workers and middle class in their own union, the Guild's Board of Directors dismissed hundreds of "incorrigibles" and organized their own loyal extras' group. Meanwhile, the Guild's chief consul, Kenneth Thomson, almost got into a fist fight with the dissidents' leader in court, and wrote a report that the insurgents were a "Frankenstein monster" which could "destroy" us.[5]

The monster, of course, did not destroy the Guild. But disruption from below did force the leaders into a new collaboration with business and their allies. Indeed, as mass strikes occurred across the country after 1945, the Board secured a union charter for its newly formed extras' group from the International Alliance of Theatrical Stage Employees (IA). Shortly thereafter, the IA president Roy Brewer and a delegation of studio leaders asked the Guild to support a lock-out of the CSU. The minutes of that secret meeting show that despite the unwillingness of a vocal minority to align with their former enemies, the Board members found that it would be "hard to refuse" in light of their "unsolicited support in the extras dispute." Though collusion between the three organizations was denied by the Guild in a congressional investigation, the results were that SAG aligned with the studios, Sorrell's members were locked out of the studios, and the actors and actresses crossed the picket lines. Over the next few months, the strikers initiated a national boycott of the stars' films and began to mobilize behind Henry Wallace's call for a "Century of the Common Man," symbolizing the unraveling of an alliance that had lasted for over a decade.[6]

By 1945 the new head of the motion picture producers association was the former President of the U.S. Chamber of Commerce, Eric Johnston. Johnston's nationalist ideology was dramatically different from the one carried by Hollywood unions and the Guilds in the New Deal era. In his anticommunism and desire for a cooperative capitalism, Johnston, of course, was not much different from earlier corporate leaders who had opposed the Guild in the Depression. Yet Johnston represented the rise of corporate leaders who saw that the consumerism unfolding in World War II had created binding ties between the immigrants and old stock Americans. To realize that unity in the future, Johnston saw that Americans had to not only eliminate poverty, but to purge political life of ideologies hostile to capitalism, ideas he equated with the "foreign" ideas of Marxism. As he observed,

> The real breeding ground of communism is in the slums. It is everywhere where people have not enough to eat or enough to wear through no fault of their own. Communism hunts misery, feeds on misery and profits by it. Freedoms walk hand in hand with abundance. That has been the history of America. It has been the American story. It turned the eyes of the world to America, because America gave reality to freedom, plus abundance when it was an idle daydream in the rest of the world.[7]

This brand of anticommunism was far from being just doctrine. It was a reformist ideology that promised to realize a final stage of the American identity pioneered by Hollywood and the Guilds over the past decade and a half. Rejecting the older antimonopoly tradition as foreign and communistic, Hollywood would now become a model of "democratic capitalism" rooted in abundance. Nowhere was the impact of that promise better illustrated than in the rise of Ronald Reagan to undisputed leadership of SAG in 1947. Like most of the Guild membership making the transition from the depression to the war years, Reagan was a New Dealer. He had inherited his loyalty to the New Deal from his father, a small businessman and Midwest Irish Catholic who was destroyed by the Depression. Coming to the film capital, Reagan performed in the most pro-Roosevelt of all the studios, Warner Brothers, and worked to advance the acceptance of the new peoples and culture advanced by the Guild. As late as 1945, Reagan could be found in organizations supporting an insurgent New Deal tradition, militant labor, and the CSU.

Ronald Reagan, however, was also different than the founding generation. His arrival in Hollywood in 1937 meant that he missed the great organizing drives of the thirties; indeed, he joined only after the Guild's closed shop agreements made it virtually mandatory. Nor did he rise to leadership by mobilizing mass support of the membership. Rather, he was appointed to the Board and later the Presidency where he ran unopposed through the early fifties. Deeply concerned with security and high level consumption—he had eight insurance policies, two Cadillacs, and a horse stable when he divorced his wife in the late forties—he saw the vision of a modern, affluent America realized less in the union struggles of the thirties than in the economic expansion spurred by the war years. The advent of the war saw him volunteering as an Army officer and dramatizing the dream of a rejuvenated middle class culture in *This is the Army*. Then, as the extras conflict erupted and Eric Johnston preached a new American Century, Reagan became an undercover agent for the FBI. He dropped his involvement in progressive groups or "communist fronts," seeing them as tools of the enemy. "I learned my lesson, the bulk of communist work is done by people who are sucked into carrying out red policy without knowing what they are doing."[8]

Anticommunism became, for Ronald Reagan, part of a struggle to "bring about the regeneration of the world I believed should have automatically appeared following the war." Seeing the CSU and their Guild supporters as thwarting the American promise, he first served on a commission to arbitrate the conflict between Sorrell, the IA, and the producers, and ended up giving a major speech persuading Guild members to cross CSU picket lines. Shortly thereafter, when the extras legitimately complained that the Board was dominated by actors who had become producers, the top leadership resigned and Reagan was appointed to the presidency. In that vacuum, Reagan, as Jack Dales recalled, not only "disliked the extras tremendously," but began to see "his own people" as "...pro-Russian Americans." Soon the Board labelled CSU supporters in the Guild as "foreign dictators" who would "enslave people," and altered the Guild's democratic procedures to limit their power, with the result that the Guild became much more bureaucratic and centralized.[9]

THE TRIUMPH OF ANTICOMMUNISM

By no means did this reorientation of democracy stay isolated to Hollywood. As the Cold War began to unfold between the United States and the Soviet Union, and domestic and anticommunist investigations started inside and outside the Truman administration, the House Un-American Activities Committee (HUAC) came to Hollywood in 1947–48 to investigate subversion in the film industry. Unlike the earlier Red Scare after World War I, Hollywood received such attention because popular culture had become identified with a new nationalism and political style. And unlike the earlier Dies Committee hearings on communism in Hollywood during the thirties, most producers and the Guilds now actively cooperated with the investigators. Soon Communist Party members known as the Hollywood Ten were discovered and sent to jail. At a time when the Soviet Union was hostile to both the United States and capitalism, the antimonopoly tradition that had justified Guild and CSU militancy was now associated with treason. As Eric Johnston pointed out, such ideas were "foreign" to "American Civilization" and its adherents were at best potential traitors or, at worst, irrational "crackpots" under the influence of a "delusion."[10]

Given that the anticommunists sought to discredit an antimonopoly ideology that had sustained national identity for over a century, the hearings also served as a large scale drama for converting Hollywood, and by implication their audiences, to a new American Way. In order to publicize that ideological transformation, the Hollywood reformers demanded that their former adversaries provide them with confessions to be widely publicized in the national press. A prime example was the noted director Edward Dymtryck's interview for the *Saturday Evening Post*. On the first page was a photo of Dymtryck holding a newspaper with the headline, "Trial Board Convicts Sorrell." As the story unfolds, the author told of being discriminated against because of his immigrant roots. In response he joined progressive causes which equated Americanism with hostility to monopoly, supported the CSU, and then joined the Communist Party in World War II. After the beginning of the Cold War, however, he realized that abundance and racial acceptance would only come through affirming the true national heritage of class cooperation and economic growth.[11]

Once this conversion process began, there could be no end to it. After all, the members of HUAC represented an older middle class that saw the entire Hollywood labor movement as morally suspect. Disliking the moral experimentation, the new peoples and unionization, they and their allies could accuse even the most loyal. Industry leaders, seeking to legitimize a new corporate hegemony, set up clearing agencies to prove that participants in the modern culture were purged of their former beliefs and associations. A telling example of this process is revealed in a letter received by the Guild from an executive at Columbia Studios in January of 1953. Written in response to a complaint by Nancy Davis, the executive apologized to the new Mrs. Ronald Reagan. Unfortunately she had been denied work because she had the same maiden name as a woman who had signed a petition supporting free speech for the Hollywood Ten. The executive explained that "as you are aware we make a check on all actors, writers, directors being considered for employment. This is a regular routine. This investigation is made by a reputable organization in New York City." Despite the fact that a mistake had been made, "I question whether your criticism of the organization that checks for us is justified. Of course we could have taken it for granted that the wife of Ronald Reagan could not be of questionable loyalty, and we could have disregarded the report." Although Nancy Reagan could prove her innocence, others were not so lucky. As the executive secretary of the Guild, Jack Dales recalled years later,

> What I have debated about since is that so many people were tarred by that brush who I don't think should have been now.... Even at the time, I'm saying my doubts came to the fore. I was not Ronnie Reagan or Roy Brewer.... I would argue about how far we were going, particularly when it got to be this clearing depot, you know, for work. I think of people who were terribly, unfairly treated like Larry Parks, Marsha Hunt, who had viewpoints that were different from the majority of the Board members, but they were far from communist agents.... They were just strong liberal people who took their lumps...the producers carried it to ridiculous extremes and we did not stand up fairly to call a fair line. A line should have been called....[12]

A line was so difficult to draw, however, because the crusaders were not just transforming politics and ideology. Rather they sought to convert the biggest prize of all—a popular culture which so many artists had identified with their personal lives. Wherever he went, for example, Eric Johnston minced no words in explaining that since films were now an agent of foreign policy, democracy and capitalism were no longer at odds, but at one with the national identity. To insure that result, Johnston, Roy Brewer and Reagan distributed a new film code written by Ayn Rand. A *Screen Guide for Americans* preached "Don't Smear the Free Enterprise System" "Don't Deify the Common Man" "Don't show that poverty is a virtue...and failure is noble." The "nobility" of the "little people" was now labelled the "drooling of weaklings." Consequently a dramatist of the little people's hostility to monopoly, like director Frank Capra, would find his security clearance taken away. Likewise, a writer whose work for years had featured American heroes whose "fortune and happiness were threatened by a banker holding a mortgage over their heads," suddenly found these themes unmarketable.[13]

Similar pressures unfolded to alter the stars' image. "We've got to resolve any conflicts," an actor remarked in 1948, "between what we are and what the public has been led to believe we are. We can't afford to have people think we're a band of strong men or crusaders." No longer did the Guild leadership use antimonopoly rhetoric, hold vast parades supporting labor insurgency, publish ads calling for boycotts, condemn anticommunist attacks, or mobilize the members in vast public gatherings. In contrast, the Guild leaders now funded industry-wide organizations to dramatize the collaboration between labor and capital, gave highly visible loyalty oaths, and produced Cold War propaganda films. Commenting on this transformation, a reporter found that "many stars are worried that the public might have received a very wrong impression about them, because of having seen them portray, say, a legendary hero who stole from the rich to give to the poor, or an honest, crusading district attorney, or a lonely, poetic, antisocial gangster."

The Guild nourished this trend by turning much of the stars' élan away from public issues and toward private life. A striking example was a series of standardized speeches produced by the Guild. These speeches emphasized the stars as models of the family life unfolding in the suburbs. As such, their charisma, their glamour, or ethnic roots and lower class manners still represented a break from the stuffy styles of Victorianism. But their vernacular or common touch was no longer a vital ideal to question established institutions and values. Rather, their democratic personalities reinvigorated a benevolent corporate consensus which found its fruits in consumer-oriented home and children. Listening to Ronald Reagan describe the new imagery, a reporter from his hometown newspaper recorded that "Dutch gave a stirring defense of his new hometown, Hollywood. He compared it with other cities in America and pointed out that it leads the nation in church attendance on a per capita basis; that its schools are among the best in the nation; that the divorce rate in Hollywood is far below the national average....He explained that it was only a few years ago that some churches wouldn't even bury an actor. That attitude he explained has changed today, because the film actors, unlike the thespians of old, now settle in one place, build homes, raise their children, attend school and churches and become part of the community. 'You certainly couldn't expect an actor to live out of a trunk to do that.'"[14]

Yet this transformation may well have killed the goose that laid the golden egg. In striking contrast to the thirties and war years, producers in 1948 found that box office receipts fell dramatically, and that membership in the Guild dropped from 7,898 in 1946 to 6,533 in 1949. Part of the erosion was due to the baby boom and the rise of television. But the family revival started as early as 1941, and it was not until 1950 that even 10 percent of American families had televisions. A more plausible explanation was that anticommunism served to diminish the appeal of mass culture and its linkage to free social space, outside power and authority. The Hollywood reformers blacklisted writers and actors, pressured film makers to alter plots, and prevented the distribution of "undesirable" films such as *Salt of the Earth*. They also attacked major box office attractions like John Garfield and Charlie Chaplin who refused to cross CSU picket lines and supported Henry Wallace in the Progressive campaign of 1948. As the Progressives were defeated and the Cold War continued to unfold at home and abroad, Garfield and Chaplin were investigated by the FBI and the IA boycotted Chaplin's films. Indeed, shortly before the great clown left the country to avoid appearing before HUAC, Roy Brewer of the IA justified these actions because, "Mr. Chaplin has shown nothing but contempt for America and her institutions. His most recent statements that Hollywood has succumbed to thought control, so far as I am concerned, confirm the fact that his thinking is still in the communist orbit of influence. This is strictly Party line....Nothing he has said or done would justify our assuming that he is on our side in this fight. Until we get such assurances, we are justified in resisting any further efforts to add to his fortune or influence."[16]

CONCLUSION

Today, of course, America's lovable tramp lies buried in Europe, and the Guild leader has become President of the United States, recently appointing the IA leader Roy Brewer to a high post in the Labor Department. Given that Hollywood gave Reagan and Brewer their political baptism, what consequences can we draw from these events? By now it should be clear that Hollywood was at the center of a struggle to determine political ideology and culture in postwar America. The industry attracted such attention because the stars were living examples of the contest between an older producer culture and a new identity rooted in affluence and city life.

When that consumer promise collapsed in the Depression, the stars aligned with workers in a radical labor movement dedicated to redistributing wealth and power. Drawing on their personification of mass culture, and reconstructing an older republican tradition hostile to capitalism, the Guild leaders created a New Deal politics intent on realizing a modern nationalism rooted in the welfare state, ethnicity, and consumption. The apolitical process of defense mobilization in World War II brought the cultural side of that promise to fulfillment, while wildcat strikes within the Guild brought the leadership into a closer relationship with big business.

Given these altered political conditions, elitists like Eric Johnston sought to reshuffle the symbols and values associated with the new Americanism. Seeking to create an unprecedented national consensus, Johnston worked to transform a democratic ideology hostile to monopoly and to generate support for economic and military expansion abroad. As the Cold War began and as the HUAC hearings served to discredit militant labor unions, the stars personified a new liberalism where labor and ethnic Americans were legitimized. Equality, however, was found now less in the work place than in a privatized consumer realm, centered in the home and children. Small wonder that when the economic growth and consensus faltered in the late sixties and seventies, Ronald Reagan should leave the film capital to save the "democratic capitalism" he helped to create. A reporter interviewing him during his successful run for the Presidency in 1980 found that postwar Hollywood was still very much on his mind:

> Reagan, with no prompting from me, in what seems in fact to be a compulsive non sequitur, had resurrected events that took place some thirty years earlier, his wounds still raw and his hatred of the enemy unyielding. Most curious of all is that his view of the Soviet menace today is so deeply colored by events that took place in Hollywood more than a generation ago, as if today's

Soviet government were simply the Hollywood communists projected on a larger screen.

Frank testimony, indeed, that the contest unfolding in postwar Hollywood continues to influence our lives.[17]

Notes

1 Ronald Reagan and Richard C. Hubler, *Where's the Rest of Me* (New York: Dell Publishing, 1981), 162–164, 189. Abraham Polansky, "How The Blacklist Worked in Hollywood," *Film Culture,* 50–51 (Fall 1970), 44.

2 Eric Johnston, "Utopia is Production," *Screen Actor,* 14(April 1946), 7, and (August 1946), 14–15. For a full exposition of these ideas, see Eric Johnston, *America Unlimited* (Garden City, New Jersey: 1942); and Karl Schriftgiesser, *Business Comes of Age: The Story of the Committee for Economic Development and Its Impact upon the Economic Policies of the United States, 1942–1960* (New York: Harper & Brothers, 1960), 13, 23, 73–75.

3 On postwar strikes, see George Lipsitz, *Class and Culture in Cold War America: A Rainbow at Midnight,* (New York: Praeger, 1983); Anthony Dawson, "Hollywood's Labor Troubles," *Industrial Labor Relations Review,* 1(July, 1948), 638–647; *Life,* (October 14, 1946), 29–33. The most influential account of Depression culture can be found in Warren Susman, *Culture as History: The Transformation of American Society in the 20th Century* (New York: Pantheon, 1984), 150–211. For a survey of the scholarship on the Hollywood Red Scare, and a welcome corrective to the traditional view, see Thom Andersen, "Red Hollywood," in Suzanne Ferguson and Barbara Groseclose, eds., *Literature and the Visual Arts in Contemporary Society* (Columbus, Ohio: Ohio State University Press, 1986), 141–196.

4 On the wartime culture, see John Morton Blum, *V Was for Victory: Politics and Culture During World War II* (New York: Harcourt Brace Jovanovich, 1979), 31–54, 90–17. *This is the Army* file, Museum of Modern Art Film Library, New York City, New York. See "Radio," *Screen Actor* (July, 1942), 4 (hereafter known as *SA*); "Mobilization," *SA* (June, 1943), 4; "Homecoming" *SA*

(January, 1944); "Marching Men," *SA* (June, 1942), 13; "SAG Cited by Army and Navy," *SA* (April, 1946), 4; and James Cagney, "Spirit of '42," *SA* (June, 1942), 9.

5 On Sorrell's wartime strikes, see testimony of Herbert Sorrell, Hearings Before a Special Committee on Education and Labor, House of Representatives, *Jurisdictional Disputes in the Motion Picture Industry,* 80th Cong. 1st Sess., 1233 (hereafter known as *Jurisdictional Disputes*). For the extras controversy, see Minutes of the Board of Directors, December 30, 1943; January 5, 1943; February 21, 1943; March 1, 1943; April 12, 1943; May 24, 1943, 2355; and Dec. 18, 1944, 2074; October 17, 1945, Screen Actors' Guild, Los Angeles, California (hereafter referred to as Minutes). The Guild executive secretary explained in reference to the extras, "there was a quite understandable feeling that we had our heads in the sand, that we really did not understand their problems...and we viewed them as a bunch of malcontents who really didn't have a stake in the business." See Jack Dales, SAG Oral History Interview, 1979, SAG; Herbert Sorrell, "You Don't Choose Your Friends: The Memoirs of Herbert Knott Sorrell," UCLA Oral History Project, 1963, Special Collections, UCLA, 70–77; Kenneth Thompson, "Report on Extras," Minutes, March 14, 1943.

6 As late as 1945 the Guild supported Sorrell; see Minutes, October 16, 1945, 2884–2892, 2915. But the Minutes, August 20, 1945, 2853–2854, show that after the producers and the IA leaders asked for cooperation against the CSU, the Board "found itself in a position of being unable to refuse...because of the unsolicited, militant support which the IA has given" their extras' union. Then the Minutes of February 18, 1946, state that the IA will give replacements for CSU jobs, (but not "if not have the support of the Guild.") Afterwards, the new Guild President, Ronald Reagan told congressional investigators, that the "charge of conspiracy and collusion between the producers and the IA" was "groundless" and "ridiculous." See Ronald Reagan to Honorable Ralph W. Gwinn, March 2, 1948, SAG Files. *CSU News,* June–August 1946, Hollywood Strike, folder 226, University of California at Los Angeles Special Collections (hereafter known as

Strike Folder) documents that for the pickets, the "actors seem to be a special object of their wrath." For the CSU and Wallace, see *CSU News,* May 24, 1947; *California Progressive Citizen,* January, 1948 in Hollywood Strike File, 226.

7 On earlier anti-communist traditions, see John Higham, *Strangers In The Land: Patterns of American Nativism, 1860–1925* (New York: Atheneum, 1971), 194–234. For the larger context of the new corporate hegemony, see Charles Maier, "The Politics of Productivity," *International Organization,* 31, no. 4(1977), 607–632. In reference to Johnston, the CSU Bulletin observed that "The boss and labor are lovers in Eric Johnston's code. But the boss gets all the kisses while the working stiff gets fired," Hollywood Strike Folder. On postwar Americanism, see Eric Johnston, *American Unlimited,* 34–60; *We're All In It* (New York: E. P. Dutton, 1948), 1–60. The Johnston quote is from "Jurisdictional Disputes," 1342. Similar expressions are in Eric Johnston, testimony, House Committee on Un-American Activities, *Hearings Regarding the Communist Infiltration of the Motion Picture Industry,* 80th Congress, 1st sess., 1947, 305–310 (hereafter known as *HUAC 1947*).

8 *Reagan versus Reagan,* Superior Court of the State of California, Los Angeles County Archives, Los Angeles, California, Case No. D360058. Testimony of Roy Brewer, Committee on Un-American Activities, House of Representatives, 82nd Congress, 1st sess., 1951, 517 (hereafter known as *HUAC 1951*). Reagan and Hubler, *Where's the Rest of Me,* 1–65, 147–230; Garry Wills, *Reagan's America: Innocents at Home* (New York: Doubleday, 1987), 247–250. Quote is from "Ronald Reagan Testifies He Didn't Know Jeffers," *Los Angeles Times,* unpaginated, undated clipping, probably January, 1951, in Ronald Reagan File, *Los Angeles Times.*

9 Reagan and Hubler, *Where's the Rest of Me,* 160–161. Dales, "SAG Oral History Project," 38; Dales, "UCLA Oral History," 34, 51. Minutes, Annual Meeting, October 2, 1946, 3092, "Special Membership Meeting," *SA* (January, 1947), 4–12. *Screen Actors' Guild Intelligence Report,* May 15, and June 16, 1947. The result was that petitions no longer could come from the floor at annual meetings; more class "A" members had to sign petitions for a meeting; no alternative recommendations to the Board were allowed on the ballots; and secret ballots, rather than public debate, determined decisions. Further, the Board also cut off the efforts of civil rights groups to pressure the producers to alter the "Sambo" type roles given to Negro actors. See Minutes, May 24, 1943 and October 20, 1947.

10 See note 3 for a survey of the literature on the Hollywood HUAC hearings. Testimony of Herbert Sorrell, "Jurisdictional Disputes," 1892. Johnston, *America Unlimited,* 152–160.

11 Richard English, "What Makes a Hollywood Communist?" *Saturday Evening Post* (May 19, 1951), 30–31, 147–148. This conversionary side of the hearings has been overlooked in previous scholarly investigations.

12 Wills, *Reagan's America,* 251–261. B. B. Kahane to Mrs. Ronald Reagan, January 7, 1953. Jack Dales, "SAG Oral History, 1979," 12–13, SAG Files.

13 For films and foreign policy imagery, see testimony of Eric Johnston, *HUAC 1947,* 305–310. Eric Johnston, *The Hollywood Hearings* (Washington, D.C.: Motion Picture Producers' Association, 1948), 1–10. *Screen Guide for Americans,* (Beverly Hills, California: Motion Picture Alliance for the Preservation of American Ideals, 1948), 1–12. Lillian Ross, "Onward and Upward With the Arts," *The New Yorker* (February 21, 1948), 32–48. Frank Capra, *The Name Above the Title: An Autobiography,* (New York: Random House, 1971), 425–430.

14 The absence of public activities is based on a survey of the *Intelligence Report,* the journal which replaced *Screen Actor* after 1946. Eric Johnston, "Motion Picture Industry Council," *New York Daily News,* unpaginated, undated article, 1948 in MPIC File, Academy of Motion Picture Arts and Sciences Library, Los Angeles, California (hereafter known as MPIC). For loyalty oaths see SAG press release, April 10, 1951; Board of Directors to Miss Gale Sondergaard, 20 March 1951: "Speakers Kit," probably designed in 1950; Ronald Reagan, "Special Editorial to the *Hartford Times,*" October 8, 1951, SAG Files. The quote is from Dixon *Evening Telegraph,* August 22, 1950, as in Wills, *Reagans' America,* 144.

15 See Michael Conant, *Anti-Trust in the Motion Picture Industry* (Berkeley, California: University of California Press, 1960), Table 1, 4, 6; and *Historical Statistics of the United States,* Part 2, 796. On the unprecedented decline in Guild membership see *Intelligence Report* (July 22, 1949), SAG Files. Herbert Biberman *Salt of the Earth* (Boston: Beacon Press, 1965); and *Salt of the Earth File,* SAG Files. For other examples, see "Film Council Asks Ban on Import of Red Movies," *Los Angeles Times,* August 26, 1952.

16 For Garfield, see Andersen, "Red Hollywood," 177–191. Stories and pictures of Chaplin supporting the CSU, see *CSU News,* May 24, 1947. On the CSU and Wallace campaign see *CSU News,* May 24, 1947, and *Hollywood Citizen,* January, 1948; *California Progressive,* June–January 1948 in Hollywood Strike File, 226, "Roy Brewer Blasts Lessing for Branding IA 'Selfish', Takes New Jab at Chaplin," *Variety,* 1952, unpaginated or dated clipping in MPIC.

17 Robert Scheer, *With Enough Shovels: Reagan, Bush and Nuclear War* (New York: Random House, 1982), 42–43. See also Bernard Weintraub, "Reagan's Early Encounters With the Left Seem to Key His Drive to Aid the Contras," *New York Times,* March 17, 1986.

THE BERKELEY FREE SPEECH
MOVEMENT

EDITOR'S INTRODUCTION

Events on the Berkeley campus of the University of California during the fall of 1964 signaled the beginning of a student movement which swept the nation in the following decade. Students at Berkeley challenged the power of the university administration and scored an impressive victory for the right of free speech. The Berkeley Free Speech Movement (FSM) provoked an impassioned national debate on higher education, student rights, and academic freedom. It also contributed to a political backlash. Conservative political candidates campaigned and were elected to high office, promising to clean up the "mess at Berkeley" and to crack down on student activists.

The events at Berkeley were perceived at the time as revolutionary. The chancellor of the Berkeley campus, Edward W. Strong, complained that "The legitimate authority of the university is being challenged and attacked in a revolutionary way." Likewise, Governor Edmund G. "Pat" Brown, who later would be severely criticized by Ronald Reagan for his handling of the crisis, warned: "We cannot compromise with revolution, whether at the University or any other place." *Life* magazine styled the student movement a "rebellion in search of a cause" and wondered whether it might result in "a genuine insurrection against society as now organized."[1]

The Berkeley FSM was viewed in such extreme terms largely because the American public had so long been accustomed to student apathy. The student movement of the 1960s came on the heels of the "silent generation" of the 1950s. Student activism and radical politics had been commonplace on college campuses in the depression, but during the war years and during the anticommunist era of the 1950s student political activity had virtually disappeared.

[1] All quotes are from Hal Draper, *Berkeley: The New Student Revolt* (New York, 1965), frontispiece and back cover.

As Lary May explained in the previous selection, the triumph of anticommunism in Hollywood was part of an effort to create in the popular culture a new, more conservative national identity. Conforming to the *Screen Guide for Americans,* endorsed by Ronald Reagan and the Screen Actors' Guild, countless Hollywood films and television programs reinforced consumerism and other middle-class values in a privatized world of home and family. Political issues and causes were out of place in the domestic world of "Ozzie and Harriet," "The Donna Reed Show," and "Father Knows Best." It was precisely that world of complacency and conformity that was crumbling in the tumult of the 1960s. Again, as Lary May has noted, it was most appropriate that Ronald Reagan would emerge from Hollywood as the leader of the forces of conservatism which were attempting to shore up that idealized world now under attack. Reagan, of course, was the prime beneficiary of the conservative backlash which followed the events at Berkeley.

The specific issue which underlay the FSM was the drive for equal rights for blacks. During the early 1960s, racial segregation and discrimination in the south were challenged by civil rights workers from throughout the country. Students from Berkeley were heavily involved in the civil rights movement, and as the university attempted to ban their activities the FSM was born. "Last summer I went to Mississippi to join the struggle there for civil rights," FSM leader Mario Savio observed in 1964. "This fall I am engaged in another phase of the same struggle, this time in Berkeley. The two battlefields may seem quite different to some observers, but this is not the case. The same rights are at stake in both places—the right to participate as citizens in democratic society and the right to due process of law."[2] The triumph of the FSM thus was not just a victory for free speech but for the civil rights movement as well.

The following selection by W. J. Rorabaugh is from a larger work in progress, a history of Berkeley in the 1960s. W. J. Rorabaugh received his Ph.D. from the University of California, Berkeley, in 1976 and is the author of *The Alcoholic Republic* (1979) and *The Craft Apprentice* (1986). He currently is a Professor of History at the University of Washington.

---

[2]Mario Savio, ''An End to History,'' in Michael V. Miller and Susan Gilmore, eds., *Revolution in Berkeley: the Crisis in American Education* (New York, 1965), 239.

READING 26

The Berkeley Free Speech Movement

W. J. Rorabaugh

In September 1964 the administration of the University of California at Berkeley suddenly banned political activists from passing out literature, soliciting funds, or organizing support at the edge of campus. This ban led the activists, largely civil rights workers, to attack the new rules and, following the administration's reprisals, to demand that all sorts of political activity be permitted throughout the campus. The activist students called themselves the Free Speech Movement (FSM). They rallied wide student support and, after the largest sit-in and mass arrest in California history, gathered overwhelming faculty support. In December the FSM triumphed. It was to be the greatest success of the student movement during the 1960s.[1]

To understand what had happened, it is necessary to go back to 1930, when California and its university faced bankruptcy, and the University's Regents desperately sought a new president. They appointed Robert Gordon Sproul, an accountant who solved the crisis without dismissing any tenured faculty. By the time he retired in 1958, Sproul had built a great university; the crown jewel campus at Berkeley boasted the world's largest number of Nobel laureates on a single campus. His one failure came in 1950, when he persuaded the Regents to require the faculty to take an anti-communist loyalty oath. The faculty protested and the ensuing controversy revealed factionalism inside the Board of Regents, showed that Sproul had lost touch with the Berkeley faculty, and led the president to insulate himself from the Berkeley campus.[2]

In 1952, trying to recover from the debacle, Sproul created the position of chancellor at Berkeley and named Prof. Clark Kerr to the post. The two were a study in contrasts. Sproul was large-bodied, loud-mouthed, ebullient, dynamic, forceful, and even physically intimidating; Kerr was quiet, cordial, cerebral, cold, and a master of detail. More to the point, Kerr had been one of the faculty leaders opposing the loyalty oath. The main reason for Kerr's appointment as chancellor was his standing with the Berkeley faculty. The professor of industrial relations had shown his ability to see all sides and to forge coalitions and compromises. Kerr, however, found the chancellorship frustrating. He saw that Sproul intended to give the post little real power, which remained with Sproul and the president's bureaucracy. Kerr and the chancellor's bureaucracy were mainly intended to protect Sproul from danger.[3]

After Sproul retired in 1958, Kerr became president. Chosen over the objections of Sproul but with support from former Gov. Earl Warren, Kerr got the presidency partly because the Regents, still divided from the loyalty oath battle, did not want to offend the prestigious Berkeley faculty, who strongly backed Kerr. The new president had both strengths and weaknesses. One of the most brilliant men in American higher education, he developed California's Master Plan, which divided responsibilities among the University, the emerging state university system, and community colleges. The Master Plan provided for orderly management of rapid growth just as the baby boom generation reached the colleges.[4] Kerr's weakness was his personality. Like many political figures, he knew that confrontation was counterproductive; to avoid confrontation he preferred to leave the impression of agreement when he encountered opposition. A journalist, George N. Crocker, noted, "At one time or another—and often at the same time—every antagonist in a controversy thinks Kerr is on his side." The difficulty, of course, came when it was necessary to make a decision. Kerr used common bureaucratic techniques to minimize offending people. He avoided meeting those with whom he disagreed, he ordered bureaucratic underlings to make the decisions that would draw the most criticism, and he maintained a low profile—becoming, at times, almost invisible.[5]

When Kerr became president, he continued Sproul's practice of running the campus through the president's office. In 1961 Edward W. Strong, a professor of philosophy, became the chancellor. Although Strong was not Kerr's first choice, the new chancellor pleased both conservative Regents and the Berkeley faculty. Strong was a contemplative, intellectual man who had won the respect of the faculty through years of service to faculty causes. One of his proudest moments came in 1962, when he helped persuade the Regents to make participation in R.O.T.C. voluntary. In that battle he made common cause with Kerr, whom Strong greatly admired. Beyond this devotion, Strong had little to offer. He was a traditionalist who turned brittle at the first sign of crisis, an almost total innocent concerning bureaucratic intrigue, and an idealist devoted to duty in a world run by accommodation and power. He lacked both the bureaucratic experience and the force of personality which would have made him effective. One suspects that Strong's limitations had led Kerr to appoint him chancellor.[6]

STUDENT ACTIVISM

During Sproul's presidency in the 1930s a communist-influenced student movement had arisen on the Berkeley campus. Sproul was anxious to keep radicalism out of the university, and so he banned political activity on campus. No longer could literature be passed out, petitions circulated, funds solicited, buttons sold, or candidates for office presented to students. The harshness of Sproul's ban was offset by geography. In those days the south boundary of the campus ended at Sather Gate, and both sides of the block of Telegraph Avenue between the gate and Bancroft Way were lined with shops. After the ban, political activists simply moved off campus into the area immediately south of Sather Gate. Since thousands of students had to funnel through Sather Gate and its adjoining footbridge over Strawberry Creek to enter campus, the movement of political activity to the Sather Gate area posed no inconvenience for student activists.[7]

During the 1940s and 1950s campus radicalism declined, and the geography of the Berkeley campus changed. The University bought the land along Telegraph between Sather Gate and Bancroft and expanded the campus southward into the city. An administration building, Sproul Hall, was built on the east side of Telegraph, and in 1961 a new student union building, largely Kerr's project, opened on the west side. The area between was closed to traffic and became Sproul Plaza. These changes took place without substantial changes in Sproul's rules banning political activity on campus. The result was to place Sather Gate inside the campus and off-limits, but the issue was more or less moot, since there were few student activists.[8]

The Left seemed to have disappeared in Berkeley, but undercurrents were to be found in the growing bohemia of coffee houses and bookstores along the deteriorated and decaying section of Telegraph between Bancroft and Dwight. In 1963 Clark Kerr led a fight inside the Regents to repeal one of the last vestiges of McCarthyism: the Regents' ban on communists speaking on any University campus. Precisely because the Left was dead Kerr felt comfortable asking the Regents to repeal the ban. But Kerr discovered, much to his annoyance, that the Regents preferred to let the regulation stand; and to get the Regents to act, he had to compromise. The old rule had banned communists but had allowed non-political student groups to invite anyone else, except political candidates, to talk on campus. The new rule allowed communists to speak but required non-political student groups to present "balanced" programs with opposing sides and a tenured faculty moderator whenever a speaker was "controversial." In practice the Kerr regulations left student groups at the mercy of the campus bureaucracy.[9]

The Kerr rules irritated a growing student movement at Berkeley. It began in 1957 with the creation of a student political party that soon took the name SLATE. The group advocated many changes and declared its contempt for the "sandbox" politics practiced by fraternity-oriented student body presidents. SLATE won few elections, but it did lead the administration to evict graduate students from student government, and SLATE leaders began to seek success elsewhere. In any event by 1960 the same students, former students, and hangers-on associated with SLATE and the growing Telegraph area bohemia were ready to organize pickets to protest the execution of Caryl Chessman at San Quentin. Just a few days later the House Un-American Activities Committee (HUAC) arrived in San Francisco to hold hearings exposing communist activity in the Bay Area. An anti-HUAC protest, largely organized by Berkeley student activists, led to dozens of students being washed down the stairs of San Francisco City Hall with high-powered fire hoses. The next day five thousand or more protesters confronted HUAC in San Francisco and chanted, "Sieg Heil!" The large turnout showed that student activists could tap mass support if they were able to identify and use popular issues.[10]

In the early 1960s the black civil rights movement in the South, led initially by the Rev. Martin Luther King, Jr.'s Southern Christian Leadership Conference (SCLC), increasingly fell under the control of black college students organized in the Student Non-Violent Coordinating Committee (SNCC). The black movement attracted the attention of Berkeley's white student activists because of the changing racial composition of the city of Berkeley. Due to black migration from the South, by 1960 the city was one-fifth black. Berkeley's blacks were confined to an area remote from the University. One seldom saw a black on campus, black shoppers were not welcome in downtown Berkeley, and both school segregation and discrimination in employment and housing were common.[11]

Student activists formed the Berkeley Congress of Racial Equality (CORE) both to aid the struggle in the south and to tackle racial problems in the Bay Area. CORE focused on job discrimination and used picketing to pressure employers into signing agreements to hire black workers. Berkeley CORE invented the "shop-in," in which protesters loaded up carts with groceries and then left them at the check-out stand. The Lucky's chain was singled out for this treatment because Lucky's had a store on Telegraph near campus. In early 1964 Berkeley CORE combined with other civil rights groups to picket the Sheraton-Palace Hotel in San Francisco. After a sit-in and numerous arrests, the hotel association agreed to CORE's terms. Sit-ins at San Francisco's auto row also produced a labor agreement. By 1964 Berkeley CORE and its allies had made an impact throughout the Bay Area. To some people, it appeared that a handful of agitators were systematically using the Berkeley campus as a staging ground for making trouble.[12]

In keeping with the Sproul and Kerr rules banning political activity on campus, for several years activists had solicited donations and sign-ups for protests from card tables set up on the city sidewalk at the edge of campus at Bancroft and Telegraph. In 1964 Alex C. Sherriffs, Vice-Chancellor for Student Affairs and a popular psychology professor among students from fraternities and sororities, became upset by the presence of the activists. Sherriffs was perhaps less worried about political activity itself than about its visibility and the effect that it had upon visitors to campus. In 1964, one of the first sights a visitor saw, at the corner of Bancroft and Telegraph, was a student, possibly blue-jeaned, bearded, and sandaled, manning a card table, jingling a can, and asking for a donation to support civil rights. To Sherriffs, this scene was appalling, because it created the image that the University was a haven for eccentrics and malcontents. The Vice-Chancellor saw himself as a moral guardian bound to protect the purity of the campus and its cleancut fraternity and sorority kids from unkempt beatniks and wild-eyed radicals. In any event, he put the issue on the agenda for discussion among a group of low-level bureaucrats in the spring of 1964, and after several postponements, the issue was aired among these administrators in July and September.[13]

NEW RULES

When the University opened that September, activists looked forward to recruitment and fund-raising. Thirty to sixty students had spent the summer working for civil rights in Mississippi, and they returned to the campus with renewed dedication and determination. These activists, including Mario Savio and Art Goldberg, were dumbfounded in mid-September when the University suddenly issued new rules that banned tables from the edge of Bancroft and Telegraph, where they had been placed in growing numbers for two or three years. When the activists tried to find out what was behind the change, they could get no answers. The Dean of Students, Katherine A. Towle, talked with the activists but declared her own lack of power, while those who held the power refused to talk. Inside the administration Towle, a former colonel in the Women's Marine Corps, had vehemently opposed the ban. The technical

reason for the ban was the University's "discovery" that the 26' x 90' area where the tables had been placed was University property and not, as previously thought, city property. In a twist of irony, years later it would be discovered that the area actually had been retained by the city of Berkeley when the city had deeded Sproul Plaza to the University. The point, of course, is that one should not make too much of the legal niceties. Neither the administration nor the activists cared about the law. This dispute, at its heart, was about power.[14]

Kerr was in Japan when the administration banned the tables, but he returned in time to have a crucial meeting with Sherriffs and Towle. Although Kerr did not wholeheartedly embrace the ban, he supported the need to restrict political activity. Towle was apprehensive, Sherriffs looked forward to throwing the radicals off campus, and Strong began to realize that he might be in for a rough time. Almost immediately the chancellor fell into an attitude of defensive legalism that he retained throughout the crisis. Paralyzed by his own fears and pushed constantly to new action by Kerr operating behind the scenes, Strong's usefulness was at an end. His tragedy was that he had to play out the role, act by act, scene by scene.

In this crisis Kerr's analytical brilliance was of no value, and his personality worked against him. Instead of marshaling his administration for war, he oscillated. At times he goaded his underlings to attack the activists but not to squash them; this had the same effect as teasing a bee. At other times he retreated into wondering what had gone wrong, how he had failed, and why his command had proved inept. It was a bit like going to war without an army, and while Kerr's instincts were warlike, he was to hand his enemy victory after victory through self-destructive bold advances alternating with paralysis and retreat.[15]

The activists were better prepared for war than Kerr. First, they knew what they wanted. Although specific demands changed over time, the basic plea was for an end to the regulation of political activity on campus. This was called free speech. Kerr, on the contrary, could only wave a sheaf of ever-changing regulations, none of which was internally logical and all of which appeared to be shifting responses to pressure. The activists identified the issue as a traditional American right in order to appeal to large numbers of students. Second, the activist leaders were battle-scarred veterans of the black civil rights movement. They knew when to advance, when to retreat, how to use crowds, how to use the media, how to intimidate, and how to negotiate. The activists understood their ultimate weapon, the sit-in, and they were prepared to use it. Kerr, on the other hand, was as unready to do battle as a southern sheriff who faced a civil rights march for the first time. Again and again, Kerr showed that he understood nothing about his opponents' tactics. Finally, the activist leaders knew how to maintain discipline over their troops. They used mass psychology, song, theater, and other techniques long favored among revivalists and street politicians. Through such techniques and by focusing on the simplicity of the demand for free speech, the activists created an environment within which followers were disciplined. They created an army. In contrast, Kerr badgered his beleaguered bureaucracy until it could barely function.[16]

Throughout September skirmishes continued as defiant activists set up tables and were cited by irritated deans. The angry students escalated the conflict by moving their tables to Sproul Plaza. This protest led to a "mill-in" inside Sproul Hall and the summary "indefinite suspension" of eight students. Finally, on October 1st, University police went to the plaza to arrest a former student, Jack Weinberg, who was manning a CORE table. The police drove a car onto the plaza to take Weinberg away to be booked, and as Weinberg got into the car, someone shouted, "Sit down." Suddenly, several hundred students surrounded the car. The police did not know what to do, because they had never encountered such massive defiance. Kerr's bureaucracy became paralyzed. It was this event that launched the Free Speech Movement.

Participants later recalled the spontaneity of the sit-down, the thrill of power over the police, and the feeling that something important was happening. For thirty-two hours Weinberg sat in the back of the police car. Although students came and went, there were always at least several hundred surrounding the car. The most significant aspect of the sit-down was the use of the roof of the police car (with police permission) as a podium to speak to the crowd. Several times a twenty-one year old junior, Mario Savio, removed his shoes to climb atop the car, and when he spoke, his words seemed especially to energize the crowd. He became a celebrity and was identified by the crowd as the leader of the activists. From then on it was to be a war between Savio and Kerr. It was not a fair match.[17]

SAVIO VERSUS KERR

Mario Savio, the devout son of Italian Catholics, had been educated at the Christian Brothers' Manhattan College until he had transferred to Queens College. In the summer of 1963 he had worked for a Catholic relief organization in rural Mexico, and that fall, after his parents had moved to Los Angeles, the former altar boy entered Berkeley as a junior. The summer of 1964 he taught a freedom school for black children in McComb, Mississippi. By the fall of 1964 this philosophy major had had unusually broad experiences that stimulated his passionate dedication to the causes he held dear. Savio's father, a machinist, was proud of his son's Catholicism and devotion to social justice. The son had begun to call himself Mario instead of the more prosaic Bob of his childhood. Perhaps it was a search for Italian roots, a rejection of a too pat Americanization, a claim of adulthood. In 1964 Savio was proud and cocky, angry and defiant. He scowled beneath longish, sandy-red hair. He was not cool. His power over the student masses came from his ability to articulate a tone that expressed the frustrations and anxieties of his generation. While others were as angry as Savio, they found it impossible to articulate their anger using words. It was Savio's gift to be able to discourse rationally while discharging an undertone of anger. This powerful projection of personality contrasted with Savio's private conversation, which was often marred by stuttering, hesitancy, and coldness. All self-doubts and inhibitions were dissolved when Savio used a megaphone or microphone to speak to the masses. An iron determination overcame inhibitions and enabled Savio to speak to crowds with apparent ease. His effectiveness came from pushing himself to the brink of losing control.[18]

While the police car was trapped, Kerr's bureaucrats dithered, and the activists came to realize that they could extract concessions from Kerr in exchange for quietly giving up the police car. Both sides picked negotiators. Kerr pushed Strong aside and took on his old role as a labor mediator to deal with the students. Kerr's terms appeared to be generous. Jack Weinberg, still in the police car, would be booked and then released with the University not pressing charges. The eight students suspended summarily by the administration for activities prior to the capture of the police car would face discipline before a faculty committee. Another committee, to be composed of administrators, faculty, and students appointed by the administration, would negotiate permanent rules for political activity on campus. Meanwhile, the administration pledged to withdraw the September regulations, and the activists promised to desist from any illegal activity. After much internal debate, the activists accepted Kerr's offer. Savio then returned to the police car to announce the settlement. He invited everyone to rise up and go home quietly. To many, the crisis appeared to be over.[19]

During October and November the agreement of October 2nd unraveled. One irritant involved a final resolution of the discipline for the eight suspended students. Kerr refused to reinstate the students pending the faculty committee's report, despite a plea from the committee. In late November, after the committee made its recommendations, Chancellor Strong, on Kerr's direct orders and after Kerr had discussed the cases in great detail with the Regents, altered the penalties by increasing them. The consequence was to suggest Kerr's contempt for judicial processes, his disdain for the faculty, and his bad faith concerning the pact of October 2nd.[20]

Meanwhile, the committee to negotiate permanent rules for political activity on campus also bogged down. The activist students on the committee rejected an administration proposal for limited political rights on campus, while an activist counterproposal that rights be based on the first amendment got no support from faculty or administration. The activists, in the end, rejected a faculty compromise.[21]

In reality, neither side was prepared to settle because each calculated that it could get more later. Kerr was convinced that time would cause support for the activists to decline, and that in the end the administration could grant limited political rights that would satisfy the administration, the faculty, and a majority of students. Kerr ignored the power of Savio and FSM to move the masses. As many as five thousand students sometimes attended the rallies that took place almost every noon in Sproul Plaza. The rallies encouraged the activists not to accept the faculty compromise, which they regarded as too restrictive because it allowed the administration to regulate the content of political activity on campus. The activist strategy was to raise student awareness until sheer numbers forced Kerr to yield. They knew, however, that student pressure alone would not suffice, and they intended to bring the faculty into the activist camp on their terms. There were several reasons why they thought this would happen. First, Kerr's support from the faculty had declined over the years, and many faculty members were ready to show their independence of the administration. Second, many faculty members were sympathetic to civil rights; since the issue of political activity on campus was seen as a question of how much civil rights activity would be permitted, the faculty could be drawn to support FSM on that basis. But most important to the activists were the twists and turns in Kerr's inconsistent and arbitrary policies, which were neither democratically enacted nor reasonable. The FSM case was stronger because it was simpler.[22]

Just as matters were quieting down, Kerr intervened maladroitly. In late November, with the disciplinary cases settled amid bitterness and the political rules committee "suspended," Kerr decided to punish the FSM leaders for their role in the events preceding and surrounding the capture of the police car. Kerr's grant of amnesty in the pact of October 2nd had carefully excluded the events that took place during the seizure and holding of the police car. Kerr now believed that mass support for FSM was waning, and he decided to act. This decision was not Kerr's alone; Strong concurred, and it was approved by the Regents at a long special meeting on November 20th. As customary, Kerr kept a low profile, and it was Strong who announced the initiation of new disciplinary proceedings. To outsiders, there was something grotesque about Strong's conduct; it destroyed the chancellor's remaining support on the campus. The administration had the law on its side, but the decision was mean-spirited. Four activist leaders were singled out, and it appears that Kerr intended to suspend Savio and Art Goldberg on the grounds that on October 1st and 2nd they had violated the terms of the probation that had been recommended by the faculty committee and imposed by the chancellor, on Kerr's orders, in late November. Kerr's petty act rallied both the faculty and large numbers of otherwise uninvolved students to the FSM cause. The activists, in a spirit of rage, decided to confront Kerr with their ultimate weapon.[23]

SPROUL HALL SIT-IN

From the beginning the activists had considered a sit-in. Now Kerr had created the circumstances that would enable the activists to recreate the spirit of the civil rights movement on the Berkeley campus. Negotiations had failed, and some activists had concluded that little could be done to gain political rights on campus. If they could not attain such rights, at least they could embarrass the man and the university that had thwarted their efforts. Other leaders, long active in civil rights, believed a sit-in would have other consequences. First, it would galvanize, mold and radicalize student opinion. One of the most important functions of sit-ins was to win converts to the cause. Friends would join, and then friends of friends, and the feeling of camaraderie experienced in the sit-in would feed the movement with what it needed most: bodies. The fellowship of a sit-in would lead to a vast expansion of the activist population on campus and the beginnings of an activist community. Berkeley would not have dozens of activists but hundreds, possibly even thousands. Second, if a sit-in brought police, and the FSM leaders calculated that Kerr was not shrewd enough to avoid this outcome, then the bringing of police onto campus would have profound consequences. The presence of police would both demonstrate Kerr's failure to manage the University and generate publicity that would bring sympathizers to Berkeley. Above all, the faculty could not tolerate the University run as a police state. Thus, a large sit-in would demonstrate widespread support for FSM and push the faculty to act. The activists set a trap for Kerr's humiliation and a faculty rescue of FSM.[24]

The sit-in was carefully planned by both sides. The activists determined to create as massive a sit-in as possible, both to show the size and depth of their support and to humiliate Kerr. At a noon rally on December 2nd Savio spoke his most memorable lines. He said,

> There is a time when the operation of the machine becomes so odious, makes you so sick at heart, that you can't take part; you can't even passively take part, and you've got to put your bodies upon the gears and upon the wheels, upon the levers, upon all the apparatus and you've got to make it stop. And you've got to indicate to the people who run it, to the people that own it, that unless you're free, the machines will be prevented from working at all.

In these few words, similar to some thoughts of Thoreau's, Savio conveyed the deep anger, the anxiety, the frustration with modern life, and the sense of powerlessness that was the undercurrent of all the turmoil of the sixties. His words were spoken calmly and dispassionately. The rally was almost dirge-like, as if the participants were embarking upon some religious ceremony that would bring about their re-births. Joan Baez closed the rally with a funereally slow rendition of the civil rights song, "We Shall Overcome," and a large portion of the crowd, more than one-thousand, made their way into Sproul Hall. They settled down for what they hoped would be a long occupation.[25]

Kerr was desperate. Criticized by many off-campus for the handling of the first large-scale demonstrations at any American university in modern times, frustrated by his own bureaucracy, burdened with an ineffective chancellor, and now faced with one of the largest sit-ins in history, Kerr felt he had no choice. Painfully aware of the faculty's disdain for the use of police on campus, a disdain enhanced by the large number of European war refugees on the faculty, Kerr kept his role in the unfolding events secret. Throughout the crisis he had consulted with the Chairman of the Regents, Edward Carter, and Carter in turn had fre-

quently talked by phone with Gov. Pat Brown. The liberal democratic governor had long been an admirer and supporter of Kerr's. Now it was agreed that the police would be called in as quickly as possible to remove the demonstrators, and that the order to do so would come from the governor, who would be portrayed publicly as taking a tough stand. Brown, a former prosecutor and attorney general, did not need to be persuaded of the virtue of law and order. His action, however, and his high visibility were politically unwise. The arrests enraged the protesters and failed to appease those Californians who came to consider Brown as part of the problem of Berkeley's disgrace. Two men played crucial roles in the police action. One was Alex Sherriffs, who had been appalled at Kerr's oscillations all fall and now grimly sought to win his battle against the activists. The other was Edwin Meese, an assistant county prosecutor who acted as liaison between the police and prosecutor's office and who during the arrests ran the operation from the campus police headquarters in the basement of Sproul Hall.[26]

The activists occupied all four floors of Sproul Hall. Different activities were held in different areas. On the second floor food was prepared, elsewhere old Charlie Chaplin films were shown, some students studied for approaching final exams, others held a Chanukah service, and still others sang folk songs. A few smoked pot, and two coeds lost their virginity on the roof. The leaders used walkie-talkies to maintain contact and discipline among their followers and with each other. Some prepared to settle down for the night, or perhaps for several nights, while others were convinced that the police might attack at any moment. At 3 A.M. Chancellor Strong appeared with a bullhorn, and carrying out one of Kerr's last directives, read a statement on each floor warning that the police were coming and would arrest anyone who remained in the building. Until this point, students had been free to leave the building, and about two hundred had done so. Then the cops came. FSM leaders had urged students who were being arrested to refuse to walk and to force the police to carry them from the building. The police obliged, although not necessarily in the gentlest manner. The purpose of forcing the police to carry students was to slow down the arrests so that students who walked past Sproul Hall in the morning could see how their classmates were being treated. This tactic was successful, for despite the 367 police who took part, the building was not cleared and the last of the 773 arrests made until 4 P.M. on the afternoon of December 3rd. It was the largest mass arrest in California history. The arrestees were put on buses and taken, for the most part, to Santa Rita, a county prison facility about twenty-five miles away. As news of what was happening spread across the campus and throughout Berkeley, faculty sympathizers organized caravans of cars to go to Santa Rita to post bail and retrieve the students from jail after they had been booked.[27]

Who sat in? The leaders are easily identified through their participation on the FSM Steering Committee. In addition to Savio, they included Bettina Aptheker, daughter of the communist historian Herbert Aptheker and herself then an unpublicized party member; Art Goldberg, a passionate although not always level-headed devotee to civil rights who planned an autobiography entitled *Commiejewbeatnick;* Art's sister Jackie Goldberg, a longtime activist in Women for Peace and delegate to that organization's Moscow conference in 1963; Suzanne Goldberg (no relation), who married Savio in the spring of 1965; Michael Rossman, a math graduate student from an old leftist family; Jack Weinberg, one of the most effective civil rights organizers, the strategist behind FSM, and author of the phrase, "You can't trust anybody over thirty"; and Barbara Garson, FSM propagandist and later playwright ("MacBird").[28]

The leftist ties are striking. These ties did not go unnoticed by Kerr, who in a press conference indicated that the FSM leaders were red. Although he later said he had been misquoted, Kerr did nothing to remove the public impression that he faced a communist revolt at the University. Kerr's remark and his subsequent refusal to attack the hysterical Right enraged the FSM leaders, who were insulted that the University's president would stoop to the sort of red-baiting once used by Sen. Joseph R. McCarthy. Part of the anger came from the fact that while the FSM leaders did not deny their Left orientations, they did not, by and large, think of themselves as leaders of Left political parties. Their radicalism was of a distinctly different type, which during the 1960s would become known as the New Left. What was most significant about the Left ties was not ideology but the legacy of McCarthyism. These activists came from families that had been persecuted or knew people who had been persecuted for their political beliefs. It made them hypersensitive about political rights and insecure and suspicious whenever someone in power behaved in such a way that rights appeared to be threatened or clouded.[29]

Except for Savio, all of the FSM leaders were Jewish. These Jewish activists had no particular interest in religion and little understanding of what their Jewishness could or should mean. Their activism was a form of self-identification. The Jewish style, at once playful and aggressive, and harkening back to working-class, immigrant roots that suggested success came only to those who struggled against power and authority, grated against the white, Anglo-Saxon, Protestant administrators who ran the University. Kerr, a practicing Quaker pacifist, disliked the activists' untidiness, their lack of self-restraint, their rudeness and disdain for propriety, their unwillingness to take rules seriously, their defiance of authority—in short, their chutzpah.[30]

The overwhelming majority of those who sat in did not resemble the radical activists who led FSM. About 85 percent were students. In most

respects the followers mirrored their fellow
students who did not sit-in. One-fifth were
graduate students. Largely from middle-class
families, the protesters had middle-class aspirations and values, were not particularly active in
politics or civil rights, and might be described
as liberal Democrats. Although many conservative students, including the Young Republicans,
supported the goals of FSM, few conservatives
believed that the issue justified illegal acts.
Indeed, it was the willingness to break a law to
protest injustice that most clearly set apart
those who sat in from those who did not. The
most striking trait of the protesters, and one
that troubled Kerr, was the fact that their
grades were higher than average. It was the
more serious and scholarly students who were
most committed to FSM.[31] Overall, Berkeley
students were split. About one-third supported
FSM goals and tactics, another third backed the
goals but rejected illegal tactics, and the remainder favored the administration view.

RESOLUTION

The sit-in destroyed Strong and ruined Kerr's
moral authority. The chancellor, already cold
and distant, had retreated into himself as the
crisis deepened. Now he felt personally be-
trayed by Kerr. Strong had thought that he had
understood Kerr and had nearly worshipped the
president. Now Strong found that the Kerr of
bold words and promised tough action was a
man of vacillation, of compromise, and of an
inappropriate toughness that spawned new cri-
ses. The chancellor saw only too clearly that he
had been used, and that now Kerr intended to
sacrifice Strong. The chancellor was hurt, and
his participation in events drifted toward unre-
ality. On the last memo in which an annotation
appears in his hand, he wrote in the margin in a
large and shaking hand, ''Niggardly.'' Strong
was not alone in his gloom. Kerr understood the
magnitude of his defeat, that the activists had
eroded his moral authority by forcing the use of

police, and that bringing police onto campus
had pushed the faculty into opposing the administration. FSM called a student strike, and
administrators painfully noted that it was surprisingly effective. Perhaps half of all students
stayed away from classes or had their classes
canceled. Kerr decided it was time for a bold
move, and so he announced a university-wide
convocation at the outdoor Greek Theatre for
Monday, December 7th.[32]

Over the weekend Kerr had consulted with a
number of faculty, especially department chairmen, and he intended to endorse a compromise
proposal on political rights sketched out by the
department chairs at the Monday meeting. But
Kerr's neglect of the faculty had taken its toll,
and a large group of younger and more liberal
faculty, the self-styled Committee of 200, many
of whom had a concern for civil rights, had
already met and prepared a set of campus
regulations that essentially granted the FSM
demands. Kerr's meeting at the Greek Theatre
was strained. He announced an amnesty in the
pending discipline cases and that students arrested in the sit-in would not face separate
University discipline. Then he let Professor
Robert Scalapino present the position of the
department chairs. As the meeting concluded, it
appeared that Kerr had won some support
among the sixteen to eighteen thousand students and faculty in attendance. At least it
seemed clear that negotiations could proceed
with the Scalapino proposals providing some
basis for discussion, and that the activists had
been reduced to a hard core that posed little
harm to the University. All Kerr had to do was
to keep things quiet, and the combination of
final exams and the winter rains would bring
FSM to an end on terms favorable to Kerr.
Then, as the meeting ended, Mario Savio
jumped onto the stage and headed for the
microphone. He later said that he planned to
announce a noon rally sponsored by FSM at
Sproul Plaza. He did not make it to the microphone, for he was tackled by campus policemen

and dragged backstage. A cry rose from the crowd. Kerr's effort had been destroyed. The symbolism was grotesque. A student leader passionately committed to free speech was physically prevented from speaking. Kerr tried to salvage the situation by allowing Savio to make his announcement, but the attack on Savio was all that most remembered of the "tragedy at the Greek Theatre."[33]

Inside the administration some urged Kerr to attend the next day's faculty senate meeting. A personal appearance and strong plea, they argued, might rescue Scalapino's plan. But Kerr chose not to appear. Perhaps he feared humiliation, or maybe he felt that the faculty had to work its own will. The faculty meeting began in Wheeler Auditorium in late afternoon. It was long and raucous. By this time most of the faculty agreed with the proposals put forward by the younger and liberal faculty who essentially endorsed the FSM demands. After several conservative amendments were defeated by wide margins, the faculty approved the liberal resolutions 824 to 115. Many voted to do so knowing that a united faculty stand was in both the faculty's and the University's best interest. Others, conservatives charged, were influenced by the presence of the 5000 FSM supporters who listened to the debate on loud speakers in the dark outside Wheeler. As the faculty exited Wheeler, FSM supporters opened a corridor through their ranks and broke into applause. Savio spoke with the press, and for the first time during the crisis, he seemed to have a grin on his face. It was his twenty-second birthday. When Kerr heard the tally, he was galled. To be attacked by a group of activist students was bad enough, but to be undercut by one's own faculty, who, in Kerr's eyes, had now played into the hands of his enemies, was almost beyond belief.[34]

The rest was anticlimax. Kerr balked at taking the liberal faculty proposals to the Regents, whom he privately described as unreasonable conservatives who would never accept such ideas. But the faculty had been talking with the Regents on their own and discovered that the Regents were anxious to settle, and if the faculty could do so, then the Regents were willing to settle on faculty terms. Indeed, by this point University attorney Thomas J. Cunningham had warned the Regents that if Sproul's old rules or Kerr's September rules were challenged in court, the University would probably lose. Although Cunningham publicly maintained a conservative, crusty posture, he was influential behind the scenes in getting the Regents to accept changes. The president, as the chancellor had predicted, sacrificed Strong, and few realized how the chancellor had been used. Kerr survived, but divisions inside the Regents grew worse, and the president remained in office primarily because of Governor Brown's support. The activists looked forward to soliciting funds and workers for civil rights, but by late 1964 white involvement in civil rights was waning in what became increasingly an all-black movement. Activists would have to find new issues. The next five years would not disappoint them.[35]

Notes

1 The following notes are illustrative; full documentation will be found in my projected book on Berkeley in the 1960s. The only full story of FSM is Max A. Heirich, *The Spiral of Conflict* (N.Y., 1971). This book, by a Berkeley graduate student in sociology, is insightful, but the author lacked access to many sources. All interviews are Regional Oral History Office transcripts. All sources are in the Bancroft Library, University of California, Berkeley.

2 On Sproul see James H. Corley interview, xii–xvi; Clark Kerr interview, 19; Donald H. McLaughlin interview, 40, 57, 68–69; Josephine Miles interview, 141; Joseph R. Mixer interview, 43; Garff B. Wilson interview, 213, 382–383; Joseph Conlin, *The Troubles* (N.Y., 1982), 114. Standard accounts for the oath are George R. Stewart, *The Year of the Oath* (Garden City, N.Y., 1950); and David P. Gardner, *The California Oath Controversy* (Berkeley, 1967).

3 *Berkeley Gazette* and *San Francisco Examiner*, Mar. 10, 1965.

4 On Kerr's appointment see Kerr interview, 13; Ida A. Sproul interview, 163–164; Transcript of Portions of Notes Taken at Regents Only Session of the Board, Feb. 19, 1965, p. 3; Ralph E.Shaffer to Savio, Dec. 5, 1964, 2:13 (indicating box: folder), FSM Arch.

5 Crocker is quoted in *San Francisco Examiner*, Mar. 21, 1965. Charles M. Otten, *University Authority and the Student* (Berkeley, 1970), 159–162; *Despite Everything,* Jan. 1965, pp. 9–11.

6 On Kerr see Elinor R. Heller interview, 483, 532–533, 544, 553, 594. On R.O.T.C. see *Daily Californian,* June 29, 1962; David Horowitz, *Student* (N.Y., 1962), 23–29, 115–120. On Strong see *Despite Everything,* 11; Alex C. Sherriffs interview, 39, 55, 78; George R. Stewart interview, 65–66; Wilson interview, 222–223; *Los Angeles Times,* Apr. 17, 1965. Strong's lack of power is noted in Kerr interview, 17, 21–22; McLaughlin interview, 67–68; David W. Reed to John H. Reynolds, Dec. 6, 1964, in "Faculty Memoranda..." (bound vol.).

7 Conlin, 114; Lewis S. Feuer, *The Conflict of Generations* (N.Y., 1969), 439–440; Heirich, 61, 68–70; Max Heirich and Sam Kaplan, "Yesterday's Discord," *California Monthly,* Feb. 1965, pp. 20–23; *American Scholar,* 34 (1965), 388–389; Dorothy N. Deane to Kerr, May 31, 1961, 1302:5, Univ. of Calif. President's Files (hereafter UCPF).

8 Heirich, 71; Heirich and Kaplan, 24–26; Sherriffs interview, 19. On the new union see *Daily Californian,* Mar. 14, 1961.

9 Repeal of the communist ban may be followed in Heirich and Kaplan, 29; *Daily Californian,* June 29, 1962; June 20, Oct. 30, 1963; Heller interview, 536; Don Mulford to Kerr, May 7, 1963; reply, Alex C. Sherriffs to file, July 1, 1963, all in 1293:1, UCPF. The effect of the new rules is shown in Michael Rossman, et al., "Administrative Pressures and Student Political Activity at the University of California" (Berkeley, 1964), introduction, pp. 3–6, Appendix D, pp. 1–2.

10 The fullest account of SLATE is in Horowitz, 18–21. The best coverage of HUAC's visit to San Francisco is in Frank J. Donner, *The Un-Americans* (New York, 1961), 1–3, 175–218.

11 On schools see Carol Sibley, *Never a Dull Moment* (Berkeley, 1972); and Neil V. Sullivan with Evelyn S. Stewart, *Now Is the Time* (Bloomington, Ind., 1969). On housing see Thomas W. Casstevens, *Politics, Housing and Race Relations* (Berkeley, 1965.)

12 See the local press, Feb.–Mar. 1964.

13 On Sherriffs see Heirich, 75, 91–93, 95–96; *California News Letter,* Oct. 5, 1964; *SLATE Supplement,* Sept. 15, 1964; Heller interview, 553; Kerr interview, 14–15; Sherriffs interview, 23–24, 27–29; Towle interview, 222–242, 291.21–291.22; Sherriffs to U.C. Vice Pres. Oswald, Mar. 5, 1963, 1293:1, UCPF; Joseph R. Mixer to Sherriffs, Aug. 3, 1964; Mixer memo, n.d.; Sherriffs to Kerr, Sept. 15, 1964, all in 3:40, University of California, Berkeley, Chancellor's Files (hereafter, UCBCF). A description is in *Commonweal,* Feb. 5, 1965, p. 603. On discussion see Arleigh Williams to Katherine A. Towle, July 31, 1964; Towle statement, Oct. 9, 1964; Towle to John Jordan, Oct. 12, 1964, all in Towle Papers.

14 The new rules and their consequences are in *Berkeley Gazette,* Sept. 17, 26, 1964; *Daily Californian,* Sept. 17–18, 21–23, 25, 29, 1964. On Towle see Heirich, 96–97, 105–106, 108–109; *New York Times,* Mar. 14, 1965; Heller interview, 541–542; Kerr interview, 14; Sherriffs interview, 26; Towle interview, passim; Towle memo, Sept. 17, 1964, 10:114, UCBCF; Towle to Strong, Oct. 12, 19, 21, 1964, Towle Papers.

15 The meeting is sketched in Kitty Malloy memo, Sept. 18, 1964; Sherriffs to Kerr, Sept. 20, 1964, both in 10:114, UCBCF. On Kerr's role see *New Politics,* 4(1965), 26–27; Heirich, 109–110; Kerr interview, 15–17; Towle interview, 242, note; Regents Committee on Educational Policy, Executive Session Minutes, Sept. 24, 1964.

16 Eugene Bardach, ed., "The Berkeley Free Speech Controversy" (Berkeley, 1964), 16; Heirich, 456, note 22, and passim. The FSM Archives are instructive. FSM retained incoming correspondence, made copies of outgoing correspondence, kept phone logs, and recorded in detail Executive Committee and Steering Committee sessions.

17 On the sit-down see Heirich, 123–130, 143–149, 154–183; *Berkeley Gate,* Oct. 12, 1964; *Berkeley Gazette,* Oct. 2, 1964; *Daily Californian,* Oct. 2,

5, 1964; McLaughlin interview, 67–69; Earl Bolton to Kerr, Oct. 2, 1964; Bolton to file, Oct. 2, 1964 (2 memos), all in 1293:13, UCPF; Sherriffs memo, Oct. 1, 1964; anon. memo, Oct. 2, 1964; Kitty Malloy memo, Oct. 2, 1964 (2 memos); Strong memo, Oct. 2, 1964, all in 3:40, UCBCF.

18 The best press biography is in *New York Herald-Tribune,* Dec. 9, 1964. See also Conlin, 123–126; Feuer, 443–444; *California Monthly,* Dec. 1984, pp. 18–20.

19 Heirich, 181–186: *Oakland Tribune,* Oct. 31, 1964; *San Francisco Chronicle,* Oct. 3, 1964; Savio remarks, Oct. 2, 1964; Kitty Malloy memo of Strong phone call, Oct. 2, 1964, 8:20 A.M.; Bolton-Lohman phone calls, Oct. 2, 1964, 5:10 and 5:45 P.M.; Bolton-Woodward phone call, Oct. 2, 1964, 5:15 P.M., all in 1293:13, UCPF; Lincoln Constance memo, Oct. 2, 1964, 3:40, UCBCF; Savio memo of Kerr-Savio conversation, Oct. 2, 1964, in 3:13, FSM Arch.; transcript of Savio's remarks, Oct. 2, 1964, approx. 7:30 P.M., 1293:13, UCPF.

20 Two key documents were issued by the University of California, Berkeley, Academic Senate's Ad Hoc Committee on Student Conduct, chaired by Ira M. Heyman. These are entitled "Materials" and "Proceedings" (both Berkeley, 1964). Regents Executive Session Minutes, Oct. 16, 1964; Transcript of Regents Informal Sessions, Nov. 19–20, 1964. On the alteration of penalties see Heirich, 227, 232, 241, 249–250; Heyman to Strong, Oct. 22, 1964; reply, Oct. 26, 1964; Kerr to Regents, Oct. 26, 1964; all in 1293:13, UCPF; Akiko memo, Oct. 23, 1964, 2:22 P.M.; Strong memo of phone call to Kerr, Oct. 23, 1964, 5:35 P.M., both in 8:90, UCBCF; Kerr to Strong, Nov. 2, 1964 (2 memos); Strong to file, Nov. 4, 1964; Strong statement (draft). Nov. 13, 1964; Heyman Communication to Kerr, Nov. 16, 1964; Kerr notes, Nov. 20, 1964, all in 1293:14, UCPF; Kerr to Regents, memo, Nov. 20, 1964, in 3:13, FSM Arch.; Strong to Academic Senate, Nov. 24, 1964, in "Faculty Memoranda."

21 Heirich, 224, 226–229, 241–242: *Daily Californian,* Oct. 14, 1964; Bolton to Kerr, Oct. 21, 1964; Kerr to Robert Brode, Oct. 26, 1964, both in 1293:13, UCPF; Kerr to Strong, Nov. 2, 1964; Frank Kidner to Kerr, Nov. 9, 1964 (2 memos), all in 1293:14, UCPF; Sherriffs Memo, Oct. 12,

1964, 11:10 A.M.; Akiko memo, Oct. 23, 1964, 3:10 P.M., both in 8:90, UCBCF; Strong call to Heyman, Nov. 9, 1964, 8:55 A.M., 8:91, UCBCF.

22 Bardach, 27–29; Heirich, 217–224; *Daily Californian,* Oct. 16, Nov. 11, 18, 24, 30, 1964; *San Francisco Chronicle,* Nov. 11, 1964; Paul Forman to Kerr, Oct. 10, Nov. 11, 1964, both in 2:18, FSM Arch.; Joe Freeman to ?, Nov. 18, 1964, 2:24, FSM Arch.; Strong to Kerr, Oct. 29, 1964; reply, Oct. 30, 1964, both in 1293:13, UCPF; Bolton record of phone call with Seymour M. Lipset, Nov. 11, 1964; Akiko to Strong, Nov. 11, 1964, both in 1293:14, UCPF.

23 Heirich, 265–266; *Daily Californian,* Nov. 30, Dec. 2, 1964; *San Francisco Chronicle,* Dec. 1, 1964; Ron Anastasi to Kerr's office, phone call, Nov. 25, 1964, 1293:14, UCPF; Bolton (?) record of phone call with Martin Roysher and Steve Weissman, Dec. 1, 1964, 1294:1, UCPF; Strong memo, Nov. 22, 1964, 3:41, UCBCF; Strong memo, Nov. 13, 1964; Lincoln Constance to Strong, Nov. 15, 1964; Kerr phone call to Strong, Nov. 17, 1964, 10 A.M.; Errol W. Mauchlan to Strong, Nov. 17, 1964; Adrian Kragen to Strong, Nov. 17, 1964; Arleigh Williams to Strong, Nov. 18, 1964, all in 8:90, UCBCF; John Landon to Williams, Nov. 30, 1964; Thomas J. Cunningham to Strong, Dec. 4, 1964, both in 8:91, UCBCF; Transcript of Regents Informal Session, Nov. 19, 1964; Regents Minutes, Nov. 20, 1964.

24 On faculty see *Graduate Student Journal,* Spring 1965, p. 25; *Spartacist,* no.4 (May–June 1965), 13; Dept. of Anthropology meeting resolves, Dec. 4, 1964, in "Faculty Memoranda."

25 Savio's speech was taped by radio station KPFA and issued as part of a recording, "Is Freedom Academic?" This excerpt is in Heirich, 271–272.

26 The evidence is contradictory and must be considered as a whole. Heirich, 274–275; *Berkeley Gazette,* Dec. 4, 1964, extra; *San Francisco Examiner,* Dec. 3, 1964; *BCU Bulletin,* Nov. 1964, p. 2; *Despite Everything,* p. 4; California Senate Fact-Finding Comm. on Un-American Activities, *Thirteenth Report* (Sacramento, 1965), 101; *Thirteenth Report Supplement* (Sacramento, 1966), 9, 17–18, 28–29, 54–55, 66–70; Hale Champion interview, 64, 69; May L. B. Davis interview, 30, 31, 33; Frederick G. Dutton interview, 146; Heller interview, 554; Richard Kline interview, 25–26;

Sherriffs interview, 37; Towle interview, 258, 291.18; Kerr statement, Dec. 3, 1964, in "Free Speech Movement" (bound vol.), handout supplement. Key documents are Strong memo, Dec. 2, 1964, 10:10 A.M.; Sherriffs memo, Dec. 2, 1964, 11 A.M., both in 4:42, UCBCF. See also Gov. Brown's phone logs and desk calendars, box 68; Fred Jordan memo, ca. Dec. 8, 1964, box 675, both in Brown papers. On Meese see *The Defender: Free Speech Trial Newsletter,* Apr. 18, 1965, pp. 3, 5–6; *San Francisco Bay Guardian,* Apr. 4, 1984, p. 9; *San Francisco Examiner,* May 4, 1965; "This World" section, *San Francisco Sunday Examiner & Chronicle,* June 22, 1986.

27 Activities are in Heirich, 275–277; *FSM, the Free Speech Movement at Berkeley* (San Francisco, 1965), 16–18; *Center Magazine,* May 1968, p. 42; *Liberal Democrat on the Pacific Scene,* Jan. 1965, p. 11; *Berkeley Gate,* Dec. 7, 14, 1964; *Daily Californian,* Dec. 4, 7, 9, 1964; *San Francisco Chronicle,* Dec. 3, 1964. On police see *Columbia Daily Spectator,* Dec. 18, 1964; *Police Chief,* Apr. 1965, p. 53. On bail see Henry N. Smith and Richard Herr memo to faculty, Dec. 3, 1964, in "Faculty Memoranda..." (bound vol.), Supplement; *Berkeley Gazette,* Dec. 4, 1964, extra.

28 The best sketches are in the *Los Angeles Times,* Mar. 24, 1982. See also *San Francisco Chronicle,* Nov. 15, 1964; and autobiographies in 1:18, FSM Arch. (BA) *Los Angeles Times,* May 2, 1965; *California Monthly,* Dec. 1984, pp. 18–20; (AG) *San Francisco Bay Guardian,* June 14, 1979, p. 10; (JG) box 677, Brown Papers; (MR) Michael Rossman's autobiography, *The Wedding within the War* (Garden City, N.Y., 1971); (JW) Bardach, 12; Feuer, 441–442, 447 (quote).

29 Kerr's remarks are noted in Robert Aronoff, "Public Opinion and the Free Speech Movement" (Berkeley, 1970), 4; *Daily Californian,* Nov. 30, 1964. Outrage is expressed in *Studies on the Left,* 5(1965), 56; *Johns Hopkins Magazine,* Oct. 1965, p. 20; Gilbert H. Robinson to Kerr, Nov. 30, 1964, 2:18, FSM Arch.

30 The shrewdest observer is Feuer, 423–429.

31 Bardach, 14, 32–33; Katherine L. Jako, *Dimensions of the Berkeley Undergraduate through the Sixties* (Berkeley, 1971), 19, 20, 23, 34, 39; Robert H. Somers, "The Mainsprings of the Rebellion: A Survey of Berkeley Students in November, 1964" (Berkeley, 1965), esp. 7–17, 21, 27; *Journal of Applied Behavioral Science,* 2(1966), 41–57; R. T. Morris and R. J. Murphy, "University of California Student Opinion Survey April 1965" (Los Angeles, 1965); Paul Heist, "Intellect and Commitment: The Faces of Discontent," paper, Center for Study of Higher Education, University of California, Berkeley, 1965; analysis of Sproul arrestees, 1294:1, UCPF; Edward E. Sampson, Jacob P. Siegel, and Alan N. Schoonmaker, "The FSM and the Berkeley Campus," paper, Western Psychological Assn. meeting, June 1965.

32 On Strong see John H. Reynolds and others statement, Dec. 9, 1964 (annotated), 4:42, UCBCF. On faculty see Mark Harris, *Twentyone Twice* (Boston, 1966), 125–126; *Berkeley Gazette,* Dec. 5, 1964; Norman Jacobson to students, Dec. 3, 1964, 3:19, FSM Arch. On the strike see Bardach, 35; *Despite Everything,* 6–7; *Graduate Student Journal,* Spring 1965, pp. 22, 25–26; Feuer, 451; Heirich, 278–279, 285–288; Political Science T.A.'s meeting, Dec. 2, 1964, "Free Speech Movement," handout supplement.

33 Bardach, 9; Harris, 133; Heirich, 291–297; *Berkeley Gazette,* Dec. 7, 1964, 2nd extra; *New York Times,* Dec. 8, 1964; Ralph J. Gleason column, *San Francisco Chronicle,* Dec. 9, 1964; Heller interview, 551; Harry R. Wellman interview, 154; Wilson interview, 224–225, 248; department chairmen's Proposal, Dec. 6, 1964; Kerr address, Greek Theatre, Dec. 7, 1964, both in "Free Speech Movement," handout supplement; John H. Rowe to Kerr, Dec. 8, 1964, 2:7, FSM Arch.; Edward S. Rogers to Charles E. Smith, Dec. 12, 1964, 1294:1, UCPF.

34 Bardach, 30–31; Nathan Glazer in Irving Howe, ed., *Student Activism* (n.p., n.d), 21–22; Heirich, 300–315; *Daily Californian,* Dec. 9–11, 1964; *San Francisco Chronicle,* Dec. 10, 1964; Heller interview, 561; McLaughlin interview, 78–79; Wellman interview, 155; Kerr statement, Dec. 8, 1964; Herbert McClosky statement, Dec. 8, 1964, both in "Free Speech Movement," handout supplement; David Pesonen to Savio, Dec. 8, 1964, 2:19, FSM Arch.

35 Heirich, 117, 319–320; *Frontier,* Apr. 1965, pp. 17–18; Lawrence H. Davis, "Report on Berkeley to the National Supervisory Board and the 18th

National Student Congress'' (n.p., 1965), 10; *Los Angeles Times,* Mar. 13, 1965; *Oakland Tribune,* Mar. 12, 1965; *San Francisco Chronicle,* Dec. 20, 1964; Mar. 13, 1965; *San Francisco News-Call-Bulletin,* Mar. 15, 1965; Heller interview, 542, 544, 547–548, 555–556; Wellman interview, 132; transcript of meeting of Regents and Emergency Executive Committee of the Berkeley Division, Academic Senate, chaired by Arthur Ross, Dec. 17, 1964; portion of transcript of Regents Informal Session, Oct. 15, 1964; transscript of Regents Informal Session, Nov. 19, 1964. See Gov. Brown phone logs and calendars, box 68; Ron Moscowitz to Brown, Dec. 16, 1964, box 724; Moskowitz to Brown, Dec. 31, 1964, box 675, all in Brown papers. Cunningham to Sherriffs, Sept. 21, 1964, in Sherriffs interview, 26a–26c; see also 43; Cunningham to Strong, Oct. 19, 1964, 1293:13, UCPF; Alan W. Searcy memo, Dec. 14, 1964; Kitty Malloy memo, Dec. 16, 1964, both in 4:42, UCBCF; Strong notes on Regents meeting, Dec. 18, 1964, 8:91, UCBCF; Strong report to Forbes Comm. of Regents, Feb. 9, 1965, 1294:1, UCPF; Kerr to Sidney Hook, Mar. 9, 1965, 1293:6, UCPF.

THE FIGHT TO SAVE LAKE TAHOE

EDITOR'S INTRODUCTION

The decade of the 1970s has defied easy generalization. Whereas the 1960s are remembered as the "protest decade," the 1970s stand as something of an enigma. One historian has summed up the period as a time when "it seemed like nothing happened."[1] Perhaps the events of the decade are too recent to allow us to place them in proper perspective.

Yet surely one of the major themes of the 1970s, in California and the nation, was the growth of the environmental protection movement. The movement was not new, but the degree of enthusiasm that it generated was unprecedented. Environmentalism became a mass movement in the 1970s, capturing the imagination of a new generation of protesters. Whereas the activists of the 1960s had rallied to protest racism, poverty, and war, their counterparts in the 1970s fought to save the wilderness, protect endangered species, and limit reckless economic development.

The struggle between the forces of environmental protection and economic development was waged on many fronts. New groups joined forces with older conservation organizations such as the Sierra Club to fight for the protection of the state's land, air, and water resources. Major battles were fought to protect San Francisco Bay and Mono Lake, the Stanislaus River and Yosemite Valley. One of the most protracted controversies centered on that jewel of the High Sierra, Lake Tahoe.

In *Tahoe: An Environmental History* (1984), Douglas H. Strong narrates the story of more than a century of contention between the forces of conservation and development. The following selection describes the controversy in the early 1970s over the newly created Tahoe Regional Protection Agency (TRPA). Because Lake Tahoe straddles the state line between California and Nevada, the agency was jointly

[1]Peter N. Carroll, *It Seemed Like Nothing Happened: The Tragedy and Promise of America in the 1970s* (New York, 1982).

operated by representatives from both states. Strong shows how environmentalists and developers viewed the role of the bistate agency with widely different expectations. He narrates the inside story of the agency, demonstrating how the prodevelopment forces gained ascendancy. Many environmentalists soon became disenchanted with the agency and began lobbying for greater federal protection of the area. Proposals were launched to create a Lake Tahoe national park, national lakeshore, or national recreation area. Local interests successfully blocked all such proposals for federal intervention.

Following the reconstitution of the TRPA in 1980, the agency began to establish more stringent guidelines for the development of the Lake Tahoe basin. The latest chapter in the Tahoe saga was TRPA's announcement in 1987 of a new regional plan for the basin. As Strong points out, in the updated version of his account that appears here, this new plan set even more rigorous standards of environmental quality. Strict limits for new construction were established for the following three years. In the fourth year, new construction would be allowed only if there was a measurable improvement in lake water quality. After that, the situation would be reassessed. While environmentalists were cautiously optimistic about the new plan, the Nevada state senate began considering legislation to secede from the bistate compact that had set up the agency.

Strong's work is representative of a new school of historiography, most commonly called "public history." As is typical of this breed of historians, Strong is primarily concerned with the workings of governmental agencies. His writings are aimed not only at general readers, but also at legislators, government officials, bureaucrats, and others involved in the formulation and administration of public policy. As a public historian, Strong is as concerned with the future of Lake Tahoe as he is with its past.

Douglas H. Strong has been visiting the Tahoe area with his family since the late 1930s. It may be of interest to readers of this anthology to note that he is the son of Edward W. Strong, the former University of California chancellor who figured prominently in the previous selection. Author of four books, Douglas H. Strong is currently Professor of History at San Diego State University.

The Fight to Save Lake Tahoe

Douglas H. Strong

The Lake Tahoe basin has been altered markedly since John Frémont first sighted the lake from a mountain peak in 1844. Although Lake Tahoe itself looks much the same today when seen from such a distance, closer inspection of the lands along its shores reveals the magnitude of human impact.

Change has come slowly. After thousands of years of summer residence at Tahoe, the Washo Indians left essentially no mark on the land, except for an occasional bedrock mortar or arrowhead. Their hunting, fishing, and gathering economy did not deplete the abundance of fish and other foods in the basin, nor did the Indians significantly alter the ecosystems of the meadows, forests, and marshes. During the early settlement of the west, whites largely bypassed Tahoe. Then construction of the Comstock Road to Nevada's mines fostered the rapid rise of a freight and tourist business in Tahoe Valley. With completion of the Central Pacific Railroad, Tahoe settled back into relative tranquility—until lumbermen invaded the basin and cut nearly all the accessible timber. Early photographs reveal the extent to which the shoreline and surrounding hills were denuded; the resulting erosion and sedimentation undoubtedly were substantial. Nevertheless, the logging era passed relatively quickly. By the early years of the twentieth century, a second growth of timber covered the mountain slopes and the lake had recuperated from most of the damage to the quality and clarity of its water.

During the next half-century, the Tahoe basin underwent slow growth as a summer resort area. Scattered cottages and a few lodges along the shoreline were served at first by trains to Tahoe City and steamships on the lake, and later by growing numbers of automobiles and a few buses. Most people assumed that Tahoe would remain a rustic, quiet summer retreat indefinitely. But then a series of events, including the population explosion in California, the completion of improved highways to the basin, the rapid expansion of winter recreation activities, and especially the construction of year-round casino-hotels, combined to produce a rate of urbanization that no one had expected or prepared for. By the early 1960s, a small city was emerging on the shores of south Tahoe. The Crystal Bay Development Company had begun the construction of Incline Village, and small communities elsewhere around the lake mushroomed in size.

As a result of this urban boom, all aspects of environmental quality within the Tahoe Basin declined. Emissions from vehicles on the congested roads created smog, reduced visibility, and often exceeded the national ambient air quality standards for carbon monoxide and ozone. Marshes and meadowlands, the habitat of many wildlife species, increasingly succumbed to the bulldozer. Even more alarming, the crystal-clear waters of Lake Tahoe revealed signs of increased pollution in spite of the introduction of a modern sewage disposal system that pumped effluent out of the basin. The growth of algae in the lake appeared to be increasing at an exponential rate, and the clarity of its water lessened.

The total impact of urbanization, like the fact of Tahoe's growth, had not been foreseen. Here was development with no apparent end in sight. The water of Lake Tahoe was given no hiatus to recover from the onslaught of nutrients from sewage, construction sites, landfills, dredging, storm run-off from parking lots, and the like. Even when the damage was not visible to the casual observer, anyone accustomed to swimming at Tahoe could not help noticing the steady accumulation of slippery green vegetation on the once clean rocks along the shoreline. Nor could one ignore the traffic congestion, or the parade of neon lights and billboards on the approach to the south shore casinos. Those who had known Tahoe in an earlier day felt deeply the loss of serenity and beauty that once had been its hallmark.

No one had proposed or consciously planned that the Tahoe Basin become urbanized; but a multitude of individual and governmental decisions—and the attraction of Tahoe's scenic wonders—inevitably flooded the basin with people. Of course alternatives have existed, then as now. But with the passage of time, setting aside all or a major portion of the basin as a public park or forest has become increasingly difficult and expensive.

THE TAHOE REGIONAL PLANNING AGENCY

Congress in 1969 launched the most important effort to protect Tahoe's natural environment by creating the Tahoe Regional Planning Agency (TRPA). Under the enabling legislation, an Advisory Planning Commission, a group dominated by local representatives, was to prepare a regional plan. The plan would be presented to a separate group, the Governing Body—representing various political entities interested in the basin—which could develop any plan it wished and alone had authority to make decisions. In addition to these two groups, the compact called for appointment of an executive officer by the Governing Body and the hiring of whatever staff was deemed necessary.

Nothing captured the hopes and aroused the suspicions of people concerned with Lake Tahoe in the 1970s as much as the newly created TRPA. The agency convened officially on March 19, 1970, following a joint proclamation

of its founding by California and Nevada governors Ronald Reagan and Paul Laxalt. Reagan called it a "milestone" that the two states "now have the means of working together to assure the beauty of Tahoe," and Laxalt cautioned that "no other single area in the country will be subject to more severe economic and ecologic pressure."[1]

The TRPA inherited an unenviable set of circumstances. In the period between congressional approval of the agency in 1969 and its first meeting, growth at Tahoe had continued at a dizzying rate. During the 1960s, assessed property values in the basin had tripled, and opportunities for profits in Tahoe real estate and land development remained substantial. A single-family lake-front lot at Incline Village that sold for $17,500 in 1960, for example, now cost $85,000. The resident population had doubled in the decade, a peak summer population now exceeded 130,000, and state and federal recreation land use had multiplied eightfold. A guidebook to Lake Tahoe published in 1971 noted that south Tahoe, once an abandoned logging area where land sold for $1.50 per acre, now had numerous motels, as well as "40 gas stations, 52 restaurants, 2 newspapers, 2 radio stations, 7 banks, 8 schools, 16 churches, a hospital, and 69 real estate offices."[2]

The TRPA needed to act quickly to impose some order on growth. The task fell to Justus K. Smith, director of the Denver Regional Council of Governments, who was selected from more than seven hundred applicants for the post of the agency's executive director. Smith clearly lacked sufficient personnel for the task assigned him: his initial staff consisted of one planner, one draftsman, an engineer, and two secretaries. Few foresaw the magnitude of the job ahead or the bold manner in which Smith would approach it. Under the enabling legislation, he had ninety days to prepare and have adopted an interim plan for the entire basin, and he had only eighteen months to develop a regional plan for the long-term development and conservation of the basin. As they set about accomplishing these tasks, Smith and his staff also had to review a continuous flow of proposals for private land development and the construction of roads, utilities, recreation facilities, shoreline development, and outdoor advertising signs. The review process alone reportedly took three-fourths of the time available to the staff.

Further, the agency suffered from a shortage of funds almost immediately; the two California counties in the basin, El Dorado and Placer, refused to contribute their share of the first year's funding. The two counties, supported by the city of South Lake Tahoe, already had filed a suit in which they challenged the constitutionality of the bi-state compact and the obligation of local government to abide by its rules. The El Dorado County supervisors claimed that the restrictive densities proposed in the interim plan constituted "inverse condemnation" for which property owners should be compensated.

Smith's idea of the mission of the TRPA differed considerably from that of many people of influence both within and outside the basin. He believed he had been hired to save Lake Tahoe from the unchecked forces of urbanization, and that a principal task would be preservation of the water and air quality of the basin. Many of his critics assumed that the legal objectives of the agency, "conservation" and "orderly development," meant at most planned growth. In their opinion, the TRPA should not act except in compliance with local wishes and should not supersede local control. In fact, the bi-state compact called for the TRPA to handle "general and regional matters," and to let the state, county, and city governments involved in the basin enact specific rules that conformed to the regional plan.

In developing the interim plan, the small staff had time only to paste together a composite of existing maps and plans from local governments. The local plans reflected local needs, did not consider the basin as a whole, and did not specify clear limits to population growth. So the loosely structured interim plan satisfied no one, providing little guidance to local developers on what to expect or help to environmentalists intent on preserving the region. As one environmentalist commented, the interim plan "can be looked upon either as a nonplan or as a blueprint for catastrophe."[3]

What lay ahead, however, was the central task—development of the regional plan. With the inadequate resources at his command, Smith turned for help to Jack W. Deincma, the regional forester. Deinema's unusual position as the nonvoting federal representative to the TRPA gave him considerable power to integrate the planning effort, coordinate federal funding, and work with state and local officials. He had already established a Forest Service team in the basin with expertise in ecology, hydrology, geology, forestry landscape, and recreational planning. This team worked closely with the TRPA staff and even shared the same building. A Federal Coordinating Committee, composed of regional representatives of all federal agencies with special interests at Tahoe, also met regularly. The federal government clearly had an important stake in the planning process: roughly 50 percent of the land in the basin remained under federal administration and ownership. In addition to this federal assistance, more than two hundred consultants, mainly from academia, provided substantial aid.[4]

Together, the Forest Service team, the TRPA staff, and consultants developed the Smith Plan, based in part on ideas popularized by Ian McHarg in his book *Design With Nature*. This was, in brief, a regional plan to regulate the size and distribution of the future population of the basin, based on levels of use that the land was capable of tolerating without sustaining such permanent damage as erosion and water degradation.

Robert G. Bailey, a Forest Service geomorphologist, devised a two-step process to measure the land's tolerance of human use. First he ranked the basin's acreage in seven classes according to the frequency and magnitude of such hazards as "floods, landslides, high water tables, poorly drained soils, fragile flora and fauna, and easily erodible soils."[5] Class one land represented areas of greatest hazard, and class seven land had essentially no hazards. Next he evaluated each unit of land on the basis of its ability to tolerate alteration by people. Bailey placed limits on disturbance of the ground surface in terms of a percentage of each area that could be used for impervious cover, that is, could be covered by buildings, parking lots, and the like.

In this classification system, 76 percent of all land in the Tahoe Basin was listed as "high hazard," 10 percent "moderate hazard," and 14 percent "low hazard." When applied to proposed development, this meant that little or no construction should take place on slopes that were subject to erosion or were in marsh and meadowland. Accordingly, under this classification, Tahoe Keys, built at the mouth of the Upper Truckee River, was most hazardous and should never have been built. And Incline Village, with its steep hillsides and construction beside streams, was already overbuilt.

The land-capability approach departed from earlier zoning practices and caused considerable controversy. Normally, planners specify tracts of land according to such designations as C (commercial), R (residential), M (industrial), and A (agricultural). This scheme has worked reasonably well in most urban and suburban areas of the country, where a major concern might be, for example, to situate homes away from factories. But Smith's chief concern was protection of Tahoe's environmental quality. His approach ran counter to that of people who believed that planners, through human ingenuity, could keep pollution and soil erosion within workable limits. Many local authorities at Tahoe held that belief. They saw no need to delay development while scientists worked on a land-capability map. Instead, they concentrated on

such immediate questions as where to place sewer lines to accommodate the anticipated influx of people.

Despite its usefulness as a planning tool, the land-capability map was no substitute for a regional plan that would include consideration of prior developments, zoning decisions, and the like. Yet Smith, pressed by an impending deadline, used the land-capability map as the basis for his plan. In the process he paid little attention to past zoning decisions, to property lines, or to who might stand to lose by application of the plan.

Increasingly, in 1970 and 1971, public interest groups that would be affected by the TRPA plan complained that their concerns were receiving little attention. Many people felt uninformed and unable to influence the work of the planning team. The lack of alternative plans also restricted discussion and a sense of public participation in the decision-making process.

Local people felt alienated. They did not trust the influx of outside experts, the use of a computer in Berkeley to quantify data, the threat of federal involvement, and what they perceived as neglect of home rule. The agency staff, busy with the scientific aspects of its planning duties, failed to acquire political support in the basin and thus became increasingly isolated. As one staff member commented: "The name of the game was persuasion. J. K. [Smith] never understood what that meant. He thought it was below his dignity to get involved in local politics and pressure groups. He shunned the political aspect and shut himself off from the public and the press."[6] As a result, Smith lost any chance of support from the TRPA Governing Body and the twenty-one-member Advisory Planning Commission.

When the staff finally unveiled its proposed regional plan to an overflow crowd at the Sahara Tahoe Hotel in May 1971, critics labeled it illogical, opinionated, utopian, and unjust. In particular, they attacked a proposal to restrict resident and visitor population to 134,000 at any given time—no more people than would already visit Tahoe on a busy summer weekend.[7] In comparison, the recently approved master plan of the city council of South Lake Tahoe would allow an ultimate population of 151,000 in that city alone, with a density two-thirds that of San Francisco.

From this point forward, the Smith Plan encountered rough sledding. At two well-attended public hearings in June, property owners, developers, and local officials complained about the impact of the plan on property rights and values, existing zoning, and sewer and other utility bonds. The TRPA Governing Body, influenced by the avid denunciation of the plan by the Advisory Planning Commission, voted unanimously to form a special subcommittee under Richard Heikka, the planning director of Placer County, to draw up an alternate plan that would be more acceptable to local interests. Smith, ordered into silence by the Governing Body, lost all hope of success and subsequently resigned.

The Governing Body hired Heikka to replace Smith. Heikka seemed better suited to work out some kind of compromise, and he and a small team of local planners worked quickly and largely in seclusion during the summer months. Perhaps to the surprise of many, Heikka incorporated much of the Smith Plan into his own proposal, adapting the land-capability system to a more conventional land-use approach. The Heikka Plan called for a maximum population of 280,000, well above the 134,000 Smith had proposed yet well below the 800,000 suggested by combination of the local plans. Of course, all population figures were only projections and had little to do with what actually might happen. Population would be concentrated at two urban cores, the north and south ends of the lake, where development already existed. In addition, the plan called for the establishment of green belts and for limits on the expansion of casinos.

After considerable debate, the Governing Body finally adopted Heikka's regional plan in December 1971. The plan gained national recognition, partly because it incorporated the innovative land-capability concept. Its implementation, however, depended on adoption of the various ordinances ordered in the original bi-state compact.

An assessment of TRPA performance before adoption of the regional plan gave reason for concern. The staff failed to halt or even seriously delay most proposed projects that it believed were destructive to Tahoe's environmental quality. Time and again it was overruled by the Advisory Planning Commission and the Governing Body, which were dominated by local members sympathetic to development. The information generated by the staff was often disregarded, and the Advisory Planning Commission increasingly based its reviews on standards set by county and city planning agencies.

Two political scientists at the University of California, Davis, provided a critical evaluation. Their conclusion was that "the expert Planning Commission proved unable to plan, the representative Governing Body acquired a clear local bias, and the neutral staff turned increasingly, if somewhat reluctantly, to advocacy."[8] As a result, the initial TRPA planning and regulatory efforts proved largely ineffective. In fact, the TRPA plan was vitiated before its approval. The Governing Body approved so many new developments during the period of preparation of the plan—reportedly 95 percent of the projects brought before it—that rapid growth was assured for years to come.

In an attempt to explain what had gone wrong, John D. Ayer, professor of law at the University of California, Davis, argued that Tahoe was engulfed in public policies that encouraged the misuse of the basin. The key problem, urbanization, exacerbated a host of related problems, such as air and water pollution, that had to be solved at public expense. Replying to the argument that events at Tahoe were simply a response to "market" conditions of what individual buyers and sellers wanted, Ayer pointed out that public policies heavily influenced these conditions.[9] For example, the real property tax made developing privately owned tracts of land especially attractive. Special assessments, such as for modern sewage disposal, also encouraged development, partly to attract more people who would help pay for the bonded indebtedness. County governments certainly encouraged such growth; they gained more in revenue than they lost in providing public service.

Ironically, the federal government also contributed to environmental problems. Despite its concern and responsibility for helping to attain and maintain air and water quality standards, federal agencies fostered growth in two important ways. First, they provided grants to facilitate construction. For example, the expenditure of federal funds for campgrounds, roads, airports, waste disposal, and other purposes contributed to further growth. Second, the agencies issued permits, such as for the Heavenly Valley ski resort, allowing construction financed by private capital on public lands.

Although federal grants and the issuance of permits were responses to perceived problems, such as crowded highways and overloaded sewage systems, they encouraged urban development. Each time the government acted to provide additional recreational facilities or expanded highways, it opened the door to more people. Since state and local governments, as well as the private sector, acted similarly, a downward spiral of environmental quality continued. As a federal task force later concluded, "Nowhere in the decision-making process were the interactions among responses or the cumulative environmental effects they caused considered."[10] As long as economic incentives pushed toward development of the basin and no governmental agency stood in the way, urbanization continued.

Deterioration of environmental quality continued throughout the 1970s, despite efforts to designate Tahoe as a national lakeshore or recreation area. An influx of goods, money, and people stimulated rapid growth in housing, transportation, public utilities, and recreational facilities. Stimulated by expansion of casinos on the Nevada shore, employment more than doubled, and the demand for goods and services maintained pressure for more development.

The permanent population of the basin by 1980 neared 60,000, and peak summer population, including tourists, may have exceeded 200,000. With more than seven million people within a four-hour drive of Tahoe, a reduction in the traffic seemed unlikely. It had in fact increased 80 percent in less than a decade.

The trend of environmental decline appeared ominous. The accumulation of seemingly minor decisions and activities had caused environmental problems of major magnitude. Since settlement first began in the basin, approximately 75 percent of all marshes, 50 percent of meadowlands, and 15 percent of forests had been converted to urban use or had been significantly damaged by human activity. And there seemed no end in sight to the process by which separate decisions, often by well-meaning people, led inevitably to the degradation of the land and the lake. Effective action was long overdue.

The 1980s witnessed a flurry of activities to resolve the numerous problems that plagued Tahoe basin. After years of negotiations, California and Nevada finally revised the bi-state compact that had created the TRPA. The new compact, approved in 1980, reduced the power of local government within the agency and changed voting procedures to make approval of development more difficult. After lengthy debate the Governing Body established threshold standards for water and air quality, soil conservation, vegetation, noise, wildlife, fisheries, recreation, and scenic resources. The next step, implementation of these standards, awaited adoption of a new regional plan that would set the parameters for growth at Tahoe in the years ahead.

The compact gave the TRPA new life; the future of the basin rested in its hands. The federal government, while remaining integrally involved in management of Forest Service lands within the basin, would play a secondary role to the TRPA. Fundamentally, decisions affecting Tahoe's future would continue to be determined by state and local governments co-operating through the reformed bi-state agency.

A new regional plan brought both hope and frustration to those concerned about Tahoe's future. Local property owners and business interests wished freedom to develop their property, while environmentalists and many people who lived outside of the basin called for more stringent protection of the basin's scenic resources. The TRPA continued to be a battle-ground for contending interest groups.

A federal judge in 1984 ruled that the TRPA's new plan would result in "deterioration of the unique environmental and ecological qualities of the region."[11] Therefore he issued an injunction to enjoin the TRPA from approving any project until the agency adopted a plan and implemented ordinances in compliance with the new bi-state compact. Finally, in 1987, a new master plan gained approval. This twenty-year plan called for limited commercial development, restoration of environmentally damaged lands within the basin, and attainment of more rigorous standards of environmental quality.

PROBLEMS AND PROSPECTS

Despite efforts to protect portions of the basin from commercial development, most of the prized shoreline remains in private hands. On these lands the urbanization has taken place and the major difficulties have arisen. Local governments have been unable to resolve the environmental and social problems resulting from the essentially unchecked growth; it was expecting too much to hope that they could solve regional problems for which they lack the political capabilities and financial means. Also,

it has become evident that political control at the local level more often than not has fallen to those whose short-term economic interests benefit from continued growth. Local government has a legitimate role at Tahoe, but only within the framework of an effective and enforceable regional plan based on the interests of a much broader spectrum of citizens and on long-term considerations.

Although Tahoe's environmental problems remain severe, much has been accomplished to protect the lake and its surroundings. The concerted efforts of many dedicated people have led to: stabilization of the lake level within a six-foot range; establishment of several state parks and extensive national forests; curtailment of highway construction throughout the basin, and protection of the mouth of Emerald Bay and its neighboring state parks from a freeway; restrictions on the expansion of new casinos; export of sewage effluent from the basin; extensive research yielding an improved understanding of the detrimental impact of people on the ecosystem of the basin; heightened public awareness of the environmental problems of Tahoe, resulting in increased political efforts to find solutions.

Some years ago, planners defined the carrying capacity of the land in the Tahoe Basin in relation to its ability to tolerate use without sustaining permanent damage. Although the concepts of environmental threshold and carrying capacity have often been disregarded by decision makers, they remain valuable. The principle of a carrying capacity could provide a workable base for the regulation of privately and publicly owned land—if it were properly understood and enforced.

Ideally, decisions affecting the environment of Tahoe should be made in accord with an environmental ethic that puts the health of the land before economic expediency. As American naturalist Aldo Leopold suggested many years ago: "Examine each question in terms of what is ethically and esthetically right, as well as what is economically expedient. A thing is right when it tends to preserve the integrity, stability, and beauty of the biotic community. It is wrong when it tends otherwise."[12]

Tahoe cannot be returned to its earlier days of quiet beauty and serenity. The demand for recreational opportunity alone precludes such a possibility. But it could evolve and be maintained in the future as an outdoor scenic and recreational area of high quality. The high-rise casino-hotels, which never should have been built in the midst of a scenic national treasure, might someday decline in importance, particularly if California decides to legalize gambling in selected locations elsewhere in the state. If that should happen, the urban problems that the casinos helped generate might be substantially reduced.

The heart of Tahoe's environmental problems is urbanization. The solution lies in the political arena. The citizen and taxpayer is the one who, ultimately, must decide what Tahoe should be. And in wrestling with the knotty problems of Tahoe they will be wrestling with but a part—albeit a dramatic part—of the larger problems of urbanization and environmental degradation that face Americans in all corners of the land. In their struggles to find solutions, as in the solutions they work out, those concerned with the Tahoe Basin are both providing warnings and pointing directions.

Notes

1 "Laxalt and Reagan Make It Official," *Tahoe Daily Tribune,* March 17, 1970.
2 Mike Hayden, *Guidebook to the Lake Tahoe Country,* 2 vols. (Los Angeles: Ward Ritchie, 1971), 2:65.
3 William Bronson, "It's About Too Late for Tahoe," *Audubon* 73 (May 1971):52.
4 For an analysis of efforts to coordinate the planning activities of the TRPA and its academic consultants, and a discussion of problems of communication with public interest groups, see James E. Pepper, "An Approach to Environmental Impact Evaluation of Land-Use Plans and Policies: the Tahoe Basin Planning Information System," Master's thesis, City Planning, University of California, Berkeley, 1972.
5 Robert G. Bailey, *Land Capability Classification of the Lake Tahoe Basin, California-Nevada* (South Lake Tahoe: USDA Forest Service in cooperation with the TRPA, 1974), p. 5.
6 Quoted in Kathleen Agena, "Tahoe," *Planning* 38 (January 1972):8.
7 The figure of 134,000 was misleading: Smith considered neither the existing density of population nor subdivisions previously approved. If he had, his estimate would have been much higher.
8 William E. Felts and Geoffrey Wandesforde-Smith, *The Politics of Development Review in the Lake Tahoe Basin* (Davis: University of California Institute of Governmental Affairs, 1973), p. 11.
9 John D. Ayer, "A Trip through the Fiscal Wilderness," *California Journal* 3 (January 1972):13–15.
10 Western Federal Regional Council Interagency Task Force, *Lake Tahoe Environmental Assessment* (1979), p. 208. See also U.S. Congress, Senate Subcommittee on Air and Water Pollution of the Committee on Public Works, Hearings, *Environmental Problems of the Lake Tahoe Basin,* 92d Cong., 2d sess., August 21, 1972, pp. 11, 17–21, 42.
11 "Judge Garcia Rules," *Tahoe World,* June 21, 1984.
12 Aldo Leopold, *A Sand County Almanac* (New York: Oxford University Press, 1949), pp. 224–225.

## CHAPTER 28

THE LEGACY OF THE TAX REVOLT

EDITOR'S INTRODUCTION

The environmental protection movement was not the only popular crusade of the 1970s. The truly *mass* movement of the decade was the revolt of the American taxpayer.

The opening shot in the tax revolt was fired on June 6, 1978, when the voters of California decisively approved a tax-cutting initiative known as Proposition 13. The initiative required that real estate taxes be limited to 1 percent of a property's assessed value. For property owners, this meant an average reduction in their taxes of more than 50 percent. For local governments, the initiative meant the loss of billions of dollars in tax revenues. Within two years of its passage, 47 other states had adopted some form of tax relief.

The causes and consequences of the tax revolt are subjects of great interest to scholars of recent California history. No complete answers are yet possible to even the most basic questions about the revolt. An important interim assessment, however, was made in 1983 by a team of researchers and reporters assembled by the *Los Angeles Times*. The *Times* project conducted an extensive survey of the response of local governments to the stringencies imposed by Proposition 13, and it gathered an enormous amount of statistical information on the impact of the initiative on a variety of local services.

The findings of the survey, published in a nine-part series in the *Times* in June 1983, revealed that Proposition 13 had caused major changes in virtually every area of public life, distributing benefits and problems across the state in ways that had not been entirely anticipated. One of the most far-reaching effects of the initiative was its impact on the state's infrastructure, the network of publicly financed services necessary for a society to function. With government revenues and spending reduced, deterioration was readily apparent in the quality of public education and in the maintenance of streets and highways, county libraries, sewers, water facilities, and flood control systems.

Concern over the damage to the state's infrastructure led the legislature and governor George Deukmejian to conduct their own investigations. The legislature's report, based on a statewide survey of cities, counties, and special districts responsible for eight public works systems, projected a $24 billion gap between the available local revenues and the amount of money needed to maintain services. The governor's report, which measured state and local needs for a wide range of services, estimated a $51 billion gap in the amount of money available and the amount required in the next decade to pay for repairs to existing public works and the construction of new facilities. Both reports warned of dire consequences for the state's economy if the deterioration in public services continued unchecked.

The *Los Angeles Times* survey was republished in 1984 as *California and the American Tax Revolt: Proposition 13 Five Years Later.* Political scientist Jack Citrin was asked to write an introductory essay to the book. In the following selection from that essay, Citrin attempts an overall interpretation of the legacy of Proposition 13. One of the most striking effects of the initiative, Citrin believes, was its impact on the "culture of policy-making." No longer could politicians blithely talk in terms of progress and social reform; they were forced to learn the more circumspect language of constraint and trade-off.

Using the findings of a California poll, Citrin also summarizes the state of public opinion on the tax revolt. Here he finds continued evidence that Californians want "something for nothing": lower taxes *and* more government services. As the tenth anniversary of Proposition 13 approached, however, a new California poll found that a growing proportion of Californians were willing to pay more taxes in order to support improved government services. More than 70 percent of the Californians polled in 1987 favored tax increases for improvements in police and fire protection, public roads, schools, and water and sewer services.[1]

Jack Citrin, a Professor of Political Science at the University of California, Berkeley, is the author of *Tax Revolt: Something for Nothing in California* (1982).

[1]"Public More Disposed to Loosen State and Local Government Purse Strings. Increase in Readiness to Pay Additional Taxes for Needed Services," *The California Poll*, April 30, 1987.

READING 28

The Legacy of the Tax Revolt

Jack Citrin

Nothing is forever. The passage of Proposition 13 in June 1978 ended an era of fiscal feast in California. The next five years were painful for those in government. Politicians used to doing good by doing more had to learn to say no, as they squirmed in a budgetary straitjacket which a suspicious electorate refused to loosen. Administrators gave up planning new programs for social betterment in order to master the intracacies of cash-flow management. With revenues scarce, costs rather than benefits dominated official thinking; and by 1983 it appeared that government spending, which had moved inexorably upward for so long, actually could come down.

Yet this slowdown too may not last. Economic recovery has relieved California's fiscal predicament, and a long line of claimants for additional funds has already formed. The prospect of burgeoning state revenues has encouraged Governor Deukmejian, a conservative whose 1983–84 budget *cut* state spending by 2 percent from the previous year's level, to propose a 1984–85 budget that would *increase* expenditures by 13 percent, without raising taxes.[1] This new shift in the turbulent budgetary climate makes it especially timely to assess the impact of the taxpayers' revolt on California politics and to ask what its legacy will be.

THE PEOPLE'S VERDICT

When Californians voted on Proposition 13, public opinion held that taxes were too high, public expenditures excessive, and government grossly inefficient, but that the level of most

Adapted from "Introduction: The Legacy of Proposition 13," by Jack Citrin, in *California and the American Tax Revolt*, edited by Terry Schwadron, pp. 1, 52–60. Copyright © 1984 by The Regents of the University of California.

specific public services should be maintained or enhanced.[2] People seemingly desired if not something for nothing, then more for less.[3] Since Proposition 13 has passed, public officials, once bitten, have been twice shy to conform more closely to popular sentiment. Fiscal developments in California thus have moved California in the direction favored by the tax rebels: taxes are much lower, the pace of government spending has slowed, and reductions in public services have been concentrated in areas with lower levels of public support. Despite a number of unanticipated consequences, these major outcomes of the tax revolt in California represent a successful translation of mass opinion into public policy.

Trends in public attitudes have tended to reflect the new fiscal realities. The most dramatic manifestation of public reactions to Proposition 13 is the drop in the proportion of the public's complaining about the level of their property taxes: In 1983 only 15 percent felt this way, compared to 60 percent in mid-1977.[4] And 78 percent of homeowners credited Proposition 13 with reducing their property taxes. Opinions about the overall state and local tax burden have softened more slowly; in 1983, 59 percent said their taxes were "somewhat" or "much" too high compared to 70 percent in 1977.[5]

Perceptions of the government as wasteful also have diminished. In May 1978, as Californians prepared to vote on Proposition 13, 38 percent believed state and local governments could be cut by 20 percent or more without reducing services. In August 1982, only 22 percent felt there was this much "fat" in state and local budgets.[6]

The syndrome of wanting lower taxes *and* more services continues to prevail. In March 1983, the California Poll once again asked California whether public spending in fourteen specific domains should be increased, held the same, or reduced. In only one instance, government regulation of business and professions, did preferences for less spending outnumber responses in favor of increases. More generally, those in favor of cutting back were always a small minority, and the proportion in favor of either the status quo or more spending had increased since May 1978.[7]

Do people who say state spending should stay the same mean they are satisfied with the cuts in services made in response to Proposition 13? The California Poll consistently has found that more people believe that the budgetary reductions have occurred in the ''wrong'' rather than in the ''right'' places, with the most common complaints that schools have been cut too much and ''bureaucracy'' too little.[8]

Five years after the passage of Proposition 13, 42 percent of Californians felt that the quality of state and local government services had declined, compared to only 6 percent who perceived improvement, with education, street maintenance, and libraries singled out as the areas of greatest decay. Interestingly, these were indeed among the areas that suffered most after Proposition 13. Thus these shifts in opinion are largely consistent with changes in the structure of expenditures, and current preferences concerning where government should now spend more come as no surprise.

When asked about the specific impact of Proposition 13 on one's personal circumstances, opinions understandably vary according to whether the focus is on taxes or services. Even in 1983, a majority of Californians (53 percent) felt Proposition 13 had had no effect on the services their family received. Those reporting unfavorable consequences have gradually increased since 1980, however. The proportion of the public that perceives positive consequences for their taxes also has slipped a little, although whether this is due to the impact of new fees or because people have come to

take the benefits of Proposition 13 for granted, one cannot say.

The recognition has spread, then, that Proposition 13 has forced a trade-off between tax relief and some loss in services. In March 1983, 30 percent of the public felt that taking all changes into account, Proposition 13 had improved their personal circumstances; 24 percent believed, on balance, they had suffered; and 45 percent reported no net effect. When asked about the impact of Jarvis-Gann on taxes and spending in California as a whole, opinion was divided evenly between those expressing satisfaction and those expressing dissatisfaction.

The growing acknowledgement that Proposition 13 has brought problems in its wake is no indication that if given a chance the electorate would reverse its decision of 1978. It is, of course, unlikely that voters would be posed the question in such a stark way, but in any event polls have continued to show a majority saying yes when asked ''Would you vote for Proposition 13 today?'' Similarly, in early 1983, the most painful moment of California's fiscal crunch, 56 percent preferred cutting services to increasing taxes in order to meet a budget deficit. This, parenthetically, was the approach adopted by Governor Deukmejian. If taxes absolutely had to be raised, only 14 percent supported the idea of higher residential property taxes.[9] Increasing taxes on alcohol, cigarettes, gasoline, crude oil, or business was more acceptable, so here too policy has followed opinion. Clearly, there are areas of concern and dissent, but the majority verdict on the tax revolt remains favorable.

With the trade-offs posed by the tax revolt in California clearer, attitudes toward the tax revolt have become somewhat more polarized on lines of interest and ideology.[10] Owners diverged more sharply from renters in 1983 than in 1978, as did people over fifty-five from those younger and conservatives from liberals.[11] Surprisingly, differences in outlook between public

employees and those working in the private
sector have actually narrowed.

Although it is commonly asserted that low-
income families and racial minorities have suffered disproportionately as a result of recent
reductions in public spending, complex statistical analyses show that in 1983 a person's race
or income did not significantly influence his
level of satisfaction with Proposition 13. But
being college-educated, particularly if someone
in one's household currently was attending a
public college or university in California,
strongly increased distaste for Proposition 13,
over and above the influence of other aspects of
background and ideology.[12] The university milieu apparently breeds a commitment to the
value of a large public sector and an accompanying antagonism toward Proposition 13 as government's symbolic foe.

MORE INEQUALITY?

It is possible to make a crude classification of
groups as "winners" or "losers" from the tax
revolt in California, but a precise accounting of
the distributional consequences of recent
changes in fiscal policy awaits further research.
For example, the net effect of the incidence of
taxation as a result of Proposition 13, the indexing of income taxes and other reforms is unknown. The best one can say is that indexing
makes the tax system more progressive,
whereas the growth in fees and the limit in
annual increases in assessed value to a flat rate
of 2 percent increase its regressivity.

It seems plausible that reduced public spending disproportionately hurts the poor, who presumably find it more difficult to pay for the
market alternatives; but there is no systematic
evidence concerning trends in the utilization of
government services across social classes. Finally, it is clear that rich and growing communities are advantaged in the search for new
revenues and that the distribution of state aid
makes no attempt to compensate for this. Im-

pressionistic evidence suggests greater inequal-
ity in the fiscal condition and services of local
governments, but, again, the magnitude of such
a trend, if any, is unmeasured.

THE QUALITY OF SERVICES

Another element in the balance-sheet for the
tax revolt is how the quality of services delivered by government has changed. Here, too,
there are conceptual and measurement problems. What constitutes the "product" of governmental activity can be elusive, and this
obviously complicates the task of linking inputs
to outputs. The roads may be bumpier in the
aftermath of Proposition 13, but has this increased the danger of accidents, or has it reduced it by encouraging slower driving? And
what about the effect of unrepaired streets on
the frequency and cost of automobile maintenance? Are mechanics unanticipated winners
from the tax revolt?

The difficulty of measuring the output of
various public agencies encourages a tendency
to equate dollars spent and services delivered.
This tempting approach, though, makes it easy
to confuse quantity and quality. It should be
possible, in principle at least, for government to
do less but to do it more efficiently. (Indeed, officials in California claim that this has occurred as
a result of Proposition 13, that of necessity all the
"fat" in government has been trimmed away.)

In an absolute sense, the quality of some
public services in California clearly has slipped
in the past five years. Roads and sewage systems have deteriorated, university buildings are
shabbier, park lawns are shaggier, and so on.
But has quality per dollar invested, if such a
concept has meaning, also declined? For example, the time it takes police to respond to calls
has grown since the passage of Proposition 13,
an apparent worsening of service. Yet, according to the Los Angeles Times survey, one cause
of this was a decision of police departments to
invest their resources more "productively."

But, since the investment in response time has declined, the response time per dollar spent may be unchanged. As this suggests, an adequate assessment of the impact of fiscal constraint on the quality of government is yet to be made.

BUSINESS AS USUAL

In meeting the challenge of fiscal stress, the dominant response of governments in California was to try and maintain organizational continuity. Self-protection motivated all participants in the process of adjustment. For example, the legislature has sheltered state spending and employment more than those of cities and counties. Changes in the structure of California government have been minimal; the proposals of the Post Commission appointed by Governor Brown to recommend changes made little or no impression. Since the passage of Proposition 13, most innovation in government has centered on pinching old pennies and finding new revenues. The purpose of a "pay as you go" mentality, however, was to minimize change.

Still, the tax revolt has influenced the political process in California in a way that transcends the outcome of the variegated efforts to cut costs or safeguard programs. In one important and pervasive sense, business is no longer as usual. Proposition 13 has modified the culture of policy-making. Austerity and self-reliance have become new symbols of legitimacy. Politicians increasingly speak the language of trade-offs and constraint, rather than progress and social reform. In the earlier era, policymakers could think first of what programs they wanted to expand and feel confident that the revenues required were available. The current mood is different. Given popular sentiments about taxes and uncertain fiscal conditions, officials must revise spending priorities to fit fixed revenues.[13]

Fiscal constraint does provide a justification for politically difficult decisions. For example, legislators blamed the tax revolt in denying requests for additional funds from the powerful special education lobby. The stated need to spend less also spurred the successful effort to reform the system of reimbursement for hospitalization under Medi-Cal. But these benefits provide little solace to the many liberal legislators who entered politics with an activist vision. One legacy of Proposition 13 is to encourage a marketing orientation toward budgeting. New programs must be "sold," since they either take money away from ongoing activities or necessitate raising fees or taxes. That disaster is at hand is a compelling argument in this contest for the taxpayers' acquiescence. When vivid examples make the need obvious, even those sympathetic to the tax rebels' cause will support more spending. This process may not make for orderly planning, but in stops and starts expenditures still can climb.

NO MORE INCREMENTALISM?

The accession of Governor Deukmejian is another influence on the future of the tax revolt in California. The governor's first budget, for 1983–84, was prepared in the context of a cash shortage so severe that the state had to resort to issuing "warrants" (IOU's). Adamant that taxes would not be raised, he dealt with the crisis by using his veto power to cut expenditures in a politically selective way. This naturally angered the governor's legislative antagonists, but his actions at least fell within the implicit rules of decremental budgeting.

Once economic recovery prepared the ground for renewed growth in government, a return to the incremental mode was possible. The 1984–85 budget disappointed those who expected the traditional norms to apply. The governor indeed proposed a large increase in spending, rather than a new reduction in taxes, but refused to apportion funds on the principle that everyone should get a fair share of the increment. Instead, his proposed allocation disproportionately increased expenditures on higher education (the University of California), highways, and prisons, thereby appealing to the middle-class constituency that provided his electoral support. To the dismay of Democratic legislators, the community colleges, environmental programs, and welfare services once again received short shrift.

Governor Deukmejian's approach therefore is to try and control the size of government by insisting on setting priorities even when growth is possible. His opponents, defenders of the incremental faith, are likely to counter by appropriating more for the programs spurned by the state administration. With the item veto on hand, the governor is likely to prevail; but whatever the outcome of this particular struggle, his decision to take fiscal limitation seriously intensifies the partisan and ideological conflicts in budgeting.

THE PROPER SIZE OF GOVERNMENT

The tax revolt in California has constrained the ability of the public sector to grow. How one appraises this historic achievement in the end depends on his beliefs about the proper functions of government. This is a question of value, not fact. Comparing the relative tax burden in California and other states cannot answer what the size of government should be: depending on one's philosophic stance, everyone's tax burden might be too high or too low. And the connections between the level of government spending, let alone specific tax-cutting measures, and the widely accepted goal of economic growth are too murky to serve as the basis for evaluation.

Government in California has proved resilient enough to stretch, though not to tear, the fabric of restrictions woven by the electorate. With this in mind, another criterion for judging the tax revolt is one's degree of confidence in the capacity for self-control among both citizens and elected politicians. The human impulse to feel entitled to something for nothing is

strong. And officials have an incentive to agree to the distinct demands of every constituency, however small. But when taxes have to be raised to pay for these decisions, satisfaction with the separate parts of the budget may coexist with disapproval of the whole.

Do sirens enchant those who sail the seas of democracy to spend and spend and spend?[14] And, if so, is it wise to use fiscal limits to lash our helmsman, like Ulysses, to the mast and put wax in our ears? These are the enduring questions raised by the tax revolt, and the search for answers goes on at every level of American government as well as among the taxpayers themselves.

Notes

This essay benefited greatly from the comments of Judith Gruber, Martin Levin, Frank Levy, and Aaron Wildavsky. I am grateful too to the many "actors" in California who were so generous with their time and material. Finally, my thanks to Ann Ben-Porat, Donald Green, and Tony Kenney for assistance in data collection and analysis and in the preparation of the manuscript.

1 State of California, *Governor's Budget 1984–85*, p. 5. This refers to both General and Special Fund expenditures. The proposed increase in General Fund spending is 10.8 percent.
2 See D. O. Sears and J. Citrin, *Tax Revolt: Something for Nothing in California* (Cambridge, Mass.: Harvard University Press, 1982), ch. 3.
3 *Ibid.*
4 *California Opinion Index*, April 1983, p. 1.
5 *Ibid.*, p. 2.
6 These data were calculated from the relevant California Polls and made available by the State Data Program, University of California, Berkeley.
7 *California Opinion Index,* April 1983, pp. 3–4.
8 Opponents of Proposition 13 complained about the damage to schools, and its supporters about the failure to cut bureaucracy.
9 *California Opinion Index,* April 1983, p. 3.
10 These are the results of the author's analysis of the March 1983, California Poll. Full results will be provided on request.

11 The first group in each pair of names was more favorable to Proposition 13.

12 This emerged from a multiple regression analysis which employed social background variables, measures of political ideology, and reports about the personal impact of Proposition 13 to predict overall satisfaction with the initiative.

13 This point is also made in J. Kirlin, *The Political Economy of Fiscal Limits* (Lexington, Mass.: D. C. Heath, 1982), p. 100.

14 See T. C. Schelling, "The Intimate Contest for Self-Command," *The Public Interest*, no. 60, Summer 1980.

CHAPTER

HIGHER EDUCATION AT THE CROSSROADS

EDITOR'S INTRODUCTION

When the California legislature approved its Master Plan for Higher Education nearly thirty years ago, expectations were high. It was widely assumed that California would soon lead the nation in the proportion of its citizens who were college-educated. Such was not to be. Fewer than one-fifth of all Californians today have completed four or more years of college, and the proportion of young people in California who have earned a bachelor's degree is well below the national average.[1]

What has gone wrong with California's much vaunted system of higher education? The Master Plan itself was hailed as a model for the rational planning of postsecondary education. Each segment of the state's higher education establishment was given a distinct mission. The University of California was to select its freshmen only from the top one-eighth of the state's high school graduates. The university was entrusted with the responsibility of conducting advanced research and awarding doctoral degrees. The "primary function" of what is now the California State University (CSU) was to provide undergraduate and graduate education through the master's degree. The campuses in the CSU system were to choose their entering students from among the top one-third of the graduating seniors. Meanwhile the two-year community colleges were to admit anyone who had graduated from high school or who was eighteen years old or older. The mission of the community colleges was to prepare students for transfer to a four-year college, to award them with an associate of arts or science degree, or to train them for employment in a vocational or technical program.[2]

[1]Michael Fallon, "Big Brother, Little Brother: The Rivalry Between the State's Two University Systems," *California Journal*, XVII (April 1986), 220.
[2]For a convenient summary see Irving G. Hendrick, *California Education: A Brief History* (San Francisco, 1980), 63–64.

Although this complex system worked well in many ways, problems soon became apparent. The two university systems engaged in a rivalry for funding, prestige, and the right to sponsor advanced research and grant doctoral degrees. The community colleges failed to transfer as many students to the four-year schools as expected, and in recent years they have suffered a significant decline in enrollment. Complaints have also been aired about the quality of undergraduate instruction at all levels of higher education. Perhaps most important, and most ominous for the future, college admissions and graduation rates for minority students have remained scandalously low.

The California legislature in 1984 created a Commission for the Review of the Master Plan for Higher Education. The "first and highest priority" of the commission was to study the community college system, deemed by many to be the segment most in need of review. The commission was then to proceed to a reexamination of the entire Master Plan.

In the following selection, William Zumeta and Priscilla Wohlstetter analyze the current status of higher education in California. They summarize the legacy of the Master Plan and look briefly at the problems and accomplishments of each of the three segments of postsecondary education. This selection pays special attention to the problems of ensuring equal access for minority students and improving the quality of undergraduate education.

Guiding their analysis is a concern for values such as *efficiency* and *equity.* By efficiency, Zumeta and Wohlstetter mean how effectively does higher education benefit the whole of society, not just the individuals being educated. Equity is achieved when all identifiable groups in the society have equal access to the educational system. As Zumeta and Wohlstetter demonstrate, sometimes these values are in conflict. The effort to impose more rigorous standards for undergraduate education, in pursuit of greater efficiency, may further limit access for some groups, thus retarding the achievement of equity.

William Zumeta is an Associate Professor in the Graduate School of Public Affairs at the University of Washington, and Priscilla Wohlstetter is an Assistant Professor of Educational Politics and Policy at the University of Southern California.

READING 29

Higher Education at the Crossroads

William Zumeta
Priscilla Wohlstetter

Higher education in California is at a crossroads. Demands on the state's postsecondary education enterprise are changing again, as they have more than once in the past, but the nature and context of these demands are qualitatively different from those in earlier times. The demand now is not for essentially more of the same as was the case in the immediate postwar period. Nor are the social consensus and financial support underpinning higher education nearly as assured as in previous periods of transition.

HIGHER EDUCATION IN CALIFORNIA

California has long been noted for its strong commitment to public higher education. Like other western states, California did not have the benefit of a large private college sector in the late nineteenth and early twentieth centuries, but unlike many others, it had both the resources and the commitment to create a large, diverse, and high-quality public higher education system. One hallmark of this now vast enterprise has been a strong belief in the benefits of broad access to higher education. This belief lay behind the expansion of the system to virtually every populated nook and cranny in the state, the early and dramatic development of the "open door" two-year college system, and the long struggle to avoid imposing tuition on students. Though student fees were finally established in the four-year institutions some

Adapted from "Higher Education at the Crossroads," by William Zumeta and Priscilla Wohlstetter, in *California Policy Choices, 1986*, edited by John J. Kirlin and Donald R. Winkler, pp. 151–202. Copyright © 1986 by the Sacramento Public Affairs Center, School of Public Administration, University of Southern California.

two decades ago and in the community colleges in 1984, these remain quite low compared with public institutions in other states.[1]

The state's current public-sector capacity in higher education spans 106 community colleges, nineteen California State University campuses, and nine University of California campuses. In fall 1985, these public institutions enrolled over 1.4 million students. Another 180,000 students were attending independent collegiate institutions, boosting the total number of students enrolled in California higher education to more than 1.6 million. In addition, approximately 468,000 were enrolled in proprietary vocational postsecondary institutions. Figure 1 displays enrollment trends by sector since 1972.

Another fundamental characteristic of California higher education has been its high quality. The University of California has long been acknowledged as the premier public university system in the country and perhaps in the world. Its Berkeley and Los Angeles campuses rank among the top five universities in the nation and, remarkably, its San Diego campus ranks among the top twenty-five universities less than two decades after its founding.[2] At least until very recently, the California State University and the community colleges have also been highly regarded in their own domains.[3]

California's private institutions of higher education have blossomed impressively, but this sector has never received much explicit attention from the state. Since the birth of the University of California in 1868, the attention of state policymakers has been focused very largely on the public institutions of higher education.

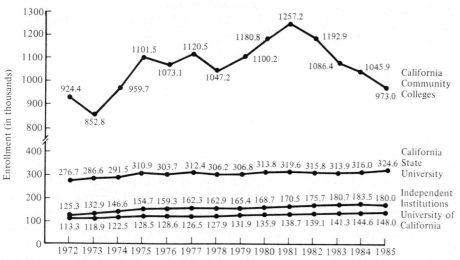

FIGURE 1   Fall Enrollments of California Higher Education Segments, 1972–1985. (Association of Independent California Colleges and Universities and California Postsecondary Education Commission.)

THE MASTER PLAN AND ITS LEGACY

Three state-level master planning efforts in higher education have been undertaken in the last quarter century. The original Master Plan Survey Team, commissioned in 1959, sought to rationalize statewide higher education planning in order to sustain the twin goals of high quality and broad access during the period of massive enrollment growth anticipated during the 1960s. At that time it was feared that, without such a broadly based and authoritative planning effort, the state would exhaust its resources on a haphazardly configured system designed to meet immediate political demands rather than long-term statewide needs.[4]

The most significant results of the Master Plan team's work were: the specification and codification of the missions (and the limitations on these) of the three public "segments," as they have come to be called; and the establishment of a permanent governmental body whose primary purpose is to monitor this division of labor. The three segments are

the University of California, the state college system (now officially called the California State University or CSU), which was taken from the jurisdiction of the State Board of Education and given its own governing board as a result of the Master Plan team's recommendations, and the junior (now community) colleges. While the community colleges did not acquire an independent statewide board and official status as a segment of the system until 1967, the Master Plan team set the stage for this development by treating them explicitly as a state resource to be governed in significant ways by statewide policies.

The Donahoe Higher Education Act of 1960, often called the Master Plan, affirmed the state's commitment to high-quality and broadly accessible public higher education and established the parameters for the development of the public system's three segments. The Master Plan had little to say about the independent sector, which was left essentially to its own devices.

THE UNIVERSITY OF CALIFORNIA

The Master Plan Survey Team both projected and prescribed enrollment parameters for the public segments. The University of California (UC) was to select its undergraduate freshmen, with minor exceptions, from the most academically qualified one-eighth of the graduates of California public high schools. It was also designated as the state's only comprehensive graduate and research university. The language of the Master Plan on this latter point reads:

> The University shall provide instruction in the liberal arts and sciences, and in the professions, including teacher education, and shall have exclusive jurisdiction over training for the professions …dentistry, law, medicine, veterinary medicine, and graduate architecture. The University shall have the sole authority in public higher education to award the doctor's degree in all fields of learning, except that it may agree with the state colleges to award joint doctor's degrees in selected fields. The University shall be the primary state-supported academic agency for research....[5]

The special status of the University of California, officially reaffirmed in the Master Plan (and each year implicitly in the state's differential budget allocations to the segments) has permitted the University to build remarkably diverse and distinguished graduate and research programs on nine campuses, and, more recently when graduate enrollments have been difficult to build, to compete successfully for academically talented undergraduates. Even as the number of California high school graduates fell by more than 11 percent between 1974 and 1984,[6] UC undergraduate enrollment has grown steadily. Most UC campuses are filled to capacity, and some 12,000 qualified undergraduate applicants each year are turned away from their first-choice campuses. The proportion of California high school graduates entering the University of California has jumped sharply in recent years, from just over 5 percent in 1974 to 7.5 percent in 1984.

It is likely that the increased concern students, employers, and the public have shown recently with the quality and marketability of academic degrees in the job market has played a role here. The University of California's success in the quality "ratings game" has been well publicized. At the same time, the university's low fee structure ($1,300 to $1,400 for full-time undergraduates in 1985–86), combined with its high academic stature, makes it a highly cost-effective investment for students.

The increased student demand was not anticipated; the Master Plan had envisioned that the proportion of students attending the University of California would remain stable. Certainly state and university planners expected student demand to slacken as the number of high school graduates fell, and it may yet as numbers of high school graduates continue to decline (after a brief surge in 1988) through 1991.[7] The university is reluctant to increase capacity substantially in the face of these demographic facts, and the state is reluctant to pay for it. Yet the public sector's fee policies, which are supported by key state policymakers, do much to fuel current enrollment pressures on the university.

THE CALIFORNIA STATE UNIVERSITY

The state colleges, which were originally the state's teacher training institutions, were granted a distinctly more limited role than the University of California by the Master Plan. Note in particular the limitations placed on the state colleges' aspirations in the areas of graduate and professional education and research:

> The state colleges have as their primary function the provision of instruction in the liberal arts and sciences and in professions and applied fields which require more than two years of collegiate education and teacher education, both for under-

graduate students and graduate students through the master's degree. The doctoral degree may be awarded jointly with the University of California, as hereinafter provided. Faculty research, using facilities provided for and consistent with the primary function of the state colleges, is authorized.[8]

To the extent they had not done so already, the state colleges were to evolve from teacher training institutions into full-fledged liberal arts colleges. They were permitted to recruit freshmen from among the top third of public high school graduates, but clearly bore a considerable status and resource disadvantage relative to the University of California in competing for the most elite group. Also, they were to continue to offer comprehensive programs through the master's degree, but not beyond (the joint doctoral program mechanism has been little used). In 1985 more than 80 percent of CSU students were undergraduates, and the system's undergraduate population was two and one-half times that of the University of California. At less than $700 per year on average for a full-time undergraduate in 1985–86, student fees in this system are well below comparable campuses in most other states and are far below those of competitive private schools, such as the universities of Santa Clara ($6,663), San Diego ($6,840), and the Pacific ($9,450).[9]

Enrollment at the California State University in the last few years has been increasing. In 1985 enrollment was up to 324,600, an increase of 8,600 students (2.7%) over the previous year (see Figure 1). Many campuses are filled to capacity, and CSU officials are now most concerned with issues of educational quality. Of primary importance has been strengthening the system's commitment to and success in its undergraduate education mission. This, of course, is in line with current concerns throughout the country,[10] but it is also in part a response to problems CSU faces at the master's program level.

Dating virtually from the time of the Master Plan, there has been an ongoing controversy over CSU's role in the California higher education system. For many years, CSU campus presidents have wanted to offer doctoral programs to enhance the system's prestige and support its claims for increased funds.[11] There also is the general feeling that, without state-supported research programs, CSU cannot attract and maintain top-quality faculty. The difference between the two segments is reflected in faculty salaries and classroom hours. At the California State University, where faculty classroom hours are about twice as heavy as at the University of California, the average salary for full professors in 1985–86 was $45,820 while the average at the University of California was $58,575, nearly 30 percent more.[12]

In November 1985 CSU announced its newest plan to offer doctoral programs, setting off a renewed turf war within higher education. Patrick Callan, then director of the California Postsecondary Education Commission, termed the plan "the most significant departure from the Master Plan that has been proposed by any segment in the past twenty-five years." As part of its review, the current Master Plan Review Commission will be asked to approve or reject the California State University proposal. However, the final decision rests with the legislature, since any expansion would add to the state's education costs.

THE COMMUNITY COLLEGES

The Master Plan provided that the two-year colleges were to continue performing their tripartite mission—i.e., providing standard collegiate courses for transfer to higher institutions, courses in vocational and technical fields leading to employment, and general or liberal arts courses. Studies in these fields may lead to the associate in arts or associate in science degree.[13] Significantly, the Master Plan gave considerable attention to facilitating the transfer function of the two-year colleges, clearly their preeminent role in the minds of the plan's framers. The current difficulties of the community colleges have much to do with their commitment to and performance in this role.

The original Master Plan gave community colleges the largest number of new campuses and the greatest possibilities for expansion of enrollment. Access to community colleges is open: anyone 18 years of age or a high school graduate may attend. Even in 1985, when enrollment was the lowest it had been since 1973, the community colleges had nearly 200,000 first-time freshmen, nearly seven times more than any other segment of California higher education.[14] Of all students enrolled in California's public institutions in 1985, 67 percent attended community colleges, compared to 23 percent in the State University system and 10 percent in the University of California.

Although community college students have always been the most numerous of any of the segments, their numbers fluctuated considerably from year to year within a generally rising trend before reaching a peak in 1981 (see Figure 1). Since then, in contrast to the four-year schools, the community colleges have faced a large enrollment decline. Between 1981 and 1985 the number of students at these colleges fell more than 22 percent from 1,257,000 to 973,000. The percentage of high school graduates enrolling in California community colleges dropped from 41.3 percent in 1974 to 36.3 percent in 1984,[15] even as the total number of high school graduates was declining. Since the funding of community colleges is closely tied to enrollment, this has created a major problem for them.

INDEPENDENT COLLEGES AND UNIVERSITIES

Over the last decade the state's private colleges and universities have enrolled a little more than one in ten students in higher education, but their share of the four-year campus population

and of graduate enrollment is much larger. Also, this sector is diverse in a way the public sector could never duplicate and includes a number of very distinguished institutions. These factors alone—in light of the cost savings and other benefits they represent to the state— would justify taking them into account in deliberations over state higher education policy. But the current demographic and fiscal squeeze on these institutions makes the urgency of a change in perspective to include them substantially greater.

EQUAL OPPORTUNITIES FOR MINORITY STUDENTS

The most profound demographic change taking place in California is the large increase in numbers of Hispanics and other minority-group members. Forecasters predict the minority population in the aggregate will become a majority in the state by the year 2010. For colleges and universities, this shift will dramatically transform the pool of potential students. This adds a new urgency to longstanding efforts to improve the access of minorities to higher education and their success in it.

Since the 1960s California's colleges and universities, along with the state legislature, have sought to increase educational opportunities for minorities. The civil rights movement imparted a sense of social and moral responsibility to educational institutions: they were to serve society by helping minorities achieve their potential. There are also efficiency reasons for these efforts. The state's economic health could be threatened if a shortage of educated and skilled workers develops, as some predict.

Unfortunately, affirmative action programs for minorities have not achieved much success thus far. In 1974 the state legislature passed a resolution (ACR 151) that directed each segment of the public postsecondary education system to develop a plan for overcoming the

underrepresentation of ethnic minorities. By
1980 the segments were supposed to have
achieved parity between proportions of minorities in their student bodies and the ethnic
composition of recent California high school
graduating classes. By all accounts little
progress was made, and underrepresentation of
Hispanics and blacks at the community colleges
and the University of California increased.[16]
The segments blamed their lack of success
mostly on factors beyond their control, namely
the legislature (unrealistic goals) and the precol-
legiate education system (minorities' low graduation rates and poor academic training). For
the most part, independent evaluators, such as
the California Postsecondary Education Commission, agreed.[17]

During this same period, independent colleges and universities were instituting affirmative action plans of their own, and with much
greater success. Between 1972 and 1977, black
and Hispanic enrollment in the private sector
grew by 50 percent. Whereas black and Hispanic students comprised about 11 percent of
the undergraduate enrollment at independent
campuses in 1972, five years later that representation had grown to over 15 percent.[18] The
increase in minority enrollment at independent
campuses was so large that by 1977 it equaled
the minority enrollment rate at the California
State University (15.5%) and far exceeded the
level at the University of California, which was
9.8 percent.[19]

State policy was a positive factor here. The
state's move in 1970 to expand the Cal Grant A
scholarship program—which lets recipients select the college (public or private) they want to
attend—was a considerable help to the indepen-
dents, according to the Association of Independent California Colleges and Universities. The
total number of these awards nearly tripled
during the 1970s. For the first time, independent campuses were able to compete with public institutions for minority students, regardless
of their economic background. By 1975 the

private sector was enrolling higher proportions
of low-income minority students than the University of California and the California State
University.[20] By 1977 the independent colleges
and universities enrolled 75 percent of the black
and Hispanic students who received Cal Grant
A awards.[21] However, during the early 1980s a
decline in Cal Grant A funding contributed to an
erosion in the gains in minority enrollment at
the independent colleges.

Affirmative action efforts in the 1980s seem
to be building on lessons from the past. The
state's new resolution (ACR 83) to improve
representation of minority students in postsecondary institutions recognizes that any plan
must be a coordinated effort reaching down into
the education system below the postsecondary
level. Accordingly, the resolution sets forth
goals for the K–12 segment (minority graduation rates), the community colleges (minority
transfer rates), and the public four-year colleges
and universities (minority enrollment rates).
The director of the California Postsecondary
Education Commission chaired a task force of
K–12 and higher education representatives
whose charge was to cooperatively adopt a
single affirmative action plan. The resolution
that resulted from this effort also sets a more
realistic time frame for achieving goals—the
1990s—than did its predecessor, which gave the
segments only five years. Finally, in response
to widespread concern about high minority
dropout rates, the resolution adds to access the
goal of improving minority success in higher
education: "By 1995, the income and ethnic
composition of baccalaureate degree recipients
from California colleges and universities is [to
be] at least equal to the income and ethnic
composition of secondary school graduates in
1990."

The segments seem also to have learned
from experience, as is reflected in their affirmative action plans. With its tough admissions
standards, the University of California emphasizes early outreach as a way to boost the

number of minorities eligible for admission. In 1983 only 3.6 percent of black graduates from California's public high schools and 4.9 percent of Hispanic graduates attained university eligibility.[22] The University of California's affirmative action plan features programs that provide services such as information dissemination, academic advising, and campus visits for junior and senior high school students. In the California State University system, where minority enrollment proportions are considerably higher than at UC but the high dropout rate among minority students has been a major problem,[23] the action plan, known as Core Student Affirmative Action, stresses retention and educational enhancement for students who are already enrolled.

The open door policy of community colleges in California has meant access for minorities,[24] but the open door has become a revolving door for many who are unprepared to handle college work. The community colleges' affirmative action projects, therefore, are aimed at increasing student success. They emphasize retention and also provide services designed to ease students' transition to employment and to four-year institutions.

The main motivation for affirmative action programs is equity, although an economic efficiency case can also be made that it is in the state's interest to increase subsidies in this area, even though progress has been sporadic at best. Cal Grant funding should be increased to a level at least commensurate with the growth in costs of attendance in California higher education (both public and private) because, as has been shown in the private sector, these monies can help increase minority enrollment. Needed also is more rigorous monitoring of the segments' progress in affirmative action projects. The legislature, moreover, must be prepared to reward the better-performing projects with state funds. To do this policymakers will need to make judgments about cost-effectiveness, so evaluations of affirmative action projects

should monitor unit costs by program in addition to the student-by-race outcome data that are routinely used to assess performance. Better data alone, however, will never be enough. State policymakers must be willing to use results to reallocate funds so that the state's large total investment begins to pay off.

Most important in this connection are state subsidies to improve minority education in elementary and secondary schools. The high dropout rate among minorities, particularly Hispanics, has eroded the pool of potential applicants for postsecondary education. The key to real progress in affirmative action is better prepared high school students and thus better performance by students who enter college.

While their high costs must be recognized, these recommendations seem politically feasible, at least in the long run. California's changing demography means there will be more minorities among the electorate and in the legislature. With this should come a renewed interest and concern for affirmative action. In any case, the moral imperative supporting such efforts is strong enough.

QUALITY OF UNDERGRADUATE EDUCATION

The agendas of the current reviews of the Master Plan for Higher Education by the independent Review Commission and the legislative joint committee to which it will report show California's concern about the quality of undergraduate education. But while California is studying the issue, many other states have policy initiatives already underway. Indeed, California has not been a leader among the states. Until quite recently, the last time the undergraduate experience was given much attention in Sacramento was during the late 1960s when students were rioting on campuses. Although times are quieter now, efforts to improve quality are complicated by simultaneous demands for increased access for and retention of disadvantaged, often poorly prepared students. Here the principles of equity and efficiency operate in some tension.

In the last few years a number of influential reports on the quality of undergraduate education in the United States have appeared.[25] These reports (one of which was written by William Bennett, who has since become U.S. Secretary of Education), along with widespread concern about how to educate people for economic growth in a time of rapid technological change, have pushed the quality issue to the forefront throughout the nation. The impetus for quality improvement in higher education has been closely linked with its predecessor movement at the elementary and secondary level by a special concern with elevating the selectivity and quality of college-level teacher education programs. California, for example, has begun testing teacher education graduates, while several other states use pre-professional skills tests with sophomores and juniors to weed out lower performing students before they major in education.

To date, the efforts in California to improve undergraduate quality have emphasized tougher admissions standards. If entering students are able to handle college work, then the institutions could stress academics over remediation and the quality of education should improve. A few years ago the University of California tightened its high school preparation standards by requiring more academic courses. The California State University followed suit recently by requiring that entering freshmen have a broader and deeper academic education during high school. Freshmen entering CSU in 1988 will be required to take four years of English and three years of mathematics in high school, as well as courses in science, history, and art.

The Master Plan Review Commission's current efforts have included proposals to tighten up academic standards in the community colleges. In addition to minimum skill levels for both academic and vocational courses, the commission has called for strengthening probation and dismissal standards for students. The commission even went so far as to recommend limiting the number of remedial education courses a student could take in the community colleges and stipulated that remediation should be offered only for no credit or non-degree credit (i.e., not applicable to the associate degree or certifiable for transfer).

These efforts to improve quality can be thought of in terms of economic efficiency. If successful, they add to the value of higher education per dollar spent, in part by increasing students' long-term career flexibility. The problem is that these standards-based efforts need to be reconciled with equity values since there is already evidence they affect minorities disproportionately.

For recommendations, we turn to the reports on the quality of undergraduate education cited earlier. They represent the distilled wisdom of the nation's best minds in the field of education, and we find little to quarrel with in their recommendations, many of which are incorporated in the discussion below. California institutions and state policymakers should begin paying more attention to these recommendations. States that already have initiatives along these lines underway provide implementation ideas.[26]

The high school/college transition is an area with great potential for bringing about real change in educational quality. The major difficulties are to be found in increasing information flow and coordination between these two organizationally separate systems. The Southern Regional Education Board suggested that, to work closely with the public schools, colleges and universities should: (1) publicize courses that should be taken and skills that should be developed in high school to prepare for college; (2) assess the skills of high school students early so that students could be informed of their deficiencies and take corrective action before graduating from high school; and (3) inform

each public school district of the college performance of its graduates, especially the numbers
requiring remedial work before placement in
college-level courses.[27] Building upon these
ideas, Ohio uses an "early assessment" program to ease the high school/college transition.
This program assesses the readiness of high
school juniors for college-level work in areas
such as writing, science, and mathematics. Students receive feedback from the college of their
choice as to their likely placement in specific
college courses. Such feedback allows students
to take appropriate corrective action during
their senior year in high school.

Educational quality can also be raised by
more and better assessments of student and
institutional performance. This is viewed as a
way to increase accountability in higher education. Reports from the National Institute of
Education and the Association of American
Colleges recommended a host of different outcome measurement activities—from narrowly
defined achievement testing to broadly defined
student assessment; from evaluating student
progress to evaluating institutional or program
effectiveness; from diagnosing student needs to
certifying   minimum   levels   of   student
achievement.[28]

New Jersey's Basic Skills Assessment Program is used statewide to counsel and place
freshmen and transfer students in courses and
programs. This type of test could be used in the
community colleges for the mandatory assessment called for by the Master Plan Review
Commission and could also be given to students
transferring to the University of California and
California State University systems to improve
student success prospects. More accurate
placement of students in courses would most
certainly help lower the dropout rate, which at
CSU in particular has been exceptionally
high.[29]

Another group of assessment initiatives
focuses on testing the basic skills and competencies of students already enrolled in college. Florida's College Level Academic Skills
Test and Georgia's Regents Exam are used to
determine whether students have mastered
basic skills and competencies before advanc-
ing to upper-division courses or programs. In
California, where community colleges have
open admissions, this type of exam could be
used to test the readiness of students for
further study or their need for remedial education.

Other assessment activities have stressed
measuring outcomes. In Tennessee public colleges and universities must measure their performance in terms of the extent to which
institutional objectives have been achieved.
Other states require their colleges and universities to show how information on a variety of
outcome measures is being used in the review
of existing academic programs. Northeast Missouri State University, for example, uses outcome data in overall institutional planning as
well as in curriculum evaluation and improvement.

Another way to improve undergraduate education is by boosting the overall quality of
college curricula, particularly in the areas of
liberal arts and teacher education. The main
thrust of a 1984 report by the National Endowment for the Humanities was that undergraduate education suffered from too much
vocationalism. That report focuses exclusively
on the humanities and what should be done to
enhance their place in higher education. Several
other reports advocate instituting more specific
academic standards and limiting remedial education, ideas that have already received considerable attention in California during the Master
Plan commission's review of the community
colleges.

Approaches to improving teacher education
also encourage broadening the curriculum to
place more emphasis on academic disciplines
for elementary and secondary education majors. A report by the Southern Regional Education Board recommends more upper-division

courses in different disciplines and more liberal arts courses for students majoring in education.[30] For elementary education majors planning to teach upper grades, the board proposes that such students complete an academic major in addition to their major in education. A more revolutionary reform for teacher education, offered recently in separate reports by the Carnegie Forum's Task Force on Teaching as a Profession and by the Holmes Group (a consortium of university education deans), advocates abolishing undergraduate degree programs in education and having professional education of teachers instead take place at the graduate level after students have received a broader undergraduate education.[31]

Some states have approached quality improvement by establishing special incentive funding for improvement efforts in undergraduate education. Florida targeted $3.5 million in 1985–86 for the reduction of class size and the strengthening of academic advising. Colorado's Quality Incentive Funding Program funds competitive grants to improve undergraduate education and to reward exemplary efforts that do so. Virginia's Funds for Excellence Program awards grants for the enhancement of undergraduate teaching and for the development of curricula in the arts and sciences. Financial incentives have also been used by some states to attract high-quality students into the teaching profession. Alabama and Kentucky, for example, offer special financial-aid packages, such as forgivable loans, to lure college students into teaching.

It is too early to evaluate the results of these state initiatives, but there is obviously no shortage of attractive ideas. Where California can take the lead is in monitoring results, continuing to support what works, and devising ways to ensure that minorities receive a better, more socially useful education from quality improvement efforts. This is how the goals of equity and efficiency can be married in this difficult area.

CONCLUSION

The policy issues identified here are not new, but many of them have reached a new level of importance. Community colleges in California do need attention, as do undergraduate education, especially training for would-be teachers, and some areas in graduate and professional education. A substantial part of the independent higher education sector, a valuable resource to the state, is on the verge of serious trouble that could cost the state dearly in the long run if not addressed soon. Student fee policy in the public sector needs to be regularized in practice as well as in official policy. Ideally, fee policy should also be more effectively coordinated with state student aid policies so as to help both needy students and the private sector without spending large sums on subsidies to students from affluent families. California also needs to consider taking steps to link appropriate parts of the higher education system more explicitly to the economy that supports it.

Of highest priority, however, is moving the entire educational system toward more effective response to the needs of minority students. In addition to the moral imperative, it is hard to see how mere rhetoric and the operation of costly programs to aid minorities can continue to suffice in a polity where the majority of voters, taxpayers, and potential students will soon be members of a minority ethnic group. Continued support for the state's higher education system commensurate with its proud traditions and aspirations probably depends on more demonstrably effective systemwide responses to this problem. Programs in higher education that work now do not generally get the increased resources they merit. Most important, the colleges and universities have thus far done too little to help teachers, schools, and education policymakers address the critical educational deficiencies of minority students in their secondary school years and earlier.

This must be the new frontier for California higher education. The future of the system depends upon it.

Notes

The authors thank William Pickens, Jack H. Schuster, Dean Stephens, and Donald R. Winkler for their helpful comments.

1 "Tuition and Fees at 2,600 Colleges and Universities, 1985–86," *Chronicle of Higher Education,* August 14, 1985, pp. 13–18.

2 Edward B. Fiske, "Berkeley Tops Scholars' Rankings of Graduate Schools' Reputations," *New York Times,* January 17, 1983, p. A-1; David S. Webster, "America's Highest Ranked Graduate Schools, 1925–1982," *Change,* 15(4):14–24, 1983.

3 Neil J. Smelser, "Growth, Structural Change and Conflict in California Public Higher Education, 1950–1970," in Smelser and Gabriel Almond (eds.), *Public Higher Education in California,* Berkeley, University of California Press, 1974.

4 Verne A. Stadtman, *The University of California, 1868–1968,* New York, McGraw-Hill, 1970.

5 Master Plan Survey Team, *A Master Plan for Higher Education in California, 1960–1975,* Sacramento, California State Department of Education, 1960, p. 2.

6 California Postsecondary Education Commission, *California College-Going Rates: 1984 Update,* Commission Report 85–34, September 1985, p. 7.

7 California Postsecondary Education Commission, *Population and Enrollment Trends: 1985–2000,* Commission Report 85-16, March 1985, pp. 30–31.

8 Supra note 5, p. 2.

9 Supra note 1, p. 13.

10 Association of American Colleges, *Integrity in the College Curriculum: A Report to the Academic Community,* February 1985; William J. Bennett, *To Reclaim a Legacy: A Report on the Humanities in Higher Education,* National Endowment for the Humanities, 1984; National Institute of Education/U.S. Department of Education, *Involvement in Learning: Realizing the Potential of American Higher Education,* October 1984.

11 The magnitude of the difference in funding between the University of California and California State University is illustrated by the incremental dollars provided by the state for each additional full-time-equivalent undergraduate student enrolled. In 1984–85 this figure was $4,539 for UC and $2,600 for CSU. (Figures provided by the California Postsecondary Education Commission.)

12 California Postsecondary Education Commission, *Faculty Salaries in California's Public Universities: 1986–87,* Commission report 85–43, December 1985, p. 11.

13 Supra note 5, p. 2.

14 Data provided by the California Postsecondary Education Commission.

15 Supra note 6, p. 7.

16 California Postsecondary Education Commission, *Equal Educational Opportunity in California Postsecondary Education: Part III,* Commission Report 80–86, March 1980.

17 California Postsecondary Education Commission, *Equal Educational Opportunity in California Postsecondary Education,* Parts I, II, and III, Commission Reports 76–6, 77–4, 80–86, 1976, 1977, and 1980.

18 Association of Independent California Colleges and Universities, *Access and Success: Equal Educational Opportunity in California's Independent Colleges and Universities,* Santa Ana, February 1980.

19 Supra note 16.

20 California Assembly Permanent Subcommittee on Postsecondary Education, *Unequal Access to College—Postsecondary Opportunities and Choices of High School Graduates,* Sacramento, California Legislature, November 1975.

21 Supra note 18.

22 University of California, Office of Admissions and Outreach Services, *University of California Undergraduate Student Affirmative Action Five-Year Plan,* February 1985, pp. 1–6.

23 For example, of black freshmen who enrolled in 1978, only 11% had earned a degree by 1983. Of Hispanics entering in 1978, only 13% had graduated five years later (David G. Savage, "Cal State Hopes to Stem Dropout Tide," *Los Angeles Times,* November 10, 1985, p. 3.).

24 The community colleges have a more ethnically diverse student population than the universities.

Black and Hispanic students accounted for about 19% of the community college population in 1984, compared to less than 14% in CSU and about 10% in the UC system. (Data provided by the California Postsecondary Education Commission.)

25 Supra note 10; Southern Regional Education Board, Commission for Educational Quality, *Improving Teacher Education: An Agenda for Higher Education and the Schools,* 1985. For a summary of these reports see Education Commission of the States, *Five Reports: Summary of the Recommendations of Recent Commission Reports on Improving Undergraduate Education,* November/December, 1985.

26 For an analysis of state initiatives to improve undergraduate education, see Carol M. Boyer and Aims C. McGuinness, Jr., "State Initiatives to Improve Undergraduate Education," *AAHE Bulletin,* 38(6):3–7, February 1986.

27 Southern Regional Education Board, Supra note 25.

28 National Institute of Education/U.S. Department of Education, supra note 10; Association of American Colleges, supra note 10.

29 Of the students who entered the California State University system as freshmen in 1978, by 1983 an average of 26% had graduated, 19% were still enrolled, and the rest had left. By contrast, 55% of students entering UCLA and 61% of those entering UC Berkeley were graduated within 5 years. Supra note 23, p. 3.

30 Supra note 25.

31 See Carnegie Forum on Education and the Economy, Task Force on Teaching as a Profession, *A Nation Prepared: Teachers for the 21st Century,* 1986; and Holmes Group, Inc., *Tomorrow's Teachers: A Report of the Holmes Group,* East Lansing, Mich. 1986.

THE CALIFORNIA ECONOMY

When describing the economy of California it is easy to get caught up in superlatives. California, with its burgeoning population of more than 27 million, is the nation's number one agricultural and industrial state, leading in almost every general manufacturing category and in the production of dozens of farm commodities. Californians produce more cotton than Egypt, more computers than Japan. If California were a separate country, its per capita GNP would rank sixth in the world—ahead of the United States itself, France, West Germany, and virtually every other industrialized nation.

So too the economic future of the state seems bright. California leads the nation in high-technology production and in such pioneering fields as bioengineering. More than 30 percent of the nation's total high-tech workforce is in California, including thousands of skilled technicians in computer and software design, robotics, space science, and telecommunications.

Michael B. Teitz, in the following selection, cautions that beneath the robust facade of the state's economy lurk many dangers. He advises his fellow Californians not to be content with the past glories of economic achievement. The future of the state is in peril, he warns, and hard choices must be made to avert disaster. It is appropriate that this anthology conclude with this selection, because Teitz touches upon and projects into the future several of the themes encountered in previous chapters.

Teitz notes that within the high-technology sector there is an almost unbridgeable gap between the elite of highly trained and well-paid technicians and the masses of low-skilled and poorly paid production workers. In the parlance of the new social history, encountered frequently in earlier selections, the typical high-tech worker faces very limited opportunities for upward mobility. Teitz finds a similar gap in the service sector.

This polarization of the work force is commonly described as the "two-tier" phenomenon. Its implications for California society as a whole are troubling. Californians are among the wealthiest of Americans, their per capita income far above the national average. Yet the proportion of Californians living in poverty is also well above average. In the 1970s the percentage of children living in households below the federally defined poverty level increased enormously. Economist John Kenneth Galbraith, in a speech at Berkeley in 1980, warned of the dangers of such polarization: "Perhaps the disadvantaged are now too few to make a revolution. But they could make life uncomfortable for all."[1]

Teitz's most valuable contribution is his discussion of the public policies that supported California's economic growth and the policy choices that now threaten it. The economic boom of the past several decades rested upon a willingness by Californians to maintain a vast infrastructure of public works and services. From freeways to public schools, this infrastructure was paid for by tax revenues. As we learned in the selection by Jack Citrin, the tax revolt of the late 1970s significantly reduced these revenues. Public services inevitably declined; the infrastructure weakened. Californians have been living off the capital of past investments in the public sector; what will be the future return on the reduced investments of today?

Teitz's discussion of economic and population growth demonstrates a conflict of values similar to those identified by William Zumeta and Priscilla Wohlstetter in their discussion of higher education. Economic growth may promote efficiency, but because its benefits are spread unequally it may also violate the principle of equity. And as we learned from Douglas H. Strong in his discussion of the Tahoe basin, economic growth often comes at the expense of the environment. How can a mature society balance concerns for economic development and environmental protection?

The most disturbing part of Teitz's analysis is his consideration of the declining quality of California education. His views are even less sanguine than those of the authors of the previous selection. The substantial decline in financial support for public education—a diminution in the state's "human capital"—clouds the future of the California economy.

Michael B. Teitz is a Professor in the Department of City and Regional Planning at the University of California, Berkeley.

[1]John Kenneth Galbraith, "Two Pleas at Berkeley," *The New York Review of Books*, July 17, 1980.

READING 30

The California Economy

Michael B. Teitz

What shapes economic development in a state or nation? Some things we know: availability of resources, capital, and skilled labor at competitive costs. Others are less tangible: enterprising spirit, absence of restraints by vested interests, the mobilization of social capacity to supply infrastructure that cannot be built by individual firms. These factors come together historically in ways always unique and, therefore, very difficult to predict. No one fully understands the process. Despite economic analyses and sophisticated models, real economies have a way of doing the unexpected.

At this point in its history, the California economy can no longer rely on what has worked in the past. So long as the U.S. is the world's leading trading nation and maintains relatively open international trade, California's huge market will be subject to fierce foreign competition. Major sectors may follow the path of decline already taken by those such as automobile assembly and tires, which were the backbone of manufacturing less than 20 years ago. At the same time, California is now a domestic market of such size and wealth that it can support levels and types of activity not previously possible. And the state's tradition of innovation in production and consumption continues with the rise of high technology industry in electronics and, in the future, bioengineering.

What seems to be clear is that California must look forward to a situation in which its own population's natural increase, together with a continuing inflow of migrants from else-

where in the U.S. and abroad, will require a dynamic economy in order to maintain employment and income. A conservative estimate suggests an average future growth rate in employment of perhaps 2 percent annually, well below the historic level. About five million *net* new jobs will be needed in the state between 1980 and 2000, if this is the case. Given the observed and very stable tendency for existing jobs to be lost for a variety of causes at about 8 percent annually on average,[1] this means that a total of about 20 million new jobs must be created in the 20-year period. Where will these jobs come from, and will they provide incomes at levels the population expects?

HIGH TECH

Two principal sources for economic growth and employment suggest themselves: high technology manufacturing, and finance and business services. Most observers have placed their hopes for California's economic future on high technology.[2] This is not an unreasonable premise. The advanced sectors of electronics, instruments, aerospace and bioengineering now account for more than 500,000 jobs, about a quarter of the state's total manufacturing employment. These are the growth sectors, dynamic in technical process innovation, and in product development. And they are growing rapidly in employment after a sharp loss in the 1980–83 recession.

More and more, it appears that electronics and solid-state technology are also keys to future modernization and survival of older sectors, perhaps giving them a new lease on life in the face of foreign competition with low-cost labor. If we believe that a powerful manufacturing base is essential to a healthy economy, then there is no alternative for California but to support high technology industry to the maximum extent possible.

However, the picture is not all roses. Recent studies have demonstrated that high technology industry will be rather specialized in its locations, and that it is a mixed blessing in terms of employment.[3] Not all areas are attractive to high technology firms. In fact, at the early stages of the product cycle, when innovation and competition are intense, they have tended to cluster in relatively few metropolitan areas, of which Silicon Valley is the most famous example. California has been fortunate in securing two of the major clusters in the U.S., in the Santa Clara Valley, and Los Angeles–Orange County. As processes involved in production, and products, become more standardized, there is a tendency for routine production to shift to lower cost (especially labor costs) sites, many outside the U.S. altogether. Although the state is not about to lose its dominance, much of the production activity in future years is likely to be elsewhere.

Even if production were more heavily concentrated in California, employment implications of high technology would not be all positive. Electronics, especially production of semi-conductors and products derived from them, requires a labor force that differs markedly from that in traditional manufacturing. The proportion of skilled technical and professional workers tends to be much higher than the average in manufacturing, and they are paid correspondingly well. However, production work is highly routinized and relatively low-skilled. Its pay has been below average for manufacturing and it tends to draw on female and immigrant labor pools that are non-unionized.

While this form of employment is undoubtedly critical for low-skilled workers, it is problematic for the long-term. It does not offer income opportunities comparable to those being lost in the older, declining industrial sectors, and therefore provides neither easy transition for displaced workers nor long-term prospects for higher income or career mobility. If anything, it has been argued that the high level of education and technical skill required by the technical/professional part of the labor force tends to decrease prospects that production workers could ever be anything more.

Requirements of these sectors for high-wage and low-wage workers presents yet another constraint, namely housing. In areas of high technology concentration, housing prices rose dramatically through the 1970s, and remain as much as twice the national average. The effect is to drive up wages for all workers, and to make it especially difficult to recruit the highly specialized labor necessary for expansion. In the face of price increases, communities have been reluctant to open up zoning for low-income and moderate-income housing that would change their character and be fiscally non-productive. It may not be too much to assert that housing costs could threaten the viability of high technology manufacturing in its core locations.

A corollary to the high cost of housing is the reluctance of many communities in the state to allow industrial development (even electronics). Although this cannot be said to be a common phenomenon, it is clearly happening in areas such as Santa Clara County, where development pressure and its environmental consequences have been most intense. As the state has grown in population and income, its urban communities have matured and have become politically adept at preventing development that would inevitably change the nature of the communities themselves. The clear conflict between tax benefits of development and its environmental consequences is observable in swings back and forth between control and development that have been quite common in recent years. Whatever the long-run implications of such on-off policies may be, in the short-run they do not inspire confidence of companies that want to establish or expand operations.

THE SERVICE SECTOR

In contrast to high technology manufacturing, finance and business services look to the service sector as a basic source of economic dynamism. It is evident that services can be a driving force in the California economy. The observed service employment growth in the 1960s and 1970s is too large and diverse to have occurred simply as a secondary result of income growth in more "basic" sectors. Thus, it is not surprising that a substantial part of the growth in service activity can be attributed to creating and selling services increasingly necessary for a complex economic system.

California is located advantageously for international trade and corporate control functions for the Western U.S. and the Pacific region. The state has also seen development of the strongest venture capital market in the world in the past 20 years. In addition, a number of major enterprises whose products are services have emerged. One example is Bechtel Corporation. Finally, whole new products, such as computer software, are now intermediate between services and conventional production.

Although the financial center of the U.S. remains New York City, Los Angeles and San Francisco have seen remarkable office building booms, reflecting the power of this sectoral growth.

The forms of employment that accompany service-based development have a good deal in common with those described above. Traditionally, office work has been divided quite sharply by sex, status and pay, with women holding lower-paid clerical positions, and men higher-paid managerial or professional roles. Thus, expansion of this sector tends to generate large numbers of low-paid to moderately-paid clerical jobs, and relatively few higher-paid positions. Such an employment structure does not address the problem of loss of secure, well-paying jobs in traditional manufacturing. Furthermore, it may not even be particularly stable employment, in the face of office automation in the next 20 years. Automation may increase wages by raising productivity, but it is also likely to demand higher-skill levels of clerical workers and reduce the total number of new jobs to be created.

Office employment expansion also faces constraints. Central cities, notably San Francisco, have been reluctant to allow development to continue unchecked. Their proportion of total office growth would, in any case, fall over time. Suburban office development has gained momentum recently, although there is no concentration of suburban corporate headquarters in California comparable to that in Fairfield County, Connecticut. We may expect to see the same type of anti-development conditions emerging in the suburbs as have occurred over moderate-income housing. Such opposition is already happening, quite strongly, in Connecticut. As development grows, it may prove stronger in California, with its traditional concern for quality of life.

Thus, it seems likely that high technology manufacturing and office development will face significant future problems of land availability and cost. In conjunction with high cost and difficulty of developing moderate-priced housing, these constraints may have complex effects. On the one hand, development could be frustrated, at least partially, and diverted to other states where the "business climate" is more welcoming. To some degree, this already accounts for rapid rates of growth in the Southeastern U.S., Texas and Arizona. On the other hand, development pressures may shift toward areas within California that have previously been less attractive, notably the Central Valley. In either case, it is unlikely that these two broad sectors alone will supply sufficient economic dynamism to maintain employment and income levels in California.

AGRICULTURE

To what other sources of growth can the state turn? One sector that has played a critical part in the state's evolution is agriculture. Together with its concomitant food processing industry, agriculture now comprises well over 500,000 workers, about 5 percent of the state's total in 1980. The productivity of California agriculture is legendary. For over 50 years, the state has been selling its produce to the U.S. and the world.

However, agriculture in California must face a new set of market conditions in coming years. The industry is a quintessential example of what can be achieved by a combination of individual enterprise and collective action. For agriculture, the collective action was creation of a plentiful and reliable supply of low-priced water, first by private districts, and later by state and federal water projects. Subsidized agricultural water is increasingly difficult to finance in an urban state, as the fate of the proposed Peripheral Canal demonstrates.

The price of delivered water will rise even as the supply of cheaper groundwater diminishes, owing to utilization beyond the natural rate of recharge. Without major new capital investments in water supply and wastewater removal facilities, agriculture will need to adapt its crops and technology to a new, higher-cost environment. Labor is also a source of cost pressure on agriculture. The trend toward increased use of machinery should hold down the growth rate of demand for labor.

At the same time, the industry will face increasing competition from foreign sources. Although world demand for food will grow in the next 20 years, as population and incomes expand, innovations in food production are now occurring worldwide with remarkable gains in productivity. These gains are now, for the most part, in basic grains and foodstuffs, but it is not unreasonable to expect that similar advances may occur in higher-value crops in which California leads. If this occurs, we may see competition from low labor-cost areas similar to that occurring in manufacturing.

In view of these constraints, it seems unlikely that agriculture and its associated sectors can be a major source of future employment and income growth. That sector will remain economically and politically potent, but it is unlikely that we will see a resurgence of massive public investment in water projects. Barring extraordinary natural disasters, there should not be a striking increase in market demand for the state's agricultural products, nor an extraordinary rise in their prices. The very productivity that has made California's agriculture so powerful an economic force ensures that prices are constantly threatened by oversupply, and federal subsidization of farm income may have reached its limits.

No other sectors are obvious candidates for massive growth. Perhaps it would be more important to concentrate instead on conditions that give rise to economic dynamism itself. Some analyses have pointed to the role of small enterprise as critical to sustaining economic momentum and, especially, creating new employment. The evidence is quite strong that small business is important for economic growth.[4] However, small business as a whole cannot be credited with this role. Most small businesses live and die in relatively static obscurity. The key to a developmental role for small business is creation of conditions that allow *new* enterprises freely to come into existence and have a reasonable probability of success. Many factors affect that probability, especially availability of capital, absence of excessive regulation, and prevention of unfair competitive practices by powerful existing interests. No one can project which businesses may fail and which may create entire new industries. Yet, support of an environment in which enterprise can flourish may be a most critical area for public policy.

POLICY CHOICES FOR CALIFORNIA

It is reasonable to argue that as the state's economy matures, constraints on development are imposed by powerful established groups for a wide variety of reasons and purposes. The great growth boom of the 1950s and its prolongation through the 1970s, however, did not occur by accident. It was crucially supported by public policy choices, such as decisions to build freeways and water systems necessary for urban growth and agricultural expansion, and creation of an unparalleled system of public education to sustain a highly productive labor force. These choices were not without costs. Physical development is expensive and creates environmental degradation. Educational systems, like other massive institutions, have a way of creating their own objectives that may diverge from what is socially desirable. Population growth inevitably changes the quality of life.

But once economic and population growth are in motion, they cannot simply be turned off without great cost and social dislocation. The state's demographic structure, and its reputation as a goal for migration, will ensure that population growth continues, albeit at a lower average rate and with fluctuations. Important policy choices in coming years must be made that will affect the economic future for that population.

What choices are there? Perhaps few that are clear-cut in the world of political reality, where interest groups struggle and negotiate to maintain or improve their relative positions. Yet, however seemingly incremental, uncoordinated, or even contradictory these decisions may be, they will reflect broader issues. Some of these we can attempt to clarify.

One such issue is California's commitment to economic growth itself. Growth means injustice. Not everyone benefits equally, and some groups usually suffer. But, to the extent that protection of existing groups' interests takes precedence over economic growth, aggregate income and employment will be lessened. This conflict takes many forms. One example is between maintenance of older sectors and locations in which workers have a long-term stake and active support of new sectors that may desire new locations and require different types of labor. A balanced industrial development policy is one of the most difficult to formulate and implement because such a policy really does have conflicting objectives.

Nonetheless, in a mature economy, it is not possible simply to write off large sections of the workforce. Some compromise between the two positions is necessary. In this respect, Massachusetts' recent formation of two industrial commissions—for mature industries and for technology—is a clear recognition that both streams of policy choice need articulation if the concerns for growth and revitalization (or, at least, humane decline) are to be addressed.

A second form of conflict occurs where localities choose to protect their current lifestyle and environment by active exclusion of development, whether it be moderate-priced housing or employment-creating activity. Again, the issue is not clear-cut, except to ardent advocates of one side or the other. Yet, without some disincentives against local rejection of development, and new sources of capital for local infrastructure, economic growth will be impeded.

Obviously it would be politically naive to suggest that the state simply override local objectives by fiat, for example, through creation of a state economic development authority with power to float bonds and negate local zoning. But it might make good sense to explore use of incentives for development, for example, in the form of capital grants for public works if a local entity accepts economic growth and zones effectively for moderate-priced housing, both ownership and rental.

California will not build another freeway system, but it could support infrastructure development necessary for growth. Such a system of incentives might be linked to regional estimates of requirements of land and facilities for future growth, together with some form of "fair share" allocation to local communities. This could avoid a sense, on their part, of carrying an undue share of the burden. Experience with such proposals for low-income housing suggests that this will never reconcile those unalterably opposed to growth, but it may create a better basis for giving the regional or statewide interest in development a voice at the local level.

Measures of this type primarily would enhance development options in metropolitan areas which have been engines of growth in the state. More venturesome would be a policy choice to actively support development of a fourth major metropolis in the state. There are strong indications that the fewest local constraints and fastest rate of urban growth in the next decade may be in the Central Valley. Given the number of cities of already substantial size, it is hardly conceivable that any one of them could be selected as the acknowledged core of growth. However, a strategy might be feasible that encourages growth of a multi-centered, regional metropolis through access to infrastructure capital, improved transportation, and adequate water and power supplies.

Such a strategy would be expensive and would most likely involve conflicts with agricultural and environmental conservation groups. To be successful, it would need to envision a more compact form of development than is now conventionally acceptable. Yet, it may be that real innovations in the physical form of development would actually be easier in an environment of new growth than in the rigidity of the major metropolitan areas.

Ultimately, the issue here is whether the state seeks actively to support future growth. The position of this chapter is that there is no option with respect to population—that will grow regardless. The real option is Californians' level of income and its rate of growth. Policies to encourage development can generate faster growth rates that translate into employment and income. The snag is that these may also enhance migration attractiveness, and therefore further population expansion. Even with effective barriers to migration, solving the problem of an adequate supply of labor and a sufficient amount of economic development simultaneously turns out to be very hard, as European countries found to their cost. California cannot close its doors, so it must take care of its economy, and also of its labor force, to ensure that its population has access to opportunities created by growth.

The question of labor is complementary to that of development. Unless California maintains the quality of its labor force, changes during the next two decades will result in a form of social disaster. During the 20 years from 1950 to 1970, massive investment in secondary and post-secondary education in California created a level of human capital that was necessary and appropriate to the remarkable development that occurred.

This investment was reinforced by migration into the state of large numbers of well-educated and trained workers. The past ten years have seen a shift in migration toward less-skilled people, and a social decision to reduce human capital investment in education substantially.

The most recent estimates by the U.S. Department of Education reveal the magnitude of this decision. As of 1982, California ranked 22nd among states in expenditure per pupil in public schools and 46th in percentage of income spent on education. In pupil-teacher ratio, California ranked 50th. Most critically, the percentage of all students graduating from high school fell from 79.9 percent in 1972 to 68.9 in 1982; the state's ranking fell from 22nd to 39th in the same decade.

At a time when the structure of employment seems to be moving increasingly toward tasks requiring verbal and quantitative skills, the state's new entrants into the labor market are decreasingly capable of reading, writing, and computation. It is an extraordinary public policy with which to enter the postindustrial era for a state that has done more than any other to create that era.

Clearly, these statistics are affected by migration into California of large numbers of poor and disadvantaged people. But the relative decline in resources allocated to public secondary education reflects also a decision to ignore the human capital needs of future generations of workers. The consequences of this choice will be very serious unless it is rectified. Unlike countries such as West Germany, where early school-leavers who work must also receive technical education, California has no requirements for its drop-outs.

The community college system is a remarkable backup for high schools, but to teach basic skills to people in their 20s and older is very inefficient. Simply dealing in a humane way with retraining displaced workers will require major post-secondary educational resources that should not be diverted from what is a task of the high schools. And, for large numbers of drop-outs, the habits and discipline of work will never be learned, if left so late.

How to provide for educating a labor force that can be productive, and command the level of income that it expects, will be a most difficult economic policy problem in California in the 1980s. Education is usually seen as a social function, providing a way for individual mobility and opportunity. Whether, in fact, it creates social mobility is questionable. Failure to educate, however, would be disastrous for workers in coming years. The state should look at its labor force as an economic resource that is renewable only with investment of capital. Further, this resource needs not only to be maintained, but also constantly improved, in order to withstand economic competition from rising productivity elsewhere in the world.

There is no obvious way to ensure a high-quality labor force in the future. More money alone is a questionable strategy in view of entrenched interests in educational institutions in the state. Partial deregulation of education has been advocated through schemes such as vouchers, but these pose grave threats to the most socially vulnerable groups, those with least access to information and capacity to choose. Still, some form of competition among secondary education providers does make sense. If we fail to maintain labor force quality, California's economic welfare will suffer as surely as if we were to allow the state's transportation system to collapse through neglect.

CONCLUSION

In economic policy, simple answers are generally wrong. Yet, the questions, once we see them, may be simple. California's economy is huge and abundant. It has made the state rich enough to understand that a good society must have many things beyond wealth. Nevertheless, the economy is not on automatic pilot, although the hidden hand of the market may work to its advantage.

What we have was created by real choices, individual and collective. The economic history of countries such as Britain demonstrates that social choices that fail to pay attention to the dynamic needs of the economy, or to distribution of its products between rich and poor—in the present and the future—can destroy what has been achieved within two generations.

Notes

I am grateful to Sabina Dietrick for her valuable assistance in gathering information for this chapter, and to the University of California, Berkeley, for research support. The ideas in this chapter draw on many discussions with colleagues and students, to whom I owe much. Of course, the views expressed remain the sole responsibility of the author.

1 See David Birch, *The Job Creation Process*. Cambridge, Mass., MIT Program in Neighborhood and Regional Change, 1979, and Michael B. Teitz, Amy Glasmeier, and Douglass Svensson, Small Business and Employment Growth in California, Berkeley: Institute of Urban and Regional Development, University of California, Working Paper No. 348, 1981.

2 See Ann R. Markusen, "High-Tech Jobs, Markets and Economic Development Prospects: Evidence from California," *Built Environment* 9 (1983) 18–28.

3 See Amy Glasmeier, Peter Hall and Ann R. Markusen, "Recent Evidence on High-Technology Industries' Spatial Tendencies: A Preliminary Investigation." Berkeley: Institute of Urban and Regional Development, University of California, Working Paper No. 417, 1983.

4 The work of David Birch has been notable in this area. See Birch, op. cit., and Teitz, Glasmeier and Svensson, op. cit.

INDEX